Administrative Law
in the Political System

ADMINISTRATIVE LAW IN THE POLITICAL SYSTEM

Fourth Edition

Kenneth F. Warren, Ph.D.

Professor of Political Science and Public Policy
Saint Louis University

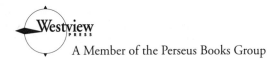

A Member of the Perseus Books Group

Copyright © 2004 by Westview Press, A Member of the Perseus Books Group

Published in the United States of America by Westview Press, A Member of the Perseus Books Group, 5500 Central Avenue, Boulder, Colorado 80301-2877, and in the United Kingdom by Westview Press, 12 Hid's Copse Road, Cumnor Hill, Oxford OX2 9JJ.

Find us on the World Wide Web at www.westviewpress.com

Westview Press books are available at special discounts for bulk purchases in the United States by corporations, institutions, and other organizations. For more information, please contact the Special Markets Department at the Perseus Books Group, 11 Cambridge Center, Cambridge, MA 02142, or call (617) 252-5298 or (800) 255-1514, or e-mail special.markets@perseusbooks.com.

Library of Congress Cataloging-in-Publication Data
Warren, Kenneth F., 1943–
    Administrative law in the political system / Kenneth F. Warren.—4th ed.
    p.   cm.
    Includes index.
    ISBN 0-8133-4116-7 (PB : alk. paper) — ISBN 0-8133-4117-5 (HB : alk. paper)
    1. Administrative law—United States.   2. Delegated legislation—
United States.   3. Administrative agencies—United States.
I. Title.
    KF5402.W37   2004
    342.73'06—dc22

                                                                        2003017960

The paper used in this publication meets the requirements of the American National Standard for Permanence of Paper for Printed Library Materials Z39.48-1984.

Design by Lisa Kreinbrink
Set in 11.5-point Adobe Garamond by the Perseus Books Group

10   9   8   7   6   5   4   3   2   1

Contents

Preface

ADMINISTRATIVE LAW IN THE POLITICAL SYSTEM, fourth edition, represents an attempt to satisfy a need in the public administration field for a comprehensive yet streamlined administrative law text written by a social scientist especially for social science students, although the book is certainly appropriate for law students. The general purpose of the book is to convey to students the role of administrative law in the American political system but, more specifically, its role in shaping, guiding, and restricting the actions of administrative agencies in order to make regulatory practices more in line with due process standards. The book is unique in that all traditional administrative law topics covered (e.g., rulemaking, adjudication, tort law) are written as much as possible in nontechnical language, with an emphasis on points of particular interest to social science students. Special attention is given to the impact politics has on efforts by administrators to comply with the dictates of administrative law. Systems theory is employed in a limited manner to stress that agency regulators must respond not only to the "demands" placed upon them by administrative law but also to the conflicting socioeconomic and political pressures stemming from their total environment.

An enormous effort has been made to make this fourth edition as up-to-date as possible. Emphasis has been placed on current trends in administrative law, recent court decisions, happenings during President George W. Bush's administration, and especially, the impact that neoconservative politics and a post–September 11 mindset have had on the development of administrative law.

In sum, this new edition should be appreciated especially by social science students, particularly in the area of public administration, because it (1) provides comprehensive yet streamlined coverage of administrative law written especially for social science students; (2) does not assume prior legal training or command of a technical legal vocabulary; (3) draws upon both the legal and social science literature to help provide insights into the nature of administrative law; (4) plays down the case approach commonly employed in law school contexts (although hundreds of cases are here covered), in favor of a more direct descriptive and analytical approach, which makes the relatively difficult subject matter of administrative law considerably easier to understand; (5) employs systems analysis, a popular analytical framework familiar to most relatively advanced social science students, so as to place administrative law in the context of the American political system; (6) relates administrative law to topics of particular concern to social science students (e.g., the impact of the USA PATRIOT Act on administrative searches, seizures, and detentions); and (7) is quite current, thus placing administrative law developments in the perspective of the 2000s.

Obviously, many people provided assistance as I struggled to finish this book. I wish to thank them for their unselfish and valuable services. First, I want to acknowledge the students in both my undergraduate and graduate administrative law classes, who, over the years, have made valuable constructive criticisms. For the first, second, and third editions of the book, valuable research assistance was provided by many loyal and dedicated people. I have already thanked them by name in those previous editions. For this fourth edition, I want to thank the following people for their technical assistance, scholarly insights, and just plain emotional support and encouragement: David Rosenbloom, John Rohr, Rosemary O'Leary, Jay Shafritz, Missouri Supreme Court Justice Mike Wolff, administrative law judge Joe Simeone, Kevin Horrigan, Tim Bagwell, Steve Puro, Tim Lomperis, Charles Kofron, Craig Fitzpatrick, Mike Schmid, Alan Lamberg, the late George Wendel, and for his continued support before his death, one of the greatest administrative law scholars, Bernard Schwartz. In particular, I want to single out and thank Phyllis Forchee, my secretary, for her dedicated efforts in typing this lengthy manuscript and helping to put this book into its final form; John Montre, the government documents librarian at Saint Louis University, for helping me with my enormous research for this book; the cartoonists, Tom Engelhardt, John Sherffius, and Daniel Pearlmutter, whose cartoons have added needed comic relief to the serious subject of administrative law; and my editor at Westview Press, Steve Catalano, who has competently guided me through this fourth edition. Finally, I want to extend a warm thanks to my wife, Annette, for her enormous patience and sacrifice and her always loving support and encouragement.

KENNETH F. WARREN
ST. LOUIS, MISSOURI
WINTER, 2004

CHAPTER 1

Administrative Law

An Introduction

OBJECTIVES OF THIS BOOK

The first edition of this book, published in 1982, was written to fill a conspicuous void in the literature of political science, public administration, public policy, and public affairs. Up to that time no comprehensive administrative law textbook had been written by a social scientist for social science students. Fortunately, since that time a few other social scientists have written administrative law textbooks specifically geared for social science students, thus helping to fill that conspicuous void.

Before these recent administrative law publications by social scientists, virtually all comprehensive administrative law textbooks were written by law professors (for example, Kenneth C. Davis, Walter Gellhorn and Clark Byse, Bernard Schwartz, and Louis Jaffe and Nathaniel Nathanson), who are indeed scholarly legal writers yet who seldom treated in any depth the relevant public policy issues quite obviously implied by administrative law questions. This is not to suggest that these writers did not on occasion entertain important policy issues. Obviously, some of them did. Davis's *Discretionary Justice* and Gellhorn's *When Americans Complain* are two excellent examples of specialized works in which the authors transcended mere technical discussion of administrative law doctrines and searched for solutions to related and obstinate public policy problems.[1] Consequently, these particular books have been widely used and applauded by social scientists.

Even a cursory inspection of these pre-1982 administrative law texts shows that they were intended primarily for students in law school. The prose reflects the technical legal language of the authors. These authors are attempting primarily not to motivate their readers to think about vital public policy questions in our society but rather to teach students how to win administrative law cases. Why, for instance, do so many of their problem-oriented discussions end with the traditional legal casework rhetoric, What judgment or what decision? While public administration students are somewhat interested in the "What judgment?" controversies, they are more concerned with administrative law issues pertaining to important public policy questions. For example, what regulatory procedures are employed by the Nuclear Regulatory Commission (NRC), the Federal Aviation Administration (FAA), and the National Aeronautics and Space Administration (NASA) when those agencies make rules and conduct hearings? And how do these regulatory procedures affect each agency's ability to prevent, for example, another Three Mile Island accident, or another fatal plane crash, or still another tragic shuttle disaster?

In sum, the foci of the lawyer and the public administrator in regard to administrative law are quite different, and an appropriate book for students in public administration should mirror this reality and emphasize pertinent subject matter. Touching on this difference in perspective, Peter Woll asserted: "Therefore, lawyers become advocates for the government as well as for private interests. Their formal training, however, fits them better for acting as advocates of private rights than of the public interest, at least of a public interest defined separately from the rights and needs of private parties. *Administrative lawyers are formally trained in how to prevent government from acting arbitrarily against private interests, rather than in how to make a government action more effective in the public interest*" (italics mine).[2]

The basic twofold goal of this book is to provide students oriented to public administration with a comprehensive coverage of administrative law fundamentals while simultaneously linking administrative law issues to relevant, topical public policy questions. For example, in discussions of the ordermaking power of agencies, a special effort is made to place ordermaking procedures and decisions in the context of rather well-publicized and relevant current events. This is done with the hope of making the somewhat difficult and tedious administrative law doctrines and principles applicable to the real world of public administration.

Another central objective is to promote among public administration students a greater appreciation of the genuine legal obstacles that must be recognized and confronted in the handling of administrative problems. Traditionally, social scientists have not given much more than a flirtatious glance at the technical legal aspects associated with public administration. Law schools, in contrast, have been content to produce graduates with a relatively solid understanding of legal doctrines, but only a flimsy grasp of the connection between technical legal doctrines and the normative operational needs of democratic government and society. While the social scientist is typically educated to reflect in a relatively abstract manner on the problems of simultaneously achieving justice for both the individual and society, the law student is trained chiefly as a legal technician whose purpose is to use the law to argue for the singular interests of a client.[3]

Thus, social scientists tend to place administrative law in the perspective of the entire political system, allowing them to examine its role in that larger system. This is obviously the chief strength of the social science or interdisciplinary approach. However, social scientists naturally tend to express this bias in their thinking, since they have been conditioned to respect and reject certain values. As far back as the days of Confucius and Plato, students have been taught to respect the knowledge of generalists over that of experts. It is this generalist bias which has unfortunately allowed those learning public administration to stress abstract theory and de-emphasize technical knowledge. Yet before the public administrator can play ball to win in our system, he or she should learn some of the finer points of the public administration game. It is hoped that this book on administrative law will help public administration students learn and apply technical administrative law factors that must be understood and employed if the students are going to be competent future participants in the serious business of administering in the public interest.

ORGANIZATION OF THIS BOOK

The book is organized to make administrative law applicable to public policy concerns. (1) Administrative law is defined and described from the perspective of the American political system. The legal and political roles governmental agencies play in the American political system vis-à-vis the Congress, the courts, the White House, the bureaucracy, the regulated industries, other interest groups, and the American public are presented, along with public policy–making implications. This systems approach should be both helpful and encouraging to social science students because many have already been exposed to and feel comfortable with this useful approach. (2) Throughout the text public policy examples and illustrations are employed to provide added insights on how administrative law applies to making and implementing public policies. (3) Comprehensive summaries are added to reiterate the major points conveyed in each chapter, especially regarding the administrative law–public policy relationship. (4) At the end of each chapter, except for Chapter 1, a case is presented along with comments and questions. Each case will help illustrate a central point in the particular chapter, helping students to understand how administrative law disputes in the context of public policy concerns are resolved by the courts. Comments and questions are designed to provide further insights into the cases and encourage students to think critically about the reasoning for the decisions.

Although there are many ways in which the chapters and chapter sections in an administrative law book could be organized, the order selected appears to be as logical as any for the stated objectives. Chapter 1 conveys the chief goals and basic approach. Systems theory and analysis are described and the rationale for selecting this particular approach is given. Students are then introduced to the fundamental character of administrative law, its scope and distinctiveness, and its growing importance in American legal and political life.

Chapter 2 focuses on the growth of administrative power and its impact on American political life. The delegation doctrine is examined early in the chapter since the great size, power, and pervasiveness of bureaucracy today stem largely from Congress's questionable delegation of quasi-legislative and quasi-judicial powers to administrative agencies. To illustrate the practical effects of administrative power, concrete examples are given that convey the tremendous impact administrative decisions may have on virtually all participants in the system. For example, the FAA's eventual decision to ground the DC-10s and NASA's unwise decisions leading to two shuttle disasters, the explosion of the *Challenger* and the disintegration of the *Columbia,* are particularly enlightening.

Because the growth of administrative power has challenged the traditional tripartite model of democratic government, traditional democratic standards are evaluated in light of the demands placed upon modern government. Logically, the chapter concludes with a treatment of the controversial subject of regulation versus deregulation. An attempt here is made to evaluate both the pros and cons of governmental regulation.

Chapter 3's focus is the relationship between Congress and the administrative agencies, with an emphasis on attempts by Congress to keep administrators responsible. Special attention is devoted to key congressional acts designed to regulate administrative procedures. Because of its critical importance to understanding prescribed administrative action, considerable space is given to the Administrative Procedure Act (APA) and its key amendments—among them, the Freedom of Information Act, the Sunshine Act, and the Privacy Act.

To ensure responsible administrative actions, administrators must be protected from unethical and illegal influence peddling from outsiders. Chapter 4 examines the various internal and external pressures placed on administrators and their likely corruptive impact. Conflict-of-interest legislation, loyalty oaths, constitutional prohibitions, and the U.S. president's appointment and removal powers are discussed in the context of administrative law and public interest theory.

Chapter 5 deals with rulemaking, a basic administrative law topic. Rulemaking is defined and justified in this chapter. APA requirements governing formal and informal rulemaking procedures are presented and assessed, especially in terms of the act's various loopholes. Particular emphasis is placed on analyzing the democratic character of rulemaking procedures and on how certain procedural steps tend to shape public policy outputs.

Administrators have the power not only to make "laws" (rules) but also to judge the appropriateness of their rules when holding hearings and issuing orders. Ordermaking, a quasi-judicial function, is covered in Chapter 6. At the beginning of the chapter, ordermaking activities are defined and distinguished from rulemaking functions. Most of the chapter is concerned with the elements considered as part of the fair hearing process, with extensive description and analysis of the differences between administrative hearings and court trials.

Chapter 7 confronts one of the most perplexing questions in administrative law: How much administrative discretion is too much? Although both formal and informal administrative activities are examined in the chapter, most of it focuses on the use and misuse of discretion. Because discretionary actions seem to conflict with the principle of the rule of law, it is vital to stress the critical importance of this issue. Richard Pierce believes this matter to be one of the most pressing administrative law issues today.[4] Because democratic government is threatened by abuses of discretionary power, different ideas for structuring and controlling administrative discretion are evaluated.

Chapter 8 focuses on the role the courts play in evaluating the appropriateness of agency actions. First, the role of judicial review in the administrative process is presented. Next, discussions center around the reviewability and nonreviewability of agency activities. The chapter makes clear that the courts do not normally want to meddle in agency affairs. Consequently, the courts have made use of several doctrines that allow them to stay clear. Court orders and their effectiveness in forcing public officials to execute sanctioned public policies (for example, school integration) are evaluated. The chapter concludes with an assessment of the overall effectiveness of judicial review on administrative action, especially during an era of conservative judicial politics.

Chapter 9 considers some of the most intriguing administrative law questions, ones that nearly always arouse intense student interest: Can the government and/or its officers be sued and under what conditions? What political and legal distinctions are made between *governmental* and *official* immunity? What justifies the existence of the sovereign immunity doctrine? How immune is the president of the United States from tort liability suits?

In the final chapter, administrative law is placed in the perspective of social contract theory, which emphasizes questions pertaining to the rights and obligations of individuals versus those of society. Because administrative law focuses largely upon the making of administrative due process, administrative law becomes caught in the middle of the perplexing and ageless political dilemma involving efforts by a constitutional government to strike an equitable balance between societal and individual rights when formulating and administering public policies. In this context administrative due process controversies are considered, especially in terms of procedural steps taken by governmental agencies when conducting administrative searches and seizures. Administrative searches and seizures have taken on a heightened interest in the early 2000s as a result of the terrorist attacks of September 11, 2001, and the quick passage of the USA PATRIOT Act (115 Stat. 272). Considerable attention is given to the emergency, yet rather draconian, provisions of the PATRIOT Act authorizing administrative searches, seizures, and detentions that under normal times would be considered flagrantly unconstitutional.[5]

THIS BOOK'S APPROACH: SYSTEMS THEORY

To study anything in the absence of a sound theoretical framework is both difficult and foolish because a well-constructed theoretical framework provides a conceptual tool that can be used to focus on particular situations (for example, agency decisionmaking) and to help interpret specific events (for example, Federal Trade Commission [FTC] orders). Social science researchers have used theoretical frameworks, or models, to help them systematically pinpoint, order, and conceptualize what they intend to study. To state it simply, models are useful because they allow one to see at a glance what variables and relationships are being considered and examined.

Thus models help to simplify, accelerate, and refine the discovery and learning process. The study of administrative law is in crucial need of theoretical approaches, approaches that can relate administrative law to real administrative behavior. Erwin G. Krasnow, Lawrence D. Longley, and Herbert A. Terry acknowledged the need for rigorous, systematic approaches to the study of regulatory behavior (the focus of administrative law) in their book on broadcast regulation. They commented: "It is remarkable that so little effort has been devoted to the systematic understanding of broad-scale regulatory systems such as those affecting broadcasting. That is not to say that people have not attempted to understand broadcasting regulation. It is to point out that they have tended to shy away from attempts to explain it in analytic systems terms."[6] This book makes an honest attempt to go beyond the formal legal approach by developing a conceptual framework (systems model) that is quite useful in analyzing administrative law in the context of actual agency actions. A next step, not taken in this book, would be to begin the empirical testing of worthwhile hypotheses implied by the various independent-dependent relationships in the model (for example, the influence of a certain interest group over the policy decisions, as seen in the rules and orders, of a particular regulatory agency).[7]

The systems approach is popular in the social sciences for good reason. Systems theory provides the learner with probably the simplest yet most revealing analytical framework or model on how participants (frequently called actors) relate functionally to one another. The *system* is defined by researchers or writers to suit their research or descriptive needs. It may be conceptualized on the micro or macro level: One might focus research on the environment of a small-town police chief or on a nation in an international setting.

Systems analysis has the advantage of often simplifying very complex interrelationships among actors in a system. *Actors* may be perceived as individuals (a judge), agencies (the Environmental Protection Agency), interest groups (the American Medical Association), and so on. They tend to influence the behavior of the focal political actor. Despite the relative simplicity of a systems model, such a heuristic model (a heuristic is, simply, a conceptual helping device) is excellent for specifying relationships between participants, as well as indicating possible hypotheses to be tested.

The systems model's conceptual strength lies in its basic isomorphic character, that is, in its ability to reflect real-world behavior in a model. For our purposes, we can use the systems framework as an analytical tool to place the administrative system into the perspective of its environment. In particular, we can demonstrate quite well the complex role administrative agencies play in the American political system.

It should be emphasized that systems analysis is excellent for stressing the functional relationships between participants in a system. Systems theory is best suited for those who want to study not static but active and continuous behavior among systemic actors. In our case we can employ systems analysis to focus on administrative law issues in the context of real administrative agencies as they interact with their environment, which at least includes the White House, the Congress, the courts, the regulated industries, other governmental agencies, the media, and the general public.

Systems theory helps to explain how agencies struggle to survive in an always potentially hostile environment while carrying out their statutory mission of making, adjudicating, and executing public policies. Systems theory accepts and assumes one basic truth: As the English philosopher Thomas Hobbes conceived it some four hundred years ago, the first instinct of any actor (our example is an administrative agency) is to survive. This maxim cannot be overemphasized. Systems analysis would have no analytical starting point without it. For centuries political theorists and sociologists have acknowledged that this fundamental instinct exists in all individuals and organizations. Self-preservation is something, then, that all administrative agencies seek, and it is impossible to understand their role in the political system without recognizing this reality.[8] For example, as explained in Chapter 11, the reaction, or possibly the overreaction, of the United States to the terrorist attacks of "9/11" is rooted in our country's basic instinct to survive in the world's always potentially hostile political system.

David Easton, who developed the systems model for political scientists, stresses that survival, or *system persistence,* is actually linked to whether the focal actor or actors (again, the example is an administrative agency) can continue to authoritatively allocate values—in this case, policy decisions or outputs. It is important to understand what Easton means by the "authoritative allocation of values." He believes that if an agency has real power within its environment, it must have the ability to force its policies (values) on others. This is really a description of power, and one must have power to survive.[9] Thus, if the FAA, for example, made policy decisions, but not authoritatively, it would presumably perish, since the allocated policies would carry no significant weight and thus would not be obeyed.

The major structural and functional features of the systems model are sketched in Figure 1.1. Basically, the conceptual design illustrates continuous reactions that must take place in a focal actor's environment if that actor is to survive as an authoritative force in the system. The actor must react properly to environmental *feedback,* which is expressed in terms of *demands* and *supports.* In systems theory, *reacting properly* to environmental stimuli (inputs) essentially means acting in a way that is consistent with furthering the actor's chances of survival. Appropriate reaction may not necessarily consist of maximizing supports, since it is not always necessary for the focal actor to have maximum support to survive. However, proper reaction does consist of action that must be committed to avoid *demand overload.* Demand overload can be conceptualized simply as a red alert situation in which the focal actor must respond immediately and appropriately to reduce the dangerous demands or, if the response is inadequate, face devastation. For example President Richard Nixon noted in his resignation speech that he was resigning because he had lost a sufficient basis of support. Nixon's description of why he felt he had to resign closely captures the essence of systems theory. Indeed, in light of the demands placed upon him by the Watergate affair, Nixon failed to respond adequately to this demand overload situation. This failure still further eroded the environmental supports he needed to survive. Finally, Nixon had no alternative but to resign because he had lost the environmental supports that were absolutely essential to sustain his survival as president. In specific systems terms, he had to step down because he could no longer authoritatively allocate values (make respected public policy decisions) in the absence of sufficient and sustaining environmental supports for his leadership. In contrast, President Bill Clinton, faced with impeachment in 1998–1999 over the Monica Lewinsky scandal, decided not to resign, because, although the Republican leadership and other groups were pressing for his resignation, his party's leadership, other groups, and his very positive job approval ratings in public opinion polls offset the demands, giving him enough support to survive.[10]

The merit of systems theory for the study of administrative law cannot be overemphasized. Administrative law involves essentially the study of the legally sanctioned procedural activities of administrative agencies as they interact with their environment. But administrative law cannot be fully appreciated and understood if it is studied only in the context of formal organizational theory—that is, in the context of how administrative organizations ought to perform in the system. Systems theory makes possible the examination of formal administrative law prescriptions in the context of actual behavior in real organizations. Every organization has what is referred to as a *natural system,* which consists of basic survival goals that often depart quite radically from the formal system's prescribed goals (for example, regulating plane safety). A major reason people often cannot comprehend why a certain decision was made is that they try to understand the decision from an unrealistically limited perspective. They tend to exclude factors that are not rational in terms of the organization's formal objectives yet nevertheless contribute rationally to the organization's ability to cope successfully with its environment.[11] Thus, administrative procedure cannot be studied realistically from the narrow perspective of what administrative law would dictate. It must instead be viewed from the perspective of the total demands placed on administrative agencies by a complex and active environment.

Simply put, agency administrators cannot respond only to what administrative law demands because they must respond to other environmental demands as well. After reading an administrative law case, a student in class will often ask me why the administrator so blatantly violated the law. My typical response is that the administrator was probably aware of what administrative law required but chose to yield to what he or she perceived as a greater pressure. Students must never ignore or underestimate the role politics can play in agency decisionmaking.

Figure 1.2 expands on Figure 1.1, applying the systems model directly to the special focus in this book—the interactions involved and interdependence between administrators within public agencies and their unique environments. The model in Figure 1.2 should still be considered a general framework because it is more useful for illustrating the systems picture for a typical administrative agency than for achieving an understanding of the specific interactions within the system of a particular agency. Figure 1.3, which depicts the unique environment of the Federal Communications Commission (FCC), is presented to show how the general systems model can be easily adapted so that the focus can be shifted readily from the general administrative system to a specific agency.

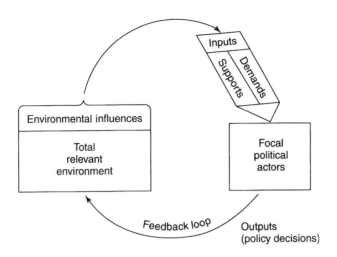

FIGURE 1.1   A General Systems Model.

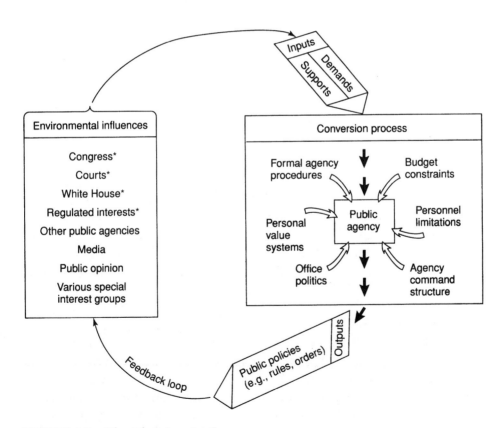

FIGURE 1.2   The Administrative System.
Note: Asterisks denote significant influence.

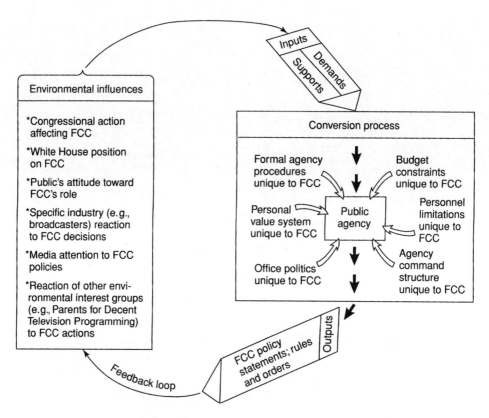

FIGURE 1.3 The Federal Communication Commission's Administrative Environment.
Note: Asterisks denote significant influence.

Figures 1.2 and 1.3 convey quickly and vividly that administrative decision-making must be viewed within the context of an agency's environment. Actually, two environments should be considered—the outer and the inner. Both environments tend to influence administrators as they formulate agency decisions.

Whether making internal procedural rules or major public policy statements, all prudent agency decisionmakers must acknowledge and respond to common outer environmental inputs (demands and supports). In the typical agency's environment, these inputs would include such major political actors as (1) Congress, (2) the courts, (3) the White House, (4) the regulated, (5) other governmental agencies, (6) the media, and (7) the public. Each of these powerful forces in the environment presents a potential threat to the survival, continued success, or at least good health of any public agency. Therefore, their messages (inputs) cannot be taken lightly or ignored. Successful agency administrators have learned to make decisions that are at least minimally acceptable to their environments. In this vein, then, it should be apparent by now that administrative law dictates constitute only one environmental demand that administrators should consider when reaching decisions. Thus, an administrative decision that complies with what legal formalism may require but is otherwise environmentally unacceptable should probably be regarded as a poor or impractical decision—a decision that would likely be ineffective when implemented.

Although not indicated in Figure 1.1, the inner environments of agency officials shown in Figures 1.2 and 1.3 also play a crucial role in shaping agency decisions. Ira Sharkansky, who has led the way in the effort to apply systems analysis to the public administration field, refers to these inner environmental factors as *with inputs* because they represent inputs into the decisionmaking process that occur "within" the agency itself during the "conversion process."[12] During the conversion process the demands and supports from the environment are transformed (converted) into outputs. These outputs represent decisions reflecting agency responses to the inputs from the outer environment and from the inner environment (with inputs) as well. That is, administrators cannot ignore realistically the inputs stemming from inside the agency itself. Internal agency stimuli typically consist of such influential forces as internal agency rules and regulations, office politics, the chain-of-command network, budgetary constraints, staff competencies, employee morale and attitudes, and the like.

It should be emphasized that the heuristic models shown are simply conceptual tools for helping an analyst to envision in a more accurate and sophisticated manner administrative agencies as they interact in a complex systems network. Any environmental force, even some forces not represented in the models, could play a key role in swaying agency decisions—for example, a major international incident. However, it makes sense to draw parameters around the causal variables so as to include only those factors that the relevant social science and administrative law literature suggests as most likely to describe agency interactions under normal systemic circumstances.[13]

It should also be noted that legal influences are not given separate, categorical status in the models. This might appear odd for a book that focuses primarily on questions pertaining to the legal relationship between administrative agencies and their environments. But there is a logical reason. Administrative agencies have only implicit constitutional status at best. While the legislative, executive, and judicial branches each have clear constitutional sanctioning as specified in Articles I, II, and III, respectively, of the U.S. Constitution, no article addresses what is perceived commonly as the fourth branch of government—the federal bureaucracy. Consequently, the legal demands and supports that tend to influence agency actions are represented in the other environmental forces indicated in the models. Of course, most of the legal parameters that tend to restrict agency behavior are imposed rather formally on agencies by Congress and the courts at the federal level. On the state level, the legislatures and the courts would restrict state agencies in a similar manner. However, the way public agencies read and actually respond to the formal legal dictates depends largely on the important signals (feedback) from other actors in an agency's environment. For instance, public opinion and media may be quite influential on a more informal level in determining agency attitudes toward how the legal mandates from the more formal institutional authorities should actually be interpreted and applied in our society.

ADMINISTRATIVE
AGENCIES PLAY THE LEAD ROLES

To obtain a realistic and insightful understanding of administrative law in the United States, it is necessary to develop an appreciation for how the American administrative system actually functions. Accordingly, a few crucial elementary questions about public agencies should be addressed, including: (1) Who are our public administrators? (2) Where do they work? (3) What do they do? (4) How do they do it? (5) What overall role do they play in our political system?

Who Are Our Public Administrators?

In many respects public administrators, at least collectively, constitute the most powerful class of workers in the United States. According to the Bureau of Labor Statistics, by the early 2000s, those working in what are regarded as traditional governmental agencies numbered just under 19 million, a sizable percentage of our entire civilian work force of about 141 million. Public administrators, especially those near the top of their respective agencies, are in reality responsible for making major policy decisions and spending most of our tax dollars, despite the fact that very few public administrators are elected. Only the president and the vice president are elected on the national level, although many more administrators are elected at the state and local levels (for example, governors, mayors, attorneys general, treasurers, auditors, sheriffs). Still, compared to the many millions of civil servants in the U.S. public bureaucracy, only a very tiny fraction of public offices are elected. Because many of these nonelected public administrators possess vast policymaking powers, many people believe that these administrators pose a potential threat to traditional democratic governmental processes in this country.

It is very difficult to generalize about the character of public servants, since their functions and backgrounds are so varied. Nearly all public servants have their occupational counterparts in private enterprise. While this was certainly not true during the nineteenth century, expanded governmental activities during the twentieth century have compelled government to employ those from all career areas ranging from such professionals as doctors, lawyers, scientists, and professors, who normally handle highly sophisticated tasks, to those needed to perform clerical and janitorial functions that may require limited talents and very little prior training. Those public servants at low employee classification levels have normally not been perceived as public administrators; yet many of them—like administrative assistants, clerks, and policemen—in fact exercise significant discretionary powers and should rightfully be viewed as part of the administrative corps, especially since they must follow certain administrative procedures as prescribed in statutes and court decisions.

Looking at job classifications and job descriptions today, one would find it challenging to discover a measurable difference between public and private bureaucracy. Only the goals that each seeks appear to be strikingly different. Generally speaking, public administrators seek to promote the public welfare by providing needed goods and services, but not necessarily or usually at a profit. Unlike private businesses, which seek to maximize profits, governmental agencies are frequently obligated because of an environmental demand to provide vital goods and services at a loss. Those administrators in the business world who criticize their public counterparts for being inefficient in handling programs often fail to realize that public administrators must administer many programs that businesses dropped because they could not operate them at a profit; the inner-city transportation services of most municipalities serve as an example.

In sum, administrators in the private and public sectors are more similar in job functions than might be expected. In many cases they have even had the same basic college preparation, although some may have placed more emphasis on one area of expertise than another. This is becoming more true because of the recent and continuing popularity of programs for the master of business administration (MBA) and the master of public administration (MPA), which often are quite similar in content, although the former is geared more toward private than public management. Commonly, because of the interdisciplinary nature of these degree programs, some even leading to joint MBA-MPA degrees, students are required to complete the same core courses (for example, organizational theory and behavior; micro- and macroeconomics) in order to satisfy the degree requirements. MBA and MPA students, those most likely to be our future leaders in private and public administration, also may focus on the same advanced areas; public finance, accounting, administrative law, labor-management relations, and management information systems are common examples. Of course, many who emerge as administrators in private and public enterprise are engineers, scientists, or others who have had little to no formal administrative training.

Private and public organizations also face common problems as they struggle to survive when interacting with their environments. There are many examples of managerial successes and failures in both sectors. Critics may find examples of poorly administered public programs (the General Accounting Office [GAO] finds several every year), but the managerial blunders that led both Lockheed and Chrysler to the brink of bankruptcy (avoided only by life-sustaining governmental loans) and, more recently, the scandals and financial collapse of such giant corporations as Enron, Worldcom, and Arthur Andersen, as well as the bankruptcies at several airlines, do not speak well for administrative efficiency in the private sector, either. Thus, we can put to rest the old yet unsubstantiated generalization that private businesses are run more efficiently than public organizations. In short, for at least the reasons noted, it is important not to put unrealistic stress on the differences between private and public administrators because of the common bonds they share in regard to administrative structure, operations, personnel, and efforts to achieve functional efficiency.

As within the American business community, those who are employed by public agencies come from all segments of society. However, evidence indicates that public agencies are actually more representative of the American people (i.e., by reflecting a more representative cross section of the diverse socioeconomic classes in America) than are business organizations or the legislative, executive, or judicial branches on the national level. Despite fair employment practices legislation that should have forced notable American businesses to open their doors to all persons, according to the 2002 *Statistical Abstract of the United States*, public sector jobs are still more open to women and minorities, especially the latter, than private sector jobs.[14] Statistics show that women and minorities stand a better chance of being hired and promoted to responsible positions in public agencies, especially at the federal level, than in private enterprise. But as Frederick C. Mosher notes, white males are still found in greater numbers in public bureaucracy and in the better positions: "There can be no doubt that there are wide statistical disparities in the employment of white males as compared with females and with blacks, Hispanics, and other minorities."[15] According to a recent U.S. General Accounting Office study, the status of women in public administration, especially management positions, has improved enormously in the past few decades. GAO reports that the percentage of women in management positions in public administration in 2000 was almost identical to that of men, with men leading by only 1.1 percent—45.1 percent to 44 percent—while women trailed men by significant percentages in most private sector employment areas (e.g., educational services, retail trade, finance, insurance, real estate, hospital and medical services).[16]

Where Do Our Public Administrators Work?

Our public administrators work in a great variety of administrative agencies. Public agencies vary in size, location, complexity of functions, and goals. Most public administrators, as common sense would dictate, are probably in agencies that reflect their particular skills, especially since the agencies have been created to handle a specific area of concern in society, such as housing, transportation, energy, or health. Thus, one would expect to find administrators with training and experience in housing matters in the U.S. Department of Housing and Urban Development (HUD), while one would expect to find a disproportionate number of energy experts working in the U.S. Department of Energy (DOE).

Especially important to the focus of this book, public agencies also vary according to their prescribed statutory status in the administrative system. An agency's defined legal status plays a major role in determining the extent of political power the agency can probably wield as it interacts with other political actors in its environment. Essentially, there are three basic types of public agencies, although their legal distinctions are commonly blurred: (1) independent regulatory agencies, (2) quasi-independent regulatory agencies, and (3) executive (cabinet) departments. After a consideration of these three agency types comes a brief discussion of other forms of public agencies in the public administrative network in which quasi-public administrators (those administrators who may be in technically private organizations but work for government in some capacity) are commonly found.

Independent Regulatory Commissions.   Although interest group theorists present credible arguments for the position that no truly independent governmental agencies exist, there are nevertheless in the U.S. administrative system public agencies commonly known as independent regulatory commissions or boards. These commissions perform powerful regulatory functions in American society, yet they exist outside the executive departments and beyond the president's jurisdiction. Congress has given commissioners in these agencies great quasi-legislative and quasi-judicial powers. They are supposed to employ these powers to create rules and orders deemed necessary to regulate specific industries. They have also been granted limited powers to determine whether the regulated have complied with the rules and orders and to punish violators, usually through fine, revocation of licenses, refusal to renew permits, and so on. Because the actions (rules, orders, and penalties) of these commissioners may result in the loss of, say, the right to operate a business, those caught in the regulatory embrace of independent regulatory commissions frequently perceive their power to be awesome. The first independent regulatory commission, the Interstate Commerce Commission, was established in 1887, about one hundred years after the founding of our republic. Other such agencies were created later, including the Federal Trade Commission (FTC), Federal Power Commission (FPC), Securities and Exchange Commission (SEC), Federal Communications Commission (FCC), National Labor Relations Board (NLRB), Federal Reserve Board (the Fed), Federal Maritime Commission, and Consumer Product Safety Commission.[17]

Actually, these independent regulatory agencies were created in response to the feedback from the environment, which placed imposing demands on Congress to create bodies of administrative experts able to deal with the varied and complex problems that plagued modern technological society. As the decades passed, it became obvious that Congress no longer had the time, patience, or special talents to regulate all of the vital activities necessary to preserve social order and prosperity in American society. Nor did the courts have the capability to settle all of the disputes between parties and agencies that emerged inevitably as a natural consequence of public policy implementation efforts.

To prevent politics from interfering with the legislative and judicial judgments of these administrative experts, Congress, when it created these agencies, took certain structural and procedural precautionary measures to help protect them from outside contaminative and disruptive political pressures. All independent regulatory commissions are multiheaded and usually consist of five to seven members, although there are exceptions to this general rule. All independent regulatory commissioners are appointed by the president with the consent of the Senate, but they cannot be removed except for *cause* (malfeasance, misfeasance, or nonfeasance). To help insulate commissioners from inappropriate White House meddling into their business affairs, the courts have ruled against presidents who have tried, without proper cause, to remove such commissioners. Political reasons are inadequate grounds for removal.

To further add to their structural independence, the president must appoint these commissioners to fixed terms that are staggered to prevent any single president from appointing too many people to the commissions. One further check—the rule that no more than a simple majority of a commission may consist of members of the same political party—has kept presidents from stacking independent commissions with appointments in their favor. The role partisan politics can play in commission decisionmaking is thus minimized.

But such independence from viable political controls has caused many critics to refer to this independent regulatory commission system as the headless fourth branch of government, and critics feel that such structure makes centralized administrative planning and coordination of policy virtually impossible.[18] Systems theory would suggest that, although the independent commissions are not immune from external environmental pressures, external influences could, nevertheless, be minimized by their particular structural arrangement. Independent regulatory commissions are never so independent, as the systems model implicitly conveys, as to be free from budgetary controls placed on them by the president and Congress, by public disclosures of their performance, by verbal reprimands from governmental and civic leaders, by congressional investigations, and by other systemic demands to which they must respond. For example, because of the wide publicity given to General Accounting Office reports (the GAO is the investigatory arm of Congress), critical GAO reports can be quite damaging to the image of any independent regulatory commission, thus tending to destroy any illusion independent regulatory commissioners may have of their actual independence from environmental forces.

Quasi-independent Regulatory Agencies.   Many writers who focus on administrative structure make no distinction between independent and quasi-independent regulatory agencies, especially since no distinction is made formally in the *U.S. Government Manual.* However, a practical distinction, important for students of administrative law, does exist. The first independent regulatory commission, the Interstate Commerce Commission, established in 1887, best exemplified the purest independent regulatory agency. The ICC (terminated on December 31, 1995) was structurally independent, not even attached to the Department of Commerce, and it was also rather well protected from outside interference by statute. But not all so-called independent regulatory agencies and commissions are so structurally or statutorily independent; thus their independent status is somewhat compromised. For example, the Federal Aviation Agency (FAA) was created as an independent regulatory commission to promote the airline industry and regulate air safety. Yet a number of experts believe that the FAA's regulatory independence is compromised somewhat because it is housed in the Department of Transportation (DOT) and is therefore under DOT's sphere of influence. Other agencies, such as the Environmental Protection Agency (EPA) and the Food and Drug Administration (FDA), were created as independent agencies with vast adjudicative powers, as is typical for the model independent regulatory commission. However, the EPA and FDA, like several other agencies, find that their regulatory independence is more imagined than real since Congress saw fit to place them within the executive branch: Their leaders are not protected by statute from removal by the president. Nevertheless, the courts have slammed the door shut on presidents who have tried to meddle with administrative officials who perform quasi-judicial functions in such agencies, regardless of whether they are specifically protected by statute from presidential intrusion (*Wiener v. United States,* 357 U.S. 349; 1958).

Executive Departments.   According to some public administration scholars, it is frequently very difficult to separate a quasi-independent regulatory agency's operational status from that of a regular executive department's, although executive departments are generally regarded as more prestigious, possibly because they have Cabinet status. However, presidential supervision over our nation's fifteen executive departments tends to make them considerably less independent than either independent regulatory commissions or quasi-independent regulatory commissions.[19]

Essentially, cabinet departments (such executive departments as the Department of Defense, Department of Transportation, Department of Health and Human Services (HHS), and the newly created Department of Homeland Security) have been created as administrative agencies to assist the president in refining and implementing public policies enacted by Congress. Thus, the Department of Homeland Security was created to help implement the goals of the USA PATRIOT Act of 2001. In contrast, independent and quasi-independent regulatory agencies play a more traditional regulatory role, thereby relying more heavily upon the standard regulatory tools of rulemaking and ordermaking. Since administrative law students have focused primarily on procedural due process procedures in agency rulemaking and ordermaking, less attention has generally been given to cabinet departments than to those agencies that are more regulatory than administrative in function and purpose. Nonetheless, administrative law pervades all governmental agencies, even those agencies or offices, such as police departments and the White House, once considered beyond the proper scope of administrative law.[20]

Other Public Agencies.   In addition to working in independent regulatory agencies and executive departments at the federal or state levels, public administrators are also found in other governmental offices, government-supported corporations, and private agencies and corporations working under government contract.

Other governmental offices range from relatively well known and important ones, such as the Small Business Administration and the National Science Foundation, to obscure and relatively inconsequential ones (for example, the American Battle Monuments Commission and the Renegotiation Board). These agencies, commissions, and boards were created as a response to special and narrow demands placed on government, and they normally function with very limited staffs and budgets, especially as compared to such giant government agencies as the HHS.

The Federal Crop Insurance Corporation, Federal National Mortgage Association, Tennessee Valley Authority, Smithsonian Institution, U.S. Postal Service, and

National Railroad Passenger Corporation (Amtrak) are examples of federal government corporations that are totally or partially owned by government and yet sell goods and services (mail delivery, electric power, bank deposit insurance, transportation) much like private businesses. Government corporations also exist at the state level, where they are frequently called authorities. These authorities must often operate turnpikes, harbors, and airports.

Before 1945 government corporations possessed a great deal of independence and flexibility and functioned practically like any business. However, increasing concern during the 1930s about the unaccountable democratic character of such corporations as the Tennessee Valley Authority (TVA) led to the passage in 1945 of the Government Corporation Control Act. Essentially, this act gives government corporations policy direction and fiscal control. Specifically, the act subjects these agencies to the usual congressional investigations and budgetary checks, such as audits, and to civil service statutes. For administrative purposes, some of these corporations are attached loosely to major departments, and their governing boards are staffed by persons appointed by the president.

The government corporations that provide goods and services at both the federal and state levels frequently cannot break even at the relatively low rates they charge (rates that private businesses, incidentally, would regard as too low to make a healthy profit). But because the goods and services provided are considered by the government to be vital to the promotion of the public welfare, they are usually supported in part by governmental subsidies. The challenge that government corporations present is to find the correct balance between granting these corporations the flexibility necessary for quick and wise business decisions in a rapidly changing environment and maintaining safeguards essential to preserving their democratically responsible character.

Such institutions as Gallaudet College, Howard University, and the American Printing House for the Blind are regarded as federally aided corporations. They function as private institutions, their boards of directors and personnel operating free from governmental intervention. However, because they are funded by tax dollars, they must be considered quasi-public agencies that must comply with numerous procedural due process restrictions required of more traditional governmental agencies. Thus, they are legitimately within the jurisdiction of administrative law, although admittedly on the fringe.

It is difficult today to judge just which organizations are beyond the scope of administrative law. The role of government expands as increasing demands are placed on it; with that role grows government pervasiveness. It appears that there are few, if any, sizable organizations left in America today that do not have to comply with required governmental procedures of some kind; equal opportunity employment requirements are frequently cited examples. Actually, some scholars argue that most of us today work for government, at least indirectly. Should those of us who work for private corporations, universities, and the like consider ourselves quasi-governmental employees? Maybe not, but the fact is that Harvard University, IBM, McDonnell Douglas, General Motors, and other such organizations must enter into certain quid pro quo agreements with government as a condition for receiving governmental contracts, grants, loans, and subsidies. Ideally, the arrangements are mutually beneficial. While the government obtains such necessary supplementary goods and services as airplanes, scientific information, transportation service, and trained future leaders, the private organizations benefit financially and in many cases receive the added benefit of prestige. Nevertheless, the bottom line is that to do business with government, these private enterprises must play by government's rules, many of which entail following elaborate procedures related to fair employment practices, work safety, use of human subjects in research, and so on. Completing compliance and various data forms to demonstrate that proper procedures are in fact being followed normally occupies a great deal of time, so much time that some administrators have seriously questioned whether playing ball with government is really worth it.

The purpose of this discussion has been to familiarize the reader with the various types of public and quasi-public administrative agencies that fall within the legitimate purview of administrative law. For the most part, however, this book will be concerned with administrators in this immense administrative system who work in the independent regulatory agencies, quasi-independent regulatory agencies, and cabinet departments. In our political system these administrators interact most with each other and the other branches of government. They also attract by far the most attention from interest groups in the administrative system's environment because these public administrators are responsible for making important policy decisions of major consequence for those affected.

What Do Our Public Administrators Do?

It is clear that if one broadly classifies as public administrators all civil servants who function as administrators (or employ administrative discretion) at least part of the time, then public administrators perform a vast array of job tasks in providing goods and services for the public. Even so, and despite the apparent similarities in employee character and structural bureaucratic features between private and public employment, for various reasons the American people do not feel that governmental employees, including public administrators, do very much. A Gallup poll once showed that 67 percent of those surveyed thought that public employees work less than those in private enterprise.[21] The pollsters also found that the public believes that civil servants not only have easier times on the job but also do so for more pay (the opinion of 64 percent) and better fringe benefits (the opinion of 77 percent).[22] Consequently, George Gallup concluded that the "federal government civilian employees—the well-known 'Washington bureaucracy'—has a giant public relations problem."[23] Despite these perceptions by the public, however, it is virtually impossible, because of the mass of intervening variables, to compare productivity accurately between "sister" industries, let alone between the public and private sector. But it is worth noting, in fairness to our public employees, that Robert Townsend, a business-efficiency expert and former president of Avis Rent-a-Car, claimed in his two books, *Up the Organization* and *Further Up the Organization*, that people in business are lazy, working at only 50 percent of their capacity, and tend to check their brains at their company's gate.[24]

Governmental administrators in general are paid to regulate. Virtually all of their job tasks relate to reaching regulatory goals assigned to them by Congress and expected of them by the general public. Despite the Gallup finding that Americans believe government is too big (67 percent of those polled held that "government employs too many people"),[25] U.S. citizens keep on asking for more to be done—and spent—in the areas of defense, education, health care, and crime prevention.[26]

Regulatory activities are designed, ideally, to aid in the promotion of the general welfare or public interest—concepts that have always eluded precise definition. Nevertheless, Congress has created virtually every department, agency, commission, board, and so on and assigned their administrators the task of performing their regulatory mandate in a manner consistent with the public interest. As the systems model demonstrates, increasing demands have caused the regulatory governmental umbrella to expand rapidly to the point where public administrators today are regulating practically all functions believed linked to the maintenance of social health and stability—energy, environment, transportation, commerce, and consumerism are some of the major examples. The English philosopher John Locke's notion of limited government was incorporated into the U.S. Constitution, but it seems to have vanished from practice long ago, replaced by the idea of the welfare state.

Essentially, public administrators regulate to protect American society from market defects and failures. Public administrators are concerned especially with preventing people from being exploited by private interests. In every society, there are those who do not mind tyrannizing and abusing others while they seek what James Madison believed every free country should permit and nurture—the right of all parties to pursue their selfish interests as long as they do not seriously jeopardize the same rights of others. Stephen G. Breyer and Richard B. Stewart believe that public administrators in their regulatory role particularly aim at (1) controlling monopoly power; (2) preventing windfall profits; (3) correcting spillover costs; (4) promoting the release of essential public or consumer information; (5) eliminating excessive, destructive, and unhealthy competition in some areas; (6) alleviating and distributing scarce resources, especially in times of crisis; and (7) regulating in other areas where the political leaders believe public administrators need to act in a parental capacity (for example, occupational and personal safety and collective bargaining).[27]

The question asked in this section's title—What do our public administrators do?—has been answered here only in very general terms (they regulate vital socioeconomic activities). The question can best be answered by examining the specific procedures public administrators employ while trying to obtain specific agency goals.

How Do Our Public Administrators Regulate?

Our public administrators employ a variety of methods to regulate, but most regulatory approaches can be classified into four general modes. Which of the basic regulatory methods is selected by administrators, or originally by Congress, depends largely on the type of activity being regulated (for example, supply of electrical power) and the specific sort of regulatory problem that needs to be addressed (for example, monopolistic or near-monopolistic dominance of a market).

The four commonly used regulatory practices are (1) licensing and granting permissions, (2) rate setting and price controls, (3) establishing and enforcing public interest standards, and (4) punishing. Naturally, most regulatory agencies use these procedures eclectically, but public administrators tend to emphasize only those regulatory techniques best suited for the type of industry that they are entrusted with regulating. Thus, because the Federal Communications Act of 1934 created the FCC to control interstate and foreign communications, mostly connected to radio, television, telephone, and telegraph communications (the Communications Satellite Act of 1962 expanded the FCC's responsibilities), the FCC commissioners have relied primarily upon the licensing method to control the communications industry. Ideally, the commissioners grant and renew licenses only to those applicants who demonstrate that they can provide, or have in the past provided, communication services in the public interest. Since the FCC cannot regulate rates that, say, television and radio stations charge their sponsors, the licensing approach is about the only viable method FCC commissioners can employ to regulate the quality of programs aired.

The idea that public administrators should be delegated the responsibility for regulating economic activities in society and should be given the necessary regulatory tools to do their jobs effectively is hardly a new one. Governments throughout history have always regulated economic activities to some extent. For example, governing authorities in ancient Egypt regulated the economic activities of the complex canal system, and during the Roman Empire the state's administrators were entrusted with regulating diverse economic activities. In 1887 the Interstate Commerce Commission, the first independent regulatory commission in the United States, was established for the general purpose of regulating interstate commerce, particularly that via the railroads—even more specifically the apparent rip-off short-haul rates charged to some farmers. These rates were criticized widely at the time by public interest groups and civic leaders as contrary to the best interests of American society. To grant public administrators the authority to establish fair rates in various industries has since become a very common practice aimed at promoting the public good.

Agency administrators have always had the regulatory authority to try to control socioeconomic activities through the practice of simply establishing compulsory standards and voluntary guidelines believed to be in the public interest. Through legislative mandates, Congress has given public agencies the power to be flexible in their particular regulatory spheres in setting standards through rules and orders to protect and promote the public interest.

Finally, public administrators have always been able to regulate through threatening or actually using the punitive measures that Congress has given them. Congress has allowed administrators to enforce their regulatory policies by permitting them, for example, to impose fines on violators or to suspend or revoke licenses permanently. Sometimes the penalties may be quite stiff if serious violations have occurred. For example, on April 28, 2003, the Securities and Exchange Commission banned two securities analysts from practicing their trade for life, while fining top Wall Street brokerage firms $1.4 billion for fraudulent business practices, especially for "issuing overly positive research" on companies or stocks to intentionally deceive investors.[28]

THE NATURE OF ADMINISTRATIVE LAW

Perspectives on Administrative Law

Since the study of administrative law involves the probing of many challenging concepts, it is ironic that one of the most difficult concepts to understand definitively is administrative law itself. One reason for the conceptual vagueness of administrative law stems from the fact that the administrative law field is still in its maturation years and is desperately trying to cut the cord from the more traditional areas of the law (constitutional, contract, tort, criminal) from which it emerged. Although it appears that most legal scholars today recognize administrative law as a fast-growing, independent legal field,[29] some still refuse to perceive it as separate from other legal fields, thus stirring mud in its definitional waters. For instance, Nathaniel Nathanson once wrote in an *Administrative Law Review* article: "I often tell my students that administrative law is nothing but a mixture of constitutional law and statutory construction, seasoned, I hope, with liberal sprinklings of common sense or sophisticated in the ways of government."[30] However, although written a few decades ago, this glib perception of administrative law not only does a disservice to its development as a separate field but is also a patently false and unfair view. In fact, not only do all developed legal areas overlap somewhat (can we separate completely criminal law from constitutional law?), but administrative law itself is a much richer and more unusual blend of various other legal fields than Nathanson acknowledges.

The term *administrative law*, like many other conceptual words—such as *love, power, justice,* and *democracy*—is a lot easier to describe than to define. Definitions have been attempted, but they always seem to lack something. Also, because the definitions are frequently so different, they sometimes only confuse the reader. For example, administrative law is defined in *Daniel Oran's Law Dictionary* as "1. Laws about the duties and proper running of an administrative agency that are handed to agencies by legislatures and courts. 2. Rules and regulations set out by administrative agencies." In the old standby, *Black's Law Dictionary,* administrative law is defined as the "body of law created by administrative agencies to implement their powers and duties in the form of rules, regulations, orders, and decisions." To Stephen G. Breyer and Richard B. Stewart, administrative law "consists of those legal principles that define the authority and structure of administrative agencies, specify the procedural formalities that agencies use, determine the validity of administrative decisions, and outline the role of reviewing courts and other organs of government in their relation to administrative agencies." One of the twentieth century's most renowned administrative law scholars, Kenneth Culp Davis, defines it as "the law concerning the powers and procedures of administrative agencies, including especially the law governing judicial review of administrative action."[31]

Together, these definitions provide some clues as to what administrative law entails. But in truth these definitions seem to raise more questions than they answer, because each definition employs words, phrases, and concepts—public law, sovereign power, administrative agencies, rules and regulations, judicial review, and so forth—that are also vague in meaning. The real role played by administrative law in our governmental system is only implied. Thus, because of acute definitional problems, it seems wiser to try to describe administrative law and its related concepts in the context of administrative law history and its modern role vis-à-vis administrative agencies, the legislatures, the courts, the White House, and outside parties.

Broadly speaking, administrative law deals with (1) how power is transferred from legislative bodies to administrative agencies, (2) how administrative agencies use power, and (3) how the actions taken by administrative agencies are reviewed by the courts. More specifically, administrative law is concerned with the legal developments that have so dramatically increased the powers and scope of the administrative branch. The law-making (technically, quasi-legislative or rulemaking) and judicial (technically, quasi-judicial or ordermaking) powers that have been delegated to administrators by the legislative branch at both the national and state levels have created an extremely powerful administrative branch, thus changing the meaning we have traditionally attributed to the separation of powers doctrine. As a result, students of administrative law have been particularly concerned over the significance of this change in the balance of power within our traditional tripartite governmental structure, especially since such alterations necessitate new interpretations of what we mean by "rule of law," "liberty," and "democracy." Consequently, administrative law scholars in recent decades have devoted much attention to evaluating the impact of the growth of administrative power on democratic society. Considerable time has been spent on seeking new and effective measures for controlling and checking the activities of administrative officials so that the public interest can be better protected. Since the 1930s, courts have been very active in reviewing agency actions and watching out for administrative abuses, although the conservative federal courts of the past two decades, led by the U.S. Supreme Court under Chief Justice William Rehnquist, have been more inclined to defer broadly to agency expertise and discretion than the more liberal federal courts of the 1960s and 1970s, encouraging, according to some critics, an increase in administrative abuses. This charge is covered at length in later chapters.

The Scope of Administrative Law

Although the scope of administrative law is impossible to determine, especially at this time in its youthful development, it is apparent that administrative law is broadly concerned with the role and power relationships of administrative agencies in society, or simply, the ways in which administrative agencies use their power in implementing public policies. One can thus expect almost all critical issues in administrative law to center ultimately on questions of power politics, which are vitally important to the character of any democratic political system. Sallyanne Payton, acknowledging that administrative law is inherently a political subject concerned primarily with procedure, puts it this way: "Procedures are power; they may assist or hinder the agencies in accomplishing their missions, may force agencies to redefine their missions or their constituencies, may provide visibility into decision-making processes and thus facilitate political accountability, and so on. . . . Preferences for one type of decision maker or process over another are at the base of political preferences."[32] More generally, Marshall Breger notes that "administrative law today deals with central issues in our political landscape. The enlarged curriculum can only spark the interest of its practitioners and scholars."[33]

The following is a relatively long list of vital administrative law questions reflecting power considerations that should provide more insights into the scope and nature of administrative law: (1) How much power should be delegated to administrative agencies? (2) How much administrative discretion is too much? (3) Does the doctrine of sovereign immunity extend too much power to governmental agencies? (4) What constitutes "arbitrary and capricious" agency decisions? (5) What are the components of a "fair hearing"? (6) How can administrative officials administer needed public policies without infringing on the rights of individuals? (7) How does an extreme interpretation of "executive privilege" square with the "rule of law," "popular sovereignty," "limited government," "separation of powers," and other notions of popular government? (8) How much "official immunity" should be extended to governmental administrators? (9) Under what circumstances should the "burden of proof" be placed on persons coming before administrative agencies? (10) How free can a country remain if administrative agencies are permitted to make laws, administer them, and decide on the appropriateness and fairness of their own laws? (11) Are administrative agencies becoming oppressive of and threatening to our freedom? (12) Is procedural due process less important than substantive law? (13) How can administrative abuses be effectively checked? (14) What internal and external safeguards can be developed to keep public administrators in line? (15) What role should the courts play in the review of agency decisions? (16) How can legislative bodies better control agency activities to guarantee that "legislative intent" is carried out responsibly in the administrative process? (17) What should be done to control the "regulators"? And (18) what limits should be placed on the exercise of emergency administrative powers, such as under the PATRIOT Act so as to prevent the awesome discretionary powers given to certain administrators (e.g., the Attorney General) from threatening our basic freedoms?

One of the best methods for gaining a quick understanding of the scope of administrative law is to scan some of the major basic textbooks on the subject.[34] Even a cursory examination of administrative law books shows that certain topics are treated by virtually all writers, while others receive little or no coverage. This can be explained easily by distinguishing between administrative law purists and nonpurists.

The purists think in an ideal mode, taking a very narrow perception of what should be regarded as legitimate areas of administrative law. They believe that administrative law should be confined essentially to the study of the independent regulatory agencies or commissions (for example, the Interstate Commerce Commission, Federal Trade Commission, Nuclear Regulatory Commission). This attitude is rooted in the argument that only these agencies have traditionally exercised quasi-legislative (rulemaking) and quasi-judicial (ordermaking) powers, while other administrative agencies (for example, the Office of the President, executive departments, police departments) do not normally possess such powers. Since administrative law focuses primarily on rulemaking and ordermaking procedures, the purists have basically concluded that only agencies that exercise such authority should be given significant attention. In short, the purists have concentrated primarily on the formal aspects of agency operations as they relate to administrative law. Specifically, they have focused mostly on the statutory authority of agencies, rulemaking and ordermaking processes, and judicial review of the "formal" actions of the independent regulatory commissions.

Unlike the purists, the nonpurists have taken a much broader view of what administrative law should entail. To the nonpurist, there is no valid reason for not studying administrative agencies of virtually all descriptions, even if these agencies perform only "purely" administrative functions. For example, to Davis, a nonpurist, police departments fall within the legitimate scope of administrative law analysis even though the police possess no formal quasi-legislative or quasi-judicial powers. However, police, as well as other purely executive officers, exercise administrative discretion when making decisions that affect the community. Because informal discretionary acts may have profound consequences for individuals and groups, Davis recommends that considerable attention be devoted to improving the quality of discretionary justice in America, especially since such informal decisionmaking makes up more than 90 percent of all agency actions. Once more, such informal agency discretionary action often falls outside the jurisdiction of the Administrative Procedure Act and the reviewing courts.[35]

The purists and nonpurists have also disagreed over whether certain executive officials, particularly the president and state governors, should be included in administrative law analysis. This controversy stems from the fact that the president and state governors do not derive their powers from legislative statutes, as do administrators in all regulatory agencies. The president of the United States draws power from Article II of the U.S. Constitution, while state governors, as well as other administrators in some states, derive their authority from their respective state constitutions. Consistent with the separation of powers doctrine, this does insulate these executives from the congressional controls that other administrators must endure. And since administrative law has focused traditionally on the relationship between legislators and administrative agencies under legislative supervision, the purists have questioned whether administrators with separate constitutional status are within the legitimate scope of administrative law or whether they should be left to the constitutional law scholars. However, the crucial point is not whether these executives are considered within the proper subject area of administrative law, but rather that students recognize the difference between these two types of administrators in the administrative system.

The purists would also maintain that elected and nonelected public administrators are not the same and that administrative law covers the latter but not the former. Once again, if the purists consider the focus of administrative law to be congressionally created regulatory commissions whose quasi-legislative and quasi-judicial officials are appointed, not elected, then applications of administrative law would hardly seem appropriate for elected officials. This is an important distinction to consider when reflecting upon the fairness of administrative actions by elected and nonelected officials: The behavior of elected officials can be checked directly by the voters, but the actions of nonelected public administrators cannot.

Additionally, the purists hold that administrative law is not concerned with substantive public policies (that is, the actual policy content of the orders and rules) but only with the procedural steps leading to orders and rules. But it is absurd to try to pretend that procedural due process can be separated from substantive due process. To do so would be like suggesting that good wine has nothing to do with the steps taken in producing and maintaining its fine quality. Chapter 5 will show how the content of rules is very much affected by the procedures adopted by agency administrators. Obviously, for example, agency officials in the rulemaking process can shape the final public policies produced by using their broad discretionary powers to determine in practice not only who participates but also what weight is given to the inputs of the different participants.

In reality, the study of administrative law, despite the purists, is like the study of almost anything else. That is, the subject's legitimate domain is open to everything sensibly pertaining to it. Robert Lorch put it this way: "One may wonder where administrative law ends and other kinds of law begin. Where, for example, does the law of civil rights leave off and administrative law begin? The answer to that cannot be supplied any more than an answer to the question where blue ends and purple begins. Administrative law is not a thing of clear boundaries, nor is any other branch of the law, for they are all *neighborhoods* in the world of law which fade into one another block by block."[36] In 1990 the administrative law section of the American Bar Association held a workshop on what should be covered in an administrative law course. The participating fifty or so administrative law professors concluded that virtually any relevant topic could be covered given how interdisciplinary administrative law has become, now legitimately including such fields as psychology, economics, organizational theory, public policy, and political science. About the only limiting factor was available time.[37]

This book takes a nonpurist approach so as to present a conceptually broad and sophisticated comprehension of the role of administrative law in our political system. It seems unwise to exclude certain subject matter from administrative law study simply because it fails to pass the administrative law purity test. Besides, many informal aspects that affect administrative law may not interest traditional law students, yet they may intrigue public administration and public policy students.

In sum, administrative law is a complicated legal field made more challenging because of its inherent linkage to the political system. Catherine Zoller describes administrative law as "a complex field replete with regulations and delicate separation of powers issues. . . . The various factors at play in administrative law make the seemingly most elementary facets hard to understand." She stresses that "the problems in administrative law are amplified by the role of politics." Quoting Associate Justice Antonin Scalia, she concludes that "indeed, 'administrative law is not for sissies.'"[38]

The Distinctiveness of Administrative Law

What makes the administrative law field distinct from other areas of law? After what has already been said about the eclectic nature of administrative law, it would now be absurd to argue that administrative law is a purebred species. It is obviously a mongrel. But even a mutt has a distinct personality.[39] And it should be reiterated that administrative law, like other law fields, is a mixture of various legal areas. (See Figure 1.4 for an illustration of this practical concept.) For some reason, however—possibly their youthful innocence—administrative law scholars are simply less secure and, therefore, less pretentious.

What makes administrative law unique is its special focus. However, probably every field of study—whether law, the social sciences, or whatever—is distinguished by its particular emphasis. Despite disagreements regarding the proper scope of administrative law, virtually all administrative law scholars focus on the makings of fair procedure in administrative agencies.

Thus, administrative law is made distinct by its attention to the procedural activities of all public administrators. Whether analysis is on agency rulemaking, ordermaking, official immunity, or judicial review of agency actions, administrative procedural due process considerations provide the chief focal points. Even after acknowledging the vague character of administrative law, Lorch nevertheless maintained that "the central business district of administrative law is fair administrative procedure."[40]

Because of administrative law's emphasis on procedural due process, as contrasted to substantive due process, its interest in the U.S. Constitution is confined mostly to sections in the Constitution or state constitutions that pertain directly or indirectly to procedural due process considerations. Therefore, in the federal Constitution, administrative law issues frequently touch upon the Fourth, Fifth, and Fourteenth Amendments. While the Fifth and Fourteenth Amendments specifically call for due process of law to be executed when governmental actions are taken, other amendments and sections of the Constitution have been interpreted by the courts to imply such a call. For example, though the Fourth Amendment says nothing about due process specifically, it prohibits unreasonable searches and seizures, thus forcing police and other administrators to follow due process procedures when carrying out searches.

Administrative law is unique, compared to other legal fields, in the sense that probably more than 90 percent of administrative law is derived from common law.[41] Common law is that body of law that accumulates over the years as the result of judicial decisions. It is judge-made law. In the case of administrative law, judges

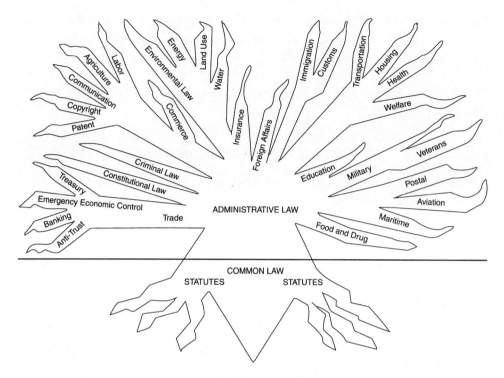

FIGURE 1.4   The Eclectic Nature of Administrative Law

over the decades have on an incremental or case-by-case basis given practical meaning to due process requirements in administrative procedure. In fact, although the Constitution mentions due process, due process is never, even weakly, defined in it. Legislative enactments, especially in such major legislation as the Administrative Procedure Act, have given some meaning to due process. However, the most authoritative and lasting insights on what due process or fair procedure should entail have come from major policy-setting court decisions, such as *Morgan v. United States,* 304 U.S. 1 (1938): *Goldberg v. Kelly,* 397 U.S. 254 (1970); *McCarthy* v. *Madigan,* 112 S.Ct. 1081 (1992); and *Demore v. Hyung Joon Kim,* 123 S.Ct. 1708 (2003). Such cases have formed the giant reservoir of common law governing administrative procedure today. Practically speaking, however, public administrators provide the everyday meaning of due process through their interpretations of statutes and court decisions. Statutes and court rulings are never so definitive that they are not open to interpretations by administrators. Consequently, unless their specific actions are overruled by the courts, administrators can employ their broad discretionary powers to determine the meaning of procedural due process in the context of the public programs that they are responsible for implementing.

The fact that administrative law today is rooted only weakly in substantive, or statutory, law also helps to give administrative law its unique character and, to some, its relative lack of respectability. Administrative law's heavily judge-made, common law backing not only makes it very difficult to understand and follow, since major changes can occur in the law with each court decision, but may also detract from its democratic soundness. That is, democratic theory holds that laws should ideally be made by elected representatives of the people. Democratic theory has never placed judges at the heart of democracy. Thus, one may ask, "How democratic is a body of laws if under 10 percent of them were made by legislators?"

The answer is self-evident, and it poses a serious threat to democratic life in the United States. Many readers may regard this contention as mere alarmist academic rhetoric. But to those a warning should be issued. Far from being impractical, theory has very practical applications. Those who continue to insist that theory and practice mix like oil and water are distorting reality. The truth is that the wisdom in democratic theory has been increasingly compromised in America for the sake of expediency. In its present form administrative law clashes too sharply with the sound principles embraced in democratic theory. Administrative law is a unique body of law that stresses procedural due process. In practice, procedural due process may mean much more to the preservation of democratic life than substantive law. Davis was absolutely correct when he noted that any person knowledgeable in the law would acknowledge this reality.[42] For example, legal experts and political scientists long recognized that the Soviet constitution was substantively more democratic than the U.S. Constitution. But what good is a democratic constitution if it is not upheld by fair procedures that in fact give constitutions their real meaning for the citizenry? In the words of Justice Robert H. Jackson, "Procedural fairness and regularity are of the indispensable essence of liberty. Severe substantive laws can be endured if they are fairly and impartially applied. Indeed, if put to the choice, one might well prefer to live under Soviet substantive law applied in good faith by our common-law procedures than under our substantive law enforced by Soviet procedural practices" (*Shaughnessy v. United States ex rel. Mezei,* 346 U.S. 206, 224 [1953]). And this perspective endures. In *Riverbend Farms v. Madigan,* 958 F.2d 1479, 1482 (9th Cir. 1992) the court exclaimed: "Procedure, not substance, is what most distinguishes our government [system] from others." (Also, see *Semtek Int'l Inc. v. Lockheed Martin Corp.,* 531 U.S. 497 [2001].)

The breakdown of the traditional tripartite model of democracy in America has resulted in a preponderance of what might be called undemocratic power in the administrative branch, with the courts trying desperately, yet futilely, to keep these new, mighty administrative agencies democratically accountable.[43] In many respects administrative law is distinct because it plays a critically important and powerful role in our society; yet its significance to the preservation of our democratic way of life has not been fully appreciated. If it were, there would be a more serious effort to develop and structure administrative law so that administrative procedures could reach higher levels of efficiency and fairness. The untidy and frequently unfair procedures followed by many of our administrative agencies in implementing public policies at all governmental levels attest clearly to our need to strengthen the procedural and substantive character of administrative law. And it should not be overlooked that citizens judge public policies not as they are written but as they take on life when implemented by administrators.

ADMINISTRATIVE
LAW'S INCREASING RELEVANCE

There is no need to spend much space noting the growing importance of administrative law in modern America. The critical nature of administrative law should be already apparent to any casual observer of governmental developments in American society, especially those advanced enough to be reading this text. Nevertheless, let me emphasize some of the factors that have made administrative law one of the more vital subjects today.

Although the development of the American administrative system is elaborated in chapter 2, it is worth acknowledging here that the expansion of public administration in the United States, starting with the presidency of Franklin Delano Roosevelt, has been enormous. This reality is the single most important reason for administrative law's rapid growth and heightened status. Since the beginning of the Great Depression, Americans have been increasingly willing to allow government to respond to and resolve a great variety of societal problems that had previously been handled outside government. This attitude has encouraged the widespread use of administrative agencies to regulate in what is considered to be the public interest.[44] Increased regulation of socioeconomic life by government has resulted in a massive number of new statutes and an especially vast quantity of agency rules and orders.

As an academic and practical field, administrative law has become more popular and relevant as the impact of public administration on American lives has become more profound. Davis claims that administrative law has passed through three stages of development and is presently, and simultaneously, entering a fourth and fifth stage.[45] Generally, as public administration activity has increased in vitality and depth in the American political system, interest in administrative law has been transformed from a more theoretical interest to serious concern for resolving the practical problems that have plagued administrative law. For example, Davis notes that the focus during the first stage was on the constitutional foundations of administrative law. A chief theoretical concern was where constitutional law ended and administrative law began. During this lengthy stage, which lasted from the beginning of the republic to about the 1920s, special emphasis was placed on issues pertaining to the separation-of-powers and delegation doctrines. Stage two, the 1920s and 1930s, was dominated by judicial review of agency actions as the courts tried to determine the constitutionality of certain new agency practices. For the courts, the central question was essentially, What role does the Constitution permit the emerging administrative state to play in our political system? Toward the end of the 1930s, at the height of agency proliferation, increased attention began to focus on formal administrative procedures, especially ordermaking and rulemaking. During this third stage, concern for fair formal administrative procedures led, in 1946, to the passage of the Administrative Procedure Act (60 Stat. 237), a major act aimed at regulating administrative behavior in virtually all federal agencies. Since the 1960s, a good deal of attention has been devoted to informal agency conduct, which makes up more than 90 percent of all agency actions.

Special focus in this fourth stage has been on increasing the fairness, efficiency, and effectiveness of informal agency decisionmaking processes. Emphasis has been placed on balancing the needs of society against the requirements of sound administrative practices. Stage five is characterized by a new concern for the technical and democratic complexities of the rulemaking process, especially since regulatory agencies in recent years have relied heavily on the rulemaking procedure to promulgate a host of new governmental regulations. The scope of these new regulations has broadened considerably during the past decade or so.[46]

According to Ernest Gellhorn in comments presented to members of the American Bar Association in the "Presidential Showcase Program," we have now passed the fifth stage and even another stage. Gellhorn contends that in what Davis calls the fifth stage (Gellhorn's second modern stage), the mood was set that virtually guaranteed swift movement to another stage. During this fifth stage governmental regulation reached its most intense and pervasive level, yet the integrity of the administrative process was doubted and challenged, especially the seemingly arrogant role played by powerful agency experts. Administrative policies were often perceived as cost-ineffective, lacking any sensible regulatory wisdom. Consequently, a new representational approach to administrative law and regulatory government developed, characterized by significant public participation in agency decisionmaking. During the late 1960s and well into the 1970s, Congress passed legislation, and the courts reached decisions, that promoted broad interest-group participation in the administrative process. The courts even liberalized standing law, making it easier for interest groups to challenge agency actions in the courts. When the courts heard administrative law cases, they employed the "hard look" rationale, scrutinizing not just administrative procedures but the quality of expertise employed by agency administrators.[47]

The sixth stage, or Gellhorn's third modern stage, emerged, then, as a reaction to the apparent runaway regulatory character of modern regulatory government. Starting around the time of President Jimmy Carter's administration, reformers began to question the reasonableness and even legitimacy of so much governmental regulation.[48] Contending generally that regulatory government had become too domineering and cost-effective, these reformers pushed for governmental deregulation and other measures to reduce the size and force of what they considered constitutionally illegitimate public administration. The deregulation movement began during President Carter's administration but picked up pace during the relatively conservative presidential administration of Ronald Reagan and George H. Bush, led by a Supreme Court dominated by Reagan and Bush appointees. Ironically, this era of serious popular skepticism and cynicism toward governmental regulation stretched into the Clinton years, causing the courts to return to fundamental administrative-constitutional law issues concerning delegation, separation of powers, and legitimacy so frequently debated before the 1930s (e.g., *INS v. Chadha*, 462 U.S. 919 [1983]; *Bowsher v. Synar*, 106 S.Ct. 3181 [1986]; *Morrison v. Olson*, 108 S.Ct. 2597 [1988]; *Skinner v. Mid-America Pipeline Co.*, 109 S.Ct. 1726 [1989]; *Touby v. United States*, 111 S.Ct. 1752

[1991]; and *Metropolitan Washington Airports Authority v. Citizens for the Abatement of Aircraft Noise*, 111 S.Ct. 2298 [1991]). Focus in the early twenty-first century, as it has been for a decade or so, is with how to uphold constitutional and procedural due process safeguards, which are time-consuming and costly, during a period of increased administrative burdens and diminishing agency resources (*Pennsylvania Bd. of Probation and Parole v. Scott*, 118 S.Ct. 2014 [1998]; and *United States v. Rangel De Aquilar*, 308 F.3d 1134 [9th Cir. 2002]).

THE REGULATORY ARM
FALLS ON GROVE CITY COLLEGE

In modern America virtually nothing seems to be immune from the far-reaching grasp of governmental regulators. Much to the dismay of laissez-faire conservatives, governmental intrusion in the private sector has become so widespread that the word *private* has been losing for decades its practical meaning, so much so that now it is becoming more popular—because it is really more accurate—to refer to many private organizations as quasi-public organizations. Quasi-public organizations can be described as organizations or companies under private ownership whose behavior is controlled rather rigorously by governmental regulations. Some examples are auto manufacturers, universities, restaurants, and advertising firms.

The controversy in the 1980s between Grove City College, a small private college in western Pennsylvania, and the U.S. Department of Education illustrates the continuing efforts of government to establish a sphere of influence in what were once considered private policy matters.[49] To put the story in a nutshell, a Department of Education (DOE) decision ordered Grove City College (GCC) to comply with a DOE regulation prohibiting sex discrimination. Asserting its independence, GCC refused to sign the DOE compliance forms in principle, arguing that it had never received a dime from federal funds. DOE, however, took the position that GCC received funds indirectly through student loans that, of course, students used to pay tuition. DOE admitted that it had no evidence that GCC was guilty of sex discrimination. In this case, the sex discrimination issue was completely beside the point. The real question being tested by GCC was whether there is such a thing as a private college or university in modern America. Even the relatively conservative Burger Court reluctantly answered that it is unlikely, because colleges and universities have to comply with Section 901 1a of Title IX (20 U.S.C., Section 1681, a). Expanding the role of governmental regulation just a bit more, the Court held that GCC was the recipient of federal financial assistance, though indirectly through a student loan program (Basic Educational Opportunity Grants), and therefore must comply with the statutory provision prohibiting sex discrimination in any of its educational programs linked to this aid *(Grove City College v. Bell*, 465 U.S. 555, 575 [1984]). In concurring, Chief Justice Burger and Justices Powell and O'Connor noted that they had no choice under law but to concur, even though in their view "the case is an unedifying example of overzealousness on the part of the Federal Government.

. . . It was and is the policy of this small college to remain wholly independent of government assistance, recognizing—as this case will illustrate—that with the acceptance of such assistance one surrenders a certain measure of the freedom that Americans have always cherished" (pp. 576–577).

Although the Grove City College case is linked specifically to the U.S. government's policies in higher education, the case obviously has widespread implications. In the GCC dispute, DOE administrators used government-sponsored student loans, a somewhat indirect source of revenue for GCC, to justify their demand for compliance with DOE standards. This justification led one scholar, after reviewing the *Grove City* decision, to conclude that "*Grove City's* expansive definition of federal financial assistance is, in effect, another step toward limiting the autonomy of private entities through further federal government encroachments."[50] *Grove City College* has remained an often cited precedent. For example, a New York court, citing *Grove City College*, held that "since Colgate is unwilling to make a change, it is the duty of this court to order change." So it ordered Colgate "to grant varsity status to the women's ice hockey program starting with the 1993/94 school year" (*Cook* v. *Colgate University*, 802 F.Supp. 737, 751 [N.D.N.Y. 1992]). In the past few years, the U.S. Supreme Court has relied upon *Grove City College* to help substantiate its rulings (*NCCA v. Smith*, 525 U.S. 459 [1999] and *Alexander v. Sandoval*, 532 U.S. 275 [2001]).

Has history not shown that federal and state agencies have employed similar techniques and rationales to enforce their will? Will not the influence of governmental bureaucracy continue to increase in the private sector as public administrators adopt an ever more prevalent parental attitude in their attempts to protect and promote the public health and safety in more and more areas of American life? Has not administrative law been thrust to the forefront by the enthusiastic encroachment of governmental regulators on the diminishing private sector? In light of these developments, would it not be wise to understand administrative law?

Some of these questions may indicate a conservative bias on the part of this author, but the questions are meant only to reflect reality. In fact, the rapid expansion of the administrative system may be perceived as part of a noble effort by government to provide Americans with a higher quality of life through increased and better regulation. And in truth, despite some administrative problems, a strong case could be made by liberal thinkers that expanded governmental regulation has indeed improved the quality of life for the average American citizen since welfare state ideas and policies began to be accepted and rapidly implemented since the New Deal. For example, governmental regulation has helped to improve working conditions, made transportation safer, curbed the marketing of dangerous consumer products, and so on. In any event, it is true that as public agencies become more involved in the areas of transportation, housing, energy, environment, communications, health, safety, education, welfare, human rights, and the like, administrative law issues will become more prevalent. Specifically, administrative law will play a greater role in helping to resolve the increasing number of disputes between the regulated and the regulators. In so doing, administrative law will have the very difficult task of fairly balancing the need for efficient and effective governmental administration with the interests and rights of the regulated.

SUMMARY

This administrative law textbook employs the noncasebook approach, making it ideally suited for students in the social sciences. Its basic purpose is to familiarize students in political science, public administration, public affairs, public policy, law, and the like with the role played by administrative law in the American political system. To fulfill this central goal, the book devotes considerable space to the examination of the major principles and issues in administrative law. This book has been written primarily for social science students; therefore, every attempt is made to apply administrative law to public policy implementation problems in the context of the realities confronted by public administrators in political life. To help clarify the role of administrative law in the political system, a systems approach, quite familiar to most social science students, is employed, on a somewhat limited basis.

Only in recent decades has the importance of administrative law been recognized by public administration scholars. However, administrative law is now perceived as so crucial to understanding the functions of administrative agencies that it has become one of the hottest fields in the public administration discipline. Modern regulatory government has become so complex and pervasive that it has strained the relationship between the regulators and the regulated. Heated disputes between these two natural rivals have increased in recent years as the regulatory arm of government has grown stronger. Recently many Americans, clinging to the freedoms that they have left, have even challenged the very legitimacy of the administrative state. To ease the tension between the regulators and the regulated, administrative law has been developing rapidly. Legislators, and especially judges, have been trying to develop an administrative law system in which administrative procedures are effective and efficient and still embrace the principles of due process under law. The developmental pace of administrative law has been so rapid that the state of administrative law is uncertain, unstable, and thus, quite difficult to understand. Administrative law in recent years has been, to quote Bernard Schwartz, in a "continual state of flux" and we are witnessing "a virtual administrative law explosion."[51]

NOTES

1. Kenneth C. Davis, *Discretionary Justice: A Preliminary Inquiry* (Westport, Conn.: Greenwood Press, 1980); Walter C. Gellhorn, *When Americans Complain: Governmental Grievance Procedures* (Cambridge, Mass.: Harvard University Press, 1966).

2. Peter Woll, *American Bureaucracy,* 2nd ed. (New York: W. W. Norton, 1977), 77.

3. For fascinating viewpoints on how administrative law should be taught, see Richard J. Pierce, Jr., "How Much Should an Administrative Law Course Accomplish?: A Response to Schotland's *Five Easy Pieces,*" *Administrative Law Review* 43 (winter 1991); Sidney A. Shapiro, "Reflections on Teaching Administrative Law: Time for a Sequel," *Administrative Law Review* 43 (summer 1991); Thomas O. Sargentich, "Administrative Law Discussion Forum: Teaching and Learning Administrative Law," *Brandeis Law Journal* 38 (winter 2000); and Gerald S. Schatz, "Comment: Health Records Privacy and Confidentiality: Pending Questions," *Journal of Contemporary Health Law and Policy* 18 (fall 2002).

4. Richard J. Pierce, Jr., *Administrative Law Treatise*, 4th ed. (New York: Aspen, 2002), vol. 111, chap. 17.

5. David Cole, "The New McCarthyism: Repeating History in the War on Terrorism," *Harvard Civil Rights–Civil Liberties Law Review* 38 (winter 2003).

6. Edward G. Krasnow, Lawrence D. Longley, and Herbert A. Terry, *The Politics of Broadcast Regulation*, 3rd ed. (New York: St. Martin's Press, 1982), p. 133.

7. Acknowledging the need for empirical studies in the area of administrative law, the editors of the *Administrative Law Review* decided to begin the 1980s with two volumes devoted to empirical research efforts. See "Symposium on Empirical Research in Administrative Law, Parts 1 and 2," *Administrative Law Review* 31, 32 (fall 1979, winter 1980). More empirical studies in administrative law have been published in professional journals since 1980, but by the early 2000s, the number was not impressive.

8. For a classic book devoted solely to explaining the survival instincts of governmental agencies, see Herbert Kaufman, *Are Government Organizations Immortal?* (Washington, D.C.: Brookings Institution Press, 1976).

9. David Easton, *A Framework for Political Analysis*, 2nd ed. (Chicago: University of Chicago Press, 1979).

10. Kenneth F. Warren, *In Defense of Public Opinion Polling* (Boulder, Colo.: Westview Press, 2003), chap. 8.

11. Judith R. Gordon, *A Diagnostic Approach to Organizational Behavior* (Boston: Allyn and Bacon, 1993), pp. 21–23.

12. Ira Sharkansky, *Public Administration: Policy-Making in Government Agencies,* 4th ed. (Chicago: Rand McNally, 1978), pp. 10–11.

13. Thomas R. Dye, *Understanding Public Policy*, 7th ed. (Englewood Cliffs, N.J.: Prentice Hall, 1992), pp. 42–44.

14. U.S. Census Bureau, *Statistical Abstract of the United States, 2002* (Washington, D.C.: U.S. Government Printing Office, 2003), no. 591, "Employment by Industry."

15. Frederick C. Mosher, *Democracy and the Public Service*, 2nd ed. (New York: Oxford University Press, 1982), p. 223. This finding is dated, yet still true today, as confirmed by 2002 government statistics as reported in the U.S. Census Bureau, *Statistical Abstract of the United States.*

16. U.S. General Accounting Office, *Women in Management* (Washington D.C., October 2001), pp. 1–23.

17. As of 2003 the *U.S. Government Manual* listed fifty-five "Independent Establishments and Government Corporations" along with another fifty-six "Boards, Commissions, and Committees" (*The United Sates Government Manual—2002/2003* [Washington, D.C.: U.S. Government Printing Office, 2003], pp. 367–556).

18. See, for example, Susan Bartlett Foote, "Independent Agencies Under Attack: A Skeptical View of the Importance of the Debate," *Duke Law Journal* (1988).

19. James P. Pfiffner, *The Modern Presidency*, 3rd ed. (Stamford, Conn.: Wadsworth, 1999), chap. 5.

20. Pierce, *Administrative Law Treatise*, 4th ed., vol. 1, chaps. 1 and 2.

21. *The Gallup Opinion Index,* report no. 146 (Princeton, N.J.: Gallup Poll, 1977), p. 23.

22. Ibid., pp. 22, 24. According to the U.S. Census Bureau, governmental employees in 1985 did average slightly greater pay when compared to "all domestic industries," a factor of $22,186 to $20,991 (*Statistical Abstract of the United States, 1987,* 107th ed. [Washington D.C.: U.S. Government Printing Office, 1986], p. 400). However, if one excludes just one of the eleven categories listed ("agriculture, forestry, fisheries"), which significantly reduces the average because of its $11,320 annual wage and salary figure, civil servants fall below the average income level, $22,186 to $24,728.

23. *The Gallup Opinion Index,* report no. 146, p. 20. For updates to 2003, go to http://www.Gallup.com and enter "Trust in Government."

24. Robert C. Townsend, *Up the Organization* (New York: Fawcett, 1978), chap. 1; and *Further Up the Organization* (New York: Alfred A. Knopf, 1984).

25. *The Gallup Opinion Index,* report no. 146, p. 20.

26. Kenneth F. Warren, "We Have Debated Ad Nauseam the Legitimacy of the Administrative State, but Why?" *Public Administration Review* (May–June 1993).

27. Stephen G. Breyer, Richard B. Stewart, et al., *Administrative Law and Regulatory Policy,* 5th ed. (New York: Aspen, 2002), pp. 4–15.

28. Reuters, "Senators Question Effectiveness of $1.4 Billion Settlement," *New York Times* (May 8, 2003), C-8.

29. Bernard Schwartz noted that "during recent years we have been in the midst of a virtual administrative law explosion" ("Recent Administrative Law Issues and Trends," *Administrate Law Journal* 3

[1990]: 543). Responding directly to Schwartz's observation, Marshall Breger agreed in "Comments on Bernard Schwartz' Essay," *Administrative Law Journal* 5 (1991); see also Breyer, Stewart, et al., *Administrative Law and Regulatory Policy,* pp. 16–35.

30. Nathaniel L. Nathanson, "Proposals for Administrative Appellate Court," *Administrative Law Review* 25 (winter 1973): 89.

31. Henry Campbell Black, *Law Dictionary,* 5th ed. (St. Paul: West, 1979), p. 22; Breyer, Stewart, et al., *Administrative Law and Regulatory Policy,* p. 3; Kenneth C. Davis, *Administrative Law Treatise,* 2nd ed. (San Diego: K. C. Davis, 1979), vol. 1, chap. 1; Daniel Oran, *Oran's Dictionary of the Law* (St. Paul: West, 1983), p. 15.

32. Sallyanne Payton, "Administrative Law: What Is It, and What Is It Doing in Our Law School?" *Law Quadrangle Notes* (fall 1983): 30.

33. Breger, "Comments on Bernard Schwartz' Essay," pp. 349–350.

34. For example, see Peter L. Strauss, *Administrative Justice in the United States,* 2nd ed. (Durham: Carolina Academic Press, 2002); Pierce, *Administrative Law Treatise,* 4th ed.; and Breyer, Stewart, et. al., *Administrative Law Regulatory Policy.*

35. Davis, *Discretionary Justice;* Kenneth C. Davis, *Police Discretion* (St. Paul: West, 1975).

36. Robert S. Lorch, *Democratic Process and Administrative Law,* 2nd ed. (Detroit: Wayne State University Press, 1980), pp. 60–61 (emphasis added).

37. For reflections on this workshop, see Roy A. Schotland, "How Much Truth Is Too Much Truth for Judicial Review? and Other *Easy Pieces* After an AALS Workshop on Teaching Administrative Law," *Administrative Law Review* 43 (winter 91); and Richard J. Pierce, Jr., "How Much Should an Administrative Law Course Accomplish?: A Response to Schotland's Five *Easy Pieces,"* *Administrative Law Review* 43 (winter 91).

38. Catherine Zoller, "The Case for Strict Statutory Construction of Mandatory Agency Deadlines Under Section 706," *William and Mary Law Review* 42 (April 2001): 1545.

39. Donald D. Barry and Howard R. Whitcomb, *The Legal Foundations of Public Administration,* 2nd ed. (St. Paul: West Publishing Co., 1987), p. 7.

40. Lorch, *Democratic Process and Administrative Law,* p. 61.

41. Davis, *Administrative Law Treatise,* 2nd ed., vol. 1, p. 140. Davis claims not only that 90 percent of administrative law is judge made but also that even the remaining 10 percent of statutory law chiefly codifies judge-made common law.

42. Kenneth C. Davis, *Administrative Law and Government,* 2nd ed. (St. Paul: West, 1975), p. 157.

43. For what I believe is still about the best analysis of the alleged collapse of the tripartite American governmental structure, see Eugene P. Dvorin and Robert H. Simmons, *From Amoral to Humane Bureaucracy* (San Francisco: Canfield Press, 1972), especially chap. 4. Also see R. Ship Melnick, "Administrative Law and Bureaucratic Reality," *Administrative Law Review* 44 (spring 1992).

44. Warren, "We Have Debated Ad Nauseam," pp. 249–254.

45. Davis, *Administrative Law Treatise,* 2nd ed., vol. 1, pp. 14–15.

46. Ibid. Davis's comments on the five stages provided the core for this summary.

47. Ernest Gellhorn, "Opening Remarks: Administrative Law in Transition," *Administrative Law Review* 38 (spring 1986).

48. Ibid. Also see Aaron Wildavsky, "Ubiquitous Anomie: Public Service in an Era of Ideological Dissensus," *Public Administration Review* 48 (July–August 1988); Brian J. Cook, "The Representative Function of Bureaucracy: Public Administration in Constitutive Perspective," *Administration and Society* 23 (February 1992); and Michael W. Spicer and Larry D. Terry, "Legitimacy, History, and Logic: Public Administration and the Constitution," *Public Administration Review* 53 (May–June 1993).

49. The dispute was originally between Grove City College and the Department of Health, Education, and Welfare. When HEW was reorganized into two agencies, the Department of Education handled the dispute.

50. Beverly Brandt Tiesenga, "Title IX and the Outer Limits of the Spending Powers: *Grove City College v. Bell,"* *Chicago-Kent Law Review* 61 (1985): 729–730.

51. Schwartz, "Recent Administrative Law Issues and Trends," p. 543.

CHAPTER 2

The Growth of Administrative Power and Its Impact on the American System

GROWTH OF THE ADMINISTRATIVE SYSTEM

A picture is worth a thousand words. In attempting to convey the dramatic growth of the administrative system since the early years of the American republic, a couple of pictures would certainly be helpful. Imagine a typical busy street in the United States during the early 1800s and compare it with a typical busy urban street today. What striking differences would be expected, reflecting changes in American living patterns that have promoted major and necessary alterations in American institutions and government? A careful scrutiny of the early-nineteenth-century street scene would show, for example, fewer people; unpaved streets; shorter and simpler building structures; no large department stores; no televisions, DVDs, dishwashers, refrigerators, or electronic games on display in store windows; fewer entertainment spots; no motorized transportation; no endless rows of street signs and lights; no planes or helicopters flying overhead; no electronic noises; no telephone poles or lines; no indications of elaborate sewer, plumbing, heating, or electrical systems; no street monitors. And other items would be missing, things that are symptomatic of the complexities in modern American life.

Selected indicators, extracted from various tables in the *Historical Abstract of the United States* and the *Statistical Abstract of the United States,* convey vividly America's rapid growth in various socioeconomic areas.[1] For example, in 1790 the total population of the United States was less than 4 million, not even the size of one major metropolitan area today. Now, in 2004, our population exceeds 260 million, about seventy-three times the 1790 figure. The growth in federal civilian employment has been even more spectacular, going from only 4,837 federal employees in 1816 to 2,697,000 by 2001—558 times the 1816 number—with state and local governmental employment increasing still more dramatically (see Table 2.1). Of course, urban growth statistics reflect the overall increase in population. For instance, in 1820 New York City's population was 123,700, while today it is more than 8 million.

TABLE 2.1:   Growth in Federal, State, and Local Civilian Employment, 1816–2001

Year	Number of federal employees	Number of state and local employees
1816	4,837	—
1831	11,491	—
1851	26,274	—
1871	51,020	—
1891	157,442	—
1911	395,905	—
1921	561,142	—
1931	609,746	2,704,000
1941	1,437,682	3,372,000
1951	2,482,666	4,287,000
1961	2,435,808	6,616,000
1971	2,862,926	8,806,000
1981	2,865,000	13,103,000
1995	2,821,000	16,457,000
2001	2,697,000	15,378,924

SOURCES: U.S. Census Bureau, Historical Abstract of the United States, Colonial Times to 1970 (Washington, D.C.: U.S. Government Printing Office, 1975), pt. 1, ser. D, specs. 139, 140, 141; and Statistical Abstract of the United States, 2001 (Washington, D.C.: U.S. Government Printing Office, 2001), section 8, no. 449.

AGENCY PROLIFERATION: THE ADMINISTRATIONS OF GEORGE WASHINGTON AND GEORGE W. BUSH

President George Washington headed the first national administration, which was tiny and very limited in powers and scope of activities. At this time in our history there was enthusiastic support for the free market system and the theory of limited government. Without doubt, governmental administration then epitomized the laissez-faire slogan: "For forms of government let fools contest; What'er is *least* administer'd is best."[2] In Washington's administration, only the basic governmental functions were performed. Only three executive departments existed. Washington's Cabinet consisted of John Jay, secretary of state (succeeded by Thomas Jefferson in 1790); Alexander Hamilton, secretary of the treasury;

and Henry Knox, secretary of war. Also part of Washington's cabinet, but not heads of departments, were Edmund Randolph, attorney general (not until 1870 was the Department of Justice established), and Samuel Osgood (succeeded by Timothy Pickering in 1791), Postmaster General (not established as a department until 1882).[3]

No "independent" regulatory agencies existed for about the first century of the republic because, to most citizens, just the thought of a governmental regulatory agency was repulsive. As noted in the last chapter, a vocal minority today still perceive any form of governmental regulation as repugnant. Nevertheless, enough public sentiment against free market abuses emerged toward the end of the1800s that the people turned to government for help. Government responded initially by creating the Interstate Commerce Commission in 1887, but this independent regulatory agency was only the first of many more to come in the twentieth century.

While virtually no governmental bureaucracy existed during the simpler times of Washington's presidency, in sharp contrast, today's administrative apparatus is gigantic, pervasive, and powerful, reflecting the complex problems and challenges of a greatly transformed American society in the new age of space exploration. President George W. Bush's administration includes fifteen huge Cabinet-level departments (including the newly created Department of Homeland Security), a large White House staff, and a host of so-called independent agencies to help in administrative and regulatory functions (see Figure 2.1).

Figure 2.2 traces the growth in the number of federal agencies from 1789 to 2004. What is not shown, however, is that our public agencies have not only increased in number but, more important, have increased in size and functions as well. Actually, the growth of the administrative system can be attributed more to increases in the functional capacity of agencies than increases in the number of agencies.

Why Have Agencies Increased in Size and Number?

Exponential Agency Growth Requires Birth Control.   Herbert Kaufman studied the life cycle of organizations for the period 1923 to 1973 to respond to the question, "Are government organizations immortal?," which is the title of his book.[4] Kaufman demonstrated the clear tendency for bureaucracy to expand in an exponential manner. He contends that once organizations are born, they tend to resist death by taking on traits of immortality. In reflecting on the growth patterns which have led to today's giant administrative system, Kaufman commented that such growth tendencies bear "some challenging implications for policymakers and managers of governmental machinery."[5] No doubt this is true, but what specifically seems to have nurtured the hearty development of the administrative system? Why has it occurred?

Kaufman cites seven reasons, all linked to an agency's bid to survive. In the first place, he points out that agencies endure after birth because they are given legal

40

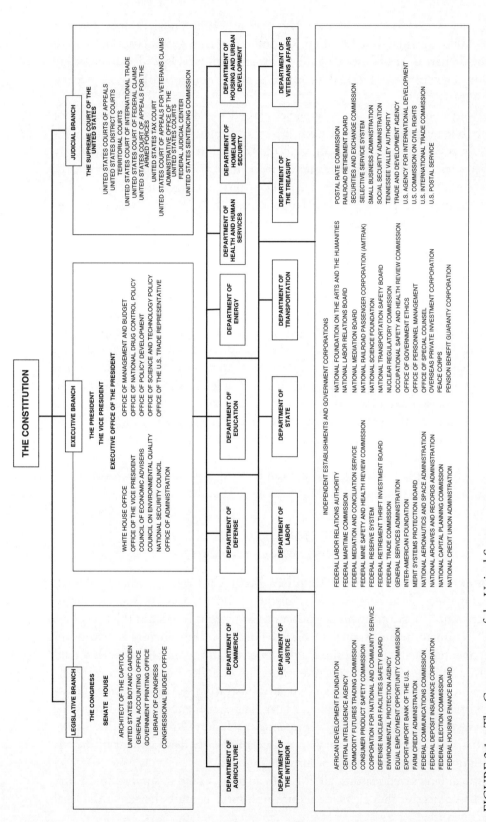

FIGURE 2.1 The Government of the United States.

SOURCE: *United States Government Manual* (Washington, D.C.: U.S. Government Printing Office, 1995–1996), p. 22.

FIGURE 2.2   Cumulative Total Numbers of Federal Agencies, 1789–2003.
SOURCES: Adapted from Herbert Kaufman, *Are Government Organizations Immortal?* (Washington, D.C.: Brookings Institution Press, 1976), p. 62. Post-1973 data, from *United States Government Manual* (Washington, D.C.: U.S. Government Printing Office, 2002–2003).

sanctioning, which provides them with formal powers. This formal authority, usually embedded in several statutes, is difficult to take away. Second, each agency has guardians in Congress, especially among powerful congressional leaders who head key congressional committees. Kaufman notes that although specific legislators may come and go, agencies retain their security by befriending congressional committees on the whole (that is, members and their staffs) so that they will survive when their particular legislative friends leave. Third, incremental budgetary procedures favor extended agency life after birth. Kaufman argues that legislators tend to become prisoners of their own creations. That is, once Congress originally approves an annual budget for an agency, the next year's budget is practically impossible to cut completely or shave: "Total elimination of funds for an agency or even massive slashes approaching total elimination are unknown, for all practical purposes."[6] Actually, agency budgets tend to increase automatically and incrementally from year to year because of "the sheer momentum of the budgetary process."[7] Agencies also benefit, Kaufman contends, from the lack of time legislators have to scrutinize the validity of submitted agency programs and budgets, thus making it exceedingly difficult for Congress to defend any cuts in the face of agency protests.

Fourth, agency expertise, protected by statutes and court decisions, provides agencies with relative independence and strength to resist hostile political attacks by intruders. Fifth, agency employees tend to fight hard to preserve the life of their agencies, and thus their jobs. Agency leaders fight not only out of loyalty to protect their agency's future but, Kaufman maintains, to protect their professional reputations and their future employability. Sixth, agency administrators learn to form strong ties with their clientele. Because many agencies were created to serve a specific clientele (for example, veterans), it would be expected that those an agency serves would likely be its most ardent supporters. And to reiterate a major point from Chapter 1, regulated industries also stand to benefit from a symbiotic relationship with regulatory agencies. Last, Kaufman holds that professional and trade associations also function to protect those agencies that tend to be supportive of their occupational interests. "When all seven of the foregoing factors are taken together," he concludes, "the contention that government agencies are virtually immortal seems incontestable."[8]

Although Kaufman acknowledges the existence of certain hazardous forces in the administrative system's environment that may serve to curb agency proliferation (competition, leadership and policy changes, alienation of key supporters, completed missions), agency expansionism appears assured because certain systemic characteristics allow many agencies to be born but few to die. Kaufman found that agency fatalities were so rare that it would probably be wise for the government to investigate different agency birth control methods. Otherwise, assuming the normal growth rate of five new agencies a year, this country can expect to have another 266 federal agencies by 2023, whether they are needed or not.[9] Reflecting on Kaufman's research, Glen O. Robinson notes that though it is risky to predict future growth trends, Kaufman appears to be right. Bureaucratic growth, Robinson acknowledges, has continued through Republican and Democratic administrations, despite political rhetoric and apparently honest efforts to stop it. Robinson comments that "there seems to be a kind of political racket at work that permits change in one direction only."[10] Figure 2.2 confirms that Kaufman's agency growth forecast, made in 1976, has proved to be remarkably accurate.

Growth Induced by Distrust and Expertise.   According to William L. Morrow, the expansion of the administrative system has emerged from a basic distrust in the ability of existing agencies to perform new functions fairly: "Distrusting existing organizations and seeking to provide new spark and thrust to new policies, interest groups, politicians, and public officials have usually preferred creating *new* organizations to the prospect of adding new policy responsibilities to existing ones."[11] A blatant example of this is the creation of the new Department of Homeland Security in 2002. The call for increased specialization has also helped to spur the creation of new agencies. John Kenneth Galbraith argues that a new elite forming a technostructure has emerged in modern industrialized countries. The *technostructure* consists of technical and managerial experts found in industry as well as in public agencies. According to Galbraith, this new technostructure, whether in industry or governmental agencies, places a high priority on productivity because increased production tends to increase and strengthen the technostructure itself.[12] Recognition of the technostructure's experts' knowledge by the other governmental branches has allowed bureaucracy to expand with little resistance.

James Q. Wilson contends that the political climate must also be conducive to stimulating waves of bureaucratic growth. He identifies four periods in our history when the political climate favored the rapid growth of regulatory agencies. To Wilson, conditions have to be just right for the creation of agencies because agency proliferation is generally resisted. He asserted that each wave

> was characterized by progressive or liberal presidents in office (Cleveland, T. R. Roosevelt, Wilson, F. D. Roosevelt, Johnson); one was a period of national crisis (the 1930s); three were periods when the President enjoyed extraordinary majorities of his own party in both houses of Congress (1914–1916, 1932–1940, and 1964–1968); and only the first preceded the emergence of the national mass media of communication. These facts are important because of the special difficulty of passing any genuinely regulatory legislation . . . without special political circumstances—a crisis, a scandal, extraordinary majorities, an especially vigorous President, the support of the media—the normal barriers to legislative innovation . . . may prove insuperable."[13]

These periods are sketched in Table 2.2. I have added to Table 2.2 a fifth stage, the "deregulation stage," that took place mostly during the Reagan and George H. W. Bush years, reflecting the sentiment that bureaucracy is "too fat" and even illegitimate (discussed in Chapter 1). This movement may have slowed the growth pace, but it flatly failed to prevent bureaucracy from expanding, especially in the area of defense and entitlement programs. Deregulation also failed because it led to financial insecurity in some industries (for example, the airline industry), public inconvenience (problems for air and bus commuters, especially on "unpopular" routes), price gouging (cable TV rate hikes), and even some outrageous and well publicized scandals (the savings and loan debacle.)[14]

Since the beginning of President Clinton's administration in 1993 through today, we have been in a sixth stage. This stage is characterized by enormous confusion over which regulatory direction to take: continued deregulation? reregulation? or just more regulation? Although continued efforts have been made to privatize and deregulate for the past dozen years, more market failures and scandals (those at Enron, Worldcom, Arthur D. Andersen, and other corporations and the plummeting stock market) have caused even the pro–big business George W. Bush administration to call for more regulatory reforms for Wall Street, accounting firms, banks, and corporations. Promoting individual freedom has continued to be an American goal, but "9/11" caused lawmakers and President Bush to reevaluate certain liberties and privacy protections, concluding that at least for the immediate future, new regulations must be imposed on various businesses and certain personal liberties must be restricted.

Attitudinal Changes Have Aided Growth.   Insights on the apparent causes of increased governmental regulation seem endless, but one can say with certainty that the public administration system grew rapidly from the late 1800s to the present simply because (1) the American people called upon government for help and (2) U.S. government officials were very eager to provide this help. Of

TABLE 2.2:   James Q. Wilson's Four Periods of Bureaucratic Growth

Period	Focus	Key acts passed
1887–90	Control Monopolies and rates	Interstate Commerce Act Sherman Anti-trust Act
1906–15	Regulate product quality	Pure Food and Drug Act Meat Inspection Act Federal Trade Commission Clayton Act
1930–40	Extend regulation to cover various socioeconomic areas, especially new technologies	Food, Drug, and Cosmetic Act Public Utility Holding Company Act National Labor Relations Act Securities and Exchange Act Natural Gas Act
1960–79	Expand regulation to make America a cleaner, healthier, safer, and fairer place to live and work	Economic Opportunity Act Civil Rights Acts of 1960, 1964, and 1968 National Environmental Policy Act Clean Air Act Occupational Safety and Health Act
1978–93	Deregulation movement as a reaction to bureaucratic overexpansion	Paperwork Reduction Act Air Deregulation Act Radio and TV Deregulation Banking Deregulation
1993–present	Deregulation, reregulation, or more regulation	Communications Decency Act of 1996 Telecommunications Act of 1996 USA PATRIOT Act of 2001

SOURCE: Based on James Q. Wilson "The Rise of the Bureaucratic State," *Policymaking*, Francis E. Rourke, ed., 4th ed. (Boston: Little, Brown, 1986), pp. 125–148; table categories and descriptions were created and supplemented by this author.

course, systems analysis theorists would expect this demand-response pattern to emerge, since acknowledging public demands would be considered the appropriate response of democratically responsible public servants, especially if they wanted to remain in office. A few decades ago Edwin W. Tucker admirably summarized the attitudinal changes that have led the American public and politicians to sanction and encourage increased governmental regulation, as well as administrative law. Although Tucker's dozen reasons overlap somewhat, he makes the clear point that the regulatory process grew because (1) the public began to change its mind and to perceive government as a viable instrument for solving many social problems; (2) public officials were willing to accept the responsibility for resolving social problems; (3) public attitudes gradually changed from a feeling of fear toward government to a more positive and euphoric attitude about the potential of public administration to cause positive social change; (4) the public began to question the conventional wisdom that government is best which governs least, arguing now that under certain conditions governmental intervention is necessary; (5) Americans started to abandon the dogmatic belief that the private sector would and could take the necessary corrective measures to alleviate problems in society; (6) public opinion began to turn against the prevailing idea that public administration can have only a negative impact on society; (7) the public adopted a more humane, welfare state concept and an accompanying rejection of the attitude that what's good for GM is necessarily good for society; (8) the public increasingly believed that certain state-of-nature liberties should be sacrificed so that social order, an important social condition, can be achieved; (9) Americans began to adopt an increasingly egalitarian philosophy that emphasized the virtues of equality over values that promoted the interests of a favored few; (10) the people felt disenchantment with property-based theory, which tends to emphasize individual property rights over social and human rights; (11) there was an increasing realization that population growth, shifts, and related issues are important matters for social planners to consider; and (12) the American people became more willing to challenge the status quo on all socioeconomic fronts in an effort to search for and establish an increasingly equitable social system.[15]

Court-Inspired Administrative Growth.   Decisions of American legislators and presidents over the decades, in their efforts to serve constituent demands, helped to shape today's large public service system. However, judicial decisions have also played a major role in expanding the size, scope, and power of the government's administrative network.[16] Examples of this type of court decision include *Munn v. Illinois,* in 1876. In this case, the U.S. Supreme Court upheld the constitutional and statutory authority of the Granger laws, thus enabling Illinois administrative agencies to regulate railroads. This case was significant because it allowed public agencies to regulate private property, so long as doing so was in the public interest. Chief Justice Waite justified governmental regulation by arguing that "property does become clothed with a public interest when used in a manner to make it of public consequence, and affect the community at large" (94 U.S. 113, 126 [1876]).

This decision helped to open the door to all sorts of regulatory measures regarded by various agencies to be in the public interest. But the *Munn* decision left an important question unanswered: Can a state regulate activities of industries that are not only engaged in *intrastate* commerce but *interstate* commerce as well? Shortly afterwards, in *Peik v. Chicago and Northwestern Railway Co.*, the Court answered yes, thus expanding state regulatory power even further and paving the way for the regulatory movement at the national level. The Court reasoned that "until Congress acts in reference to the relations of this company to interstate commerce, it is certainly within the power of Wisconsin to regulate its fares, etc. so far as they are of domestic concern. With the people of Wisconsin this company has domestic relations. Incidentally, these may reach beyond the State" (94 U.S. 164, 178 [1877]). Although the railroads and other industries attempted to thwart governmental efforts to regulate their businesses, eventually the courts supported critics who argued that the public interest would suffer if government failed to regulate socioeconomic activities to some extent. In reviewing the growth of regulation in the United States, Stephen G. Breyer and Richard B. Stewart concluded that "the decisions of federal and state courts reviewing the actions of these early regulatory agencies laid the foundations of modern administrative law."[17]

Despite some court support for governmental regulation before the New Deal, significant judicial sanctioning for administrative regulations did not come until the impact of the Great Depression on society became so crippling as to create a critical need for governmental intervention in the economy. Breyer end Stewart point out that at first the federal courts sided with the critics of the New Deal's regulatory programs, but "in a relatively short time, the Supreme Court (and with it, much of the lower federal judiciary) swung from almost undisguised hostility toward the new programs of administration to conspicuous deference. The availability of judicial review of administrative action was curtailed, and particular agency decisions were frequently sustained with judicial obeisance to the mysteries of administrative expertise."[18] Evidence of this can be seen in the following Court decisions: *NLRB v. Jones and Laughlin Steel Coup.,* 301 U.S. 1 (1937); *Steward Machine Co. v. Davis,* 301 U.S. 548 (1937); *Switchmen's Union v. National Mediation Board,* 320 U.S. 297 (1943); and *NLRB v. Hearst Publications, Inc.,* 322 U.S. 111 (1944). The Court's increasing willingness to bow to agency expertise, as we shall see, has played a major role in the development of agency dominance today.

The strength and pervasiveness of the administrative system were developed in other, rather typical court rulings. Recognition of the legitimacy and power of the administrative process was given by Justice Robert Jackson in *FTC v. Ruberoid Co.,* when he wrote, "The rise of administrative bodies probably had been the most significant legal trend of the last century and perhaps more values today are affected by their decisions than those of all the courts, review of administrative decisions apart" (343 U.S. 470, 487 [1952]). In *U.S. v. Caltex,* 344 U.S. 149 (1952), Chief Justice Fred Vinson strengthened the power of administrative action during times of emergency. Specifically, Justice Vinson fortified the government's police power by giving administrative agencies total immunity from suits filed under the just compensation clause of the Fifth Amendment challenging the legitimacy of certain administrative actions taken while responding to an emergency, such as the destruction of property. Vinson noted in his opinion that "the common law had long recognized that in times of imminent peril—such as when fire threatened a whole community—the sovereign could, with immunity, destroy the property of a few that the property of many and the lives of many more could be saved" (p. 154). In *Heart of Atlanta Motel, Inc. v. U.S.* (379 U.S. 241 [1964]), Justice Tom Clark significantly broadened the scope of federal administrative authority under the commerce clause. Essentially Clark held that federal agencies can regulate any activity that is related directly or indirectly to commerce, so long as Congress has sanctioned such regulation. Justice Clark "argued that Congress could have pursued other methods to eliminate the obstructions it found in interstate commerce caused by racial discrimination. But this is a matter of policy that rests entirely with the Congress, not with the courts. How obstructions in commerce may be removed—what means are to be employed—is within the sound and exclusive discretion of Congress" (pp. 261–262). This decision has enabled federal agencies to use the threat of the commerce clause to regulate virtually any business activity occurring within states that has possible interstate impact. Drug trafficking, prostitution, gambling, deceptive sales practices, professional sports, and racial discrimination in businesses are a few examples.

Various court decisions more recently have added still further to the growing strength of both national and state administrative agencies. In *Vermont Yankee Nuclear Power Corp. v. Natural Resources Defense Council*, 435 U.S. 519 (1978), the U.S. Supreme Court was not impressed with the public interest intervenor's argument that the courts should make administrative agencies employ stricter rulemaking procedures when dealing with complicated scientific matters that could lead to the promulgation of potentially dangerous rules or public policies. The Court held that agency officials have the discretion to follow only rulemaking procedures required specifically by the Administrative Procedure Act or other pertinent statutes. It stressed that to require more elaborate procedures "almost compels the agency to conduct all rulemaking proceedings with the full panoply of procedural devices normally associated only with adjudicatory hearings" (p. 525). In brief, the Court said Congress would have to limit the discretionary power of agency administrators when drafting rules, because the courts have no business in this area. Six years later, in *Chevron, U.S.A. v. National Resources Defense Council*, 104 S.Ct. 2778 (1984), the Supreme Court reiterated its position by stating in essence that courts should defer to agency expertise or discretion as long as that discretion is based on a "permissible" application of what a law permits. In the words of the Court, "a court may not substitute its own construction of a statutory provision for a reasonable interpretation made by the administrator of an agency" (p. 2782).

According to Michael Herz, the *Chevron* decision "has become perhaps the central case of modern administrative law."[19] The case was cited by over 2,000 federal courts by 1992, only eight years after it was decided, and has caused much heated debate.[20] By 2003 a LEXIS-NEXIS legal search revealed that *Chevron* had been cited by almost 7,000 federal courts and close to 4,000 state courts. In *Yellow Transportation, Inc. v. Michigan* 123 S.Ct. 371 (2002), a unanimous U.S. Supreme Court again used *Chevron* to scold and overrule the Michigan Supreme Court for inappropriately intruding on administrative process. The Court held: "Because the ICC's interpretation of ISTEA's fee-cap provision is consistent with the language of the statute and reasonably resolves any ambiguity therein (see *Chevron*), . . . the Michigan Supreme Court erred in declining to enforce it" (p. 389). In "Deference Running Riot: Separating Interpretation and Lawmaking Under *Chevron*," Herz contends that *Chevron* goes too far, permitting administrators to exercise too much power without subjecting the exercise of such power to judicial review. To Herz, application of the *Chevron* doctrine, which permits broad and possibly irresponsible deference to public administrators, tends to make public agencies too powerful, illegitimate, and unaccountable.[21]

Legal scholars argue that nothing has contributed more to the growth of administrative power than decisions such as *Chevron* because the *Chevron* doctrine sanctions broad deference to administrative expertise by the courts, thus severely limiting which administrative action or decisions will be subjected to judicial review. Once more, *Chevron* also endorses broad, vague, and frequently irresponsible delegations of legislative power by Congress to public agencies, tending to strengthen even more the "independent" power of administrators, causing an increasing number of citizens to question the very legitimacy of the power they hold.[22]

But critics charge that, making matters worse, too many state and federal courts have been too quick to embrace and even expand *Chevron*. In 1991 the U.S. Supreme Court itself expanded the *Chevron* doctrine in *Rust v. Sullivan*, 111 S.Ct. 1759, holding that the *Chevron* doctrine requires deference to the agency's interpretation of a statute—not just a *reasonable* agency interpretation, as originally held in *Chevron*, but an interpretation that is merely *plausible*. Critics, already bothered that *Chevron* had caused courts to retreat from their obligation to review agency action, became more disturbed by *Rust*. One leading scholarly critic, Bernard Schwartz, exclaimed: "Now *Rust* transforms the reasonableness requirement to one of plausibility—a test met by an interpretation that has only an appearance or show of truth—i.e., it is only superficially fair or reasonable. In this respect, *Rust* makes for a dilution in scope of review even beyond that made by *Chevron* itself."[23] Originally applied only to rulemaking, *Chevron* now applies to all agency interpretations of statutes, including adjudicatory decisions. In short, *Chevron*, as applied by the courts, has greatly expanded the power of the administrative state.

There is an irony to this development. During the New Deal, FDR and his liberal supporters fought the conservative courts fiercely, eventually persuading them to defer more to agency expertise and discretion. Of course, this deference allowed for the growth of the administrative state and the emergence of awesome administrative power. However, by the mid-1960s political observers, especially liberal critics led by such public interest groups as Common Cause and Union of Concerned Scientists and by consumer advocate Ralph Nader, became disillusioned and distrustful of "unfettered" administrative actions and began to urge the courts to reassert their power of judicial review to check abuses of administrative power. Generally, for the next dozen years or so, the courts did respond, overruling various agency actions that seemed to undermine the public interest, especially when related to safety, civil rights, and environmental hazards. The courts seemed determined to make public administration "more democratically accountable." But by the mid-1980s, under the influence of a more conservative public and Reagan administration politics, state and federal courts, led by the U.S. Supreme Court, started once again to defer to agency expertise and discretion, with *Chevron* dramatically and emphatically "kicking off" the movement. Courts were responding to outcries, mostly from conservatives, that the courts had been violating the separation-of-powers doctrine by meddling too much in the administrative process and making too many public policy decisions that should be made by legislators and public administrators. President Clinton, through administrative politics and judicial appointments, tried to reverse this conservative trend of judicial self-restraint, but he was largely unsuccessful because Republican resistance proved too formidable. The Bush administration, especially since the Republicans took total control of Congress in 2002, has been in a solid position to ensure the continuation of the Reagan–Bush I judicial politics of the 1980s and early 1990s.

On the whole, court decisions in various legal areas related to public administration (for example, hearing rights, rulemaking, torts, delegation, judicial review of agency actions, administrative searches and seizures) have had the impact of increasing the power and scope of administrative action. These specific legal areas will be the focus of later discussions. In a real sense, the courts have had little practical choice but to sanction the development of the administrative state because the growth of American society has unquestionably demanded a greater role be played by our public administrators at all levels of government.

A Concluding Macro View.   Obviously, numerous factors have caused the expansion of the administrative system; yet mere bureaucratic inertia has probably been the most crucial factor. Rapid bureaucratic expansion has not been confined only to the public sector. Red tape, the unfortunate symbol of modern bureaucracy, has engulfed private enterprise as well. Nor has swift bureaucratic growth been limited to the American system. Henry Jacoby, in *The Bureaucratization of the World,* makes it quite clear, as Max Weber did before him, that bureaucratization is a natural process that eventually invades the private and public institutions of all nations.[24]

Despite much well-publicized public opinion against bureaucratic growth, Americans have turned continually to government for helpful services, thus stimulating the growth of the public administration system. It also seems true that modern bureaucracy, as conceptualized by Max Weber (that is, a structure in which administration is meritorious and separated from flagrant political manipulation by nonexperts), can survive only in a fairly wealthy country with a relatively stable socioeconomic, legal, and political order. Certainly, administrative law cannot be expected to mature in a volatile environment. Thus, despite some of the administrative system's shortcomings (for example, too many and confusing procedures, abuses of administrative discretion), public agencies overall have increased the quality of American life.

A SIGNIFICANT HISTORICAL DEVELOPMENT: THE DELEGATION OF POWER TO ADMINISTRATIVE AGENCIES

The American colonists fought against what they considered an abuse of power by British governors in the American colonies. As a result, the founding fathers made sure after the Revolutionary War that the powers granted to the executive branch were limited and controllable. This pattern was also established in the states. In some states governors were not even given enough power to govern properly, a fact of political life that still plagues some state executives today. But despite the fact that most state governors and even city mayors are still relatively weak, most governmental administrators today enjoy tremendous power—power that would almost certainly make our constitutional writers gasp with alarm. What has happened between then and now? Should Americans fear the trend toward more and more powerful administrators who cannot be checked through the ballot box?

The demand for public services caused government to increase, especially after President Franklin D. Roosevelt was elected and given a mandate by the people to employ administrative machinery to end the suffering caused by the Great Depression. As government expanded its operations and agency tasks became more specialized, legislators lost the ability and enthusiasm to scrutinize administrative activities as closely as they had done when governmental bureaucracy was smaller and simpler. To allow the president to lead and the government's bureaucracy to administer public programs expeditiously, U.S. legislators increasingly began to delegate and subdelegate their legislative powers to agency heads and their subordinates. But could legislative power be so delegated? Did this transfer of power from one branch to another violate the separation-of-powers doctrine, which seemed to be such a vital part of the U.S. Constitution?

Glen O. Robinson asserts that delegating legislative power to administrators has always presented a problem to liberal constitutionalists because concepts of trusteeship, rooted in English common law and Lockean theory, strictly prohibits the entrusted lawmaking power to be delegated away to undemocratically accountable administrators. Robinson notes that trusteeship "is a simple notion that requires no elaborate legal or political theory to defend, at least in principle. If the legislature is truly a trustee, any general transfer of entrusted power would seem a plain evasion of responsibility. The irresponsibility is heightened by the transfer of powers to a politically unresponsible bureaucracy."[25] Of course, delegation is also restricted in theory by the separation-of-powers doctrine, which the founding fathers regarded as fundamental to the U.S. Constitution.

A literalist look at the Constitution seems to indicate that the constitutional framers did not intend for the legislative branch to weaken itself by giving away its policymaking powers. The framers clearly made the legislative branch the strongest of the three branches, at least rhetorically. Article I, Section 1, of the U.S. Constitution states clearly that "all legislative powers herein granted shall be vested in a Congress of the United States, which shall consist of a Senate and House of Representatives." Section 8 of the same article also makes clear that "the Congress shall have . . . to make all laws which shall be necessary and proper for carrying into execution" all the enumerated powers listed in the section.

Article I, Section 8, specifically grants to Congress the powers to "collect taxes," "borrow money," "regulate commerce," "coin money," "establish Police offices and post roads," "declare war," "raise and support armies," "provide and maintain a navy," and so on. Could these specific powers be legally delegated to an administrative branch, thus encouraging the growth of vast bureaucratic power? Why did the constitutional framers enumerate what powers the Congress should have if they did not really care who, for example, regulated commerce or maintained a navy? These questions are tough ones to answer comfortably, especially since what was said in the Constitution and what was practiced by the constitutional framers clashed so sharply in the early years of the republic, when many who developed the Constitution served as congressmen. Despite what was written in the Constitution, as soon as the framers became congressmen, they enacted legislation that had the effect of giving away some of their legislative powers. For example, they authorized the president to regulate the provision of military pensions and establish pay scales for injured or disabled soldiers as he saw fit.

Before Curtiss-Wright: *Court Ambivalence Toward Delegation*

Ironically, especially in light of the rocky history of the delegation doctrine until well into the twentieth century, the first real challenge to the legitimacy of Congress to delegate legislative powers to administrators was overruled. In *The Cargo of the Brig Aurora, Brunside, claimant v. United States,* 11 U.S. (7 Crunch) 382 (1813), it was charged that the president should not be able, even under statutory authority, to determine when the Non-intercourse Act of 1809 should come into force because this task is legislative in nature and not purely executive in function. Justice William Johnson held, however, that it would be improper for such discretion not to be granted to a president: "We can see no reason, why the legislature should not exercise its discretion in reviewing the act . . . either expressly or conditionally, as their judgment should direct." In an extremely perceptive decision that even today sounds contemporary, Chief Justice John Marshall gave more support to the delegation doctrine in 1825, although his insightful decision was later overruled but then restored to some extent during the 1930s. In reflecting on the ability of Congress to handle *all* legislative tasks itself, Marshall commented: "It will not be contended that Congress can delegate to the courts, or to any other tribunal, powers which are strictly and exclusively legislative. But Congress may certainly delegate to others, powers which the legislature may rightfully exercise itself; the line has not been exactly drawn which separate those important subjects, which must be entirely regulated by the legislature itself, from those of less interest, in which a general provision may be made, and power given to those who are to act under such general provisions to fill up the details" *(Wayman v. Southward,* 23 U.S. [10 Wheat] 1, 15–16). When Marshall talked about distinguishing between "important subjects" and those that amount only to "provisions to fill up the details," he put his finger on the basic delegation doctrine controversy that is still argued heatedly among some scholars today.[26] That is, what constitutes significant legislative activity by administrators? What types of legislative functions by administrators seem truly minor or quasi-legislative in character? This is an important distinction, especially for those persons who are interested in preserving the democratic operating procedures in government, because different answers to the question make meaningful differences in how our system approaches the making of public policies.

The key to settling the dispute really centers around what the framers meant by *law* and what they felt constituted the "lawmaking" function. In 1852 a judicial attempt was made to distinguish between laws that should be made only by legis-lators and those "laws" (actually rules) that could be made by administrators. The position was taken that only legislators have the authority to make basic laws or determine which laws Americans should live under. It was argued that the power to decide on what "shall be" our laws should not be delegated: "The true distinc-tion is between the delegation of power to make the law, which necessarily in-volves a discretion as to what it shall be, and conferring authority to discretion as to its execution to be exercised under and in pursuance of the law" (*Cincinnati, W. & Z. P. Co. v. Commissioner,* 1 Ohio St. 77, 88).

The *Cincinnati* case had the effect of helping to develop a nondelegation doc-trine because it was held that legislators should not be allowed to permit those outside the legislative branch to engage in meaningful rulemaking that might in-fringe, even slightly, upon their policymaking powers. The opinion that signifi-cant legislative power should not be delegated was developed further in *Field v. Clark,* 143 U.S. 649 (1892) and *United States v. Shreveport Grain and Elevator Co.,* 287 U.S. 77 (1932). In these two cases the principle of nondelegation was upheld, although specific limited delegations were allowed. In *Field* the U.S. Supreme Court permitted the president to alter import duties at his discretion, yet acknowledged: "That Congress cannot delegate legislative power to the Presi-dent is a principle universally recognized as vital to the integrity and maintenance of the system of government ordained by the Constitution" (p. 1692). In *Shreve-port Grain and Elevator,* a relatively recent case in terms of the long court history of delegation disputes, the Court paid lip service to the virtues of nondelegation yet allowed "reasonable variations" so that the specific delegation could be up-held: "That the legislative power of Congress cannot be delegated is, of course, clear" (p. 85). But Kenneth C. Davis argues that such court decisions have befud-dled the status of delegation before the judiciary: "It is statements of this kind that have caused much of the difficulty in law development. Congress persisted in delegating, and the Court perceived that delegation was often necessary if the tasks of government were to be performed."[27] Nevertheless, there exists a long list of cases, even since 1930, in which the courts have allowed the specific delegation and yet opposed delegation in principle.

But for practical reasons—and the courts admitted this by their actions—the nondelegation doctrine could not survive in a climate which demands that admin-istrative agencies must occasionally act alone and devise "rules and regulations" so that the administrative process does not break down when implementing public programs. Administrators simply must make "shall be" policies themselves if their agencies are to be effective.

Since Schechter: *Toward Broad Delegation*

Today, various applications of doctrines limiting delegation are yielding to doc-trines permitting broad delegation; the latter take into account the limited capa-bilities of legislators in watching over administrative activities and the problems of administering public programs if the administrator's hands are tied. Only twice in American legal history did the courts find it appropriate to absolutely invalidate Congress's delegation of power to public officials. And in both cases unusual circumstances prevailed because power was not delegated to a normal administrative agency that functioned according to established procedures. In *Panama Refining Co. v. Ryan,* 293 U.S. 388 (1935), unusual administrative chaos prevailed, while in *Schechter Poultry Corp. v. United States,* 295 U.S. 495 (1935), an unreasonable, excessive amount of delegated authority was involved. Nevertheless, in these cases the Supreme Court did declare the National Industrial Recovery Act of 1933 unconstitutional, arguing that it authorized the unconstitutional delegation of legislative powers to the president and an executive agency. At this point, there was significant confusion over how far Congress could go in delegating its powers to the administrative branch.

But starting with *United States v. Curtiss-Wright Export Co.,* 299 U.S. 304 (1936), the courts have ruled consistently in favor of Congress's right to delegate authority, as long as Congress sets forth some meaningful standards to guide administrators in their efforts to implement governmental policies. For example, in *Sunshine Anthracite Coal Co. v. Atkins* (310 U.S. 381 [1940]), the Court noted that Congress must delegate some of its legislative powers to escape legislative futility. In *SEC v. Chenery Corp.,* 332 U.S. 194 (1947), the Court took the position that the delegation of legislative power is acceptable if administrators "strive to do as much as they reasonably can to develop and to make known the needed confinements of discretionary power through standards, principles, and rules." In *United States v. Southwestern Cable Co.,* 392 U.S. 157 (1968), the Court vaguely interpreted "standards" as administering in a manner consistent with law as "public convenience, intent, or necessity requires."

It is interesting to note that frequently, the courts bend to allow the inevitable to happen. During the New Deal, governmental bureaucracy was expanding rapidly to respond to public demands caused by the Great Depression. While the courts initially fought the trend, which involved a major transfer of public policy–making power from the legislative to the executive branch and the creation of an enormous, powerful public service system, they eventually yielded. It has often been said that courts tend to lead and shape society, but here was a vivid example of where the courts followed.

On the question of delegation, the reasoning behind the *Chenery* and *Southwestern Cable Co.* decisions has by now been widely accepted by the courts. These decisions, without doubt, have allowed administrative power to reach new heights in American society because although judges paid lip service to proper standards, their holdings did not define standards in a way that could effectively control abuses of administrative discretion. This has caused many legal scholars to worry over the possible emergence of uncontrollable, irresponsible, and oppressive administrative power, especially in light of a federal district court's upholding of the constitutionality of the Economic Stabilization Act of 1970. This act gave to the president sweeping powers to "issue such orders and regulations as he may deem appropriate to stabilize prices, wages and salaries at levels not less than those prevailing on May 25, 1970." On August 17, 1971, President Nixon did freeze all prices in the absence of any significant standards laid down by Congress. Believing that Nixon's actions were without precedent and clearly unconstitutional, the Amalgamated Meat Cutters Union brought suit, but the suit was flatly rejected by the court on the grounds that Congress had provided sufficient standards (*Amalgamated Meat Cutters v. Connally*, 337 F.Supp. 737, D.D.C. [1971]).

In 1974, in *National Cable Assn. v. United States*, 415 U.S. 336, the U.S. Supreme Court held that delegation of legislative power to administrative agencies was acceptable as long as "an intelligible principle" is attached. In this case Justice Thurgood Marshall seemed to even want to bury the nondelegation idea forever when he commented that nondelegation "was briefly in vogue in the 1930s, has been virtually abandoned by the Court for all practical purposes," and today "is surely as moribund as the substantive due process approach of the same era" (pp. 352–353). The spirit of Marshall's position was reiterated in *Algonquin SNG, Inc. v. Federal Energy Administration*, 518 F.2d 1051, 1063 (1975): "Here the delegated power is broad, and Congress has had repeated opportunities to limit it or withdraw it altogether. It has not done so, and I think this court should not do so." Although this was said by Judge Robb in dissent, the U.S. Supreme Court later upheld the wisdom of this opinion in overturning the appeals court's majority (426 U.S. 548 [1976]).

Justice Marshall is unquestionably right. The nondelegation doctrine is and has been dead since 1935. In fact, fifteen years after Marshall pronounced the nondelegation "very dead," the Supreme Court reaffirmed Marshall's pronouncement by noting: "After invalidating in 1935 two statutes as excessive delegations, . . . we have upheld, again without deviation, Congress' ability to delegate power under broad standards" (*Mistretta* v. *United States*, 109 S.Ct. 647, 655 [1989]).

Ironically, however, despite the "deadness" of the nondelegation doctrine, the Supreme Court agreed to hear several cases that focused upon the basic constitutional issues pertaining to delegation and the directly related issue of separation of powers. Presumably, the high court heard such cases because the conservative political climate during these years encouraged such old, basic constitutional questions pertaining to the very legitimacy of administrative power to be asked once again. The Court responded, but even this quite conservative court could not bring itself to reverse a well-established legal trend in complete support of broad delegation.

In *Mistretta*, for example, the Supreme Court upheld a broad delegation of discretionary legislative power to a sentencing commission, consisting of three federal judges, three academics, and one prison warden, all appointed by the president subject to Senate confirmation. Prisoners (Mistretta and others) argued that the Sentencing Reform Act (18 U.S.C.A., Section 3551 *et req.*) allowed Congress to delegate excessive legislative or policymaking discretion to the commission in violation of Article I, Section 1, of the U.S. Constitution, which prohibits Congress from delegating such basic lawmaking powers to another branch. But the Supreme Court disagreed, arguing "that the separation-of-powers principle, and the nondelegation doctrine in particular, do not prevent Congress from obtaining the assistance of its coordinate branches" (p. 654). As long as an "intelligible principle" is attached to congressional delegations, the Court asserted, the delegation, however broad, is constitutional (p. 654). The Court concluded "that in creating the Sentencing Commission . . . Congress neither delegated excessive legislative power nor upset the constitutionally mandated balance of powers among the coordinate Branches" (p. 675).

In 1991, in *Touby* v. *United States* (111 S.Ct. 1752), the Supreme Court upheld another broad delegation, one that granted the attorney general, under the provisions of the Comprehensive Drug Abuse Prevention and Control Act of 1970 [21 U.S.C.A., Sections 811(h), 812(b)], the discretionary authority to temporarily designate new controlled substances or "designer drugs" in order to avoid an "imminent hazard to the public safety." Petitioners argued that "more than an 'intelligible principle' is required when Congress authorizes another Branch to promulgate regulations that contemplate criminal sanctions." However, the Supreme Court concluded that the intelligible principle "passes muster even if greater congressional specificity is required in the criminal context" (p. 1756). Reiterating what it said in *Mistretta*, the court argued that "the nondelegation doctrine does not prevent Congress from seeking assistance, within proper limits, from its coordinate branches. Thus, Congress does not violate the Constitution merely because it legislates in broad terms, leaving a certain degree of discretion to executive or judicial actors" (p. 1756).

But even the "intelligible principle" doctrine carries little clout today. In 2001 a unanimous Supreme Court in *Whitman v. American Trucking Associations, Inc.*, 121 S.Ct. 903, upheld a very broad delegation of legislative power to Christine Whitman, head of the Environmental Protection Agency, allowing her to exercise vast discretion in promulgating national ambient air quality standards regarding air pollutants under the Clean Air Act, even though apparently no "intelligible principle" seemed to exist to help guide Whitman under the controversial provision, Section 109. The Court seemed to give almost no weight to the intelligible principle standard. Justice Thomas, in concurring, said, "I agree with the majority that Section 109's directive to the agency is no less an 'intelligible principle' than a host of other directives that we have approved" (p. 919). Thomas even argued that even though "this Court since 1928 has treated the 'intelligible principle' requirement as the only constitutional limit on congressional acts of power to administrative agencies, . . . the Constitution does not speak of 'intelligible principles'" (p. 921). So, reasoned Thomas, why should the Court? Thus, he concluded: "I am not convinced that the intelligible principle doctrine serves to prevent all cessions of legislative power" (p. 921).

Systems analysis can help us understand what happened to the nondelegation doctrine. In 1831 Justice Story exclaimed in *Shankland v. Washington*, 5 Pet. 390, 395 (U.S. 1831): "The general rule of law is, that a delegated authority cannot be delegated." In 1892 Justice Harlan noted similarly: "That Congress cannot delegate legislative power . . . is a principle universally recognized as vital to the integrity and maintenance of the system of government ordained by the

Constitution" (*Field v. Clark*, 143 U.S. 649, 692). And in 1989 Justice Scalia, dissenting in *Mistretta*, stressed that the courts "must be particularly rigorous in preserving the Constitution's structural restrictions that deter excessive delegation. The major one . . . is that the power to make law cannot be exercised by anyone other than Congress" (p. 678).

Bernard Schwartz points out that "the law on delegation has moved from the theoretical prohibition against any delegation of legislative power . . . to a rule against unrestricted delegations (i.e., those that are not limited by *standards*)."[28] But the question remains, how could such a basic constitutional principle of nondelegation reach a point where it plays virtually no role in our constitutional system? Actually, the reasons are quite clear and, from a system's perspective, very understandable. One reason is that the judiciary really cannot practically develop meaningful tests to distinguish permissible delegations from nonpermissible ones. But second, and much more important, our governmental system simply could not and cannot function efficiently and effectively unless broad delegations of legislative powers are permitted. In other words, broad delegations are upheld by the courts, not because they are technically constitutional, but because practicality or sound government requires such broad delegations to administrators. Possibly Justice Blackmun, writing for the majority in *Mistretta*, said it best: "Our jurisprudence has been driven by a practical understanding that in our increasingly complex society, replete with ever changing and more technical problems, Congress simply cannot do its job absent an ability to delegate power under broad general directives"(p. 654).

Delegation of Judicial Powers

Most delegation cases deal with the issue of whether Congress can delegate legislative power to administrative agencies, but agency power has increased through Congress's delegation of adjudicative powers as well. Article III, Section 1, of the Constitution clearly states that "the judicial power of the United States shall be vested in one Supreme Court and in such inferior Courts as the Congress shall from time to time ordain." In this light, can Congress legally bestow judicial powers on nonjudicial bodies or administrative agencies? The answer is yes. Actually, the delegation of judicial power to administrative agencies has never caused the same intense concern as when legislative powers have been delegated, despite the similar encroachment upon the separation-of-powers doctrine. This is probably largely due to the fact that legislative acts, whether by Congress or public agencies, have normally and traditionally had a much greater impact on society than judicial acts. It is true that although federal appellate and U.S. Supreme Court holdings have had profound social consequences (for example, in the areas of education, housing, criminal procedure, and civil rights), agency-adjudicated decisions in general have had comparatively minor impact. This is not to suggest that agency adjudications have not significantly affected some industries. But agency rulemaking is macro-oriented, while ordermaking is more micro-oriented. Thus, as methods for promulgating public policies, the former would likely cause more public concern than the latter.

However, it is also important to emphasize that agency rules are generally less reviewable than agency orders. This makes the delegation of judicial power much less threatening to those concerned about the undermining of the separation of powers. As long as judicial review is not precluded, the Court argued in the precedential case *Cromwell v. Benson*, 285 U.S. 22 (1932), the delegation of judicial power to administrative agencies seems both reasonable and necessary. In judging the constitutionality of delegated judicial power to public agencies, the Court held that "Congress did not attempt to define questions of law, and the generality of the description leaves no doubt of the intention to reserve to the Federal court full authority to pass upon all matters which this Court has held to fall within that category. There is thus no attempt to interfere with, but rather provision is made to facilitate, the exercise by the court of its jurisdiction to deny effect to any administrative finding which is without evidence, or 'contrary to the indisputable character of the evidence,' or where the hearing is 'inadequate,' or 'unfair,' or arbitrary in any respect" (pp. 49–50). In *City of Waukegan v. Pollution Control Board*, 57 Ill. 2d 170 (1974), Justice Ward argued that the U.S. Supreme Court has never found it appropriate to rule that judicial power had been vested improperly in a public agency. In addition, he contended, citing several administrative law experts, any delegation of authority, whether legislative or judicial, does not violate the separation-of-powers doctrine as long as effective legislative or judicial checks exist. "It may be irrelevant if an agency has legislative or judicial characteristics," he maintained, "so long as the legislature or the judiciary can effectively correct errors of the agency" (p. 175).[29]

However, in *Northern Pipeline Construction Co. v. Marathon Pipe Line Co.*, 458 U.S. 50 (1982), the Court handed down a decision that created some confusion regarding the delegation of adjudicative powers to administrative agencies. In *Northern Pipeline* the Court's plurality vaguely applied the old, public rights/private rights test to agency adjudicative authority, apparently arguing that questions of public rights can be heard in agency adjudications but those involving private rights must be heard before a regular court established under Article III of the U.S. Constitution. Parenthetically, although not always easy to distinguish, an issue involving a public right involves the government and another party (for example, the Federal Communications Commission and a TV station), while a private right involves a question between private parties only (for example, TWA and a mechanic's union). Administrative law critic Bernard Schwartz, as well as many others, severely criticized this decision, arguing that the employment of the public rights/private rights test to determine adjudicative authority was rejected nearly a century ago. "It is too late in the development of our administrative law for there to be any question of the legislative power to delegate adjudicatory power to agencies. Adjudications of both public and private rights may be committed to administrative agencies, as long as their decisions are subject to judicial review. To indicate otherwise, as *Northern Pipeline* did, is to go back almost a century in administrative law development."[30] Fortunately, three years later in *Thomas v. Union Carbide Agricultural Products Co.*, 105 S.Ct. 3325 (1985), the Supreme Court rectified its apparent error in judgment by flatly rejecting the public rights/private rights test and reaffirming the long-established judicial opinion that the legislature has the authority to delegate adjudicative powers to administrative agencies, regardless of whether public or private rights are involved, as long as agency adjudicative decisions are subject to judicial review.

However, in 1989 the Supreme Court, in *Granfinanciera S.A. v. Nordberg*, 109 S.Ct. 2782, relied again on the public right/private right distinction, causing more confusion regarding when agency adjudications are unconstitutional because a party is entitled to a jury trial in an Article III court versus when they are constitutional because no jury trial is required. In *Granfinanciera* the court held that the Seventh Amendment's jury trial requirement applies because the disputes pertaining to a bankruptcy involve only private parties. Thus, as a result of inconsistent reliance on the public right/private right test by the Supreme Court when reviewing the constitutionality of agency adjudicative authority, it is not clear today exactly what delegations of judicial powers to agencies are constitutional. Nonetheless, as a general rule, as developed in *Cromwell*, it can be said that most agency adjudications are constitutional under the separation-of-powers doctrine, as long as the delegation of judicial power to administrative agencies in the statutory scheme permits judicial review (*Glenborough New Mexico Assoc. v. Resolution Trust*, 802 F.Supp. 387, 391 [D.N.M. 1992]; *Whitman v. American Trucking Associations*,121 S.Ct. 903 [2001]).

In conclusion, it should be noted that the courts will continue to permit agencies to adjudicate a variety of disputes, even when they involve only private parties, because our courts simply don't have the time or expertise to settle such disputes. The fact is that the Social Security Administration alone adjudicates about 300,000 cases each year, or over ten times the total caseload of all federal judges. According to Kenneth C. Davis and Richard J. Pierce, Jr., agency adjudications are preferable because they (1) cost far less than court trials, (2) yield more consistent and accurate results, and (3) relieve the courts of an enormous burden that they could not possibly handle.[31]

Delegation at the State Level

The judiciary has in general significantly contributed to the growth of administrative power by upholding broad delegations of power from legislatures to administrators. Although for a few decades after *Curtiss-Wright* (1936) the courts timidly espoused the principle that broad delegation was only acceptable if meaningful standards were attached, by the 1970s the federal courts seemed to have abandoned any serious effort to make legislators comply with the meaningful standard requirement. Even though the prevalent judicial mood appears to indicate that the nondelegation doctrine is dead, there are definite signs at the state level that some questions pertaining to the legitimate limits of delegated authority still exist.

State courts, following the trend set by the federal courts, have normally upheld broad delegations (*Manduley v. Superior Court*, 27 Cal. 4th 537 [2002]), but occasionally they have refused to uphold the constitutionality of broad delegations when the legislative body failed to attach any meaningful standards to guide administrative actions. The fact is that state judges are more likely than federal judges to question the competence of state and local administrators and trust them. Of course, most states, particularly the more rural ones, have simpler regulatory problems and can afford to insist that state legislatures attach more meaningful standards. Also, state courts have invoked a fundamental administrative law principle that agencies, including municipalities, are mere creatures of statutory powers delegated to them by the state legislative branch, since they have no inherently independent or common law powers. In *Subcontractors Trade v. Koch*, 62 N.Y. 2d 422 (1984), a New York court held that Mayor Koch was not delegated the legislative power to mandate that "locally based enterprises" must get at least 10 percent of all construction contracts awarded by New York City. "In order for the executive to lawfully mandate the award of construction contracts to a particular group or category of business enterprise, the legislature must *specifically* delegate the power to him and must provide adequate guidelines and standards for the implementation of that policy" (p. 429). In *State Dept. of Env. Reg. v. Puckett Oil*, 577 So. 2d 988 (Fla. App. 1 Dist. 1991), a Florida court struck a blow against broad delegation by overruling a state agency's actions that were "in excess of any express or reasonably implied delegated legislative authority" (p. 991). The court noted that "it is well recognized that the power of administrative agencies are measured and limited by statutes or acts in which such powers are expressly granted or implicitly conferred" (p. 991). While in *Klein v. Leis*, 146 Ohio App. 3d 526 (2002), an irritated Ohio court said that "this court cannot rule on the propriety or efficacy" of new laws dealing with concealed weapons because the laws are much too vague, thus constituting an unconstitutional delegation. The court noted that "vague statutes are open to subjective interpretation, rather than objective application. The result, which is confusing or opaque to the average citizen—and to police officers, lawyers, judges, and jurors—is an unconstitutional delegation of public policy matters. When the police, the citizens, and the courts all must guess at the meaning of a criminal statute, subjective and arbitrary enforcement results" (pp. 538–539). Consider how far this opinion is from the opinions of the U.S. Supreme Court on broad delegations.

Subdelegation

All experienced administrative practitioners know that, as a matter of necessity, authority granted to those at the top of the organizational hierarchy must be delegated to subordinates. If this were not done, little could be accomplished, simply because the chief executive officer, the person at the top, is technically the only nonsubordinate in the pyramidal structure. This chief could not be expected to carry out all functions. The justification for subdelegating authority to subordinates was stated decades ago by Commissioner Eastman of the Interstate Commerce

Commission: "Sound principles of organization demand that those at the top be able to concentrate their attention upon the larger and more important questions of policy and practice, and that their time be freed, so far as possible, from consideration of smaller and less important matters of detail."[32] Presidents, state governors, agency heads, and the like clearly cannot be expected to personally handle all tasks legally delegated only to them.

As early as 1839 the Supreme Court upheld the rights of a president to informally subdelegate powers to his department heads, even though the statutes did not technically permit such a delegation. For decades during the nineteenth century, presidents did not push the subdelegation doctrine too far, mostly because the mood of the day seemed to forbid irresponsible subdelegation to those to whom legislators did not formally grant power. In 1887 the U.S. Supreme Court ruled that a president cannot subdelegate a power to a subordinate if a statute requires a president to employ his personal judgment *(Runkle v. United States,* 122 U.S. 543). However, for many decades now "subdelegation has become a mainstay of government operation."[33] For example, in *United States v. Cottman Co.,* 190 F.2d 805, 807 (1952), the court reasoned: "It is manifestly necessary that he [the secretary of the treasury] delegate duties of this sort [remitting custom duties] to subordinate officials."

The general rule pertaining to subdelegation is that the subdelegation is allowed if the legislative body has specifically authorized it or if the statute is silent on the issue. For instance, in *In Re Advisory Opinion to Governor,* 627 A.2d 1246 (R.I. 1993), the Supreme Court of Rhode Island opined that "the test for determining whether a subdelegation is valid is primarily a question of statutory interpretation. . . . Our obligation is to determine whether the General Assembly fairly intended to grant the director of the DOT the power to subdelegate" (p. 1250). In this case the court upheld the subdelegation not only because the statute in part specifically permitted it but also because, even where the statute was silent on the subdelegation question, at least the statute did not prohibit the subdelegation (p. 1250).

Occasionally, a statute may prohibit subdelegation because the legislature believes that the specific duty is too important to subdelegate to subordinates. For example, in *United States* v. *Giordano,* 416 U.S. 505 (1974), the Supreme Court ruled against a subdelegation by the U.S. attorney general to his executive assistant. The court held that a fair reading of the statute limited the power "to the Attorney General himself" (p. 514).

Subdelegation Issues

Most legal scholars argue that it makes little sense to continue to debate whether powers should be subdelegated, but they do voice serious concern over how effectively and responsibly authority is subdelegated to subordinates by superiors. Kenneth C. Davis, who is known best in the administrative law field for his research into the proper limits of administrative discretion, believes that subdelegated authority not accompanied by meaningful standards poses a threat to rational administrative processes and should therefore be forbidden: "When the discretion of officers in individual cases is insufficiently confined and insufficiently guided by standards, a subdelegation which fails to do what reasonably can and should be done to confine and to guide discretion may well be held invalid."[34]

Subdelegation of authority to those who are technically not supposed to wield such power raises other serious questions for legislators, administrators, and the American public. If you were a legislator held politically accountable for your actions, would you feel uneasy about delegating lawmaking powers to agency heads, knowing that these public policy–making powers will quite possibly be subdelegated to those far down in the agency's decisionmaking pyramid? If you were an agency administrator, would you feel comfortable delegating vital policymaking assignments to those who are not ultimately responsible for seeing to it that the job tasks are handled properly? As for the public, should it feel content with a subdelegation process in which important public policy decisions are sometimes made by lower-level personnel? Do you think it is wise for relatively low-ranking agency officials with less training and relevant experience in, say, the U.S. Department of Housing and Urban Development to draft housing policies that affect millions? Do such things in fact happen, at more than one agency? Do you believe that it is sensible for lowly administrators in the field to employ their subdelegated authority under existing legislation to propose (that is, virtually to make) rules and regulations that will eventually govern industry behavior, knowing their rules will probably be accepted in a pro forma manner only by their superiors? How adequately can superiors be expected to supervise and scrutinize the work of their subordinates when it involves reviewing relatively important, informally promulgated rules or adjudicated decisions? How far down the organizational ladder should subdelegation authority pass before democratic decisionmaking processes are threatened, thus jeopardizing democratic accountability in the American political system? But regardless of the democratic accountability problems posed by subdelegation, do we have any practical choice but to subdelegate powers to our public administrators and trust them to act responsibly?

Conclusion

In sum, the extremely permissive position taken by the courts regarding the delegation, as well as the subdelegation, of legislative power to administrative agencies since the mid-1930s has expanded the scope and powers of administrators beyond limitations that the Founders would have perceived as tolerable. The typical administrative agency today makes, administers, and adjudicates its own policies, and these agency policies frequently have significant social consequences. Theodore Lowi, like many others, looks with disfavor on this development because he holds that it is irresponsible for Congress to delegate broad legislative powers without attaching clear and useful guidelines. This present trend toward broader and broader delegation, Lowi maintains, cannot but reduce the policymaking input and impact of Congress to a relative insignificance.[35] Joseph Harris, however, argues that Congress should grant vast policymaking powers to public agencies, leaving the authority broad and vague enough that administrators can make appropriate policies to resolve particular program problems.[36] Despite the extensive policymaking powers of agencies today, administrative actions are no longer so carefully scrutinized, either by legislators or judges. Neither the courts nor legislative bodies seem to have the time, will, or expertise to do the supervising. This seems to leave the United States in a potentially dangerous position.

Administrators cannot be led to believe that just about anything they do may be considered acceptable. Discretionary power must be controlled if freedom is to survive. However, at the same time we cannot turn back the clock to days when life was simpler. No longer are there only a few million Americans living in the United States; the population is approaching 300 million. Such a large population and the problems that go with a vast and complicated technological society necessitate an enlarged government to operate and coordinate needed programs in a complex society. Administrators need to have enough freedom and flexibility to implement programs successfully. The solution is to seek a sensible and viable balance that will permit administrators to function without crippling handcuffs yet still to work under the scrutiny of legislators, judges, or newly created watchdog agencies that have power to provide realistic vital checks. And because legislators cannot possibly be expected to draft legislation and attach meaningful standards to every phase (unanticipated and critical policy questions will always be left for administrators to resolve), less emphasis should be placed on seeking standards. More attention, however, should be placed on training public officials in and sensitizing them to principles of democratic accountability and on developing broad institutional safeguards to aid in preventing unnecessary, uncontrollable, and abusive administrative discretion.

THE POWER OF ADMINISTRATIVE
OFFICIALS AND AGENCIES

The powers originally assigned to the administrative system were quite limited, at least in a formal sense. Informally, of course, administrative agencies have always exercised more power than the statutes seemed to permit. Nevertheless, public agencies had a very limited role in the legislative and judicial areas of policy formation. Today, however, administrative agencies actually make more public policies than the legislative branch and decide more legal issues than the courts. It was once popular to suggest that administrative agencies possess quasi-legislative and quasi-judicial powers in addition to their normal executive powers. But in recent years it has been commonly argued among legal scholars that the prefix *quasi-* is a misnomer because it creates a misconception regarding the real authority administrative agencies have in the legislative and judicial areas. *Quasi-* implies that administrators have only the appearance of possessing such powers, but this is bogus, argues Justice John Stevens, concurring in *Whitman v. American Trucking Associations*, 121 S.Ct. 903, 920 (2001), at least regarding agency rulemaking power: "I am persuaded that it would be both wiser and more faithful to . . . admit that agency rulemaking is legislative power."

Although a case can still be made for calling the legislative and judicial powers of administrative agencies quasi-legislative and quasi-judicial, it is no longer realistic to do so. For all practical purposes, administrators nowadays are allowed to make significant public policies in some areas, to judge the merits of their laws, and even to hand out penalties to those who do not comply with their policies. James Burnham has referred to bureaucrats as the new ruling class of all advanced nations, while Eugene P. Dvorin and Robert H. Simmons have argued that misguided and inhumane public administrators have inherited so much power that the traditional, tripartite model of government, with powers divided among the legislative, executive, and judicial branches, has lost its functional meaning.[37]

Examples of the Power of Administrators

And why should people not cry out against the expanding role of bureaucratic power? After all, with the odds greatly against any administrator's being stopped by legislators or judges from executing some action (implying that administrators may in certain cases actually possess de facto rather than de jure powers), bureaucrats have relatively broad discretionary power. For example, they can (1) give or deny persons welfare benefits; (2) grant or deny licenses involving great financial investment and careers; (3) prosecute or not prosecute felonious crimes; (4) expel students from public schools; (5) deport persons from the United States; (6) close down businesses; (7) seize a person's parked car for payment of back taxes; (8) take certain children away from their parents; (9) decide to demand or dismiss taxes that they consider due the government; (10) take away individually owned land and homes and build highways on their sites; (11) hold innocent people in jail cells as material witnesses for long periods of time; (12) strip people down at airports without genuine probable cause to carry out humiliating searches of their naked bodies; (13) prevent families from moving into their newly purchased homes until they comply with "occupancy permit" demands that frequently involve minor, yet expensive and inconvenient repairs; (14) forbid home owners from changing such things as a simple electrical switch in their own houses until they purchase permits; (15) prevent persons from parking particular motor vehicles in their own driveways; (16) forbid entrepreneurs from placing advertising signs beyond a certain size in their store windows; (17) prevent landlords from raising rents or even from expelling tenants; (18) fine companies for not complying with safety or anti-pollution standards; (19) require certain private businesses to hire minority-group persons as employees; (20) force parents to send their children to schools far away from their own neighborhoods; and (21) implement Homeland Security measures denying individuals freedoms and personal privacy protections.

It should be acknowledged that some of these powers rightfully belong to legislators and judges, but the point is that administrators, for all practical purposes, possess sufficient discretionary power to give concrete meaning to laws and orders. For example, John Ashcroft, as head of the Justice Department, and Tom Ridge, as head of the Department of Homeland Security, honorable intentions aside, have enormous discretionary power to promulgate regulations that could severely restrict our basic civil liberties. As a practical matter, legislators have already delegated this awesome discretionary authority to promulgate such restrictive policies, while the courts believe that they should defer to agency interpretations of statutes as long as Congress has not specifically prohibited the discretionary action.

Do Administrators Possess Too Much Power?

Not surprisingly, many scholars today characterize the United States as an administrative state. Legal experts have estimated (see Chapter 1) that more than 90 percent of the laws that regulate American life are made by nonelected career bureaucrats with extreme job security. Is our democratic heritage threatened by the emergence of the administrative state? Is America sacrificing democratic political controls for administrative efficiency? These very critical questions need serious attention, especially in view of such statements on democracy as this one by Lewis Mainzer: "Elected officials rightly claim to be, more truly than bureaucrats, in the democratic stream. In formulating a democratic theory of political control of bureaucrats, the first rule must be that any fundamental rejection of political control is antidemocratic."[38]

The power of elected administrators (the president, state governors, state attorneys general, sheriffs, auditors, and so on) and top administrative appointees, as well as that of career civil servants, has also increased dramatically in recent decades. Although the voters have more direct control over elected officials and their appointees, problems of control exist here also. Methods such as the recall to unseat irresponsible elected officials are not very effective. Recently a rare event took place in California: Governor Gray Davis was removed from office by recall. Yet Davis is the only governor in California's history to be successfully recalled and only the second governor to be removed by this means in U.S. history. Elected officials who direct powerful administrative apparatus can do much harm if they abuse their positions of power. Presidents, of course, serve four-year terms, and some state officials serve as long as six years before they have to run for reelection. It is easy to find instances when presidents have strengthened their power positions, potentially threatening the constitutional system of democratic checks and balances they are sworn to uphold. Presidents can expand their powers (and have done so) in the American system simply by stepping a little further than previous presidents who had also exceeded their formal, constitutional powers. In the political science classroom today it is next to useless to try to explain presidential power to students by way of the U.S. Constitution. Professors must instead talk in terms of the president's informal powers. The president now initiates most legislation in the domestic sphere and drafts practically all bills in the foreign policy area. Treaties, which were once the exclusive domain of Congress, are now made by the president, under the name of executive agreements.

Examples of the Impact of Administrative Decisions: The FAA's Decision to Ground and NASA's Decision to Launch

Federal Aviation Administrator Langhorne Bond stated publicly on June 5, 1979: "Overnight my certitude has switched from the position of high likelihood of no risk to sufficient likelihood of risk and that's enough to put the planes on the ground."[39] Bond's decision to ground DC-10s for an indefinite period after investigations into the airworthiness of this aircraft helps to demonstrate the mighty, though frequently justifiable, powers regulatory administrators may wield. Eleven days before Bond issued the temporary order, a DC-10 had crashed in Chicago, killing 279 persons, making it the worst air disaster in the history of U.S. aviation. The DC-10 had also been involved in other serious accidents in the 1970s, including a major crash that killed 346 people near Paris. Nevertheless, despite these human tragedies and Bond's obligation as FAA chief to protect the public's safety, complaints about his decision to ground the DC-10s were heated and plentiful.

Bond was criticized by those who had to cope with inconveniences caused by flight cancellations but mainly by those who stood to suffer great financial losses as a result of the DC-10s being declared not airworthy. The McDonnell Douglas Corporation, manufacturer of the DC-10, stood to lose hundreds of millions of dollars in decreased sales and millions more for repairs, as well as suffer costly damage to its image as a reputable aircraft company. Bond's decision would also place a hardship on domestic and foreign airlines, although these were technically out of his jurisdiction. U.S. airlines were expected to lose millions of dollars daily, based on 1978 airline profits, which showed DC-10 flights generating earnings of approximately $6 million per day in gross revenues. Since a significant percentage of passenger seat miles would be affected by the grounding, the loss estimates indeed appeared to place these U.S. airlines under financial stress, possibly jeopardizing their ability to stay in business. Shippers, travel agents, the hotel and motel industry, and many other businesses that depend on the transportation of air passengers would undoubtedly also feel the effects of Bond's grounding order.[40]

Top-level public administrators frequently find themselves caught between a rock and a hard place. NASA administrators found themselves in such a precarious position in the weeks before they gave the fatal OK to launch the space shuttle *Challenger* on that cold, icy Florida morning of January 28, 1986. About seventy-three seconds after ignition, combustion gas leaked through faulty O-ring seals in the right booster rocket and caused the shuttle to explode, killing the entire crew, destroying the costly spacecraft and its valuable payload, severely damaging the image of U.S. space technology, and indefinitely postponing America's space program.

As is often said after a tragedy, this was an accident just waiting to happen. In a situation similar to Bond's, Arnold Aldrich, the space shuttle program manager,

and other top NASA officials were constantly pressured to place financial and political considerations before safety concerns. According to the *Report of the Presidential Commission on the Space Shuttle Accident* (popularly known as the Rogers
Commission Report), pressure to produce in a cost-effective manner and NASA's
accommodating "can-do" attitude led NASA to increase its flight rate schedule
unrealistically, compromising safety standards.[41] Testifying before the Rogers
Commission, Leonard Nicholson, manager of Space Transportation System Integration and Operations at Johnson Space Center, said that attempts were made
to voice concerns about the shuttle launch, "but the political aspects of the decision are so overwhelming that our concerns do not carry much weight," and the
"political advantages of implying those late changes outweighed our general objections."[42] In response, the Rogers Commission recommended: "It is important
to determine how many flights can be accommodated, and accommodated safely.
NASA must establish a realistic level of expectation, then approach it carefully.
Mission schedules should be based on a realistic assessment of what NASA can
do safely and well, not on what is possible with maximum efforts."[43]

It is clear that the space shuttle *Challenger* disaster was caused more by administrative shortcomings than design or mechanical failures, since technical problems can be resolved through thoughtful administrative actions. The Rogers
Commission Report concluded "that there was a serious flaw in the decision
making process leading up to the launch. . . . A well structured and managed system emphasizing safety would have flagged the rising doubts about the Solid
Rocket Booster joint seal," making the launch unlikely. "The waiving of launch
constraints appears to have been at the expense of flight safety."[44]

It is easy to criticize NASA officials in retrospect for succumbing to the political and financial pressures to launch, but the pressures were severe. NASA's
budget was lean, shuttle missions were behind schedule, and *Challenger*'s launch
had already been delayed three times, important future missions faced long delays, grumblings were heard from legislators, impatient private clients wanted
their satellites placed in orbit, and President Reagan was scheduled to deliver his
State of the Union message that evening and comments about the *Challenger*
mission were in his speech.[45] Given these acute demands, it is not hard to understand why administrators often take risks that compromise safety, especially when
questions of safety involve speculative judgments. The odds of a serious accident
happening "this time" are normally very low, while economic and political realities are usually quite clear. Given so many environmental demands, it is also easy
to understand, as mentioned previously, why the procedural due process dictates
of administrative law are sometimes not given the attention they deserve by administrators desperately trying to survive.

In the winter of 2003 the shuttle *Columbia* burned up and disintegrated upon
reentering the earth's atmosphere, killing the entire crew. NASA has apparently
not learned from the *Challenger* disaster. According to physicist and Nobel Prize
winner Richard Feynman, who served on the Rogers Commission, NASA tends
to play "Russian roulette" when it makes decisions. Years after the *Challenger*

tragedy, NASA again began to get involved in serious conflicts of interest that placed financial priorities above safety. For example, the only review for possible wing damage caused by tank debris on liftoff was conducted by engineers for Boeing, which makes about $2 billion a year from NASA contracts. NASA gambled on the O-ring problem in 1986 with the *Challenger,* and it gambled with the "tank debris" problem in 2003 with the *Columbia.* Just as engineers and other experts warned NASA about likely O-ring failures under cold temperature conditions in 1986, engineers and other experts warned NASA about tank debris falling off and damaging heat-resistant wing tiles, which is what led to the *Columbia* tragedy. A March 9, 2003, *St. Louis Post-Dispatch* editorial concluded that NASA had changed certain safety procedures since *Challenger,* but the *Columbia* disaster occurred because NASA had not changed its "institutional culture," and "that lesson should not have to be learned twice."

As these three tragic cases demonstrate, public administrators sometimes make decisions that have an enormous impact on various interests in our society. Obviously, agency heads such as FAA's Langhorne Bond and NASA's Arnold Aldrich make billion-dollar decisions, ones that can lead to jubilant celebrations or mournful funeral processions. Some, usually those who have suffered the consequences of adverse agency decisions, feel that billion-dollar and life-or-death decisionmaking power should not be left to agency regulators who function relatively independent of viable political oversight. But the hard truth is that someone or some decisionmaking body must make these tough decisions if public policy goals are to be reached. Thus far Congress has found it appropriate to delegate such decisionmaking authority to agency administrators because legislators believe that agency experts are in the best position to reach intelligent decisions.

Some Serious Concerns About Administrative Power

Elected, appointed, and regular career administrators have inherited vast powers through one channel or another. Over time administrative powers have expanded in scope and intensity. Despite all the attempts to limit and control the power of administrators through various pieces of legislation and court decisions, there has undoubtedly been a significant net gain in power for administrative agencies. This enormous growth in the power of governmental agencies has without doubt upset the traditional constitutional power allocations among governmental branches and increased the probability of oppressive and unpopular government.

Regardless of these contentions, Walter Gellhorn argues that the power of administrators has been exaggerated and that it is not nearly so great as many observers suspect. Actually, Gellhorn noted to this author, most administrators he has known over the decades who have left Washington posts did so because they felt they had too little power and were frustrated in their efforts to perform their jobs adequately.[46] Gellhorn may be right, but if questions are posed that put administrative power in perspective, it is easier to assess the relative power of administrators. Compared with the powers of individual legislators and judges, how would you rank the power position of administrative chiefs today? How has the power of individual administrators grown since 1789, as compared with the power of legislators and judges? In light of the historical facts, it would be difficult to argue persuasively that individual legislators or judges are, on the whole, more powerful and influential than top-level administrators, especially in view of the impact these administrators have today on determining the content of social programs. Also, it would be virtually impossible to argue credibly that growth in administrative power since 1789 has not far outstripped gains in power among legislators and judges. In short, it may be correct to hold, as Gellhorn does, that administrators are frequently frustrated by checks that tend to undermine their authority, but it is probably also true that the powers of legislators and judges are checked even more rigorously.

Some readers may be thinking that the U.S. is not so bad and that they have not been treated very unfairly, if unfairly at all, by public administrators. Because most administrators have a sense of right and wrong, adhere to a professional code of conduct, and face performance reviews, or at least the threat of review, administrative behavior in America has probably been relatively honorable. But in this frank discussion of administrative power, what is being mainly addressed is not how administrators have performed, but how they could function if they had no scruples or public conscience. As it stands right now, the potential for abuse by administrators is great because our political system has thus far probably granted too much power to administrative agencies. But this is so only because power has been extended without arranging for adequate checks or taking the time to consider seriously the grave consequences of allowing so much power to pass to the administrative branch.

There are additional reasons for concern over the potential for executives and administrative agencies to misuse their powers. Much administrative behavior is protected under various interpretations of the sovereign and official immunity doctrines. Even if the questionable behavior of administrative agencies is challenged in the courts, the odds of a successful appeal are low. Also, despite the unfair treatment a person may experience from a public administrator, it is virtually impossible to get an incompetent and irresponsible civil service employee dismissed. Classified civil service employees are well protected by a so-called merit system that needs fundamental revision if these administrators, as contrasted to politically appointed administrators, are to be made more responsible to the public.

ADMINISTRATIVE GROWTH, THE PUBLIC INTEREST, AND ADMINISTRATIVE LAW CONSIDERATIONS

Introduction: Growth, Administrative Law, and the Public Interest

Ideally, the central purpose of government is to promote the public interest. This point is made clear in the writings of most political theorists over the centuries. American administrative law deals essentially with the propriety of the procedures used by public administrators to implement policies designed to promote the public interest. More specifically, administrative law provides the standards that must be incorporated into the methods employed by regulatory agencies in their attempts to regulate societal activities in the public interest. As discussed earlier in this chapter, dramatic changes in the complexity of social functions have caused the demands on government to increase at an accelerated pace, thus giving birth to the reality of the administrative state in our political system. But this new administrative state has needed to be controlled. Consequently, administrative law surfaced as a pervasive legal check to help ensure that the rise of the administrative state would not be accompanied by the demise of democratic institutional practices necessary to protect the public interest.

However, despite the emergence of procedural due process protections stemming from the growth of administrative law, many citizens, some of them scholars, have questioned the legitimacy of the major role played by the administrative system in public policy making, as well as the ability and willingness of public agency officials to represent the general public fairly and to regulate in the public interest in a democratically responsible fashion. Consequently, in the 1970s a reform movement began aimed at forcing public agencies to act more within the public interest. When, over a quarter century ago, the editors of the *Public Administration Review* devoted their attention to the problem of public interest representation in the federal bureaucracy, symposium editor Edgar Shor commented: "In a remarkably short time, the remedy of public interest representation has gained wide acceptance as a way of increasing administrative responsiveness and accountability to the public. Indeed, for the persistently suspect administrative process, and recurrently questioned bureaucratic exercise of vast discretionary power, the representativeness of agency proceedings conceivably could become a touchstone of their legitimacy. At any rate, political and executive leaders, along with administrators, can expect continuing demands for the further institutionalization of public interest advocacy."[47] The institutionalization of public interest advocacy has continued into the twenty-first century, but the movement has been weakened significantly by diminished resources, political conservation, and new, urgent political priorities, especially since September 11, 2001.

Defining the Public Interest

For administrative agencies to work toward fulfilling the public interest, that interest must be reasonably identified. Public interest goals must be defined clearly enough so that agencies can pursue understandable and relatively concrete objectives (for example, the reduction of environmental pollution to "acceptable" levels), while genuine public interest groups must be recognizable. But can this be done? Arguments over definitions of the public interest have bothered social scientists for literally centuries and, in the past fifty years, have severely hampered the positive development of administrative law and governmental regulatory practices. The root of the definitional problem seems to be buried in the fact that the term *public interest* has been defined in radically different and often contradictory ways. Several definitions of the concept have been attempted, but it appears that no definition has been broadly accepted. In what is nonetheless something of a classic definition, Walter Lippman has been quoted as defining public interest as "what men would choose if they saw clearly, thought rationally, and acted disinterestedly and benevolently."[48] J. A. W. Gun believes that the public interest is similar to what Jeremy Bentham meant by *utilitarianism,* while J. W. R. Coy believed that majority will was the guts of public interest.[49] However, many have argued, including Robert Miewald, Frank Sorauf, and Glendon Schubert, that the concept of public interest is much too vague to have any practical utility for public administrators.[50] In fact, Miewald poses this disturbing question: "What about the possibility that there is no such thing, at least not in the sense of an operational standard against which specific administrative acts can be measured before the fact?"[51] Miewald humorously adds: "It should be quite clear that on the bureaucrat's first day on the job, the orientation officer is not able to say, 'There's the washroom, there's the water cooler, and over there in the corner is the public interest.'"[52] Despite Miewald's strong feeling that it would certainly be helpful if agency rulemakers could be guided by an identifiable public interest, he concludes, as do most public interest group theorists, that "there is no public interest—not in the sense of an identifiable, enduring 'thing.' The closest one can come to it is the will of the majority of voters at any particular time."[53]

Those who argue that the public interest cannot be operationalized meaningfully so that the concept can provide worthwhile guidance for agency regulators in promulgating rules (public policies) may be right, but it appears silly to argue that nothing exists that American administrators can understand and appreciate as the public interest. Although it is difficult to talk about the public interest in the abstract, just as it is to discuss the concept of justice in the abstract, it appears that the public interest, like justice, comes into sharper focus when one deals with specific social issues (for example, environmental pollution). To determine what is or is not in the public interest requires that one employ reason—sometimes plain, logical, insightful common sense. If Leo Strauss, one of the most famous neo-Platonic thinkers of the twentieth century, were alive today, he would compel students of public administration to employ Platonic reasoning to improve the understanding of public interest. Strauss would pose some provocative questions, such as, Should we have to question whether allowing industries to pollute the environment is offensive to the public interest? Employing commonly accepted moral and ethical democratic values, would America as a society have to question whether promulgating agency rules, which tend to favor only a select few at the expense of the vast majority of Americans, promotes the public interest? Are not certain business activities obviously contrary to what the public interest would demand? In even modern behaviorist terms, cannot systems analysis be employed by agency evaluators to detect activities that will obviously have a negative impact on our entire social system? Should not these activities be considered by U.S. governmental regulators as activities that should be banned because they threaten the public interest? Would it be in the public interest for FDA administrators to allow obviously deadly foods to be sold by businesses to consumers?

For many specific regulatory problems, though admittedly not all, probably a simple cost-benefit formula could be used by systems evaluators to determine the public interest content of some actions or some product. Only a few vital questions would have to be posed within a framework of basic democratic values. What are the costs? To whom? What are the comparative benefits? These questions need not imply a zero-sum game, because virtually all could gain or lose from some activities or products. However, when special interest groups would obviously benefit at high costs to the general public, administrators should be able to draw the reasonable conclusion without any difficulty that the activity or product would be detrimental to the public interest. Too often in our society common agreement on what is consistent with the public interest is frustrated by only a few, speaking for only a tiny percentage of the American public—frequently only a single industry or company. Unanimous agreement on anything is virtually impossible to attain, given human nature. But this should not imply that a clear consensus cannot be obtained. Unfortunately, in the U.S. political system, special interest group lobbyists have been allowed to have a disproportionate say in determining what is in the public interest. An important challenge for agency regulators is to discover what is genuinely in the public interest versus what interest group lobbyists claim is in the public interest but really favors only their selfish interests.[54]

The Impact of Administrative Growth on Democratic Ideals and Administrative Law

What are the democratic ideals that Americans cherish dearly?[55] Have they been threatened by the emergence of the modern administrative state? If so, how and to what extent? In particular, have particular agency practices helped to destroy the functional meaning of the U.S. democratic tradition? What relevance do these questions have to students of administrative law?

The democratic ideals embodied in the Constitution of the United States reflect the thinking of countless political theorists who contributed in various ways over the centuries to the development of democratic theory. However, the U.S. Constitution appears to most reflect the writings of Aristotle, John Locke, the Baron de Montesquieu, Jean Jacques Rousseau, John Stuart Mill, James Madison, Thomas Jefferson, and Alexander Hamilton. Together, these great theorists designed and refined the basic democratic principles of the U.S. Constitution, namely, (1) constitutionalism, (2) shared governmental powers, (3) popular government, (4) individualism, and (5) political equality. Actually, it is very difficult to separate these democratic principles into neat categories because of their obviously interrelated character. Constitutionalism, in particular, naturally implies the other four democratic ideals listed. Nevertheless, for the sake of clarity, these five democratic ideals are reviewed separately. Administrative law, an offspring of constitutional law, reflects these democratic ideals.

Constitutionalism.   Constitutionalism is the most basic, as well as the broad-est, democratic ideal. Aristotle was probably the first political theorist to discuss the concept in great depth. Constitutionalism is rooted in the Aristotelian princi-ple of the rule of law, the basic underpinning for democratic constitutionalism. The rule of law stresses the supremacy of the law (constitutional law and all other lesser laws sanctioned by the constitution), thus prohibiting illegal actions, espe-cially arbitrary and capricious behavior, by all public officials. Not unexpectedly, an obvious outgrowth of the rule of law, developed quite well by John Locke and other social contract theorists, is the notion of limited government. Basically, the contract theorists held that a contractual agreement was created among members of a society who sought to establish an orderly society. The contract, usually in the form of a written document (for example, a constitution), forms the basis of the government. In the contract, the rights and powers of the government and the cit-izenry are enumerated and implied. A constitutional government such as ours passes one test of political legitimacy because it is based upon popular consent. It is also a limited government because U.S. governmental officials have specified powers; thus the breadth of their activities and power is limited. Some have there-fore viewed governmental regulation as illegitimate, because they believe govern-ment's regulatory activities go beyond the scope of our government's limited and legitimate role. American constitutional government was developed by persons who found obnoxious the unlimited and tyrannical powers of governmental dicta-tors. In a constitutional governmental system, the people, not the government, are regarded as sovereign. U.S. federal courts ideally serve to preserve this constitu-tional principle of limited government by reviewing acts perceived by petitioners to be beyond the scope of the government's restricted powers.

Shared Powers.   Another democratic ideal in the American political system is the idea that governmental powers should be shared. The concept of shared powers also serves as a protection against excessive and illegitimate governmental power. The shared-powers principle is rooted in the compatible doctrines of separation of pow-ers and checks and balances. The separation-of-powers doctrine demands, of course, that governmental powers be divided among different governmental branches and units. Thus, a concentration of governmental power in the hands of one or a few is prevented by distributing governmental decisionmaking power not only among the chief executive, administrative, legislative, and judicial branches but among the different governmental levels as well. Governmental powers are still further divided in several ways within the specific political branches and units; for example, congressional powers are separated by the House and the Senate, while specific administrative powers are divided between independent agencies. In theory, this diffusion of governmental powers allows them to be checked and balanced be-cause each political entity has a limited check over the powers of other authoritative actors in the governmental system (for example, judicial review of agency actions, legislative oversight of agency behavior, presidential veto of congressional bills). James MacGregor Burns believed that a decisional deadlock was created because this system of checks and balances worked too well.[56] To most American government experts, the notion of shared powers, incidentally, is preferable to the notion of a separation of powers because it is more accurate to perceive the government's powers as shared, since, as the courts have often stressed, the Constitution does not endorse a strict separation of powers between the branches.

Popular Government.   The principle of popular government may be the democratic ideal cherished most by the average American. A popular government implies democratic government, which in turn implies that the ultimate political power to determine public policy directions should reside with the people. The idea of popular sovereignty is expressed in the Declaration of Independence and the U.S. Constitution but is seen in practice in our representative political institutions. The theory of popular government is linked closely to the attitude that all governmental officials should be held accountable to the people for their behavior because they are in reality the people's servants. This representative, popular-government theory clashes sharply with the theory of absolutism, under which dictators create and define the depths of their political powers, with the people serving as subjects, lacking the authority to check the unrestrained powers of government. In contrast to absolutism, popular-government theory stresses the role of majority will, individual rights, and liberty.

Individualism.   A particularly important aspect of popular government, especially to Americans, is the concept of individualism. Individualism is a socioeconomic political concept that stresses the right of individuals to determine their own destinies. Individualism, as opposed to collectivism, emphasizes the importance of freedom, personal well-being, and individual capabilities. The idea of individualism, especially before the New Deal, promoted the political and economic theories of laissez-faire. Because the doctrine of individualism has tended to reinforce certain notions that may conflict with public interest or national goals, a major governmental problem in any democratic system has always focused on how to balance societal rights with individual rights.

Political Equality.   Ideally, democratic constitutionalism implies the principle of political and, to some degree, social equality. Many critics of American government charge that this democratic ideal has not been achieved as well as the other ideals in our system. Political equality suggests that all persons should be treated and represented equally by government. Although identical treatment is not required by the Constitution, it does require that reasonable due process and equal protection guarantees be rendered to all persons. Because political equality is rooted in the democratic principles of equality under the law, as well as equal opportunity for all persons, arbitrary treatment of citizens by governmental officials is strictly forbidden by various laws. Legislation, court rulings, and a mass of administrative regulations have functioned in recent decades to make persons more truly equal under the law.

Challenges to Democratic Ideals

The growth of the administrative system in the United States, as elsewhere and throughout the history of the bureaucratization of the world, was largely a governmental response to the basic need to structure, order, and regulate society. Many social thinkers have held that the emergence of public bureaucracy in capitalist America resulted mainly because the capitalist class believed that it could benefit by having the state stabilize business activities through regulating the economic climate. This would help to reduce business risks involving vast sums of capital. Ralph P. Hummel described the growth phenomenon:

> Modern bureaucracy in the public service arose out of the need of private groups—industrial entrepreneurs, financiers, and merchants—to have the state regulate the world so that the huge investments and reinvestments characterizing modern capital enterprise could be justified. Out of this came rationalized state administration of the legal system (emphasizing the enforcement of contract), the regulation of labor, the state supervision of commerce and finance, and finally state stabilization of markets. Today we criticize bureaucracy for its inflexibility, stability, and immutability in the face of change. But in the past these qualities perfectly reflected the purpose for which it was set up—to provide controls over a society that had, from the viewpoint of capital enterprises, too much change in it.[57]

A less cynical viewpoint suggested earlier is that the state's administrative apparatus, as well as administrative law, grew in response to the demands placed upon American government by the citizenry. It is also possible that bureaucracy, as an institution, unfortunately expands in an effort to support its own weight. Although the precise causes of the growth of the public regulatory system remain a mystery, there is little doubt that the expansion of administrative power has jeopardized the welfare of the five cherished democratic values just described. To what extent have these democratic ideals survived the emergence of administrative power?

Challenges to Democratic Constitutionalism.   Clearly, the growth of administrative expertise has posed the greatest threat not only to democratic constitutionalism, but also to virtually all our democratic ideals. Basically, this is true because the public policy making undertaken by administrative experts, especially those who are removed from direct political controls, tends to undermine the fundamental maxims of democratic constitutionalism. Constitutionalism assumes the supremacy of the rule of law, but our public agencies hold to this principle only in theory. In practice, few written rules and regulations guide the day-to-day decisions made by administrators. In fact, it is argued, administrative discretion is so broad that the United States is ruled by public administrators. Kenneth C. Davis believes that this allows administrators to have the power of choice, thus permitting them to select and determine important public policy directions, as well as to render injustices to individuals contrary to what the rule of law would sensibly demand.[58] Specifically, observers have discovered that public administrators can jeopardize rule of law precepts by informally promulgating rules and orders in the absence of a clear, written, and reviewable record.

Constitutional democracy is additionally compromised by the undemocratic character of administrative experts. James O. Freedman acknowledged that possibly too much reliance is placed upon agency experts at the expense of more open and democratically controlled decisionmaking.[59] To some scholars, this new class of governmental experts constitutes an administrative elite—a new oligarchical structure that appears democratically irresponsible. This evolution is justified, according to Felix Frankfurter, because the framers believed the power of administrative expertise could be controlled by demanding (1) high professional performance standards, (2) the use of elaborate procedural safeguards, (3) open criticism of expert opinions and decisions, and (4) reservation of important decisions for the elected leaders.[60] But the public's refusal to believe that these experts can be adequately controlled, as well as its refusal to believe that these officials are indeed experts, has caused the public to question, according to Freedman, the very legitimacy of the power of these regulatory experts in a political system that is supposed to be guided by the principles of democratic constitutionalism.[61]

Challenges to the Concept of Shared Powers.   The constitutional framers established a tripartite system of government specifically designed to make public policy decisionmaking a shared governmental function. The purpose of this plan was to ensure that decisionmaking power was not monopolized by a single governmental branch but shared among three branches. This separation of powers was intended to promote democratic decisionmaking by balancing governmental powers among legislators, justices, and the president. However, the rise of the administrative system as the fourth branch of government has possibly damaged the tripartite decisionmaking system beyond repair, especially since this fourth branch is likely the most powerful. "By 1970," Eugene P. Dvorin and Robert H. Simmons claimed, "any pretense by public servants of maintaining their former disclaimers to dominance could only border on the ludicrous. Possibly the only faith in the traditional idea of a balanced, tripartite government remained in those civics courses taught by home economic teachers and football coaches."[62]

Despite the apparent threat to the traditional democratic decisionmaking model, experts hold that the expansion of administrative policymaking powers has actually been encouraged by the other branches. Past presidents, legislators, and court judges have asked public administrators to do more and more. Dvorin and Simmons believe the new powers and responsibilities that have been inherited by administrators have caused a crisis of imbalance. These critics question in particular whether U.S. public administrators have accepted the moral responsibilities that come with the new powers that have destroyed what was left of tripartite power: "The combination of power and responsibility now vested in the executive branch contrasts dangerously with the scant attention paid by public administrators to questions of moral principles."[63]

The erosion of the doctrine of shared powers symbolized by the tripartite model represents to many people the end of a democracy. A long list of cynics and fatalists compete in the public administration and administrative law literature to convey in the most eloquent prose how the consolidation of powers in the administrative branch is causing the fall of democracy. While Dvorin and Simmons point to the amoral or even immoral character of administrators who have obtained such vast powers in recent times, Hummel has concluded, in the most pessimistic tone, that the growth of administrative power threatens democratic decisionmaking processes because the public administration system is, he believes, a closed political system, in contrast to the open decisionmaking structure forged by the constitutional framers. Hummel contends that no matter how hard people may argue that the administrative system is open, it is unquestionably and exceptionally undemocratic and closed, a condition he perceives as a very poor substitute for the more democratic political process:

> In combination with science, bureaucracy can calculate the cost of pursuing certain society-wide goals against others. In combination with technology, bureaucracy can administer most efficiently the pursuit of one set of goals against others. But there is nothing in the social relations, culture, psychology, language, and thought of the bureaucrat that gives him the capacity to replace the political philosopher or the political process. Unfortunately, there is, of course, all the power in the world available to him and no reason to think that the bureaucrat will restrain himself from the use of power any more than any of the rulers who preceded him.[64]

However, Louis L. Jaffe and Nathaniel L. Nathanson regard such pessimism as an overreaction to the nation's increasing reliance on agency experts. They do not believe that the shared-powers doctrine has been seriously threatened by the growth of administrative expertise. In fact, Jaffe and Nathanson argue that those who contend that the separation-of-powers doctrine has been eroded by the new policymaking role given to administrators fail to understand the intended purpose of the doctrine: "We should in sum keep in mind that the great end of the theory is, by dispersing in some measure the centers of authority, to prevent absolutism. It is not eternally to stratify our governmental arrangements in the particular mold of 1789, or any other date."[65]

Challenges to Popular Government.   Naturally, the trend toward depoliticizing the public policy–making process, as Hummel suggests, would have to challenge the democratic ideal of popular government as conceptualized by the founding fathers. But the growth of administrative expertise has created a question: How popular can a government be if public policy choice is largely left in the hands of administrators, not popularly elected political leaders? Clearly, according to the principles of popular-government theory, public policy decisions should be made by political leaders under the watchful eye of the public. But

Freedman holds that the arena for political debate and political decisions has shifted from true political institutions to administrative agencies.[66]

However, even if policy decisions have been transferred to nonelected governmental officials as the administrative state has developed, the popular-government ideal could still remain in salvageable condition as long as the public could exert reasonable influence and retain sufficient control over the policymaking processes of public administrators. But scholarly opinion raises great doubt about such a possibility. In general, scholars hold that despite efforts to promote public participation and control over administrative decisionmaking so as to preserve democratic accountability, public bureaucracy has been successful in resisting attempts by freedom lovers to open the administrative process to the public. Indeed, the critics claim, the Freedom of Information Act, "sunshine" laws in general, citizen groups, liberal politicians condemning closed-door bureaucratic decisionmaking, efforts to create effective ombudsman offices, notice and comment rulemaking (even including subsidized citizen commentary), and the like have all failed to keep open the doors of bureaucracy.[67] To Robert Alford, efforts to make public agencies an open forum for debating public policy issues have failed, simply because "the principles of bureaucracy and participation are to some extent incompatible."[68] He contends, in what is basically an old Weberian insight, that public participation tends to undermine administrative expertise: "Bureaucratization implies the insulation of decisionmakers from outside influences, by definition not as competent as experts are to judge the relevant range of facts, nor to balance the objectives desired. Participation implies the right and duty of the public to intervene in the determination of decisions."[69]

However, Guy Benveniste, in *The Politics of Expertise*, made clear that the public is largely to blame for promoting what has become known as "anemic democracy," a condition in which the people distrust their government yet create a "demand overload" situation for it by expecting government to tackle and cure all conceivable social ills.[70] Benveniste says (echoing of Freedman) that this places administrative experts in a no-win situation because their regulatory expertise is demanded but the use of their apolitical expertise is considered illegitimate. A real challenge for our political system, if it is in fact possible—and some observers feel it is not—is to develop a capacity for limited and meaningful public participation in the administrative process without destroying the obvious advantages of expertise. Weber's insight that specialists have been employed by bureaucracy because of their expert knowledge should not be played down; if it is, another brand of spoils government will emerge that will be even more democratically irresponsible.

Challenges to Individualism.   Americans have always, at least in spirit, cherished the principle of individualism. As children, we were taught that rugged individuals built the United States from nothing. Individualism is what has made this nation great! We were told further that dependence on others is a sure sign of weakness. We should learn to go it alone and to stand tall, on our own two feet. The mark of a successful individual has been one who has found financial independence

by no later than age twenty-five. Americans have traditionally condemned social-
ism and communism for various reasons, but probably a major reason was that
these economic and political systems restrict individual choice. (Administrative law
in the American political system cannot be understood clearly unless its applications to administrative regulatory behavior are perceived within the capitalist, free
market ideals that Americans still endorse.) At least in principle Americans still support capitalism, the theory of which emphasizes the virtues of individualism. No
wonder, in this light, the American people in general are so afraid of what governmental regulations may do to them as individuals. In a capitalist country such as
the United States, regulatory agencies represent nothing more than an assault on
individualism and, if not on private individuals, certainly on private businesses.

It should not be forgotten that bureaucracy emerged out of the need to regulate society. Control is what regulatory agencies seek. Thus, administrative agencies may pretend to be otherwise, but they are control agents that, in order to
reach their regulatory goals, must to some extent destroy the freedom of individuals. Defenders of the growth of the public administrative system argue that public agencies are needed to protect individuals from stronger and potentially
dangerous threats. To a certain extent administrative agencies do accomplish this
end, but governmental efforts to protect individuals from others (for example,
from future terrorist attacks) have simultaneously, and often justifiably, encroached upon the freedom and privacy of individuals. The Bush administration,
for instance, since September 11, 2001, has imposed all sorts of new regulations
to protect Americans against terrorism that certainly may be justified yet,
nonetheless, have had the impact of further restricting the freedoms and privacy
rights that we once enjoyed. To Ralph Hummel, governmental regulation has
succeeded in destroying an individual's ability to regulate him- or herself. The
regulators in bureaucracy, he asserts, have caused individuals to lose their integrity: "The bureaucratic relationship has trained us to look always upward toward superiors. Culturally, what we look to them for is the answer to the question
what is good or bad for us; bureaucracy has made it impossible to maintain personal norms. Psychologically, the process of bureaucratization has destroyed the
integrity of the individual, made him into a being of dependency, and opened up
his reservoir of human needs (the id) to direct manipulation from the outside."[71]

Lewis Mainzer also entertains the possibility that administrative agencies have
tended to destroy the democratic individualism. Focusing mostly on the effects of
rules and regulations upon agency employees themselves, he notes that "regulations
replace judgment in bureaucracy, thereby permitting equal treatment of citizens
and lessening the talent or experience required for reaching a judgment. Reliance
on precedent and rules seems to deprive the bureaucrats of creative possibilities, of
personal judgment."[72] The bureaucratic hierarchy, as well as bureaucracy's rules and
regulations, may be functioning to the detriment of individualism, but Mainzer
concludes that the charges against bureaucracy have been greatly exaggerated.

Mainzer is most likely correct. Despite talk about the government's regulatory machinery sapping the minds of America's rugged individualists, hard evidence does

not suggest this to be true. The regulated have in general been able to exert their individual preferences and manipulate the regulators. Private businesses are still quite independent (maybe too independent, as the Enron, Worldcom, and other recent corporate scandals would suggest), despite some successful regulatory efforts, and individual citizens still remain quite free to do what they like as far as should be permitted in any society that places some reasonable emphasis on social order.[73]

Challenges to Political Equality.   Political equality does not imply that the polity must or should treat everyone identically under law. Obviously, various forms of political inequalities have been sanctioned by U.S. political leaders (some very sensitive to democratic values), upheld by the courts, and given tacit approval by the general public. Clearly, our federal income tax system, which is based roughly on one's ability to pay, runs contrary to the equal protection principle. That is, in a sense, some must pay more than others for equal political representation. The U.S. governmental system has also denied political equality to certain groups. For example, those under eighteen are forbidden the right to vote in federal elections.

However, denial of equal protection under law has been prohibited by the courts in cases in which unreasonable classifications of people have been used to deny persons or groups equal protection due process rights. (Originally, the concept applied only to the states under the Fourteenth Amendment, but in several decisions the courts have consistently applied the concept to the federal government through the due process clause of the Fifth Amendment.) Consequently, while the government has been allowed to place taxpayers in different income categories so that they can be taxed unequally, according to their different tax classifications, the courts have forbidden the government from classifying persons into groups according to race, religion, national origin, sex, or social class for the purpose of subjecting particular groups of people to unequal treatment. Some critics consider such classifications unreasonable, whether devised by legislators or administrators, since they are related neither to legitimate governmental functions nor to the proper ends of government in this constitutional democracy.

Although political inequality has been outlawed as an unconstitutional principle, in practice U.S. governmental institutions, including administrative agencies, have historically not granted complete political equality to all persons or groups. The history of sexual and racial discrimination in the United States is well known and has tarnished the image of America as a nation that should be respected for upholding the principle of political equality. Even a cursory examination of the latest *Statistical Abstract of the United States* clearly reveals that, despite efforts to reverse the historical trend, the impact of discriminatory practices against women, blacks, and other underrepresented groups has placed them in inferior positions today, as compared with other groups that have historically enjoyed a favored position in our society. For example, the employment, job status, and pay of women, blacks, and other groups that have historically been discriminated against make a poor showing when compared to those of white males, especially outside the federal civil service system.[74]

Inequality under the law led to the development of various plans aimed at eliminating political and social inequality in our society. Affirmative action programs have tried to rectify past sexual and racial discriminatory practices by government and by society in general. In sum, affirmative action programs, administered by a variety of governmental agencies, required all governmental agencies or any private institutions receiving public funds (for example, large companies on governmental contracts or universities receiving governmental grants) to design, implement, and evaluate in good faith a program aimed at compensation for past discriminatory practices. Affirmative action should not be confused with equal opportunity legislation, an example of which is fair housing laws, since equal opportunity laws only prohibit unequal treatment, while affirmative action calls for special compensatory measures aimed at correcting past mistreatment of certain groups. Affirmative action has been vehemently opposed by those who argue that the concept is based upon the erroneous assumption that two wrongs make a right. Specifically, opponents of affirmative action hold that its programs amount to nothing more than what they call reverse discrimination, which violates the due process and equal protection clauses of the Fifth and Fourteenth Amendments. The federal courts had pretty much struck the final blows to affirmative action by the mid-1990s, holding that affirmative action was constitutional under the equal protection clause only as long as it was considered temporary. The courts now required organizations to look hard for alternative remedies, using affirmative action only as a last resort. In 2003 President George W. Bush tried to score a knockout punch against affirmative action by asserting that a University of Michigan affirmative action program, which gave some preferences to African Americans in their admissions policies in order to achieve more diversity, was illegal because the university should have adopted only "race-neutral alternative" policies to promote diversity.[75]

Administrative Law and
Political Equality: A Concluding Note

Although administrative law focuses frequently on the procedural problems pertaining to equal protection provisions of statutes and internal agency rules and regulations, considerable attention is devoted to how equally agency administrators treat those who deal with their agencies. The democratic ideal, eloquently set forth in the writings of Max Weber, is that administrators should treat all persons having business with their agencies in an objective, professional, and impersonal fashion.[76] According to democratic theory, the paying of special favors to individuals or groups, in the context of modern bureaucracy, is not only unprofessional and unethical but also flatly illegal. According to Victor A. Thompson, this is so because modern bureaucracy is not a compassionate human system but an impersonal formal system rooted in the rule of law. The rule of law compels bureaucrats to treat all individuals equally, thus making the granting of a favor an illegitimate act.[77]

However, administrators do not always act impartially but in fact favor certain parties over others. James Freedman has commented that the preferential treatment given to special interests, commonly leading to eventual control by specific industries over particular agencies, has long been recognized and, unfortunately, "has had a deleterious effect on the legitimacy of the administrative process by calling into question its independence and integrity."[78]

Political scientists have held since day one that the social inequality so blatant in our society stems largely from the inability of certain groups to influence the governmental decisionmaking process to their benefit. As the argument goes, groups in society cannot logically expect to be given a fair shake unless they are allowed an equal opportunity to influence our government's decisionmakers. Formally, of course, the U.S. political system seems to allow relatively equal access and participation in the decisionmaking processes. But as Jeffrey L. Jowell stressed in *Law and Bureaucracy,* "the mere existence of formal channels does not itself ensure democratic decision making. Rulemaking procedures, for example, ideally allow consultation of affected interests and an implicit assurance that the rules will substantially reflect the merits of the arguments presented."[79] He concluded that "rulemaking procedures may be used by an administrative agency to give an impression of participation, whereas no more than *pro forma* adherence to an empty democratic ritual was involved."[80] Jowell's contention that the rulemaking process is in reality not very open is supported by Murray Edelman's thesis that the myth of open rulemaking represents just another "symbolic reassurance" employed by our government to deceive the public into believing that the U.S. political system is functioning in a more democratic manner than it really is.[81]

Jowell asked, "How can the opportunity of access to bureaucracy be equalized in fact?"[82] This is a crucial question that the United States must address as a society in the future—one that poses special challenges for students of administrative law as agency power increases in degree and scope—because it will remain highly unlikely that the social benefits can be expected to be fairly and equally distributed if de facto equal access to the politicoadministrative decisionmaking process remains closed.

REGULATING IN THE PUBLIC INTEREST: REGULATION VERSUS DEREGULATION

No one living in the United States today can truly imagine what it would be like to live in a society where no form of governmental regulation exists, for it was popular demand for an orderly society that gave rise to the proliferation of governmental regulations. In the absence of any state regulation, all reasonable persons should conclude, a society would be in constant chaos. Obviously, a degree of governmental regulation serves the public interest, and the promotion of the public interest is the most basic reason that can be given to justify state regulatory activities. It should be quite clear by now that the administrative system's growth was largely due to government's efforts to regulate those activities that society believed should be regulated.

But precisely what is governmental regulation, and what are the chief goals of our regulators? Governmental regulation basically consists of any efforts aimed at resolving various defects or failures in the open, or free, marketplace. Governmental regulation is especially concerned with protecting businesses from ruthless, cutthroat competition; blocking the emergence of monopoly power; and protecting consumers from rip-off prices for merchandise (especially due to price fixing among producers and sellers), unsafe products, and unfair and illegal business practices in general. But all governmental regulation is directed to some extent at controlling the selfish interests of private parties in the social system so that the larger public interest will not be placed in serious jeopardy.[83] Louis M. Kohlmeier, Jr., though acknowledging that governmental regulation is quite varied and can mean many things, stressed that "all regulation is government direction of private economic endeavor and all regulation tends to produce similar economic consequences which are in conflict with the basic definitions of competition and with antitrust law."[84] To Kohlmeier, the original purpose of federal regulation in the United States was to keep prices lower, but this modest objective was soon abandoned for more comprehensive and ambitious regulatory goals. Consequently, according to Kohlmeier, individual freedoms guaranteed in the Bill of Rights have been compromised by congressional and judicial approval of regulatory expansionism: "Thus has the Constitution been read and reread over nearly two hundred years to gauge the power of the federal government to regulate the nation's commerce and to discipline the exercise of that power within the government. As it turns out, there are in the Bill of Rights no absolute guarantees of freedom of private conduct from government interference."[85] Although governmental regulation in the United States has been more confined to the control of the ownership and management of private property, particularly in connection with business endeavors, virtually all social activities have come under government's regulatory sphere. Nevertheless, as Kohlmeier recognized, "freedom of private conduct is a relative matter. Freedom of speech, of the press and of religious practice were and are relatively more absolute than freedom to own and manage private property."[86] To many persons this may appear ironic since so many scholars have held that the Constitution was designed largely by the economic elite, influenced heavily by the leading capitalist theorists, primarily to protect and promote private property rights. However, others do present credible arguments supporting the contention that businesspeople seeking a relatively stable and predictable marketplace favored a constitutional system from the very beginning that permitted at least limited regulation of business use of private property.

However, in keeping with the belief during the late 1700s that government should play a restricted regulatory role, the laissez-faire philosophy, symbolized by the expression *caveat emptor* ("let the buyer beware"), dominated the thinking of that era.[87] But by the 1960s the *caveat emptor* philosophy had been replaced by the functional doctrine of *caveat venditor* (let the seller beware). *Caveat venditor,* in many respects a symbol of the modern welfare state, stands in firm opposition to the principles of laissez-faire capitalism, which promoted relatively free-swinging, selfish, exploitive, and even cruel business practices during the nineteenth century. At least according to public opinion, *caveat venditor* is presently a broadly accepted ideology that embraces the attitude that economic life is too critical to society's general well-being to be left unregulated. For example, even though during the Reagan years a less pro-regulatory attitude existed than just years before, toward the end of the Reagan era only a minority of Americans (38 percent in 1987), probably shaken by what deregulation apparently caused in the savings and loan industry, believed we had "too much" governmental regulation. In a June 28–30, 2002, Gallup poll, respondents blamed decreased governmental regulation of corporations a "great deal" (26 percent) or a "moderate amount" (44 percent) for the recent corporate scandals. Another 18 percent said "not much," while only 8 percent answered "not at all." These poll data, as well as other polls over the past few decades, have disclosed that Americans generally favor rather widespread governmental regulations to protect them, including the new and pervasive anti-terrorism or homeland security regulations. But what has caused Americans over the decades to change their minds so much about government and to support such extensive governmental regulation?

Arguments for Governmental Regulation

Historically speaking, governmental regulation has, of course, always existed because, as recognized by Carol Tucker Foreman and Maureen S. Steinbruner, "almost every human activity has the potential to injure someone."[88] As nations developed at different times in world history, governmental regulation expanded to bring order to the increasing complexities in society. Thus, although the colonists came to North America largely to escape the various regulatory controls imposed on them in their native countries, as America matured, this nation also was destined to follow the same historical course. Societal complexity simply requires relatively comprehensive governmental regulation. Henry Jacoby has written at some length on the phenomenon of increased governmental regulation as an inevitable outgrowth of a developing society.[89] Certainly, expanding governmental regulation can be witnessed in developing Third World nations today. Like it or not, modern life demands some national, centralized control and organization; this translates into governmental regulations. For a sophisticated argument on the need for governmental regulations, one does not need to consult the writings of contemporary political scientists or administrative law scholars. Plato, in the *Republic*, presented a superb argument for the absolute necessity of governmental regulation if the polity is to achieve at least some degree of vital social harmony. Plato reasoned that the parts of the state must be coordinated for the good of the whole (that is, the public interest).[90]

Kaufman on Regulation.   In *Red Tape: Its Origins, Uses, and Abuses,* Herbert Kaufman presents an impassioned argument in defense of the need for governmental regulation, or red tape. Kaufman asserts that while everyone seems to abhor their existence, regulations are everywhere. This mystery led him to pose and research the question "How can any product of the human mind be so unpopular yet so widespread and enduring?"[91] In general, Kaufman concluded, as have so many, that popular demand justified comprehensive governmental regulation. Specifically, Kaufman discovered that regulations can be justified because governmental regulatory efforts have increased the compassion, fairness, and democratic accountability of American government.[92]

Kaufman believes a compassionate government cannot sit back and allow members of society to exploit one another. Selfish acts by individuals can cause harm to come to other persons, especially those who are not capable of protecting themselves. Consequently, a compassionate government must devise and employ regulations to protect people from other members of society. He emphasizes in particular that red tape should be used to regulate relations between buyer and seller with an eye toward "preventing injuries *before* they occur."[93] The FAA and NRC are just two highly visible federal regulatory agencies that are largely responsible for preventing dangerous accidents from occurring. Regulations were also promoted by the government's interest in protecting people from hardships—many due to circumstances beyond the affected individuals' control. Thus, regulatory government grew because the government has tried to help, for instance, the victims of natural disasters; unnatural disasters (for example, victims of 9/11); farmer victims of shifting economic policies; handicapped veterans; and mothers with dependent children. The government's efforts to prevent such painful disruptions to the social system as worker strikes, inflation, and unemployment have also required the institution of certain regulations.[94]

The public's insistence that government act in a fair manner when executing its tasks provides still another reason for governmental regulations. Due process procedures (regulations), an admirable and vital trait of democratic government, fill seemingly endless volumes in the *Federal Register* and the *Code of Federal Regulations.* (The Administrative Procedure Act of 1946 requires federal agencies to publish, among other things, their rules and regulations. These rules and regulations are then codified in the *Code of Federal Regulations.*) But these regulations provide essential safeguards for persons interacting with government and for those who may be affected by the implementation of certain public policies, thus justifying their usefulness. Of course, Kaufman contends, the demand for an open, representative, and democratically accountable government has increased the regulatory burden of government. Nevertheless, fundamental fairness, he holds, must bow to simplicity of implementation in a pluralist society: "Old or new, the methods of interest group representation generate more directives and controls, more steps in the forging of governmental policies, more bargaining before decisions are reached, and more postdecision litigation than would otherwise develop. Fairness, comprehensiveness, and community acceptance of policy decisions obviously rate higher than administrative simplicity and speed."[95]

Gellhorn on Regulation.   Over two decades ago the eminent administrative law scholar Walter Gellhorn presented a still memorable lecture entitled "Deregulation or Delusion" in which he argued persuasively for the need for governmental regulations by sharply attacking the proponents of deregulation.[96] Gellhorn noted that most deregulation arguments stem from a simplistic belief that the United States can feasibly return to a laissez-faire governmental process. Bureaucrats have grown in number, he stressed, because they are needed to assist government in coping with the various social problems that have emerged. He was quick to point out that more societal problems emerge when regulatory controls are absent than when they exist. Our administrative agencies are unlikely to win popularity contests, Gellhorn asserted, despite the fact that they are very necessary. To Gellhorn, administrators are the consequence of our society's problems, certainly not the cause.

Gellhorn conveyed his great respect for the capabilities of public administrators and the positive contributions of U.S. regulatory agencies. He essentially argued that administrative experts have been given a bum rap and have not been appreciated, despite their successful regulatory accomplishments. But Gellhorn was not blind to the problems that prevail in our administrative system. Obviously, he acknowledged, some regulations are ill designed and archaic. Such regulations should be either abandoned or redesigned so that they are up-to-date. From the very first year of the republic, Gellhorn maintained, public administrators have been called upon to cope with social problems. A systems theorist would say that Gellhorn argued that public dissatisfactions led to the demand for regulatory control; thus our regulatory agencies indeed reflect a responsible and appropriate democratic response to popular demands on government. Unquestionably, he implied, U.S. public agencies are legitimate, democratically sanctioned institutions supported by a popular mandate. Gellhorn believes that administrative tinkering has brought more overall good than harm to this country. The Great Depression, he noted, was so severe because governmental manipulation of the economy was virtually nonexistent. But since the government's regulators have been tinkering with the economy, he exclaimed, the United States has not had very steep inflations or deep recessions, despite claims to the contrary. Parenthetically, I wonder how Gellhorn, now deceased, would categorize the stock market's relative free fall after January 2000.

"Should we allow the market to regulate itself naturally?" Gellhorn asked. In some cases he feels the market should be permitted to self-regulate freely, but he urged that society must be selective in what the market is allowed to control. Surely, Gellhorn asserted, we cannot safely rely on the market to regulate in society's best interest. Too many horror stories remind us of how special interests have acted selfishly and in a fashion contradictory to the nation's general welfare (some current examples: Enron, Worldcom, Arthur D. Andersen). Unfortunately, Gellhorn noted, businesses have assumed the dangerous attitude that what no agency regulation forbids should be left to free market decisions. But he warned that private entrepreneurial decisions normally focus on the short run, while governmental planners tend to focus on the long-term consequences of contemplated actions. Free market regulation cannot work, Gellhorn argued, if essential information required for intelligent social planning is held in secret by various private enterprises. Even consumers cannot make wise market choices if they cannot obtain the necessary information about services and products. (Perhaps that's why 58 percent of the American people in a June 28–30, 2002, Gallup poll said, in light of lies about earnings by corporate executives, they would be "less likely to invest in the stock market.") It cannot be forgotten, Gellhorn underscored, that businesses are primarily concerned with making high profits. Strip-mining businesses were not run by evil people, he pointed out, but by people who did what was natural to get coal out of the ground as cheaply as possible. Governmental regulation is needed to check such short-term business ventures. Gellhorn does not want selfish business motives to determine, for example, the future condition of this nation's environment. Regulation, he insisted, is required before irreparable damages occur.

Breyer on Regulation.   Walter Gellhorn certainly presented some credible justifications for governmental regulation. Stephen Breyer, who was appointed by President Clinton to the U.S. Supreme Court, also defends the need for governmental regulation, although he argues, like Gellhorn, that there is much room for improving traditional regulatory methods.[97]

Breyer's starting point in justifying the need for regulation is not unique. His framework for examining various regulatory methods assumes "that regulation is *justified* only if it achieves without too great a corresponding cost policy objectives that a consensus of reasonable observers would consider to be in the public interest."[98] Breyer is open to the question of what should be considered to be in the public interest. In analyzing the worth of regulatory approaches (programs), he holds that they should ultimately be evaluated on the basis of their public interest content, even if they also happen to benefit special interests. In his analytical framework, Breyer assumes that the unregulated marketplace should be considered the norm. Thus it becomes essential for all governmental regulation to be justified by demonstrating that the regulatory activity can accomplish important public policy objectives that the unregulated market cannot bring about. However, certain market failures have justified to Breyer the need for governmental intervention because the regulatory action appears clearly to promote the public welfare.[99]

Controlling monopoly power can be justified on the grounds that regulation can keep prices and profits of the "natural monopolists" within reasonable public interest limits. Specifically, regulation here is aimed at achieving "allocative efficiency," in which the costs of producing the product or service are linked to the price of these products or services if they were sold in the competitive marketplace. Despite arguments by free market advocates that natural monopolists would keep prices and profits down naturally by charging only what the market would tolerate, thereby maximizing allocative efficiency, Breyer is not convinced that the public would be protected. "Nonetheless," he says, "as long as one believes that, without regulation, the firm will raise prices substantially, one can reasonably argue that regulated prices will *help* achieve allocative efficiency."[100]

Breyer's second point is that preventing windfall profits is also a noble regulatory end. In essence, windfall profits are made by "lucky" changes in the marketplace that cause owners of a commodity to make "excessive" profits. Breyer points out that such windfalls are normally allowed, but when they "are great in amount and do not reflect any particular talent or skill on the part of producers, there is sometimes a demand for regulation. The object of the regulation is to transfer these 'undeserved windfall profits' from producers or owners of the scarce resources to consumers or taxpayers."[101]

Breyer's third point is that regulation should be employed to correct spillover costs. Spillovers are really additional costs to society (for example, pollution of the air and waters) that have not been absorbed by the companies, but instead have been imposed on society. Why should society pay for such social costs as cleaning up rivers and lakes if private companies, not society, are responsible for them? Breyer argues that it should not. Governmental regulators such as the Environmental Protection Agency are needed to make producers include reasonable social costs (for example, the cost of anti-air pollution scrubbers) in their total costs of production.[102]

Breyer's fourth point is that regulation is necessary to force private enterprises to release certain information that the public has a right to know. To Breyer information itself should be regarded as a valuable commodity. The public needs information to help it evaluate various services and products in the competitive marketplace. The release of information helps to keep the marketplace competitive, thus leading to more intelligent consumer purchases, which in turn should keep prices down. Disclosure of information is particularly useful to guard against sellers purposefully misleading consumers. Information may also be required to be released in a certain form so that it can be more easily understood; for example, in recent years states have been requiring insurance companies to write their policies so that it doesn't take a Philadelphia lawyer to decode what is in the policy.[103]

Breyer's fifth point is that governmental regulation should also be used to prevent excessive and counterproductive competition. His chief argument is that under certain conditions it is in the public interest to protect particular firms from excessive competition so that needed businesses will not be bankrupted. For example, the railroads have often argued that their competitive decline in the 1970s and 1980s was largely due to the government allowing truckers to go virtually unregulated, thus permitting the trucking industry to steal from them their most profitable business. Regulating against excessive competition, Breyer adds, has also been employed to stop predatory pricing. Predatory pricing, as seen in price wars, has been used by financially powerful and stable companies to drive competitors out of business. Regulations have also been used to keep new competition from entering the market if the regulators believed that increased competition would actually create unnecessary hardships on the existing companies (for example, public utilities with fixed operating costs and investments to protect), as well as consumers (who, in the case of utilities, might have to pay higher prices in the long run). However, Breyer does not generally feel that rigorous agency regulations should be used to prevent excessive competition. He contends that the public interest could be served better by deregulation in this one area, as long as anti-trust laws are enforced to guard against the unlikely possibility that excessive competition may eventually lead to the creation of natural monopolies.[104]

Breyer's sixth point recognizes the argument that regulations should be improved to guard against "moral hazards" that occur when "someone other than a buyer pays for the buyer's purchases."[105] Because the buyer is not responsible for the payment, he or she may irresponsibly purchase goods and services. Breyer notes that soaring medical costs are due in part to irresponsible and excessive use of medical services. This has placed a great financial burden on government resources since the government has become increasingly obligated to pick up the tab.[106]

Breyer's last major justification for governmental regulation is that the government, through regulatory supervision and coordination, can stimulate industry-wide rationalization. Breyer's main contention here is that the public would benefit if the government in general managed industry-wide development. Governmental intervention could lead to sensible cooperative planning and growth, which inevitably could yield increased efficiency and lower costs.[107]

In summary, Breyer enthusiastically supports traditional governmental regulatory methods, as long as they further the promotion of the public interest. He concludes that regulatory reform is required and that the reform measures should entail generally "less restrictive alternatives" to classical regulatory approaches, including in some cases partial deregulation.[108]

Anti-Regulation and Deregulation Arguments

Few today, whether scholars or everyday citizens, believe that governmental regulation is not essential. Evidently, experience and the weight of pro-regulation arguments have been persuasive. Nevertheless, some still argue that governmental regulation is not necessary or at least that only very limited regulation of the private sector is warranted. Even the most vocal supporters of governmental regulation would have to admit that it has not always served this nation well. According to Herbert Kaufman, our regulatory processes have been generally criticized for imposing too many pointless, irrelevant, duplicative, contradictory, and inconsistent constraints. Some frustrated business executives have even exclaimed that it is impossible to comply with one agency's regulations without violating another's requirements. Once more, Kaufman acknowledges, many outdated regulations are kept alive by simple bureaucratic inertia. Regulations are also linked to program failures and perceived as awkward, too slow, and oppressive. Kaufman states that regulation horror stories are so commonplace among the regulators and the regulated that sound regulations are not noticed or appreciated.[109] Even if some worth is seen in the regulations, critics frequently charge that the regulations are too costly to justify it. James G. Cook, a specialist in technological development, has been quoted as arguing that regulations have stifled creativity and innovation in American business, thus making it difficult to justify the cost effectiveness of the regulations. Cook believes governmental regulations have hindered individual and corporate creativity at a time when "our country's continued prosperity depends on a renewed leadership in technology and science to keep pace with strides being made by other nations."[110] However, Robert B. Reich does not blame public administrators for the voluminous, nit-picking regulations. "The underlying problem has nothing to do with nefarious forces hidden within regulatory agencies; it is inherent in the American regulatory process itself."[111] He specifically contends that businesses, employing their lawyers to take advantage of every loophole in governmental regulations, cause agencies to respond with more detailed regulations year after year in an effort to close the loopholes.[112] For example, in 1992 the government, reacting to soaring cable television rates under deregulation, reregulated the cable television industry, devising new regulations to curb "runaway" basic-cable rate hikes. However, exploiting the regulatory loopholes, the cable industry shocked most cable subscribers by raising their cable rates even more. In response, the regulators in 1994 promulgated more elaborate regulations to close the loopholes to stop the "excessive" charges.

Private Property Should Not Be Regulated.   Since the first attempts to regulate the use of private property, people have opposed such regulation on the grounds that it violates Bill of Rights guarantees, especially the Fourth and Fifth Amendments. To these people, private property is sacred, and as far as they are concerned, the Constitution was originally drafted to protect property rights. The argument that the regulation of private property is sometimes necessary to protect the public interest means virtually nothing to them, for they strongly believe that private property rights should not be sacrificed for public welfare goals. They also tend to cling to Adam Smith's notion, articulated in the late eighteenth century, that the pursuit of private interests is consistent with the public interest.[113] Foreman and Steinbruner concluded that the Reagan administration seemed to think that society's needs could "be served by the unfettered pursuit of private interest"; thus it opposed "the very idea of regulation."[114] Today, a relatively small but vocal percentage of Americans even associate government regulation with communism. It is from this extreme position that some particularly emotional protests against governmental regulation must be understood.

The courts, however, have not been very sympathetic with the claim that private property rights should come before the welfare of the general public. In an early case, *Charles River Bridge v. Warren Bridge,* 11 Peters 420, 548 (1837), the U.S. Supreme Court did maintain that property rights should be "sacredly guarded," but concluded, nevertheless, that "we must not forget that the community also have rights, and that the happiness and well being of every citizen depends on their [the community's] faithful preservation." Chief Justice Roger Taney's position in the *Charles River Bridge* case was affirmed in *Munn v. Illinois,* 94 U.S. 113 (1876). According to Louis Kohlmeier, Jr., the *Munn* case represents a "major decision in the definition of private property and public rights," and this precedential decision has supported "all the regulation of business that has come after."[115] The Court in *Munn* also emphasized the primary importance of the public welfare, arguing that the Granger laws were justified because they sought to regulate private property rights (the business operations of elevators and railroads) that were crucially linked to public interest rights. Particularly disturbing to those who opposed the regulation of private interests was the Court's opinion that states should be able to regulate any business operations significantly affecting the public interest, regardless of the monopolistic status of the enterprise or state franchise laws. This holding expanded *Charles River Bridge* since in this case Chief Justice Roger Taney upheld as constitutional the power of a state to regulate businesses only because they were monopolies or franchises. In *Cottonwood Mall Shop Ctr., Inc. v. Utah Power and Light Co.,* 440 F.2d 36, 43, 1971 (certiorari denied, 404

U.S. 857), the court once again relied upon *Munn* to justify the legislative trend, which has given to regulatory agencies "almost limitless power to regulate private commercial activity" over the years. Thus, happily or unhappily, the regulation of private property rights for the purpose of prompting the public interest has had strong consistent court support for more than a century and two-thirds.

The Free Market Is the Best Regulator.   It is difficult for me, as well as the vast majority of social scientists, to remain emotionless when discussing the contentions of those who argue that the free market system can provide regulations that are in the best interests of our society. Clearly, governmental regulators have not always served us well, but the natural regulatory failures of the free market system have been demonstrably worse, bringing terrible hardships and suffering to Americans, as seen in cases of child abuse, exploitation of adult workers, consumer rip-offs, formation of tyrannical commercial enterprises, pollution of our environment by selfish profiteers, and the like. Few social scientists are convinced that free (that is, unregulated) competition among selfish interests could yield anything but chaos in a nation as large and complex as ours, or accept the patently absurd argument, epitomizing free market economics, that what's good for GM is good for America. Peter L. Kahn maintains that anti-regulation arguments are rooted in the assumption that free market competition can produce desirable results for society. However, he asserts, when the free marketplace fails to produce attractive results, governmental regulation becomes suddenly quite appealing. Kahn concludes that governmental regulation may not always be perfect, but it may on occasion serve society better than the sometimes "flawed alternative" of the free market.[116]

It should be made clear that some of the anti-regulation arguments do make theoretical and practical sense, especially on a micro level, but they generally fail to adequately consider the broader implications for the entire social system. That is, one could concede that free market competition would eventually provide checks against fluctuation in the natural business cycle (between inflations and depressions), but what effects would the extremes of the natural business cycle have on the people? One could also find plausible the free market theorists' argument that protective tariffs, Federal Reserve Board monetary controls, the imposition of price ceilings, and so on, simply provide artificial checks, as opposed to natural free market controls, which can only forestall the inevitable—for example, an inflation—from occurring. Nevertheless, governmental tinkering with the economy, as Walter Gellhorn asserted, seems to prevent the cruel excesses of the economic cycle.

One of the most popular and basic arguments in favor of deregulation has always been that open-market competition will naturally lead to the most efficient production of quality merchandise or services at the lowest competitive cost to consumers. In 1958, in *Northern Pacific Railway Co. v. U.S.,* 356 U.S. 1, 4, Justice Hugo Black wrote in defense of the free market system that it "rests on the premise that the unrestrained interaction of competitive forces will yield the best allocation of our economic resources, the lowest prices, the highest quality and the

Reprinted with permission of Tom Engelhardt and the *St. Louis Post-Dispatch,* September 25, 2000.

greatest material progress, while at the same time providing an environment conducive to the preservation of our democratic, political and social institutions." It is doubtful that any empirical evidence could be offered to support the claim that free market competition leads "to the preservation of our democratic, political and social institutions," especially since free market competition inevitably tends to lead to the development of monopoly power by those who have over the decades survived the forces of free-wheeling, cutthroat competition. Social Darwinism suggests that survival-of-the-fittest competition among firms in an industry produces monopoly control or at least oligarchical control over goods production or service delivery. Since monopoly or oligarchical power means power by one or a few, respectively, the ends of free market competition could hardly be consistent with democratic or social principles. Also, history has shown that once markets are dominated by one or a few companies, prices soar while service and product quality tend to decline because, it is suspected, the necessary competitive forces do not exist to keep prices down (informal price-fixing can easily take place among a few competitors). Ironically, Justice Black, despite his praise for the free market system, held that regulation is required to keep the free market free! Of course, the implication here is that the free market is not capable of keeping itself free. Thus, Justice Black upheld the regulatory powers of the Sherman Anti-trust Act, declaring the act to be "a comprehensive charter of economic liberty" (p. 84). Black thus echoed the wisdom of Jean Jacques Rousseau, who in essence argued in *On the Social Contract* that men must be forced (regulated) to be free.[117]

Free market competition advocates argue that governmental regulation has unfortunately promoted the welfare of special interests by allowing the regulated industries to capture and dominate the regulatory agencies. Peter Kahn summarizes quite well the argument of the anti-regulation advocates: "In the gritty real world, the theory goes, democratic government serves the interests of whichever interest group turns out to be the most powerful. Unfortunately, the dominant interest group is unlikely to be the general public. Economic regulation, as a result, . . . will not serve the public interest because it is not designed to do so."[118] No doubt this argument has some validity because the typical life cycle of a regulatory agency seems to end in the capture of the agency by the industry. Much to the dismay of the general public, this has allegedly permitted regulated industries to increase prices unjustifiably and with the protective blessings of the regulatory agency. Legislation presented for the deregulation of the airline and trucking industries, sponsored by a unique and powerful liberal-conservative coalition, was rooted in the fundamental contention that deregulation would help encourage healthier competition once freed from the anti-competitive clutches of the Civil Aeronautics Board (CAB) and the ICC.

Airline Deregulation: An Assessment.   About a quarter of a century has passed since the airlines were deregulated in 1978, giving us enough time to evaluate the impact of deregulation. I concluded in the second edition of this book (1988) that airline deregulation had met with "moderate success." This tentative conclusion was reached because, despite many existing problems, the airline industry was showing healthy profits during the mid-1980s and air fares had generally fallen, while the number of flights to at least the major cities had increased.

However, by the third edition, published in 1997, many negative developments had occurred in the airline industry, causing this author and many other observers to question the wisdom of airline deregulation. Paul Dempsey concluded at that time that the airline industry must be reregulated "since deregulation has been a catastrophic failure, for creditors, stockholders, labor, and yes, consumers."[119]

But profits dipped sharply between 1990 and 1992, reaching a record low of $2.444 billion in 1992, in part due to a sluggish economy and large-scale purchases of new airplanes by airlines determined to build up their fleets with better and new aircraft. By 1992, according to Dempsey, the troubled airline industry had "lost all the profits it had earned since the Wright Brothers' flight at Kitty Hawk in 1903, plus $2 billion more."[120] At the same time, many analysts were attributing a significant percentage of airline losses to destructive unregulated competition that had forced some airlines to charge unprofitably low fares to compete with Chapter 11 airlines, which were able to charge ridiculously low fares because they were protected from their creditors by Chapter 11 bankruptcy provisions. Also, megacarriers were permitted under deregulation to engage in predatory pricing to drive the smaller and financially weaker airlines out of business.

Figure 2.3 shows, however, that by 1993 the airline industry was again earning profits, which continued to the end of the century, although consumer complaints were increasing as a result of a dramatic decline in "frill" services; inconvenient, time-consuming, and absurd nondirect routes (for example, flying from St. Louis to Denver via Dallas); related connection and layover problems; and increased departure and landing delays. The prosperous economy during the Clinton years nonetheless seemed to indicate that deregulation had worked and the airline industry was overall quite healthy.

However, the health of the airline industry was more imagined than real. According to the Air Transit Association's 2002–2003 report, "State of the U.S. Airline Industry," the airlines accumulated massive debt during the 1990s into the early twenty-first century. This left them in a weak position to cope with a worsening economy before September 11, 2001, and no realistic chance of dealing with the really catastrophic economic and regulatory conditions after 9/11. Of course, 9/11 has caused passenger travel to decline dramatically, causing enormous revenue losses to the airlines. At the same time the carriers have been hit with new and costly government security regulations, higher jet fuel prices, and new and expensive "war risk insurance" premiums. Even worse, airlines have had to reduce fares to levels not seen since 1998 to attract passengers, yet fares do not appear lower to travelers because the government has added new taxes and fees to help cover the costs of improved security. "Once a small fraction, federal taxes and fees now constitute 25 percent of the cost of a low-priced ticket. Based on a total round-trip ticket price of $200, with one connection each way, an airline would receive $149, while $51 in taxes and fees would go to the government."[121]

The impact deregulation has had on air fares is difficult to assess because the proliferation of so many "special" fares has confused not only travelers but analysts as well. It is true that many passengers today obtain discounted fares, yet such fares are based upon full fare rates that have increased dramatically since deregulation. Unquestionably, discount fares can be terrific bargains, but various restrictions apply involving restricted flight times and destination cities, Saturday night stayovers, nondirect and often very indirect flights, and prepurchase of tickets with nontransfer and nonrefund stipulations that can prove inconvenient and sometimes very costly to travelers. In addition to extra travel burdens placed on passengers by post-9/11 policies, restrictions under deregulation have made flying today complicated at times and not necessarily a great travel bargain when cost and inconveniences are considered.[122]

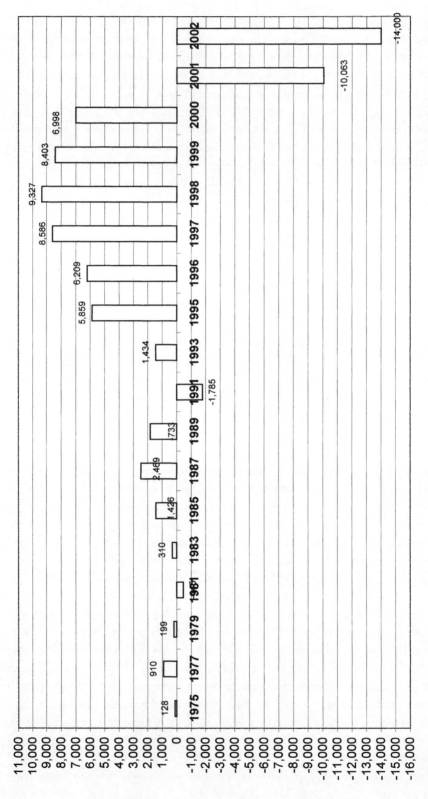

FIGURE 2.3   Net Profit/Loss for U.S. Airlines, 1975–2002. SOURCE: Air Transport Association (Washington, D.C., 2003). NOTE: The 2003 profit/loss figure was unavailable at time of publication, but it is expected to exceed the 2002 figure.

Airline safety has been a concern since airline deregulation in 1978. However, statistics on airline safety tracked since 1978 show that air safety has actually increased, making air travel still the safest way to travel. For example, for the decade ending in 2000, passenger deaths per million passenger miles was only 0.02. Naturally, the three airline crashes caused by the terrorists on September 11 increased passenger fatalities per million passenger mile, but it would make little sense to count these murders of passengers and crew against the quite impressive history of airline safety.[123]

The impact of deregulation on smaller airlines and on "non-hub" cities has not been good. Over the past twenty-five years since airline deregulation cutthroat competition caused the weaker airlines, as expected, to collapse, give way to hostile takeovers, or to operate in the red as long as they could. To meet the competition, airlines dropped their unprofitable routes to medium-sized and smaller cities, inconveniencing passengers and businesses dependent on air service. However, in recent years, discount airlines not carrying the heavy debt burden of the larger airlines, such as Southwest and Jetblue, entered the competition and began providing air travelers with more travel opportunities, forcing the traditional "hub-and-spoke" airlines to compete by offering more routes, even to smaller cities, at reasonable prices. In short, just before "9/11" most critics, despite some "predatory pricing" by some carriers and other problems during the 1990s causing President Clinton to consider re-regulating the airlines in 1998, believed airline deregulation to be a qualified success since the most critical barometric indicators of air travel appeared healthy (airline profits, air passenger miles, air safety, and reasonable air fares).

But the impact of the "9/11" terrorist attacks has thrown the airline industry into financial chaos. Every airline has been affected by the economic downturn. Bankruptcies have occurred and more are expected. Serious domestic economic problems and international political and financial instability will likely cause the situation to worsen for at least the next few years. The Air Transport Association concludes candidly: "There are few bright spots in the industry. In an effort to reduce costs, carriers have streamlined operations, lowered distribution costs, simplified fleets, and negotiated labor concessions."[124]

Unquestionably, the health of the airline industry is essential to the health of the U.S. economy overall. For example, civil aviation in 2000 accounted for about 11 million jobs, roughly 9 percent of our gross domestic product (GDP), and approximately $800 billion in direct and indirect economic activity.[125] Local, state, regional, national, and international economics are linked and promoted by the airline industry. Consequently, some analysts argue that the vital importance of the airlines suggests that we cannot afford to permit airline deregulation to continue.[126] However, others agree that the airlines are presently in financial chaos, but airline deregulation cannot be blamed.[127]

So what can be concluded twenty-five years after airline deregulation? Has it been successful or not? Probably the only safe answer is that no definitive answer can be given because 9/11 had such an unusual and unexpected catastrophic impact on the airlines. Certainly, even if the government were still regulating the airlines, 9/11 would still have caused enormous economic hardships to the airlines.

Airline Bankruptcies. Reprinted with permission of John Sherffius and the *St. Louis Post-Dispatch,* August 14, 2002.

Critics will still debate the wisdom of airline deregulation, but in 2004 the truth seems to be that competition in the airline industry has probably proved overall good for the airlines and consumers. No airline has been successful in monopolizing the industry and charging predatory prices for long. Yes, competition, expectedly, has driven some airlines into bankruptcy, but many bankrupt airlines "deserved" this fate since their executives had unwisely given in to too many costly labor and other demands during the good years, causing their operating costs to be far too high to get them successfully through the lean years, causing many heavily debt-burdened airlines to go bankrupt.

Bankruptcy is not necessarily a bad thing for an airline, however, and may prove to be a much better alternative than a government loan bailout. For example, United Airlines was turned down by the Air Transportation Stabilization Board when seeking a $1.8 billion loan guarantee in late 2002. If United had been given the loan but could not repay, the taxpayers would be stuck with the bill. Additionally, government loans may simply postpone the inevitable financial death of an airline hopelessly debt ridden. Chapter 11 bankruptcy protection allows a struggling airline a more realistic chance of long-term survival because bankruptcy laws allow it to renegotiate labor contracts and the like to permit necessary cost-cutting restructuring so it once again can compete. The reality is that airline deregulation is very likely here to stay and forcing existing airlines to adopt competitive measures so they will be equipped to compete with new competitors will prove healthy for the industry and consumers.[128]

Regulatory Reform and the Future of Regulation

Many attempts at regulatory reform have been made since the New Deal. The deregulation reform movement, starting with airline and transportation deregulation in 1978, quickly spread to deregulation in telecommunications, cable television, banking, and electric power. But not all has gone well, causing critics of deregulation to call for reregulation of industries where deregulation failures are apparent.

Over the decades, regulatory forms have taken many broad forms. Thomas O. McGarity has classified regulatory forms into four types—substantive, procedural, structural, and cognitive.[129] *Substantive regulatory reform* aims at changing public policy outputs in administrative agencies through lawmaking and rulemaking. Since the 1960s, substantive changes in regulatory policy have had the objective of making more progress in civil rights, consumerism, and environmental protection. An example of substantive reform is the Environmental Protection Agency's 1994 rule, authorized by the 1990 Clean Air Act, requiring an unprecedented reduction in the air toxins that can be released from chemical plants.[130] *Procedural regulatory reform* has focused on improving agency procedures in implementing regulatory policies. For example, procedural reform has led to negotiated rulemaking. *Structural* reforms have stressed restructuring agency decisionmaking to allow environmental political actors greater or lesser influence over agency decisionmaking. Such restructuring allows President George W. Bush to use the Office of Management and Budget to exert more control over agency rulemaking. *Cognitive regulatory reform* focuses on the way agencies perceive and assess regulatory problems. For example, cost-benefit analysis has been used in recent decades to determine the potential costs and benefits of proposed agency rules.[131]

So how should we evaluate regulatory reform leading to deregulation? McGarity holds that one lesson that can be learned from the deregulation movement "is that there is no inevitable march forward of the positive state."[132] However, the reality is that deregulation represents only a temporary retreat from the onward march of the positive state, which, out of necessity, will inevitably become a more pervasive regulator. The deregulation movement is really best characterized as *reduced* regulation because virtually no socioeconomic or political activities go totally unregulated. And Paul Teske has noted that the reduced regulatory role played by federal regulators during deregulation "led to an even more prominent role for the states in many regulatory arenas."[133]

A consensus of observers of the regulatory climate believe that we can expect to see deregulation continue, but with some reregulation in industries where well-publicized "failures" have caused public outcries and politicians to respond. For instance, in light of the corporate scandals that had such a negative impact on Wall Street, New York Attorney General Eliot Spitzer, with support in D.C., called for reregulation measures to be taken by the Securities and Exchange Commission to force corporate heads and auditors to disclose the truth in their reports about their corporate earnings or losses.[134]

In conclusion, most people and businesses have learned to accept the "necessary evil" of governmental regulation. We should expect that in the future a stronger regulatory alliance will be formed between the government and regulated businesses. In fact, this is exactly what the Air Transportation Association said was needed to ensure the future well-being of the airlines and America.[135] Individuals will also be subjected to more red tape as government's obligation to promote the public interest intensifies. Many will continue to complain about how big the government is and how un-American the regulators are. Yet the public will not, as individuals or groups, stop demanding that our government regulate to promote the public interest.

SUMMARY

The administrative system President George W. Bush inherited is enormous, complex, and costly, especially when compared to the bureaucratic apparatus under President George Washington. But much has changed in America since the late 1700s, and these changes have necessitated the growth of public bureaucracy and the eventual maturation of administrative law. Systems theorists provide a solid conceptual framework for understanding why the administrative system developed as it did. Although many specific reasons can be cited to explain administrative growth, these theorists contend that the administrative system grew largely in response to the increasing demands placed upon government by various interests in society that were concerned about various social and economic problems. Government tried to resolve the different problems by creating public agencies. As U.S. socioeconomic institutions became more complex as American society matured, an increasing number of administrative agencies were created to regulate in the public interest.

The demand for more public services at both the national and state levels created a demand overload situation for legislators, who initially tried in vain to handle most of the regulatory problems themselves. It soon became apparent that legislators had to delegate the regulatory function to public administrators. At first, during the 1800s and early 1900s, administrators were given very limited powers to shape and implement public policies, but as pressures on Congress continued to mount, especially as a result of the massive socioeconomic problems of the 1930s, legislators expressed a strong desire to delegate significant policy-making powers to agency administrators, including vast authority to design, adjudicate, and implement agency policies. In 1936 in *Curtiss-Wright,* the U.S. Supreme Court permitted Congress to delegate broad powers to administrators as long as they attached meaningful standards to guide agency actions. However, for the past several decades the courts have allowed Congress to delegate broad policymaking powers to public administrators without the requirement of attaching meaningful standards. Although some state courts have been reluctant to permit such delegation, most have followed the path of the federal courts by upholding the constitutionality of standardless statutes that allow state administrators to assume powerful policymaking roles.

Consequently, administrative power in the early 2000s is awesome. To some, the emergence of the new administrative state has eroded the principles of democratic governance and usurped individual liberties. One of the hottest political topics today centers on what role government should play in regulating socioeconomic activities. This issue has been a major campaign issue in recent political campaigns and will continue to dominate political debates for the foreseeable future. Defenders of widespread governmental regulation basically argue that the regulators are necessary to protect and promote the public interest in modern society, especially by protecting the public from the selfishness of large and mighty special interests. Those opposed to governmental regulations espouse a modified laissez-faire philosophy. They hold that the free market system is capable of providing the necessary regulatory controls. Besides, they maintain, the government has no right to encroach upon private property interests protected by the Constitution. Although there are few left who advocate no governmental regulation of private life, there are many who believe that governmental regulation is too extensive, too expensive, and too threatening to individual liberties.

The complexities of modern living have made extensive governmental regulation necessary. But the question of *how* extensive governmental regulation should be will continue to be hotly debated in the years to come. Nevertheless, the future will likely bring additional bureaucratic growth, reregulation, and more regulations. It will also bring stronger ties between the business community, especially big business, and government since tomorrow's problems will demand that government and business resolve challenging socioeconomic problems together.

WHITMAN, ADMINISTRATOR OF ENVIRONMENTAL PROTECTION AGENCY V. AMERICAN TRUCKING ASSOCIATIONS

531 U.S. 457; 121 S.Ct. 903 (2001)

Facts

The Clean Air Act (CAA) in Section 109(a) requires the EPA administrator to set national ambient air quality standards (NAAQS) for different air pollutants. Section 109(b) requires EPA's administrator to establish these standards within a tolerable safety margin. Subpart 2 of Part D restricts the administrator's discretion in promulgating rules pertaining to ozone NAAQS. However, in 1997, EPA's administrators used their discretion in revising and implementing new ozone standards, ignoring essentially Subpart 2 of Part D. Some private companies and states brought suit, contending, inter alia, that Section 109(b), as applied by the EPA, was an unconstitutional delegation of power under Article I, Section 1, of the U.S. Constitution. The U.S. Court of Appeals for the D.C. Circuit agreed, arguing further that the EPA could have avoided the unconstitutional delegation by applying Section 109(b) in a more restrictive manner. The EPA appealed and the Supreme Court granted certiorari.

Justice Scalia delivered the opinion of the Court with justices Thomas, Stevens, Souter, and Breyer concurring in part. Only the delegation question is reproduced below. Since only Thomas, Stevens, and Souter address the delegation issue in their concurring opinions, only their opinions are included.

(Note: This case, as well as those appearing at the ends of other chapters, has been pared down to exclude elements nonessential to the decision.)

Section 109(b)(1) of the CAA instructs the EPA to set "ambient air quality standards the attainment and maintenance of which in the judgment of the Administrator, based on [the] criteria and allowing an adequate margin of safety, are requisite to protect the public health." 42 U.S.C. §7409(b)(1). The Court of Appeals held that this section as interpreted by the Administrator did not provide an "intelligible principle" to guide the EPA's exercise of authority in setting NAAQS. "[The] EPA," it said, "lacked any determinate criteria for drawing lines. It has failed to state intelligibly how much is too much." The court hence found that the EPA's interpretation (but not the statute itself) violated the nondelegation doctrine. Id. at 1038. We disagree.

In a delegation challenge, the constitutional question is whether the statute has delegated legislative power to the agency. Article I, Section 1, of the Constitution vests "all legislative Powers herein granted . . . in a Congress of the United States." This text permits no delegation of those powers, *Loving v. United States*, 517 U.S. 748 (1996); . . . and so we repeatedly have said that when Congress confers decisionmaking authority upon agencies Congress must "lay down by legislative act an intelligible principle to which the person or body authorized to [act] is directed to conform." *J. W. Hampton, Jr., & Co. v. United States*, 276 U.S. 394 (1928). We have never suggested that an agency can cure an unlawful delegation of legislative power by adopting in its discretion a limiting construction of the statute. Both *Fahey v. Mallonee*, 332 U.S. 245 (1947), and *Lichter v. United States*, 334 U.S. 742 (1948), mention agency regulations in the course of their nondelegation discussions, but *Lichter* did so because a subsequent Congress had incorporated the regulations into a revised version of the statute, ibid., and *Fahey* because the customary practices in the area, implicitly incorporated into the statute, were reflected in the regulations. The idea that an agency can cure an unconstitutionally standardless delegation of power by declining to exercise some of that power seems to us internally contradictory. The very choice of which portion of the power to exercise—that is to say, the prescription of the standard that Congress had omitted—would itself be an exercise of the forbidden legislative authority. Whether the statute delegates legislative power is a question for the courts, and an agency's voluntary self-denial has no bearing upon the answer.

We agree with the Solicitor General that the text of §109(b)(1) of the CAA at a minimum requires that "for a discrete set of pollutants and based on published air quality criteria that reflect the latest scientific knowledge, [the] EPA must establish uniform national standards at a level that is requisite to protect public health from the adverse effects of the pollutant in the ambient air." Requisite, in turn, "means sufficient, but not more than necessary." These limits on the EPA's discretion are strikingly similar to the ones we approved in *Touby v. United States*, 500 U.S. 160 (1991), which permitted the Attorney General to designate a drug as a controlled substance for purposes of criminal drug enforcement if doing so was "'necessary to avoid an imminent hazard to the public safety.'" They also resemble the Occupational Safety and

Health Act provision requiring the agency to "set the standard which most adequately assures, to the extent feasible, on the basis of the best available evidence, that no employee will suffer any impairment of health." . . .

The scope of discretion §109(b)(1) allows is in fact well within the outer limits of our nondelegation precedents. In the history of the Court we have found the requisite "intelligible principle" lacking in only two statutes, one of which provided literally no guidance for the exercise of discretion, and the other of which conferred authority to regulate the entire economy on the basis of no more precise a standard than stimulating the economy by assuring "fair competition." See *Panama Refining Co. v. Ryan*, 293 U.S. 388 (1935); *A. L. A. Schechter Poultry Corp. v. United States*, 295 U.S. 495 (1935). We have, on the other hand, upheld the validity of §11(b)(2) of the Public Utility Holding Company Act of 1935, 49 Stat. 821, which gave the Securities and Exchange Commission authority to modify the structure of holding company systems so as to ensure that they are not "unduly or unnecessarily complicated" and do not "unfairly or inequitably distribute voting power among security holders." *American Power & Light Co. v. SEC*, 329 U.S. 90 (1946). We have approved the wartime conferral of agency power to fix the prices of commodities at a level that "will be generally fair and equitable and will effectuate the [in some respects conflicting] purposes of the Act." *Yakus v. United States*, 321 (1944). And we have found an "intelligible principle" in various statutes authorizing regulation in the "public

interest." In short, we have "almost never felt qualified to second-guess Congress regarding the permissible degree of policy judgment that can be left to those executing or applying the law." *Mistretta v. United States*, 488 U.S. 361 (1989).

It is true enough that the degree of agency discretion that is acceptable varies according to the scope of the power congressionally conferred. While Congress need not provide any direction to the EPA regarding the manner in which it is to define "country elevators," which are to be exempt from new-stationary-source regulations governing grain elevators, see §7411(i), it must provide substantial guidance on setting air standards that affect the entire national economy. But even in sweeping regulatory schemes we have never demanded, as the Court of Appeals did here, that statutes provide a "determinate criterion" for saying "how much [of the regulated harm] is too much." In *Touby*, for example, we did not require the statute to decree how "imminent" was too imminent, or how "necessary" was necessary enough, or even—most relevant here—how "hazardous" was too hazardous. Similarly, the statute at issue in *Lichter* authorized agencies to recoup "excess profits" paid under wartime Government contracts, yet we did not insist that Congress specify how much profit was too much. It is therefore not conclusive for delegation purposes that, as respondents argue, ozone and particulate matter are "nonthreshold" pollutants that inflict a continuum of adverse health effects at any airborne concentration greater than zero, and hence require the EPA to make judgments of degree. "[A] certain degree of discretion, and thus of law-making, inheres in most executive or judicial action." *Mistretta v. United States, supra*, at 417 (SCALIA, J., dissenting) (emphasis deleted); see 488 U.S. at 378–379 (majority opinion). Section 109(b)(1) of the CAA, which to repeat we interpret as requiring the EPA to set air quality standards at the level that is "requisite"—that is, not lower or higher than is necessary—to protect the public health with an adequate margin of safety, fits comfortably within the scope of discretion permitted by our precedent.

We therefore reverse the judgment of the Court of Appeals remanding for reinterpretation that would avoid a supposed delegation of legislative power. It will remain for the Court of Appeals—on the remand that we direct for other reasons—to dispose of any other preserved challenge to the NAAQS under the judicial-review provisions contained in 42 U.S.C. §7607(d)(9).

The final two issues on which we granted certiorari concern the EPA's authority to implement the revised ozone NAAQS in areas whose ozone levels currently exceed the maximum level permitted by that standard. The CAA designates such areas "non-attainment," §107(d)(1), 42 U.S.C. §7407(d)(1); and it exposes them to additional restrictions over and above the implementation requirements imposed generally by §110 of the CAA. These additional restrictions are found in the five substantive subparts of Part D of Title I, 42 U.S.C. §§7501–7515. Subpart 1, §§7501–7509a, contains general nonattainment regulations that pertain to every pollutant for which a NAAQS exists. Subparts 2 through 5,

§§7511–7514a, contain rules tailored to specific individual pollutants. Subpart 2, added by the Clean Air Act Amendments of 1990, §103, 104 Stat. 2423, addresses ozone. 42 U.S.C. §§7511–7511f. The dispute before us here, in a nutshell, is whether Subpart 1 alone (as the agency determined), or rather Subpart 2 or some combination of Subparts 1 and 2, controls the implementation of the revised ozone NAAQS in nonattainment areas.

The Administrator first urges, however, that we vacate the judgment of the Court of Appeals on this issue because it lacked jurisdiction to review the EPA's implementation policy. Section 307(b)(1) of the CAA, 42 U.S.C. §7607(b)(1), gives the court jurisdiction over "any . . . nationally applicable regulations promulgated, or final action taken, by the Administrator," but the EPA argues that its implementation policy was not agency "action," was not "final" action, and is not ripe for review. We reject each of these three contentions.

At the same time the EPA proposed the revised ozone NAAQS in 1996, it also proposed an "interim implementation policy" for the NAAQS, see 61 Fed. Reg. 65752 (1996), that was to govern until the details of implementation could be put in final form through specific "rulemaking actions." The preamble to this proposed policy declared that "the interim implementation policy . . . represents EPA's preliminary views on these issues and, while it may include various statements that States must take certain actions, these statements are made pursuant to EPA's preliminary interpretations, and thus do not bind the States and public as a matter of law." Ibid. If the EPA had done no more, we perhaps could accept its current claim that its action was not final. However, after the agency had accepted comments on its proposed policy, and on the same day that the final ozone NAAQS was promulgated, the White House published in the Federal Register what it titled a "Memorandum for the Administrator of the Environmental Protection Agency" that prescribed implementation procedures for the EPA to follow. 62 Fed. Reg. 38421 (1997). . . . The EPA supplemented this memorandum with an explanation of the implementation procedures, which it published in the explanatory preamble to its final ozone NAAQS under the heading, "Final decision on the primary standard." "In light of comments received regarding the interpretation proposed in the Interim Implementation Policy," the EPA announced, it had "reconsidered that interpretation" and settled on a new one. The provisions of "subpart 1 of part D of Title I of the Act" will immediately "apply to the implementation of the new 8-hour [ozone] standards." . . . Moreover, the provisions of subpart 2 "will [also] continue to apply as a matter of law for so long as an area is not attaining the [old] 1-hour standard." Once the area reaches attainment for the old standard, however, "the provisions of subpart 2 will have been achieved and those provisions will no longer apply."

We have little trouble concluding that this constitutes final agency action subject to review under §307. The bite in the phrase "final action" is not in the word "action," which is meant to cover comprehensively every manner in which

an agency may exercise its power. It is rather in the word "final," which requires that the action under review "mark the consummation of the agency's decisionmaking process." Only if the "EPA has rendered its last word on the matter" in question is its action "final" and thus reviewable. That standard is satisfied here. The EPA's "decisionmaking process," which began with the 1996 proposal and continued with the reception of public comments, concluded when the agency, "in light of [these comments]," and in conjunction with a corresponding directive from the White House, adopted the interpretation of Part D at issue here.

Since that interpretation [was] issued, the EPA has refused in subsequent rulemakings to reconsider it, explaining to disappointed commenters that its earlier decision was conclusive. Though the agency has not dressed its decision with the conventional procedural accoutrements of finality, its own behavior thus belies the claim that its interpretation is not final.

The decision is also ripe for our review. "Ripeness 'requires us to evaluate both the fitness of the issues for judicial decision and the hardship to the parties of withholding court consideration.'" *Texas v. United States*, 523 U.S. 296 (1998) (quoting *Abbott Laboratories v. Gardner*, 387 U.S. 136 [1967]). The question before us here is purely one of statutory interpretation that would not "benefit from further factual development of the issues presented." Nor will our review "inappropriately interfere with further administrative action" since the EPA has concluded its consideration of the implementation issue. Finally, as for hardship to the parties: The respondent States must—on pain of forfeiting to the EPA control over implementation of the NAAQS—promptly undertake the lengthy and expensive task of developing state implementation plans (SIP's) that will attain the new, more stringent standard within five years. See 42 U.S.C. §§7410, 7502. Whether or not this would suffice in an ordinary case brought under the review provisions of the APA, we have characterized the special judicial-review provision of the CAA, 42 U.S.C. §7607(b), as one of those statutes that specifically provides for "preenforcement" review. Such statutes, we have said, permit "judicial review directly, even before the concrete effects normally required for APA review are felt." The effects at issue here surely meet that lower standard.

Beyond all this, the implementation issue was fairly included within the challenges to the final ozone rule that were properly before the Court of Appeals. Respondents argued below that the EPA could not revise the ozone standard, because to do so would trigger the use of Subpart 1, which had been supplanted (for ozone) by the specific rules of Subpart 2. The EPA responded that Subpart 2 did not supplant but simply supplemented Subpart 1, so that the latter section still "applies to all nonattainment areas for all NAAQS, . . . including nonattainment areas for any revised ozone standard." The agency later reiterated that Subpart 2 "does not supplant implementation provisions for revised ozone standards. This interpretation fully harmonizes Subpart 2 with EPA's clear authority to revise any NAAQS." In other words, the EPA was arguing that the revised standard could be issued,

despite its apparent incompatibility with portions of Subpart 2, because it would be implemented under Subpart 1 rather than Subpart 2. The District of Columbia Circuit ultimately agreed that Subpart 2 could be harmonized with the EPA's authority to promulgate revised NAAQS, but not because Subpart 2 is entirely inapplicable—which is one of EPA's assignments of error. It is unreasonable to contend, as the EPA now does, that the Court of Appeals was obligated to reach the agency's preferred result, but forbidden to assess the reasons the EPA had given for reaching that result. The implementation issue was fairly included within respondents' challenge to the ozone rule, which all parties agree is final agency action ripe for review.

Our approach to the merits of the parties' dispute is the familiar one of *Chevron U.S.A. Inc. v. Natural Resources Defense Council, Inc.*, 467 U.S. 837 (1984). If the statute resolves the question whether Subpart 1 or Subpart 2 (or some combination of the two) shall apply to revised ozone NAAQS, then "that is the end of the matter." But if the statute is "silent or ambiguous" with respect to the issue, then we must defer to a "reasonable interpretation made by the administrator of an agency." We cannot agree with the Court of Appeals that Subpart 2 clearly controls the implementation of revised ozone NAAQS because we find the statute to some extent ambiguous. We conclude, however, that the agency's interpretation goes beyond the limits of what is ambiguous and contradicts what in our view is quite clear. We therefore hold the implementation policy unlawful.

The text of Subpart 1 at first seems to point the way to a clear answer to the question, which Subpart controls? Two sections of Subpart 1, 7502(a)(1)(C) and 7502(a)(2)(D), contain switching provisions stating that if the classification of ozone nonattainment areas is "specifically provided [for] under other provisions of [Part D]," then those provisions will control instead of Subpart 1's. Thus it is true but incomplete to note, as the Administrator does, that the substantive language of Subpart 1 is broad enough to apply to revised ozone standards. To determine whether that language does apply one must resolve the further textual issue whether some other provision, namely Subpart 2, provides for the classification of ozone nonattainment areas. If it does, then according to the switching provisions of Subpart 1 it will control.

So, does Subpart 2 provide for classifying nonattainment ozone areas under the revised standard? It unquestionably does. The backbone of the subpart is Table 1, printed in §7511(a)(1), which defines five categories of ozone nonattainment areas and prescribes attainment deadlines for each. Section 7511(a)(1) funnels all nonattainment areas into the table for classification, declaring that "each area designated nonattainment for ozone . . . shall be classified at the time of such designation, under table 1, by operation of law." And once an area has been classified, "the primary standard attainment date for ozone shall be as expeditiously as practicable but not later than the date provided in table 1." The EPA argues that this text is not as clear or comprehensive as it seems, because the title of §7511(a) reads "Classification and attainment

dates for 1989 nonattainment areas," which suggests that Subpart 2 applies only to areas that were in nonattainment in 1989, and not to areas later designated nonattainment under a revised ozone standard. The suggestion must be rejected, however, because §7511(b)(1) specifically provides for the classification of areas that were in attainment in 1989 but have subsequently slipped into nonattainment. It thus makes clear that Subpart 2 is not limited solely to 1989 nonattainment areas. This eliminates the interpretive role of the title, which may only "shed light on some ambiguous word or phrase in the statute itself."

It may well be, as the EPA argues. The concurring opinion below on denial of rehearing pointed out that some provisions of Subpart 2 are ill fitted to implementation of the revised standard. Using the old 1-hour averages of ozone levels, for example, as Subpart 2 requires, see §7511(a)(1); 44 Fed. Reg. 8202 (1979), would produce at best an inexact estimate of the new 8-hour averages, . . . and App. I (1999). And finally, Subpart 2's method for calculating attainment dates—which is simply to count forward a certain number of years from November 15, 1990 (the date the 1990 CAA Amendments took force), depending on how far out of attainment the area started—seems to make no sense for areas that are first classified under a new standard after November 15, 1990. If, for example, areas were classified in the year 2000, many of the deadlines would already have expired at the time of classification.

These gaps in Subpart 2's scheme prevent us from concluding that Congress clearly intended Subpart 2 to be the exclusive, permanent means of enforcing a revised ozone standard in nonattainment areas. The statute is in our view ambiguous concerning the manner in which Subpart 1 and Subpart 2 interact with regard to revised ozone standards, and we would defer to the EPA's reasonable resolution of that ambiguity. We cannot defer, however, to the interpretation the EPA has given.

Whatever effect may be accorded the gaps in Subpart 2 as implying some limited applicability of Subpart 1, they cannot be thought to render Subpart 2's carefully designed restrictions on EPA discretion utterly nugatory once a new standard has been promulgated, as the EPA has concluded. The principal distinction between Subpart 1 and Subpart 2 is that the latter eliminates regulatory discretion that the former allowed. While Subpart 1 permits the EPA to establish classifications for nonattainment areas, Subpart 2 classifies areas as a matter of law based on a table. . . . Yet according to the EPA, Subpart 2 was simply Congress's "approach to the implementation of the [old] 1-hour" standard, and so there was no reason that "the new standard could not simultaneously be implemented under . . . subpart 1." To use a few apparent gaps in Subpart 2 to render its textually explicit applicability to nonattainment areas under the new standard utterly inoperative is to go over the edge of reasonable interpretation. The EPA may not construe the statute in a way that completely nullifies textually applicable provisions meant to limit its discretion.

The EPA's interpretation making Subpart 2 abruptly obsolete is all the more astonishing because Subpart 2 was obviously written to govern implementation for some time. Some of the elements required to be included in SIP's under Subpart 2 were not to take effect until many years after the passage of the Act. . . . A plan reaching so far into the future was not enacted to be abandoned the next time the EPA reviewed the ozone standard—which Congress knew could happen at any time, since the technical staff papers had already been completed in late 1989. Yet nothing in the EPA's interpretation would have prevented the agency from aborting Subpart 2 the day after it was enacted. Even now, if the EPA's interpretation were correct, some areas of the country could be required to meet the new, more stringent ozone standard in at most the same time that Subpart 2 had allowed them to meet the old standard. . . . An interpretation of Subpart 2 so at odds with its structure and manifest purpose cannot be sustained.

We therefore find the EPA's implementation policy to be unlawful, though not in the precise respect determined by the Court of Appeals. After our remand, and the Court of Appeals' final disposition of this case, it is left to the EPA to develop a reasonable interpretation of the nonattainment implementation provisions insofar as they apply to revised ozone NAAQS.

To summarize our holdings in these unusually complex cases: (1) The EPA may not consider implementation costs in setting primary and secondary NAAQS under §109(b) of the CAA. (2) Section 109(b)(1) does not delegate legislative power to the EPA in contravention of Art. I, §1, of the Constitution. (3) The Court of Appeals had jurisdiction to review the EPA's interpretation of Part D of Title I of the CAA, relating to the implementation of the revised ozone NAAQS. (4) The EPA's interpretation of that Part is unreasonable.

The judgment of the Court of Appeals is affirmed in part and reversed in part, and the cases are remanded for proceedings consistent with this opinion.

It is so ordered.

CONCUR BY: THOMAS; STEVENS; BREYER

CONCUR: JUSTICE THOMAS, concurring.

I agree with the majority that §109's directive to the agency is no less an "intelligible principle" than a host of other directives that we have approved. I also agree that the Court of Appeals' remand to the agency to make its own corrective interpretation does not accord with our understanding of the delegation issue. I write separately, however, to express my concern that there may nevertheless be a genuine constitutional problem with §109, a problem which the parties did not address.

The parties to this case who briefed the constitutional issue wrangled over constitutional doctrine with barely a nod to the text of the Constitution. Although this Court since 1928 has treated the "intelligible principle" requirement as the only constitutional limit on congressional grants of power to administrative agencies, the Constitution does not speak of "intelligible principles." Rather, it speaks in much simpler terms: "All legislative Powers herein granted shall be vested in a Congress." U.S. Const., Art. 1, §1. I am not convinced that the intelligible principle doctrine serves to prevent all cessions of legislative power. I believe that there are cases in which the principle is intelligible and yet the significance of the delegated decision is simply too great for the decision to be called anything other than "legislative."

As it is, none of the parties to this case has examined the text of the Constitution or asked us to reconsider our precedents on cessions of legislative power. On a future day, however, I would be willing to address the question whether our delegation jurisprudence has strayed too far from our Founders' understanding of separation of powers.

JUSTICE STEVENS, with whom JUSTICE SOUTER joins, concurring in part and concurring in the judgment.

Section 109(b)(1) delegates to the Administrator of the Environmental Protection Agency (EPA) the authority to promulgate national ambient air quality standards (NAAQS). In Part III of its opinion, the Court convincingly explains why the Court of Appeals erred when it concluded that §109 effected "an unconstitutional delegation of legislative power." *American Trucking Assns., Inc. v. EPA*, 175 F.3d 1027 (CADC 1999) (per curiam). I wholeheartedly endorse the Court's result and endorse its explanation of its reasons, albeit with the following caveat.

The Court has two choices. We could choose to articulate our ultimate disposition of this issue by frankly acknowledging that the power delegated to the EPA is "legislative" but nevertheless conclude that the delegation is constitutional because adequately limited by the terms of the authorizing statute. Alternatively, we could pretend, as the

Court does, that the authority delegated to the EPA is somehow not "legislative power." Despite the fact that there is language in our opinions that supports the Court's articulation of our holding, I am persuaded that it would be both wiser and more faithful to what we have actually done in delegation cases to admit that agency rulemaking authority is "legislative power."

The proper characterization of governmental power should generally depend on the nature of the power, not on the identity of the person exercising it. . . . If the NAAQS that the EPA promulgated had been prescribed by Congress, everyone would agree that those rules would be the product of an exercise of "legislative power." The same characterization is appropriate when an agency exercises rulemaking authority pursuant to a permissible delegation from Congress.

My view is not only more faithful to normal English usage, but is also fully consistent with the text of the Constitution. In Article I, the Framers vested "All legislative Powers" in the Congress, Art. I., §1, just as in Article II they vested the "executive Power" in the President, Art. II, §1. Those provisions do not purport to limit the authority of either recipient of power to delegate authority to others. . . . ([Although] "'All legislative powers herein granted shall be vested in a Congress of the United States,' it is far from novel to acknowledge that independent agencies do indeed exercise legislative powers"); . . . Surely the authority granted to members of the Cabinet and federal law enforcement agents is properly characterized as "Executive" even though not exercised by the President.

It seems clear that an executive agency's exercise of rulemaking authority pursuant to a valid delegation from Congress is "legislative." As long as the delegation provides a sufficiently intelligible principle, there is nothing inherently unconstitutional about it. Accordingly, while I join Parts I, II, and IV of the Court's opinion, and agree with almost everything said in Part III, I would hold that when Congress enacted §109, it effected a constitutional delegation of legislative power to the EPA.

COMMENTS AND QUESTIONS

Delegation cases are both fascinating and somewhat amusing because it is so obvious to any legal observer that the courts must engage in quite imaginative "Alice in Wonderland" thinking to rationalize the constitutionality of delegating legislative power to agency administrators. Clearly, the delegation of legislative power to the EPA administrator to set national ambient air quality standards within "an adequate margin of safety" that "are requisite to protect the public health" constitutes a blatant delegation of legislative power in violation of Article I, Section 1, of our Constitution, if literally interpreted.

However, the unanimous Supreme Court held that Section 109(b) of the Clean Air Act was a constitutional delegation. The Court reasoned that the broad delegation of "decisionmaking authority" was constitutionally permissible because Congress attached "an intelligible principle to which the person or body authorized to [act] is directed to conform." Yet the only principle—which would not actually seem to constitute an "intelligible principle" to a reasonable person—was the extremely vague requirement that the EPA had to set air quality standards at a "requisite" level, which the Court interpreted to mean a level that is "not lower or higher than is necessary—to protect the public health within an adequate margin of safety."

Now let's face the realities of this decision. This so-called "intelligible principle standard" really provides no meaningful guidance to EPA administrators at all. For all practical purposes, EPA administrators under Section 109(b) have virtually total discretion to promulgate basic laws or public policies on a national level regarding NAAQS. Congress has delegated away these basic legislative powers to the EPA because legislators simply do not have the time, will, or expertise to indulge in such public policy making. The Courts naturally understand this and, thus, out of practical necessity, are quick to rationalize or justify such delegations of legislative power to administrators because our political system simply requires it, regardless of the technical constitutionality of such delegations under Article I, Section 1, which vests "all legislative powers . . . in a Congress of the United States." In *American Trucking Associations*, the Court argues that "requisite" is just as much an "intelligible principle" as it has allowed in so many other delegation cases over the years, such as "necessary to avoid an imminent hazard to the public safety"; "set the standards which most adequately assures, to the extent feasible"; "generally fair and equitable"; and "regulation in the public interest."

In his concurring opinion, Justice Thomas agrees that the "intelligible principle" in this case "is no less an 'intelligible principle' than a host of other directives that we have approved." However, he contends that the use of the "intelligible principle" rationale to uphold delegations of legislative powers to agencies has likely gone too far to justify obviously unconstitutional delegations of legislative power. He claims that delegations may have attached "intelligible principles" yet may still be unconstitutional. He is very concerned that the Court over the years has simply used an unconstitutional standard, the "intelligible principle" standard, while ignoring the obvious constitutional requirement that "all legislative powers herein granted shall be vested in a Congress."

Justices Stevens and Souter in their concurring opinion address the issue head on. They argue that the Court can either admit that it is allowing the delegation of legislative power or continue to pretend that it isn't. They assert that the Court should simply acknowledge that it is approving the delegation of legislative powers to administrators and stop playing judicial games, especially since they maintain that Article I, Section 1, does not necessarily prohibit Congress from delegating some of their legislative powers away to administrators.

Do you think that Article I, Section 1, allows Congress to delegate away certain legislative powers, if it wishes? If so, why have the federal Courts used the "intelligible principle" standard to justify delegations? Do you really think that these "intelligible principles" provide any meaningful guidance to administrators or can be used to check administrators from abusing their discretion when making "law"? Given the history of constitutional disputes over delegation, don't you think that the Supreme Court, in upholding all delegations of legislative power to administrative agencies since the historic *Curtiss-Wright Export Co.* decision in 1936, is simply doing what expediency and practicality require to permit American government to function effectively and efficiently? Why do you think no justices dissented in *American Trucking Associations*?

NOTES

1. U.S. Census Bureau, *Historical Abstract of the United States: Historical Statistics, Colonial Times to 1970* (Washington, D.C.: U.S. Government Printing Office, 1976), pt. 1, specs. A, F, H; pt. 2, sec. Y; and *Statistical Abstract of the United States, 2001* (Washington D.C: U.S. Government Printing Office, 2001), pp. 1–67.

2. Peter Woll, *American Bureaucracy,* 2d ed. (New York: W. W. Norton, 1977), p. 1.

3. This department ceased to be a part of the president's Cabinet on July 1,1971, when it was made into a quasi-independent nonprofit corporation.

4. Herbert Kaufman, *Are Government Organizations Immortal?* (Washington, D.C.: Brookings Institution Press, 1976).

5. Ibid., p. 11.

6. Ibid., p. 7.

7. Ibid.

8. Ibid., p. 11. The literature is replete with organizational theorists making this contention. See, for example, John Marini, *The Politics of Budget Control: Congress, the Presidency, and the Growth of the Administrative State* (Washington, D.C.: Crane Russak, 1992); and Glen O. Robinson, *American Bureaucracy: Public Choice and Public Law* (Ann Arbor: University of Michigan Press, 1991), pp. 9–17.

9. Kaufman, *Are Government Organizations Immortal?* pp. 73–77.

10. Robinson, *American Bureaucracy: Public Choice and Public Law,* pp. 18–19.

11. William L. Morrow, *Public Administration: Politics, Policy and Political Systems,* 2nd ed. (New York: Random House, 1980), p. 10.

12. John Kenneth Galbraith, *The New Industrial State,* 4th ed. (Cambridge, Mass.: Harvard University Press, 1985).

13. James Q. Wilson, "The Rise of the Bureaucratic State," *The Public Interest* 41 (fall 1975); reprinted in Francis E. Rourke, ed., *Bureaucratic Power in National Policy Making,* 4th ed. (Boston: Little, Brown, 1986), p. 143.

14. For a thorough treatment of a deregulation failure, see James R. Barth, *The Great Savings and Loan Debacle* (Washington, D.C.: American Enterprise Institute, 1991).

15. Edwin W. Tucker, *Administrative Law, Regulation of Enterprise, and Individual Liberties* (St. Paul: West, 1975), pp. 1–2. Also see George Berkeley, John Rouse, and Stanley Baran, *The Craft of Public Administration,* 9th ed. (New York: McGraw Hill, 2004), chap. 2.

16. David H. Rosenbloom and Robert S. Kravchuk. *Public Administration: Understanding Management, Politics, and Law in the Public Sector,* 5th ed. (New York: McGraw-Hill, 2001), pp. 62–68; David H. Rosenbloom, "The Judicial Response to the Bureaucratic State," *American Review of Public Administration* 50 (spring 1981); and Harold Seidman and Robert Gilmour, *Politics, Position, and Power: From the Positive to the Regulatory State,* 5th ed. (New York: Oxford University Press, 1997), chap. 7.

17. Stephen G. Breyer and Richard B. Stewart, *Administrative Law and Regulatory Policy,* 3rd ed. (Boston: Little, Brown, 1992), p. 18.

18. Ibid., p. 22.

19. Michael Herz, "Deference Running Riot: Separating Interpretation and Lawmaking Under *Chevron,*" *Administrative Law Journal* 6 (1992), p. 187.

20. Ibid.

21. Ibid., pp. 187–233.

22. Ibid. Also see Peter H. Schuck and E. Donald Elliott, "To the Chevron Station: An Empirical Study of Federal Administrative Law," *Duke Law Journal* (1990); Cass R. Sunstein, "Law and Administration After *Chevron,*" *Columbia Law Review* 90 (1990); and Bernard Schwartz, "Administrative Law Cases During 1992," *Administrative Law Review* 45 (summer 1993).

23. Schwartz, "Administrative Law Cases During 1992," p. 648.

24. Henry Jacoby, *The Bureaucratization of the World*, trans. Eveline Kane (Berkeley: University of California Press, 1973), especially introduction and chap. 6.

25. Robinson, *American Bureaucracy: Public Choice and Public Law*, p. 70.

26. See, for example, Robinson, *American Bureaucracy: Public Choice and Public Law*, chap. 3; Richard B. Stewart, "Beyond Delegation Doctrine," *American University Law Review* 36 (1987); and Richard J. Pierce, Jr., "Political Accountability and Delegated Power: A Response to Professor Lowi," *American University Law Review* 36 (1987).

27. Kenneth C. Davis, *Administrative Law: Cases, Text, Problems,* 6th ed. (St. Paul: West, 1977), p. 34.

28. Bernard Schwartz, *Administrative Law*, 3rd ed. (Boston: Little, Brown, 1991), p. 44.

29. For a good analysis of *Waukegan* in the perspective of other related cases, see Davis, *Administrative Law: Cases, Text, Problems*, pp. 28–32.

30. Bernard Schwartz, "Administrative Law Cases During 1985," *Administrative Law Review* 38 (summer 1986): 295.

31. Kenneth C. Davis and Richard J. Pierce, Jr., *Administrative Law Treatise*, 3rd ed. (Boston: Little, Brown, 1994), vol. 1, pp. 90–91.

32. Eastman, testimony at the hearing on H.R. 7432, before House Committee on Interstate and Foreign Commerce, 72nd Congress, end Session 7 (1933).

33. Davis and Pierce, *Administrative Law Treatise*, 3rd ed., vol. 1, p. 87.

34. Davis, *Administrative Law: Cases, Text, Problems*, p. 51.

35. Theodore Lowi, *The End of Liberalism*, 2nd ed. (New York: W. W. Norton, 1979), pp. 92–127.

36. Joseph Harris, *Congressional Control of Administration* (New York: Doubleday, Anchor Press, 1965), especially chap. 10.

37. James Burnham, *The Managerial Revolution: What Is Happening in the World* (New York: Praeger, 1960); and Eugene P. Dvorin and Robert H. Simmons, *From Amoral to Humane Bureaucracy* (San Francisco: Canfield Press, 1972).

38. Lewis C. Mainzer, *Political Bureaucracy* (Glenview, Ill.: Scott, Foresman, 1973), pp. 72.

39. "DC-1O Grounding: The Ripples Spread," *U.S. News and World Report*, June 18, 1979, p. 126.

40. Ibid., pp. 25, 26; Jane See White, "FAA Role Questioned in Aftermath of Mishaps, Disasters," *St. Louis Post-Dispatch*, September 23, 1979, p. 44D.

41. William P. Rogers, *Report of the Presidential Commission on the Space Shuttle* Challenger *Accident* (Washington, D.C., 1986), pp. 171–73.

42. Ibid., p. 173.

43. Ibid.

44. Ibid., p. 104.

45. Also, rumor had it that a live communication hookup with the *Challenger* crew was to take place during the State of the Union address. However, the Rogers Commission could not substantiate this rumor. Ibid., p. 176.

46. Walter Gellhorn, personal interview, Saint Louis University, March 5, 1980.

47. Edgar Shor, "Public Interest Representation and the Federal Agencies: Introductory Comments," *Public Administrative Review* 37 (March–April 1977): 132.

48. J. D. Williams, *Public Administration: The People's Business* (Boston: Little, Brown, 1980), p. 532.

49. Ibid., pp. 532–533.

50. Robert Miewald, *Public Administration: A Critical Perspective* (New York: McGraw-Hill, 1978), pp. 68–70.

51. Ibid., p. 69.

52. Ibid.

53. Ibid.

54. For a brief review of cost-benefit analysis, see Rosenbloom and Kravchuk, *Public Administration: Understanding Management, Politics, and Law*, pp. 55, 319, 320, 393–395, 448, 451, 464.

55. It should be noted at the outset that public opinion polls have consistently shown that Americans fail to understand the meaning of democratic ideals in practice. They may embrace democratic ideals in theory, but they reject them in practice. For example, Americans would likely indicate, if asked, that they believe in free speech but would then in the same questionnaire state that they feel it is wrong to allow avowed Communists to speak at public meetings in the United States. See William H. Flanigan

and Nancy H. Zingale, *Political Behavior of the American Electorate,* 10th ed. (Washington, D.C.: Congressional Quarterly Press, 2002), chap. 1.

56. James MacGregor Burns, *Deadlock of Democracy: Four-Party Politics in America* (Englewood Cliffs, N.J.: Prentice-Hall, 1967).

57. Ralph P. Hummel, *The Bureaucratic Experience,* 4th ed. (New York: St. Martin's Press, 1994), p. 219.

58. Kenneth C. Davis, *Discretionary Justice in Europe and America* (Urbana: University of Illinois Press, 1976), pp. 1–4.

59. James O. Freedman, "Crisis and Legitimacy in the Administrative Process," *Stanford Law Review* 27 (April 1975).

60. Felix Frankfurter, *The Public and Its Government* (New Haven: Yale University Press, 1930), p. 160.

61. Freedman, "Crisis and Legitimacy in the Administrative Process."

62. Dvorin and Simmons, *From Amoral to Humane Bureaucracy*, p. 1.

63. Ibid., p. 4.

64. Ralph P. Hummel, *The Bureaucratic Experience*, 2nd ed. (New York: St. Martin's Press, 1982), pp. 207–208.

65. Louis L. Jaffe and Nathaniel L. Nathanson, *Administrative Law*, 4th ed. (Boston: Little, Brown, 1976).

66. Freedman, "Crisis and Legitimacy in the Administrative Process," p. 1063.

67. Frederick C. Mosher, *Democracy and the Public Service,* 2nd ed. (New York: Oxford University Press, 1982); and Francis E. Rourke, *Bureaucracy, Politics and Public Policy*, 3rd ed. (Boston: Little, Brown, 1984).

68. Robert Alford, *Bureaucracy and Participation: Political Culture in Four Wisconsin Cities* (Chicago: Rand McNally, 1969), p. 52. Also see Seidman and Gilmour, *Politics, Position and Power,* p. 76; and Norma M. Riccucci, *Managing Diversity in Public Sector Workforces* (Boulder, CO: Westview Press, 2002).

69. Alford, *Bureaucracy and Participation*, p. 52.

70. Guy Benveniste, *The Politics of Expertise*, 2nd ed. (San Francisco: Boy and Fraser, 1977), pp. 228–239.

71. Ibid., p. 220.

72. Mainzer, *Political Bureaucracy*, p. 9.

73. For an insightful analysis of the regulatory process today, see Sydney Shapiro, "Political Oversight and the Deterioration of Regulatory Policy," *Administrative Law Review* 46 (winter 1994).

74. U.S. Census Bureau, *Statistical Abstract of the United States, 2003* (Washington, D.C.: U.S. Government Printing Office, 2003), esp. secs. 12–13.

75. Tony Mauro, "What Will Court Think of SG's Position?" *Legal Times* (January 20, 2003), Court Watch sec., p. 8.

76. Max Weber, *The Theory of Social and Economic Organization*, trans. A. M. Henderson and Talcott Parsons (London: Oxford University Press, 1947), especially sec. 3, chaps. 4, 5, and 6.

77. Victor A. Thompson, *Bureaucracy and the Modern World* (Morristown, N.J.: General Learning Press, 1976), pp. 111–115.

78. Freedman, "Crisis and Legitimacy in the Administrative Process," p. 1056.

79. Jeffrey L. Jowell, *Law and Bureaucracy: Administrative Discretion and the Limits of Legal Action* (New York: Irvington, 1984), p. 199.

80. Ibid.

81. Murray Edelman, *The Symbolic Uses of Politics* (Urbana: University of Illinois Press 1967), pp. 56–61.

82. Jowell, *Law and Bureaucracy*, p. 199.

83. For an overview of the issues of governmental regulation, see Robert Langren and Martin Schnitzer, *Government, Business, and the American Economy* (Upper Saddle River, N.J.: Prentice-Hall, 2001).

84. Louis M. Kohlmeier, Jr., *The Regulators: Watchdog Agencies and the Public Interest* (New York: Harper and Row, 1969), pp. 83–84.

85. Ibid., pp. 25–26.

86. Ibid., p. 26.

87. Thomas O. McGarity, "Regulatory Reform and the Positive State: An Historical Overview," *Administrative Law Review* 38 (fall 1986); and Organization for Economic Cooperation and Development (OECD), *Regulatory Reform in the United States* (Washington, D.C., 2000).

88. Carol Tucker Foreman and Maureen S. Steinbruner, "Righting the Record on Regulation: An Introduction," in Foreman, ed., *Regulating for the Future* (Washington, D.C.: Center for National Policy Press), p. 12.

89. Jacoby, *Bureaucratization of the World*, especially chaps. 10–13.

90. For an excellent commentary on Plato's emphasis on social harmony and its application to modern America, see William T. Bluhm, *Theories of the Political System*, 3rd ed. (Englewood Cliffs, N.J.: Prentice-Hall, 1978), chap. 3.

91. Herbert Kaufman, *Red Tape: Its Origins, Uses, and Abuses* (Washington, D.C.: Brookings Institution Press, 1977), p. 1.

92. Ibid., chap. 2.

93. Ibid., p. 31.

94. Ibid., pp. 39–41.

95. Ibid., p. 49.

96. Walter Gellhorn, *Deregulation or Delusion* (Richard J. Childress Memorial Lecture, St. Louis, Mo., March 4, 1980).

97. Stephen G. Breyer, "Analyzing Regulatory Failure: Mismatches, Less Restrictive Alternatives, and Reform," *Harvard Law Review* 92 (January 1979). For updates, see Stephen G. Breyer, Cass R. Sunstein, Matthew L. Spitzer, and Richard B. Stewart, *Administrative Law and Regulatory Policy*, 4th ed. (New York: Aspen, 1998), chap. 1.

98. Breyer, "Analyzing Regulatory Failure," 553.

99. Ibid., pp. 549–560.

100. Ibid., p. 554.

101. Ibid., p. 555.

102. Ibid.

103. Ibid., p. 556.

104. Ibid., pp. 556–557.

105. Ibid., p. 557.

106. Ibid., p. 558.

107. Ibid.

108. Ibid., pp. 604–609.

109. Kaufman, *Red Tape*, pp. 4–28.

110. James G. Cook, quoted in Bill Bogota, "Is the U.S. in an Innovative Recession?" *St. Louis Post-Dispatch*, July 24, 1979, p. 8A.

111. Robert B. Reich, "How Nit-Picking Regulations Get That Way," *Harper's Magazine* (February 1987): 18.

112. Ibid., pp. 18–22.

113. This perspective is very well expressed by the Supreme Court in *Boyd v. United States*, 116 U.S. 616 (1886).

114. Foreman and Steinbruner, "Righting the Record on Regulation: An Introduction," pp. 19 and 24.

115. Kohlmeier, *Regulators,* p. 22.

116. Peter L. Kahn, "Regulation and Imperfect Democracies," in Foreman, ed., *Regulating for the Future*, p. 31.

117. Jean Jacques Rousseau, *On the Social Contract,* trans. Maurice Evanston (1762; Baltimore: Penguin Books, 1968), pp. 49–50.

118. Kahn, "Regulation and Imperfect Democracies," pp. 29–30.

119. Paul S. Dempsey, "Deregulation and Reregulation: Policy, Politics, and Economics," in David H. Rosenbloom and Richard D. Schwartz, ed., *Handbook of Regulation and Administrative Law* (New York: Marcell Dekker, 1994), p. 198.

120. Ibid., p. 180.

121. Air Transport Association, "State of the U.S. Airline Industry: A Report on Recent Trends for U.S. Air Carriers: 2002–2003" (Washington, D.C.: 2002), pp. 1–11.

122. See, Marilyn Geewax, "Deregulation Harms Public, Group Claims," *Atlanta Journal and Constitution,* June 11, 2002, p. 1C; and Robert Kuttner, "The Scam of Airline Deregulation," *Boston Globe,* April 17, 2002, p. A19. For a related story, see Christopher Carey, "Free and Not So Easy: Airlines Make Bonus Flights Harder to Win," *Saint Louis Post-Dispatch,* February 27, 1994, p. 1E.

123. Air Transport Association, "Airline Safety" (Washington, D.C.: 2002), www.airlines.org/public/industry/display1.asp?nid=1036.

124. Air Transport Association, "State of the U.S. Airline Industry," p. 11.

125. Ibid.

126. Geewax, "Deregulation Harms Public," p. 1C.

127. Michael E. Levine, "No Clear Way Forward for Airlines," *New York Times,* December 6, 2002, p. 35A

128. Ernest Holsendolph, "United's Travails Teach an Excruciating Lesson: Deregulation Is Here to Stay," *Atlanta Journal and Constitution,* December 15, 2002, p. 1G.

129. Thomas O. McGarity, "Regulatory Reform in the Reagan Era," *Maryland Law Review* 45 (1986).

130. Associated Press, "EPA Issues Cleaner Air Regulations," *Saint Louis Post-Dispatch,* March 2, 1994, p. 3A.

131. Bruce D. Fisher, "Controlling Government Regulation: Cost-Benefit Analysis Before and After the Cotton-Dust Case," *Administrative Law Review* 36 (spring 1984).

132. McGarity, "Regulatory Reform and the Positive State," p. 411.

133. Paul Teske, "The State of State Regulation," in Rosenbloom and Schwartz, eds., *Handbook of Regulations and Administrative Law,* chap. 3.

134. "Too Late to Matter," *The Economist,* December 14, 2002, p. 1.

135. Air Transport Association, "State of the U.S. Airline Industry," p. 1–11, esp. 11.

CHAPTER 3

Legislative Attempts to Achieve Democratic Accountability in the Administrative Process

KEEPING ADMINISTRATORS ACCOUNTABLE

Demands on the U.S. political system have naturally led to the development of a gigantic public service system. Most informed observers agree that an extensive regulatory network is necessary but disagree over the feasibility of specific regulatory approaches and the proper scope of regulatory activities. Administrative growth and regulatory powers will inevitably continue to increase because this modern nation can no longer rely on obsolete institutional structures and processes not designed or equipped to handle the demands placed upon government by a society in the twenty-first century. In the insightful words of the famed statesman Elihu Root in an address to the American Bar Association in 1916: "We shall go on; we shall expand them, whether we approve theoretically or not, because such agencies furnish protection to rights and obstacles to wrongdoing which under our new social and industrial conditions cannot be practically accomplished by the old and simple procedures of legislatures and courts as in the last generation."[1] But Root emphasized that it would be democratically irresponsible to allow this newly emerging administrative power to go unchecked. To preserve popular government, he maintained, public administrators must be held democratically accountable for their actions: "If we are to continue a government of limited powers, these agencies of regulation must themselves be regulated. . . . The rights of the citizen against them must be made plain. A system of administrative law must be developed, and that with us is still in its infancy, crude and imperfect."[2]

Although Elihu Root warned in 1916 that the United States should develop methods to keep administrative power accountable, the early general reaction was simply to resist the growth of administrative power. Not until after World War II was any serious attention given to the problem of keeping administrators democratically responsible. The administrative law field in the United States has developed primarily since 1945, and the concern with controlling the behavior of public administrators since that time has been well documented in the professional literature.[3] It should be inferred from this, not that public administrators are any more or less unethical or corrupt than other workers, but that their jobs are unique. Democratic theory demands that all public servants, elected or nonelected, be accountable to the people. Obviously, this requires the creation of certain oversight mechanisms so that administrative behavior can be watched and controlled.

Control Mechanisms

A great variety of control mechanisms exist. Some controls can be categorized as informal, internal, or natural, while others can be classified as formal, external, or artificial. Internal checks mostly originate from within an agency or its employees. Some idealists, who place great faith in the virtues of human nature, believe that a person's own desire to perform according to ethical, moral, and professional codes of conduct can provide the best check against administrative misconduct. But others, especially those realists who take a dimmer view of human nature, feel that more formal, institutionalized checks are absolutely necessary to force employees to perform in an efficient, honest, and professional manner. The framers of the Constitution were realists about human nature because our constitutional democracy seems at times plagued by a crippling system of frustrating checks and balances that tend to hinder decisionmaking capabilities. Traditionally, legislators, judges, and presidents have exerted external controls over public administrators in our political system, although other institutionalized checks exist. (For example, communications media, which obtain most of their formal powers from the First Amendment, have played a powerful role in overseeing and checking administrative action.) This chapter examines congressional attempts to keep public administrators democratically accountable. Other formal and informal checks over the bureaucracy are reviewed in subsequent chapters.

When we say we want our public administrators to be controlled, what should we have in mind? First, we should be prepared to admit, as James Madison did in *The Federalist,* no. 51, that "if men were angels no government would be necessary. If angels were to govern men, neither external nor internal controls on government would be necessary."[4] However, it does not follow that we should seek more controls over public officials than are absolutely necessary. Too many controls can be counterproductive because they can serve to frustrate attempts by dedicated public servants who are simply trying to do their jobs. Needless controls can waste the time of everyone involved, thus creating morale problems and adding to the taxpayer's burden. Unnecessary checks can disrupt the administrative process, rendering it unable to handle vital governmental tasks effectively. Ideally, controls should be aimed at simply promoting responsible behavior and guarding against irresponsible behavior.[5]

Seeking Democratically Responsible Behavior

To generalize, democratically responsible behavior by public agency employees is any legally and procedurally proper action that leads to the efficient accomplishment of publicly sanctioned and desired goals. Responsible administrative behavior by public administrators could be conceptualized as moral, ethical, honest, lawful, courteous, and productive actions aimed at conscientiously serving the public. While negative controls (forms of punishments) are aimed at checking irresponsible employee or agency actions, positive controls (various rewards and incentive measures) are used to promote responsible conduct. Critics have maintained that entirely too much emphasis has been placed on checking administrative behavior through the use of various negative micromanagement control mechanisms, while not enough attention has been given to how agency administrators can be kept accountable and productive through positive approaches.[6]

Possibly one reason for this criticism is that irresponsible conduct is more striking or detectable than responsible behavior. We expect responsible behavior from employees. As a somewhat paradoxical consequence, we have concentrated on devising mechanisms to prevent irresponsible behavior. Irresponsible conduct has many faces. Generally, according to various statutes, those civil servants who are guilty of nonfeasance, malfeasance, or misfeasance of office are guilty of irresponsible behavior, thus justifying their removal from office. In practice, **nonfeasance** translates into doing nothing. Since few employees simply do nothing at all, claims of irresponsibility due to nonfeasance are rarely made against civil servants. Charges of **malfeasance** (evil or wrongful behavior that is wholly unlawful) are also made infrequently, simply because few employee acts can be classified as evil or positively unlawful. Allegations of **misfeasance** (improper performance of duties that a person may do lawfully) are much more common, although only seldom do such charges lead to dismissals. Misfeasance, or employee incompetence, is not only difficult to define in context but also very difficult to substantiate in practice, largely because civil service procedures seem to function more to protect employee rights than to combat worker incompetence and promote overall efficiency and effectiveness in the public service system.[7]

In practice, irresponsible administrative behavior can be seen when an administrator (1) abuses discretionary powers, (2) reaches arbitrary and capricious decisions, (3) grossly ignores facts and reason when making decisions, (4) acts contrary to constitutional and statutory dictates, (5) violates established due process standards, (6) goes beyond lawful authority, or (7) fails to act or respond in a reasonable time. All of these irresponsible administrative actions fall into the category of malfeasance. The Administrative Procedure Act, in Section 706, "Scope of Review," specifically prohibits, as do many other statutes and agency rules and regulations, such unlawful administrative conduct. It should be understood that, because of the evidentiary problems involved in making misfeasance charges stick in the public service system, efforts at holding public administrators accountable have mostly centered around preventing obviously illegal and corrupt administrative practices.

Indeed, administrative law focuses almost exclusively on illegal—not unethical, unprofessional, or poorly performed—administrative actions. It appears tough enough to keep agency officials functioning within the law. Practitioners of administrative law feel that it is up to others (perhaps public administration scholars, organizational theorists, management experts, or investigative journalists) to help solve the problems associated with misfeasance.

Because this is an administrative law book, it is concerned primarily with how well public administrators uphold the law when serving the public. However, particular emphasis is given to the problem of controlling the discretionary power of administrators, not only because abuses of discretion tend to be the root cause of all irresponsible and/or illegal administrative acts but also because discretionary practices seem to conflict so blatantly with the rule of law and democratic accountability maxims.

The Congressional Watchdog Role: An Overview

Despite frequent criticisms of the watchdog functions of Congress, probably the most effective external controls over administrative agencies come from this source. According to James W. Fesler, Congress in its watchdog role has the duty to identify all errors and irresponsible administrative actions and, when possible, the obligation to correct them.[8] This is the ideal. In reality, Congress does not have the resources to carry out day-to-day supervision of administrators. And close daily monitoring of administrative work would be undesirable anyway, since it would likely disrupt normal administrative processes. Thus, the monitoring of administrative behavior must be done on a selective basis.

According to Fesler, legislators have adopted three general supervisory approaches, employing them as they deem appropriate. The first is *reactive monitoring*. Reactive monitoring is a passive approach; the legislators react only when some administrative wrongdoing is somehow called to their attention, often through complaints. Reactive monitoring seems to work best for responding to specific charges of illegal administrative acts. The second is *sampling monitoring*. Sampling monitoring is aimed at discovering through various sampling procedures the reasons for the poor administration of particular agency functions. Thus, to find out why welfare cases are being mishandled, Congress may decide to sample a certain number of the cases administered randomly and periodically. The third is *concentrated monitoring*. Concentrated monitoring works well for close supervision of administrative functions or programs that pose higher-than-normal risks for corrupt or unethical activities.[9]

Despite the existence of these monitoring approaches, the possibility is always present that Congress may fail in its watchdog role. In the first place, the supervisory methods may not be used when needed. When they are employed, they may fail to provide useful information. As a matter of fact, the problems Congress has had in controlling administrative power, especially during the 1960s and 1970s, led critics to call for Congress to reinvigorate its watchdog powers. These critics think that the dramatic rise of the administrative state has been encouraged by positive congressional action, through vast delegation, and by negative inactions, such as the failure to use constitutionally sanctioned oversight powers to thwart efforts by administrators to increase their powers. Congress's failure to deploy necessary control efforts has prompted some critics to conclude that it may be too late to regain directional control over the bureaucratic leviathan. However, other observers, such as Joel D. Aberbach, conclude that Congressional oversight "is far from perfect, not even pretty or neat, but we could be far worse."[10]

A famous Latin quotation—"*Quis custodiet ipsos custodes?*"—translates colloquially as "Who is to watch the watchdogs?"[11] The answer is a lot of watchdogs. In the case of U.S. administrative agencies, the more there are, the greater the odds that effective checks over public administrators will prevail, despite the fact that some of the watchdogs will fall asleep while others will be bribed with one bone or another.

The search for ways to promote democratic accountability in the U.S. administrative system has been both challenging and frustrating. Each watchdog institution has taken a different approach, and none has been totally successful in preventing foul administrative acts.[12] While the media, for example, have tried to check abusive administrative activities by alerting the public to the behavior, Congress has traditionally attempted to keep administrators accountable to the democratic faith by focusing upon three basic areas of responsibility in the administrative process. Specifically, congressional controls have been aimed at achieving (1) fiscal responsibility, (2) procedural responsibility, and (3) program responsibility. In recent times Congress has been concerned with achieving a fourth goal as well, systems responsibility. Of course, keeping the hands of public servants out of the tax dollar till has always been a fundamental legislative watchdog task. Congress has also been traditionally concerned with making sure that administrators do not waste tax dollars simply through blundering. Additionally, legislators have been concerned with the procedures employed in the implementation of public policies. Specifically, the legislative watchdogs watch to make certain that administrative agencies perform efficiently and fairly.

Obviously, it is not sufficient for congressional watchdogs to merely monitor the fiscal and procedural practices of administrators, especially since these practices represent only a means to an end. As citizens and scholars, we are all interested primarily in evaluating the administrative agency's end product, their programs. When Congress evaluates administrative programs, it is interested particularly in the effectiveness of these programs. That is, Congress seeks primarily to answer the question, Do these programs fulfill the policy goals intended by Congress? In relatively recent times, policy evaluation has taken a sensible additional step. Programs have been assessed in terms not only of particular successes and failures but also of how the programs affect the entire system.

With every passing year the watchdog role of Congress expands, as does the corps of public administrators it must supervise. Traditional controls were originally established to monitor a relatively small group of regular public administrators. However, Congress today is responsible for holding accountable to the public a large variety of administrators who have joined the public administration system, even those in private industry who are linked to the public sector by governmental contracts and grants. With such changes from the original administrative system, it is conceivable that the traditional legislative control mechanisms may be inadequate to keep the various public and quasi-public administrators democratically accountable.

Richard E. Neustadt recognized years ago that the Constitution has provided Congress with four specific oversight powers: "organization, authorization, financing, and investigation. Departments and agencies—the operating arms of the 'executive branch'—are created by acts of Congress. They gain operational authority, programmatic jurisdiction, from laws passed by Congress. They gain funds to pay for personnel and programs from congressional appropriations. And their use of both authority and money is subject to 'oversight,' to inquiry in Congress."[13] Are these constitutionally sanctioned oversight powers effective? This chapter breaks down each congressional oversight power into similar functional areas in order to evaluate the capabilities of each to monitor and control administrative behavior in the public interest.

TRADITIONAL CONGRESSIONAL OVERSIGHT POWERS

Three traditional congressional oversight powers are (1) the power to create and organize, (2) the power to control agency budgets, and (3) the power to investigate agency activities. A fourth legislative oversight mechanism, the power to control agency performance through general guidance legislation (the Administrative Procedure Act is an example), is given separate treatment later in the chapter. Because of the relevance to administrative law, separate coverage is also given to the legislative power to create and organize. In evaluating the overall worth of these congressional oversight functions, it is unwise to use snap judgments. As the systems model makes quite evident, actions by any actor in the political system must be assessed on the basis of their impact upon the whole system. Thus, the method is always to evaluate the effectiveness of a control or the extent to which an oversight method is used by our legislators from the perspective of total costs and benefits to society.

Naturally, each examiner weighing the costs and benefits of various congressional oversight measures would undoubtedly reach different conclusions about their appropriateness; we all have different value systems. For instance, some Americans feel that it is very important for Congress to watch administrators closely, to limit administrative discretion severely, and in general, to keep the scope and powers of regulators stunted. However, other Americans believe that it is of utmost importance to free administrators from close supervision, to allow administrative specialists broad discretionary powers, and to increase the scope and strength of regulatory activities. Generally speaking, the politically conservative would most likely adopt the former attitude, and the politically liberal would probably share the latter view. Such differences in our open, pluralist system of politics led to political debate and to the formation of political parties. Since the 1930s, these basic viewpoints regarding the proper relationship between Congress and the bureaucracy, conservative and liberal, have provided one fundamental division between most Republicans and most Democrats. Therefore, within reasonable democratic constitutional standards, many conclusions regarding the adequacy of legislative controls over administrative officials can have more to do with a person's politics than with what appears to be right or wrong. However, constitutional democracy does demand reasonable use of oversight powers by Congress so that the public service system can be held at least minimally accountable to the people.

With this in mind, it should be mentioned that plenty of critics feel that legislators have not even performed up to minimal standards. Stephen K. Bailey, a scholar of the Congress, noted in 1970 that a whole generation of political scientists believe that Congress has performed its watchdog function very poorly.[14] Since the early 1970s, Congress, reacting to harsh criticism, has tried to reinvigorate its watchdog role, but its efforts have received mixed reviews. Some scholars suggest that the reason the watchdog role is weak is that legislators simply prioritize other interests. In a 2002 textbook assessment, the authors noted that too frequently, legislators undermine their watchdog responsibilities because they are too obsessed with getting reelected and gaining partisan advantage, causing Americans to "often characterize Congress as a bickering, timid, ignorant, selfish, or narrow-minded body."[15] In fact, many critics maintain that legislators have contributed to the runaway growth of bureaucracy by responding to constituent demands. Since such legislative responses normally necessitate more bureaucratic action, it can "be argued that Congress itself has a vested interest in the continued growth of bureaucracy. The more agencies there are for constituents to deal with, the more important becomes the Congressional role as intermediary between the citizen and bureaucracy. From this perspective Congress becomes the protagonist rather than the antagonist of bureaucracy in government."[16]

However, other observers feel that Congress is performing its watchdog function well. For instance, Cathy Marie Johnson believes that it simply is not true that Congress is unable to control the federal bureaucracy. She holds that "the legislature has the necessary control devices to prevail in any dispute with the bureaucracy."[17] Moreover, she feels that increasing "legislative control could be detrimental to the political system because the ability of the bureaucracy to contribute to policy making would be curtailed."[18] In a 1987 interview, veteran congressman William Clay (D.–Mo.) noted that the congressional oversight function was not working very well in checking administrative actions.[19] However, in a follow-up interview in 1994, Congressman Clay stressed that "although the system isn't perfect, in just the past five years appreciable improvements have been made [in the watchdog function] and Congress has been doing a progressively better job in uncovering waste and mismanagement."[20] In the early 2000s, many scholars and political practitioners agree with Clay's revised assessment. However, the SEC's failure to competently regulate in the public interest accounting practices by Arthur D. Andersen, leading to the filing of "cooked books" by Enron, Worldcom, and others, suggests that Congress still needs to improve its watchdog role.[21]

The Power to Create and Organize

Probably the most rudimentary congressional oversight powers stem from Congress's authority to create and organize agencies, departments, and the like as it sees fit. In Article I, Section 8, of the Constitution, Congress is given the power to create agencies legislators believe to be "necessary and proper" to help with the tasks of government. This basic constitutional power to create agencies allows Congress to become the sole architect, through its enabling legislation, of an agency's power structure. This further confers on Congress—to reiterate an earlier point—the design flexibility necessary to make some agencies stronger or more independent than others. Such power can be perceived as a fundamental, preoversight power, since it provides Congress with the opportunity to structure agencies so that they can be made more or less susceptible to various legislative oversight controls. Ideally, the power to create, if properly employed by Congress, should prevent Congress from giving life to uncontrollable Frankenstein monsters, because wise legislators should be able, with foresight, to eliminate or restrict from the very beginning potentially dangerous agency powers. For example, Congress, in the statutes that enable agencies to be created, can limit agency jurisdiction, attach appropriation ceilings to discourage agency expansionism, dictate specific procedural steps to be followed when implementing legislated policies, limit administrative discretion, and spell out program content and expected policy goals in detail. Because it perceives Internal Revenue Service activities as critical to its function, Congress has, in fact, done a fairly good job through enabling statutes (original and subsequent) to keep the discretionary power of IRS administrators within limited and equitable bounds, thus making effective legislative oversight a reality in this case. However, this type of motivation among legislators probably should be considered atypical. In other cases, and in probably too many cases, Congress has created administrative agencies too hastily and in the absence of sufficient thought. The result has been the creation of poorly developed, skeletal enabling legislation that tends to encourage the development of irresponsible administrative power—power that quickly becomes too well fortified to be realistically challenged by any legislative oversight mechanisms.

Authorization Committees.   Both the House and Senate have autonomous standing committees that specialize in substantive policy areas. Most of the legislative work in Congress is done in these committees, but their primary tasks center on establishing initial programs and agencies to run them and assuring, through subsequent statutory review, that the programs and agencies are being run up to expectations. Because these substantive committees have the power to authorize, kill, modify, amend, or alter program directions and agency operations in any way, these committees were labeled *authorization committees* in the Legislative Reorganization Act of 1946 (60 Stat. 24, Section 138). This same act also described the role of two other congressional committees with watchdog functions, the *government operations committees* and the *appropriation committees.*

Authorization committees have at least six specific watchdog powers: to (1) authorize, (2) reauthorize, (3) amend, (4) confirm appointments, (5) conduct investigatory research, and (6) veto proposed administrative actions. It should be clear by now that the power to authorize potentially carries great clout. Agencies cannot act without congressional authorization; thus, if the authorization committees choose to do so, they can detail in their authorization legislation specific courses of action for agency administrators to follow. Even if legislators fail to provide the proper mandates while drafting the initial legislation, they are provided with another opportunity to reflect upon the adequacy of the original enabling law during the reauthorization process. Although agencies are not always subject to routine renewal or reauthorization procedures, those agencies that are can be placed in precarious positions because legislators, with the advantage of hindsight, have a second chance to impose restrictions on the power of administrators.

Some agencies have the questionable luxury of functioning under permanent statutory authorization. Statutory legislative oversight can also be implemented through amending the initial legislation. Lawrence C. Dodd and Richard L. Scott have described the process: "In situations where agency or program mandates are too broad, where agencies implement programs in ways that Congress did not intend, or where evidence exists that initial statutory language is producing undesired consequences, the authorization committees can propose that Congress change statutory language by amendments to the original act."[22] Some critics argue that just the threat of the authorization committee's ability to propose amending the current enabling legislation is enough to scare agency administrators into using their power responsibly. In reality, however, it is hard to believe that the threat to amend legislation could serve as an effective oversight check, especially since most administrators realize how difficult it is for amendments to be approved by Congress. Commenting on the viability of the amending process as an effective oversight weapon, Dodd and Scott asserted that "despite its potential significance, the amending process has real limits as an oversight technique. It is time-consuming, and necessitates considerable agreement within Congress on specific matters of agency behavior. Without general congressional consensus, it may be difficult to pass amendments because a small fraction can filibuster them in the Senate or often delay committee or subcommittee action. For these reasons, members of Congress seeking to exert control or influence on administration in particular areas often prefer less time-consuming and more informal methods."[23]

But authorization committees have still other watchdog powers. Senate authorization committees have the power to screen persons nominated by the president to head various departments and agencies. In the confirmation hearing, committee members can obligate nominees to honor certain procedures, goals, and the like.

Even so, the plain truth is that the confirmation process has turned out to be a practically useless oversight tool because legislators do not have the time to scrutinize nominees, thus making the confirmation process, with rare exception, a mere formality. But one may ask how it could be anything else, since presidents may submit over 100,000 military and about 8,000 civilian nominations during a single congressional session. Nominations for major governmental posts may receive more attention, but evidence indicates that even these nominees receive only scant review. Since the passage of the Ethics in Government Act of 1978, 92 Stat. 1824–1836, the Senate has spent a little more time evaluating at least the more important senior-level nominees for possible conflicts of interest, outside-income violations, and "problem" backgrounds.[24] However, Presidents Reagan, Bush, Clinton, and Bush have had virtually all of their nominees quickly and routinely confirmed.

Another power all standing committees have is the power to conduct research to obtain information necessary to the performance of their functions. Legislators are concerned especially with whether their constituents have been treated fairly by governmental agencies. If they find that problems exist through their casework probing, authorization committee members can compel agencies to respond to the problems.

The Legislative Veto.   Because of its extremely controversial nature, the legislative veto oversight technique deserves special attention. Although controversy over its use has been brewing for decades, since the late 1970s the legislative veto issue has been the focus of increased attention and hot debate, even though some scholars feel the Supreme Court ended the debate in 1983 when it ruled a legislative veto provision unconstitutional in *Immigration and Naturalization Service v. Chadha,* 462 U.S. 919 (more on this case later). It is highly debatable whether the legislative veto can be considered a traditional legislative oversight approach, especially since it has been plagued by hostile attacks since it first appeared in a federal statute in 1932 (Legislative Appropriations for Fiscal Year 1933, 47 Stat. 382). Despite its late and slow start, use of the legislative veto as a control device increased steadily. Between 1932 and 1975, 295 legislative vetoes were imposed.[25] From the mid-1970s to around the time of the *Chadha* decision, about half of the legislative veto provisions were enacted.[26]

During the 1970s efforts were made to expand the use of the legislative veto by amending the Administrative Procedure Act so that all agency rulemaking would be subject to a legislative veto. However, since it was first employed to oversee agency decisionmaking, opposition to the legislative veto has remained fierce. The strongest resistance to the veto's use seems to come from those who contend that the legislative veto is unconstitutional, although it is attacked on many other grounds. For reasons to be discussed, virtually all presidents have assailed the legislative veto, holding that it represents an unconstitutional legislative encroachment upon the domain of the executive branch.

What is a legislative veto, and why all the fuss? Basically, a legislative veto provision in a statute requires that certain agency actions, usually rules, be subject to the review of Congress before they can take effect; thus Congress is given the opportunity to veto any planned activity. The general purpose of the legislative veto is to provide Congress with an opportunity to block agency or presidential actions that legislators feel exceed statutory authority or are unsound. The legislative veto gives legislators flexibility to void administrative actions by cutting corners (by allowing legislators to bypass those formal processes many believe to be required by the Constitution). Legislative vetoes have been used to overturn virtually all administrative acts, but not adjudicative decisions, since such direct legislative intrusions in the administrative process appear to be clearly unconstitutional (see *Pillsbury Co. v. FTC,* 354 F.2d 952 [1966]). There are four basic versions of the legislative veto: (1) veto by both houses, (2) veto by only one house, (3) veto by a single committee (rare), and (4) veto by just a single committee chairman (very rare).[27] Although the legislative veto has been attacked in general, critics intensify their protests as the veto power is exercised by a decreasing number of the entire membership of Congress.

What have been the major arguments in support of the legislative veto as a tool for overseeing agency conduct? Proponents of the legislative veto argue that its purpose is a noble one—to keep administrators democratically accountable by making them more answerable to Congress. A specific objective of the legislative veto, supporters assert, is to ensure that promulgated rules are in line with congressional intent. The legislative veto, it is held, helps to compensate for the trend toward broad delegation. Proponents hold that the legislative veto represents an honest attempt by Congress to reinvigorate its oversight powers—something critics of Congress have urged for a decade or more.

In regard to the constitutional status of the legislative veto, proponents contend that the Constitution never imposed a rigid legislative-administrative relationship. Therefore, it cannot be validly argued that the Constitution prohibits the use of the innovative oversight measure. Supporters counter the claim that the legislative veto violates the separation-of-powers doctrine by pointing out that the Constitution calls for shared powers, not strict separation. Proponents further assert that Congress has every right to attach strings (that is, the legislative veto provision) when delegating legislative powers to nonelected administrators who serve in agencies created by Congress. After all, they maintain, a president has the opportunity to meddle in the affairs of Congress in the exercise of presidential veto power. The fact that the whole Congress may not participate when administrative action is vetoed should not imply, proponents contend, that the legislative veto is undemocratic. For the whole Congress to delegate veto authority to a single chamber or committee only reflects current and sensible managerial practices. Congress, it is maintained, is already too busy and certainly does not have time to scrutinize every administrative action subject to the legislative veto as an entire assembly.

But critics of the legislative veto charge that this power is in fact unconstitutional, especially when only a single authorization committee has the power to veto an agency action. Opponents argue that Congress should not have the right to circumvent the channels for amending legislation established by the framers of the Constitution. The legislative veto function violates the separation-of-powers and checks-and-balances doctrines by permitting Congress to encroach upon the powers of the president and the courts. By use of the legislative veto, Congress fails to provide the president with an opportunity to use his constitutional power to veto an act of Congress. Since opponents insist that the legislative veto power can be employed to change policies and previous legislative intent, they argue that the president's constitutional role in the public policy–making process should not be bypassed. Critics charge that the legislative veto also undermines the role of the courts, for if administrative rules exceed statutory authority or are inconsistent with legislative intent, then the courts should have the power to review the legality of the promulgated rules.[28]

Aside from the opposition stemming from the alleged unconstitutionality of the legislative veto generally, opponents note that it provides only a negative force against public policymaking through rulemaking, failing to show how to improve rulemaking procedures, and thus also failing to encourage rulemakers.[29] This negativism, it is maintained, can discourage agency administrators from proposing new and needed rules, to say nothing about what the legislative veto does to the morale of conscientious agency rulemakers.

When campaigning in the 1980 presidential primaries, President Carter charged that the legislative veto would destroy regulatory enforcement, turning it "into an endless process of capricious negotiation with special interests."[30] Others argue that the legislative veto causes unnecessary delays in program implementation, adds to administrative legislative and social costs, burdens both legislators and administrators, and inconveniences the beneficiaries of agency rules.

The *Chadha* Decision: A Critical Analysis.   Exactly fifty years after the first legislative veto provision took effect, the Supreme Court in *Chadha* finally ruled on the constitutional status of the legislative veto. In writing the majority opinion, Chief Justice Warren Burger admitted that the Supreme Court felt compelled to rule on the constitutionality of the legislative veto because so many legislative vetoes had been added to statutes in recent years. The high court ruled that the one-house legislative veto provision in the Immigration and Nationality Act of 1952, Section 244(C)(2), was unconstitutional because it generally violates the separation-of-powers doctrine (pp. 951–959). Claiming that the framers of the Constitution regarded legislative tyranny as a possibility, the Court specifically argued that the legislative veto constitutes an unconstitutional encroachment on the executive branch by the legislative branch because it essentially permits Congress to legislate activities outside its constitutional domain. In this particular case, the Court noted that the one-house legislative veto allowed the House of Representatives to override a decision by the attorney general, working with the INS (Immigration and Naturalization Service), not to deport Chadha. This legislative action, the Court asserted, altered Chadha's deportation status. Justice Burger held that such action by the House violated the separation-of-powers doctrine because it voided the constitutional principles of bicameralism (Article I, Section 1) and presentment (Article I, Section 7). That is, in simple language, before Congress can take such action against the president or an administrative agency, Congress must pass a bill by a majority of both houses and present it to the president for his approval or disapproval. "Disagreement with the Attorney General's decision on Chadha's deportation—that is, Congress' decision to deport Chadha—no less than Congress' original choice to delegate to the Attorney General the authority to make that decision, involves determination of policy that Congress can implement in only one way; bicameral passage followed by presentment to the President" (pp. 954–955). In explanation, the Court noted further:

> The bicameral requirement, the Presentment Clauses, the President's veto, and Congress' power to override a veto were intended to erect enduring checks on each Branch and to protect the people from the improvident exercise of power by mandating certain prescribed steps. To preserve those checks, and maintain the separation of powers, the carefully defined limits on the power of each Branch must not be eroded. To accomplish what has been attempted by one House of Congress in this case requires action in conformity with the express procedures of the Constitution's prescription for legislative action: passage by a majority of both Houses and presentment to the President. [pp. 957–958]

In reaching its 7–2 decision in *Chadha*, the Supreme Court also made a few other points. The Court acknowledged that the framers authorized only one of the houses to act alone under four clear circumstances, and specific procedures for such unicameral actions were made explicit (provisions allowing the House to initiate impeachment and the Senate to conduct impeachment trials, act on presidential appointments, and ratify treaties). Conceding that the legislative veto appears to be an efficient mechanism for checking administrative actions, the Supreme Court said that nevertheless, this does not mean that efficiency measures should be ranked over constitutional principles. Thus, the Supreme Court concluded: "With all the obvious flaws of delay, untidiness, and potential for abuse, we have not yet found a better way to preserve freedom than by making the exercise of power subject to the carefully crafted restraints spelled out in the Constitution. . . . We hold that the Congressional veto provision . . . is severable from the Act and that it is unconstitutional" (p. 959).

How important was the *Chadha* decision? Some legal scholars believe that *Chadha* was the most significant decision handed down in the areas of constitutional and administrative law in many years, because the ruling struck at the basic constitutional relationship between Congress and the administrative branch. In particular, some thought it would affect the way Congress delegates discretionary administrative powers to administrative rulemakers, including the president, and how Congress oversees administrative actions. The *Chadha* holding led one analyst to conclude soon after the decision that it "stands out as the most significant of the last 10 years."[31] In dissent, Justice Byron White argued that the majority decision was irresponsible because it overruled "nearly 200 separate laws over a period of 50 years" (p. 977). He added: "Today's decision strikes down in one fell swoop provisions in more laws enacted by Congress than the Court has cumulatively invalidated in history" (p. 1002). The *Chadha* holding also casts doubt on the constitutionality of major acts, such as the War Powers Resolution of 1973 (500 U.S.C., Section 1544[C]), the Congressional Budget and Impoundment Control Act of 1974 (31 U.S.C., Section 1403), the National Emergencies Act (50 U.S.C., Section 1622), and the International Security Assistance and Arms Export Control Act (22 U.S.C., Section 2776[b]), that were designed to resolve serious conflicts between Congress and the president over the president's exercise of broad powers in the areas of impoundment, war, national emergency, and international security and arms exports.[32]

In *Chadha* the Supreme Court declared unconstitutional only the legislative veto section of the Immigration and Nationality Act, thus upholding the validity of the rest of the act on the grounds that the specific legislative veto provision is "severable." However, legal scholars assert that the *Chadha* decision has made the legal and functional status of entire acts questionable, because certain legislative veto provisions cannot be easily severed from the rest of an act without destroying the act's functional effectiveness. That is, in some cases Congress allowed administrators to exercise certain powers under an act only as long as such powers could be checked through the legislative veto provision (i.e., recognition is given to a dependent association between practically unseverable sections of the act). Many scholars claim that this is especially true for the War Powers Resolution. Regarding this act, Daniel Franklin commented: "The Court determines the severability of a provision by determining if the deletion of that unconstitutional part alters legislative intent. Even a cursory examination of the legislative history of the War Powers Resolution shows that Congress would have never delegated the authority for unilateral presidential actions without some kind of veto."[33] It is worth noting that the War Powers Resolution, with its constitutionally dubious two-house legislative veto that has never been tested in the courts, still commanded respect by President George H. W. Bush during the Gulf War and by President George W. Bush in Iraq.

In the *Administrative Law Review* in 1991 Bernard Schwartz wrote: "The Legislative Veto may turn out to be an administrative law version of Hamlet's father—a ghost that refuses to remain in repose."[34] And a decade later, in 2001, in a *Duke Law Journal* article, James F. Blumstein did not dispute that the "ghost of the legislative veto" still walks, concluding that Congress uses "the legislative veto as a political tool."[35] But the reality is that the legislative veto's ghost today is dressed in more friendly constitutional clothes because Congress, finally addressing the Court's position in *Chadha*, passed the Congressional Review Act of 1996 (Administrative Procedure Act, 5 U.S.C., Sections 801–808), which creates a two-house legislative veto that cannot take effect unless it is presented to the President for his approval or rejection. Richard J. Pierce, Jr., contends that this kind of legislative veto would very likely be held constitutional because it resolves the constitutional problems cited by the Supreme Court in *Chadha*, making "the veto process indistinguishable from the process of enacting a statute."[36] Ironically, however, these corrections to the legislative veto make it practically useless as a veto weapon because it is quite inconvenient and politically unfeasible to obtain passage of a legislative veto in both houses of Congress. Additionally, Pierce points out: "Congress rarely will be successful in convincing the President to sign a joint resolution of disapproval of an agency rule or in overriding the President's veto of such a joint resolution."[37]

Of course, *Chadha* does not apply to the states, so many states use legislative vetoes as an oversight tool. In *Mead v. Arnell*, 791 P.2d 410 (1990), the Idaho court relied heavily upon Justice White's dissent in *Chadha* to uphold the constitutionality of a legislative veto under Idaho's constitution, holding basically that the legislative veto does not violate presentment or the separation-of-powers doctrine. And in 2001 in *Carmel Valley Fire Protection District v. California*, 25 Cal. 4th 287, the California Supreme Court, in upholding a two-house legislative veto, argued that the *Chadha* decision did not apply.

SEEKING ADMINISTRATIVE ACCOUNTABILITY THROUGH GUIDANCE LEGISLATION

This section examines the effectiveness of general statutes passed by Congress to guide and compel certain administrative behavior. By and large, these laws have proved quite effective in keeping administrative actions consistent with the democratic rules of the game. However, legislated statutes are hard-core laws. Although legislators, politicians, interest groups, and agency administrators may play selfish games with vague authorization statutes (often those that inform administrators simply that they must act in the public interest), agency budgets, and politicized investigatory committees, they cannot take the same liberties with certain laws that clearly dictate which administrative acts are or are not legally permissible. Of course, all laws contain some loopholes, and the Administrative Procedure Act certainly has its share. Nevertheless, many laws like the APA, which are aimed at controlling administrative behavior, consist of provisions that leave little room for interpretation. For the most part, in U.S. politics, tactical political maneuvers to gain a power advantage have usually stopped short of flagrantly breaking the law. Well-documented exceptions exist, such as the infamous Teapot Dome, Watergate, Iran-contra, saving-and-loan, and corporate scandals that rocked the Harding, Nixon, Reagan, George H. W. Bush, and George W. Bush administrations. In short, laws have been at least modestly successful in curbing wrongful administrative conduct because rule-of-law restrictions have been generally honored by all the players. Also, the courts have been available to punish those who want to play by different rules.

A great number of laws restrict and order administrative behavior. In general, these laws are directed toward restraining democratically irresponsible and illegal administrative practices. To achieve this end, legislation has been aimed specifically at achieving procedural due process, limiting administrative discretion, making the administrative process more efficient and meritorious, insulating administrators from corruptive political pressures, terminating unwanted agencies and programs, and opening administrative decisionmaking to public scrutiny. The following brief review considers only two types of laws: those believed to have had the greatest impact on structuring and controlling administrative behavior and those most relevant to administrative law.

Legislative Efforts Aimed at Depoliticizing and Professionalizing the Administrative Process

As acknowledged, the field of administrative law developed rather recently in political history, not getting significantly started until after World War II. But public administration as a recognized profession and academic discipline also received a very late start. After George Washington was elected as the first U.S. president in 1789, nearly a century elapsed before any serious attempt took place to structure a professional civil service system in America. Somewhat illogically, public administration, once it started to take on a professional character, existed for close to a half century before any clear indications appeared that public administration had emerged as a distinct field of study. In 1926 Leonard D. White published *Introduction to the Study of Public Administration*, the first book devoted solely to the study of the principles of public management.[38] The first comprehensive administrative law casebook did not appear until 1940.[39]

The Spoils System.   Our government's early administrators were well educated, but certainly not in public administration and administrative law. By and large, early presidents hired persons as civil servants on the basis of how well they reflected the president's political views. Although political historians have generally credited President Andrew Jackson as the designer of the spoils system in American politics, the practice of presidents appointing those to office who agree with them was a common custom long before the Jackson presidency. In fact, appointing persons to and removing them from administrative posts on grounds of shared political beliefs was so common in Thomas Jefferson's administration that Paul Van Riper, a renowned civil service political historian, claimed that Jefferson could easily be "considered the founder of the spoils system in American politics."[40]

However, the administrative personnel system, which developed under administrations before Jackson's presidency began in 1829, was radically different. While President Jackson was an egalitarian, presidents Washington, John Adams, Jefferson, Madison, Monroe, and John Quincy Adams appointed to administrative positions only persons who had socioeconomic status similar to their own. Appointing commoners to governmental jobs at the federal level was unthinkable before Andrew Jackson's administration. But Jackson's brand of spoils, or patronage politics, buried elitist public administration forever in America. Since Jackson's time, there has been an unabated movement toward opening up the civil service system to virtually all classes.

Because President Jackson so deeply loathed what he perceived as the decadent traits of the Federalist civil servants, who still occupied many administrative positions at the time he assumed office, his spoils politics probably evolved into an overreactive force directed at purging the federal bureaucracy of all Federalist remnants, especially leftover Federalist employees. Assuming that governmental work was easy and anyone could handle the simple tasks of government, Jackson proceeded to replace the remaining well-educated, upper-class Federalist administrators with his friends, relatives, and supporters, placing little emphasis on their educational merits or professional experience, especially if they had helped in his bid for the presidency. Such personnel recruitment practices soon gave great popularity to the phrase, "to the victor belong the spoils," which epitomizes spoils politics.

For the record, however, it is worth noting that Jackson did not believe that patronage jobs should be filled only by loyal supporters. He felt that they should also be reasonably capable persons. It was really his successors who employed the spoils system in its worst form.

In any event, versions of the Jacksonian meritless spoils system soon became quite popular. Jackson's successors engaged in spoils politics to staff the federal bureaucracy after their election triumphs. The spoils system idea spread rapidly to state and local governments as well, although spoils administrations had been functioning on a limited basis before Jackson's presidency. By the 1860s, spoils politics had become so pervasive, yet inefficient and corrupt, that it motivated President Abraham Lincoln to declare to a group of eager patronage seekers who had assembled in his outer office that this "spoils system might in the course of time become far more dangerous to the Republic than the rebellion itself."[41]

The Pendleton Act of 1883.   The pertinent point is that before the Civil War's end, there had never existed a systematic and relentless attempt to professionalize public administration. Specifically, no concerted effort had been made to seek efficiency, effectiveness, integrity, and procedural due process (the chief focus of administrative law) in governmental administration. However, after the Civil War, reformers set out to destroy machine government, which had achieved its strength and cohesiveness from the spoils system. The reform movement quickly picked up momentum as the press began to wage an unyielding attack against various political machines—the most notable being the one against the Tweed machine of the late 1860s and early 1870s, which had thoroughly corrupted municipal administration in New York City.

Generally, the reformers' central goal was to make government more democratically accountable to the people. However, they were concerned in particular with governmental administration since patronage politics had succeeded in filling national, state, and local governments with blatantly unqualified administrators. These administrators, more loyal to the machine than to constitutional principles, had little understanding of the significance of due process and equal protection under the law. Consequently, those who came before them were likely to be treated in an arbitrary and capricious manner. Friends of the machine may have benefited, but others tended to be denied their rights and privileges.

Past attempts by reformers to obtain reform civil service legislation had failed at the federal level. In 1881 the contention by the reformers that patronage politics was severely out of control obtained instant credibility when Charles Guiteau, angered because President James A. Garfield had not given him the patronage job he sought, shot and killed Garfield. "Enough is enough!" cried the reformers. Civil service reform, which for years had drawn only modest attention, suddenly became a national issue. Less than two years later, the Pendleton Act, or the Civil Service Act of 1883 (22 Stat. 403), represented an attempt by reformers to depoliticize and professionalize the administrative process at the national level. Endorsed enthusiastically by the newly formed National Civil Service Reform League, the Pendleton Act became the first civil service law enacted by Congress. Congress had taken its first major step toward making public administration a professional and respectable profession. However, during the decades to follow, similar civil service acts were enacted in states and municipalities.

The original Civil Service Act, which has been amended several times since 1883, contained many provisions aimed at promoting a more professional federal administrative system by making administrative work more politically neutral, but especially more independent of the corruptive influences of spoils politics. Accordingly, the act's major provisions required that (1) employees be selected through open and competitive examinations; (2) civil service workers be protected from various outside political influence peddling and solicitations; (3) civil servants be given meaningful job tenure and protected against removal for political reasons; (4) allocation of federal civil service jobs to the states and U.S. territories be done according to population (thus geographically spreading the influence of merit employees); (5) a three-member Civil Service Commission responsible for regulating the civil service system be created (replaced in 1979 by the Merit Systems Protection Board), of whose members only two could be from the same political party; and (6) the president determine through executive order the administrative employee classifications under the commission's authority. Also evident in these provisions is an attempt to encourage careerism and administrative expertise in the federal civil service. The reformers believed these were needed if governmental administrators were to become more efficient and responsive.

In actuality, however, the Pendleton Act had only a limited impact on federal administrative practices. Stiff opposition from spoils politicians, who struggled to retain the personal advantages of the patronage system, caused the original Civil Service Act to be limited to less than 11 percent of all civilian federal employees. Although states, cities, and counties began to pass civil service legislation (New York in 1883, Massachusetts in 1884, Albany and New York City in 1884, and Cook County, Illinois, in 1895), even cursory observation of American politics shows that in all of these areas machine politics flourished, despite the existing civil service legislation.

Woodrow Wilson was probably the first distinguished scholar to condemn public administration at all governmental levels in America, even after civil service reform had started. Wilson exclaimed: "The poisonous atmosphere of city government, the crooked secrets of state administration, the confusion, sinecurism, and corruption ever and again discovered in the bureau of Washington forbid us to believe that any clear conceptions of what constitutes good administration are as yet very widely current in the United States." To Wilson, it was essential that a science of public administration be developed, especially since the tasks of public policy making and execution were growing more complex with each passing day. He believed a science of administration was vital "to straighten the paths of government, to make its business less businesslike, to strengthen and purify its organization, and to crown its duties with dutifulness."[42] More specifically, Wilson argued that it was necessary to discover a science of administration "to rescue executive methods from the confusion and costliness of empirical experiment and set them upon foundations laid deep in stable principle." Accordingly, he maintained, "we must regard civil-service reform in its present stages as but a prelude to a fuller administrative reform."[43]

To build a democratically responsible administrative network, Wilson contended that administrators must be placed in their proper role in the political system. But what the proper role of public administrators should be is a tough question, one that has not yet been resolved by public administration and administrative law scholars. Despite the complexity of the issue, Wilson agreed with the reformers that governmental administration could be improved if administrative and political functions were separated from each other. For him it was patently obvious that "administration lies outside the proper sphere of *politics*. Administrative questions are not political questions. Although politics sets the tasks for administration, it should not be suffered to manipulate its offices."[44] Consequently, Wilson concluded that "this discrimination between administration and politics is by now, happily, too obvious to need further discussion."[45]

Wilson's basic claim that administration could be made more scientific, and thus more professionally efficient, if it were separated from politics gained broad support from the reform-oriented public during his day. Max Weber, in particular, described as ideal a public bureaucracy that recruited and promoted personnel on the basis of merit examinations and that is subject only to general political controls. Weber also suggested, as did Luther Gulick years later, that certain discoverable administrative principles tended to promote administrative expertise.[46] Daily political meddling in administrative affairs would tend only to disrupt technical, nonpolitical administrative operations. In numerous decisions, the courts have generally upheld the notion that needless political meddling serves only to disrupt the administrative process.

By the 1940s, the ideas of these reformers began to come under severe attack, especially their notion that administrators should be separated from politics. Now the claim was that administrators had become too powerful and too independent of traditional democratic controls; for example, nonelected city managers had replaced elected mayors, while independent regulatory commissions were now performing legislative tasks once carried out by Congress. Some critics continue to believe reform has gone too far. The most prevalent arguments presented recently against reform government are that (1) administrators now have too much neutral power that cannot be held democratically accountable; (2) administrative discretion is so broad that it challenges the principles of democratic constitutionalism; (3) administrators are cold, aloof, and insensitive; and (4) it is patently absurd to argue that politics can be separated from administration since administration is inherently a part of the political process. No doubt there is some validity in the contention that administration cannot be functionally separated from politics, but students of administrative law are confronted with the problem of figuring out just how much interplay should exist between politicians and administrative experts.[47]

In any event, the arguments presented by the reformers have been largely persuasive and have inspired Congress to enact legislation over the decades aimed at upgrading the original 1883 act; for example, the Lloyd-LaFollette Act of 1912,[48] Hatch Act of 1939, Civil Service Act of 1940,[49] Federal Salary Reform Act of 1962,[50] Civil Service Reform Act of 1978,[51] and revised Hatch Act of 1993.[52]

However, despite specific attempts by reformers to eliminate patronage politics in public employment and despite two Supreme Court decisions, *Branti v. Finkel,* 445 U.S. 507 (1980), and *Rutan v. Republican Party of Illinois,* 110 S.Ct. 2729 (1990) (which essentially prohibits nonmeritorious patronage hiring and firing practices for virtually all public employees unless they are in high policy-making positions requiring "trust" and "confidentiality"), politicians, especially at the state and local levels, have somehow kept patronage politics healthy. In studying the persistence of patronage politics in Illinois, David K. Hamilton noted that "a personnel code with rules and regulations to foster merit and a supposedly independent commission to monitor compliance are no match for a determined assault on merit hiring by the political leadership of the government."[53]

Legal Challenges to the Civil Service System: Merit versus Employee Rights

The development of the federal civil service system based on meritorious service, as contrasted to a public administration system rooted in patronage, has not evolved free from legal challenges that questioned the merit system's constitutional and statutory legitimacy. Vehement protests have been made over the years by various activist groups charging that federal civil service policies serve to restrict constitutionally sanctioned participation in politics, prohibit equal opportunity in federal agencies, prevent effective collective bargaining, and in other ways deny public employees certain rights and privileges. Similar charges have been lodged against state civil service systems. The claims against the merit system raise some interesting constitutional-administrative law questions in regard to how far legislators can go in passing restrictive legislation engineered to make civil service more professional and accountable.

Restricting Political Activities.   The Hatch Act of 1939 has been by far the most controversial piece of civil service legislation passed since the Pendleton Act.

As Karl T. Thurber, Jr., asserts, "The Hatch Act long has represented contentious public policy, public administration, constitutional, and political participation issues."[54] In 1907 President Theodore Roosevelt, a Progressive who was sympathetic to the struggles of the reformers to free public service employment from undesirable political influence, issued Executive Order 642. In this order Roosevelt stated that civil service employees should be restricted from playing any active role in campaign management or campaign politics, although they were entitled to retain their constitutional rights as citizens to vote freely and to express privately their political beliefs. The executive order had limited impact, so in 1939, during Franklin Roosevelt's term, the Hatch Act was passed as a more forceful effort to take politics out of administration. The original Hatch Act prohibited civil service employees from (1) using their "official authority or influence for the purpose of interfering with or affecting the result of an election"; (2) taking "an active part in political management or in political campaigns"; but it (3) allowed such an employee to retain "the right to vote as he chooses and to express his opinion on political subjects and candidates." However, the 1939 Hatch Act allowed employees to participate in nonpartisan political activities. Violation of the act's prohibitions could result in removal from office.

Since its initial enactment, the Hatch Act has been controversial, basically because it did in fact forbid certain political activities of employees simply because they happen to work for the federal civil service system. The courts did not deny that the act actually took away political rights held by non-civil-service employees but rather argued that such denials were a reasonable price to pay to protect the civil service system from political pressures that could undermine professional public administration practices. In *United Public Workers v. Mitchell*, 330 U.S. 75 (1947), the Supreme Court upheld the act's provisions that allowed civil service employment to be terminated if an employee chooses to participate in political activities in violation of the act. Again in 1973, in *United States Civil Service Commission v. National Association of Letter Carriers, AFL-CIO*, 413 U.S. 548, 567, the Court upheld the Hatch Act's validity, concluding that "plainly identifiable acts of political management and political campaigning on the part of federal employees may constitutionally be prohibited." In reaching this decision, Justice Byron White, writing the Court's opinion, noted that the Act's purpose is to ensure the government's noble end—"the impartial execution of its laws." Although Congress has placed some restrictions on free speech, the Court maintained the Act does not "seek to control political opinions or beliefs, or to interfere with or influence anyone's vote at the poll." Further, the Court held that Congress should have the right to strike a balance between the interests of employees as citizens and the interests of the government as an employer determined to promote efficiency in the federal civil service. The Court cited five justifications for the act's restrictions, thus enabling this reasonable balance to be achieved. The Court argued that (1) civil service employees "should administer the law in accordance with the will of Congress, rather than in accordance with their own or the will of a political party"; (2) it is essential that the civil service remain, in fact as well as in appearance, politically neutral "if confidence in the system of representative Government is not to be eroded to a disastrous extent"; (3) given the large number of governmental employees on tap, it is imperative that they not be manipulated by political parties wanting to "build a powerful, invincible and perhaps corrupt political machine . . . paid for at public expense"; (4) employment and promotional opportunities should "not depend on political performance"; and (5) such employees should remain "free from pressure and from express or tacit invitation to vote in a certain way or perform political chores in order to curry favor with their supervisors rather than to act out their own beliefs." In *William M. Broadrick v. Oklahoma*, 413 U.S. 601 (1973), a companion case to the *Letter Carriers'* case, the Court upheld restrictions placed on Oklahoma state employees that were similar to the limitations placed on federal workers under the Hatch Act.

In 1990 President George H. W. Bush vetoed a Hatch Act reform bill, contending that the bill would undermine meritorious employment in the federal service. While the Republicans argued that the existing Hatch Act served to protect federal employees from political pressures, the Democrats held that the act unfairly and unconstitutionally restricted unnecessarily the right of their employees to participate in political activities.[55]

The persistence of the Democrats, led by Senator John Glen (D.–Ohio) and Congressman William Clay (D.–Mo.), finally prevailed once Bill Clinton was elected president. On October 6, 1993, President Clinton signed into law PL 103-94, a new law that significantly alters the old 1939 Hatch Act. The 1993, revised Hatch Act actually tightens on-the-job restrictions placed on most federal and postal employees but lifts many restrictions previously placed on these employees while they are off duty. Under the amended, 1993 Hatch Act, most federal employees and postal workers while on the job may not engage in any political activities. This includes even wearing campaign buttons, which the old Hatch Act actually allowed. Yet when off duty, these employees may actively participate in partisan politics. Specifically, for example, they can now participate in political campaigns; manage campaigns; organize and participate in political meetings, fund-raisers, and rallies; carry posters, distribute campaign literature, and solicit votes; run and participate in phone banks; publicly support and endorse candidates; and solicit contributions for the political action committee of the employee's organization from the organization's other members, as long as the employees targeted are not subordinates of the employee doing the soliciting. The 1993 Hatch Act does prohibit these employees from soliciting contributions from the general public; running for partisan political office; using their official position to influence the results of an election; and soliciting or discouraging any political activities with any persons having business with the employee's office or with any persons under investigation, audit, or enforcement action by the employee's office. The 1993 Hatch Act also does not apply to many senior executive officials (for example, those in the Executive Office of the President, departmental heads and assistants, and presidential appointees requiring Senate confirmation), nor to federal employees in "sensitive positions" (in, for example, the

Federal Elections Commission, Defense Intelligence Agency, Merit Systems Protection Board, and Administrative Law Judges).[56]

The real irony is that most surveys showed that federal employees overwhelmingly opposed Hatch Act reform, fearing increased political pressures and compromises to meritorious job performance.[57] Additionally, in a Merit Systems Protection Board survey of personnel specialists, 36 percent believed that Hatch Act reform would have a negative impact on federal employment, only 11 percent felt it would have a positive effect, and the rest thought it would have no impact or were undecided.[58] Skeptics then feared that the 1993 Hatch Act represented a step backward because it had the potential of once again exposing federal workers to political coercion and undermining the civil service system, but over a decade later there have been no signs of any problems.

Labor Grievances.   Consistent with the purposes of civil service legislation in general and the Lloyd-LaFollette Act (5 U.S.C., Section 7501a) in particular, "an individual in the competitive service may be removed or suspended without pay only for such cause as will promote the efficiency of the service." The Lloyd-LaFollette Act, under Section 7501(b), outlines the extent of procedural due process rights that must be accorded when an employee is dismissed or suspended without pay. When such actions are taken, a civil service employee "is entitled to reasons in writing and to: (1) notice of action sought and of any charges preferred against him; (2) a copy of the charges; (3) a reasonable time for filing a written answer to the charges, with affidavits; and (4) a written decision on the answer at the earliest practical date." The act also makes clear that "examination of witnesses, trial, or hearing is not required but may be provided in the discretion of the individual directing the removal or suspension without pay" (Section 7501, b, 4).

In *Arnett v. Kennedy,* 416 U.S. 134 (1974), Wayne Kennedy, a dismissed civil service employee who had been accorded the rights he was entitled under the Lloyd-LaFollette Act, charged that the act's protections failed to provide him with the due process protections guaranteed to him under the Constitution. Specifically, Kennedy claimed that he should be given a pretermination "trial type hearing before an impartial hearing officer before he could be removed from his employment." His employment constituted a property interest, which entitled him to elaborate due process rights under the Fifth Amendment. The practical question for the Court was whether Kennedy should be entitled to constitutional protections beyond those granted to him by statutes. Because the Court acknowledged that property rights are not determined by the Constitution but protected by it only when the property rights have been created by statutory entitlement or rules, the Court ruled that civil service employment should not be considered a property right unless Congress wants to make it one. The Court reasoned that Congress is entitled to establish the procedures that can be used to determine the cause for a civil service employee's dismissal or suspension. Pretermination hearings are not mandated by the Constitution, the Court held. Although an employee's interest may be in job security, the government's interest is in promoting efficiency in the administrative system. Accordingly, Congress had the authority, in the interests of administrative efficiency, to legislate procedures to provide for fair dismissal review without placing a detrimental burden on the administrative process (p. 152).

However, two cases in the 1980s flatly overruled the reasoning employed by Justice Rehnquist's plurality opinion in *Arnett* that a property interest (right or entitlement) can be conditioned by a statute that places restrictions on due process protections. In holding that a state employee had a property interest in using the Illinois Fair Employment Practices Act's adjudicatory procedures that was protected by the due process clause of the Fourteenth Amendment, the Supreme Court in *Logan v. Zimmerman Brush Co.,* 102 S.Ct. 1148 (1982), rejected the Arnett-based contention that the state legislature has the prerogative to limit due process protections connected with property entitlements simply because a state statute had created the property interest in the first place. The Court reasoned that once the legislature confers a property interest entitlement, it must safeguard the property interest with the mandated constitutional due process protections. "Indeed, any other conclusion would allow the State to destroy at will virtually any state-created property interest" (p. 1156). Quoting from *Vitek v. Jones,* 445 U.S. 480, 490–491 (1980), the Court noted: "While the legislature may elect not to confer a property interest, . . . it may not constitutionally authorize the deprivation of such an interest." Three years later in *Cleveland Board of Education v. Loudermill,* 105 S.Ct. 1487 (1985), the Supreme Court reiterated its legal position taken in *Logan* by holding that Loudermill, an employee dismissed by the Cleveland Board of Education for filling out his employment application dishonestly, had a property interest in continued employment and, therefore, had a right to due process protections. The Court said that minimum due process in this case would not require a full evidentiary hearing, but at least "some kind of hearing" so that Loudermill would not be deprived of a significant property right without an opportunity to be heard. At the very least, the Court asserted, Loudermill "is entitled to oral or written notice of the charges against him, an explanation of the employer's evidence, and an opportunity to present his side of the story" (p. 1495).

Loudermill is an important precedent, yet it should not be interpreted as a liberal decision, since it provides for extending only minimum due process hearing protections even when property or liberty interests are involved. In some cases, the informal, "some kind of hearing" rights have not seemed to provide very meaningful due process protections. For example, in *Goff v. Dailey,* 991 F.2d 1437 (8th Cir. 1993), the court, citing *Loudermill,* held that a prisoner's due process hearing rights may be satisfied by simply providing "notice and an opportunity for the claimant to tell the decisionmaker his side of the story. No more is required here" (p. 1441). And in *O'Neill v. Baker,* 210 F.3d 41, 15, 16 (2000), the U.S. Court of Appeals for the First Circuit held that under *Loudermill,* even a tenured state employee with due process property rights in her employment is still entitled only to "a very limited hearing prior to termination." Quoting *Loudermill,* the court argued that O'Neill was only "entitled to the constitutional minimum of 'some kind of hearing' and 'some pre-termination opportunity to respond'" (p. 48).

Probably the greatest complaint voiced by public employee unions against civil service employment in the past several decades is that public employees have been generally deprived of the most persuasive collective bargaining tool—the right to strike. In the private sector, in contrast, the Taft-Hartley Act (National Labor Relations Act of 1947, 61 Stat. 136) gave workers the right to strike. Because strikes by public employees have been thought to jeopardize the public interest, such strikes have been traditionally prohibited by common law. On the state level, strikes by public employees have been outlawed by statute. Some states, however, have passed laws allowing restricted strike powers to public employees, usually those service areas perceived as nonessential. On the federal level, all public employee strikes are strictly forbidden, and consequently, civil service employees feel discriminated against. These workers argue that effective collective bargaining negotiations cannot be carried out if the government's managers know that employees cannot actually strike to win their demands. Others contend, however, that public employees are, in fact, different from workers in the private sector. Public employees, they maintain, should not be given the power to strike, because strikes by civil servants could throw government and society into chaos. It is also maintained that public employee strikes would cause the costs of running government to skyrocket because government would eventually have to surrender to the strikers' pay demands to continue operating. In contrast, in the private sector, labor unions know that they cannot ask for demands that the company cannot afford in the competitive marketplace. Thus, demands are limited by natural market forces. But unrealistic public employee demands could be placed on government because the government provides vital public services that must be continued. Further, the government is not perceived to be constrained by the normal competitive market forces.

In *United Federation of Postal Clerks v. Blunt,* 404 U.S. 802 (1971), the Supreme Court rejected the contention of public employees that the right to strike was a constitutionally protected right. Specifically, the United Federation of Postal Clerks held that their constitutional rights had been violated by federal statutes prohibiting strikes because anti-strike clauses take away public employees' rights of free speech and assembly and deny them equal protection under law, given that private employees have the statutory right to strike. However, the Court asserted that neither private nor public employees have a constitutional right to strike under common law doctrine. Private workers were given a specific statutory right to strike when Congress legislated the Taft-Hartley Act. Congress's legislative intent was clear. But Congress has never found it appropriate to provide federal employees with the strike power. Given the reality that the power to strike is not a fundamental right, plus the fact that no statutes grant this right to federal employees, the Court failed to see how it could rule against congressional intent.[59]

Some Other Questions Pertaining to Public Employment Rights.   In the twenty-first century, questions regarding the rights of public employees still require much attention. Concerns about public employment rights range from equal opportunity in obtaining public service employment, to issues of proper dress, to the rights of sexual minorities and Americans with disabilities in the civil service. Because the issues are numerous and since many of the employment rights disputes are treated elsewhere in the book, only a few issues are noted here as examples.

To combat the ruination of public administration by spoils politics, Congress initially proceeded in the late 1800s to make the civil service system more professional by simply legislating measures designed to promote meritorious administrative behavior in public agencies. One way to accomplish this objective was to make certain that only the best-qualified applicants were permitted to enter public service. Merit examinations seemed to provide a safe path to this goal. Test results allowed governmental recruiters to screen and select applicants on the basis of their performance on the examinations. Promotions were also based almost solely on past performance and new testing. Tests seemed to be the solution to virtually all staffing problems, while democratic accountability in administration was almost exclusively measured in terms of efficiency criteria.

But starting with the 1960s, this all began to change as different groups challenged the legitimacy and fairness of the merit system's values and procedures. The fundamental claim was made that the merit system discriminated unfairly against various social groups. Women charged that the system discriminated against them because of their sex, while minorities, especially African Americans, claimed that institutional racism prevented them from having equal access to public employment. Minorities, particularly blacks and Latinos, held that even the civil service examinations were unfair because they had a class and subcultural bias.

Minority group and women's rights activism succeeded in persuading legislators, agency rulemakers, and judges at the national, state, and local governmental levels that civil service personnel policies were discriminatory. Congress passed the Civil Rights Act of 1964 (78 Stat. 241), the Equal Employment Opportunity Act of 1972 (86 Stat. 103), and a host of affirmative action laws, while administrative rulemakers promulgated rules intended to equalize employment and promotional opportunities in public jobs. Special federal attention was focused on placing minorities and women in higher classification levels, and state governments and local communities tended to follow suit.

The courts generally affirmed the legality of the actions taken by legislators and administrators. In *Griggs v. Duke Power Company,* 401 U.S. 424 (1971), the Supreme Court held that employers must not use selection criteria that discriminate in regard to race, religion, or national origin. Any screening or testing methods must be demonstrably job related. In this case the Court emphasized that selection criteria are illegal if they have a negative discriminatory *effect* in regard to race, sex, religion, or national origin, even if the selection methods did not have that *intent.* Parenthetically, legal experts point out that an effects test is a considerably stronger measure than an intent test for the simple reason that it is difficult to prove intent (for example, to prove that racial discrimination was the intent) but relatively easy to show the effects of some policy (for example, that measurable discrimination regarding race resulted). But in *Washington, Mayor of Washington, D.C., et al. v. Davis,* 426 U.S. 229 (1976), the Court modified the *Griggs* holding in ruling on the constitutionality of recruiting practices employed by the District of Columbia. Here the justices argued that the Court did not embrace "the proposition that a law or other official act, without regard to whether it reflects a racially discriminatory purpose, is unconstitutional *solely* because it has a racially disproportionate impact" (p. 239). However, in *U.S. v. Paradise,* 107 S.Ct. 1053 (1987), Justice Brennan made clear in his plurality opinion that promotion procedures will likely be overruled as unconstitutional if they are found to have an "adverse impact on blacks" (p. 1067). In recent affirmative action cases, it is quite evident that the courts have not taken a firm and definitive stand on the extent to which the merit principle should be compromised where the federal government is attempting to provide greater opportunities in employment, school admissions, and the like to those who are less qualified and have been discriminated against as a class in the past.

In recent affirmative action cases the federal courts have tended to support the principles of equal protection and merit, not affirmative action programs designed to advantage minorities and women, whether in employment, school admissions, or other areas. For example, in *City of Dallas v. Dallas Firefighters Association,* 119 S.Ct. 1349 (1999), justices Breyer and Ginsburg criticized the majority for voting to not even review the legitimacy of the Dallas Fire Department's affirmative action plan even though credible evidence, including findings of a history of discrimination by the Department of Justice, seemed to suggest that blacks, Latinos, and women continue to be victimized by the Dallas Fire Department's hiring practices.

To some critics, the real issue of affirmative action or any compensatory program, such as veterans' preferences, is this: Although compensatory programs for women and minorities may be justified on humanitarian grounds, such programs nevertheless tend to undermine the merit system, and thus governmental performance. To these critics, the merit system should not be compromised, because, as Max Weber held many decades ago, a meritorious civil service system is superior to all other kinds. And it should be remembered that the argument for a merit system is not an argument against equal opportunity in Weber's thinking. In fact, Weber and his followers have maintained that an administrative system rooted in the principles of merit tends to be more open and classless (more consistent with democratic ideals) because opportunities are based on objective performance measures, not on social considerations.

Still another public employees' rights question pertains to the role an employee's personal behavior should play in agency decisions regarding recruitment, promotion, and dismissal. The courts have been fairly clear on this issue, having taken the general position in recent years that employees' personal lives should be separated from their professional lives as far as the public employer is concerned. In *Norton v. May,* 417 F.2d 1161, 1165 (1969), in a precedent-setting decision, the Court of Appeals for the District of Columbia ruled that proof must be given to substantiate the charge that an employee's personal conduct has "an ascertainable deleterious effect on the efficiency of the service." Otherwise, the court maintained, the Constitution protects the right of an individual in his or her personal affairs. Thus, this decision places the burden of proof on the agency to show that a person's dress, personal appearance, sexual preference, disability, or the like has such a negative effect on agency operations that the individual should not be employed, promoted, or retained by the agency. Employers have had limited success in demonstrating such. For example, in *Equal Employment Opportunity Commission v. Waffle House, Inc.*, 122 S.Ct. 754 (2002), the U.S. Supreme Court ruled that EEOC could pursue victim-specific judicial remedies against an employer who violated the Americans with Disabilities Act even though the fired employee had signed an agreement to arbitrate any employment dispute. In *Chevron, U.S.A., Inc. v. Echazabel*, 122 S.Ct. 2045 (2002), the Supreme Court held that an employer cannot refuse to hire an otherwise qualified applicant with HIV, using the excuse that it is just trying to protect the person from diseases that he might be exposed to in his employment.

THE ADMINISTRATIVE PROCEDURE ACT:
AN OVERVIEW OF ITS ROLE IN CONTROLLING
ADMINISTRATIVE BEHAVIOR

An administrative agency may be referred to as an administration, agency, board, bureau, commission, corporation, department, division, office, officer, and so on. The titles have been applied casually and rather arbitrarily. Consequently, no substantive differences exist between, say, the Office of Family Services and the Division of Family Services, especially from the perspective of administrative law. They are both welfare agencies providing the same basic services to the public and obligated by statutes to follow prescribed procedures. Thus, the names assigned to them are inconsequential. What is important, as noted in Chapter 2, is that these agencies have been created at an increasing rate since July 31, 1789, when the first administrative agency was created at the federal level. Before 1900 only about one-third of present federal agencies existed; within another thirty years, supposedly during an era of conservatism, another third of the present number was added.[60] A similar proliferation took place on the state level, although the number of state and municipal agencies has really soared in recent decades, while the rate of growth on the national level seems to have leveled off.

But counting heads provides only one side of the story. Public agencies have not only increased in number but also expanded in size, scope, and procedural complexity, especially since 1932. Because of the rapid expansion of the administrative system, many Americans became alarmed during the New Deal. Pressured to investigate the possible exploitations of unchecked administrative power, FDR in the late 1930s was moved to form a commission to deal with the problems of procedural reform in public administration at the federal level. The Brownlow Commission prepared a comprehensive report on procedural problems confronting the federal administrative system. The Brownlow Commission's 1937 recommendations for procedural reform, along with reports by the American Bar Association on the state of administrative law and the 1941 report of the attorney general's Committee on Administrative Procedure, inspired Congress after World War II to draft and unanimously pass the Administrative Procedure Act of 1946.[61] Although by 1959 only five states followed the 1946 Model State Administrative Procedure Act, today the vast majority of states follow wholly or in part the Revised Model State Administrative Procedure Act of 1981 or the original 1946 act, as amended, while other states follow administrative plans of some kind.[62] The federal APA, as amended, is in the Appendix of this book.

According to Richard J. Pierce, Jr., "The major effects of the Act were to satisfy the political will for reform, to improve and strengthen the administrative process, to enhance uniformity in the administrative process, and to preserve the basic limits upon judicial review of administrative action."[63] In many respects, the federal APA symbolizes American commitment to fair administrative processes. Or in the court's words in *Riverbend Farms, Inc. v. Madigan*, 958 F.2d 1479 (9th Cir. 1992), "The Administrative Procedures Act ensures that the massive federal bureaucracy remains tethered to those it governs, or so the theory goes" (pp. 1483–1484). Actually, much of what is said in the APA simply reiterates and elaborates on fair governmental standards already in the Constitution, especially under the due process clauses of the Fifth and Fourteenth Amendments. The act also reflects the attitudes toward administrative due process reflected in prior court decisions involving questions of due process, particularly the famous *Morgan* cases.[64]

Despite the APA's weaknesses, mostly attributed to its vagueness and loopholes that tend to protect agency interests, the act does represent the most meaningful piece of federal legislation in the field of administrative law. The APA is the most comprehensive, authoritative, and enduring legislation governing administrative practice in the United States today. To preserve the APA's probity, the courts, ad hoc committees, and Congress (the act has been amended several times) have spent considerable time since its passage attempting to resolve inherent legal difficulties and generally upgrading and refining its functional effectiveness. Critics of the APA have charged that the act needs additional overhauling. However, the latest revised APA shows that no drastic revisions have been made to the act.

In general, the Administrative Procedure Act is a legislative weapon employed by Congress to promote democratic responsibility in administrative agencies, especially by limiting arbitrary and capricious agency actions and generally opening the administrative process to public scrutiny. Basically, the intent of Congress was to apply rule-of-law principles to the administrative process. Thus, the APA is aimed largely at making administrative behavior consistent and predictable over time and doing away with whimsical, unpredictable, and constitutionally repulsive administrative decisionmaking. More specifically, major provisions in the APA are aimed at making the administrative process more democratically accountable. Some examples of methods include (1) requiring administrators to make public their proposed procedures and activities; (2) permitting those affected by rules and orders to testify in their own defense; (3) allowing persons who are compelled to appear before an agency to be represented and advised by counsel; (4) forcing agency administrators to disclose to concerned parties designated "unclassified" materials for inspection; (5) placing the burden of proof on administrators in specific cases; (6) allowing affected persons the right to submit reasonable information and arguments for the purpose of influencing agency decisions; (7) demanding that agencies keep adequate records so that their decisions can be easily reviewed if appealed to higher levels; (8) providing for appellate remedies within the agency; (9) creating a quasi-independent status for administrative law judges to better ensure impartial hearings; (10) allowing for judicial review of agency actions; and (11) generally limiting unnecessary and undesirable administrative discretion.

Each of these procedural safeguards is described and evaluated in some detail in later chapters. However, it should be acknowledged here that there exists much criticism regarding the APA's effectiveness in practice, although on the whole the act has done a reasonably good job in preventing flagrant violations of administrative due process norms. Probably the chief general criticism that has been lodged against the APA is that the act has numerous loopholes that allow determined administrators to use the letter of the law to avoid having to uphold its spirit. But one thing is for certain: If the APA is to control administrative behavior in a respectable fashion in the twenty-first century, it will have to be modernized so that it can realistically respond and adjust to the many changes that have taken place in public administration and administrative law over the past few decades. The most notable recent changes in public administration, which have obvious administrative law implications, include (1) increased reliance on administrators to resolve socioeconomic crises; (2) greater administrative roles in public policy making; (3) increased openness in agency activities; (4) the new demands placed on domestic administrative decisionmaking by the pressures of international politics and terrorism; (5) the blurring of the line between what may be considered rightfully public versus private administration; (6) the intensifying controversy between public versus private rights; (7) the frustrating pressures to accommodate the simultaneous demands for equal rights and opportunities, affirmative action, and meritorious administrative service; (8) experimental deregulation and reregulation in selected industries (for example, transportation, telecommunications, and banking); (9) new statutory demands for administrators to employ complex, sophisticated, and controversial evaluation techniques to determine the worth (costs and benefits) of proposed agency rules; and (10) growing problems associated with new regulatory challenges (e.g., nuclear power, chemicals, homeland security, multinational corporations) that, frankly, our public administrators do not fully understand.

Dramatic developments have also occurred in recent decades in administrative law, including (1) the rapid increase in the number of rules promulgated by governmental agencies; (2) the emergence of new conflicts due to the passage of the

Freedom of Information, Privacy, Sunshine, and Ethics Acts; (3) new statutory provisions sanctioning more public participation in agency decisionmaking; (4) the increasing vulnerability of federal and state agencies to lawsuits following the abolition of sovereign immunity and the erosion of official immunity for public officials; (5) diminished judicial scrutiny of administrative actions due to greater judicial deference to administrative expertise; (6) the new judicial challenge to competently review cases involving extremely complicated technological questions of fact; and (7) sweeping and abrupt doctrinal changes (for example, the presumption in favor of hearing rights for those exercising new "property" and "liberty" interests and, in light of the September 11, 2001, terrorist attacks, the new "nation at war" mentality that has caused our government to perceive our Fourth and Fifth Amendment privacy rights from a more liberticidal perspective.

The Freedom of Information Act

Despite the fact that disclosure of information about governmental operations is consistent with democratic theory, apparently many public administrators resist almost instinctively any efforts by those who wish to make administrators disclose any more information than they must to information-seeking parties. On July 4, 1966, President Lyndon B. Johnson signed into law the Freedom of Information Act (80 Stat. 383), which constituted a progressive amendment to the public information section of the 1946 APA. In signing the legislation, President Johnson declared, "I have always believed that freedom of information is so vital that only the national security, not the desire of public officials or private citizens, should determine when it must be restricted."[65]

In passing the Freedom of Information Act (FOIA), Congress had as its main goal—as the Supreme Court reiterated in *Department of Interior and Bureau of Indian Affairs v. Klamath Water Users Protective Association,* 532 U.S. (2001)—to ensure that "any person" could obtain information from public agencies about the operations of the government. Congress did not demand in the act that genuinely sensitive or personal information be released. So why were administrators so upset about the prospect that they would have to live with the constitutionally sanctioned FOIA? Could they not see that a viable democratic system cannot function if the people are unable to obtain the information necessary to intelligently scrutinize governmental operations? Does not popular government theory rest on the assumption that for the people to maintain popular control over their government, they must be able to know what their government is doing? Does not the viability of the First Amendment ultimately depend upon reasonably open access to governmental information? In a letter on August 4, 1822, to W. T. Barry, James Madison placed the need for open disclosure in vivid perspective: "A popular government without popular information, or the means of acquiring it, is but a Prologue to a Farce or a Tragedy, or perhaps both. Knowledge will forever govern ignorance: And a people who mean to be their own Governors, must arm themselves with the power which knowledge gives."[66]

Reasons for Administrative Resistance to the FOIA.   Regardless of the persuasive popular-government arguments in support of freedom of information legislation, the FOIA was, and continues to be, resisted by some agency administrators, although in recent years some evidence has indicated that an increasing percentage of administrators have learned to accept it.

In investigating the reasons for administrator opposition to the FOIA, scholars have found that fear of what this new legislation would bring constituted administrators' fundamental concern. Specifically, some administrators felt that the act would (1) cost them too much time in handling FOIA requests; (2) reduce their position of importance and authority by forcing them to release bureaucratic secrets, the real source of their power; (3) open their files and their own work to public scrutiny; (4) prevent them from hiding from public view any of their mistakes, especially their procedural errors and wrongdoings—probably justification enough for the FOIA as far as journalists and scholars are concerned; (5) in light of reasons 3 and 4, threaten their job security; and (6) place agency behavior in a fish bowl, thus inviting unnecessary trouble, especially in the form of bothersome FOIA lawsuits.[67]

FOIA's Major Provisions.   In the spirit of open government and joint administrative procedure, a provision was attached to the 1946 Administrative Procedure Act that was aimed at preventing administrators from operating in unnecessary secrecy. Because governmental secrecy is the antithesis of democratic government, this provision almost had to be attached to the 1946 APA, especially since people at that time dreaded the consequences of the growth in administrative power. The thought of such awesome administrative power being wielded outside the view of the public eye and its control was even more alarming. However, Congress's original attempts to guarantee that nonsensitive administrative action would be kept aboveboard failed miserably because the legislators were either naive or never intended the provisions to accomplish the task of curbing secrecy in public agencies. The 1946 APA obligated agency officials to make available all agency records for public inspection unless they believed there was good cause for keeping records or information confidential.[68] But how could any realistic person expect this provision to work if administrators were left with the total discretion to determine good cause? Obviously, the 1946 Administrative Procedure Act had to be amended.[69]

The 1967 FOIA (80 Stat. 383) amended Section 552 of the 1946 APA. The FOIA's major provision is found in Section 552(a)(3), where Congress intended, except for limited exceptions, that "each agency, on request for identifiable records made in accordance with published rules stating the time, place, fees to the extent authorized by statute, and procedure to be followed, shall make the records promptly available to any person." Also, in Section 552(a)(4)(B), Congress placed the burden of proof on the agency to justify why information should not be released and provided for court review of unsatisfied requests for information by persons, and punishment for agency noncompliance with FOIA dictates:

"On complaint, the district court of the United States in the district in which the complainant resides, or has his principal place of business, or in which the agency records are situated, has jurisdiction to enjoin the agency from withholding agency records improperly withheld from the complainant. In such a case the court shall determine the matter de novo and the burden is on the agency to sustain its action. In the event of noncompliance with the order of the court, the district court may punish for contempt the responsible employee, and in the case of a uniformed service, the responsible member."

But the 1967 Freedom of Information Act, plagued by enfeebling political compromise measures, was doomed from the start to fail. Section 552(b) contained nine exemptions to the seemingly strong disclosure provision of Section 552(a)(3). The exemptions offered administrators who did not wish to disclose information under Section 552(a)(3) a plethora of golden opportunities to avoid disclosing any information. Three exemptions were popularly used to avoid disclosure because they could be rationalized by administrators to relate (1) "solely to the internal personnel rules and practices of an agency"; (2) to "trade secrets and commercial or financial information obtained from a person and privileged or confidential"; and (3) to "personnel and medical files and similar files the disclosure of which would constitute a clearly unwarranted invasion of personal privacy" (Section 552[b][2, 4, 6]). Other problems also emerged as administrators strengthened their resistance. In general, even if they knew that they would eventually have to release the requested information, many administrators tried their best to make it as difficult and expensive as possible for persons to obtain such information. Cherishing so-called official secrets, administrators commonly responded very slowly to requests for information. They often refused to release information that was not *specifically* requested. This made it very difficult for investigative reporters and academic researchers to obtain information since, never having been able to study it, they often could not identify the specific information they sought. Excessive fees for copying data could be charged, also for the purpose of discouraging the disclosure. Stubborn administrators could even force those requesting information to go to court to obtain the information.

Upgrading the FOIA.   Within a half-dozen years or so after the FOIA became law on July 1, 1967, it was obvious that the act had to be revised. Originally, Congress had intended the FOIA to be used by the press, scholars, and other citizens in the spirit of popular and open government; but the great inconveniences, delays, and costs discouraged this. Consequently, the FOIA's primary users became businesses seeking to obtain confidential information that they could use to gain an advantage over their competitors.[70] By the early 1970s several official reports had severely criticized the effectiveness of the FOIA and urged major revisions. The Library of Congress Task Force study, which had examined the act's successes and failures from its inception through 1971, and a 1972 House Committee Report emphasized the FOIA's general inability to compel administrators to release requested information.[71]

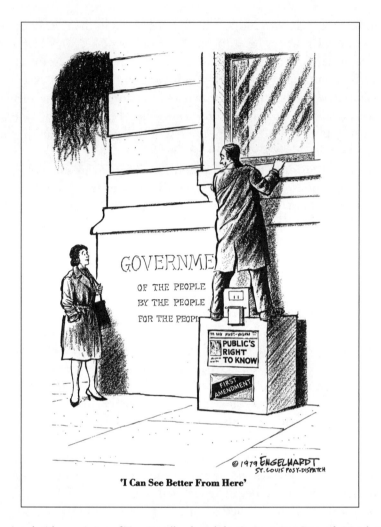

'I Can See Better From Here'

Source: Reprinted with permission of Tom Engelhardt and the *St. Louis Post-Dispatch,* March 25, 1979.

Congress responded in 1974 by making major revisions to the FOIA in Public Law 93–502 (88 Stat. 1561). Key amendments: (1) forced agencies to respond to requests for information within ten days, to answer all administrative appeals within twenty days, and permitted agencies to take an extra ten days to respond in extreme cases (Section 552[a][6][A][B]); (2) forbade agencies from charging research and copying fees above actual costs of the services, while requiring agencies to charge no fee if the general public would benefit (Section 552[a][4][A]); (3) allowed the district court, upon complaint, to determine through *in camera* (private) inspection whether classified agency materials should be kept classified, and to order improperly classified (held) materials to be disclosed (Section 552[a][4][B]); (4) reduced exemptions to only six categories of information which the agencies could withhold (Section 552[b][7]); (5) made the agency liable for court costs and attorneys' fees if it lost its FOIA dispute (Section 552[a][4][E]); and (6) allowed a court to order the U.S. Civil Service Commission to compel disciplinary measures to be taken against any administrators who arbitrarily and capriciously withhold information which should have been released (Section 552[a][4][F]).

However, Congress did not stop its efforts to open the files of all federal administrators, including presidents, with Public Law 93–502 in 1974. In that same year Congress passed the Privacy Act (88 Stat. 1896; 5 U.S.C. 552[a]) to help ensure that disclosures of information would not unnecessarily encroach upon persons' right to privacy. In 1976 Congress drafted the Government in the Sunshine Act (90 Stat. 1241; 5 U.S.C. 552[b]), which requires, although with many exceptions, for all portions of all meetings of an agency, where the meetings are led by a collegial body and where most of the members have been appointed by the president and confirmed by the Senate, to "be open to public observation." And in 1978 Congress approved the Presidential Records Act (92 Stat. 2523), which provides for the preservation of presidential records and public access to them. This Act, for example, afforded the public opportunity to gain access to the much-sought Watergate tapes, a source of information about the Nixon presidency that former President Nixon tried in vain to keep from the public eye.

Amendments to the FOIA in 1986 included waivers for attorney fees and the costs of obtaining information for non-commercial, educational, and media requesters. Congress's assumptions behind these amendments was that commercial requesters have ample resources and seek "selfish" information (e.g., trade secrets), while non-commercial requesters (e.g., reporters, scholars, public interest groups) generally have limited resources, yet seek information (e.g., scandals within public agencies) that, if disclosed, could promote the public interest.

The FOIA has received mixed reviews. By 1980 most critics were applauding the FOIA. Kenneth C. Davis noted: "The Act as amended and interpreted has become a highly successful piece of basic legislation."[72] Samuel Archibald asserted that "information may not be completely free but it is much more reasonably accessible."[73]

However, by the mid-1990s, the FOIA had attracted many harsh critics. Davis and Pierce now pointed out that one basic problem was that Congress seriously underestimated the burden FOIA requests would place upon federal agencies. "Agency compliance costs have been estimated at 50 to 200 million dollars per year, about 100,000 times Congress' original estimate."[74] Responding to this burden, many agencies just started ignoring the 20–30-day legal time limit for responding to FOIA requests. In turn, the courts responded to this practical problem by employing a balance doctrine, which essentially allowed an agency to take a very long time to respond as long as it showed "due diligence" and the requester could not show "exceptional circumstances" or an "urgent need" for the information. Robert G. Vaughn contends that "users of the FOIA face delays that limit the usefulness of the FOIA."[75] Vaughn claims that delays discourage requesters, cost them too much time and money, and engender hostility between the requesters and the agency, as well as toward the FOIA's noble goals.[76]

Although such a result was not anticipated when the FOIA first became law almost four decades ago, the FOIA has developed into a very complicated law attracting a variety of lawsuits. Most of the legal challengers focus upon (1) what constitutes an agency record, (2) what constitutes an agency, (3) what constitutes an exemption to the disclosure requirements, and (4) how long an agency can take in responding to an FOIA request. To take a few recent FOIA cases, in *National Sec. Archive v. Archivist of the United States*, 909 F. 2d 541, 545 (D.C. Cir. 1990), the court held that "the White House Counsel Office is not a FOIA agency" because it is part of the president's "immediate personal staff," which only advises and assists the president but does not function independently. Independence seems to be the key because in *Meyer v. Bush*, 981 F.2d 1288, 1297 (D.C. Cir. 1993) the court ruled that the Task Force on Regulatory Relief, which serves the president by advising the Office of Management and Budget, is also not an FOIA agency because it is "not a body with 'substantial independent authority' to direct executive branch officials." In *Department of Justice v. Tax Analysts*, 492 U.S. 136 (1989), the Supreme Court decided that FOIA disclosure requirements apply only if the agency creates or retains materials and is in "control" of the records at the time of the request. An agency may be in control even if it must direct the requester to another source that actually holds physical possession of the records. And in *U.S. v. Landano*, 113 S.Ct. 2014 (1993), the Court held that the FBI cannot use "ease of administration" to justify nondisclosure. Justice Sandra Day O'Connor, writing for the court, noted that the FBI is not entitled to a blanket exemption from disclosing sources it uses when conducting criminal investigations. She argued that circumstances or a "more particularized approach" should be taken in deciding whether sources should be disclosed, because FBI communications "range from the extremely sensitive to the routine" (p. 2038). Thus, in *Wisconsin Project on Nuclear Army Control v. United States Department of Commerce*, 317 F.3d 275 (D.C. Cir. 2003), the Court upheld the decision by the Department of Commerce not to disclose to the public, under the FOIA, personal information contained in applications for export licenses.

Freedom of Information versus Privacy: An Administrative Dilemma

The general praise for the FOIA as amended should not suggest that problems do not exist. In fact, as we begin the twenty-first century, legislators, administrators, and courts will face a difficult challenge in trying to reconcile the somewhat conflictual goals of the Freedom of Information Act and Privacy Act of 1974 (88 Stat. 1897; amended into the Administrative Procedure Act, 5 U.S.C. 552[a]). As David Rosenbloom simply puts it: "The fit between the [Privacy] Act and the FOIA can be complicated."[77] The legal dilemma created by the seemingly conflicting acts was addressed by the Supreme Court in *Department of Air Force v. Rose*, 425 U.S. 352 (1976) shortly after the Privacy Act took effect. Although the Court's majority ruled in favor of disclosure regarding the records of Air Force cadets, Chief Justice Burger in dissent argued that the majority had given insufficient weight to the cadets' privacy interests. Specifically, Congress must attempt to achieve "a proper balance between the protection of the individuals' right to privacy and the preservation of the public's right to Governmental information by excluding those kinds of files the disclosure of which might harm the individual."[78] However, for years some administrators tried to use the Privacy Act to hold back information, so in 1984 Congress amended the Privacy Act to promote a presumption of disclosure under Section 552 when questions arise about whether an agency should hold back or disclose information. "No agency shall rely on any exemption contained in Section 552 of this title to withhold from an individual any record which is otherwise accessible to such individual under the provisions of this section" (98 Stat. 2209, 2211).

The 1984 amendments to the Privacy Act favoring disclosure of nonexempt information under the FOIA provided agency administrators with a meaningful policy guideline, yet administrators still face frustrations trying to decide whether certain information should be disclosed or withheld. Parenthetically, the Privacy Act does not apply to corporations or other business organizations but only to records kept on individuals. Over a quarter century after *Rose,* in *Owasso Independent School District v. Falvo,* 122 S.Ct. 934 (2002), the Supreme Court ruled against a mother who argued that her children's privacy rights were violated under the Privacy Act because their teachers allowed other students to see and grade her children's tests in a "peer grading" process in which students exchange their work with other students and then grade the papers as the teacher provides the right answers. In a rather technical decision, the court reasoned that "peer grading" did not violate the Privacy Act because the act protects individuals only against the disclosure of their personal "educational records," whereas the peer-graded tests did not technically become records until the teacher "maintained them" by collecting and recording them in her grade book.

It shall be noted that the USA PATRIOT Act of 2001 has eroded some of the privacy protections under the Privacy Act and other laws, as well as the Fourth and Fifth Amendments of the U.S. Constitution. For example, the Justice Department is now able to access students' educational records under the rationale that the search and seizure of the records is related to a terrorist investigation. A comprehensive analysis of the PATRIOT Act's impact on privacy rights is presented in Chapter 11, which deals with administrative searches and seizures.

The FOIA and the Privacy Act embrace two cherished yet conflicting American values that administrators must protect. While the FOIA essentially calls for disclosure of information, the Privacy Act pleads for agency protection of an individual's personal privacy by requiring agency officials to restrict the collection, maintenance, and release of information that is in clear violation of a person's privacy rights. Specifically, subsection e of the Privacy Act obligates agencies to, among other requirements, maintain only "necessary" records on individuals, obtain as much information from individuals as practical when the information may be considered adverse, explain to individuals how the information will be used, try to maintain accurate and fair records, and preserve the security and confidentiality of records on individuals. A still-valid insight by David O'Brien is that problems exist because the requirements of each act, which administrators are entrusted with upholding, "are in many ways discordant: legitimation only of rights of access would require disclosure of all information, whereas maximum privacy protection would require that personal information never be disclosed."[79] Obviously then, administrators, who must comply with the dictates of both acts, become frustrated when, as they see it, compliance with one act appears to violate the provisions of the other.

Each act gives administrators broad discretionary powers to resolve the dilemma, but neither act provides them with meaningful guidelines to be used in resolving apparent contradictions found in these acts. Not only are statutory guidelines conspicuously absent, but even the Constitution fails to provide any clear clues for administrators. "Moreover," says O'Brien, "the particular problems which confront an agency when determining whether to grant or deny access to personal information are exacerbated by the ambiguous nature of the problem of information control and the absence of any specific constitutional guarantee of either a right of access or personal privacy." In his opinion, "without a perspicuous view of an individual's interests in both access to government records and personal privacy, development of a comprehensive policy framework for reconciling both interests and regulating agencies' information practices is impossible."[80]

According to the old Privacy Protection Study Commission, no serious conflict exists between the FOIA and the Privacy Act if only administrators understand their proper discretionary powers under each act. The commission believed that agency administrators were most bothered by the exemption in the FOIA that prohibited disclosure of information if such disclosure would clearly "constitute an unwarranted invasion of personal privacy" (Section 552[b][7][c]). The commission pointed out that before the Privacy Act was passed, administrators under the FOIA *could* use their discretion to withhold information that they believed constituted an obvious "unwarranted invasion of personal privacy." But under the Privacy Act "an agency is still *required,* by the Freedom of Information Act, to disclose information that would *not* constitute a 'clearly unwarranted invasion of personal privacy,' but now an agency no longer has the *discretion* to disclose information it believes would constitute such a clearly unwarranted invasion."[81]

However, this commission failed to focus on the real problem. The chief problem for administrators is defining what constitutes a clearly "unwarranted invasion of personal privacy." This problem is not new to administrative law, nor to law in general. In the absence of meaningful guidelines, administrators will continue to be frustrated in their attempt to define and implement statutory phrases as nebulous as "for good cause," "unwarranted invasion of personal privacy," "the public interest," and the like. If Congress refuses to provide more meaning for these vague standards and legislative intent is difficult to determine, the courts will also be unable or unwilling to provide helpful guidance. Not only do courts tend to interpret vague standards differently, but judges frequently refuse, in the absence of clear legislative standards, to go further than Congress in clarifying those standards. Witness, for example, this unhelpful Supreme Court riddle: "Exemption six ('constitutes a clearly unwarranted invasion of personal privacy') does not protect against disclosure of every incidental invasion of privacy—only such disclosures as constitute 'clearly unwarranted' invasions of personal privacy" (*Department of Air Force v. Rose,* 425 U.S. 352, 382 [1976]).

Many experts feel that injustices will occur if administrators are not provided with standards that can be used to guide their discretionary decisions when they are asked to release information. Despite the conflict that appears to exist between the Freedom of Information Act and the Privacy Act, the administrative and legal problems resulting from the apparent conflict should not be exaggerated. Indeed, administrators who employ common sense should in most cases have little difficulty deciding whether requested information should be released or withheld under these acts. Nevertheless, the government and concerned citizens should still try in the future to minimize the conflict. Virtually all states today have followed the federal example and have adopted freedom-of-information and privacy legislation.[82]

SUNSHINE AND SUNSET LEGISLATION

Sunshine Laws

In 1976 Congress drafted the Government in the Sunshine Act (90 Stat. 1241) as an amendment to the Administrative Procedure Act (5 U.S.C., Section 552b). To allow the sun to shine on official meetings where important public policy decisions are made (for example, state hearings regarding the proposed construction of a nuclear power plant, a city planning board meeting involving zoning issues), states have also passed sunshine legislation. In fact, in an unusual occurrence, states led the way; by the time the federal Sunshine Act was enacted by Congress in 1976, every state had passed sunshine laws.[83] *Sunshine laws* are aimed chiefly at keeping administrative decisions aboveboard. The underlying assumption of sunshine laws is that it is unwise to permit our administrators to make public policy decisions behind closed doors. In the more specific words of a specialist on the act: "The assumptions underlying the Sunshine Act were that increased openness would improve public knowledge of government programs, encourage higher quality work by government officials, stimulate public debate about government policies, and enhance public confidence in government actions. In short, open meetings were viewed as an integral part of the democratic process."[84]

Opponents of sunshine legislation, however, contend that such laws impede governmental decisionmaking and drive up the costs of government. Although they concede that some decisions are important enough to involve the public, they hold that it is a waste of time and money for administrators to have to consult the public (hold open meetings) on minor policy issues. After all, they maintain, administrators are held accountable for their decisions by the appropriate legislative bodies. Supporters of sunshine laws concede that requiring decisional meetings in the sunshine may slow down the decisionmaking process somewhat, but, they argue, this is a small price to pay for keeping governmental decisionmaking open and democrat-ically accountable. Besides, they point out, open decisionmaking can expose prob-lems that would not have been revealed if the decisions were not made in public. Proponents argue that a thorough ventilation of relevant issues early in the game re-duces the odds of running into major unanticipated problems later, thus saving the government money in the long run. It should be noted that specific provisions in statutes and ordinances already require open meetings in regard to certain issues. Sunshine laws, which differ from state to state, have had the effect of opening up some meetings that used to be closed to the public.

The courts have had to resolve some problems created by some of the vague pro-visions in the otherwise detailed Sunshine Act, yet since "the federal Sunshine Act has been in effect since 1977, it has spurred little litigation."[85] In fact, a 2003 Lexis-Nexis legal search of "sunshine act" turned up no citations by the U.S. Supreme Court since 1984 and only nine citations in all the federal appellate courts in the past five years. Although the act established the presumption that agency meetings should be held in the open, ten exemptions (see 552b[c]) allow federal agencies to avoid holding meetings in public when "sensitive matters" are at stake (for example, national defense and foreign policy, internal personnel rules, trade secrets, police records [under certain circumstances], information regarding the regulation and su-pervision of financial institutions). Parenthetically, some critics maintain that fail-ure to hold open meetings on the financial status of the savings and loan industry, as well as exemptions from disclosure of financial information under the FOIA, helped a great deal to cause the savings and loan crisis of the late 1980s and early 1990s. In *Common Cause v. Nuclear Regulatory Commission*, 674 F.2d 921 (D.C. Cir. 1982), the D.C. circuit court had to settle a controversy regarding when an agency can legally use one or more of the exemptions. But the two most common legal challenges have stemmed from what is meant under the act by "agency" and "agency meeting." The act defines "agency" as "headed by a collegian body com-posed of two or more individual members, a majority of whom are appointed to such position by the President with advice and consent of the Senate, and any sub-division thereof authorized to act on behalf of the agency" (Section 552b[2][1]). In *Symons v. Chrysler Corporation Loan Guarantee Board*, 670 F.2d 238 (D.C. Cir. 1981), the D.C. circuit court accepted the argument by the Chrysler Loan Guaran-tee Board, created by Congress to help monitor the government loan given to Chrysler Corporation, that it should not be subject to the Sunshine Act, because, even though members of the board consisted of members appointed by the presi-dent to certain governmental posts (for example, secretary of the treasury), they served only as ex officio board members and were not specifically appointed to it by the president. The court noted: "When Congress wishes to extend Sunshine cover-age to ex officio agencies, it will do so" (p. 244).

In *Federal Communications Commission v. ITT World Communications, Inc.*, 104 S.Ct. 1936 (1984), the Supreme Court focused on the question of what con-stitutes a meeting under the Sunshine Act. Specifically, the Court had to decide whether certain preliminary consultative meetings held by the FCC's Telecommunications Committee could include representatives of foreign telecommunications governing authorities but exclude ITT World Communications, Inc. ITT charged that its exclusion violated the Sunshine Act. The Supreme Court ruled that preliminary meetings held by agency "subdivisions" that produce only general background information and do not play "an integral role in the . . . policy making process" or "effectively predetermine official actions" cannot be considered a meeting under the Sunshine Act (p. 1941).

In 2000 the D.C. Circuit Court of Appeals made very clear that the Supreme Court's definitions of *agency* and *meeting* still stand. In *Natural Resources Defense Council v. Nuclear Regulatory Commission,* 216 F.3d 1180, the court, rejecting a petition by the NRDC for judicial review of the NRC's definition of *meeting,* argued that the NRC's definition should not be reviewed since their definition was taken "*in haec verba* from the Supreme Court's decision in the precedential *ITT* case. In *ITT,* the high court defined 'meeting' under the Sunshine Act to mean discussions which are '. . . sufficiently focused on discrete proposals or issues as to cause or to be likely to cause the individual participating members to form reasonably firm positions regarding matters pending or likely to arise before the agency'" (pp. 1187–1188). Regarding *agency,* the D.C. court, citing *ITT,* defined *agency* under the federal Sunshine Act as "an executive branch authority or independent regulatory agency 'headed by a collegial body composed of two or more individual members, a majority of whom are appointed to such a position by the President with the advice and consent of the Senate.'" Also, the court noted that "'agency' extends to 'any subdivision thereof authorized to act on behalf of the agency'" (pp. 1182–1184).

In his 2002 *Administrative Law Treatise,* Richard J. Pierce, Jr., argues that the Sunshine Act has had the unfortunate effect of preventing frank, insightful, and productive discussions at multimember agency meetings because the act prohibits "pre-decisional deliberations." He holds that commissioners "often make important decisions through notational voting with no prior deliberation; and communications at open meetings are grossly distorted by the presence of the public. Commissioners are reluctant to express their true views for fear that they will expose their ignorance or uncertainty with respect to issues of fact, policy and law."[86] But wait a minute! Isn't the obvious rebuttal to this criticism that commissioners, to avoid showing ignorance at open meetings, would be compelled to do their "homework," so that they would come to meetings more prepared, so, in fact, the deliberations would be more substantive and fruitful? Overall then, despite criticism, the Sunshine Act has helped to democratize agency decisionmaking by bringing the decisionmaking process from behind closed doors into the "sunlight."

Sunset Laws

Dismayed at the inability to determine effectively whether certain public agencies and programs were worth funding for still another year, political leaders, trying to live within a reasonable budget, have searched desperately in the past few decades for a way to make budgetary decisions easier and more rational. As Georgia's newly elected governor, Jimmy Carter thought he found the solution to his problems in zero-based budgeting (ZBB), a technique created by Peter Pyhrr, a treasurer for Texas Instruments, who presented his idea in the *Harvard Business Review*.[87] Very simply, zero-based budgeting requires a systematic evaluation of agencies and programs, usually once each fiscal year, to determine whether continued funding is justified, especially in light of the need to finance other agencies and programs within a limited budget. The approach is given the name "zero-based budgeting" because, before the agency or program can be considered worthy of continued funding, it is assumed that *no* monies have been budgeted for the agency or program. Soon after bringing Pyhrr to Georgia and implementing ZBB, Carter claimed that the budgetary technique was a huge success. When Carter became president, he brought ZBB with him, and it was widely publicized and tried at all governmental levels.

The ZBB concept was implemented in the form of sunset laws at a great pace in the states, especially between 1976 and 1981, yet only a few sunset laws were passed at the federal level.[88] Sunset laws, as ZBB tools, require laws, agencies, and their rules and programs to be evaluated, usually at set intervals (for example, every four years), to ascertain whether they should be given new life through continued financial support. Specifically regarding agencies, sunset laws provide for the automatic termination of (or the sun to set on) an agency, program, or rule unless new funds are appropriated at the end of the specified period of years. Therefore, sunset laws, in effect, provide the legislature with potent veto power. In theory, sunset laws compel legislators to give serious consideration to the worth of agency functions and programs to society before funding is reauthorized. Sunset laws are also supposed to force legislators to review the adequacy of agency procedures and the overall performance of agency administrators. Thus, the sunset review process provides legislators (different legislative committees are assigned specific agencies and programs) an opportunity to scrutinize agencies, rules, and programs at regular intervals and propose necessary changes, termination, or unaltered continuance.

The threat of having their agencies abolished or their programs suddenly cut is supposed to cause administrators to act more responsibly. However, many observers are convinced that sunset laws have proved, and will continue to prove, ineffective. One reason given is that many statutes already provide for programs to be terminated after a certain number of years unless new funds are appropriated. Another reason is that the legislature has always reserved the right to investigate and terminate agencies and programs. Thus, sunset laws seem to be a new way to do an old thing. But pressure groups have usually been very effective in persuading legislators to preserve existing agencies and programs. Should legislators be expected to respond differently under sunset legislation? For example, Colorado's experience with sunset laws years ago has shown that they are not very effective. The Colorado legislature reviewed thirteen state agencies during the first year its sunset legislation was in effect. Although it did eliminate three agencies, the $11,000 this saved was offset by the $212,000 in reviewing costs (the total annual budget for three agencies).[89] Rosalie Schiff, then director of Colorado's Common Cause, contended that Colorado's sunset law had proved ineffective thus far because influential lobbyists were able to convince legislators that their particular agencies and programs should be retained.[90] Nevertheless, proponents insist that sunset laws require systematic program evaluation after a certain number of years, keeping administrators on their toes. Without sunset laws, they assert, legislators can always elect to avoid the chore of taking the time to review agency performance and the costs and benefits of agency programs.

Recently, responding to concerns over the "anti-privacy" provisions in the 2001 USA PATRIOT Act (115 Stat. 272), legislators placed sunset provisions in the act to appease critics and guarantee passage. However, civil libertarians, led by the American Civil Liberties Union, contend that not only have sunset laws proved quite ineffective in the past in terminating agency programs and laws, but the sunset provisions in the PATRIOT Act, calling for the sun to set on surveillance provisions on December 31, 2005, apply only to some of the surveillance provisions.

In conclusion, sunset laws today are not very well respected. What Kenneth J. Meier concluded almost two decades ago seems still to be the opinion of a large consensus of critics: "Sunset's performance . . . has been less than its promise."[91] Sunset laws have never been adopted broadly on the federal level, while state enthusiasm for sunset statutes has declined sharply in the past two decades. Florence Heffron acknowledges that at one time all fifty states considered adopting sunset laws and, in fact, thirty-six did by 1982, but soon many states started to repeal their sunset laws because "sunset provisions quickly proved to be an expensive, cumbersome, and disappointing method for enhancing legislative control."[92] By 1988 six states had repealed their sunset laws, while six others simply permitted them to become dormant. Nonetheless, almost a majority of states today have sunset provisions, despite their dubious effectiveness, including Colorado, which even proudly advertises on its Web site its comprehensive sunset review process and its importance in promoting the public interest: "These reviews seek to balance the need for regulation to protect the public interest with the need to ensure that state agencies, industry and the professions, and the functions of government are not over-regulated."[93]

SUMMARY

In the early years of the twentieth century, Elihu Root, speaking to the American Bar Association, declared that the public administration machinery had to expand to meet the growing demands of modern government, but he warned that Congress had to keep administrative power democratically accountable to the people. It appears that Congress failed to heed Root's warning, because, since at least the mid-1930s, congressional controls over the emerging administrative state have become weaker and weaker, despite some honest congressional attempts to keep administrative activities under its firm control. However, this is not to suggest that Congress does not provide the best check against possible abuses of administrative power. The congressional watchdog may not be as powerful as it once was, but it still seems better equipped to preserve the democratic character of administrative action than any other watchdogs in the American political system, and there are signs in the twenty-first century that Congress is using micromanagement to better oversee the bureaucracy. It may be that bureaucratic power has become so strong that it is now beyond the realistic control of all existing external systemic checks.

The vast majority of critics argue that the traditional congressional controls over bureaucracy have become conspicuously less effective as the scope and strength of the administrative state has developed. All these control mechanisms have been found to be fairly inadequate for effectively controlling administrative behavior. Specifically, Congress's ability to create agencies and organize administrative business through enabling legislation provided Congress from the beginning with the potential to restrict administrative power. However, since the 1930s, Congress has tended to draft skeletal statutes that have provided agency administrators with vast discretionary powers to mold and implement public policies as they like. Realizing in the 1970s and early 1980s that it had not used its "preoversight" power very well, Congress increasingly turned to the legislative veto so it could check administrative actions it believed to be unacceptable. Unfortunately for Congress, the Supreme Court declared the legislative veto unconstitutional in 1983, yet Congress has largely ignored the decision, continuing to include "more constitutional" legislative veto provisions in new laws. In 1996 Congress passed the Congressional Review Act, which supposedly creates a "constitution-proof" legislative veto. This new legislative veto probably will survive a constitutional test, but it is unlikely to be an effective watchdog tool, because it is virtually identical to the lawmaking process, making its use awkward legislatively and politically challenging.

The purse-string power used to be considered Congress's strongest weapon against public agencies stepping out of line. However, controlling agency expenditures is much more difficult than it would seem. The huge size and complexity of most agency operations work in favor of the agency. Because Congress does not have time to study complex agency operations and budgets in detail, it usually does not know where to begin in slashing agency appropriations. Besides, all agencies have friends inside and outside Congress who will fight hard to make certain that funds for their particular programs are not cut. Virtually the same reasons can be given for why Congress's investigatory power has also proved quite ineffective in discovering and checking misuses of administrative power. Ideally, congressional investigations are used to discover administrative problems in various governmental agencies. However, even with the help of the General Accounting Office, legislators do not have the time to conduct many congressional investigations or to carry out thorough investigations after they do decide to investigate certain agency practices. GAO reports are frequently very good, but Congress typically has very little time to study the hundreds of reports that GAO conducts every year, each one focusing on a problem that probably needs considerable attention.

In an attempt to make public administration more democratically responsible to the American public, Congress passed various pieces of guidance legislation. The Pendleton Act of 1883 represented a modest effort to take unnecessary and disruptive politics out of public administration at the federal level. Later acts were also aimed at professionalizing the federal civil service system. The states passed similar legislation. However, legislative attempts to make public service more responsible and meritorious have created some problems. The most serious problem has stemmed from the charge that the merit system has encroached upon the constitutional rights of individuals in various ways. Reacting to past criticism of procedural problems in the administrative system, Congress passed the Administrative Procedure Act in 1946. The APA is the most comprehensive statute in administrative law. It is designed to make administrative procedures fairer. More specifically, the APA functions to make administrators honor constitutional due process and rule of law principles, especially by prohibiting arbitrary and capricious administrative behavior. On the whole, the APA is a reasonably sound law that has probably done much to improve the quality of administrative practices in the United States, despite the fact that it fails to apply to roughly 90 percent of informal, discretionary, administrative actions. Several major amendments, including the Freedom of Information Act, have done much to improve the original APA. Nevertheless, the APA has come under attack from critics who hold that vague standards and numerous exemptions have done much to weaken the authoritative potential of the law by allowing determined administrators to use the broad discretionary powers granted to them under the act to escape having to uphold the true spirit of many of its provisions.

In recent decades state legislatures and, infrequently, the U.S. Congress have implemented new ideas aimed at keeping the administrative process more democratically responsible. The FOIA has been a qualified success in opening up government records to the public, and the Privacy Act has been used to protect certain personal and confidential information from public disclosure. Passage of the USA PATRIOT Act in 2001 presents new challenges to privacy protections and will no doubt be debated in American society and the courts in the immediate future. Sunshine laws have been employed to keep administrators from making important policy decisions in private; sunset legislation has been used to force legislators to evaluate agencies and programs to determine at specified intervals whether they are satisfactory enough to warrant continued funding. Although sunshine laws have attracted criticisms, overall they have proved relatively successful in making agency decisionmaking more open and democratic. Sunset legislation, in contrast, has received mostly negative assessments, critics asserting that sunset reviews have been cost-ineffective. Several states have even repealed or made dormant their sunset provisions.

RUTAN V. REPUBLICAN PARTY OF ILLINOIS

497 U.S. 62; 110 S.Ct. 2729 (1990)

Facts

Present and former lower-level Illinois public employees and a job applicant charged that Governor James Thompson's executive order, issued November 12, 1980, proclaiming a hiring freeze for every agency, board, and so forth under his control, along with a specific order prohibiting state officials from hiring, promoting, transferring, or recalling any employees without his approval, violated their First Amendment freedoms to believe and associate. The district court dismissed the complaint. The court of appeals affirmed and reversed in part, and remanded the case to the district court. After a rehearing en banc, the Supreme Court granted certiorari.

Justice BRENNAN delivered the plurality opinion, and Justice SCALIA wrote the dissent. Key passages from the dissent are included.

To the victor belong only those spoils that may be constitutionally obtained. *Elrod v. Burns*, 427 U.S. 347 (1976), and *Branti v. Finkel*, 445 U.S. 507 . . . (1980), decided that the First Amendment forbids government officials to discharge or threaten to discharge public employees solely for not being supporters of the political party in power, unless party affiliation is an appropriate requirement for the position involved. Today we are asked to decide the constitutionality of several related political patronage practices— whether promotion, transfer, recall and hiring decisions involving low-level public employees may be constitutionally based on party affiliation and support. We hold that they may not.

The petition and cross-petition before us arise from a lawsuit protesting certain employment policies and practices instituted by Governor James Thompson of Illinois. On November 12, 1980, the Governor issued an executive order proclaiming a hiring freeze for every agency, bureau, board, or commission subject to his control. The order prohibits state officials from hiring any employees, filling any vacancy, creating any new position, or taking any similar action. It affects approximately 60,000 state positions. More than 5,000 of these become available each year as a result of resignations, retirements, deaths, expansions, and reorganizations. The order proclaims that "no exceptions" are permitted without the Governor's "express permission after submission of appropriate requests to his office." . . .

Requests for the Governor's "express permission" have allegedly become routine. Permission has been granted or withheld through an agency expressly created for this purpose, the Governor's Office of Personnel (Governor's Office). Agencies have been screening applicants under Illinois' civil service system, making their personnel choices, and submitting them as requests to be approved or disapproved by the Governor's Office. Among the employment decisions for which approvals have been required are new hires, promotions, transfers, and recalls after layoffs.

By means of the freeze, . . . the Governor has been using the Governor's Office to operate a political patronage system to limit state employment and beneficial employment-related decisions to those who are supported by the Republican Party. . . .

Five people (including the three petitioners) brought suit against various Illinois and Republican Party officials in the United States Court for the Central District of Illinois. They alleged that they had suffered discrimination with respect to state employment because they had not been supporters of the State's Republican Party and that this discrimination violates the First Amendment. Cynthia B. Rutan has been working for the State since 1974 as a rehabilitation counselor. She claims that since 1981 she has been repeatedly denied promotions to supervisory positions for which she was qualified because she had not worked for or supported the Republican Party. Franklin Taylor, who operates road equipment for the Illinois Department of Transportation, claims that he was denied a promotion in 1983 because he did not have the support of the local Republican Party. Taylor also maintains that he was denied a transfer to an office nearer to his home because of opposition from the Republican Party chairmen in the counties in which he worked and to which he requested a transfer. James W. Moore claims that he has been repeatedly denied state employment as a prison guard because he did not have the support of Republican Party officials.

The two other plaintiffs, before the Court as cross-respondents, allege that they were not recalled after layoffs because they lacked Republican credentials. Rick Standefer was a state garage worker who claims that he was not recalled, although his fellow employees were, because he had voted in a Democratic primary and did not have the support of the Republican Party. Dan O'Brien, formerly a dietary manager with the mental health department, contends that he was not recalled after a layoff because of his party affiliation and that he later obtained a lower paying position with the corrections department only after receiving support from the chairman of the local Republican Party. . . .

Rutan, Taylor, and Moore petitioned this court to review the constitutional standard set forth by the Seventh Circuit. . . . We granted *certiorari* . . . (1989) to decide the important question whether the First Amendment's proscription of patronage dismissals recognized in *Elrod v. Burns* . . . (1976) and *Branti v. Finkel* . . . (1980) extends to promotion, transfer, recall, or hiring decisions involving public employment positions for which party affiliation is not an appropriate requirement.

In *Elrod,* . . . we decided that a newly elected Democratic sheriff could not constitutionally engage in the patronage practice of replacing certain office staff with members of his own party "when the existing employees lack or fail to obtain requisite support from, or fail to affiliate with, that party." . . . The plurality explained that conditioning public employment on the provision of support for the favored political party "unquestionably inhibits protected belief and association." . . . It reasoned that conditioning employment on political activity pressures employees to pledge political allegiance to a party with which they prefer not to associate, to work for the election of political candidates they do not support, and to contribute money to be used to further policies with which they do not agree. The latter, the plurality noted, had been recognized by this Court as "tantamount to coerced belief." . . .

The Court then decided that the government interests generally asserted in support of patronage fail to justify this burden on First Amendment rights because patronage dismissals are not the least restrictive means for fostering those interests. . . . The plurality acknowledged that a government has a significant interest in ensuring that it has effective and efficient employees. It expressed doubt, however, that "mere difference of political persuasion motivates poor performance" and concluded that, in any case, the government can ensure employee effectiveness and efficiency through the less drastic means of discharging staff members whose work is inadequate. . . . The plurality also found that a government can meet its need for politically loyal employees to implement its policies by the less intrusive measure of dismissing, on political grounds, only those employees in policymaking positions. . . . Finally, although the plurality recognized that preservation of the democratic process "may in some instances justify limitations on First Amendment freedoms," it concluded that the "process functions as well without the practice, perhaps even better." Patronage, it explained, "can result in the entrenchment of one or a few parties to the exclusion of others" and

"is a very effective impediment to the associational and speech freedoms which are essential to a meaningful system of democratic government." . . .

Four years later, in *Branti*, . . . we decided that the First Amendment prohibited a newly appointed public defender, who was a Democrat, from discharging assistant public defenders because they did not have the support of the Democratic Party. The Court rejected an attempt to distinguish the case from *Elrod,* deciding that it was immaterial whether the public defender had attempted to coerce employees to change political parties or had only dismissed them on the basis of their private political beliefs. We explained that conditioning continued public employment on an employee's having obtained support from a particular political party violates the First Amendment because of "the coercion of belief that necessarily flows from the knowledge that one must have a sponsor in the dominant party in order to retain one's job." . . . "In sum," we said, "there is no requirement that dismissed employees prove that they, or other employees, have been coerced into changing, either actually or ostensibly, their political allegiance." . . . To prevail, we concluded, public employees need show only that they were discharged because they were not affiliated with or sponsored by the Democratic Party. . . .

We first address the claims of the four current or former employees. Respondents urge us to view *Elrod* and *Branti* as inapplicable because the patronage dismissals at issue in those cases are different in kind from failure to promote, failure to transfer, and failure to recall after layoff. Respondents initially contend that the employee petitioners' and cross-respondents' First Amendment rights have not been infringed because they have no entitlement to promotion, transfer, or rehire. We rejected just such an argument in *Elrod* . . . and *Branti,* . . . as both cases involved state workers who were employees at will with no legal entitlement to continued employment. . . .

Likewise, we find the assertion here that the employee petitioners and cross-respondents had no legal entitlement to promotion, transfer, or recall beside the point.

Respondents must argue that the employment decisions at issue here do not violate the First Amendment because decisions are not punitive, do not in any way adversely affect the terms of employment, and therefore do not chill the exercise of protected belief and association by public employees. This is not credible. Employees who find themselves in dead-end positions due to their political backgrounds *are* adversely affected. They will feel a significant obligation to support political positions held by their superiors, and to refrain from acting on the political views they actually hold, in order to progress up the career ladder. . . .

The same First Amendment concerns that underlay our decisions in *Elrod* . . . and *Branti* . . . are implicated here. Employees who do not compromise their beliefs stand to lose the considerable increases in pay and job satisfaction attendant to promotions, the hours and maintenance expenses that are consumed by long daily commutes, and even their jobs if they are not rehired after a "temporary" layoff.

These are significant penalties and are imposed for the exercise of rights guaranteed by the First Amendment. Unless these patronage practices are narrowly tailored to further vital government interests, we must conclude that they impermissibly encroach on First Amendment freedoms. . . .

We find, however, that our conclusions in *Elrod* . . . and *Branti* . . . are equally applicable to the patronage practices at issue here. A government's interest in securing effective employees can be met by discharging, demoting, or transferring staff members whose work is deficient. A government's interest in securing employees who will loyally implement its policies can be adequately served by choosing or dismissing certain high-level employees on the basis of their political views. . . . Likewise, the "preservation of the democratic process" is no more furthered by the patronage promotions, transfers, and rehires at issue here than it is by patronage dismissals. First, "political parties are nurtured by other, less intrusive and equally effective methods." . . . Political parties have already survived the substantial decline in patronage employment practices in this century. . . .

Second, patronage decidedly impairs the elective process by discouraging free political expression by public employees. . . . Respondents, who include the Governor of Illinois and other state officials, do not suggest any other overriding government interest in favoring Republican Party supporters for promotion, transfer, and rehire.

We therefore determine that promotions, transfers, and recalls after layoffs based on political affiliation or support are an impermissible infringement on the First Amendment rights of public employees. In doing so, we reject the Seventh Circuit's view of the appropriate constitutional standard by which to measure alleged patronage practices in government employment. The Seventh Circuit proposed that only those employment decisions that are the "substantial equivalent of a dismissal" violate a public employee's right under the First Amendment. . . . We find this test unduly restrictive because it fails to recognize that there are deprivations less harsh than dismissal that nevertheless press state employees and applicants to conform their beliefs and associations to some state-selected orthodoxy. . . . The First Amendment is not a tenure provision, protecting public employees from actual or constructive discharge. The First Amendment prevents the government, except in the most compelling circumstances, from wielding its power to interfere with its employees' freedom to believe and associate, or to not believe and not associate. . . .

Petitioner James W. Moore presents the closely related question whether patronage hiring violates the First Amendment. Patronage hiring places burdens on free speech and association similar to those imposed by the patronage practices discussed above. A state job is valuable. Like most employment, it provides regular paychecks, health insurance, and other benefits. . . .

Nonetheless, respondents contend that the burden imposed is not of constitutional magnitude. Decades of decisions by this Court belie such a claim. . . .

Almost half a century ago, this Court made clear that the government "may not enact a regulation providing that no Republican . . . shall be appointed to federal office." . . . What the First Amendment precludes the government from commanding directly, it also precludes the government from accomplishing indirectly. . . . Under our sustained precedent, conditioning hiring decisions on political belief and association plainly constitutes an unconstitutional condition, unless the government has a vital interest in doing so. . . . We find no such government interest here, for the same reasons that we found that the government lacks justification for patronage promotions, transfers, or recalls. . . .

The court below, having decided that the appropriate inquiry in patronage cases is whether the employment decision at issue is the substantial equivalent of a dismissal, affirmed the trial court's dismissal of Moore's claim. . . . The Court of Appeals reasoned that "rejecting an employment application does not impose a hardship upon an employee comparable to the loss of a job." . . . *Wygant v. Jackson Bd. of Education* . . . (1980). . . . The plurality said that race-based layoffs placed too great a burden on individual members of the non-minority race, but suggested that discriminatory hiring was permissible, under certain circumstances, even though it burdened white applicants, because the burden was less intrusive than the loss of an existing job. . . .

Wygant has no application to the question at issue here. The plurality's concern in that case was identifying the least harsh means of remedying past wrongs. It did not question that *some* remedy was permissible when there was sufficient evidence of past discrimination. In contrast, the Governor of Illinois has not instituted a remedial undertaking. It is unnecessary here to consider whether not being hired is less burdensome than being discharged, because the government is not pressed to do *either* on the basis of political affiliation. The question in the patronage context is not which penalty is more acute but whether the government, without sufficient justification, is pressuring employees to discontinue the free exercise of their First Amendment rights.

If Moore's employment application was set aside because he chose not to support the Republican Party, as he asserts, then Moore's First Amendment rights have been violated. Therefore, we find that Moore's complaint was improperly dismissed.

We hold that the rule of *Elrod* and *Branti* extends to promotion, transfer, recall and hiring decisions based on party affiliation and support and that all of the petitioners and cross-respondents have stated claims upon which relief may be granted. We affirm the Seventh Circuit insofar as it remanded Rutan's, Taylor's, Standefer's, and O'Brien's claims. However, we reverse the Seventh Circuit's decision to uphold the dismissal of Moore's claim. All five claims are remanded for proceedings consistent with this opinion.

It is so ordered.

Justice SCALIA, with whom The Chief Justice and Justice KENNEDY join, and with whom Justice O'CONNOR joins as to Parts II and III, dissenting.

Today the Court establishes the constitutional principle that party membership is not a permissible factor in the dispensation of government jobs, except those jobs for the performance of which party affiliation is an "appropriate requirement." . . . It is hard to say precisely (or even generally) what that exception means, but if there is any category of jobs for whose performance party affiliation is not an appropriate requirement, it is the job of being a judge, where partisanship is not only unneeded but positively undesirable. It is, however, rare that a federal administration of one party will appoint a judge from another party. And it has always been rare. . . . Thus, the new principle that the Court today announces will be enforced by a corps of judges (the Members of this Court included) who overwhelmingly owe their office to its violation. Something must be wrong here, and I suggest it is the Court. . . .

The choice between patronage and the merit principle—or, to be more realistic about it, the choice between the desirable mix of merit and patronage principles in widely varying federal, state, and local political contexts—is not so clear that I would be prepared, as an original matter, to chisel a single, inflexible prescription into the Constitution. Fourteen years ago, in *Elrod v. Burns,* . . . the Court did that. *Elrod* was limited however, as was the later decision of *Branti v. Finkel* . . . to patronage firings, leaving it to state and federal legislatures to determine when and where political affiliation could be taken into account in hirings and promotions. Today the Court makes its constitutional civil service reform absolute, extending to all decisions regarding government employment. Because the First Amendment has never been thought to require this disposition, which may well have disastrous consequences for our political system, I dissent.

Once it is acknowledged that the Constitution's prohibition against laws "abridging the freedom of speech" does not apply to laws enacted in the government's capacity as employer in the same way that it does to laws enacted in the government's capacity as regulator of private conduct, it may sometimes be difficult to assess what employment practices are permissible and what are not. That seems to me not a difficult question, however, in the present context. The provisions of the Bill of Rights were designed to restrain transient majorities from impairing long-recognized personal liberties. They did not create by implication novel individual rights overturning accepted political norms. Thus, when a practice not expressly prohibited by the text of the Bill of Rights bears the endorsement of a long tradition of open, wide-spread, and unchallenged use that dates back to the beginning of the Republic, we have no proper basis for striking it down. . . .

I will not describe at length the claim of patronage to landmark status as one of our accepted political traditions. Justice Powell discussed it in his dissenting opinions in *Elrod* and *Branti.* . . . Suffice it to say that patronage was, without any thought that it could be unconstitutional, a basis for government employment from the earliest days of the Republic until *Elrod*—and has continued unabated *since Elrod,* to the extent still permitted by

that unfortunate decision. . . . Given that unbroken tradition regarding the application of an ambiguous constitutional text, there was in my view no basis for holding that patronage-based dismissals violated the First Amendment—much less for holding, as the Court does today, that even patronage hiring does so.

Even accepting the Court's own mode of analysis, however, and engaging in "balancing" a tradition that ought to be part of the scales, *Elrod, Branti,* and today's extension of them seem to me wrong.

The Court limits patronage on the ground that the individual's interest in uncoerced belief and expression outweighs the systemic interests invoked to justify the practice. . . . The opinion indicates that the government may prevail only if it proves that the practice is "narrowly tailored to further vital government interests." . . .

The Court holds that the governmental benefits of patronage cannot reasonably be thought to outweigh its "coercive" effects (even the lesser "coercive" effects of patronage hiring as opposed to patronage firing) not merely in 1990 in the State of Illinois, but at any time in any of the numerous political subdivisions of this vast country. It seems to me that that categorical pronouncement reflects a naive vision of politics and an inadequate appreciation of the systemic effects of promoting political stability and facilitating the social and political integration of previously powerless groups.

The whole point of my dissent is that the desirability of patronage is a policy question to be decided by the people's representatives; . . .

It is self-evident that eliminating patronage will significantly undermine party discipline; and that as party discipline wanes, so will the strength of the two-party system. But, says the Court, "[p]olitical parties have already survived the substantial decline in patronage employment practices in this century." . . . Parties have assuredly survived—but as what? As the forges upon which many of the essential compromises of American political life are hammered out? Or merely as convenient vehicles for the conducting of national Presidential elections?

Equally apparent is the relatively destabilizing nature of a system in which candidates cannot rely upon patronage-based party loyalty for their campaign support, but must attract workers and raise funds by appealing to various interest groups. . . . There is little doubt that our decisions in *Elrod* and *Branti*, by contributing to the decline of party strength, have also contributed to the growth of interest-group politics in the last decade. . . . Our decision today will greatly accelerate the trend.

Patronage, moreover, has been a powerful means of achieving the social and political integration of excluded groups. . . . By supporting and ultimately dominating a particular party "machine," racial and ethnic minorities have—on the basis of their politics rather than their race or ethnicity—acquired the patronage awards the machine had power to confer. . . .

In emphasizing the advantages and minimizing the disadvantages (or at least minimizing one of the disadvantages) of the patronage system, I do not mean to suggest that that system is best. It may not always be; it may never be. To oppose our *Elrod-Branti* jurisprudence, one need not believe that the patronage system is *necessarily* desirable; nor even that it is always and everywhere *arguably* desirable; but merely that it is a political arrangement that may sometimes be a reasonable choice, and should therefore be left to the judgment of the people's elected representatives. . . .

This uncertainty and confusion are not the result of the fact that *Elrod*, and then *Branti*, chose the wrong "line." My point is that there is no right line—or at least no right line that can be nationally applied and that is known by judges. . . . The appropriate "mix" of party-based employment is a political question if there ever was one, and we should give it back to the voters of the various political units to decide, through civil service legislation crafted to suit the time and place, which mix is best.

The Court's opinion, of course, not only declines to confine *Elrod* and *Branti* to dismissals in the narrow sense I have proposed, but . . . even extends those opinions beyond "constructive" dismissals—indeed, even beyond adverse treatment of current employees—to all hiring decisions. In the long run there may be cause to rejoice in that extension. When the courts are flooded with litigation under that most unmanageable of standards (*Branti*) brought by that most persistent and tenacious of suitors (the disappointed office seeker) we may be moved to reconsider our intrusion into the entire field.

In the meantime, I dissent.

COMMENTS AND QUESTIONS

The *Rutan* case is another in a barrage of attacks on patronage politics as contrary to both constitutional process and meritorious principles. A decade before, the Supreme Court extended the famous *Elrod* decision by holding in *Branti v. Finkel* that lower-level governmental officials cannot be fired or threatened to be discharged solely because they are not supporters of or affiliated with the particular political party in power. Such, argued the Court, violates their rights of freedom of speech and association under the First Amendment. The *Rutan* decision is particularly devastating to the tradition of patronage politics in America because the Court extended *Branti* to apply to basic political patronage employment practices involving promotions, transfers, and recalls. With the comprehensiveness of the *Rutan* holding, the Supreme Court has practically closed the door on "job-oriented" patronage politics for lower-level employees.

The high court does not reject patronage politics per se but argues that it cannot allow constitutional principles to be crushed by the practices of patronage politics. According to the court's plurality, the government, as an employer, cannot erode the freedom of employees to associate and speak unless it can show a vital governmental interest for doing so.

Justice Scalia, joined by justices Rehnquist, Kennedy, and O'Connor, wrote an unusually long and emotional dissent, contending mainly that the judiciary has no legitimate right to strike down the long, widespread, and accepted tradition of patronage politics that dates back to our republic's beginning unless the Constitution specifically prohibits it. Stressing the positive contributions of patronage politics to our democratic system and the public support for it, Justice Scalia argues that civil service reform should be left to legislators, not judges. Scalia also points out the interesting irony that the court's majority, although determined to destroy patronage politics, consists, in fact, of patronage appointees.

Curiously, Justice Scalia suggests that the Court's majority has unfortunately ruled against an old and popular tradition that has served democracy quite well. However, although he makes a few reasonable points, his dissent would probably attract only feeble support among public administration scholars and practitioners, as well as the American public, despite his assertion that patronage politics has public support. The public administration literature is replete with attacks on the corrupt and inefficient nature of patronage politics and how it has undermined the development of honest, efficient, and meritorious public administration, while journalists and the American people have overwhelmingly voiced their disgust for the evils of patronage. But clearly, given the divided Court (remember that four justices dissented), not all are convinced that patronage politics is bad for our governmental system. What do you think? Which side in the traditional American controversy presents the most sensible arguments? How can you reconcile the legal with the practical arguments in *Rutan*?

NOTES

1. *American Bar Association Bulletin* (1916), pp. 355, 368–369.

2. Ibid.

3. Kenneth C. Davis and Walter Gellhorn, with Paul R. Verkuil, moderator, "Present at the Creation: Regulatory Reform Before 1946," *Administrative Law Review* 38 (fall 1986). In remarks originally presented to the spring 1986 American Bar Association Council's meeting, administrative law section, it was made clear that, although regulatory groundwork was laid before 1945, serious regulatory reform efforts came after 1945. Also see David H. Rosenbloom, "The Evolution of the Administrative State and Transformations of Administrative Law," in David H. Rosenbloom and Richard D. Schwartz, eds., *Handbook of Regulation and Administrative Law* (New York: Marcel Dekker, 1994), pp. 3–36.

4. Jacob F. Cooke, ed., no. 51, *The Federalist* (Cleveland: World Publishing, 1961), p. 349.

5. Cathy Marie Johnson, *The Dynamics of Conflict Between Bureaucratic and Legislators* (New York: M. E. Sharpe, 1992), pp. 138–159.

6. Kenneth R. Mayer, "Policy Disputes as a Source of Administrative Controls: Congressional Micromanagement of the Department of Defense," *Public Administration Review* 53 (July–August 1993).

7. Steven W. Hays and Richard C. Kearney, eds., *Public Personnel Administration: Problems and Prospects*, 4th ed. (Upper Saddle River, N.J.: Prentice-Hall, 2002), chaps. 3, 7, and 11.

8. James W. Fesler, *Public Administration: Theory and Practice* (Englewood Cliffs, N.J.: Prentice-Hall, 1980), p. 311.

9. Ibid., pp. 313–314.

10. Joel D. Aberbach, *Keeping a Watchful Eye: The Politics of Congressional Oversight* (Washington, D.C.: Brookings Institution Press, 1991), p. 213. For a more recent overview, see James N. Burns et. al., *Government by the People*, brief 4th ed. (Upper Saddle River, N.J.: Prentice-Hall, 2002), pp. 228–233.

11. Juvenal, *Satires,* 347, quoted in Fesler, *Public Administration,* p. 315. Neither Fesler nor I give the literal translation of the Latin, but the purpose is served.

12. Kenneth F. Warren, "The Search for Administrative Responsibility," *Public Administrative Review* 34 (March–April 1974). Also see Terry L. Cooper, *The Responsible Administrator*, 4th ed. (San Francisco: Jossey-Bass, 1998).

13. Richard E. Neustadt, "Politicians and Bureaucrats," in Frederick S. Lane, ed., *Current Issues in Public Administration* (New York: St. Martin's Press, 1978), p. 51.

14. Stephen K. Bailey, *Congress in the Seventies* (New York: St. Martin's Press, 1970), p. 92.

15. James M. Burns, et. al., *Government by the People*, pp. 228–232.

16. Francis E. Rourke, *Bureaucracy, Politics, and Public Policy*, 3rd ed. (Boston: Little, Brown, 1984), p. 72.

17. Johnson, *The Dynamics of Conflict Between Bureaucrats and Legislators*, p. 159.

18. Ibid.

19. Congressman William Clay, personal interview with the author, February 17, 1987.

20. Congressman William Clay, personal interview, March 10, 1994.

21. Roberta S. Karmel, "Securities Regulation: Enron and the Accounting Profession," *New York Law Journal* 227 (February 21, 2002).

22. Lawrence C. Dodd and Richard L. Scott, *Congress and the Administrative State* (New York: Wiley, 1979), p. 163.

23. Ibid., pp. 163–64.

24. Randall B. Ripley and Grace A. Franklin, *Congress, the Bureaucracy, and Public Policy*, 5th ed. (Washington, D.C.: International Thompson, 1999), chaps. 2–3.

25. Richard Cohen, "Junior Members Seek Approval for Wider Use of the Legislative Veto," *National Journal,* August 6, 1977, pp. 1228–1232.

26. Michael Saks, "Holding the Independent Agencies Accountable: Legislative Veto of Agency Rules," *Administrative Law Review* 36 (winter 1984): 42; and Joseph Cooper and Patricia Hurley, "The Legislative Veto: A Policy Analysis," *Congress and the Presidency* 10 (spring 1983).

27. The one- and two-house legislative vetoes are common, but legislative vetoes from a committee in one house are rare. The Future Trading Act of 1978, 7 U.S.C., Sec. 6c(c), provides an example of a committee veto, while the Supplemental Appropriations Act of 1953, Ch. 758, 66 Stat. 637, allowed the chairman of the House Appropriations Committee to exercise a legislative veto.

28. Harold H. Buff and Ernest Gellhorn, "Congressional Control of Administrative Regulation: A Study of Legislative Vetoes," *Harvard Law Review* 90 (May 1977). Also, see Cornelius M. Kerwin, *Rulemaking: How Government Agencies Write Law and Make Policy* (Washington, D.C.: Congressional Quarterly Press, 1994), pp. 225–229.

29. Buff and Gellhorn, "Congressional Control of Administrative Regulation," pp. 1373–1397.

30. *Wall Street Journal,* February 8, 1980, p. 7.

31. Rowland L. Young, "Supreme Court Report: The Court Vetoes the Legislative Veto," *American Bar Association Journal* 69 (September 1983): 1288.

32. Incidentally, in the Iran-contra affair, President Reagan was charged with violating the International Security Assistance and Arms Export Control Act by having arms shipped to Iran and the Nicaraguan contras without notifying Congress.

33. Daniel P. Franklin, "Why the Legislative Veto Isn't Dead," *Presidential Studies Quarterly* 26 (summer 1986): 486.

34. Bernard Schwartz, "Administrative Law Cases During 1990," *Administrative Law Review* 43 (summer 1991): 477.

35. James F. Blumstein, "Politics and Policy: Presidential Administrations and Administrative Law," *Duke Law Journal* 51 (December 2001): 851, n. 203.

36. Richard J. Pierce, Jr., *Administrative Law Treatise*, 4th ed. (New York: Aspen, 2002), vol. 1, p. 57.

37. Ibid.

38. Leonard D. White, *Introduction to the Study of Public Administration* (New York: Macmillan, 1926).

39. Walter Gellhorn, *Administrative Law: Cases and Comments* (Mineola, N.Y.: Foundation Press, 1940).

40. Paul Van Riper, *History of the United States Civil Service* (New York: Harper and Row, 1958), p. 23.

41. Ibid., pp. 43–44; see also Ronald D. Sylvia, *Public Personnel Administration* (Belmont, Calif.: Wadsworth, 1994).

42. Woodrow Wilson, "The Study of Administration," *Political Science Quarterly* 16 (December 1941).

43. Ibid., p. 485.

44. Ibid., p. 484.

45. Ibid., p. 495.

46. Fesler, *Public Administration,* pp. 26–29.

47. See, for example, President's Advisory Council on Executive Organization (Roy L. Ash, chairman), *A New Regulatory Framework* (Washington, D.C.: U.S. Government Printing Office, 1971) (known as the Ash Council Report); and the American Bar Association's administrative law section's report, reprinted in Peter L. Strauss and Cass R. Sunstein, "The Role of the President and OMB in Informal Rulemaking," *Administrative Law Review* 38 (spring 1986); and Marianne K. Smythe, "An Irreverent Look at Regulatory Reform," *Administrative Law Review* 38 (fall 1986).

48. 37 Stat. 555.

49. 53 Stat. 1147.

50. 54 Stat. 1211.

51. 78 Stat. 412.

52. PL 103-94.

53. David K. Hamilton, "The Staffing Function in Illinois State Government after *Rutan,*" *Public Administration Review* 5 (July–August 1993).

54. Karl T. Thurber, Jr., "Revising the Hatch Act: A Practitioner's Perspective," *The Public Manager* (spring 1993): 43.

55. Ibid., p. 46. Republicans also feared that Democrats would benefit the most from Hatch Act reform because more federal workers are Democrats, thus creating the potential to increase public union control over the federal government.

56. Jenne Ponessa, "The Hatch Act Rewrite," *Congressional Quarterly,* November 13, 1993, pp. 3146–3147.

57. Thurber, "Revising the Hatch Act," pp. 43–46.

58. Ibid., p.45.

59. For a recent review of the right to strike, see Michael H. LeRoy and John H. Johnson, IV, "Death by Lethal Injunction: National Emergency Strikes Under the Taft-Hartley Act and the Moribund Right to Strike," *Arizona Law Review* 43 (spring 2001).

60. Herbert Kaufman, *Are Government Organizations Immortal?* (Washington, D.C.: Brookings Institution Press, 1976), pp. 34–63.

61. For a most enlightening informal discussion of the events leading up to the passage of the APA by two of the key participants in its creation, Walter Gellhorn and Kenneth C. Davis, see their remarks delivered at the spring 1986 Council Meeting of the American Bar Association in celebration of the fortieth anniversary of the APA, reprinted as "Present at the Creation"; see also David H. Rosenbloom, *Building a Legislative-Centered Public Administration: Congress and the Administrative State, 1946–1999* (Tuscaloosa: University of Alabama Press, 2000).

62. Arthur Bonfield, "The Federal APA and State Administrative Law," *Virginia Law Review* 72 (March 1986). The states that have adopted the Revised Model State Administrative Procedure Act of 1981 (13 Uniform State Laws Ann. 347) in whole or in part, or the original Model State APA or its 1961 revision, include Alabama, Arkansas, Connecticut, Georgia, Hawaii, Idaho, Illinois, Iowa, Louisiana, Maine, Maryland, Michigan, Mississippi, Missouri, Montana, Nebraska, Nevada, New Hampshire, New York, North Carolina, Oklahoma, Oregon, Rhode Island, South Dakota, Tennessee, Vermont, Washington, West Virginia, Wisconsin, and Wyoming.

63. Pierce, *Administrative Law Treatise*, 4th ed., vol. 1, p. 15.

64. *Morgan v. United States*, 298 U.S. 468 (1936); *Morgan v. United States*, 304 U.S. 1(1938), and *United States v. Morgan*, 313 U.S. 409 (1941).

65. Quoted in Harold C. Relyea, "The Freedom of Information Act," *Public Administration Review* (July–August 1979): 310.

66. Gaillard Hunt, ed., *The Writings of James Madison* (New York: G. P. Putnam's Sons 1910), vol. 9, p. 103.

67. Frances E. Zollers, "The Implementation of the Consumer Product Safety Act Section 6(b) and the Conflict with Freedom of Information Act Policies," *Administrative Law Review* 38 (winter 1987).

68. Ibid., pp. 311–15.

69. Ibid., p. 314.

70. Russell M. Roberts, "Faithful Execution of the FOI Act: One Executive Branch Experience," *Public Administration Review* 39 (July–August 1979).

71. House Committee on Governmental Operations, V:S. *Governmental Information Policies and Practices-Administration and Operation of Freedom of Information Act, Hearings,* 92nd Cong., 2nd sess. (Washington, D.C.: Government Printing Office, 1972), pp. 8, 15.

72. Kenneth C. Davis, *Administrative Law Treatise*, 2nd ed. (San Diego: K. C. Davis, 1979), vol. 1, p. 309.

73. Samuel Archibald, "Freedom of Information Act Revisited," *Public Administration Review* 39 (July–August 1979): 316.

74. Davis and Pierce, *Administrative Law Treatise*, 3rd ed., vol. 1, p. 194.

75. Robert G. Vaughn, "Federal Information Policy and Administrative Law," in Rosenbloom and Schwartz, eds., *Handbook of Regulation and Administrative Law*, p. 479.

76. Ibid., pp. 478–481.

77. David H. Rosenbloom, *Building a Legislative-Centered Public Administration* (Tuscaloosa: University of Alabama Press, 2000), p. 59.

78. House Report 1497, 89th Cong., 2nd sess., p. 11.

79. David M. O'Brien, "Freedom of Information, Privacy, and Information Control: A Contemporary Administrative Dilemma," *Public Administration Review* 39 (July–August 1978): 324.

80. Ibid., pp. 323–324.

81. U.S. Privacy Protection Study Commission, *Personnel Privacy in an Information Society* (Washington, D.C.: U.S. Government Printing Office, 1977), p. 520.

82. Arthur Earl Bonfield and Michael Asimow, *State and Federal Administrative Law* (St. Paul: West, 1989), pp. 589–590.

83. Howard I. Fox, "Government in the Sunshine," *1978 Annual Survey of American Law* (1979): 305–306.

84. Larry W. Thomas, "The Courts and the Implementation of the Government in Sunshine Act," *Administrative Law Review* 37 (summer 1985): 260. Also see Alfred C. Aman, Jr., and William T. Mayton, *Administrative Law*, 2nd ed. (St. Paul: West Group, 2001), pp. 728–739.

85. Aman and Mayton, *Administrative Law*, p. 728.

86. Pierce, *Administrative Law Treatise*, 4th ed., vol. 1, p. 296.

87. Peter A. Pyhrr, "Zero-Base Budgeting," *Harvard Business Review* 48 (November–December 1970).

88. Kenneth J. Meier, *Politics and the Bureaucracy*, 3rd ed. (Pacific Grove, Calif.: Brooks/Cole, 1993), pp. 158–159.

89. Kenneth J. Meier, *Regulation: Politics, Bureaucracy, and Economics* (New York: St. Martin's Press, 1985), p. 296.

90. George E. Berkley, *The Craft of Public Administration*, 3rd ed. (Boston: Allyn and Bacon, 1981), pp. 291–292; Meier, *Regulation: Politics, Bureaucracy, and Economics,* pp. 296–297.

91. Meier, *Regulation: Politics, Bureaucracy, and Economics*, p. 159.

92. Florence A. Heffron, "Legislative Review of Administrative Rules Under the Idaho Administrative Procedure Act," *Idaho Law Review* 30 (1994): 371.

93. State of Colorado, www.state.co.us/gov_dir/leg_dir/lcsstaff/2001/research/01sunsetproc.htm.

CHAPTER 4

Protecting Administrators from Undue Interference and Harassment

LEGITIMATE VERSUS ILLEGITIMATE MEDDLING IN THE ADMINISTRATIVE PROCESS

Public administrators should not be insensitive to all pressures from their environment. Popular government and democratically accountable public administration require that public officials be reasonably responsive to the legitimate demands placed upon them by various political actors. Systems theory makes clear that all public administrators, whether in totalitarian or democratic governments, must be somewhat responsive to environmental demands to survive. Because of the openness in democratic administrations, their administrators are placed under even more pressure to respond to external demands. In fact, a vital function of administrative law is keeping open the channels of communication and influence between public administrators and concerned individual and group interests and their political representatives. For example, when promulgating administrative rules, agency rulemakers are required under the Administrative Procedure Act to provide an opportunity for interested parties to submit comments on the proposed rules.

However, while democratic government is enhanced by a certain degree of input in the administrative process, administrative actions are harmed by undue interference. Undue interference in the administrative process takes many forms, but in general any intervention that is inappropriate, improper, excessive, unethical, or illegal can be classified as **undue.** Civil service reformers, elected political officials, court justices, public administration scholars, and public administrators themselves have all noted how administrative behavior can be undermined by unnecessary and counterproductive intrusions. Edwin Tucker stressed over two decades ago that for public administrators to perform their jobs in a democratic and professionally objective manner, "it is imperative that an administrator's actions be determined by the Constitution, legislative mandates, judicial pronouncements, agency rules and practices, and the administrator's personal impartial judgment."[1] Accordingly, Tucker concluded, "the shaping of administrative behavior by corrupting extra-legal interference, however beneficent the motivation of the corrupter may be, disparages government and denies justice to the party who is adversely affected because of covert tampering."[2]

The vast majority of public administrative theorists have argued persuasively that although general political controls should guide administrative decisionmaking, daily and routine administrative work is best handled by objective and professional administrators. To prevent the disruption of normal administrative processes, our political leaders have structured the administrative system so that administrators can enjoy a certain degree of independence from outside forces, particularly interest group and political pressures. The underlying assumption is that structural independence can help to promote efficient, effective, and responsible public administration through generally reducing biases, costs, and malfeasance in the planning and execution of public policies. In this chapter the focus is on the thin line that separates acceptable influence (oversight) by political actors from unacceptable and illegal harassment of administrative officials. Attention is paid to how interest groups, legislators, and presidents have tried to peddle influence to gain special favors from administrators. The legitimacy of such transactions is assessed from the perspective of what administrative law and democratic government permit.

PROTECTING ADMINISTRATORS FROM THEMSELVES AND OTHERS: CONFLICT-OF-INTEREST LAWS

Most public administrators seem to be honest, but are they honest because they want to be or because they have to be? This philosophical question deserves the special attention of organizational theorists. It is true, however, that the vast majority of political theorists, in contemplating human nature, have concluded that because people are inherently selfish creatures, they probably would commit dishonest and profitable acts if given the opportunity. Generally, these political theorists have pointed out that moral character can be genuinely tested only under very unrealistic circumstances. For instance, Plato, in *The Republic,* essentially posed this question: How honest would a person be if he had the opportunity to act as he wished, in the absence of laws, and with the absolute knowledge beforehand that, if he acted dishonestly, he would not be caught or punished for his actions?[3]

Only extremely naive idealists could construct a governmental system on the assumption that if unchecked by laws and the threat of punishment, people would instinctively act in consistent honesty. Successful laws are based on fear and can only remain effective as long as they are respected. If laws are perceived by people to pose no real threat to them, whether because they are not enforced or only feebly enforced, fear of the consequences of violation diminishes, along with the effectiveness of those laws.

Laws are designed with the specific intention of reducing the risk that social disruption will occur, because people left to their own devices will act in ways contrary to the interests of others and thereby jeopardize the public interest. Simply, laws are employed to establish order. Conflict-of-interest laws have been legislated to better ensure that actions by public officials are objective, untainted by personal interests. Herbert Kaufman contends that conflict-of-interest laws are necessary in order "to keep the government from turning into an instrumentality of private profit for those in its employ or those with private fortunes at their disposal."[4] Specifically, Kaufman believes that conflict-of-interest laws are needed to control administrative behavior because administrative officers possess so much power and are confronted with so many temptations. And some scholars argue that conflict-of-interest laws are needed even more in modern American society than when our Republic first began, because as a society we have increasingly devalued the public sector and have unfortunately become obsessed with promoting our selfish financial and career interests.[5] ABC correspondent Sam Donnelson noted on *Weekend with David Brinkley*, in response to the seventeen corruption charges faced by Representative Dan Rostenkowski (D.–Ill.) in 1994, that misusing public office for private gain has become so commonplace that part of Rostenkowski's defense will probably be to claim that he only did "what everyone is doing."[6]

What Are Conflicts of Interest?

Conflicts of interest for governmental employees—according to various federal, state, and local statutes and ordinances, as well as agency rules and regulations—in general exist when a public servant uses an office for personal gain by paying special favors to private interests in exchange for payments of some kind (money, products, services). A conflict of interest also exists when a public official uses governmental position to benefit individual private interests (commonly, private business interests) or the interests of the government worker's family or friends. Administrators, although largely unelected public officials, still are responsible for promoting the public interest. Accordingly, public administrators must avoid real as well as apparent conflicts of interest. A person does not have to benefit personally from a conflictual situation for a conflict of interest to exist. Getting into a position where one could potentially benefit from the conflict of interest is enough to make a person guilty of violating a conflict-of-interest law. For example, in *United States v. Mississippi Valley Generating Co.* (364 U.S. 520 [1961]), the Supreme Court held that a conflict of interest existed between a consultant for the government and the consultant's regular employer because an atmosphere was created that tended to invite unnecessarily biased and dishonorable decisions:

The statute does not specify as elements of the crime that there be actual corruption or that there be any actual loss suffered by the Government as a result of the defendant's conflict of interest. This omission indicates that the statute establishes an objective standard of conduct, and that whenever a government agent fails to act in accordance with that standard, he is guilty of violating the statute, regardless whether there is positive corruption. The statute is thus directed not only at dishonor, but also at conduct which tempts dishonor. This broad proscription embodies a recognition of the fact that an impairment of impartial judgment can occur in even the most well-meaning men when their personal economic interests are affected by the business they transact on behalf of the Government." (pp. 549–550)

In *In re Berger Co. Util. Auth.* (553 A.2d 849, 853 9 N.J. Super. [1989]), the New Jersey Superior Court held that a hearing official should have disqualified himself from hearing a utility case because a clear conflict of interest existed since he had inquired about a job possibility with the very utility company his commission later required him to adjudicate. In *Sanjour v. E.P.A.*, 984 F.2d 434 (D.C. Cir. 1993) the court upheld a government ethics law that prohibited EPA employees from receiving reimbursement and pay for unofficial writing and speaking engagements, even though they related to their official duties, because such compensation created at least the appearance of a conflict of interest. And in a 2003 case a Texas court ruled in *Lewis v. Austin Independent School District*, 2003 Tex. App. Lexis 310, that an administrative law judge was not in a conflict of interest and therefore could still judge impartially even though she was once employed by the law firm that had previously represented the Austin Independent School District. The court reasoned that her prior employment with this law firm could have created a conflict of interest, but no such conflict existed because it was not shown or even contended that "the ALJ [administrative law judge] or her law firm were employed on or had knowledge of the controversy at issue here" (p. 13).

The Court in *Mississippi Valley* acknowledged that biased judgments, leading possibly to personal gain, can occur among even "the most well-meaning men." In so holding, the court answered the question posed by Plato, noted previously. Plato, of course, answered his own question in the *Republic*. He believed that the conflict-of-interest problem among governmental decisionmakers, at least the top-level administrators responsible for making important public policy decisions, could be eliminated by taking away all of their private property. Plato believed private property interests tended to corrupt governmental administration because they generated too much temptation.

Of course, Plato's solution to the conflict-of-interest problem in government would hardly be acceptable in a capitalist country such as the United States. However, U.S. lawmakers have realized that private property interests are at the root of the conflict-of-interest controversy because conflict-of-interest laws in this country are aimed primarily at preventing public servants from using their office to secure unethical and illegal economic advantages.

Specific examples of economic conflicts of interest are numerous. They are directed more at benefiting a public official personally than the public. Nonelected administrative officials, because they hold so much discretionary power and commonly serve out of the limelight, are likely to be exposed to the most tempting conflict-of-interest situations. The range of conflicts of interest among public administrators is so great that U.S. conflict-of-interest laws are not even aimed at eliminating all such instances, but only those that appear to pose potentially significant threats to fair and objective governmental decisionmaking.[7] It seems clear that all persons possess conflicts of interests of some kind in their jobs. For example, people of different religious and ethical beliefs work for public agencies in which they are entrusted with implementing public policies that may conflict with their beliefs (an emotional example is that of a pro-life advocate working for a public hospital that provides abortion services). In numerous decisions the courts have said that the government does not seek to regulate, through the conflict-of-interest laws, the role that public employees' religious or personal beliefs may play in their performance as governmental employees.[8] It seeks rather to regulate blatant conflict-of-interest situations, especially where unscrupulous administrative officials solicit favors of value in exchange for, to cite a few examples, (1) approving permits and licenses, (2) overlooking license violations, (3) awarding contracts or grants, (4) giving tax breaks, (5) not enforcing code violations, (6) releasing privileged information, (7) approving applications from aliens seeking permanent residency, and (8) granting any other special requests and privileges that would probably be denied on the basis of the facts by objective and honest administrative decisionmakers.

Conflict of interest problems have plagued government in America since its beginning. The first widespread scandal was the Yazoo Land Fraud of 1795 in Georgia. During the past few decades, disclosures of conflicts of interest have appeared frequently on the front pages of the newspapers. Watergate, involving numerous conflict-of-interest violations in the Nixon White House, was, of course, the most publicized governmental scandal of the 1970s. Conflict of interest scandals plagued Presidents Reagan and George H. W. Bush, involving the military, the Environmental Protection Agency, Housing and Urban Development, and the regulators of the savings and loan industry. Conflict-of-interest accusations regarding Whitewater plagued President Clinton's administration, while one of Clinton's aides was forced to resign after using a presidential helicopter to take him on a golf trip.

Of course, many conflicts of interest—especially what at least appear to be conflicts of interest—have surfaced during George W. Bush's presidency, involving elected officials, as high as the president and vice president, and governmental regulators closely connected to banking interests, securities, accounting firms, the oil industry, and large corporations in general. More specifically, Vice President Dick Cheney, former head of Halliburton, has had to deny conflicts of interest because of his close associations to oil interests, while Harvey Pitt was forced to resign as head of the Securities and Exchange Commission because his critics charged that he was simply incapable of regulating impartially the very industry that he once represented as an attorney. The *New York Times* reported that Harvey Pitt exhibited blatant conflict of interest as head of the SEC because, for one thing, "in the fall of 2001, at the outset of his tenure, Mr. Pitt told a prominent group of accountants that he once represented in private practice that he planned to reduce what he saw as the hostile tone of the agency toward the profession."[9] Pitt's conflicts of interest not only lowered the morale of SEC personnel but caused many Americans and investors to distrust the SEC, corporate financial reports, and the stock market in general. Pitt's conflicts of interest, along with others involving accounting practices of big corporations, contributed significantly to 63 percent of the Americans polled by Gallup between July 26 and 28, 2002 to say that they are "not too confident" (41 percent) or "not confident at all" (22 percent) that reports by accountants of a "corporation's financial situation" are accurate, while 71 percent felt that the way large corporations are audited need either a "complete overhaul" (28 percent) or "major reforms" (43 percent); only 22 percent said "minor reforms" and only an insignificant percentage (3 percent) responded that "no reforms" were needed.[10] Having focused on conflicts of interest at the national level, we should note that conflicts of interest in government have historically been worse on the local level.[11]

Official Attempts to Control Conflicts of Interest

Without much question, blatant conflicts of interest involving public employees were more prevalent decades ago, especially during the heyday of machine politics, but widespread publicity given to conflict-of-interest scandals in our media age has prompted renewed efforts by legislators, presidents, and rulemakers to squelch conflicts of interest in government. A few major efforts warrant mention. Federal conflicts-of-interest law (18 U.S.C.S., Section 201) as of 2003 states that anyone who

(1) directly or indirectly, corruptly gives, offers or promises anything of value to any public official or person who has been selected to be a public official to give anything of value to any other person or entity, with intent—
    (A) to influence any official act; or
    (B) to influence such public official or person who has been selected to be a public official to commit or aid in committing, or collude in, or allow, any fraud, or make opportunity for the commission of any fraud, on the United States; or
    (C) induce such public official or such person who has been selected to be a public official to do or omit to do any act in violation of the law or duty of such official or person;
(2) being a public official or person selected to be a public official, directly or indirectly, corruptly demands, seeks, receives, accepts, or agrees to receive or accept anything of value personally or for any other person or entity, in return for:
    (A) being influenced in the performance of any official act;
    (B) being influenced to commit or aid in committing, or to collude in, or allow, any fraud, or make opportunity for the commission of any fraud, on the United States; or

Harvey Pitt, watchdog

Source: Reprinted with permission of John Sherffius and the *St. Louis Post-Dispatch,* July 9, 2002.

 (C) being induced to do or omit to do any act in violation of the official duty of such official or person;

(3) directly or indirectly, corruptly gives, offers, or promises anything of value to any person, or offers or promises such person to give anything of value to any other person or entity, with intent to influence the testimony under oath or affirmation of such first-mentioned person as a witness upon a trial, hearing, or other commission, or officer authorized by the laws of the United States to hear evidence or take testimony, or with intent to influence such person to absent himself therefrom.

(4) directly or indirectly, corruptly demands, seeks, receives, accepts, or agrees to receive or accept anything of value personally or for any other person or entity in return for being influenced in testimony under oath or affirmation as a witness upon such trial, hearing, or other proceeding, or in return for absenting himself therefrom;

shall be fined under this title not more than three times the monetary equivalent of the thing of value, whichever is greater, or imprisoned for not more than fifteen years, or both, and may be disqualified from holding any office of honor, trust, or profit under the United States.

(c) Whoever

(1) otherwise than as provided by law for the proper discharge of official duty—
    (A) directly or indirectly gives, offers, or promises anything of value to any public official, former public official, or person selected to be a public official, for or because of any official act performed or to be performed by such public official, former public official, or person selected to be a public official; or
    (B) being a public official, former public official, or person selected to be a public official, otherwise than as provided by law for the proper discharge of official duty, directly or indirectly demands, seeks, receives, accepts, or agrees to receive or accept anything of value personally for or because of any official act performed or to be performed by such official or person;
(2) directly or indirectly gives, offers, or promises anything of value to any person, for or because of the testimony under oath or affirmation given by such person as a witness upon a trial, hearing, or other proceeding, before any court, any committee or either House of both Houses of Congress, or any agency, commission, or officer authorized by the laws of the United States to hear evidence or take testimony, or for or because of such person's absence therefrom;
(3) directly or indirectly demands, seeks, receives, accepts, or agrees to receive or accept anything of value personally for or because of the testimony under oath or affirmation given or to be given by such person as a witness upon any such trial, hearing, or other proceeding, or for or because of such person's absence therefrom;
(4) shall be fined under this title or imprisoned for not more than two years, or both.

During the Carter administration, the Ethics in Government Act was enacted.[12] This 1978 act was aimed primarily at restricting postemployment contacts between former top-level administrators now working in the private sector and their former agencies so as to reduce the revolving-door syndrome. Title 5 of this act makes it unlawful for former agency executives to *ever* try to influence any "particular matters" in the agency where they once were "personally and substantially" involved, either formally or informally. Other bans prohibit them from getting involved in certain matters for one-to-two-year periods after they have left their particular agency. The act also includes financial disclosure provisions for all employees classified GS-16 and higher in order to guard against blatant economic conflicts of interest. However, under the act, former employees may appear and participate in business matters before their former agencies as long as their business does not involve the "particular matters" excluded by the act and as long as the former employees are not subject to the one-to-two-year bans precluding employees from engaging in any business dealings with the agency. And since the act applies only to the particular former employee, it does not prevent a business associate of the former employee from dealing with his or her former agency; nor does it stop the former agency employee, once his or her one- or two-year ban has expired, from *assisting* a business associate in dealings with the former agency, even when they concern "particular matters" (ah—there's the loophole!).

In 1987 Michael K. Deaver, a friend and former aide to President Ronald Reagan, became, after a special prosecutor's investigation, the first high-ranking White House official to face criminal charges under the Ethics in Government Act. The investigation evidently disclosed that Deaver had violated conflict-of-interest provisions of the Ethics in Government Act, especially by making contacts with top White House officials, including President Reagan, on behalf of his clients less than one year after leaving the White House on January 4, 1985.[13] The Deaver case stimulated thought on the usefulness of the Ethics in Government Act. That is, it must be made clear that ironically, after the special prosecutor's office spent 4,200 work days on the Deaver investigation, Special Prosecutor Whitney Seymour, Jr., was unable to convince the grand jury to indict Deaver on violations of the act. He had to settle for two counts of perjury. According to rumors from the special prosecutor's office, "loose" provisions under the act made it difficult to obtain indictments on specific violations. To William Safire, a noted Washington columnist, this strongly suggests that the Ethics in Government Act has no teeth and in the future the act would prove feeble in deterring influence peddling.[14] Safire's insight proved prophetic. In 1989 Congress tried to strengthen the 1978 Ethics Act by passing the Government Ethics Reform Act. This Ethics Reform Act (1) limited outside income for members of Congress and noncareer executive branch officials, (2) placed greater restrictions upon postemployment lobbying activities, (3) created uniform acceptance rules pertaining to gifts, (4) established stricter financial disclosure laws, and (5) authorized significant salary increases for high executive branch officials and House members, presumably to reduce the reliance on outside income that too often engendered conflicts of interest that tend to undermine the public interest.

The Ethics in Government Act of 1978 was controversial from the start, mostly because it created an Office of the Independent Counsel with practically unbridled powers to conduct lengthy and very costly investigations of high-ranking governmental officials, including the president. The independent counsel provision was created in response to the "Saturday night massacre" during the Watergate investigation of President Nixon, when two attorneys general resigned because they refused to fire Special Prosecutor Archibald Cox, whom Nixon wanted removed because Cox was pressing relentlessly forward in his investigation of the president. But according to critics such as George Washington Law School professor Mary Cheh, the independent counsel law created "a constitutional gremlin unleashed to work in behalf of the president's opponents."[15] Most Republicans, Democrats, and the public eventually called for an end to this law, which by its "death" on June 30, 1999, had cost taxpayers $150 million for twenty-one investigations, including those of the Iran-contra affair during the Reagan and George H. W. Bush administrations and endless probes into Whitewater, Travelgate, and the Lewinsky affair during the Clinton presidency. Only seven convictions, some fairly minor, were obtained during the Independent

Counsel Act's twenty-one-year history at a "bargain" price of only $21.4 million per conviction.[16]

Most of the provisions in the Ethics in Government Act remain, and they will probably help to prevent conflicts of interest and other unethical and illegal acts by lower-level public officials, especially by having a "chilling effect" on any who contemplate unethical conduct. However, the demise of the independent counsel provision, returning responsibility for official misbehavior to the Department of Justice, should raise concern because of the obvious structural conflicts of interest that this creates. It is for this reason that some observers believe that the independent counsel law should have been amended, not abandoned completely, because now we still are faced with the same problems of trying to hold high public officials ethically accountable as we faced during the Watergate era, although some scholars question whether laws can bring ethics to government anyway.[17]

Executive orders have also been used in attempts to improve ethics in governmental service. President Lyndon B. Johnson's Executive Order 11222, known as "Standards of Ethical Conduct for Government Officers and Employees," states: "Where government is based on the consent of the governed, every citizen is entitled to have complete confidence in the integrity of his government. Each individual officer, employee, or advisor of government must help to earn and must honor that trust by his own integrity and conduct in all official actions" (Section 201).[18] (This order was revised by President Richard Nixon's Executive Order 11590.)[19] The Johnson order also prohibits any governmental official or adviser from soliciting or accepting in either a direct or indirect manner "any gift, gratuity, favor, entertainment, loan, or any other thing of monetary value, from any person, corporation, or group which—(1) has, or is seeking to obtain, contractual or other business or financial relationships with his agency; (2) conducts operations or activities which are regulated by his agency; or (3) has interests which may be substantially affected by the performance or nonperformance of his official duty" (Section 201[a]). Under Section 201(b), agencies, with the approval of the Civil Service Commission, are allowed to make exceptions to the requirements of Section 201(a) as long as they are "necessary and appropriate in view of the nature of their agency's work and the duties of their employees."

Because of the unique regulatory situation of some agencies, agency rulemakers have promulgated rules directed at preventing conflicts of interest among their employees. Some of these conflict-of-interest regulations appear stricter than the general federal statutes. Enabling legislation that gives birth to the agency may contain provisions focusing on conflicts of interest that would probably be peculiar to the agency. For example, as of 2003, federal trade commissioners are not permitted to engage "in any other business, vocation, or employment" (15 U.S.C., Section 41).

The Effectiveness of Conflict-of-Interest Prohibitions

Conflict-of-interest statutes, executive orders, and agency rules generally call for severe punishments for those governmental employees found guilty of violating conflict-of-interest prohibitions. Punishments range from stiff fines and lengthy prison sentences to simple removal from office. Overall, conflict-of-interest laws appear to be comprehensive, clear, and well written. Few loopholes can be found, and the courts have generally given strong support to their usefulness. Therefore, if public employees in fact read and believed the documents stating that violators would be discovered and punished, the completeness and forcefulness of the conflict-of-interest provisions would surely scare employees into dutiful compliance.

But the problem is that the conflict-of-interest bark has historically been much greater than its bite. What is worse is that many public employees are not very frightened by this dog anymore. The truth is that conflict-of-interest laws are virtually impossible to enforce unless governmental employees flagrantly violate them. Elaborate, time-consuming, and expensive schemes to catch those who are using their public office for such personal gains as payoffs (e.g., the Deaver case) have demonstrated how difficult it is to catch and prosecute those who have violated conflict-of-interest prohibitions. From a systems perspective, the additional time and costs to the political system would probably preclude the guilty employee's being prosecuted and punished in full accordance with the law.

In sum, laws can remain effective only as long as they are feared. Because conflict-of-interest laws are difficult to enforce, they should not be perceived as the most effective instruments for combating unethical and illegal employee conduct. Most critics feel that in the final analysis, honorable public employee behavior must be motivated from within. From Confucius and Plato to more modern democratic theorists such as Thomas Jefferson, the thinking has been that a person's inner attitudes toward governance, not conflict-of-interest or other similar statutes, provide the best guidance for proper conduct. The National Academy of Public Administration's report quotes a 1785 letter to Peter Carr, in which Thomas Jefferson wrote: "Whenever you are to do a thing, though it can never be known but to yourself, ask yourself how you would act were all the world looking at you, and act accordingly."[20] To obtain responsible behavior in governmental administration, it is necessary to place less emphasis on restrictive laws and more emphasis on the early ethical training of children, on conveying the importance of upholding ethical standards in professional degree programs where future public servants are educated, and on careful public service recruitment. All this is much easier to advocate than to accomplish.

CONGRESSIONAL INFLUENCE PEDDLING

Clearly, legislators have a right to try to influence the directions of the administrative branch. The Constitution, especially in Article I, Section 8, clearly provides certain formal and informal powers to Congress so it can exert its influence in shaping the administrative system. When legislators act within these constitutionally sanctioned powers, no ethical or legal problems emerge. But too often legislators believe that they own administrators and thus can manipulate the administrative process in any way they see fit to accomplish their goals. The famed

Speaker of the House Sam Rayburn made this point crystal clear when he embraced Newton Minow, who had just been appointed to the Federal Communications Commission, and said to him: "Just remember one thing, son. Your agency is an arm of the Congress; you belong to us. Remember that and you'll be all right."[21] There is a sense in which Rayburn could not have been more wrong. Although it is necessary to recall Rayburn's immense success and longevity in office and the vast numbers of legislators who have emulated him, if the constitutional checks-and-balances system rooted in the separation-of-powers doctrine is to function properly, other governmental branches must remain relatively independent of one another. In short, influence peddling among the governmental branches must have its limits.

There are proper and improper ways for legislators to influence administrative actions. Authorized methods for shaping and controlling administrative behavior include legislating enabling statutes that include policy and procedural guidelines, confirming key administrative appointments, making appropriations, investigating agency activities, and using other such orthodox techniques that the Constitution regards as necessary and proper legislative intrusions in administrative business. But fortunately, this constitutionally democratic system frowns upon congressional attempts to influence administrative decisions in unethical ways and outlaws congressional influence peddling that is, besides being flatly dishonest, in blatant violation of separation-of-powers mandates.

Illegal legislative influence peddling before administrative agencies is rather easy to define, understand, and analyze; but it is very difficult to pinpoint what constitutes such action. Consequently, those who are determined to stop legislators from using unethical means to influence administrators are frustrated. Using bribes, blackmail, and physical threats to motivate administrators to make them comply with a legislator's will are clearly illegal criminal acts that are prohibited by criminal and administrative law statutes. But virtually all other legislative methods for pressuring administrators to meet the demands of legislators fall into a huge gray area where it is frequently very difficult to distinguish illegal from unethical acts and unethical acts from those that are acceptable within the democratic rules of the game.[22]

Influence Peddling as Part of Representative Democracy

These gray areas are of considerable interest. In the first place, it should be recognized that in the U.S. democratic system, politics plays a crucial role in governmental decisionmaking. Nothing in this open political system prohibits legislators or other politicians from representing the interests of their constituents. Indeed, as delegates of their constituencies, they have a democratic commitment to represent their concerns and to try to fight for their interests. In the words of former senator Paul Douglas (D.–Ill.), the American people "distrust and dislike a self-perpetuating bureaucracy, because they believe that ultimately it will not reflect the best interest of the people. They therefore turn to their elected representatives to protect their legitimate interests in their relation-ship with the public administrators."[23]

What is wrong, then, with legislators who want to do the best job they can to represent in Washington those interests that were primarily responsible for send-ing them to Congress? Why shouldn't they persuade administrators to make deci-sions that help promote the welfare of their constituents? Is anything wrong with the following attitude by former senator Mike Mansfield (D.–Mont.): "I would be remiss in my duty if I did not try to do for my constituents everything I possi-bly could to comply with their legitimate requests. I certainly think this is a part of the job of being a Senator."[24] The answer is that probably nothing is wrong with legislative influence peddling as long as it does not undermine ethical and constitutional principles of due process and equal protection and as long as legis-lators represent their entire constituency fairly. In theory at least, this sort of rep-resentative democracy makes sense.

In practice, unfortunately, legislative influence peddling commonly falls far short of the normative standards set forth in the ideal model of representative democracy. In reality, the motives of the legislators may not be as innocent and noble as implied by the previous quotations. Too much evidence exists to suggest that sometimes legislators seek to influence administrative action for the most selfish and irresponsible reasons. That is, some legislators must obey the com-mands of special interests (for example, the oil industry) because they owe their past electoral success and their continued political survival to them. Retired sena-tor Thomas F. Eagleton (D.–Mo.) has charged that control over congresspersons by special interests, especially as a result of campaign contributions, has become an ever increasing democratic accountability concern, as the costs of political campaigns continue to skyrocket.[25] Of course, campaign finance reform has been pushed to rectify this accountability problem, but as of 2004 still no campaign fi-nance reform measures have been passed that have been effective in stopping the influence of special interests in political campaigns.

How gray are the democratic ethics of a situation in which legislators selfishly peddle influence before administrative agencies as loyal lobbyists for special inter-ests, not as representatives striving to serve their constituents' general welfare? For instance between 1964 and 1969 Russell Long, a Democrat and "oil senator" from Louisiana, had a $1,196,015 income from oil interests. Of that amount, $329,151 was nontaxable because of the oil depletion allowance in tax laws Long helped to write and push through Congress as chairman of the mighty Senate Finance Com-mittee.[26] But in lobbying for the oil interests before administrative officials and his fellow congresspersons, Long did not believe he was peddling influence in a man-ner that denied his constituents equal representation, because he equated oil inter-ests with the general interests of the people of Louisiana. Nor did he perceive any conflict of interest between his oil holdings and his role as a senator.[27]

Congressional influence peddling assumes many forms, and it is sometimes very difficult to judge, and especially to prove, whether it is carried out in the best interests of a legislator's constituency or not. To achieve their objectives, legislators have on occasion misused congressional committees, have purposely seen to it that legislation is vague and filled with loopholes, have misused their investigatory powers to harass and threaten administrators, have made unethical and sometimes illegal ex parte contacts with administrators to promote special interest causes, and have used other means to manipulate the administrative process.[28] In so doing, they have violated the separation-of-powers doctrine by getting involved in matters that should be decided by administrative experts, not by politicians. A 1979 report by Ralph Nader argued that congressional partisan politics has made a shambles out of administrative decisionmaking, especially in the Federal Trade Commission (the focus of the report): "Even more destructive to the sense of purpose and nonpolitical ideals of the Commission are the Congressional politics that permeate it. Congressional pressures have made nonsense of priorities for action which related only in theory to the importance of the social issue involved."[29] The 1993 Gore Report concluded similarly that professional, efficient administration is too often compromised by illegitimate influence peddling.[30] Legitimately or not, it was widely reported in 2002 that the Bush administration was blatantly encouraging special interests representing big business energy executives (coal, gas, oil, and nuclear power) to peddle influence, with the help of key congressional supporters, among energy administration officials, compromising national energy policy in the public interest by leaving "environmentalists and consumers out of its national energy equation." Accurately or not, the Bush administration was portrayed as being "preoccupied with big oil, big business, and influence peddling."[31]

The Courts on Congressional Meddling in the Administrative Process

Some legislators use their personal legislative powers to cajole, harass, and pressure administrators in other ways in an attempt to win administrative decisions favorable to the special interests to which they owe their political careers. But Congress as a whole may also occasionally overstep its constitutional powers in an effort to influence specific administrative action. The systems model of the administrative system vividly conveys that certain demands other than the constitutional kind place pressures on legislators that help mold their perceptions and decisions. Thus, the decisions of legislators are on occasion motivated by their personal convictions. These may be particularly rooted in their religious and nationalistic beliefs, in their sense that special circumstances warrant such decisions, or possibly in a feeling that modern demands justify particular action. But when legislative decisions are motivated by such forces, frequently the actions are found to be unconstitutional by the courts.

It can be said at the outset that the courts have often permitted Congress to intervene in the business of public administrators. Judging from what has been said in court decisions over the years, especially since the 1930s, one might say the courts perceive Congress as the creator and caretaker of the administrative ma-

'You Don't Mind If I Look Over Your Shoulder, Do You?'

Source: Reprinted with permission of Tom Engelhardt and the *St. Louis Post-Dispatch,* March 26, 1982.

chinery. Consequently, the courts have allowed Congress to do what it believes is necessary and proper in regard to delegating power to administrators and even judges. In general, in the past half century the courts have not ruled that a sharp separation of powers should exist between the administrative branch and its creator, the Congress. However, in recent years, the Supreme Court has occasionally surprised the legal community by employing a rather strict interpretation of the separation-of-powers doctrine to prevent Congress from encroaching on the administrative branch (*INS v. Chadha*, 462 U.S. 919 [1983]; *Bowsher v. Synar*, 106 S.Ct. 3181 [1986]; *Metropolitan Washington Airports Auth. v. Citizens*, 111 S.Ct. 2298 [1991]; and *Clinton v. City of New York*, 524 U.S. 417 [1998]). Despite the high court's occasional rulings that apparently endorse a rather strict application of the separation of powers doctrine, the Supreme Court's prevailing position supports a flexible, shared-powers doctrine as exemplified in *Mistretta v. U.S.*, 109 S.Ct. 647 (1989); *Touby v. U.S.*, 111 S.Ct. 1752 (1991); and *Whitman v. American Trucking Association*, 121 S.Ct. 903 (2001). In *Mistretta*, for example, the Court argued that James Madison had a "flexible approach to separation of powers" because he rejected, as did the Framers in general, "the notion that the three Branches be entirely separate and distinct" (p. 659). Consequently, the court held in *Mistretta* that Congress did not violate the separation-of-powers doctrine when it established a Sentencing Commission in which sentencing power is shared by federal judges and nonjudges.[32]

Congressional Influence Peddling from the Perspective of Legislative and Administrative Roles: *D.C. Federation of Civic Associations v. Volpe.*   *D.C. Federation of Civic Associations v. Volpe,* 459 F.2d 1231 (1972), is an excellent case for understanding how the courts view the different roles played by legislators and administrators in the U.S. political system, especially in light of their roles as political actors under the influence of virtually omnipresent political pressures.[33] In this case, the U.S. Court of Appeals for the District of Columbia Circuit essentially held that legislators are free to exert strong, persuasive political pressure on administrative officials—short, of course, of illegal pressure—but administrators are not free to yield to such political influence when making administrative decisions.

The *Volpe* case involved a situation in which Representative William Natcher (D.–Ky.), then an influential member of the House Appropriations Committee and the District of Columbia subcommittee, threatened Secretary of Transportation John Volpe with withholding funds for a much needed District of Columbia subway transit system unless Volpe approved the construction of the proposed Three Sisters Bridge. Because the proposed bridge would affect the Georgetown Historic District and would also use part of Overton Park, Volpe was required by statute to carry out an environmental impact study to determine the extent to which the building of the bridge would harm the historic site and parkland (23 U.S.C.A., Section 138). However, in the absence of any environmental impact data or any record (a record is required by the APA, Sections 556 and 557), Volpe bowed to the political pressures of Representative Natcher and his supporters and announced on August 12, 1969, that he had approved the construction of the proposed Three Sisters Bridge. The case presents two interesting questions. First, could Representative Natcher, playing the role of a legislator, legally exert such political pressure on an agency administrator? Second, could Volpe, playing the role of an agency administrator, allow his decision to be influenced by political pressures?

In the first place, agreeing with the district court's findings, Chief Judge Bazelon, writing for the appellate court, acknowledged "that the pressure exerted by Representative Natcher and others did have an impact on Secretary Volpe's decision to approve the bridge" (p. 1246).[34] Despite the strong political pressures placed on Volpe by Natcher, the court did not find that Natcher acted beyond the scope of his powers as a congressman. Evidently, the court viewed such influence peddling as a natural function of the political process: "To avoid any misconceptions about the nature of our holding, we emphasize that we have not found— nor, for that matter, have we sought—any suggestion of impropriety or illegality in the actions of Representative Natcher and others who strongly advocate the bridge. They are surely entitled to their own views on the need for the Three Sisters Bridge, and we indicate no opinion on their authority to exert pressure on Secretary Volpe" (p. 1249). It is important to note, however, that if the court believed that Volpe was acting in a quasi-judicial capacity in reaching his decision on the bridge, as contrasted to a legislative-administrative capacity, Representative Natcher's ex parte communications (contacts) with Volpe would likely have been condemned by the court since the court earlier noted (p. 1246) that such influence peddling was prohibited in *Sangamon Valley Television Corp. v. United States,* 106 U.S. App. D.C. 30 (1959). (Later the D.C. circuit court condemned ex parte contacts with quasi-judicial officials in *Professional Air Traffic Controllers Organization v. Federal Labor Relations Authority,* 685 F.2d 547 [1982].)

The court held, however, that Volpe, as an administrator bound by statutory obligations, could not let his decisions be swayed by political considerations. In testifying before the district court, Volpe asserted that his "decision was based on the merits of the project and not *solely* on the extraneous political influence" (p. 1246). However, Judge Bazelon ruled that Volpe's decision must be made "strictly on the merits and completely without regard to any consideration not made relevant by Congress in the applicable statutes" (p. 1246). The court did acknowledge that the error in decisionmaking would have been "more flagrant, of course, if the Secretary had based his decision solely on the pressures generated by Representative Natcher. But it should be clear that his action would not be immunized merely because he also considered some relevant factors" (p. 1248). Bazelon believed such political pressures were not intended by Congress to be considered in reaching such decisions (p. 1247). However, the court confused its decision somewhat by noting that if Volpe's action had been *purely* legislative, the court might have reached a different conclusion. Judge Bazelon perceived Volpe's decision as one involving a mixture of legislative, judicial, and administrative functions.

It is worth noting that in *United States ex rel. Parco v. Morris,* 426 F.Supp. 976 (1977), District Court Judge Becker, citing Bazelon's decision in the *Volpe* case, ruled against petitioners, who maintained that an administrator's decision should not stand because it violated the separation-of-powers doctrine since it rested on a congressman's influential recommendation. But Judge Becker emphasized that his holding was consistent with Bazelon's decision, because here the administrator was performing a purely legislative act, thus making it irrelevant that the administrative decision may have been motivated by a legislator's weighty recommendation. In so holding, Becker noted that "when the agency action is purely 'legislative,' as in the informal rulemaking involved here, the decision 'cannot be invalidated merely because the . . . action was motivated by impermissible considerations' any more than can that of a legislature" (p. 982). Furthermore, Judge Becker found "no Constitutional violation in a Congressional attempt to influence the regulatory interpretation of statutes. Interrogation of agency officials at Congressional hearings often serves such a purpose and is part of the give and take of democratic government. We think that the contention the Parcos seek to raise is really one of administrative law, i.e., that an agency decision may be invalid if induced by secret or otherwise improper influence" (p. 982).

The *Volpe* decision still stands as law today. More recently, in *Town of Norfolk v. U.S. Army Corps of Engineers*, 968 F.2d 1438 (1st Cir. 1992), the First Circuit court relied heavily upon *Volpe* in upholding a controversial decision by the Army Corps of Engineers pertaining to discharge of fill at an artificial wetland site. Reflecting on the *Volpe* case, the court in *Town of Norfolk* condemned Volpe's reliance on the political influence peddled by Representative Natcher, concluding that "the defects in the Secretary's decision in *Volpe* were colossal, including his failure to compile an administrative record" (p. 1459).

To conclude, it should be stressed that the courts since *Volpe* have been insisting that administrators reach decisions on the basis of the merits and in the context of a written, reviewable record even indicating the date and nature of any ex parte contacts. Judges note that agency decisionmaking cannot be reviewed properly unless a meaningful, complete record is kept. A comprehensive record would show the role played by political influence peddling in agency decisionmaking.

The Limitations of the Speech or Debate Clause. The speech or debate clause found in Article I, Section 6(1), of the U.S. Constitution grants certain liberties to congresspersons in their role as legislators, but some congresspersons have on occasion abused these liberties to meddle in the administrative process. When this has happened, the courts have objected. The Constitution is very vague as to exactly how the speech or debate clause should be applied to legislators. All that is written is that "Senators and Representatives . . . for any speech or debate in either House . . . shall not be questioned in any other place." However, court opinions have clarified its meaning. In *Gravel v. United States,* 408 U.S. 606 (1972), the Supreme Court contended that the speech or debate clause "was designed to assure a coequal branch of the government wide freedom of speech, debate and deliberation without intimidation or threats from the Executive Branch. It thus protects members against prosecutions that directly impinge upon or threaten the legislative process" (p. 616). But the Court was quick to point out that senators and representatives are not protected in acts that are nonlegislative in nature. That is, wrote Justice Byron White, "members of Congress are constantly in touch with the Executive Branch of the Government and with administrative agencies—they may cajole, and exhort with respect to the administration of a federal statute—but such conduct, though generally done, is not protected legislative activity" (p. 625). The purpose of the clause, White argued, is not to protect legislators who try to influence agency decisions. Rather, it is to protect normal legislative functions or those "deliberative and communicative processes by which . . . [congresspersons] participate in committee and [congressional] proceedings with respect to the consideration and passage or rejection of proposed legislation or with respect to other matters which the Constitution places within the jurisdiction of either House" (p. 625). Only on rare occasions have the courts extended the scope of the speech or debate clause, Justice White noted, but then only out of an effort to preserve necessary legislative proceedings. This clause, according to the 1972 Court, gives immunity to legislators and their aides in regard to speech, voting, and various other legislative functions, but it does not permit legislators or their assistants "to violate an otherwise valid criminal law in preparing for or implementing legislative acts" (p. 622).

In *United States v. Brewster,* 408 U.S. 501 (1972), the Supreme Court rejected Senator Daniel B. Brewster's argument that he should be immune from prosecution on bribery charges because he was protected from prosecution under the speech or debate clause. Specifically, Brewster was charged with soliciting and accepting a bribe in exchange for promising to carry out a legislative function that would violate federal law. But Chief Justice Warren Burger, evidently outraged by such an abuse of the speech or debate clause, wrote: "The immunities of the Speech or Debate Clause were not written into the Constitution simply for the personal or private benefit of Members of Congress, but to protect the integrity of the legislative process" (p. 507). Burger emphasized that the clause applies only to "those things 'generally done in a session in the House by one of its members in relation to the business before it,' . . . or things 'said or done by him as a representative, in the exercise of the functions of that office'" (p. 512). Burger noted that the clause does not extend immunity to those acts that cannot be considered proper functions of the legislative process, but its purpose is certainly not "to make Members of Congress super-citizens, immune from criminal responsibility" (p. 516). The Speech or Debate Clause immunity privilege, Burger concluded, is "broad enough to insure the historic independence of the Legislative Branch, essential to our separation of powers, but narrow enough to guard against the excesses of those who would corrupt the process by corrupting its members . . . taking a bribe is, obviously, no part of the legislative process or function; it is not a legislative act" (p. 526).

In recent cases, the courts have built upon *Gravel* and *Brewster* to expand the scope of qualified immunity for legislators under the speech or debate clause so as to immunize "members of Congress against both criminal and civil liability based on their legislative conduct, whether the action is for prospective relief or damages" (*Montgomery County v. Schooley,* 627 A.2d 69, 74 [Md. App. 1993]). Clearly, the key is to determine the boundaries of legislative conduct because there is legal precedent now to protect legislators from being held liable for criminal acts if somehow the conduct can be construed as "within the sphere of legitimate legislative activity" (p. 75). The Second Circuit Court of Appeals in *X-Men, Inc. v. Pataki,* 196 F3d 56, emphatically upheld *Gravel* in 1999, arguing that political communications by legislators may not be purely legislative in nature, yet such communications are still "'entirely legitimate' acts . . . performed in the legislator's 'official' capacity'" (p. 69). Hopefully, the courts in the future will not find forms of illegal influence peddling by legislators before our public administrators, such as bribery, conduct that is within the scope of "legitimate legislative activity."[35]

The Use and Misuse of Loyalty Oaths. Basically, loyalty oaths have been used to force individuals to disavow certain associations, beliefs, and principles. Although the use of loyalty oaths at the national and state levels has been on a general decline in recent times because of many serious legal challenges to their constitutionality, they nevertheless have a long history in America, being first employed to compel allegiance during the Revolutionary War.[36] They were also used extensively during the Civil War and during the Red Scare of the 1920s. During the 1940s and 1950s, in response to Cold War mania, people were forced to sign loyalty oaths in exchange for privileges such as government jobs, swearing that they did not advocate the violent overthrow of the American government or belong to any organization that did. Some loyalty oaths, especially at the state and local levels, were directed more toward making people disavow any attachment to communism.

The general purpose of the loyalty oath in public personnel practices is to ensure that governmental employees, paid out of the public treasury, will not use their employment to undermine the American government. Various loyalty and security programs have been used in conjunction with loyalty oaths since 1947 in an effort to purge the government of disloyal persons who pose unnecessary security risks. For example, in 1947 President Harry S. Truman, in initiating a federal government security program, ordered that governmental workers be dismissed if evidence existed that cast doubt on their loyalty. This security program applied to governmental employees as well as to many quasi-governmental workers (employees working for private companies under government contract). It is of special interest to students of administrative law that the various governmental security programs allowed discharged persons the right of appeal yet did not always permit them to confront and challenge the sources of the incriminating evidence.

During the late 1940s and early 1950s, the misuse of loyalty oaths and security programs reached its peak. The word *McCarthyism* symbolizes the shame of this era in American history, an era in which real or imagined Communist threats caused some of our government leaders to place on the back burner the constitutional principles that they claimed they wanted to preserve. The leader behind this movement was Senator Joseph R. McCarthy (R.–Wis.), a man who recklessly charged numerous public employees and private citizens with being Communists without being able to substantiate the charges. (McCarthy, by the way, used the speech or debate clause's immunity privilege to protect himself from lawsuits.) But Americans who were more truly American than McCarthy finally brought the senator down. However, this is not to suggest that traces of McCarthyism do not still persist. Eventually, McCarthy was charged by his Senate colleagues with acting in a manner unbecoming a senator. On December 2, 1954, a special Senate committee officially condemned his conduct in two senatorial committees. With that, Senator McCarthy, as a major force, faded rapidly.

But before this, even the courts tended to uphold the constitutionality of very questionable loyalty oaths and security programs. For example, in 1951, in *Garner v. Board of Public Works,* 341 U.S. 716, the Supreme Court ruled that compelling prospective public employees to sign a non-Communist affidavit constituted a reasonable public employment prerequisite. In 1952, in *Adler v. Board of Education,* 342 U.S. 485, the high court held that a state law can be used to disqualify from public service employment any person who advocates the overthrow of the American government by violence or any other illegal means or is a member of any organization that advocates such. Three years after the Senate censured Senator McCarthy, the Supreme Court began a dramatic reversal of its previous position. In *Yates v. United States,* 354 U.S. 298 (1957), a case which did not directly involve loyalty oaths, the Court, drastically modifying its decision in *Dennis v. United States,* 341 U.S. 494 (1951), ruled that a distinction must be recognized between believing in something versus acting upon those beliefs. The *Yates* ruling had immediate practical significance for those who had held that forcing people to take loyalty oaths violated the First Amendment guarantees of freedom of speech, association, and assembly. Because the *Yates* decision in effect requested that a "clear and present danger" should be established between beliefs and the threatening use of these beliefs (for example, acting on Communist beliefs by trying to violently overthrow the American government), it now became very difficult for the government to require loyalty oaths that essentially asked if prospective governmental employees or those in public employment advocated the violent overthrow of the American government or belonged to any organizations that did.

Beginning with *Speiser v. Randall,* 357 U.S. 513 (1958), the Supreme Court, under Chief Justice Earl Warren, handed down a series of decisions aimed at eliminating the unconstitutional use of loyalty oaths. In *Speiser* the Court ruled, in a related matter, that loyalty test oaths could not be required as a condition for obtaining government benefits. In *Baggett v. Bullitt,* 377 U.S. 360 (1964), the Supreme Court struck down a loyalty oath because it was too vague. In 1966 in *Elfbrandt v. Russell,* 384 U.S. 11, the Warren Court overruled the 1951 *Garner* decision by holding that a state loyalty oath that forbade state employees becoming Communist Party members was unconstitutional on the grounds that the law was not related to specific illegal actions and, in addition, was rooted in the unconstitutional doctrine of guilt by association. The *Elfbrandt* case established that loyalty oaths may not abridge First Amendment freedoms. A year later, in *Keyishian v. Board of Regents of New York,* 385 U.S. 589 (1967), the Warren Court struck down a loyalty-security law directed at disqualifying from state governmental employment any person who advocated the overthrow of the government by force or by any other illegal means or belonged to any association that did. In overturning the 1952 *Adler* holding, the Court in *Keyishian* determined that such loyalty-security laws violated First Amendment protections guaranteeing persons freedom of speech and association. In *Keyishian,* the Court stressed that a person should not be expected to give up his or her constitutional rights to obtain government employment.

However, the unpopular Vietnam War, chaotic student demonstrations, violent minority protest movements, and other such occurrences identified with the 1960s evidently caused a conservative shift in the electorate, which apparently helped Richard Nixon reach the White House. Within a few years, given his unusual opportunity to appoint so many justices to the high court, President Nixon turned the relatively liberal Warren Court into the relatively conservative Burger Court. Before long the new Court started reversing some earlier Warren Court decisions. In regard to loyalty oaths, for example, the Burger Court shocked many constitutional and administrative law experts by upholding, in *Cole v. Richardson,* 405 U.S. 676 (1972), a Massachusetts loyalty oath that required state employees to swear that they would "uphold and defend the Constitution of the United States of America and the Constitution of the Commonwealth of Massachusetts" and would "oppose the overthrow of the government of the United States of America or of this Commonwealth by force, violence, or by any illegal or unconstitutional method" (p. 677). As to the first requirement of the oath, the Court held that the oath, similar to the oaths required by the U.S. Constitution in Article II, Section 1, Clause 7 (applicable to the president) and Article VI, Clause 3 (applicable to federal and state public officials) is constitutional because it simply asks "for an acknowledgement of a willingness to abide by 'constitutional processes of government'" (p. 682). In writing the decision, Burger reasoned that a state oath "need not parrot the exact language of the constitutional oaths to be constitutionally proper" (p. 682). Regarding the more controversial part of the Massachusetts loyalty oath, which required an employee to swear that he or she "will oppose the overthrow of the government of the United States of America or of this Commonwealth by force, violence, or by any illegal or unconstitutional method," the Court found that such was a reasonable extension of the first part of the oath, requiring only that Massachusetts public employees were "willing to commit themselves to live by the constitutional process of our system" (p. 682). The oath did not, Burger argued, "require specific action in some hypothetical or actual situation" (p. 683).

Furthermore, the Court held that the oath was sufficiently clear and thus could not be overturned on the grounds that it was too vague, as had been the situation in the 1964 *Baggett* case, 377 U.S. 360. Also, the Court recognized that since no evidence existed to show that the oath had been used to harass public employees since its enactment in 1948 (in fact, nobody had been prosecuted under the oath), there existed no real cause to exaggerate its role. If the oath had been employed to harass public employees, Burger noted, the Court would have been confronted with a different issue. However, despite some rulings in which courts have upheld rather inconsequential loyalty oaths, the federal courts in the past few decades have struck down virtually all loyalty oaths of any significance (for example, loyalty oaths as a condition for public employment, union membership, "certain professions," or running for public office or qualifying as new political party).[37]

Using Bills of Attainder and Ex Post Facto Laws to Punish Administrators. In drafting the Constitution, the Founders gave broad powers to the legislative branch, apparently because they believed that if tyrannical power were to emerge within a branch, it would most likely be in the administrative branch, not within an assembly, where so many voices are heard. In *Fletcher v. Peck,* 6 Cranch 87, 136 (1810), the Court noted that though this reasoning might be valid, Congress was "not so numerous as to be incapable of pursuing the objects of its passions," and thus "barriers had to be erected to ensure that the legislature would not overstep the bounds of its authority and perform the functions of the other departments." Accordingly, the constitutional framers, among other restrictions they imposed on congressional power, prohibited the U.S. Congress and state legislatures from legislating any bills of attainder or ex post facto laws: "No bill of attainder or ex post facto law shall be passed" (Article I, Section 9, Clause 3).[38]

But what is a bill of attainder? An ex post facto law? Simply, a **bill of attainder** is a legislative act directed toward an individual that pronounces the person guilty of an offense without the benefit of due process procedures (a trial). But in *Springfield Armory, Inc. v. City of Columbus*, 805 F. Supp. 489, 493 (S.D. Ohio 1992), the Ohio court noted that "a legislative act does not automatically violate the prohibition against bills of attainder merely because it places some burden upon an identified individual or group. That is, specificity alone does not establish that a law is an unconstitutional bill of attainder. Rather, the burden imposed by the legislature must constitute punishment." Historically, bills of attainder were directed at serious offenses, especially treason, with sentences usually resulting in death. Milder forms of bills of attainder, not resulting in death sentences, are known as *bills of pains and penalties,* but both forms are strictly prohibited by the Constitution *(Losier v. Sherman,* 157 Kans. 153; 138 F.2d 272 [1943]). If legislators had the power to employ bills of attainder to convict persons of crimes, such power would encroach upon the rightful powers of the judiciary, thereby undermining the democratic forces believed to exist in the separation-of-powers doctrine. In *Fletcher v. Peck,* the Court asserted that "the Bill of Attainder Clause not only was intended as one implementation of the general principle of fractionalized power, but also reflected the Framers' belief that the Legislative Branch is not so well suited as politically independent judges and juries to the task of ruling upon the blameworthiness of, and levying appropriate punishment upon, specific persons" (6 Cranch 87, 136). The constitutional ban on bills of attainder has generally been considered essential to the preservation of liberty. The Supreme Court in 2000, upholding the wisdom of the framers of the U.S. Constitution, reiterated how essential to "every principle of sound legislation" prohibiting bills of attainder are to preserving "liberty and republicanism" (*Carmell v. Texas*, 120 S.Ct. 1620).

But the constitutional prohibition of ex post facto laws has likewise been regarded as absolutely necessary to the promotion of liberty and justice in a free society. In banning the use of ex post facto legislation, the constitutional framers guaranteed that a person would be able to perform activities that are not prohibited by existing laws without the fear of being punished under new laws at sometime in the future. In *People of U.S. ex rel. Umbenhowar v. McDonnell,* 11 F.Supp. 1014, 1015 (1934), the court defined an **ex post facto law** as "one which renders an act punishable in a manner in which it was not punishable when it was committed, or which deprives [the] accused of any substantial right or immunity possessed by him before its passage to prior offenses." While in *Strong v. State,* 1 Black, Ind., 196 (1822), the court noted that "the plain and obvious meaning of prohibition is that the legislature shall not pass any law, after a fact done by any citizen, which shall have relation to that fact, so as to punish that which was innocent when done; or to add to the punishment of that which was criminal; or to increase the malignity of a crime; or to retrench the rules of evidence, so as to make conviction more easy." And recently, in *Johnson v. United States*, 120 S.Ct. 1795, 1801 (2000), the Supreme Court struck down an ex post facto law, reminding the litigants: "The *Ex Post Facto* Clause raises to the constitutional level one of the most basic presumptions of our law: legislation, especially of the criminal sort, is not to be applied retroactively." Although ex post facto legislation may strike today's Americans as obviously unfair, such laws have been used throughout history by many dictators, who did not question their character. However, these dictators were not bound by the rule of law, which under the U.S. Constitution, places law above the arbitrary and capricious personal decisions of whimsical leaders. Ex post facto laws are inconsistent with rule-of-law principles and, accordingly, cannot be tolerated in a nation that cherishes due process of law. In American society the ex post facto principle is so commonly accepted that virtually any law, rule, or the like applied ex post facto is simply regarded as patently unfair.

Despite the relatively respectable due-process-of-law tradition in the United States, on occasion national and state legislators have trespassed on the domain and rights of administrators by passing unconstitutional bills of attainder and ex post facto laws. In 1866 the Supreme Court ruled that laws legislated after the Civil War to prevent former Confederate soldiers from obtaining governmental benefits were bills of attainder (*Cummings v. Missouri*, 4 Wallace 277 [1866], and *Ex parte Garland*, 4 Wallace 333 [1866]). In *United States v. Lovett*, 328 U.S. 303 (1946), the Supreme Court found a congressional act to be an unconstitutional bill of attainder because Congress specifically intended for three named individuals, whom Congress regarded as subversives, to be punished by removing them from government employment without a trial. Speaking for the Court, Justice Hugo Black maintained that the clear goal of Congress was to "permanently bar" the three named individuals from further government employment because Congress, not the courts, decided that they were "unfit." Ruling that the issue at hand was justiciable because the Constitution prohibits the passage of any bills of attainder, Justice Black held that the act must be regarded as an unconstitutional bill of attainder if it applies "to named individuals or to easily ascertainable members of a group in such a way as to inflict punishment on them without a judicial trial" (p. 315), as was the situation here.

In *United States v. Brown*, 381 U.S. 437 (1965), Chief Justice Earl Warren ruled that a provision in the Landrum-Griffin Labor Act was an unconstitutional bill of attainder because it made it a crime for Communists to hold office in labor unions. The Court found that this provision violated the separation-of-powers doctrine by promoting the "legislative exercise of the judicial function, or more simply—trial by legislature" (p. 442). Chief Justice Warren stressed that the separation-of-powers doctrine "was obviously not instituted with the idea that it would promote governmental efficiency. It was, on the contrary, looked to as a bulwark against tyranny" (p. 443).

In a highly publicized case, *Hiss v. Hampton,* 338 F.Supp. 1141 (1972), Circuit Judge Robb (U.S. Dist. Ct. D.C.) ruled that a 1954 federal statute, popularly known as the Hiss Act, was unconstitutional on the grounds that it was an ex post facto law.[39] Alger Hiss and Richard Strasburger had applied for retirement annuities under the Civil Service Retirement Systems, but they were informed that under the Hiss Act they were ineligible to receive benefits because they were in violation of specific provisions of the act. However, Judge Robb, citing the opinion in *Cummings v. Missouri,* argued that "a statute is an *ex post facto* law, and invalid, if its purpose and effect are to punish for past conduct and not to regulate a profession, calling or present situation" (p. 1148). According to the legislative history of the Hiss Act, Judge Robb concluded that without any question, the purpose of the act was to punish specific former federal employees and not to regulate future conduct: "There is substantial evidence in the 'objective manifestations of congressional purpose' that the primary target of the Act was Alger Hiss and not general regulation of the federal service" (p. 1149).

Judge Robb scolded Congress for enacting a law with no apparent legitimate regulatory purpose: "Neither Hiss nor Strasburger was a federal employee at the time the Act was passed, and we do not understand how the conduct of federal employees could be regulated or their moral standards elevated by imposing a financial penalty for their prior conduct upon men who were not federal employees or likely ever again to become federal employees. Retroactive punishment of former employees for their past misdoings has no reasonable bearing upon regulation of the conduct of the presently employed. The proper function of regulation is to guide and control present and future conduct, not to penalize former employees for acts done long ago" (p. 1149). Judge Robb concluded that the only important question to decide in this case "is simply whether the Constitution permits Congress to deprive them of their annuities by retroactive penal legislation. We conclude that it does not. We hold that as applied retroactively to the plaintiffs the challenged statute is penal, cannot be sustained as regulation, and is invalid as an *ex post facto* law prohibited by the Constitution" (p. 1153).

TINKERING WITH ADMINISTRATORS: THE PRESIDENT'S APPOINTMENT AND REMOVAL POWERS

If a U.S. president could at will appoint and remove administrators, he or she would have the capacity to virtually destroy the efficiency and effectiveness of the administration process through reckless manipulation of agency administrators. A president is entrusted with controlling and leading the administrative system and should possess reasonable powers over it, along with the freedom to appoint and remove administrators as seems advisable. The complete freedom to appoint and remove, at the president's personal pleasure, would undoubtedly prove extremely disruptive to normal administrative operations. Consequently, presidential appointment and removal powers have been restricted by various constitutional provisions, federal statutes, and court rulings. Generally, the limitations placed on the president's appointment and removal powers have been directed at stabilizing the administrative process, professionalizing its character, and protecting public administrators from undue interference and harassment. Of course, efforts aimed at confining the president's power to appoint and remove administrative officials are consistent with the constitutional framers' chief objective of keeping all governmental powers shared and limited.

The President's Appointment Power

The Constitution states in Article II, Section 1, Clause 1, that "the executive power shall be vested in a President of the United States of America." So that the president could function as the chief executive, the framers in Article II, Section 2, Clause 2, provided that the president "shall nominate, and by and with the advice and consent of the Senate, shall appoint ambassadors, other public ministers and consuls, judges of the Supreme Court, and all other officers of the United States, whose appointments are not herein otherwise provided for, and which shall be established by law: but the Congress may by law vest the appointment of such inferior officers, as they think proper, in the President alone, in the courts of law, or in the heads of departments."

As interpreted by the courts, this constitutional provision vests exclusive powers in the president to appoint persons to all major executive posts in the government, so long as the nominees meet with the approval of the Senate. Essentially, this appointment power provides presidents with the authority to select those high-level administrators whom they want in their administrations. Generally, high-level administrators are distinguished from those lower down in that the former normally possess considerably greater discretionary policymaking powers than the latter. Consequently, most lower-level governmental administrators—as permitted by Article II, Section 2, Clause 2—have been placed by Congress under the civil service system. With the expansion of the administrative system, presidents have been given the rightful authority to appoint members to the independent and quasi-independent regulatory commissions. The appointment powers of governors and mayors in the strong mayoral system are similar, although their appointment powers are generally considerably more limited.

In *Buckley v. Valeo*, 424 U.S. 1 (1976), the Supreme Court, reaffirming the holding in *Springer v. Philippine Islands*, 277 U.S. 189 (1928), held essentially that the Constitution did not permit Congress to usurp the president's appointment powers. In *Buckley*, it was charged, inter alia, that the Federal Election Campaign Act of 1974 (2 U.S.C., Section 437h) violated Article II, Section 2, Clause 2, of the Constitution because the act permits Congress, not the president, to appoint four members to the six-member Federal Elections Commission. The Court ruled that although the Constitution does not call for a rigid separation of powers between the governmental branches, it does forbid Congress from appointing its own members to administrative positions (those in which officers perform the normal administrative functions, including rulemaking and ordermaking within the scope of Article II).

In 1991 the Supreme Court in *Freytag v. Commissioner of Internal Revenue*, 111 S.Ct. 2631, held that Congress could use its discretion under the appointments clause to allow the chief justice of the Tax Court, not the president, to appoint special trial judges (formerly called commissioners) because the court said they were "inferior officers," not "officers of the United States." This decision has proved very "difficult to interpret," according to administrative law scholars Kenneth C. Davis and Richard J. Pierce, Jr., because "its reasoning could require major restructuring of the administrative state."[40]

The reason legal scholars are bothered by the Court's holding in *Freytag* is that the Court's majority, to justify permitting the Tax Court's chief justice appointment power, argued that the Tax Court was *not* an agency but a "court of law." Of course, by labeling the Tax Court a "court of law," the appointment of "inferior officers," according to Article II, Section 2, Chapter 2, could be assigned to the Tax Court's chief justice by Congress since Congress has the discretion to delegate this appointment power to the president alone, courts of law, or heads of departments. In this case the Congress selected to give the appointment power to the "court of law."

The problem is, however, that few legal and political scholars appear to regard the Tax Court as a constitutionally sanctioned court of law for the purpose of applying Article II, Section 2, Chapter 2, including even the four justices concurring in this case. Ironically, both sides in the case even argued that the appointments clause applied only to Article III courts. It was only the Supreme Court's majority which held that "Congress' consistent interpretation of the appointments clause evinces a clear congressional understanding that Article I courts could be given the power to appoint" (p. 2645).

The point is that most scholars still regard the Tax Court as an agency similar to many other agencies in the executive branch that exercise judicial or quasi-judicial powers, such as the Occupational Safety and Health Regulatory Commission, all of which are under the president's appointment authority. "*Freytag* illustrates the surprising extent to which the entire modern structure of government rests on an uncertain and controversial constitutional footing," Davis and Pierce maintain.[41] Since the Tax Court is similar to hundreds of other agencies in our administrative system that exercise judicial power, the *Freytag* decision seems to call into question the broad applicability of the president's appointment powers, especially regarding quasi-judicial, independent regulatory agencies.

Unquestionably, Davis and Pierce are right, but their point should not be exaggerated. The truth is that the constitutionality of well over 90 percent of the presidential appointments is quite clear because it is normally very obvious which officers are major or minor officers in the federal system. However, the courts are still struggling with criteria to resolve the constitutionality of presidential appointments in cases in which it is not absolutely clear whether the officers are major or inferior officers (*Weiss v. United States*, 510 U.S. 163 [1994]; *Ryder v. United States*, 515 U.S. 177 [1995]; *Crawford v. Commissioners of Internal Revenue*, 266 F.3d

1120 [2001]; and *Riley v. St. Luke Episcopal Hospital,* 252 F.3d 749 [2001]) or even if the nonpresidential appointment of a major officer is constitutional (e.g., U.S. attorney) so long as the appointment is only temporary (*U.S. v. Hilario,* 218 F.3d 19 [2001]).[42]

The Appointment Power's Limitations

Despite the broad presidential appointment powers, it would be a mistake to assume that the president could blatantly abuse this power to the flagrant detriment of the administrative process. As noted previously, presidents have almost routinely managed to obtain confirmation of those they have nominated, although confirmation is certainly not automatic.[43] Remember recently the problems Presidents G. H. W. Bush, Clinton, and G. W. Bush had with some of their nominees. The president's appointment power is limited by the Senate's negative confirmation power. The president may have absolute power to appoint, but the Senate has absolute power to refuse confirmation.

Arthur S. Miller, in *Presidential Power,* points out that the president's appointment power is also restricted by congressional statutes, thus forcing the appointment power to be shared.[44] Justice Louis Brandeis, Miller acknowledged, cited many examples of Congress placing restrictions on whom presidents could appoint to administrative positions. In a dissenting opinion in *Myers v. United States,* 272 U.S. 52 (1926), Brandeis noted that Congress in the past had limited the appointment power by requiring appointees to (1) be citizens, (2) be residents of specific geographical regions, (3) possess particular professional qualifications and experience, (4) pass qualification tests, and (5) be representatives of various political, professional, age, sex, race, and property groupings. Under Article II, Section 2, the president is given the authority "to fill up all vacancies that may happen during the recess of the Senate by granting commissions which shall expire at the end of their next session."

On the informal side, senatorial courtesy has always played a role in limiting presidents' flexibility in appointing anyone they wished to various administrative offices. For example, in 1789, during the very first presidential appointments, President George Washington had to withdraw an appointment to a naval post because he did not observe senatorial courtesy.[45] "Failure of the Executive to follow the wishes of a Senator (or Senators) of the state from which a nominee is selected or where he will serve," Miller asserts, "will usually defeat the appointment."[46]

Nevertheless, the power to make appointments has allowed presidents to change the bureaucratic perspective. In regard to the judiciary, for example, President Richard Nixon changed the philosophical perspective of the Supreme Court in a short time. Presidents Ronald Reagan, George H. W. Bush, and Bill Clinton also left their mark on the high court as well as the lower courts through their many appointments. Of course, President Bill Clinton, being the only Democrat to hold the presidency since 1969 except for Jimmy Carter, tried his best to replace the relatively conservative Republican appointees with more liberal Democrats. Likewise, key top-level appointments throughout a president's administration can dramatically shift the philosophical position of the administration. Naturally, President George W. Bush has been doing the best he can to reverse the ideological direction of the Clinton administration with his conservative appointments.

The President's Limited Removal Powers

In a sense, presidential appointment power is restricted most by the limitations placed upon the president's removal powers. That is, to appoint persons to administrative posts, the president must first remove those already occupying the positions. If the president had unlimited appointment and removal powers in combination, presidential influence over the administrative apparatus would be awesome. But presidential appointment and removal powers are limited by both formal and informal checks. In regard to removal powers, the president's authority is curtailed considerably more. From the administrators' perspective this is fortunate because, if presidents were allowed to remove administrators and appoint replacements at their whim, administrators could never function without worrying about whether their actions would lead to their dismissal by an irate president. In the words of Justice Felix Frankfurter, they would have to fear being removed "by the Damocles sword . . . for no reason."[47]

The Constitution is silent on the president's role in regard to removing administrative officials. Of course, according to the Constitution, any federal administrator, including the president, can be removed by impeachment, but the impeachment process is strictly a legislative function.[48] In *Myers v. United States,* 272 U.S. 52 (1926), William Howard Taft, at the time the chief justice of the Supreme Court, argued that under Article II of the Constitution the president had the power to remove those "executive officers appointed by him" and Congress had no constitutional authority to prohibit such presidential action. Although Myers was a purely executive officer (a postmaster), Taft contended that the Constitution gave the president the power to remove even those administrators who "perform duties of a quasi-judicial character . . . whose decisions after a hearing affect interests of individuals, the discharge of which the President can not in a particular case properly influence or control" (p. 135). If this decision stood today, the relationship between the president and the administrative regulatory system would be radically different, especially because the president would be able to remove commissioners from the independent regulatory agencies at will.

The *Humphrey's* Precedent.   Court sanctioning of the legitimacy of the headless governmental branch came less than a decade after *Myers* in *Humphrey's Executor v. United States,* 295 U.S. 602 (1935), with the Court holding that the president could not remove independent regulatory commissioners except for good cause. Since the president could not control (head) such regulatory commissions, these agencies became known as headless.

Unlike Myers, Humphrey was not a purely executive official but rather a member of the Federal Trade Commission (FTC). As a member of this independent regulatory agency, Humphrey performed quasi-judicial functions in hearing and deciding cases. To protect the independence of these quasi-judicial officials, Congress specifically prohibited the president from removing these commissioners except "for inefficiency, neglect of duty or malfeasance in office" (Federal Trade Commission Act of 1914, Section 1; 15 U.S.C., Section 41). Therefore, the question for the Court became whether Congress, under the Constitution, could validly place such a restriction on the president's removal power.

In delivering the opinion of the Court, Justice George Sutherland stressed that a regulatory agency such as the FTC, which performs quasi-legislative and quasi-judicial functions, "cannot in any proper sense be characterized as an arm or an eye of the executive. Its duties are performed without executive leave and, in the contemplation of the statute, must be free from executive control" (p. 628). The Court argued that it is plain that the Constitution did not assign illimitable removal powers to the president, especially in the case of administrators performing quasi-legislative and quasi-judicial tasks. Consequently, Congress has the power to restrict the president's removal powers in regard to independent regulatory agencies (p. 629).

Once again, the perceived supreme importance to democratic government of keeping governmental powers comfortably separated played a major role in the Court's holding in *Humphrey's*. Justice Sutherland contended that the necessity of preserving a separation of powers between the governmental branches has never been challenged seriously. Sutherland considered that the principle of separation of powers would be violated if presidents were permitted to remove independent regulatory commissioners without sound cause, since such removal authority would threaten "the independence of a commission, which is not only wholly disconnected from the executive department, but which, as already fully appears, was created by Congress as a means of carrying into operation legislative and judicial powers, and as an agency of the legislative and judicial departments" (p. 630).

In concluding, Justice Sutherland made very clear that the removal powers of the president depend on the specific functional classification of the administrators in question. Sutherland expressed the emphatic point that the *Myers* decision applied only to those administrations performing purely executive functions. However, as to quasi-legislative and quasi-judicial administrators such as Humphrey, the Court held that "no removal can be made during the prescribed term for which the officer is appointed, except for one or more of the causes named in the applicable statute" (p. 632).

Today, the *Humphrey's* decision stands on firmer turf than it did when the decision was handed down in 1935. This is true because in *Wiener v. United States*, 357 U.S. 349 (1958), the Court, praising the wisdom of Justice Sutherland in *Humphrey's*, gave solid endorsement to the *Humphrey's* ruling. Although the Court noted that the *Humphrey's* case was a cause célèbre (p. 353), it felt that it should hear the *Wiener* case "because it presents a variant of the constitutional issue decided in *Humphrey's Exr. v. United States*" (p. 351). In *Wiener*, Justice Frankfurter, writing the unanimous opinion, made clear that the circumstances surrounding the removals of both Humphrey and petitioner Wiener, both quasi-legislative and quasi-judicial officers, were virtually the same: "The ground of President Eisenhower's removal of petitioner was precisely the same as President Roosevelt's removal of Humphrey. Both Presidents desired to have commissioners, one on the Federal Trade Commission, the other on the War Claims Commission, 'of my own selection.' They wanted these Commissioners to be their men." However, one notable difference distinguished the two cases. While Humphrey's removal without good cause (for political reasons) was prohibited by statute (15 U.S.C., Section 41), Wiener was not specifically protected from removal by the War Claims Act of 1948 (62 Stat. 1240). Nevertheless, the Court asserted, since Congress created the War Claims Commission to adjudicate claims, it became a quasi-judicial body with officials to be protected from removal by the president except for good cause. Thus, the Court concluded: "Judging the matter in all the nakedness in which it is presented, namely, the claim that the President could remove a member of an adjudicatory body like the War Claims Commission merely because he wanted his own appointees on such a commission, we are compelled to conclude that no such power is given to the President directly by the Constitution, and none is impliedly conferred upon him by statute simply because Congress said nothing about it. The philosophy of *Humphrey's Executor,* in its explicit language as well as its implications, precludes such a claim" (p. 356).

The Impact of *Humphrey's.* The significance of the *Humphrey's* decision, as upheld and expanded in *Wiener,* must not be underestimated. Few decisions in American history have had more of an impact on administrative structure than these two decisions. And of course, court decisions regarding structure carry with them meaningful procedural implications. If the Courts in *Humphrey's* and *Wiener* had upheld Taft's broad interpretation of presidential removal powers in *Myers,* which permitted quasi-legislative and quasi-judicial administrators to be subject to unrestricted presidential removal as long as the president had authority to appoint them, the entire independent regulatory system would have developed much differently. For one thing, independent regulatory commissions would not exist today, except in a nonindependent, politicized capacity with status similar to that of the executive departments. Obviously, this would tend to make these regulatory commissions highly partisan agencies, filled with the sitting president's own supporters. As a result, the public policy perspective of the regulatory administrators would be expected to change dramatically and suddenly from one presidential administration to the next. Whether impartial adjudicative proceedings could take place would be highly questionable since the influence and pressures of partisan politics would tend to bias agency proceedings and decisions.

But the Courts in *Humphrey's* and *Wiener* did not uphold the *Myers* decision. Consequently, a rather large and powerful independent regulatory system has developed since the 1935 *Humphrey's* decision, and it has not been very vulnerable to White House political pressures or controls. But is this necessarily good? Was Justice Sutherland right in *Humphrey's* when he asserted unequivocally that an agency such as the FTC "cannot in any proper sense be characterized as an arm or an eye of the executive" (p. 628)? Many, especially in the field of public administration, question the insightfulness of Sutherland's contention because such regulatory agencies are obviously very much a part of the administrative system, which the president is held responsible for administering.[49] Do these regulatory administrators not make significant public policy decisions that influence the directions of presidential administrations in attempting to resolve this nation's socioeconomic problems? How can a president be expected to successfully tackle complex public policy problems like inflation if top-level administrators in the administrative system (for example, the chair of the Federal Reserve Board) can make major policy decisions (such as a monetary decision causing banks to drop their interest rates) that are independent and frequently contrary to the policy directions taken by the president? Can an administrative system be efficient and effective if all the independent regulatory agencies are pulling in opposite directions under no central or authoritative leader?

Recent Supreme Court Cases
Upholding Humphrey's and Wiener

For about three decades after *Wiener,* the Supreme Court entertained no serious challenges to the constitutional legitimacy of independent regulatory agencies or to the limitations placed upon the president's removal powers. However, the appointment of new conservative justices to the Supreme Court by Presidents Reagan and G. H. W. Bush evidently encouraged new challenges. But despite the rehashing of essentially the argument presented by Chief Justice Taft in the *Myer* case, the Supreme Court ended up reaffirming the legitimacy of the independent agencies and the president's limited removal powers.

In *Bowsher v. Synar,* 106 S.Ct. 318 (1986), the Supreme Court upheld the right of Congress to delegate powers to independent regulatory agencies and to protect their independence. However, the Court refused to permit Congress to use the removal powers to manipulate executive officials. In *Morrison v. Olson,* 487 U.S. 654 (1988), the high court once again affirmed the constitutional status of independent agencies, as it did in *Mistretta v. United States,* 488 U.S. 361 (1989). In *Morrison* the Court's majority ruled that the Congress did not violate the separation-of-powers doctrine by drafting an independent counsel provision that allowed the president to remove the independent counsel only for cause. The Court did agree that the investigative and prosecutorial functions were inherently executive functions normally under a president's control, but it reasoned that since the independent counsel was assigned the task of investigating for prosecution any wrongdoing in the executive branch, it only made sense to not allow the president to exercise "at will" removal powers. Concurring, Justice Antonin Scalia charged that the Court's majority ignored established law that placed limits on what Congress could do to limit presidential power over the executive branch.

Kenneth C. Davis and Richard Pierce, Jr., sympathize with Scalia's criticism because, they assert, "the opinion does not state any justiciable standard for determining the limits on Congress's power to limit presidential control of Executive Branch officers." Specifically, they maintain, the Court has not specified "the type of Executive Branch officers that must be subject to presidential power to remove 'at will' or what constitutes adequate 'cause' for removal of officers who can be removed only 'for cause.'" Davis and Pierce conclude: "Without some judicially enforced limit on Congress' power to limit the President's power to control Executive Branch officers, Justice Scalia's concern that Congress will emasculate the presidency seems plausible."[50]

Justice Scalia's major concern is with accountability. His basic argument is that if the president is going to be held accountable for activity in "his" executive branch, he should be placed into a position to control it. To Scalia, administrative agencies and the public policies they promulgate should be under the direction and control of the president. To Scalia it is that simple! The president should have the power to appoint and remove all administrative officials in the executive branch who make public policy. To Scalia the Court made a grave mistake in *Humphrey's*, so grave in fact that he suggests strongly in his concurring opinion in *Freytag v. Commissioner of Internal Revenue*, 111 S.Ct. 2631 (1991), that the *Humphrey's* decision should be reversed. He argues that the consequence in *Humphrey's* was to create a "headless Fourth Branch" that prevents the president from diminishing the very officers he or she appointed to the Federal Trade Commission or other such "independent" agencies. To Scalia, such a scheme makes "agencies less accountable to him, and hence he less responsible for them" (p. 2660). And Scalia adds: "Depending upon how broadly one reads the President's power to dismiss 'for cause,' it may be that he has no control over the appointment of inferior officers in such agencies; and if those agencies are publicly regarded as beyond his control—a 'headless Fourth Branch'—he may have less incentive to care about such appointments" (pp. 2660–2661). In concluding, Justice Scalia suggests that the Court should admit to being wrong in *Humphrey's Executor* yet concludes that "adjusting the remainder of the Constitution to compensate for *Humphrey's Executor* is a fruitless endeavor" (p. 2661).

Even though Justice Scalia raises some points worthy of further scrutiny, his viewpoints on agency independence and presidential removal powers are definitely in the minority because most scholars and practitioners apparently believe that independent regulatory agencies should remain fairly independent of presidential manipulation. Specifically reacting to Scalia's comments in *Freytag*, Bernard Schwartz concludes: "To most of us . . . *Humphrey's* was correctly decided and remains under *Freytag* and other recent decisions, the bastion of the necessary independence of agencies such as the FTC, which can be insulated from political pressures because they are not subject to direct presidential control."[51]

SUMMARY

Responsive and accountable public administration in a democratic country demands that the administrative process be kept reasonably open to those who want to influence administrative decisionmaking. Nevertheless, the integrity of democratic administration can be jeopardized if public administrators are not protected from undue interference and harassment from those special interests in their environment. Specifically, unethical and illegal influence peddling tends to bias administrative decisions in favor of those special interests that are peddling the influence. This chapter gave special attention to various kinds of meddling in the administrative process that undermine the ability of agency officials to develop and administer public policies in an objective, fair, efficient, and effective manner.

The lines between permissible, unethical, and illegal tampering with the administrative apparatus are often very thin, but steps have been taken to make unlawful influence peddling that obviously disrupts the administrative machinery and contravenes the public interest. To protect administrators from themselves, various conflict-of-interest statutes have been legislated. Conflict-of-interest laws make it illegal for public officials to accept things of value in exchange for preferential treatment. These laws also make it a crime for parties to offer gifts to public administrators.

To protect the independence and righteousness of the administrative process, some modest limits have been placed on legislative influence peddling. For example, in *D.C. Federation of Civic Associations v. Volpe,* 459 F.2d 1231 (1972), the Supreme Court held that administrators cannot make policy decisions based upon political influence pressures alone but must reach decisions in light of relevant facts. The wisdom of *Volpe* has been upheld many times by the courts. In *Gravel v. United States,* 408 U.S. 606 (1972), and *United States v. Brewster,* 408 U.S. 501 (1972), the Court argued that the Constitution's speech or debate clause cannot be used to protect illegal legislative influence peddling, especially such activities as are not legislative in function or are criminal in character (for example, soliciting, accepting, or offering bribes). The courts have also struck down bills of attainder and ex post facto laws (for example, the Hiss Act of 1954 and the Urgent Deficiency Act of 1943), which have no regulatory purpose but have been passed to harass and punish administrators (e.g., *Hiss v. Hampton,* 338 F.Supp. 1141 [1972]; *Ethics Com'n v. Collusion,* 850 P. 2d 1069 [Okla. 1993]; and *Springfield Armory, Inc. v. City of Columbus,* 805 F. Supp. 489 [S.D. Ohio 1992]). In addition, the courts have overruled the constitutionality of loyalty oaths, which have been required by legislators, especially at the state level, as a condition of employment and used, in general, to keep administrative officials in line. In 1970 the Civil Service Commission dropped the loyalty oath requirement for federal employees.

In the final analysis, all these measures have done little to protect administrators from undue congressional meddling in the administrative process. Democratic procedures permit legislators to lobby administrators, but unethical ex parte contacts are discouraged. But the distinction between unethical and ethical legislative lobbying practices is extremely nebulous, and this has allowed legislators to manipulate administrative actions unfairly. Congress is unlikely to pass meaningful legislation that would tend to restrict its influence over administrative conduct. Political scientists for decades have asserted that the big interest groups in America "own" legislators and, as a result, compel those legislators to pressure administrators to make decisions that favor their respective special interests.

To prevent the president from harassing and politically manipulating certain administrative officials at personal discretion, the Supreme Court has ruled that the president's power to appoint major "officers of the United States" is virtually absolute (*Buckley v. Valeo*, 424 U.S. 1 [1976]), yet Congress has the discretion to delegate the appointment of "inferior officers" to the president alone, courts of law, or heads of departments (*Freytag v. Commissioner of Internal Revenue*, 111 S.Ct. 2631 [1991]), while presidential removal powers are limited to the removal of those administrators who perform purely executive functions. In *Humphrey's v. United States* and *Wiener v. United States,* 357 U.S. 349 (1958), the high court held that a president cannot remove, except for good cause, administrators who perform quasi-legislative and quasi-judicial functions. These decisions have made administrators who perform legislative and judicial functions in independent and quasi-independent regulatory agencies (the Federal Trade Commission and the War Claims Commission are examples) virtually unremovable until their set terms expire.

In *Freytag v. Commissioner of Internal Revenue*, 111 S.Ct. 2631, 2660 (1991) Justice Scalia attacked the *Humphrey's* decision, arguing vehemently that *Humphrey's* created a "headless Fourth Branch" that made independent "agencies less accountable to [the president], and hence he less responsible for them." Many sympathize with Scalia's argument that *Humphrey's* has created serious accountability problems, yet *Humphrey's* has survived a recent flurry of legal challenges because most seem to believe that, all things considered, independent regulatory agencies should remain fairly protected from corruptive political pressures.

WIENER V. UNITED STATES

357 U.S. 349; 78 S.Ct. 1275 (1958)

Facts

Wiener was appointed to the War Claims Commission by President Harry Truman and began serving on June 8, 1950. The War Claims Commission was created by the War Claims Act of 1948 (62 Stat. 1240). Its purpose was "to receive and adjudicate according to law" various personal injury and property damage claims caused by the enemy during World War II. The three-member commission was to reach "final" decisions, not subject to any other official or court review. The commissioners' terms were to last for the commission's life and the act contained no provision regarding removal. However, after Wiener refused to resign voluntarily, President Dwight Eisenhower removed him on December 10, 1953, stating that he felt it was "in the national interest to complete the administration of the War Claims Act . . . with personnel of [my] own selection." Wiener filed suit in the court of claims for recovery of his salary from the time of his removal to the end of the commission's existence, but his petition was dismissed. Because the Supreme Court believed it presented an important variant to the constitutional issue decided in *Humphrey's Executor,* it granted certiorari.

Justice Frankfurter delivered the unanimous Court opinion.

Controversy pertaining to the scope and limits of the President's power of removal fills a thick chapter of our political and judicial history. The long stretches of its history, beginning with the very first Congress, with early echoes in the Report of this Court, were laboriously traversed in *Myers v. United States* . . . and need not be retraced. . . . Speaking through a Chief Justice who himself had been President, the Court did not restrict itself to the immediate issue before it, the President's inherent power to remove a postmaster, obviously an executive official. As of set purpose and not by way of parenthetic casualness, the Court announced that the President had inherent constitutional power of removal also of officials who have "duties of a quasi-judicial character . . . whose decisions after hearing affect interests of individuals, the discharge of which the President can not in a particular case properly influence or control." This view of presidential power was deemed to flow from his "constitutional duty of seeing that the laws be faithfully executed."

The assumption was short-lived that the *Myers* case recognized the President's inherent constitutional power to remove officials, no matter what the relation of the executive to the discharge of their duties and no matter what restrictions Congress may have imposed regarding the nature of their tenure. The versatility of circumstances often mocks a natural desire for definitiveness. Within less than ten years a unanimous Court, in *Humphrey's Executor v. United States,* narrowly confined the scope of the *Myers* decision to include only "all purely executive officers." The Court explicitly "disapproved" the expressions in *Myers* supporting the Presi-

dent's inherent constitutional power to remove members of quasi-judicial bodies. Congress had given members of the Federal Trade Commission a seven-year term and also provided for the removal of a Commissioner by the President for inefficiency, neglect of duty or malfeasance in office. In the present case, Congress provided for a tenure defined by the relatively short period of time during which the War Claims Commission was to operate. . . . But nothing was said in the Act about removal.

This is another instance in which the most appropriate legal significance must be drawn from congressional failure of explicitness. Necessarily this is a problem in probabilities. We start with one certainty. The problem of the President's power to remove members of agencies entrusted with duties of the kind with which the War Claims Commission was charged was within the lively knowledge of Congress. . . .

Humphrey's case was a cause and not least in the halls of Congress. And what is the essence of the decision in *Humphrey's* case? It drew a sharp line of cleavage between officials who were part of the Executive establishment and were thus removable by virtue of the President's constitutional powers, and those who are members of a body "to exercise its judgment without the leave or hindrance of any other official or any department of the government. . . . " This sharp differentiation derives from the difference in functions between those who are part of the Executive establishment and those whose tasks require absolute freedom from Executive interference. "For it is quite evident," again to quote *Humphrey's Executor*, "that one who holds his office only during the pleasure of another, cannot be depended upon to maintain an attitude of independence against the latter's will."

Thus, the most reliable factor for drawing an inference regarding the President's power of removal in our case is the nature of the function that Congress vested in the War Claims Commission. What were the duties that Congress confided to this Commission? And can the inference fairly be drawn from the failure of Congress to provide for removal that these Commissioners were to remain in office at the will of the President? For such is the assertion of power on which petitioner's removal must rest. The ground of President Eisenhower's removal of petitioner was precisely the same as President Roosevelt's removal of Humphrey. Both Presidents desired to have Commissioners, one on the Federal Trade Commission, the other on the War Claims Commission, "of my own selection." They wanted these Commissioners to be their men. The terms of removal in the two cases are identical and express the assumption that the agencies of which the two Commissioners were members were subject in the discharge of their duties to the control of the Executive. An analysis of the Federal Trade Commission Act left this Court in no doubt that such was not the conception of Congress in creating the Federal Trade Commission. The terms of the War Claims Act of 1948 leave no doubt that such was not the conception of Congress regarding the War Claims Commission.

The history of this legislation emphatically underlines this fact. . . . The Commission was established as an adjudicating body with all the paraphernalia by which legal claims are put to the test of proof, with finality of determination "not subject to review by any other official of the United States or by any court by mandamus or otherwise, . . . " The claims were to be "adjudicated according to law," that is, on the merits of each claim, supported by evidence and governing legal considerations, by a body that was "entirely free from the control or coercive influence, direct or indirect," *Humphrey's Executor v. United States*, . . . of either the Executive or the Congress. If, as one must take for granted, the War Claims Act precluded the President from influencing the Commission in passing on a particular claim, *a certiori* must it be inferred that Congress did not wish to have hang over the Commission the Damocles' sword of removal by the President for no reason other than that he preferred to have on that Commission men of his own choosing?

For such is this case. We have not a removal for cause involving the rectitude of a member of an adjudicatory body, nor even a suspensory removal until the Senate could act upon it by confirming the appointment of a new Commissioner or otherwise dealing with the matter. Judging the matter in all the nakedness in which it is presented, namely, the claim that the President could remove a member of an adjudicatory body like the War Claims Commission merely because he wanted his own appointees on such a Commission, we are compelled to conclude that no such power is given to the President directly by the Constitution, and none is impliedly conferred upon him by statute simply because Congress said nothing about it. The philosophy of *Humphrey's Executor*, in its explicit language as well as its implications, precludes such a claim.

The judgment is Reversed.

COMMENTS AND QUESTIONS

Few court rulings in administrative law are so easy to understand as the *Wiener* decision. The Supreme Court held, simply, that the Constitution does not authorize presidents to remove administrative officials who perform quasi-judicial functions, nor do congressional statutes confer such removal powers upon presidents just because they are silent about removal procedures. In *Wiener* the Court felt it was only affirming what it had clearly established in *Humphrey's* more than two decades before. Essentially, the Court in *Wiener* held that presidents cannot interfere in the administrative process by tampering with administrators who perform adjudicative functions. Despite the relative simplicity of the legal issues in *Wiener,* it stands as one of the most important rulings in administrative law because it places severe restrictions on the political muscle presidents can exert over the bureaucracy. It is puzzling, in light of the clarity of the *Humphrey's Executor* ruling, that the court of claims supported Eisenhower's removal of Wiener, who was obviously appointed to his position by Truman to perform almost exclusively adjudicative tasks. Should Congress specify every intention, even when its intentions are explicit? The *Wiener* Court acknowledged that Congress failed to specify the conditions of removal but argued that the *Humphrey* decision was common knowledge to Congress when it drafted the legislation. Therefore, the Court concluded that it was reasonable to assume that Congress did not intend for members of the War Claims Commission, created to perform adjudicative functions, to be removed for reasons other than *good cause.* Thus, the Court made it clear that Congress need not always be explicit when drafting statutes when common knowledge about certain matters should provide sufficient guidance.

But it was evidently not common knowledge to the court of claims that presidents should not be permitted to remove quasi-judicial officials from office for political reasons. Was it confused as to what sort of quasi-judicial administrators should be given independence from the president's removal authority? What differences exist between the Federal Trade Commission and the War Claims Commission to justify the fact that a president is unable to remove a member for political reasons from the FTC but not from the WCC? There is no doubt that members of traditional independent regulatory commissions are fully protected against being removed by a president except for good cause, but to what extent can the *Wiener* ruling be applied to other administrators who perform quasi-judicial functions? Many administrators in nonindependent regulatory agencies perform primarily adjudicative functions (deciding, for example, whether benefits should be granted), although the adjudicative proceedings are normally far less formal than those held by regulatory commissions. To preserve the integrity of judicial proceedings inside executive departments and other nonindependent regulatory agencies, to what extent should non-civil-service administrators be given independence from removal or threats of removal by a president determined to exert political influence over quasi-judicial decisionmaking? Preserving the integrity of informal agency adjudications (as compared to formal agency trial-like hearings) by minimizing presidential meddling appears important, but how wise is it to make quasi-judicial officials so free from presidential influence that they may reach adjudicative decisions that undermine presidential programs?

NOTES

1. Edwin Wallace Tucker, *Administrative Law, Regulation of Enterprise, and Individual Liberties* (St. Paul: West, 1975), p. 1975.

2. Ibid.

3. *The Republic of Plato*, trans. Francis M. Cornford (New York: Oxford University Press, 1945), chap. 5. Plato entertained the thought that even good men may not have the will to resist evil acts if they have no fear of being punished. He pondered: "Surely this would be strong proof that men do right only under compulsion; no individual thinks of it as good for him personally, since he does wrong whenever he finds he has the power" (p. 45).

4. Herbert Kaufman, *Red Tape: Its Origins, Uses, and Abuses* (Washington, D.C.: Brookings Institution Press, 1977), p. 50.

5. Terry L. Cooper, *The Responsible Administrator*, 3rd ed. (San Francisco: Jossey-Bass, 1990), p. 109.

6. Sam Donaldson, *Weekend With David Brinkley,* June 12, 1994.

7. Walter Gellhorn et al., *Administrative Law: Cases and Comments,* 8th ed. (Mineola, N.Y.: Foundation Press, 1987), pp. 982–984.

8. Ibid.

9. Stephen Labaton, "S.E.C. Choice Says He's No Harvey Pitt," *New York Times,* February 6, 2003, sec. C, p. 1.

10. Ibid. Also see Gallup and other polls conducted on the impact of corporate corruption and the failure of government to properly regulate corporate bookkeeping and reporting practices on investors and Americans (for example, go to Gallup.com or CNN.com).

11. Robert Roberts, "The Public Integrity Quagmire," in Carolyn Barr and Norma M. Riccucci, ed., *Public Personnel Management: Current Concerns—Future Challenges* (New York: Longman, 1991), p. 144.

12. Public Law 95-521; 18 U.S.C., Sec. 207.

13. "Deaver Named in Indictment," *St. Louis Post-Dispatch,* March 19, 1987, pp. 1, 16.

14. William Safire, "A Weak Indictment Against Mike Deaver," *St. Louis Post-Dispatch,* March 24, 1987, sec. B, p. 3.

15. AP, "Independent Counsel Law Dies Today With Few Eulogies; Even Kenneth Starr, The Latest To Hold Title, Favors Its Abolition," *St. Louis Post-Dispatch* (June 30, 1999), p. A5.

16. "From Watergate to Whitewater: History of the Independent Counsel," CNN.com, June 30, 1999, http://www.cnn.com/ALL POLITICS/stories/1999/06/30/ic.history/.

17. G. Calvin Mackenzie with Michael Hafken, *Scandal Proof: Do Ethics Laws Make Government Ethical?* (Washington, D.C.: Brookings Institute Press, 2002).

18. 30 Fed. Reg. 6469, May 8, 1965.

19. 36 Fed. Reg. 7831, April 23, 1971.

20. In Frederick C. Mosher et al., *Watergate: Implications for Responsible Government* (New York: Basic Books, 1974), p. 126.

21. Newton Minow, Review of *Politics and the Regulatory Agencies* by William Cary, *Columbia Law Review* 68 (February 1968): 383–384.

22. For an article that puts this gray area into context see "The Other Scandal," *The New Republic,* March 23, 1987, p. 6.

23. Paul H. Douglas, *Ethics in Government* (Cambridge, Mass.: Harvard University Press, 1952), pp. 85–88.

24. 105 *Congressional Record* (July 23, 1959), p. 12883.

25. Senator Thomas Eagleton, remarks at "How the Senate Works," conference at Clemson University, aired on C-Span, November 11, 1986.

26. Carl E. Lutrin and Allen K. Settle, *American Public Administration: Concepts and Cases,* 3d ed. (Palo Alto, Calif.: Mayfield, 1985), p. 336.

27. Ibid.

28. Stephen G. Breyer and Richard B. Stewart, *Administrative Law and Regulatory Policy: Problems, Text, and Cases*, 3rd ed. (Boston: Little, Brown, 1992), pp. 660–685.

29. E. Cox, R. Fellmeth, and J. Schultz, "The Consumer and the Federal Trade Commission," in Stephen G. Breyer and Richard B. Stewart, eds., *Administrative Law and Regulatory Policy* (Boston: Little, Brown, 1979), p. 773.

30. Al Gore, "Creating a Government That Works Better and Costs Less" (Washington, D.C.: U.S. Government Printing Office, 1993).

31. Jennifer Harper, "Energy Pile-On Ignores the Facts," *Washington Times,* March 3, 2002, p. A6.

32. For a recent review of separation of powers in the context of case law, see Peter L. Strauss, *Administrative Justice in the United States*, 2nd ed. (Durham: Carolina Academic Press, 2002), pp. 17–26.

33. Certiorari denied, 405 U.S. 1030 (1972).

34. *D.C. Federation of Civil Associations, Inc. v. Volpe,* 140 U.S. App. D.C. 162, 434 F.2d 436 (1970).

35. See also, *U.S. v. Vasquez,* 985 F.2d 491 (10th Cir. 1993); *Ethics Com'n v. Cullison,* 850 F.2d 1069 (Okla. 1993); *Kamplain v. Curry County Bd. of Com'rs,* 159 F.3d 1248 (10th Cir. 1998); and *Powell v. Ridge,* 247 F.3d 520 (3rd Cir. 2001).

36. In 1970 the Civil Service Commission dropped the loyalty oath as a requirement for federal employment. Loyalty oaths have also been eliminated for Job Corps members, Medicare recipients, and for students receiving federal financial assistance.

37. *Plelan v. Laramie County Cmty. College Bd. Of Trustees,* 235 F.3d 1243 (2000); *EEOC v. Union Independiente,* 279 F.3d 49 (2002); *Seariver Maritime Financial Holdings, Inc. v. Mineta,* 309 F.3d 662 (2002); *Rutan v. Republican Party of Illinois,* 110 S.Ct. 2729 (1990); and *Chandler v. Miller,* 117 S.Ct. 1295 (1997) are just a few of the federal cases that have struck severe blows to various loyalty oaths.

38. Article 1, Section 10, Clause 1, specifically prohibits states from passing any bill of attainder or ex post facto law.

39. The Hiss Act (Pub.L. no. 83-769; 68 Stat. 1142) was originally enacted on September 1, 1954, but amended on July 31, 1956 (Pub.L. no. 84-854; 70 Stat. 761) and again on September 26, 1961 (Pub.L. no. 87-299; 75 Stat. 640). On September 6, 1966, the whole act was codified as 5 U.S.C., Secs. 8311–8322 (Pub.L. no. 89-554; 80 Stat. 557).

40. Kenneth C. Davis and Richard J. Pierce, Jr., *Administrative Law Treatise*, 3rd ed. (Boston: Little, Brown, 1994), vol. 1, p. 65.

41. Ibid.

42. Also see Richard J. Pierce, Jr., *Administrative Law Treatise*, 4th ed. (New York: Aspen, 2002), vol. 1, pp. 41–51, for an analysis of the constitutionality of various appointments of major and inferior officers.

43. Norman C. Thomas, Joseph A. Pika, and Richard A. Watson, *The Politics of the Presidency*, revised 3rd ed. (Washington, D.C.: Congressional Quarterly Press, 1994), pp. 256–258.

44. Arthur S. Miller, *Presidential Power in a Nutshell* (St. Paul: West, 1977), p. 42.

45. Ibid., p. 41.

46. Ibid., p. 44.

47. *Wiener v. United States,* 357 U.S. 849, 349–356 (1958).

48. Federal judges can also be removed by the impeachment procedure.

49. Once again, the Ash Report provides an excellent argument in defense of the position that independent regulatory commissions are part of the administrative system and, therefore, should be under presidential control.

50. Davis and Pierce, *Administrative Law Treatise*, 3rd ed., vol. 1, pp. 52–53.

51. Bernard Schwartz, "Administrative Law Cases During 1991," *Administrative Law Review* 44 (summer 1992): 632.

CHAPTER 5

Rulemaking

Agencies as Legislative Bodies

THE GROWING IMPORTANCE OF
AGENCY RULEMAKING

If the field of administrative law has a primary focal point, it would have to be rulemaking. Rulemaking is at center stage among other administrative topics since virtually every discussion involving administrative law issues would almost have to be rooted in the rulemaking process. This is so because the vast majority of agency policies are the product of the rulemaking process. To Cornelius M. Kerwin, who has written many scholarly works on the rulemaking process, "rulemaking is the single most important function performed by agencies of government."[1]

The legislative branch, with the blessing of the courts, has transferred much of its lawmaking power to administrators simply because legislators felt compelled to delegate such power to meet the increasing demands placed upon government by the citizenry. But regardless of why lawmaking powers were so delegated, the fact is that administrative agencies have been created and expanded at an accelerated pace. Over the past half century, legislative bodies at all governmental levels were eager to allow administrators to have primary responsibility for making all decisions they deem necessary for implementing general public policies. In reality, lawmaking by agency administrators has become so prevalent that some scholars assert that the change constitutes de facto amendments to the U.S. Constitution and state constitutions that we must recognize and accept, and as best we can, let this new reality of the administrative state work for us.[2]

The subtitle of this chapter, "Agencies as Legislative Bodies," was selected because I think it best encapsulates the role of modern administrative agencies.

Although public administrators also perform adjudicative and purely administrative functions, probably their most important task is making rules to govern society. When making rules, public administrators in fact interpret general congressional statutes and assign them their real meaning by giving them life in society. Or as Kerwin asserts, "Rules, like legislation, attempt to structure the future. By creating new conditions, eliminating existing ones, or preventing others from coming into being, rules implement legislation that seeks to improve the quality of life."[3] Although some laws are more precise in their language and intent than others, legislatures are increasingly cranking out pieces of legislation that leave the precise intentions of their public policy statements quite unclear. In fact, the courts have recognized this trend but have refrained, in general, from compelling Congress or state legislatures to draft legislation with clearer standards. Of course, these developments have placed administrators in a very powerful position; they can design and execute public policies according to what within reason they perceive as being good or bad for society. Actually, if a top-level administrator opposes a certain piece of legislation, for whatever reason, the odds are low indeed that that agency will make efforts to see that the particular public policy is successfully implemented. Many instances of this can be seen, but one example should illustrate the point.

It should be stressed that administrative power is determined largely by the amount of rulemaking authority delegated to administrators by legislators. Congress remains the primary source of administrative power and the chief watchdog overseeing agency behavior. If legislators are content with delegating away the most fundamental governmental power, that of lawmaking, to administrative agencies, and if the courts continue to give their approval, then this change in governmental structure will simply have to be accepted. No other authoritative vehicle in our system is capable of reversing this trend. However, most scholars in the field believe that despite the fact that the delegation of significant lawmaking powers to public administrators represents a threat to traditional democratic practices,[4] such delegation seems to have been almost inevitable, given the mounting demands on modern government, especially since rulemaking practices can prove advantageous to the system of government. Some scholars also maintain that rulemaking can be kept within the democratic limits if determined efforts are made to carefully structure and check rulemaking so that the process complements democratic government. This chapter examines rulemaking in relative detail, especially with an eye on how fair and democratic rulemaking procedures are in molding U.S. public policies.

WHAT IS RULEMAKING?

Actually, answering this question in a definitive manner presents quite a challenge, mostly because of problems in both rulemaking terminology and in the way rulemaking processes are implemented by various governmental agencies. Administrative law is a relatively new field that has not developed in a very logical or systematic way. Actually, the laissez-faire attitude prevalent in America before the New Deal played an instrumental role in deterring the development of a set of administrative laws designed to regulate the behavior of public agencies. Consequently, and predictably, during the 1930s and 1940s, when New Deal challenges and World War II demands stimulated the rapid growth of bureaucracy, public agencies began to function chaotically in the absence of a comprehensive body of laws designed to regulate administrative procedure. By the time the Administrative Procedure Act was passed in 1946 in response to the obvious need to control and regularize agency actions in the public interest, administrative law nomenclature had already been developed in a random and unstructured way by individual public agencies and through common law, which reflected the inconsistent usage and application of administrative law terminology by both administrators and judges.

Because of America's administrative law history before the passage of the Administrative Procedure Act, the APA's attempt to standardize administrative law terminology has met with only partial success. Today administrative law scholars and practitioners are still frustrated by the inconsistent meanings given to administrative law terms, especially when clear distinctions and applications are considered very crucial, as with rules and orders. Since orders and rules normally carry different weight before the courts and their penalties for noncompliance may be very different, it is necessary that the distinction between rules and orders be more definitive and useful. For example, in a frequently cited case, an automobile driver argued that his speeding ticket conviction should be overruled by the court because the speed limit in question had been set by an "order" of the New York State Traffic Commission, not filed as a rule, and therefore was not applicable to him. The court ruled that despite the fact that the commission called it an "order," it was really a rule because it was a "legislative or quasi-legislative norm or prescription which established a pattern or course of conduct for the future" (*People v. Cull*, 10 N.Y.2d 123, 126 [1961]).

Despite the acute need to make a sharper distinction between the meanings and significance of rules and orders, public agencies, courts, and legislators continue to employ the terminology inconsistently, thus causing confusion for outsiders and themselves. For instance, the Treasury Department has a tradition of referring to rules as "decisions," which it publishes as "Treasury Decisions," while regulatory commissions such as the FTC and FCC like to shape public policy through "orders," which they apply as general rules or regulations.[5] The state of confusion over the status of rules and orders motivated Bernard Schwartz to write in 1991: "Today the administrative law student too often feels like Alice after going through her looking glass; he yearns for that *other* room where chairs are actually chairs and tables, tables—and rules and regulations are rules and regulations and orders, orders."[6] Richard J. Pierce, Jr., however, acknowledges the definitional problem, but plays it down, remarking: "Notwithstanding the theoretical difficulty of distinguishing between rulemakings and adjudications and unsatisfactory APA definitions, agencies and courts have experienced little difficulty in practice."[7]

Despite the terminological problems, administrative law terms and processes are defined by the federal APA. Although definitions of rulemaking, ordermaking, and the like must be employed when the act specifically applies, APA terminology and procedures are not considered mandatory outside the APA's specific jurisdiction. Since the APA's jurisdiction is largely limited to situations involving formal administrative decisionmaking, agencies have a great many opportunities to simply ignore APA definitions and requirements. Judging from the large number of suits filed against public agencies for flagrantly violating APA requirements, many public administrators evidently know little or nothing about APA's requirements, or they choose to ignore them. Nevertheless, it appears that with each passing year, APA terminology and procedures are becoming more accepted, especially as the APA is refined by further amendments.

According to the Administrative Procedure Act, **rulemaking** means an "agency process for formulating, amending, or repealing a rule," and *rule* means "the whole or a part of an agency statement of general or particular applicability and future effect designed to implement, interpret, or prescribe law or policy or describing the organization, procedure, or practice requirements of an agency" (Section 551). In simple language, a rule is a law made in an administrative agency. When an administrative agency engages in rulemaking, it is legislating policy. In fact, Kerwin notes that "the history of rulemaking is the history of American public policy."[8] Rules are designed to regulate both the internal operations of administrative agencies and to help implement the broad public policies assigned to government agencies by the legislature.

Depending on the statutory base of agencies, some agencies have potent rulemaking strength, while others are severely limited in their rulemaking powers. Congress, in the process of creating administrative agencies over the decades, allocated some agencies, such as the Environmental Protection Agency, vast lawmaking powers, while it severely restricted the legislative function of others, such as the Internal Revenue Service. The IRS may be one of the most feared agencies in the federal government; yet IRS employees actually have fewer rulemaking and discretionary powers than most government departments.

Frequently, the Congress has actually specified the kind of weight the rules should carry, as well as whether the courts should have the right to review the rules made by agencies. Because of this, Congress has, in effect, created first-class and second-class agencies in governmental bureaucracy. Consequently, public agencies have unequal status, powers, and influence in the American political system.

Although the distinction is often blurred and the courts frequently fail to recognize it, it is nevertheless valuable to note the difference in status between *legislative* (substantive) and *interpretative* rules. As one might suspect, legislative rules carry much more clout than interpretative rules. "First-class agencies," because of their statutory foundation, have been given the legal and undisputed authority to draft *legislative rules*, which carry the thrust of law (*New Jersey v. Department of HHS*, 670 F.2d 1262, 1282 [3rd Cir. 1981]). Normally, legislative rules are not open to interpretation or invalidation by the courts, as are interpretative rules. Commenting on the status of legislative rules, Kenneth C. Davis wrote that, as long as such rules are otherwise constitutional, "a court may no more substitute its judgment as to the content of a legislative rule than it may substitute its judgment as to the content of a statute."[9] Because *interpretative rules* (also spelled *interpretive*) are made by agencies without the advantage of direct statutory sanctioning to make rules with the force of law, such rules are weaker and considered open to the courts. The courts can readily interpret and invalidate these rules; thus interpretative rules receive less deference or respect by the courts than legislative rules (*Krzabic v. Republic Title Co.*, 314 F.3d 875 [7th Cir. 2002]). However, the strength of interpretative rules increases the more they are (1) backed by demonstrated legislative intent, (2) long-standing, (3) supported by agency expertise, and (4) supported by any other factors that strengthen their reasonableness before the courts (*National Muffler Dealers Association, Inc. v. United States*, 99 S.Ct. 1304, 1307 [1979]). Theoretically, interpretative rules are supposed only to *interpret* existing provisions in statutes, not to add to, or make new, substantive law (*Nat'l Family Planning and Reproductive Health Ass'n v. Sullivan*, 979 F.2d 227, 237 [D.C. Cir. 1992]).

For example, the court in *Rocky Mountain Helicopters, Inc. v. F.A.A.*, 971 F.2d 544, 547 (10th Cir. 1992) ruled that an interpretative rule must satisfy three requirements: "(1) the factual findings underlying the interpretation must be supported by substantial evidence, . . . (2) the agency must offer a satisfactory explanation for its actions, . . . and (3) the interpretation must be consistent with the statute, rule, or regulation being interpreted."

The Supreme Court, in *Chevron v. Natural Resources Defense Council*, 467 U.S. 837 (1984), has probably given more strength to interpretative rules because some courts have applied *Chevron* to interpretative rules, even though apparently most legal scholars think that *Chevron* should apply only to legislative rules.[10] In *Chevron* the court held basically that courts should defer to an administrative interpretation of a statute in the event that legislative intent is ambiguous or silent, as long as the statute does not clearly prohibit it. Consequently, Richard Pierce, Jr., takes the position that the *Chevron* doctrine may apply to interpretative rules: "Legislative rules and formal adjudications are always entitled to *Chevron* deference, while less formal pronouncements like interpretative rules and informal adjudications may or may not be entitled to *Chevron* deference."[11]

Despite the fact that legislative bodies have granted some agencies stronger rulemaking power than others, legislative assemblies at every level in American government have allowed all agencies to make rules the public must obey. The rulemaking function is probably the most basic power of any public agency. Surely no agency could operate if it had to obtain congressional clearance before it could ever act. But because agency-made laws have the potential to be arbitrary, capricious, or unjust in a number of ways, steps have been taken to guard against administrators who may abuse their rulemaking powers and draft rules that rub abrasively against the American spirit of fairness and due process. Not only are all rules ultimately subject to legislative oversight and judicial review, but various acts, especially the Administrative Procedure Act, and court decisions have also established legal guidelines for administrators to follow in legislating rules.

APA Notice-and-Comment Rulemaking

Section 553 of the APA in essence requires administrative agencies to follow fair and reasonable procedures when they make rules. Although liberal exceptions exist for particular agencies and under certain conditions (mostly foreign affairs agencies working with sensitive national security data or domestic agencies dealing with "private and secret" information), the APA requires administrators to follow several important procedural steps when making rules. First, administrators are required to give public notice of proposed rulemaking by publishing the proposal in the *Federal Register* (an official daily government publication). To be proper, the notice should include (1) the "time, place, and nature" of the proposed rulemaking proceedings; (2) the legal basis on which the rules are proposed; and (3) a general description of the proposed rule along with an explanation of the issues involved. Second, agencies are compelled to provide opportunities for "interested persons" to take an active part in the rulemaking process by allowing them to submit "written data, views, or arguments with or without opportunity for oral presentation." Third, the act specifies that a "substantive rule" should not be allowed to take effect until at least thirty days have elapsed after its public notice. Fourth, administrators are legally obligated to grant concerned parties "the right to petition for the issuance, amendment, or repeal of a rule." Figure 5.1 visually demonstrates this process.

Formal Rulemaking

Only three kinds of rulemaking are acknowledged by the Administrative Procedure Act: informal (notice-and-comment rulemaking), formal (trial-like hearing rulemaking), and a new rulemaking approach, called negotiated rulemaking, codified in Sections 561–583 of the APA in 1990 (negotiated rulemaking is an experimental approach with limited application and is discussed later in the chapter). Informal, notice-and-comment rulemaking, which simply provides notice and an opportunity for interested parties to make comments on the proposed rule, is by far the most common procedure. However, the APA provides for formal rulemaking to be employed "when rules are required by statute to be made on the record after opportunity for an agency hearing" (Section 554). When formal rulemaking is required by statute, the APA sections governing adjudications must be followed. In *Vermont Yankee Nuclear Power Corp. v. Natural Resources Defense Council*, 435 U.S. 519, 547 (1978), the Supreme Court noted that when formal rulemaking is required, administrative agencies are expected to promulgate rules employing "the full panoply of procedural devices normally associated only with adjudicatory hearings." Among other things, this entails the submission of evidence and opportunity to cross-examine it.

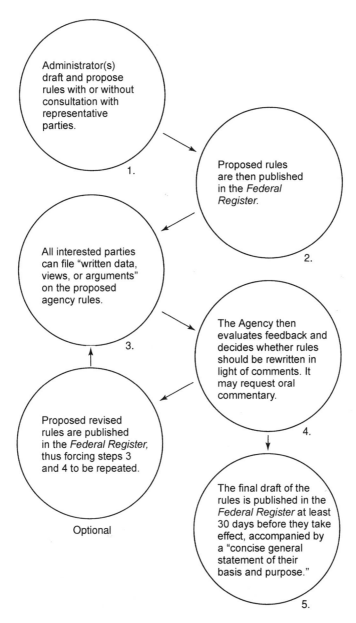

FIGURE 5.1   The Normal APA Rulemaking Process: Notice-and-Comment Rulemaking

In reality, however, very few statutes call for trial-like hearings in the making of rules. The most familiar statute requiring formal rulemaking procedures is the Food, Drug, and Cosmetic Act of 1938, 21 U.S.C., Section 371(e)(3). Under the act, before issuing a rule, the Food and Drug Administration must (1) hold a public hearing affording interested parties an opportunity to be heard, (2) base decisions on substantial evidence in light of the record, (3) structure the order (rule) to include findings of fact based upon the formal hearing record, and (4) provide for review of adjudicatory proceedings before agency findings of fact substantiating the rule can be considered conclusive or final. These elaborate formal rulemaking procedures have been sharply criticized because such procedures tend to cripple the rulemaking process. One critic of formal rulemaking, Bernard Schwartz, asserts in vivid prose that formal trial-like procedures "are out of place in rulemaking. They imprison a legislative process within a formal strait jacket designed for an entirely different type of proceeding and may produce a virtual paralysis of the administrative process."[12] Criticizing the Food, Drug, and Cosmetic Act in particular, he claims that the formal rulemaking requirement has caused long delays, with all rules taking at least two years to promulgate and some taking over ten years. One hearing, which focused on whether peanut butter should contain 87.5 percent or 90 percent peanuts, produced a weighty 7,736-page transcript and lasted about nine years.[13] Richard J. Pierce, Jr., is just as direct, concluding that there is "solid evidence" proving "that the formal rulemaking procedure simply does not work."[14] Also citing the fiasco of the long peanut butter proceedings, Pierce notes that most issues are much more complex than determining the percent of peanuts that should be in peanut butter. He claims that the typical controversy involves more difficult questions of fact and policy, thus creating the real possibility that many formal rulemaking proceedings could last even longer than the peanut butter case. To these scholars, "it is simply impossible to complete a major rulemaking in a timely manner through the use of formal adjudicatory proceedings."[15]

The reality is that legislators, as well as judges, realize that formal rulemaking normally "does not work"; consequently legislators have tried to write legislation that does not statutorily require formal rulemaking, while judges have handed down decisions allowing agencies to escape having to employ formal rulemaking. *United States v. Florida East Coast Railway Co.*, 410 U.S. 224 (1973), has had the greatest impact on severely limiting agency use of formal rulemaking, because the court held essentially that informal notice-and-comment rulemaking could usually be substituted for the formal hearing requirement. Specifically, the Supreme Court in *Florida East Coast* applied the hearing requirement very loosely, arguing that a "proper hearing" could result from the written comments submitted in the notice-and-comment process, thus establishing a record and satisfying the APA's "on the record after hearing" requirement. Despite the questionable legal rationale employed in *Florida East Coast*, this case has set strong precedent because of the almost universal agreement that the formal rulemaking process is not viable in most rulemaking situations (e.g., *Bell Telephone Co. of Pennsylvania v. FCC*, 503 F.2d 1250 [3rd Cir. 1974]; *United Airlines v. CAB*, 766 F.2d 1109 [7th Cir. 1985]; *Quivara Mining Co. v. NRC*, 866 F.2d 1246 [10th Cir. 1989]).

As a result of *Florida East Coast*, courts very rarely compel an agency to employ formal rulemaking; they do so only when (1) a specific statute clearly requires formal rulemaking; (2) an oral, evidentiary hearing is mandated by statute; and (3) adjudicative facts specific to an individual involving "property" or "liberty" interests must be resolved through a due process, formal-rulemaking agency hearing.[16]

RULEMAKING:
LOOPHOLES AND THEIR SIGNIFICANCE

Some may be disturbed by the apparent burden placed on administrators by certain APA requirements, yet others may be encouraged by such rulemaking requirements, which seem to compel administrators to promulgate rules in an open, fair, and democratic manner that encourages public participation. After all, as Cornelius Kerwin stresses, rulemaking has inherent democratic problems, simply because rulemakers are not elected and, therefore, not directly accountable to the American people. Thus, "the legitimacy of the rulemaking process is clearly linked to public participation."[17]

However, despite APA requirements, most rules are made behind closed doors by administrative agencies without any input at all from interested persons. Lewis Mainzer once noted, even during the 1970s, the alleged height of the participatory movement in rulemaking: "Agencies no doubt make vast numbers of rules day by day with nothing but internal procedure, but others affect outsiders as well or primarily."[18] Yet Kerwin makes clear that public participation is essential for making sound rules, since rulemakers "rely on the public for much of the information they need to formulate rules. Therefore, if participation is hampered by hostility, intransigence, secrecy, or incompetence on the part of the agency, the rule will be deprived of information that is crucial in establishing its authority with the affected community. Put another way, stupid rules do not beget respect."[19]

The problem is that the APA simply permits its general requirements too many exceptions, which have the effect of permitting administrators to take the easy way out by interpreting vague clauses in the act so that they will not have to be inconvenienced. Unfortunately, some administrative officials seem to have a natural instinct to protect agency operations from public view by unnecessarily classifying material and functions from public scrutiny, thereby avoiding uninvited headaches. However, if government is to be democratic and accountable, as many operations as is reasonable should be conducted in the open. Because of APA loopholes, rulemaking and other important administrative activities have sometimes been kept too secretive.

In 1967 the Freedom of Information Act, an amendment to the APA, was passed to help force public agencies to become more public. Amendments have strengthened the originally rather weak FOIA over the years, although critics still contend that serious loopholes effectively prevent it from accomplishing its lofty objective of keeping *public* policy in the public eye. In a democracy public policy decisions should ideally involve the public. Delegating lawmaking powers to administrators is acceptable under most circumstances, but allowing administrators to make laws in secrecy appears contrary to popular-government theory. Democratic theorists maintain that secretive decisionmaking tends to encourage the growth of tyranny in government. Critics claim the Central Intelligence Agency and Federal Bureau of Investigation, two American public agencies, have for decades managed to operate quite undemocratically outside the public eye. Because of the nature of these public institutions, it seems that a certain degree of operative secrecy should be considered tolerable. For example, a spy can't spy if everything is known about the spying agenda. But it has been alleged that these agencies have frequently abused their privileged position and that lessons should be drawn from their abuses. It is true that the FBI (Federal Bureau of Investigation) and CIA (Central Intelligence Agency) have been rather successful in keeping their policies and practices not only from the American people but also from interested legislators and presidents (i.e., away from popular governmental machinery).

Pressure on these agencies to disclose publicly some of their controversial in-volvements—agency-head turnovers, leaks to the press, and books published by former CIA and FBI agents—combined, before September 11, 2001, to force these agencies' doors open just a bit to allow us to at least peek at some of the ac-tivities of the CIA and FBI, with shocking results. Evidently, these agencies have (1) carried out political assassinations (CIA); (2) acted to overthrow foreign gov-ernments (CIA); (3) blackmailed presidents (FBI); (4) worked as partners with the Mafia (FBI); (5) had prior associations with Lee Harvey Oswald, the assassin of President Kennedy (CIA and FBI); (6) sabotaged the 1972 presidential elec-tion (FBI); (7) illegally invaded the privacy of persons by breaking into their homes and private offices to obtain personal information (FBI); and (8) secretly helped build up the political and military power of President Saddam Hussein of Iraq, only for the U.S. to later topple Hussein's regime in 2003.[20]

Of course, since 9/11 much has changed. The USA PATRIOT Act of 2001 has allowed our government, once again, to conduct much of its anti-terrorist opera-tions, especially related to administrative and criminal searches and seizures, in relative secrecy. Attorney General John Ashcroft argues that such secrecy meas-ures are necessary to fight terrorism effectively. Civil libertarians naturally dis-agree vehemently. Fortunately, however, most agency actions, including rulemaking, are reasonably open to public participation and scrutiny because most agencies are not very involved with intelligence or security matters related to fighting terrorists.

The Rulemaking Power Rationale

How can the delegation of vast rulemaking powers to public administrators who are not subject to direct check by the voters be justified in a democratic nation? Although the extensive legislative powers granted to administrative agencies are feared by those who believe that administrative processes in a democratic country should closely reflect the prescriptions of democratic theory, an overwhelming majority of onlookers persuasively argue that modern government could not pos-sibly handle the burdens placed on it by a demanding public if legislators had to call all the shots or even most of them. There is some evidence that Americans ex-pect their government to cope with the problems that plague their daily lives but really don't seem to care how this is done.[21] By and large, administrative regula-tors have been accepted as legitimate by a public whose attitudes are rooted in a pragmatic philosophy. The pragmatic character of the American people has yielded the commonly accepted belief that theory is fine but only as long as it is as practical as it is elegant.[22]

Because the public tends to uphold democratic theory in the abstract but not altogether on practical grounds, it was easy for democratic theory to be compromised over the decades for better or for worse, so that it supports a modern, technological society that demands a fleet of regulators to guide and protect the public interest. Despite the fact that the U.S. Constitution does not, at least literally, allow administrators to act as legislators, the public has been quite willing to rationalize the granting of these legislative powers to public administrators. Probably the most basic insight offered to justify the rulemaking function of administrative agencies is that rulemaking, in fact, cannot be equated with the lawmaking function of legislators. Lawmaking is lawmaking and rulemaking is rulemaking—and that's that! While lawmaking is the drafting of basic public policies or laws by democratically elected legislators, it is held that rulemaking constitutes, in actuality, only a quasi-legislative power, not a genuine legislative power that can lead to the formation of fundamental public policies. Contrary to fact, proponents of the delegation doctrine suffer from the illusion that rulemakers do not engage in basic public policy making, but only in the making of those rules necessary to order the internal administrative procedures in their agencies and to make operational general congressional legislation already entrenched in legislative standards.

Practical considerations tend to dominate the reasons for allowing administrators to play such an assertive legislative role in the governmental system. A trite, yet valid, contention is that legislators simply do not have the time, will, or expertise to draft detailed legislation. Thus, public policies are purposely left vague by legislators so that administrators in the field and close to the action can have the flexibility to make any rules to implement public policies, as long as those quasi-legislative measures are consistent with legislative intent and proper procedure. Many critics also believe that administrators, not legislators, are in the best position to make meaningful public policies, because administrators can employ their plentiful field experiences to mold abstract, congressionally mandated public policies into practical public programs that stand a realistic chance of working in the field. It is also maintained that administrators, by virtue of their positions, are the real experts in their specialized areas and, therefore, should be accorded the power and flexibility they need to administer public policies in an insightful and responsive manner. Overall, administrators are perceived by many scholars, especially political scientists and sociologists, as being in a better position than legislators to make rules (policy statements) that reflect rational adjustments to environmental pressures.

But aside from the practical aspects of rulemaking for society, most observers probably do not see the rulemaking function as being particularly threatening to the U.S. democratic system. In the first place, as noted, administrators are not free to make general, or even rather specific, public policies as they see fit. Agency activities are watched not only by Congress, the courts, and the president but also by the public, guided by the news and editorial opinions in the newspapers and on television and radio. CBS's *60 Minutes* news magazine show, now in its thirty-sixth season, is an enlightening example of the impact such a show can have on shaping public opinion and checking agency behavior.[23] Despite the occasional scandal and discoveries of mismanagement, critics generally think that government administration is basically sound and responsible, especially at the national level. Political scientists have traditionally been more critical of public administration at the state and local levels.[24] It is held that professionalism, reflecting both expertise and a professional code of ethics, seems to keep most administrators accountable to the public. Rulemaking, especially the notice-and-comment kind, is thought by many to be a reasonably fair and open process.

Various pieces of legislation, especially the Administrative Procedure Act, help to define and structure rulemaking procedures so that the process is fair to the citizenry. Such amendments to the APA as the Freedom of Information Act, Privacy Act, Sunshine Act, and Negotiated Rulemaking Act of 1990 were all passed, it is argued, to guarantee administrative due process in rulemaking, as well as in other areas. The APA in Sections 552, 553, and 706 also compels agencies to obey their own rules, while other sections require agencies to reach decisions based on "substantial evidence" (556, 557, and 706) and not to make "arbitrary and capricious" decisions (706[2][a]). Although not all these sections apply to rulemaking specifically, they represent basic principles that pervade rulemaking, tending to make rules reasonable and dependable from the public's standpoint.

However, these arguments used to justify the very powerful legislative role played by administrators are not accepted as valid by many critics. Such experts assert that those who support without worry the trend toward increased delegation of legislative powers to administrative agencies are closing their eyes to rather blatant realities. It is foolish to suggest, these critics contend, that when agencies make rules, they are only carrying out the will of the legislators. The legislators do not attach meaningful guidelines (standards) to their mandated public policies; in recent years the trend has been for the legislature to pass public policy statements on to public agencies virtually without any meaningful guidelines in terms of their guidance capabilities (clearly indicating legislative intent). Consequently, rulemakers have been given the awesome power to design and implement fundamental public policies that have a profound impact on the American way of life, and Congress has not been reluctant to provide administrators with this authority.[25]

Theodore Lowi held in his classic work, *The End of Liberalism*, written over three decades ago, that legislators had irresponsibly delegated too broad lawmaking powers to agency rulemakers.[26] By the mid-1990s, he argued more vehemently that such irresponsible delegation, the source of power for rulemakers, constitutes a clear "derangement" of our Constitution.[27]

Another argument espoused by those who endorse a liberal application of the delegation doctrine asserts that administrators, because they are close to people and happenings in the field, are in the best position to obtain information and develop the insights necessary to shape sound public policies. But the critics maintain that these administrators frequently get too close to the field operations to regulate objectively in the public interest, thus failing to take the needs of the whole system into account. This charge is highly debatable, especially since no conclusive evidence exists suggesting that it is contrary to the intent of the system for people to fight for and protect, to the best of their abilities, their programs and clients.[28] It is also true that many of the regulatory agencies are obligated by statute to oversee, as well as promote, the welfare of those regulated. For example, the Federal Trade Commission promotes private business interests by dedicating itself not so much to protecting consumer interests, as many seem to believe, as to defending the right of business to function in the marketplace in relative freedom. Thus, in many instances, unless evidence is clearly to the contrary, it is difficult to contend that if rules favor the healthy development of an industry (for example, airlines), these rules necessarily are detrimental to the public interest.

However, in the absence of a convincing amount of evidence, a more credible charge is that field administrators use informal rulemaking processes to make rules that benefit, at least in the short run, the regulated interest at the expense of the public. Close ties, even friendship associations, can impair administrators' objectivity and cause them to grant to the industry concessions that can jeopardize the public safety. Evidence suggests, for example, that such was a contributing factor in the Three Mile Island nuclear plant meltdown, the DC-10 air disasters, the 9/11 terrorist hijackings and attacks,[29] and the deadly disintegration of the space shuttle *Columbia*.[30]

Opponents of the exaggerated application of the delegation doctrine also attack the proponents' contention that the public welfare is protected from irresponsible rulemaking because the rulemakers are adequately checked through both internal and external controls. But how effective are these controls? Norton Long argued over a half century ago that administrators are ultimately checked by themselves—that is, by prior training and a professional code that provides them with a value framework which guides their behavior.[31] However, rule-of-law advocates have always felt particularly uneasy with this position, especially since history has shown that people are not always capable of governing themselves. Besides, these critics maintain, what is honorable and professional to one public servant may not be perceived as such to another. Surely the 1973 Senate Watergate hearings give much credibility to this viewpoint, as well as testimony given during the Iran-contra and Whitewater investigations during the 1980s and 1990s. Thus, it does not seem illogical to hold that those who believe that administrative behavior can be effectively checked through administrators' adherence to professional codes of conduct are only engaging in wishful thinking. Responsibility in governmental administration cannot rest securely over time on the hope that civil servants will act responsibly, guided largely by an abstract professional code in, say, drafting rules to promote the public interest. The problem is that professionalism cannot be concretely defined and thus is incapable of providing the clear guidelines necessary to guarantee democratically responsible agency action.

Professionalism guided by concrete and elaborate external and internal statutes and rules would be consistent with the notion of "officialdom" as developed in Max Weber's famous and respected classical model on the ideals of bureaucracy. In Weber's thinking, professionalism should be guided by rigid and comprehensive statutes and rules that define the duties and obligations of the office. In this way, professionalism would be confined and structured and thus safer and more useful for governing administrative behavior. However, in the American administrative system, flexibility in administration has been wholeheartedly promoted as a virtue, thus preventing the development of essential statutes and rules necessary to prohibit the sometimes outrageous interpretations given to the professional code by irresponsible public administrators. To some, the argument that rulemakers should be granted great flexibility in administration is basically rooted in a lazy unwillingness on the part of legislators and administrators to become involved in the hard work vitally necessary to provide reasonable structuring of and limitations on delegation and rulemaking. Theodore Lowi, for example, acknowledges that it is unwise to handcuff administrators unnecessarily with inflexible statutes and rules. Nevertheless, he notes that the need-for-flexibility argument, although basically sound, has been "overused as an alibi for malfeasance in legislative drafting. Social pressure for some kind of quick action also interferes with drafting of a proper rule, even though this too is a much overused alibi."[32] Kenneth Culp Davis, condemning the broad discretionary flexibility given administrators in the absence of meaningful legislative guidelines and agency rules, tersely wrote: "Perhaps nine-tenths of injustice in our legal system flows from discretion and perhaps only one-tenth from rules."[33] Davis has always had a way of making his words count. This leading administrative law scholar has spent much of his academic career probing the ways in which discretion in decisionmaking, especially rulemaking, can be "confined, structured, and checked." Davis is very critical of those who assert that present rulemaking procedures represent a fair and open process in the American governmental system. Formal rulemaking procedures are relatively fair and open, Davis admits, but most rulemaking is very informal. Unfortunately, this too often leads to gross abuse of the rulemaking power and the drafting of informal rules (public policy statements) in the absence of meaningful input by the public.[34] Lowi agrees, adding that the ideal of relatively formal procedures leading to orders and rules in administrative agencies is largely a myth: "In practice, agencies end up with the worst of case-by-case adjudication and of rulemaking."[35]

THE DEMOCRATIC CHARACTER OF RULEMAKING PROCEDURES AND PUBLIC POLICY OUTPUTS

How democratic is the rulemaking process? In answering this question, the most popular approach, taken mostly by law-oriented writers, has been to analyze the nature of rulemaking procedures. They would focus essentially on the legislative statutes and agency procedures outlining rulemaking steps and on the question, How closely do these steps follow prescribed democratic standards? Realizing that attention to only formal or ideal requirements and procedures of rulemaking would be shortsighted, these scholars also spend considerable time examining informal aspects of rulemaking. As far as these critics go, they do an admirable job, particularly when they point to the notable differences between what formal rulemaking demands and which actual rulemaking procedures are practiced by administrators.

Unfortunately, the analysis of the democratic character of rulemaking normally stops here. An in-depth analysis of the democratic character of rulemaking requires that the ends and means of rulemaking be meaningfully linked to each other. That is, legal scholars seem to become so involved with the technical legal requirements of rulemaking (the means) that they either ignore or fail to emphasize the vital social purpose of rulemaking (the ends). It is absolutely impossible to reach intelligent conclusions regarding how democratic our current rulemaking practices really are unless rulemaking procedures are carefully scrutinized in the context of the actual public policies they produce. Thus, two additional questions need to be stressed: Who participates meaningfully in the rulemaking process? And probably of greater social importance, who really benefits from the public policies created by rulemakers? For certain, democratic theorists are most interested in the answers to these two questions. They would contend that formal and informal procedures mean very little in a democratic country if, in the final analysis, the general public is not provided with ample and genuine opportunity to influence public policy making while it must nonetheless stand to become the chief beneficiary of implemented public programs (the product of final rules in our case). Before addressing the issues surrounding these questions, it is appropriate to address some other points related to this question: Is rulemaking consistent with democratic government?

Are Rulemaking Procedures Developed and Structured Enough?

A popular argument has been made that rulemaking is safe for democracy because the delegation of this lawmaking function by legislators to administrators has not been done in the absence of reasonable checks. It appears that despite the importance of the rulemaking power, legislative assemblies were content to delegate the most fundamental governmental power (the legislative power) without attempting to confine this power by limiting its use through viable restrictions. As Robert S. Lorch points out, despite the vital importance of the rulemaking function to the preservation of democratic procedures in governance, only about one-tenth of the Administrative Procedure Act focuses on rulemaking standards. Nor do the agencies themselves devote much attention to developing rulemaking standards, although the time devoted to developing standards depends upon the nature and purposes of each agency.[36]

The relatively unstructured condition of rulemaking has been further compounded by the steadfast reluctance of the courts to demand that agencies develop and structure rulemaking procedures, especially when Congress has not requested agencies to do so through statutes (*Lopez v. Davis*, 121 S.Ct. 714 [2001]). Although rulemaking procedures lack meaningful structural guidelines at the national level, the situation is even worse at the state and local levels. Although the situation is improving, too many states have still not passed legislation adequate to reasonably guide their administrators when they are engaged in agency rulemaking. Although local governments are often compelled to follow the federal APA and their state's administrative procedure acts when they have jurisdiction (for example, federally funded programs in a local community normally require the recipient communities to honor federal procedures such as notice), they have developed virtually no rules governing administrative procedure. This is unfortunate because democracy probably acquires its most practical meaning at the local governmental level, where the average citizen has the most frequent confrontation with administrators. Yet citizens are most likely to be denied administrative due process by rather undistinguished local officials who are more geared to personalized administration than their typically more qualified, federal counterparts. In this sense, impersonalization is regarded as a virtue in public administration because it implies that all those who come before an administrative agency are given the same equal treatment according to established rules and regulations.

Of course, many vehemently argue that democracy would not be well served by rigidly structured rulemaking procedures that were too inflexible for quick and decisive responses to problems that plague the democratic state. Generally, these critics hold that a simple and flexible rulemaking system avoids procedural arthritis, which can stifle administrative efforts to generate needed public programs in response to public demands. They also maintain that complex procedures can confuse the public, thus discouraging citizens from participating in the rulemaking process altogether.

These arguments have some validity and point to a serious problem unique to democratic, as opposed to totalitarian, countries. They are, nevertheless, unconvincing. They are not convincing because democratic countries, if democratic practices are to be preserved, must resolve democratic problems with democratic solutions. The streamlining of rulemaking procedures may make it easier for administrators to propose, draft, and implement rules; but if the procedures are undemocratic, the likelihood that the resulting public policies would reflect majority will would diminish. There seems to be little question among democratic theorists that, logically, democracy is best preserved by the continuance of democratic decisionmaking. Consequently, those who cherish democratic institutions must seek a way to allow essential flexibility in rulemaking while simultaneously guaranteeing that rulemakers remain democratically accountable to the public.

Public Participation in
Rulemaking: Myth versus Reality

Ideally, the public can meaningfully participate in the rulemaking process. On paper, rulemaking is a relatively open process. In *Riverbend Farms, Inc. v. Madi-*

gan, 958 F.2d 1479, 1483–1484 (9th Cir. 1992), the court exclaimed: "The Administrative Procedure Act ensures that the massive federal bureaucracy remains tethered to those it governs—or so the theory goes." According to the APA (Section 553), as well as state APAs, proposed rules are announced to the public by being published in the *Federal Register* or a similar governmental news source on the state level. After such notice, agencies are required, under "normal" circumstances, to "give interested persons an opportunity to participate in the rulemaking through submission of written data, views, or arguments with or without opportunity for oral presentation" (Section 553[c]). Agencies are also required to "consider relevant matter presented" before drafting their final rules, and such adopted "substantive" rules shall not become effective for at least thirty days after passage (Section 553[d]). Finally, to protect against the possibility of unsound rules being kept in force, "each agency shall give an interested person the right to petition for the issuance, amendment, or repeal of a rule" (Section 553[e]). It would appear that even a devout cynic would have to admit, after reading Section 553 of the APA, that rulemaking is fair and open to democratic participation.

Unfortunately, however, this rulemaking section is so plagued with exceptions and loopholes that it turns out to be a cynic's paradise. For example, after evaluating the difference between what ought to be and what is in rulemaking, Jeffrey F. Jowell concluded that formal rulemaking prescriptions, as developed in the APA, amount to not much more than what Murray Edelman several years ago referred to as "symbolic reassurances"—myths, symbols, rituals, and the like used by states to appease the public.[37] Jowell wrote summarily: "In other words, rulemaking procedures may be used by an administrative agency to give an impression of participation, whereas no more than pro forma adherence to an empty democratic ritual is involved."[38]

This cynical perspective on the openness of rulemaking to meaningful participation by interested persons is shared by many, and apparently for good reason. Careful examination of all exceptions or loopholes in the rulemaking section of the prototypical APA shows that there are enough loopholes in the legislation to allow administrators ample opportunities to undermine what the section ideally promotes. A leading administrative law scholar supports this insight by his assertion that "the strength of [Section] 553 may lie in the procedure marked out for rulemaking when the exceptions do not apply. Experience for a quarter of a century or more fully confirms that strength. The weakness of 553 may lie in the extensive exceptions."[39] For instance, although on the surface public notice of rulemaking is required, notice does not apply to "interpretative rules, general statements of policy, or rules of agency organization, procedure, or practice" (Sec. 553[b][3][A]).[40]

This means that agencies have broad discretion. They can select from various rule types, as well as rulemaking methods that do not require notice. Rules may be promulgated by a variety of informal and formal methods in which (1) absolutely no participation by affected or interested persons is involved, (2) participation is limited to consultation or conferences between the interested persons and the agency, (3) consultation takes place with advisory committees, (4) formal written arguments and facts are solicited and submitted to the agency, or (5) trial-like hearings are conducted. Any of these rulemaking procedures can be used more or less formally. But the bottom line is that by promulgating interpretative rules and policy statements, rulemakers can quite easily avoid the making of substantive or legislative rules, of which the granting of notice is much more common but not necessarily required. Notice is never absolutely required. There are enough loopholes in the rulemaking legislation that notice as well as comment can almost always be avoided by an administrator determined to foreclose public participation. And, according to Richard Pierce, Jr., exploiting the loophole of notice has negative democratic consequences because the "elimination of notice and comment procedure invariably detracts from the fairness, wisdom, and political legitimacy of a rule."[41]

But why should certain rules be exempt from requiring notice and allowing interested parties to participate? Anyone who is familiar with administrative law understands that interpretative rules may carry considerable weight. It was noted earlier in this chapter that interpretative rules (agency "laws" which have resulted from interpretations of legislative statutes entrusted to the agency), in fact, constitute agency policy; and such policy is normally upheld by the courts. The application of an interpretative rule by an agency could cause an industry, for example, to incur substantial unanticipated expenses (for example, the EPA decides that waste includes certain dangerous substances that, therefore, cannot be emitted into the atmosphere). Consequently, it seems only fair that affected parties be given notice and provided an opportunity to present arguments in their behalf.

The problem is further compounded by Congress's failure to pass clear and well-developed legislation. It has been especially the case in recent decades that Congress passes the most general legislation, allowing administrative agencies great latitude in giving functional meaning to legislative policies through their interpretations. Consequently, most rules made by administrators can be regarded as interpretative rules, although distinguishing between an interpretative rule and a legislative rule, as indicated previously, is not always an easy task.[42] The charge has been made that administrators too often abuse their rulemaking powers by relying too heavily on the interpretative rule loophole, thus weakening the democratic fabric of rulemaking by eliminating notice, an obvious prerequisite to meaningful participation in the shaping of public policy. The wisdom of excluding interpretative rules from notice requirements is also suspect on the grounds that interpretative rules are very likely to be durable as well as unreviewable. In criticizing case law on interpretative rules, Michael Asimow concluded: "Interpretative rules are usually neither tentative nor temporary. Finally, even if their effect on the regulated parties is subject to a probably illusory administrative reconsideration, their effect on others, such as consumers or competitors, may be definitive and virtually unreviewable."[43]

Policy statements by administrative agencies are also issued without the benefit of notice, despite the fact they too carry great clout. It is sometimes difficult to distinguish between legislative and interpretative rules; yet it is no less of a chore to distinguish policy statements from legislative rules. *Policy statements* are supposed to be more tentative than legislative rules; yet policy statements are expected to be developed enough to provide a genuine guide for agency behavior in executing public policy. Critics have held that policy statements are to be both tentative and concrete, but this, they acknowledge, is a contradiction. Nevertheless, policy statements, as exempted interpretative rules, can and have played a significant role in shaping public policies that determine in part the way Americans can live. Therefore, agency policy statements also should not be exempt from the notice requirements, and healthy democratic participation should not be blocked.

Notice is also not required when agencies issue rules pertaining to agency procedure, organization, and practice. Such appears to be an unjustifiable exemption, even if notice involves inconveniencing agency officials somewhat. Max Weber reasoned decades ago that the operating procedures of public bureaucracies should be made known to the public. In a democracy, this guarantees that bureaucracy functions in the context of the rule of law. Fundamental fairness, Weber argued, demands that the public be notified about the rules and regulations that govern administrative procedure so that the public is protected from arbitrary and capricious agency practices that can promote unreliable, irresponsible, and unstable agency behavior. To Weber, the importance of properly drafting and publicizing bureaucratic rules and regulations in a "legal-rational" system of government, such as that of the United States, could not be overemphasized.[44] It seems only fair that people who come before administrative agencies should be able to rely on relatively consistent agency practices over time. Surely, agencies must be allowed to make necessary procedural adjustments from time to time, but such changes in operational procedures should be made public so that persons counting on certain established procedures are not unfairly inconvenienced.[45]

Although the APA does not require notice to be given when agencies issue interpretative rules, policy statements, or rules regarding agency organization, procedures, and practices, some federal agencies give notice anyway. However, democracy will not be properly served unless the APA is amended to require all federal agencies, except for those involved in sensitive policy areas, such as the CIA, to issue notice for such proposed rules. In a democracy, the first impulse should be to open the door to participation in the making of virtually any kind of public policy, not to close it. If genuine public policies in the form of rules are to be generated by rulemakers, then the rulemakers should be compelled to open rulemaking to interested parties as much as possible. It is reasonable to assume that public policy outputs will generally reflect the public policy–making inputs. Thus, undemocratic inputs will yield undemocratic outputs.[46]

The APA provision that requires public agencies to solicit and consider all relevant material in the drafting of a final substantive rule has attracted considerable criticism, not so much because of what Section 553(c) says but for what actually goes on in practice. The consensus is that participation in the rulemaking process is far from equitable and democratic. It is important to emphasize that Section 553(c) requires administrative agencies to consider only relevant materials presented. It does not require administrators to actually be influenced by submitted data and arguments. Under this section agency officials are also given the discretion to decide what constitutes relevant submitted information. This gives agency officials great power because, as organizational theorists have long pointed out, those who control the information can control the situation. To Weber, this was the real source of power for bureaucracy.[47] Thus, for all practical purposes, when making rules, administrators have absolute discretionary power to ignore or honor any or all inputs from interested parties attempting to shape the rules in their favor. (It must be said, however, that Congress had no real choice but to give administrators such discretion, because realistically it would create a potentially chaotic, disruptive, and inefficient situation if rulemakers were legally obligated to respond formally to every "comment" and piece of "relevant materials" submitted.) And the courts, especially since *Chevron*, have been very willing to accept the expertise of administrators in determining the relevancy of submitted data. Obviously, then, two intriguing questions emerge. First, to whom do agency rulemakers tend to listen and respond? Second, why?

A preponderance of credible evidence presented by social scientists suggests strongly that rulemakers are influenced much too much by the powerful special interest groups and not enough by those forces that are more representative of the public interest.[48] This reality was acknowledged in *Riverbend Farms* when the court said that "usually special interest groups influence the rulemaking process, even though the process is open to 'members of the public'" (p. 1484). One problem in interest group theory has always been the inability of the observers to define the public interest definitively enough that general agreement could be reached on its meaning. Trying to block the merger of the International Telephone and Telegraph Corporation with the Hartford Fire Insurance Company in the early 1970s, Ralph Nader and Reuben B. Robertson argued before the federal district court (D. Conn.) that the merger, among other things, was contrary to the public interest. District Judge Blumenfeld, however, did not sympathize with Nader and Robertson's claim that they represented the public interest, especially since the public interest could not be satisfactorily defined.[49] But if the public interest cannot be defined, then why does Congress assign to regulatory agencies the task of regulating within the public interest?

Only a naive observer of the American system could conclude that all interest groups have equal access and influence on U.S. decisionmakers, whether they are lawmakers or rulemakers. Real pluralist politics in America tends to substantiate the realist's belief that life is unfair. It only makes sense, despite the obvious inequities, that the most powerful interests are in the best position to influence policy decisions so that they can become even more powerful and secure. This reality is well documented and is even championed by social Darwinists, who hold that the social system is strengthened by allowing the strong to survive and the weak to perish.

This is the key point. For all practical purposes, the power game that started during the colonial period is now over. Victors and vanquished, so to speak, have emerged. The big, rich, powerful interests are the winners. These interests, exerting their great influence, have been able to change the original rules of the game to favor their privileged position, thus ensuring no serious threat from competitors and, thereby, effectively destroying what was left of the free marketplace in the United States. Therefore, weaker interests today (many small businesses, consumer groups) have very little chance of influencing, say, rulemaking in their favor over the wishes of the powerful interests (for example, IBM, General Motors, ITT, AMA), because virtually all the wild cards in the game have already been dealt to the big interests. That is, in this context the powerful interest groups today could be accused of cheating because they are playing with a stacked deck that makes fair competition among pluralist interests impossible. This stacked deck has given the powerful interest groups the cards they need to make them formidable lobbyists before the rulemakers. As compared to lesser opponents in this modern influence-peddling game, the big interests are in an advantageous position because they have well-organized, well-financed, stable lobbying organizations that are staffed by well-paid, full-time professionals who are able to tap a stockpile of in-house information. According to Robert S. Lorch, this gives the powerful interests strong teeth with which to bite agency rulemakers. Although he somewhat overstates himself here, Lorch claims "teeth are all that count in politics."[50]

Some observers of the power game argue that the big interests are not only too much for their competitors but too much for the regulatory agencies as well. Legal obstacles and lack of personnel and necessary technical knowledge and data, particularly when some interests have seemingly endless resources with which to fight agencies with limited budgets, inspired at least one federal rulemaker to say, in a remark quoted by Caroline E. Mayer, "We're no match for the people we're supposed to regulate."[51] Summarizing the chief argument of the critics in 1978, Robert A. Kagan noted that a serious problem exists in achieving democratic rulemaking in America, because "regulatory agencies are not too stringent but overly accommodative to the businesses they are supposed to control; they become 'captives' of the dominant firms in the regulated industry, protecting their interests rather than preventing or redressing injuries to the public."[52] Evidently, nothing has changed. In a recent law review article on the 9/11 terrorist attacks and airline security, Mark Niles acknowledges that the airline industry's dominance or capture of the Federal Aviation Administration arguably contributed to the failure of the FAA to promulgate safety rules that might have prevented the terrorists from so easily hijacking four planes and carrying out their deadly attacks. Focusing on the role that the FAA's "regulatory structure" may have played in 9/11 and other recent airline disasters, he observed: "Specifically, scholars have pointed to the FAA as a victim of the phenomenon of 'agency capture,' and at least one agency veteran was quoted in a national news magazine in 1995 as saying: 'To tell the truth, the industry, they really own the FAA.'"[53]

In a card game the players can start over again after throwing out the cheaters, but real-life contenders cannot start over; they must cope with the players already in the game and do the best to make the game fairer. Davis contends that "probably most rulemaking is still done with little or no party participation of any kind."[54] But this seemingly undemocratic practice should not be taken so pessimistically. Formal party participation is certainly excluded from the making of most rules, but one should not infer that rulemakers are not listening or are insensitive to the pressures coming from their environment through the normal feedback cycle. Systems theory makes clear that all capable decisionmakers read and respond to input from their respective environments. In this case, rulemakers are normally informed enough to anticipate at least the basic reactions to their proposed and final rules from various interest groups. A plethora of studies of interest group politics by social scientists over the past few decades have demonstrated that most governmental decisionmakers, including agency rulemakers, tend to favor the powerful interest groups in their policy outputs, even in the absence of any evidence of formal participation in the decisionmaking process by the always pervasive big interests.[55] In regard to agency rulemaking, this happens if for no other reason than that the rulemakers do not want to ruffle the feathers of those who can relentlessly fight back.

In summary, if the rulemakers feel pressured more by the well-organized, well-financed, and determined special interests, then it is only logical to assume that agency policies will tend to favor these special interests. But when decisionmakers (rulemakers) in a political system favor special interests over the public interest, the system ceases to be a democratic one rooted in the rule of law. Plato argued in the *Laws* that such politics function more like parties than governments because parties normally favor special interests but governments should not.[56] Jean Jacques Rousseau argued similarly in *Social Contract* that democracy is undermined when special interests dominate the general will.[57] In *The Federalist* James Madison argued that democratic liberty allows for the pursuit of selfish interests by private parties—but not to the point that the public interest is jeopardized. Madison considered the preservation of relative freedom by preventing any single or few interests from destroying the larger public interest a critical role of government.[58] Thus, the consensus among theorists seems to be that promoting the public interest, not special interests, is government's rightful role. Therefore, Americans should seek to equalize group inputs in the rulemaking process and design rulemaking techniques so that the public interest is better represented and democracy can be preserved. But is it naive to assume, given the tremendous influence big interests already have over agency policymaking today, that this goal can be achieved? Maybe this country will never be able to release the tightening grip the powerful interests already have on its rulemakers. In this era of corporate takeovers and mergers creating giant global companies, it appears that the most powerful interests are becoming even more powerful, promising to make it even more difficult for agency administrators to protect and promote the public interest over the wants of the newly emerging "super special interests."

But maybe this rhetoric is too alarming. Kerwin notes that although 84.1 percent of the interest group lobbyists report that their participation influences rulemaking "half of the time" (40.9 percent), three-quarters of the time (42.4 percent), or "always" (0.8%), agency rulemakers claim in another survey that they make few changes to proposed rules because of interest group participation and do not show any significant preference for comments by special interests over the general public. Although Kerwin questions claims of the lobbyists because he believes they have an interest in exaggerating their effectiveness, he really doubts the survey responses of the agency rulemakers because he thinks that "rulemakers are by now quite sensitive to charges of 'unresponsiveness' and 'capture' by special interests." Consequently, he concludes that rulemakers would not want to give answers to questions about the influences of the big special interest group lobbyists which could make agency rulemakers look like they serve as doormats for these special interests.[59]

More Exemptions to the APA

There are still more exemptions to Section 553 of the APA; they also tend to close rulemaking from open, democratic participation. Although these exemptions deserve comment, what has just been said about the interactions between rulemakers and various interest groups helps to explain the whys of these exemptions too. Most, if not all, of the exemptions tend to favor administrators and certain special interests—probably not the general public. Administrators benefit directly from the freedom they are given to draft rules, thus sparing themselves many headaches. The powerful interest groups, in contrast, benefit indirectly because they are the most capable in dealing with the complex, time-consuming, and expensive rulemaking process, with its confusing and inconsistent procedures.

Section 553(e) allows interested persons "the right to petition for the issuance, amendment, or repeal of a rule." However, the APA does not require agencies to do anything more than *receive* these petitions. Administrators are given total discretion in deciding what attention they should give certain inputs. Systems theory suggests that administrators would not likely ignore those inputs that could pose serious problems to the agency. It should be recalled that it is very important in systems theory that agency leaders respond properly to feedback from their environment so that the smooth continuance of agency operations can be assured. But it is logical to conclude that the rhetoric of Section 553(e) creates another significant loophole. Though certainly reasonable in that administrators should not be compelled to act on every petition submitted, the loophole nevertheless permits agencies to treat submitted petitions unequally. It is only sensible to assume, especially in the context of systems theory, that agencies would likely honor most of those petitions, regardless of their objective merits, which place the greatest demands upon the agencies.

Military or foreign affairs functions (Section 553[a][1]) and matters relating to "agency management or personnel or to public property, loans, grants, benefits, or contracts" (Section 553[a][2]) are also exempt from the general APA rulemaking requirements. While some of these exemptions seem justified, others are questionable, especially since the exemptions are allowed to apply under all circumstances, regardless of the democratic fairness and reasonableness of their application. Probably those military and foreign affairs functions actually linked to national security interests, especially in legitimate classified areas, should be excluded from the Section 553 requirements. But what about those military and foreign affairs activities that cannot reasonably be considered sensitive or meaningfully related to national security? It is true that the defense of the United States should be given high priority, especially since the 9/11 terrorist attacks, but the importance of defense matters should not blind the country so that it allows the Homeland Security Department, for example, to carry out any policy it sees fit without public comment. There is no reason to exclude the public from rulemaking leading to important, nonsensitive policy decisions. For example, should not the public have a right to object to a proposed rule that calls for nuclear missile tests or the dangerous dumping of nuclear waste close to large population centers? Did this nation not learn decades earlier that certain Defense Department decisions placed the lives of innocent persons in jeopardy (for example, atomic bomb tests in the 1950s in Utah leading to radiation sickness in the 1980s and 1990s) when an open airing of the proposed test sites could have prevented unnecessary risks? These past decisions are costing taxpayers millions of extra dollars today in tort liability suits against the federal government.

It would seem democratically justifiable to amend Section 553(a)(1) of the APA so that only those military and foreign affairs matters considered sensitive or those that place in jeopardy national security interests are exempted from normal rulemaking procedures established in the act. In addition, it might even be a good idea to request the rulemakers taking the exemption to note in writing, for the record, why taking the exemption is justified.

Similarly, why should the public not be allowed to express opinions regarding matters related to "agency management or personnel or to public property, loans, grants, benefits, or contracts" (Section 553[a][2])? Under certain circumstances, it would be unwise and unethical for agencies to open the rulemaking process in these areas to the public, especially if by doing so, they would disclose business secrets or endanger the public interest. For instance, under special circumstances, it would be detrimental to the public interest, in a financial sense, for an agency to disclose prematurely the intention of building a road through a particular area, because such notice would undoubtedly cause speculators to buy key property so that they could make it difficult for the government to obtain the needed property at a reasonable price.

For purposes of privacy, there are reasons to keep personnel records secret, but possibly not when employee performance becomes a significant factor. The business of awarding loans, grants, and contracts has become quite controversial, especially since so much money is involved. Although Congress has dealt with some of these matters in such transactions as the Lockheed and Chrysler loans, most are negotiated directly with administrative agencies. Richard P. Nathan pointed out that during the Nixon presidency Nixon reached the conclusion that the bureaucracy had tremendous powers to influence public policy directions because these agencies were directly responsible for awarding billions of dollars in federal loans, grants, and contracts each year.[60] On a lower level, state and local agencies also wield such power. Does not the public have a right during rulemaking to question, for example, the intention of public agencies to award costly contracts? Or as Robert S. Lorch sarcastically asserted in this regard, "I can imagine that some people might be interested in knowing in advance that the Park Service is about to sell Old Faithful to a steam generating company."[61]

Finally, the APA, under Section 553(b)(A), allows agencies to prevent participation by not giving notice if agency officials believe that to do so would be "unpracticable, unnecessary, or contrary to the public interest." However, the agency must show "good cause" when invoking this exemption, stating the reasons. In 1992 in *Riverbend Farms*, the Ninth Circuit court recognized the importance of the good cause exception, but stressed that the "exception goes only as far as its name implies: It authorizes departures from the APA's requirements only when compliance would interfere with the agency's ability to carry out its mission" (p. 1485). Despite the fact that this loophole could be abused by those administrators determined to limit participation by using an unreasonably broad interpretation as to when notice seems "unpracticable, unnecessary, or contrary to public interest," the exemption is acceptable since the abuse could not likely be carried too far. Justifying "good cause" too often could muster suspicion and create cause for investigation.

In *Natural Resources Defense Council v. Evans*, 316 F.3d 904 (2003), the same Ninth Circuit court, building on their *Riverbend Farms* decision, upheld the argument by the NRDC that the National Marine Fisheries Service misused the good cause exception under the APA by using it to avoid providing notice and allowing comment before issuing specifications and management regulations applying to Pacific Coast Groundfish Fishery. The court argued that the good cause exception should be used rarely or only when legitimate reasons exist (for example, genuine emergencies) to justify the agency not using notice-and-comment rulemaking procedures, because not permitting notice and comment can actually change "the substance of the decision reached" (p. 912). In sum, the court reasoned: "We need not determine the precise contours of what constitutes good cause in this context. We simply hold that NMFS failed to make a sufficient showing that good cause existed for 2001, as the agency did not demonstrate that some exigency apart from generic complexity of data collection and time constraints interfered with its ability to promulgate specifications and management measures" (p. 912). There are times when inviting unnecessary participation through notice may be disruptive to the administrative process; for example, notice could lead to time-consuming participation at a moment when administrators need to respond quickly to alleviate a serious social problem. But to reiterate, as demonstrated in Evans, the exemption does not seem to be contrary to democratic principles as long as the withholding of participation is modest and truly within the public interest—an expediency in the administrative process, particularly in times of emergency, seems to be within the public interest.

SENSIBLE SUGGESTIONS FOR
MAKING RULEMAKING MORE DEMOCRATIC

One thing becomes evident from reading the literature pertaining to rulemaking: A great number of administrative law critics have been quite displeased with the state of rulemaking for many years. They argue that rulemakers have essentially been given carte blanche discretionary powers to implement and eventually judge the appropriateness, effectiveness, and fairness of their own administratively constructed public policies, under which the public must live. These scholars are particularly upset with the position taken by the spokespersons for another point of view, who hold that public administrators should be given the necessary flexibility (discretion) to implement and adjudicate public policies, since they are real experts. Because external checks on administrative actions have proved to be quite ineffective in practice, these critics are quick to point out that the future of democratic policymaking in the United States is in real jeopardy. They claim that any semblance of democratic procedure in rulemaking today is missing.

Richard Pierce, Jr., points out in his 2002 *Administrative Law Treatise* that the rulemaking process suffers from a variety of problems, one of the most serious stemming from the many APA exemptions that allow public administrators the discretionary power to avoid more open democratic rulemaking procedures. He stresses that the Administrative Conference of the United States has recommended to Congress that significant changes in rulemaking should be made to make it fairer, more responsive, and essentially more democratically accountable; yet by 2002, he reported, "Congress has not chosen to follow those ACUS Recommendations."[62]

Basically, the scholars advocate three chief suggestions for improving the democratic character of rulemaking. One is to improve the delegation of lawmaking or rulemaking powers to administrative agencies by attaching standards and guidelines that can be effective in guiding rulemakers. The second is to confine and structure internal rulemaking procedures so that procedural due process and rule-of-law principles are honored in the making of rules. Third, the scholars advocate that better review of agency actions be provided, in the area of rulemaking in particular, by improving supervisory methods that can be employed by legislative assemblies, courts, and the public. The by now renowned ideas of Theodore Lowi and J. Skelly Wright on rulemaking reform tend to encapsulate very well the opinions of many others.[63]

Lowi: Today's Rulemaking Is Undemocratic

In his classic work, *The End of Liberalism*, Theodore Lowi set forth a forceful, scholarly argument that holds basically that our rulemaking practices are undemocratic and contrary to the public interest. His argument is as valid today in the 1990s as it was when he first made it in the 1960s, especially since overall delegation has become broader. He contends that administrators have written very poor laws, laws so vague and inconsistent that they cannot convey legislative intent to administrators. Although Lowi is opposed to the practice of legislators delegating broad legislative powers to administrative agencies through undeveloped, skeletal statutes, he nevertheless feels that improving delegation through designing better laws is one way to make rulemaking more consistent with juridical democracy. Lowi contends that rulemaking could be made more democratic if increased "administrative formality" were in practice, by which he means, simply, the adherence by administrators to internal agency rules and regulations governing the promulgation of substantive agency policies (rules). More specifically, administrative formality in rulemaking would obligate rulemakers to follow more prescribed written rules. Such rulemaking formality would curtail the use of administrative discretion and produce more formalized, written rules. Lowi contends that the present rulemaking process encourages bargaining between agency leaders and privileged interests, ending in rules that are implicit or in reality even nonexistent but, in any event, crippling to the public interest.[64]

Lowi further maintains that "early and frequent administrative rulemaking" is a necessary requisite in administrative formality.[65] In other words, the frequent making of needed rules tends to formalize administrative procedure because it leads to a body of written rules that provides general guidelines for future internal or external agency policy standards. In short, such formalization tends to give the public agency structure and consistency. According to the Supreme Court, structure and consistency must be promoted in public agencies so that the agencies act reliably (*Heckler v. Community Health Services of Crawford*, 104 S.Ct. 2218 [1984]). Formalization also necessarily limits discretionary actions since agencies, by law, are compelled to comply with their own rules. Lowi submits that the promulgation of "early rules" (those drafted by an agency early in the life of a mandating statute) is in the best interests of democratic government because the procedure permits a relatively quick evaluation of whether legislative intent is reasonably represented by agency interpretations of specific statutes. Early rulemaking also is sensible, according to Lowi, because it facilitates legislative and judicial review of agency rulemaking and the relevance of agency actions.[66]

Lowi believes administrative formality, fostered by "early and frequent rulemaking," promotes administrative centralization. He believes that this makes sound managerial sense because it provides "unity of direction" to rulemaking. He contends that if enough procedural and substantive rules to form a "guiding light" are promulgated by an agency, then administrative decisionmaking at all hierarchical levels within the agency could reflect prescribed general organizational goals in a more consistent manner. This would make agency decisions not only quicker and more decisive but also more reliable and responsible and, thus, more in line with democratic accountability in decisionmaking.[67]

Lowi holds that the democratic nature of rulemaking could also be improved significantly through codification. He asserts that present administrative law is in such a mess that codification could serve to clarify ambiguities, remove inconsistencies, and generally resolve many of the administrative law problems due chiefly to disorganization. Essentially, *codification* is a process whereby centralized organization is achieved through systematic categorization. In administrative law, the systematic recording and indexing of pertinent statutes, rules, judicial decisions, and the like into a comprehensible and accessible source would help to make administrative law in general, but rulemaking in particular, more consistent and accessible. In addition, Lowi argues that codification would help to restore democratic control over agency practices. In particular, it would tend to restore healthy legislative dominance over administration by presenting administrative law in a practical, understandable, and useful package. A unified code of administrative law would allow legislators to delegate powers, such as rulemaking powers, more broadly to administrators yet still retain basic control over administrative actions because legislators would be left with a current, comprehensible, and practical administrative law code that they could employ to manage and oversee administrative behavior. Lowi thinks codification could eventually evolve into an adequate substitute for what he perceives as "the futile oversight process."[68]

Judge Wright: Rulemakers Must Keep Adequate Records, Especially of Ex Parte Contacts

J. Skelly Wright, former chief judge of the U.S. Court of Appeals for the D.C. Circuit, argues persuasively that rulemaking could be made more equitable and democratic if rulemakers only kept a reasonable record during informal rulemaking. Informal rulemaking, commonly known as the notice-and-comment approach, is the most popular APA-sanctioned rulemaking procedure used by administrative agencies, except when specific agency statutes require rulemaking "to be on the record after opportunity for hearing" (Section 553[c]).

Wright is appalled at the way rulemaking is carried out by federal agency officials, especially since the APA's rulemaking requirements are so straightforward. He notes that "the procedure under the APA for informal rulemaking is so simple that it is unfortunate what has been done to it by the agencies and by the courts. All that is required by the statute is that the proposed rules and supporting data be published in the *Federal Register* with notice that comments and counter-comments on the proposed rules will be received by the agency during a stated limited period."[69] Unfortunately, Wright adds, agencies frequently make rules in the complete absence of adequately kept records.

Wright asserts that surely there can be no question as to what should constitute a proper record for informal rulemaking. A proper record would simply include (1) the published proposed agency rule with its relatively detailed description; (2) the final rule with written agency justification for it; and (3) the comments and countercomments, documents, and so on submitted as a response to the proposed published rule. Such would constitute a proper record unless testimonial transcripts or special hearing records are involved.

Despite the Supreme Court's decision in *Citizens to Preserve Overton Park, Inc. v. Volpe*, 401 U.S. 402 (1971), to require agencies in the future to keep a proper record, most agencies by the early 2000s still do not do so, although improvements have been made. What agency administrators must understand, Wright exclaims, is that agencies are now compelled to keep a record of informal rulemaking. He asserts: "We are not mind readers; nor are we unduly impressed by pretensions of agency expertise unsupported by the record. . . . It is with respect to this record that we must review the reasons given by the agency for proposing the rule initially, and approving it finally."[70]

However, Wright argues, the failure to keep an adequate record not only precludes intelligent review of agency rulemaking but also is patently undemocratic and detrimental to the promotion of the public interest. The reasons are obvious. Rulemaking in the absence of a decent record keeps rulemaking, a very important policymaking process, "behind closed doors." The keeping of a record is consistent with popular government theory because it assures that decisionmakers are allowed to see the light of day, in the forms of further comment, analysis, and review, if deemed necessary.[71]

Wright expresses particular concern for unethical and undemocratic ex parte contacts (contacts made to benefit the *present* party, usually at the expense of the *absent* party or parties), which can easily be carried out between privileged parties and agencies if all their dealings remain totally out of public view and thus off the record. If an interested party wants to influence rulemaking, Wright argues that their contributions should properly be placed in the record so that all other interested parties have an opportunity to respond. Wright asks: "Why should only some parties have private access to the eye or ear of the decision-maker during rulemaking? What conceivably acceptable reason can there be for such private access during rulemaking? If there is a reason, can it be strong enough to overcome the damage to the rulemaking proceeding caused by the appearance of preference and prejudice created by the *ex parte* contacts if disclosed, and the damage to the other interested parties, to the record, and therefore to judicial review, if the *ex parte* contacts remain undisclosed?"[72]

Ex parte contacts are such one-sided affairs, Wright concludes, that they give unfair preference to the special interests and undermine the public interest. This is a dangerous practice to continue in a democratic society, because public policies can be easily warped by ex parte contacts with our rulemakers; yet reviewing courts would never be able to determine what inputs actually shaped the final rules. Wright takes this view:

> Unless *ex parte* contacts during rulemaking are avoided, in addition to keeping the public and other parties in the dark, the reviewing court is denied access, not only to the contents of the contacts, but also to whatever response those contacts would have triggered were their contacts known. How is a court to make in-depth review of the record when some parts, perhaps some important parts, have been withheld—from it, from the public, and from other interested parties? How is a court to know—how is anyone to know—whether an undisclosed *ex parte* contact with the decisionmaker tilted his decision one way or another?

Whatever the law was with respect to *ex parte* contacts during informal rulemaking proceedings before *Overton Park*, in my judgment a reviewing court acting under the mandate of *Overton Park* can no longer accept a record flawed by such practices? . . . Why—why the *ex parte* contacts?"[73]

It seems that the vast majority of administrative law scholars and political scientists condemn ex parte contacts in principle. However, there are those who argue that ex parte contacts constitute a legitimate aspect of pluralist, democratic politics. They argue, as Judge Wald did in *Sierra Club v. Castle*, 657 F.2d 298 (D.C. Cir. 1978), that Congress prohibited ex parte contacts only on communications in formal rulemaking proceedings, not in informal rulemaking. Proponents contend that rulemakers need to listen to lobbyists who make ex parte contact with them in order to promulgate intelligent, responsible rules. Advocates acknowledge that ex parte contacts could lead to biased agency rules that serve more to promote the welfare of special interests than the public interest, but they believe that if adequate records are kept on such contacts, reviewing courts could always judge whether biased, irresponsible decisions on rules were made. However, such may be wishful thinking because certainly agency administrators, if they wanted to hide biased agency rulemaking, could easily construct a record of the ex parte contacts that buries the truth.[74]

Recently, the Supreme Court revisited the question of ex parte communications in *United States v. Navajo Nation*, 123 S.Ct. 1079 (2003). In this case the Court rejected the argument by the Navajo nation that ex parte communications during an administrative appeals process unduly influenced the interior secretary's decision, because the process was informal, permitting ex parte communications and the secretary to rely on "any information available . . . whether formally part of the record or not." The Court added that if the dispute was heard before the Board of Indian Appeals, it "would have triggered review of a more formal character, in which *ex parte* communications would have been prohibited" (p. 1095).

Negotiated Rulemaking:
An Effort to Promote Consensual Rulemaking

In 1990 Congress passed the Negotiated Rulemaking Act (104 Stat. 499), and in 1996 the experimental act was reauthorized permanently by the Administrative Dispute Resolution Act (110 Stat. 3870). This reform measure was designed to bring together representatives of various organizations that agency administrators believe will be impacted the most by proposed agency action leading to a promulgated rule. Ideally, these representatives would work together with agency rulemakers to negotiate a settlement on a proposed rule that all parties having a major stake in the outcome could "live with." Starting in the 1980s, negotiated rulemaking—popularly called "Reg-Neg"—was sold as a reform rulemaking approach that would greatly improve the quality of participation in the rulemaking process and, as a consequence, also improve the substance of the actual rules promulgated. Proponents also held that Reg-Neg would significantly reduce lawsuits resulting from the promulgation of rules, because Reg-Neg participants, having participated in the negotiation of the rule and now having a vested interest in making it work, would not likely want to sue.[75]

The concept of negotiated rulemaking, endorsed in the literature by a weighty consensus of scholars (practitioners, especially the rulemakers themselves, are more ambivalent about the idea), is, of course, rooted in a very old and tested technique for reaching decisions—employed for many decades for mediating and resolving labor disputes. For instance, in the 1930s the Fair Labor Standards Act established a process whereby interested parties were brought together in committees to negotiate settlements to labor disputes. In the 1960s Charles Lindbloom, a public administration scholar, advanced an idea for improving decisionmaking in public agencies by proposing the concept of partisan mutual adjustment (PMA),[76] which embraces virtually all of the components of and basic arguments for Reg-Neg. Lindbloom argued, as do proponents of Reg-Neg, that decisions reached through negotiation or through interested parties mutually working out differences between them (i.e., through PMA) are much more likely to gain participants' respect and honor than when decisions are "crammed down their throats." Philip Harter, who wrote "Negotiating Regulations" in 1982, is credited the most for promoting the Reg-Neg concept. In this article Harter applies essentially Lindbloom's arguments in trying to persuade the reader that negotiated rulemaking should frequently be substituted for traditional notice-and-comment rulemaking. To Harter, traditional rulemaking is characterized by an adversarial process in which special interests ruthlessly pressure rulemakers to promulgate rules that favor their particular interests at the expense of the public interest, while the rulemakers create records to avoid being sued. Harter contends that traditional notice-and-comment rulemaking usually produces long delays in the issuance of rules, substantively flawed rules, and rules that fail to gain respect and compliance from the regulated. Reg-Neg, in contrast, promotes negotiation, or Lindbloom's PMA process, which, Harter maintains, tends to lead to informed, intelligent rules that the regulated, whose representatives participated in the process, are willing to uphold (see Figure 5.2 for an example of Reg-Neg).[77]

On the surface, Reg-Neg looks like a desirable alternative to notice-and-comment rulemaking, particularly because it has the promise of promoting more "informed" rules that will likely enjoy wide acceptance and voluntary compliance, as well as significantly reduce lawsuits caused by the promulgation of "insensitive" rules by agency rulemakers. Reg-Neg enjoyed initial acceptance because of its promise. By the mid-1990s, most federal agencies had at least experimented with Reg-Neg, especially after President Clinton's Executive Order 12866 in 1993 encouraged the use of negotiated rulemaking. However, despite being permanently authorized in 1996, Reg-Neg will probably face a rocky road in the future. The basic problem with Reg-Neg is that it can work only under ideal conditions, which of course limits its ability to be used very broadly by agencies to promulgate rules. First, negotiated rulemaking will succeed only if the potential exists for a negotiated settlement or rule. This means that the stakes cannot be too high or issue conflict too intense. For example, it would likely prove futile to use Reg-Neg to promulgate a rule on abortion procedures at clinics because of the intensity of the moral issue. Second, the regulatory objectives must be clear; yet in reality agency rulemakers themselves are often not sure what their objectives should be. Third, the regulatory issues must be ripe for resolution, whereas a host of problems may prevent maturation (e.g., insufficient data on the issue exist, not every participating organization may be "ready"). Fourth, the "right" participants must be selected as negotiators. They must be willing to compromise and have the authority to do so (i.e., they must be able to speak for their organizations). Fifth, agency rulemakers must avoid selecting too few or too many Reg-Neg participants yet somehow assemble an ideal number that truly reflects those interests that a negotiated rule would affect. Certainly Reg-Neg cannot work in a large assembly hall filled with participants, yet it would also fail if only, say, four participants were supposed to represent a large diversified field of interests. Parenthetically, the ideal Reg-Neg committee is "limited to twenty-five members drawn from the agency, citizen groups, regulated entities, trade unions, and associations."[78] Sixth, Reg-Neg will work only if participants perceive advantages to participating in Reg-Neg. The truth is that many organizations may rather stick with their sophisticated lobbyist network already in place rather than rely upon the risky Reg-Neg process whereby each organization would have very limited control. Seventh, organizations must have not only the will to participate but also the time and resources to do so. The typical Reg-Neg process would likely take many negotiating sessions spread over a period of at least several months, if not years. Small organizations, therefore, may not be able to commit the time and financial resources to Reg-Neg, even though they may have a great stake in the rule eventually promulgated by Reg-Neg. Such small organizations would probably rather participate in the much less costly notice-and-comment rulemaking process. Eighth, agencies must be able to select very skilled convenors with considerable mediation experience to handle participants who may have more advanced negotiating skills than the convenors. Convenors must achieve a consensus among the Reg-Neg participants so a rule can be promulgated; yet this will rarely be an easy task. Ninth, and very important, agencies must be willing to accept the negotiated rule, which means that the agency must be willing to "give up" a lot of its rulemaking power. If participants ever suspect that their input is just a waste of time because the agency will simply promulgate the rule it really wants, the Reg-Neg process will immediately be perceived as a farce and break down. Ultimately, Reg-Neg can succeed only if the participants honestly feel that their input is really going to be considered by the agency rulemakers because, legally speaking, only the agency administrator can make the final decision since, "as President George Bush emphasized upon signing the act, 'Under the Appointments Clause of the Constitution . . . governmental authority may be exercised only by officers of the United States.'"[79]

EVALUATION
• Identify issues and deadlines
• Identify interested parties
• Compare to selection criteria
• Confirm management interest
• Select convenor

CONVENING—PHASE 1
• Identify additional parties
• Discuss RegNeg with parties
• Discuss issues with parties
• Determine willingness of parties to negotiate
• Report to agency
• Obtain agency management commitment
• Preliminary selection of 15–25 participants

CONVENING—PHASE 2
• Obtain parties commitment to negotiate
• Publish "notice of intent to negotiate"
• Process FACA charter
• Select facilitator/mediator
• Respond to public comments on "notice"
• Adjust committee membership if necessary
• Arrange organizational meeting
• Arrange committee orientation/training

NEGOTIATIONS
• Establish groundrules/protocols
• Define "consensus"
• Set meeting schedule
• Publish notices of meetings
• Review available information and issues
• Review draft rule or proposals, if available
• Establish work groups or subcommittees as necessary
• Negotiate text or outline of proposed rule

RULEMAKING
• Negotiations concluded

• If consensus is reached on language of rule:
   • Agency circulates draft for international/external review
   • Agency publishes consensus as draft rule

• If consensus is reached only on issues or outline:
   • Agency drafts proposed rule
   • Agency circulates draft for internal/external review
   • Agency publishes NPRM

• If consensus is not reached:
   • Agency proceeds with rulemaking using discussions as a guide
   • Agency drafts and publishes NPRM

• Draft rule is subject to public comment
• Committee notified of public comment
• Agency revises rule, if necessary
• Agency publishes final rule

FIGURE 5.2   Negotiated Rulemaking at the EPA

Ironically, the first Reg-Neg case to reach a federal circuit court in fact involved a charge by a participant that the agency negotiated in bad faith. In *USA Group Loan Services v. Riley*, 82 F.3d 708 (7th Cir. 1996), USA Group Loan Services, a participant on the Department of Education's Reg-Neg committee trying to negotiate a rule pertaining to student loan servicers' liability for student loan defaults, argued that DOE negotiated in bad faith because it included in its final rule a cap on liability after the cap had been proposed by the agency and rejected and withdrawn during Reg-Neg. The court held that even though DOE reneged on a promise to comply with any consensus reached by the Reg-Neg committee, "the Negotiated Rulemaking Act did not make the promise enforceable. . . . The practical effect of enforcing it would be to make the Act extinguish notice-and-comment rulemaking in all cases in which it was preceded by negotiated rulemaking; the comments would be irrelevant if the agency were already bound by promises that it had made to the industry. . . . Unlike collective bargaining negotiations, . . . the Act does not envisage that the negotiations will end in a binding contract. The Act simply creates a consultative process in advance of the more formal, arm's length procedure of notice and comment rulemaking" (pp. 714–715).

It is worth noting that this court showed its dislike for Reg-Neg. Believing that the Negotiated Rulemaking Act of 1990 was going to expire in 1996, the court criticized the act, contending that it seems to allow agencies to promise what they cannot and should not promise—that is, it allows participants in Reg-Neg to really make the rules. To the court this seemed "an abdication of regulatory authority to the regulated, the full burgeoning of the interest-group state, and the final confirmation of the 'capture' theory of administrative regulation" (p. 714). Although this dicta by the court caused considerable controversy and prompted defenders of Reg-Neg to bash the court, the court's insights are quite valid but somewhat exaggerated. Phil Harter claimed the court misrepresented Reg-Neg because the act requires the Reg-Neg committee "to ensure that the full range of concerns, facts, and issues will be raised while developing a rule."[80] However, Harter seems to ignore the obvious, what the court in *USA Group Loan Services* could not ignore. That is, the special interests, at the expense of the public, tend to dominate rulemaking in general, and Reg-Neg is no exception. For example, in the case before this court, the Reg-Neg committee consisted not of a diverse group of interested parties but "principally, if not exclusively, of loan servicers" lobbying for their special interest.[81] Richard Pierce, Jr., asserts that "the Court's description of the process is more realistic than Harter's description." He is right because, typically, participants in Reg-Neg do not reflect fairly the diverse interests that should be represented ideally in democratic decisionmaking. Pierce concludes: "Most rulemakings [a]ffect both the interests of small groups of firms, each of which has a great deal at stake, and large groups of people, each of whom has a small amount at stake. The small groups have an enormous practical advantage over the large groups when an agency uses a decisionmaking procedure like Reg-Neg that puts a premium on the amount of resources groups are willing to commit to the decisionmaking process."[82]

The main reason Reg-Neg will probably either fail as a common procedure for promulgating rules or be used on a very limited basis is that most of the conditions cited above describe most rulemaking situations. After acknowledging a long list of conditions that must be satisfied for Reg-Neg to succeed, Pierce, who is more pessimistic about the future of Reg-Neg than most scholars, concludes:

"Unfortunately, most major rulemakings involve all of these conditions. Thus, most major rulemakings are poor candidates for resolution through Reg-Neg, which has succeeded in only about 20 percent of the rulemakings in which it has been tried."[83] Pierce stresses that Reg-Neg has little chance of succeeding because it is virtually impossible to get all parties to agree on anything when "the stakes are high, and a large number of parties will be affected in disparate and complicated ways."[84]

Others attack Reg-Neg because it has proved cost-ineffective. For instance, Cary Coglianese, rooting his opinion in empirical research on the effectiveness of negotiated rulemaking, concludes that it has not saved agencies tax dollars, resources, or time; nor curbed rulemaking conflicts between parties; nor reduced litigations.[85] He is probably right, given the circumstances in *USA Group Loan Services* and the reality that Reg-Neg disputes are becoming much more commonplace in federal courts.[86] Ellen Siegler, providing an industry perspective, criticizes Reg-Neg for demanding too much counterproductive time and resources from participants.[87] Another opponent, William Funk, opposes Reg-Neg because he believes that the process prioritizes consensus agreements among the often unrepresentative participants at the expense of sound law rooted in the facts that promotes the larger public interest.[88] Jack Beermann agrees, arguing that negotiated rulemaking presents a threat to democratic accountability practices, undermining the public interest. "From an accountability standpoint," Beermann writes, "there is some concern that the negotiations simply will degenerate into horse trading among interested parties who may ignore the overall public interest." The reality, he notes, is that most interested parties are not Reg-Neg participants and, therefore, "the negotiation process still may excite suspicion from those not involved in the negotiations."[89]

Cornelius Kerwin is much more optimistic about the future of Reg-Neg. Although he recognizes the many problems associated with Reg-Neg, he nonetheless concludes that "regulatory negotiation is a permanent part of contemporary rulemaking."[90] He is right that it is a part of today's rulemaking, but as he admits, it will remain only a small part: "Because of the time and resource costs, negotiated rules will continue to represent a small percentage of all rules developed by agencies." Nonetheless, Kerwin stresses that "it would be a serious mistake to measure the influence of this innovation solely on the basis of the volume of rules produced in accord with the Negotiated Rulemaking Act of 1990. In fact, agencies with Reg-Neg have convincingly demonstrated the efficacy of open bargaining."[91] In some cases Reg-Neg has been used successfully, no doubt, but Kerwin is unquestionably giving Reg-Neg a positive spin. The hard reality is that Reg-Neg has many obvious flaws and is a process that can be used only under ideal conditions and, even when used, has reportedly an 80 percent failure rate. Given the time, energy, and resources that must be devoted to negotiated rulemaking, this constitutes an alarming failure rate that will discourage the future use of Reg-Neg and continue to raise the eyebrows of Reg-Neg's numerous critics.

SUMMARY

The lawmaking power is the most basic of governmental powers. Although the constitutional framers originally assigned this function to Congress, that body eventually delegated away much of the authority to public administrators. A similar course of action has taken place at the state level. In agencies, lawmaking is called rulemaking. It would be wrong to assume that promulgated rules do not often carry the same force as laws drafted by legislators. In fact, the courts have insisted that they would not set aside a legislative rule any more than they would overturn a law passed by Congress. Interpretative rules are also quite authoritative, although they stand more of a risk of being overruled by the courts when challenged. The truth, even though it might gravely shock those who wrote the Constitution, is that more than 90 percent of modern American laws are rules (public policies) promulgated by agency administrators.

To guide the rulemaking process, Congress has drafted specific provisions in the Administrative Procedure Act. Basically, these provisions have been designed to make agency rulemaking fair by opening up the process to all interested parties. But critics charge that the democratic character of rulemaking procedures under the APA is more apparent than real. They point to major loopholes in the APA rulemaking requirements that permit agency rulemakers the discretion to favor certain interest groups over others. Systems theorists contend that public administrators would have a tendency to favor those powerful interests in the political system that could jeopardize agency security, because agency leaders are naturally concerned about responding appropriately to those environmental demands that pose the greatest threat to agency well-being.

Social scientists' consensus is that present agency rulemaking practices do, in fact, favor the powerful interests at the expense of the weaker interest groups and the general citizenry. If an effects test is applied, the interest group theorists argue, it is clear that agency rules have mostly benefited the *haves* to the detriment of the *have-nots*. To improve the democratic nature of rulemaking, several suggestions have been proposed. Most notably, it has been suggested that more formal procedures should be incorporated into the rulemaking process to further structure rulemaking so that the uncertainties and inequities associated with agency discretion could be minimized. In an attempt to make rulemaking more substantively sound and fairer to the parties who ostensibly would be most affected by agency rules, reformers managed to get the Negotiated Rulemaking Act passed in 1990. This new law encourages rulemakers, using agency intervenors working with representatives from "key" organizations, to negotiate proposed rules. Reg-Neg, as it is called, shows some promise, but skeptics believe it will ultimately fade away as a viable rulemaking approach, mainly because the process is too costly and time-consuming and can be employed only under ideal conditions. Also, cynics claim that Reg-Neg is structured to better serve special interests than the general public. Reformers in general have argued that agency rulemaking could be improved if rulemakers limited ex parte contacts with outside parties and, at the very least, kept better records of any ex parte contacts.

MOTOR VEHICLE MFRS. ASS'N V. STATE FARM MUTUAL

463 U.S. 29; 103 S.Ct. 2856 (1983)

Facts

Under the National Traffic and Motor Vehicle Safety Act of 1966, the secretary of transportation is entrusted with issuing motor vehicle safety standards that "shall be practicable, shall meet the need for motor vehicle safety, and shall be stated in objective terms." The secretary must consider, when implementing these standards, "relevant available motor vehicle safety data"; whether a proposed standard is "reasonable, practicable and appropriate" for a specific vehicle; and the extent to which a proposed standard contributes to the act's goals. Judicial review of "all orders establishing, amending, or revoking" any vehicle safety standard is authorized under the Administrative Procedure Act. The National Highway Traffic Safety Administration (NHTSA), under the secretary's delegated authority, rescinded Modified Standard 208, which required new motor vehicles made after September 1982 to be equipped with passive restraints (i.e., automatic seat belts or air bags). NHTSA justified the rescission of the safety standard by arguing that it could no longer show, as it could when the rule was first issued in 1977, that the passive restraints would yield significant safety benefits. Also, NHTSA maintained that many consumers would perceive the safety requirement as just another example of ineffective regulation, given the high cost of the passive restraints. State Farm Mutual Automobile Insurance Company et al., objecting to the rescission, petitioned the D.C. Circuit Court of Appeals for review. The court ruled that rescission was arbitrary and capricious, arguing, inter alia, that NHTSA failed to provide sufficient reasons for the rescission. The Supreme Court granted certiorari.

Justice White delivered the opinion of the Court.

The ultimate question before us is whether NHTSA's rescission of the passive restraint requirement of Standard 208 was arbitrary and capricious. We concluded, as did the Court of Appeals, that it was. We also conclude, but for somewhat different reasons, that further consideration of the issue by the agency is therefore required. We deal separately with the rescission as it applies to airbags and as it applies to seatbelts.

The first and most obvious reason for finding the rescission arbitrary and capricious is that NHTSA apparently gave no consideration whatever to modifying the Standard to require that airbag technology be utilized. Standard 208 sought to achieve automatic crash protection by requiring automobile manufacturers to install either of two passive restraint devices: airbags or automatic seatbelts. There was no suggestion in the long rulemaking process that led to Standard 208 that if only one of these options were feasible, no passive restraint standard should be promulgated. Indeed, the agency's original proposed standard contemplated the installation of inflatable restraints in all cars. Automatic belts were added as a means of complying with the standard because they were believed to be as effective as airbags in achieving the goal of occupant crash protection, 36 Fed. Reg. 12,858, 12,859 (July 8, 1971). At that time, the passive belt approved by the agency could not be detached. Only later, at a manufacturer's behest, did the agency approve of the detachability feature—and only after assurances that the feature would not compromise the safety benefits of the restraint. Although it was the foreseen that 60% of the new cars would contain airbags and 40% would have automatic seatbelts, the ratio between the two was not significant as long as the passive belt would also assure greater passenger safety.

The agency has not determined that the detachable automatic belts will not attain anticipated safety benefits because so many individuals will detach the mechanism. Even if this conclusion were acceptable in its entirety, see infra, at 2871–2872, standing alone, it would not justify any more than an amendment of Standard 208 to disallow compliance by means of the one technology which will not provide effective passenger protection. It does not cast doubt on the need for a passive restraint standard or upon the efficacy of airbag technology. In its most recent rulemaking, the agency again acknowledged the lifesaving potential of the airbag. Given the effectiveness ascribed to airbag technology by the agency, the mandate of the Safety Act to achieve traffic safety would suggest that the logical response to the faults of detachable seatbelts would be to require the installation of airbags. At the very least this alternative way of achieving the objectives of the Act should have been addressed and adequate reasons given for its abandonment. But the agency not only did not require compliance through airbags, it did not even consider the possibility in its 1981 rulemaking. Not one sentence of its rulemaking statement discusses the airbags-only option. Because, as the Court of Appeals stated, "NHTSA's . . . analysis of airbags was nonexistent." We have frequently reiterated that an agency must cogently explain why it has exercised its discretion in a given manner, *Atchison, T. & S.F.R. Co. v. Wichita Bd. of Trade*, 412 U.S. at 806 (1965); and we reaffirm this principle again today.

The automobile industry has opted for the passive belt over the airbag, but surely it is not enough that the regulated industry has eschewed a given safety device. For nearly a decade, the automobile industry waged the regulatory equivalent of war against the airbag and lost—the inflatable restraint was proven sufficiently effective. Now the automobile industry has decided to employ a seatbelt system which will not meet the safety objectives of Standard 208. This hardly constitutes cause to revoke the standard itself. . . . If, under the statute, the agency should not defer to the industry's failure to develop safer cars, which it surely should not do, *a fortiori* it may not revoke a safety standard which can be satisfied by current technology simply because the industry has opted for an ineffective seatbelt design. Although the agency did not address the mandatory airbags option and the Court of Appeals noted that "airbags seem to have none of the problems that NHTSA identified in passive seatbelts," petitioners recite a number of difficulties that they believe would be posed by a mandatory airbag standard. These range from questions concerning the installation of airbags in small cars to that of adverse public reaction. But these are not the agency's reasons for rejecting a mandatory airbag standard. Not having discussed the possibility, the agency submitted no reasons at all. The short—and sufficient—answer to petitioners' submission is that the courts may not accept appellate counsel's *post hoc* rationalizations for agency action. *Burlington Truck Lines v. United States, supra*, 371 U.S., at 168, 83 S.Ct., at 245. It is well-established that an agency's action must be upheld, if at all, on the basis articulated by the agency itself. . . .

Petitioners also invoke our decision in *Vermont Yankee Nuclear Power Corp. v. NRDC*, 435 U.S. 519, 98 S.Ct. 1197, 55 L.Ed.2d 460 (1978), as though it were a talisman under which any agency decision is by definition unimpeachable. Specifically, it is submitted that to require an agency to consider an airbags-only alternative is, in essence, to dictate to the agency the procedures it is to follow. Petitioners both misread *Vermont Yankee* and misconstrue the nature of the remand that is in order. In *Vermont Yankee*, we held that a court may not impose additional procedural requirements upon an agency. We do not require today any specific procedures which NHTSA must follow. Nor do we broadly require an agency to consider all policy alternatives in reaching decision. It is true that a rulemaking "cannot be found wanting simply because the agency failed to include every alternative device and thought conceivable by the mind of man . . . regardless of how uncommon or unknown that alternative may have been, . . ." 435 U.S., at 551, 98 S.Ct., at 1215–1216. But the airbag is more than a policy alternative to the passive restraint standard; it is a technological alternative within the ambit of the existing standard. We hold only that given the judgment made in

1977 that airbags are an effective and cost-beneficial life-saving technology, the mandatory passive-restraint rule may not be abandoned without any consideration whatsoever of an airbags-only requirement.

Although the issue is closer, we also find that the agency was too quick to dismiss the safety benefits of automatic seatbelts. NHTSA's critical finding was that, in light of the industry's plans to install readily detachable passive belts, it could not reliably predict "even a 5 percentage point increase as the minimum level of expected usage increase," 46 Fed.Reg., at 53,423. The Court of Appeals rejected this finding because there is "not one iota" of evidence that Modified Standard 208 will fail to increase nationwide seatbelt use by at least 13 percentage points, the level of increased usage necessary for the standard to justify its cost. Given the lack of probative evidence, the court held that "only a well-justified refusal to seek more evidence could render rescission non-arbitrary."

Petitioners object to this conclusion. In their view, "substantial uncertainty" that a regulation will accomplish its intended purpose is sufficient reason, without more, to rescind a regulation. We agree with petitioners that just as an agency reasonably may decline to issue a safety standard if it is uncertain about its efficacy, an agency may also revoke a standard on the basis of serious uncertainties if supported by the record and reasonably explained. Rescission of the passive restraint requirement would not be arbitrary and capricious simply because there was no evidence in direct support of the agency's conclusion. It is not infrequent that the available data does not settle a regulatory issue and the agency must then exercise its judgment in moving from the facts and probabilities on the record to a policy conclusion. Recognizing that policymaking in a complex society must account for uncertainty, however, does not imply that it is sufficient for an agency to merely recite the terms "substantial uncertainty" as a justification for its actions. The agency must explain the evidence which is available, and must offer a "rational connection between the facts found and the choice made." *Burlington Truck Lines, Inc. v. United States, supra,* 371 U.S., at 168, 83 S.Ct., at 246. Generally, one aspect of that explanation would be a justification for rescinding the regulation before engaging in a search for further evidence.

In this case, the agency's explanation for rescission of the passive restraint requirement is *not* sufficient to enable us to conclude that the rescission was the product of reasoned decisionmaking. To reach this conclusion, we do not upset the agency's view of the facts, but we do appreciate the limitations of this record in supporting the agency's decision. We start with the accepted ground that if used, seatbelts unquestionably would save many thousands of lives and would prevent tens of thousands of crippling injuries. Unlike recent regulatory decisions we have reviewed . . . (1981), the safety benefits of wearing seatbelts are not in doubt and it is not challenged that, were those benefits to accrue, the monetary costs of implementing the standard would be easily justified. We move next to the fact that there is no direct evidence in support of the agency's finding that detachable automatic belts cannot be predicted to yield a substantial increase in usage. The empirical evidence on the record, consisting of surveys of drivers of automobiles equipped with passive belts, reveals more than a doubling of the usage rate experienced with manual belts. Much of the agency's rulemaking statement—and much of the controversy in this case—centers on the conclusions that should be drawn from these studies. . . . We believe that it is within the agency's discretion to pass upon the generalizability of these field studies. This is precisely the type of issue which rests within the expertise of NHTSA, and upon which a reviewing court must be most hesitant to intrude.

But accepting the agency's view of the field tests on passive restraints indicates only that there is no reliable real-world experience that usage rates will substantially increase. To be sure, NHTSA opines that "it cannot reliably predict even a 5 percentage point increase as the minimum level of increased usage." But this and other statements that passive belts will not yield substantial increases in seatbelt usage apparently take no account of the critical difference between detachable automatic belts and current manual belts. A detached passive belt does require an affirmative act to reconnect it, but—unlike a manual seat belt—the passive belt, once reattached, will continue to function automatically unless again disconnected. Thus, inertia—a factor which the agency's own studies have found significant in explaining the current low usage rates for seatbelts—works in *favor* of, not *against*, use of the protective device. Since 20 to 50% of motorists currently wear seatbelts on some occasions, there would seem to be grounds to believe that seatbelt use by occasional users will be substantially increased by the detachable passive belts. Whether this is in fact the case is a matter for the agency to decide, but it must bring its expertise to bear on the question.

The agency is correct to look at the costs as well as the benefits of Standard 208. The agency's conclusion that the incremental costs of the requirements were no longer reasonable was predicated on its prediction that the safety benefits of the regulation might be minimal. Specifically, the agency's fears that the public might resent paying more for the automatic belt systems is expressly dependent on the assumption that detachable automatic belts will not produce more than "negligible safety benefits." 46 Fed.Reg., at 53,424. When the agency reexamines its findings as to the likely increase in seatbelt usage, it must also reconsider its judgment of the reasonableness of the monetary and other costs associated with the Standard. In reaching its judgment, NHTSA should bear in mind that Congress intended safety to be the preeminent factor under the Motor Vehicle Safety Act. . . .

The agency also failed to articulate a basis for not requiring nondetachable belts under Standard 208. It is argued that the concern of the agency with the easy detachability of the currently favored design would be readily solved by a continuous passive belt, which allows the occupant to "spool out" the belt and create the necessary slack for easy extrication from the vehicle. The agency did not separately consider the continuous belt option, but treated it together with the ignition interlock de-

vice in a category it titled "option of use-compelling features." The agency was concerned that use-compelling devices would "complicate extrication of [a]n occupant from his or her car." . . . "To require that passive belts contain use-compelling features," the agency observed, "could be counterproductive [given] . . . widespread, latent and irrational fear in many members of the public that they could be trapped by the seat belt after a crash." . . . In addition, based on the experience with the ignition interlock, the agency feared that use-compelling features might trigger adverse public reaction.

By failing to analyze the continuous seatbelt in its own right, the agency has failed to offer the rational connection between facts and judgment required to pass muster under the arbitrary and capricious standard. We agree with the Court of Appeals that NHTSA did not suggest that the emergency release mechanisms used in nondetachable belts are any less effective for emergency egress than the buckle release system used in detachable belts. In 1978, when General Motors obtained the agency's approval to install a continuous passive belt, it assured the agency that nondetachable belts with spool releases were as safe as detachable belts with buckle releases. 43 Fed.Reg. 21,912, 21,913–14 (1978). NHTSA was satisfied that this belt design assured easy extricability: "the agency does not believe that the use of [such] release mechanisms will cause serious occupant egress problems . . ." 43 Fed.Reg. 52,493, 52,494 (1978). While the agency is entitled to change its view on the acceptability of continuous passive belts, it is obligated to explain its reasons for doing so.

The agency also failed to offer any explanation why a continuous passive belt would engender the same adverse public reaction as the ignition interlock, and, as the Court of Appeals concluded, "every indication in the record points the other way." We see no basis for equating the two devices: the continuous belt, unlike the ignition interlock, does not interfere with the operation of the vehicle. More importantly, it is the agency's responsibility, not this Court's, to explain this decision.

"An agency's view of what is in the public interest may change, either with or without a change in circumstances. But an agency changing its course must supply a reasoned analysis. . . . " *Greater Boston Television Corp. v. FCC*, 444 F.2d 841, 852 (1971). We do not accept all of the reasoning of the Court of Appeals, but we do conclude that the agency has failed to supply the requisite "reasoned analysis" in this case. Accordingly, we vacate the judgment of the Court of Appeals and remand the case to that court with directions to remand the matter to the NHTSA for further consideration consistent with this opinion.

So ordered.

Justice REHNQUIST, with whom THE CHIEF JUSTICE, Justice POWELL, and Justice O'CONNOR join, concurring in part and dissenting in part.

. . . In particular, I agree that, since the airbag and continuous spool automatic seatbelt were explicitly approved in the standard the agency was rescinding, the agency should explain why it declined to leave those requirements intact. In this case, the agency gave no explanation at all. Of course, if the agency can provide a rational explanation, it may adhere to its decision to rescind the entire standard.

I do not believe, however, that NHTSA's view of detachable automatic seatbelts was arbitrary and capricious. The agency adequately explained its decision to rescind the standard insofar as it was satisfied by detachable belts.

The statute that requires the Secretary of Transportation to issue motor vehicle safety standards also requires that "[e]ach such . . . standard shall be practicable [and] shall meet the need for motor vehicle safety." 15 U.S.C. 1392(a). The Court rejects the agency's explanation for its conclusion that there is substantial uncertainty whether requiring installation of detachable automatic belts would substantially increase seatbelt usage. The agency chose not to rely on a study showing a substantial increase in seatbelt usage in cars equipped with automatic seatbelts and an ignition interlock to prevent the car from being operated when the belts were not in place and which were voluntarily purchased with this equipment by consumers. See *ante*, at 2870, n.15. It is reasonable for the agency to decide that this study does not support any conclusion concerning the effect of automatic seatbelts that are installed in all cars whether the consumer wants them or not and are not linked to an ignition interlock system.

The Court rejects this explanation because "there would seem to be grounds to believe that seatbelt use by occasional users will be substantially increased by the detachable passive belts," *ante*, at 2872, and the agency did not adequately explain its rejection of these grounds. It seems to me that the agency's explanation, while by no means a model, is adequate. The agency acknowledged that there would probably be some increase in belt usage, but concluded that the increase would be small and not worth the cost of mandatory detachable automatic belts. 46 F.R. 53421–54323 (1981). The agency's obligation is to articulate a "rational connection between the facts found and the choice made." *Ante*, at 2866–2867, 2871, quoting *Burlington Truck Lines v. United States,* 371 U.S. 156, 168, 83 S.Ct. 239, 246, 9 L.Ed. 2d 207 (1962). I believe it has met this standard.

The agency explicitly stated that it will increase its educational efforts in an attempt to promote public understanding, acceptance, and use of passenger restraint systems. 46 F.R. 53425 (1981). It also stated that it will "initiate efforts with automobile manufacturers to ensure that the public will have [automatic crash protection] technology available.

If this does not succeed, the agency will consider regulatory action to assure that the last decade's enormous advances in crash protection technology will not be lost." *Id.,* at 53426.

The agency's changed view of the standard seems to be related to the election of a new President of a different political party. It is readily apparent that the responsible members of one administration may consider public resistance and uncertainties to be more important than do their counterparts in a previous administration. A change in administration brought about by the people casting their votes is a perfectly reasonable basis for an executive agency's reappraisal of the costs and benefits of its programs and regulations. As long as the agency remains within the bounds established by Congress, it is entitled to assess administrative records and evaluate priorities in light of the philosophy of the administration.

COMMENTS AND QUESTIONS

State Farm, 103 S.Ct. 2856 (1983), stands as one of the most important rulemaking decisions ever handed down by the Supreme Court. This is because the Court addressed and upheld in articulate fashion a fundamental principle that administrative agencies in a rule-of-law nation must honor. That is, the Court held essentially that public agencies must be bound by their own rules. In *Reuters Ltd. v. FCC,* 781 F.2d 946, 947 (D.C. Cir.1986), Judge Starr stressed that this "elementary" precept "lies at the foundation of the modern administrative state." It is a "block-letter principle" which holds that "properly enacted regulations have the force of law and are binding on the government until properly repealed" (p. 950).

In *State Farm* the Court made clear that an agency does not have the freedom simply to abandon a prior policy course by suddenly rescinding a rule that has guided its previous policy and has been relied upon by those dealing with the agency. To the Court, a public agency such as the NHTSA may rescind a rule or its current policy, but in reversing its policy position, it is legally obligated to provide an explanation ("reasoned analysis") for the policy reversal beyond that required when an agency had no prior policy course. In *State Farm* the Court believed that the NHTSA was very negligent in this respect, so it concluded that the agency's "explanation for rescission of the passive restraint requirement is *not* sufficient to enable us to conclude that the rescission was the product of reasoned decisionmaking" (p. 2871). Therefore, the Court found the NHTSA's rescission of Standard 208 to constitute an arbitrary and capricious action.

Why do you suppose the NHTSA abruptly decided to reverse policy directions, knowing that its action would anger many and violate basic administrative procedure? The truth is that the NHTSA's decision to rescind was probably more political than administrative. Under pressure from the new Reagan administration, the NHTSA made the policy shift in order to comply with President Reagan's deregulation philosophy. Is it responsible for federal agencies to reverse established policy directions dramatically in order to conform to a newly elected president's political philosophy? Although the Supreme Court's majority in *State Farm* thought not, unless the agency roots its policy change in reasoned analysis supported by the rulemaking record, the four dissenters (justices Rehnquist, Powell, and O'Connor and Chief Justice Burger) felt otherwise. They argued that it is "perfectly reasonable" for an executive agency to reappraise the costs and benefits of programs and rules and then change policy directions in response to the democratic election of a new president (p. 2875). The dissenters probably have a point regarding broad policy decisions, but could this be carried too far? To what extent should agency decisionmaking be politicized? For many scholars, including Max Weber, responsible, efficient, and professional public administration requires a reasonable separation between administration and politics. Should our implementation of tested safety standards that protect human lives rest on whether the safety standard is politically popular at the time? Which sort of administrative decisions legitimately belong in the political arena, and which kind should be kept politically neutral?

NOTES

1. Cornelius M. Kerwin, "The Elements of Rulemaking," in David H. Rosenbloom and Richard D. Schwartz, ed., *Handbook of Regulation and Administrative Law* (New York: Marcel Dekker, 1994), p. 345. For a comprehensive analysis of the importance of rulemaking, see Cornelius M. Kerwin, *Rulemaking: How Government Agencies Write Law and Make Policy*, 2nd ed. (Washington, D.C.: Congressional Quarterly Press, 1999), chap. 1.

2. Susan Sommer, "Independent Agencies as Article One Tribunals: Foundations of a Theory of Agency Independence," *Administrative Law Review* 39 (winter 1987). Also see, Donald E. Elliott, "*INS v. Chadha:* The Administrative Constitution, the Constitution, and the Legislative Veto," *Supreme Court Review* 183 (1983).

3. Kerwin, *Rulemaking*, p. 6.

4. Theodore J. Lowi, "Two Roads to Serfdom: Liberalism, Conservatism and Administrative Power," *American University Law Review* 36 (winter 1987).

5. This regulatory agency practice has been severely criticized by administrative law scholars since both "rules" and "orders" yield public policies. Yet participation in rulemaking is generally considered more consistent with democratic norms since in theory the processes are much more open to interested parties seeking to influence the content of the final rule.

6. Bernard Schwartz, *Administrative Law,* 3rd ed. (Boston: Little, Brown, 1991), p. 162.

7. Richard J. Pierce, Jr., *Administrative Law Treatise,* 4th ed. (New York: Aspen, 2002), vol. 1, p. 303.

8. Kerwin, "The Elements of Rulemaking," p. 348.

9. Kenneth C. Davis, *Administrative Law and Government*, 2d ed. (St. Paul: West, 1975), p. 119. Also, see Robert A. Anthony, "'Interpretive' Rules, 'Legislative' Rules and 'Spurious' Rules: Lifting the Smog," *Administrative Law Journal of the American University* 8 (spring 1994).

10. Robert Anthony, "Which Agency Interpretations Should Bind Citizens and Courts?" *Yale Journal on Regulation* 1 (1990).

11. Pierce, *Administrative Law Treatise*, 4th ed., Supp. 2003.

12. Schwartz, *Administrative Law*, 3rd ed., p. 193.

13. Ibid., pp. 170–171. Also see Pierce, *Administrative Law Treatise*, 4th ed., vol. 1, pp. 416–417.

14. Pierce, *Administrative Law Treatise*, 4th ed., vol. 1, p. 416.

15. Ibid.

16. Ibid., pp. 419–420.

17. Kerwin, *Rulemaking*, p. 157.

18. Lewis Mainzer, *Political Bureaucracy* (Glenview, Ill.: Scott, Foresman, 1973). p. 39.

19. Kerwin, *Rulemaking*, p. 158.

20. See, for example, David Wise and Thomas Ross, *The Invisible Government* (New York: Random House, 1964); Frederick C. Mosher et al., *Watergate: Implications for Responsible Government* (New York: Basic Books, 1974); Dan Rather and Gary P. Gates, *The Palace Guard* (New York: Harper and Row, 1974); Philip Agee, *Inside the Company: CIA* (New York: Stonehill, 1976); David Nachmias and David H. Rosenbloom, *Bureaucratic Government: USA* (New York: St. Martin's Press, 1980); Paul R. Pillar and Michael H. Armacost, *Terrorism and U.S. Foreign Policy* (Washington, D.C.: Brookings Institution Press, 2001).

21. Pollsters have found that Americans do not condone unethical behavior in their public officials but seem to be more concerned with officials' possessing strong leadership than high personal morals and ethics. For example, in polls after the Monica Lewinsky scandal became news, President Clinton consistently received high job approval and leadership scores from the public yet relatively low morality/character ratings. See Kenneth F. Warren, *In Defense of Public Opinion Polling* (Boulder, CO: Westview Press, 2002), chap. 8.

22. For a fascinating and enlightening behavioral analysis showing how Americans seem to support various democratic ideas only in the abstract see, William H. Flanigan and Nancy H. Zingale, *Political Behavior of the American Electorate*, 10th ed. (Washington, D.C.: Congressional Quarterly Press, 2002), chaps. 1 and 6.

23. Russell H. Weigel and Richard Jessor, "Television and Adolescent Conventionality: An Exploratory Study," *Public Opinion Quarterly* 37 (spring 1973). Also see Elissa Haney, "The Top 10 TV Shows of the Century," Information Please, March 6, 2003, infoplease.com/spot/toptv1.html.

24. Ira Sharkansky, in *The Maligned States*, 2nd ed. (New York: McGraw-Hill, 1977), esp. chap. 1–2, tries in this classic work to defend the states against the criticisms of the political science community. However, even in the early twenty-first century, most political scientists and public administration scholars still find more public administration problems at the state and local levels.

25. Eric A. Posner and Adrian Vermeule, "Interring the Nondelegation Doctrine," *University of Chicago Law Review* 69 (fall 2002).

26. Theodore Lowi, *The End of Liberalism* (New York: W. W. Norton, 1969), pp. 302–303.

27. Theodore J. Lowi, "Two Roads to Serfdom"; and Lowi, "Legitimizing Public Administration: A Disturbed Dissent," *Public Administration Review* 53 (May–June 1993).

28. Aaron Wildavsky, in *The Politics of the Budgetary Process*, 4th ed. (Boston: Little, Brown, 1983), argues that it is healthy for the system when each department, agency, or interest has to fight for its own welfare. The net result, he maintains, is stronger parts that contribute to a stronger whole.

29. Mark C. Niles, "On the Hijacking of Agencies (and Airplanes): The Federal Aviation Administration, 'Agency Capture,' and Airline Security," *American University Journal of Gender, Social Policy and the Law* 10 (2002).

30. Helen Thomas, "Shuttle Panel Could Use a Few Detached Outsiders," *Houston Chronicle,* February 16, 2003, Outlook, p. 3; and Editorial, "The Columbia Disaster: NASA Roulette," *St. Louis Post-Dispatch,* March 9, 2003, p. B2.

31. See Norton E. Long, "Bureaucracy and Constitutionalism," *American Political Science Review* (September 1952).

32. Theodore Lowi, *The End of Liberalism*, 2nd ed. (New York: W. W. Norton, 1979), p. 302.

33. Kenneth C. Davis, *Discretionary Justice: A Preliminary Inquiry* (Urbana: University of Illinois Press, 1969), p. 25.

34. Ibid., chap. 1.

35. Lowi, *End of Liberalism*, 2nd ed., p. 303.

36. Robert S. Lorch, *Democratic Process and Administrative Law*, rev. ed. (Detroit: Wayne State University Press, 1980), p. 95.

37. Murray J. Edelman, "Symbols and Political Quiescence," *American Political Science Review* 54 (September 1960).

38. Jeffrey J. Jowell, *Law and Bureaucracy: Administrative Discretion and the Limits of Legal Action* (New York: Dunellen, 1984), p. 199.

39. Davis, *Administrative Law and Government*, p. 122.

40. Florence Heffron, with Neil McFeeley, *The Administrative Regulatory Process* (New York: Longman, 1983), chap. 9.

41. Pierce, *Administrative Law Treatise*, 4th ed., vol. 1, p. 506.

42. Ibid. For a dated but solid treatment of this issue, see Michael Asimow, "Interpretive Rules and Agency Statements," *Michigan Law Review* 75 (January 1977). It should be noted that the words *interpretative* and *interpretive* (for the rules) have been used interchangeably in the literature. The word *interpretative* appears in the Administrative Procedure Act, but since it is grammatically incorrect, *interpretive* has been substituted for *interpretative* by some scholars.

43. Ibid., pp. 531–532.

44. See Reinhard Bendix, *Max Weber: An Intellectual Portrait* (New York: Doubleday Anchor Books, 1978), chaps. 12–13.

45. Scott H. Ainsworth, *Analyzing Interest Groups: Group Influence on People and Policies* (New York: W. W. Norton, 2002), chap. 7.

46. Ibid., esp. chaps. 1–5, 7, 8, 10. Also see George E. Shambaugh IV and Paul J. Weinstein, Jr., *The Art of Policymaking* (New York: Longman, 2003), esp. chaps. 1–4, 6.

47. H. H. Gerth and C. Wright Mills, eds., *From Max Weber: Essays in Sociology* (New York: Oxford University Press, 1946), chap. 8.

48. See Thomas R. Dye, *Who's Running America?: The Conservative Years* (Englewood Cliffs, N.J.: Prentice-Hall, 1986); Kerwin, *Rulemaking*, 2nd ed., chap. 5; and Alan Ramo, "California's Energy Crisis: The Perils of Crisis Management and a Challenge to Environmental Justice," *Albany Law Environmental Outlook* 7:1 (2002).

49. *United States v. International Telephone and Telegraph Corp.* and the *Hartford Fire Insurance Co.*, 349 F.Supp. 22 (1972).

50. Robert S. Lorch, *Democratic Process and Administrative Law* (Detroit: Wayne State University Press, 1969), p. 103.

51. Ibid. See also Caroline E. Mayer, "Too Much Regulation? Not as Regulators Tell It," *U.S. News & World Report*, October 8, 1979, p. 74.

52. Robert A. Kagan, *Regulatory Justice* (New York: Russell Sage Foundation, 1978), p. 74.

53. Mark C. Niles, "On the Hijacking of Agencies (and Airplanes)," p. 384.

54. Davis, *Administrative Law and Government*, p. 121.

55. Some good sources are Philip Selznick, *TVA and the Grass Roots* (Berkeley: University of California Press, 1949); Marver Bernstein, *Regulating Business by Independent Commissions* (Princeton, N.J.: Princeton University Press, 1955); C. Wright Mills, *The Power Elite* (New York: Oxford University Press, 1959); Murray Edelman, *The Symbolic Uses of Politics* (Urbana: University of Illinois Press, 1964); Peter Woll, *American Bureaucracy*, 2nd ed. (New York: W. W. Norton, 1977); Lowi, *The End of Liberalism*, 2nd ed.; James E. Anderson, *Public Policy Making*, 2nd ed. (New York: Holt, Rinehart and Winston, 1979); Martha Derthick and Paul J. Quirk, *The Politics of Deregulation* (Washington, D.C.: Brookings Institution Press, 1985); Robert A. Leone, *Who Profits: Winners, Losers, and Government Regulation* (New York: Basic Books, 1986); B. Guy Peters, *American Public Policy: Promise and Performance*, 2nd ed. (Chatham, N.J.: Chatham House, 1986); Randall B. Ripley and Grace A. Franklin, *Congress, The Bureaucracy and Public Policy*, 4th ed. (Chicago: Dorsey Press, 1987); Kenneth J. Meier, *Politics and the Bureaucracy: Policymaking in the Fourth Branch of Government*, 3rd ed. (Pacific Grove, Calif.: Brooks/Cole, 1993); and Ainsworth, *Analyzing Interest Groups*.

56. Plato, *Laws,* in *The Dialogues of Plato*, trans. Benjamin Jowell (London: Oxford University Press, 1953), vol. 4 pp. 284–285.

57. Jean Jacques Rousseau, *On the Social Contract*, trans. Maurice Cranston (Baltimore: Penguin Books, 1968), esp. books 2 and 3.

58. James Madison, Alexander Hamilton, and John Jay, *The Federalist Papers* (New York: Random House, 1937), no. 10, pp. 48–51.

59. Kerwin, *Rulemaking*, pp. 200–221.

60. Richard P. Nathan, *The Plot That Failed: Nixon and the Administrative Presidency* (New York: Wiley, 1975), esp. chap. 5.

61. Lorch, *Democratic Process and Administrative Law*, p. 104. Although Lorch says this, he is technically incorrect (and he probably knows it; the irony was the point). Because Old Faithful is located in a national park, the Park Service would probably have to obtain congressional approval before the sale.

62. Pierce, *Administrative Law Treatise*, 4th ed., vol. 1, p. 504.

63. See Lowi, *End of Liberalism*, 2nd ed.; Lowi, "Two Roads to Serfdom"; Schwartz, *Administrative Law*, 3rd ed., chaps. 2 and 4; Pierce, *Administrative Law Treatise*, 4th ed., vol. 1, pp. 301–528, 559–704; and J. Skelly Wright, "Rulemaking and Judicial Review," *Administrative Law Review* 30 (summer 1978).

64. Lowi, *The End of Liberalism*, 2nd ed., pp. 36–38, 302–305.

65. Ibid., pp. 302–303.

66. Ibid., p. 304.

67. Ibid., pp. 304–305.

68. Ibid., pp. 305–307.

69. Wright, "Rulemaking and Judicial Review," p. 465.

70. Ibid.

71. Ibid.

72. Ibid., p. 466.

73. Ibid.

74. See Pierce, *Administrative Law Treatise*, 4th ed., vol. 1, pp. 478–484, for a good legalistic review of how the courts have regarded ex parte contacts.

75. Kerwin, *Rulemaking*, pp. 185–191.

76. Charles E. Lindbloom, *The Intelligence of Democracy* (New York: Free Press, 1965).

77. Phillip Harter, "Negotiating Regulations: A Cure for the Malaise," *Georgetown Law Review* 71 (1982).

78. David H. Rosenbloom, *Building a Legislative-Centered Public Administration* (Tuscaloosa: University of Alabama Press, 2000), p. 44.

79. Ibid.

80. Cited in Pierce, *Administrative Law Treatise*, 4th ed., vol. 1, p. 525.

81. Ibid., p. 524.

82. Ibid., p. 525.

83. Ibid., p. 524.

84. Ibid.

85. Cary Coglianese, "Assessing Consensus: The Promise and Performance of Negotiated Rulemaking," *Duke Law Review* 46 (April 1997).

86. A Lexis-Nexis search with the keywords "negotiated rulemaking" generated twenty-three cases, ten at the court of appeals level and thirteen in the district courts.

87. Ellen Siegler, "Regulatory Negotiations and Other Rulemaking Processes: Strengths and Weaknesses from an Industry Viewpoint," *Duke Law Journal* 46 (April 1997).

88. William Funk, "Bargaining Toward the New Millennium: Regulatory Negotiations and the Subversion of the Public Interest," *Duke Law Review* 46 (April 1997): 1351, 1387.

89. Jack M. Beermann, "Privatization and Political Accountability," *Fordham Urban Law Journal* 28 (June 2001): 1536.

90. Cornelius M. Kerwin, *Rulemaking*, p. 183.

91. Ibid.

CHAPTER 6

The Public Policy–Making Tug-of-War

Between Rulemaking and Ordermaking

WHAT IS ORDERMAKING?

Public administration agencies today, as a result of broad delegation of both rule-making and ordermaking powers, have the legal authority to make "laws," or the public policies that govern socioeconomic and political activities in the United States. In fact, scholars estimate that well over 90 percent of the laws that regulate our lives, whether at work or at play, are now made by our public administrators, not by our legislators or traditional lawmakers. These administrators promulgate public laws or policies through either rulemaking or ordermaking (adjudication), although frequently a combination of the processes is employed to make and fine-tune agency policies. Agency policies may target the whole society (e.g., homeland security regulations), an entire industry (passive safety restraints for all automobiles), particular companies or a single company (safety regulations directed at a specific nuclear power plant), or even an individual (a termination hearing decision involving a public employee).

Agency policy decisions may grant or deny benefits (e.g., permit an industry to operate or not operate under certain conditions; grant or deny a license to a business or an individual; grant or deny a welfare recipient, farmer, or veteran a benefit). Whether benefits are given or taken away, agency actions are ideally supposed to be guided by due process considerations. In agency rulemaking, due process may mean allowing all interested parties ample opportunity to respond to a proposed rule, while in an agency adjudication it may mean allowing a person in a termination hearing sufficient time to examine and respond to allegations of misconduct.

As noted, our public administrators make public policies through agency rule-making and agency adjudications (ordermaking). Formally, according to the language of the Administrative Procedure Act (APA), Pub.L. no. 404, 60 Stat. 237, Section 551 (1946), as amended, "rulemaking means agency process for formulating, amending, or appealing a rule," while "adjudication means agency process for the formulation of an order." While rulemaking is a quasi-legislative process, adjudication is a quasi-judicial process. In technical terms, when a public agency engages in rulemaking the result is a rule. When the agency employs **adjudication (ordermaking)**, the product is an **order.** According to the specific language of the AAP,

> a rule means the whole or part of an agency statement of general or particular applicability and future effect designed to implement, interpret, or prescribe law or policy or describing the organization, procedure or practice requirements of an agency and includes the approval or prescription for the future of rates, wages, corporate or financial structures or reorganizations thereof, prices, facilities, appliances, services or allowances therefor or valuations, costs, or accounting, or practices bearing on any of the foregoing.

In contrast, the APA states that an "order means the whole or a part of a final disposition, whether affirmative, negative, injunctive, or declaratory in form, of an agency in a matter other than rule making but including licensing."

When a public agency **adjudicates** (judges), it issues an order that represents a judgment in favor of one party or the other in a dispute. Just as U.S. Supreme Court decisions establish policies to be followed (e.g., court-ordered school desegregation), agency orders also set policies and establish precedents that commonly have the impact of law. The need for agency adjudication arises normally when a dispute touches on a policy area within the regulatory jurisdiction of a particular public agency. The dispute may be between the agency and a private party (e.g., the Federal Communications Commission and a television station); between private outside parties (two television networks) seeking new policies or policy clarifications affecting operations in their industry; or between an intervenor, or "party of interest" in a hearing involving an agency, and a regulated company (an environmental group, such as the Union of Concerned Scientists, intervening in a licensing hearing involving the Nuclear Regulatory Commission and a utility company).

Adjudications are mostly retrospective in focus. That is, agency adjudicative actions are aimed at trying to settle unresolved past conflicts between specific parties. Consequently, as Cornelius Kerwin points out, in comparing rulemaking with adjudication, "adjudication works best with two-sided issues."[1] Because participation is limited only to those parties involved in the agency's adjudicative proceedings, ordermaking is not supposed to lead to the development of broad public policies for the future. However, despite widespread criticism, some regulatory agencies have preferred to employ ordermaking to make prospective agency orders of general applicability. When orders play this role, they are made to function more like rules than orders. Critics claim that orders should be restricted in their application so that they are not used simultaneously as retrospective orders and broad prospective rules. That is, critics feel that administrators should not try to use the order-making process to kill two birds with one stone. Ordermaking is designed to deliberate adjudicative, not legislative, facts. When an agency is considering *adjudicative* facts during adjudicative proceedings, either informal or formal, it is concerned with determining who did what to whom and for what reasons in order to settle a dispute between specific parties. Under normal conditions it would be inappropriate during adjudication to entertain *legislative* facts, which relate only to general public policy considerations but are irrelevant to the specific dispute. (An example of legislative facts is public attitudes toward subsidized housing. An example of a specific dispute about legislative facts is a determination of a housing agency illegally denying subsidy payments to a claimant.)

In sum, since administrative orders are supposed to be directed toward particular parties involved in a controversy, participation excludes the general public, and only adjudicative facts should be seriously entertained. The vast majority of administrative law experts, among them Kenneth C. Davis, Richard J. Pierce, Jr., Henry J. Friendly, David Shapiro, J. Skelly Wright, Richard K. Berg, David H. Rosenbloom, Cornelius M. Kerwin, and Peter L. Strauss, believe that it is foolish under most circumstances to promulgate general public policies through the ordermaking process.[2]

DIFFERENTIATING ORDERMAKING FROM RULEMAKING

Definitive guidelines to determine when issues appear appropriate for the adjudicative process simply do not exist. However, a few very rough guidelines that administrative agencies and courts have generally endorsed may be helpful. In general, the ordermaking process (frequently referred to as the case-by-case approach to formulating regulatory policies) is used in lieu of the rulemaking process when (1) the issue in question involves specific parties in a dispute; (2) the matter concerns past behavior and is not future oriented (although orders do set precedents); (3) the issues or problems could not have been reasonably anticipated by the agency; (4) the agency wants to reach only a tentative decision because its administrators lack sufficient knowledge, experience, and confidence at the time in the specific area; and (5) the matter is simply too esoteric, complex, and varied to be resolved by the formulation of a general rule.

It is not always easy to differentiate between ordermaking and rulemaking, nor is it easy to judge when ordermaking or rulemaking should be employed to promulgate regulatory policies. The truth is that the legislative rulemaking and judicial ordermaking functions in administrative agencies are frequently juxtaposed in practice. Adding to the confusion, asserts Edwin J. Madaj, "is the anomaly that formal rulemaking is in many ways more procedurally like an adjudication than an informal adjudication."[3] Trying to differentiate between the two processes often turns out to be a futile academic exercise. For example, when the Federal Trade Commission (FTC) reviews the advertising practices of a certain company, concludes that the practices are deceptive, and orders the company to retract its earlier contentions publicly, is the agency functioning in a purely judicial capacity? The fact is that FTC decisions or orders (such as forcing a company to carry out corrective advertising) almost always shape FTC policy toward certain business practices. In many instances FTC hearing decisions establish rules that businesses dare not overlook.

In 1908, in *Prentis v. Atlantic Coast Line Company*, 211 U.S. 210, the Supreme Court tried to make a practical distinction between rulemaking and ordermaking activities. The Court said that "the establishment of a rate is the making of a rule for the future, and therefore is an act legislative, not judicial in kind" (p. 226). But only a year later the New York Court of Appeals in *People ex rel. Central Park, N. and E.R.R. Company v. Willcox*, 194 N.Y. 383 (1909), complicated the definitional problem by contradicting the Supreme Court's interpretation of rulemaking. The appeals court contended respectfully that the Supreme Court's definition ran contrary to established judicial authority in New York and added that it was not "convinced that the function of prescribing a rate is necessarily nonjudicial solely because it enforces a rule of conduct for the future" (p. 386). Thus, because of the definitional problems, the courts have made a common practice of deciding administrative law cases, especially if the functions are hazy, without ever attempting to differentiate between judicial and legislative activities.

The failure to draw a distinction presents legal problems and causes some confusion because the APA specifies the procedural obligations of administrative agencies under sections of the act labeled "Rulemaking" and "Adjudications." It may be difficult to establish an authoritative position and reach a respected decision based on certain procedural requirements or points of law in the APA if the courts cannot decide which sections of the act to apply because they are uncertain as to which agency processes are in question.

Two simple tests have been used to try to determine whether agency decisions should have followed rulemaking or ordermaking processes. Both tests fail as reliable measures, although they should not be discarded as useless, since most agencies probably try to comply with the test requirements in general when promulgating policies. The first is the *past-future test,* which poses the question, Is the agency policy concerned with regulating past or future practices? If the regulatory policy is aimed at controlling future conduct, the policy should have been promulgated through rulemaking procedures. However, if the policy is directed primarily at resolving a dispute involving past behavior, the policy position should have been the consequence of adjudication. The second test, called the *specific-general test*, seeks essentially to discover whether the promulgated agency policy is directed toward a specific or a general audience. If agency policy is aimed at regulating the activities of no specific parties but rather parties in general, the policy should have been generated through rulemaking. If the policy decision is directed toward specific parties (frequently even named parties in a controversy), the policy should have been developed through adjudication.

Unfortunately, however, agency policies almost never tend to be wholly past-specific or future-general in content or application. What compounds this problem further is that agencies have the legal, discretionary authority to decide whether they should employ the rulemaking or ordermaking approach when making agency policies. Agency discretion is especially well respected by reviewing courts if agency officials take care to rationalize their approach selection as necessary to achieving a particular agency goal. About the only time courts would find an abuse of agency discretion in this matter would be in a situation in which an agency promulgated a policy through adjudication and then applied the new policy in such a way that serious adverse consequences resulted or the retroactive application obviously caused more harm than good (*SEC v. Chenery Corp.*, 332 U.S. 194 [1947]; *NLRB v. Bell Aerospace Co.*, 416 U.S. 267 [1947]; *First Bancorporation v. Board of Governors*, 728 F.2d 434 [10th Cir. 1984]; *District Lodge 64 v. NLRB*, 949 F.2d 441 [D.C. Cir. 1991]; and *United States v. Mead*, 533 U.S. 218 [2002]).

For all practical purposes, such discretionary power has allowed agencies to ignore the general-specific and past-future tests when making policies, although most agencies do take these tests into account because of external pressures to conform to what is expected. Nevertheless, agency leaders frequently decide to choose either rulemaking or ordermaking procedures to promulgate policies, not because one procedure may be more appropriate but because one process may be perceived as more convenient by the agency officials. For instance, some agency administrators believe they can control the development of their regulatory policies better if they use the more flexible case-by-case approach, since the courts have generally allowed agencies to change policy directions with each case. The courts have been much more insistent, however, that policies resulting from rulemaking be honored by agencies for the purpose of keeping these policies consistent over time (*Vitarelli v. Seaton*, 359 U.S. 535 [1959]; *Motor Vehicle Mfrs. Ass'n v. State Farm Mutual*, 463 U.S. 29 [1983]; *South Cent. Terminal Co. v. U.S. Dept. of Energy*, 728 F.Supp. 1083, 1096 [D. Del. 1990]; and *United States v. Mead*, 533 U.S. 218 [2002]).

PROS AND CONS OF ORDERMAKING AND RULEMAKING IN AGENCY POLICYMAKING

It is very important to comprehend the character of ordermaking and rulemaking if one is to develop conceptually strong insights into the agency policymaking process. After all, formal agency policies, which essentially represent the regulatory role played by an agency, are made either through the rulemaking or ordermaking processes. David Rosenbloom characterizes agencies as "legislative-centered extensions of Congress" in which Congress has prudently given agency administrators various means for making public policies, particularly rulemaking and ordermaking processes.[4] Consequently, a great deal can be learned about agency behavior and its relationship to its external environment if these basic processes are contrasted. This section compares the more important features of ordermaking and rulemaking, with an eye to their relative merits in generating sound regulatory policies rooted in democratic procedures fundamental to the maintenance and promotion of administrative due process. Special attention is devoted to how the public, regulated industries, and agency administrators perceive the comparative advantages and disadvantages of rulemaking and ordermaking. Justifications are then presented to explain why a large number of administrative law critics prefer rulemaking to ordermaking for the promulgation of most regulatory policies, and why they frequently become irritated at regulators who keep insisting on promulgating policies through adjudication.[5]

Procedural Differences

There are several basic procedural differences between rulemaking and ordermaking. Although some of the these differences have been made apparent in previous discussions, a brief review is helpful. The basic procedural difference between the two is that the rulemaking process is legislative in character, while ordermaking is judicial in nature. Of course, this basic procedural difference makes these two approaches to administrative policy formation fundamentally distinct. While rulemaking typically involves the notice-and-comment approach, ordermaking procedure is supposed to be trial-like, meaningfully reflecting procedures followed in regular court trials. Thus, unlike rules, hearing orders impose penalties and rewards directed at particular parties involved in the hearing proceedings. Hearing decisions (orders) must be based wholly on the hearing record. Specifically, this means that administrative law judges who preside over agency hearings must root their orders in evidence presented at the hearings. The bulk of hearing evidence results from written and oral testimony and cross-examinations involving specific questions pertaining to a particular dispute.

Final rules do not have to be based on the varied information and arguments submitted to the rulemakers in response to publication of a proposed rule in the *Federal Register*. Rulemakers have only the legal obligation to accept comments. They do not actually have to be influenced by these comments or data in drafting rules, although the courts, especially since *Overton Park*, have been insisting that rulemakers avoid "arbitrary and capricious" rulemaking by rooting their decisions in substantial evidence based "on the record," especially after holding public hearings. The Court's position has probably forced many agency decisionmakers to pay more attention to submitted comments, but discretion remains a powerful tool on the side of administrators because it takes very little in practice for rulemakers to defend their rules against charges that they were arbitrarily and capriciously drafted.

Differences in Uniformity and Consistency

Because rulemaking procedures are designed to facilitate the making of generally applicable rules that help to shape an overall regulatory game plan, attempts have been made to promote uniformity and consistency in agency policies. As a result of agency attempts to develop policies that can be applied in a uniform and consistent manner to those who will come under their regulatory umbrella, little effort is made to address unique objections and problems that some of those to be regulated might have. Thus, rulemaking procedures are designed primarily to produce broad, sweeping regulatory policies that are not particularly sensitive to individual cases or problems. In contrast, ordermaking, which utilizes the case-by-case approach, has the advantage of developing policies incrementally over time by addressing individual cases. Therefore, the real strength in the ordermaking approach lies in its emphasis on tailoring decisions (policy outputs) to special circumstances. In this sense, ordermaking is more compassionate than rulemaking, at least for the individual parties involved. In fact, adjudicative procedures are sometimes much more elaborate than rulemaking procedures, simply because sincere efforts have been made to promote administrative due process during adjudication so that the rights of individuals are protected. The obvious disadvantage, however, is that this case-by-case approach may cause agency policies to fluctuate in an unpredictable manner over time, preventing the development of a stable and uniform policy climate for the regulated.

One serious problem with making policies through the ordermaking process is that resulting agency decisions come without warning, sometimes creating great hardships for those who must comply with the orders even though they were not parties in the dispute and who therefore did not have the opportunity to present data and arguments. Rules, in contrast, are proposed in the *Federal Register* before they become law (a final rule). Despite the fact that some rulemaking gives little attention to comments by outsiders on proposed rules, all interested parties are at least afforded the opportunity to provide input.

In addition, because agencies are compelled under Section 553(b) of the APA to publish their proposed agency rules in the *Federal Register*, agencies are obligated to spell out their policy intentions rather clearly for all to scrutinize. This has the obvious advantage of forcing agencies not only to clarify their policy positions but also to justify them in anticipation of challenges to their position. Many people think this prevents rulemakers from hiding the ball from interested parties, helping to ensure democratically accountable agency actions.[6] Such an open policy-making process, as contrasted to adjudication, allows judicial review of proposed agency policy before it is too late, as long as the petitioning party can show the court that it would suffer unfairly if the proposed action were carried out. The ordermaking process clearly fails to provide these advantages to affected parties.[7]

Policy Planning

Intelligent administrative policy planning demands that agency regulators develop a comprehensive game plan so that rational actions can be taken by the regulatory agency for the purpose of reaching desired goals. Agencies can rely on either rulemaking or ordermaking approaches to achieve their regulatory ambitions. When facts and arguments are considered, rulemaking appears to be preferable to ordermaking for policy planning by an administrative agency. The most persuasive reason, noted previously, is that in general, rulemaking tends to be general-future oriented, while ordermaking is more specific-past in focus.

Planning through rulemaking allows agency planners to obtain varied feedback from a diverse environment every time the agency proposes a rule. This ability to build a comprehensive database to aid future planning decisions is one of the key advantages of rulemaking over adjudication in the area of policy planning.[8]

In contrast, the adjudicative process in administrative agencies is poorly de-signed for wise agency planning, not only because the process has a past-specific orientation but also because the focal policy areas are left too much to chance se-lection. That is, some agencies (for example, the NLRB) cannot adjudicate unless outside parties raise the issue in a dispute. This causes agency planning, Shapiro once wrote, to "depend [more] on the accident of litigation than on conscious planning."[9] In fact, this largely causes agency planning to be left somewhat ran-domly to outsiders who are in no way concerned about an agency's efforts to de-velop sensible, long-range regulatory policies. It is true, however, as noted previously, that some agencies, like the FTC and the Environmental Protection Agency (EPA), do possess the power to initiate cases for the purposes of settling disputes and/or making and clarifying policies. This is considered overall to be a haphazard, inefficient, and ineffective way to approach agency policymaking, es-pecially in view of the fact that the typical regulatory agency must confront mas-sive regulatory problems with its very limited resources. In "Policy Oscillation at the Labor Board: A Plea for Rulemaking," Samuel Estreicher argues that the ad-judicative approach to policymaking by the National Labor Relations Board has turned labor law into a "nightmare." He concludes by noting that the NLRB should "take its policymaking responsibility more seriously" by relying on the rulemaking approach. Its use "should improve the quality of the Board's decision, its success rate in the courts, and, ultimately, its institutional standing."[10]

Rulemaking or Ordermaking? Three Perspectives

It is accurate to say that the perceived advantages and disadvantages of rulemak-ing or ordermaking as policymaking approaches depend largely on how particu-lar parties believe specific rulemaking or ordermaking practices will benefit or harm their interests. Three broadly defined groups have a stake in agency policy-making procedures, and each perceives the pros and cons of rulemaking and or-dermaking procedures quite differently. This should be expected since the regulated, the general public, and the agencies themselves have radically different selfish interests to protect and promote.

The Regulated.   Of course, the regulated seek to secure their position in society by attempting to influence administrative policymakers to see things their way. Big, wealthy, and powerful interest groups have succeeded in persuading rulemakers to see it their way. For this reason, the regulated industries generally prefer rulemaking to ordermaking. Rulemaking provides the regulated with advance notice and a chance to submit viewpoints for the purpose of altering a proposed rule more to the industry's liking. Since rulemakers do not want to promulgate policies that might meet with forceful resistance, including lawsuits, agencies frequently respond to the so-called "suggestions" of the regulated. The regulated also favor rulemaking over adjudication because the process generally leads to quickly promulgated rules, uniformly applied in the industry. This has the advantages of minimizing unnecessary delays in the implementation of policies deemed necessary by a regulated industry and reducing business uncertainties and promoting fair competition among industry competitors. In sharp contrast, adjudication is generally perceived by the regulated as a closed, expensive, time-consuming process leading to uncertain and sudden policy stands. In the view of the regulated, the incremental ordermaking process excludes the general industry from agency policy decisions, leads to unnecessary litigations, and tends to promote instability and industry-wide inequities. However, at times, particular industry competitors may prefer adjudication to serve their special interests. For example, companies with vast financial resources may want to delay the implementation of agency policies they believe to be unfavorable, particularly those they feel will prove costly or give their competitors a better position in the marketplace. Individual corporations, or groups of them, have been known to delay agency implementation efforts for many years, sometimes a decade or more.

The General Public.   The general public, who frequently regards the regulated as its nemesis and perceives the regulators as captives of those that they are entrusted with regulating, also favors administrative rulemaking to administrative adjudication. In the first place, if policymaking through adjudication is perceived as expensive, unpredictable, and impractical by the regulated, one can imagine how the general public would react. The public, probably best represented by underfunded and understaffed consumer groups such as Common Cause and Nader's Raiders, do not commonly look with favor on fighting for their interests via the agency ordermaking process. Agency adjudicative processes are simply too complex, costly, and time-consuming; and the resulting orders frequently have limited applicability or social impact.

The resources of consumer or citizen action groups are generally so scarce that these organizations have learned that they can usually be more cost-effective in shaping agency policy development if they concentrate their efforts on influencing agency rulemaking. The rulemaking process ideally permits any interested party to present information and arguments for or against a proposed agency rule. Compared with agency adjudicative procedures, rulemaking steps are simple and easy to understand. For example, after reading the proposed rule in the *Federal Register*, all a party has to do is write, call, fax, or e-mail the contact person at the agency cited along with the proposed rule. The example from the *Federal Register* shown in Box 6.1 displays the apparent simplicity and openness of rulemaking, naturally making it appealing to the general public, especially since access appears as open to the little person as to corporate giants.

Big money or a high-priced lawyer do not appear to be necessary to influence agency rulemaking decisions. This public perspective is true as long as agency decisionmakers do not play favorites when weighing submitted comments. It should be noted, however, that in reality the average person is very unlikely to read the *Federal Register* or even to be aware of its existence. This fact works to the

Rulemaking Versus Ordermaking
Source: Reprinted with permission of Daniel Pearlmutter.

advantage of special interests, which pay much more attention to proposed rules published in the *Federal Register*, thus placing themselves in a better position to react to proposed agency rules they oppose.

Nevertheless, on its face, the rulemaking process seems to embrace the democratic principles of fair play more than agency adjudication. Rulemaking is comprehensible, relatively quick, and democratically accountable, especially in the sense that decisionmaking is kept aboveboard and equal access is provided to all. As Professor Estreicher asserted while making his plea for the use of the rulemaking process at the NLRB: "Rulemaking ensures a level of public participation in the policymaking process not currently available. The opportunity for public participation is automatic with each notice of rulemaking, and open to all concerned."[11] Pluralist interests are fairly represented also. Despite political interest group realities that suggest otherwise, the general public is probably correct in assuming that public policies are more fairly promulgated through rulemaking than ordermaking and that their interests will probably be best represented by agency rulemaking.

Agency Officials.   It is difficult to state generally whether most agencies prefer rulemaking or ordermaking for formulating agency policies. From the perspective of agency officials, there are obvious advantages and disadvantages of each approach. Rulemaking allows agencies to propose and implement rules rather

BOX 6.1   A Proposed Rule Published in the *Federal Register,* May 5, 2003

Federal Register: May 5, 2003 (Volume 68, Number 86); Rules and Regulations; Pages 23851–23873.

DEPARTMENT OF HOMELAND SECURITY: Transportation Security Administration

49 CFR Parts 1570 and 1572, [Docket No. TSA-2003-14610; Amendment No. 1572-1], RIN 1652-AA17

Security Threat Assessment for Individuals Applying for a Hazardous Materials Endorsement for a Commercial Drivers License

AGENCY: Transportation Security Administration (TSA), Department of Homeland Security (DHS).

ACTION: Interim final rule; request for comments.

SUMMARY: The Transportation Security Administration (TSA) is amending the Transportation Security Regulations to establish security threat assessment standards for determining whether an individual poses a security threat warranting denial of a hazardous materials endorsement for a commercial drivers license (CDL). TSA is also establishing procedures for seeking a waiver from the standards and for appealing a security assessment determination. TSA is issuing this interim final rule in coordination with a separate interim final rule being issued by the Federal Motor Carrier Safety Administration (FMCSA). The FMCSA rule amends the Federal Motor Carrier Safety Regulations governing commercial drivers licenses to prohibit States from issuing, renewing, transferring, or upgrading a commercial drivers license with a hazardous material endorsement unless the Department of Justice has first conducted a background records check of the applicant and the TSA has determined that the applicant does not pose a security threat warranting denial of the hazardous materials endorsement. These interim final rules implement the background records check requirements of section 1012 of the Uniting and Strengthening America by Providing Appropriate Tools Required to Intercept and Obstruct Terrorism Act of 2001 (USA PATRIOT Act), and also establish requirements regarding the transportation of explosives in commerce.

DATES: This final rule is effective May 5, 2003. Comments must be received on or before July 7, 2003.

ADDRESSES: Comments Submitted by Mail: Address written, signed comments to the Docket Management System, U.S. Department of Transportation, Room Plaza 401, 400 Seventh Street, SW., Washington, DC 20590-0001. You must identify the docket number TSA-2003-14610 at the beginning of your comments, and you should submit two copies of your comments. If you wish to receive confirmation that TSA received your comments, include a self-addressed, stamped postcard on which the following statement is made: "Comments to Docket No. TSA-2003-14610." The postcard will be date-stamped and mailed to you.

Comments Filed Electronically: You may also submit comments through the Internet at http://dms.dot.gov.

Reviewing Comments in the Docket: You may review the public docket containing comments on this proposed rule in person in the Dockets Office between 9 a.m. and 5 p.m., Monday through Friday, except Federal holidays. The Dockets Office is on the plaza level of the NASSIF Building at the Department of Transportation at the above address. Also, you may review public dockets on the Internet at http://dms.dot.gov

FOR FURTHER INFORMATION CONTACT: For technical issues, Stephen Sprague, Office of Maritime and Land, Transportation Security Administration Headquarters, West Building, Floor 9, 400 Seventh Street, SW., Washington, DC 20590; e-mail: patriotact@tsa.dot.gov; telephone: 571-227-1500.

For legal issues, Dion Casey, Office of Chief Counsel, Transportation Security Administration Headquarters, West Building, Floor 8, TSA-2, 400 Seventh Street, SW., Washington, DC 20590; e-mail: Dion.Casey@tsa.dot.gov; telephone: 571-227-2663.

quickly; yet only under ideal circumstances is the process free from headaches for agency rulemakers. If the proposed rules are significant or controversial, agency administrators can expect vehement commentary protests from interests in their environment, some of which are very powerful and influential. Despite the total discretionary power of agency officials to consider or ignore submitted comments, agency leaders are always fearful of powerful protests to proposed agency actions that might jeopardize the stability and welfare of their agency.

Agency officials also see the difficulty of promulgating general policies through rulemaking that will be fair to all affected parties. One chief advantage to rulemaking, as contrasted with agency adjudication, is that it is quite cost-effective in the sense that it allows an agency to make efficient use of its limited resources, since blanket rules are made that can be applied, for example, industry-wide to resolve many questions all at once.

Because of the inequities inevitably involved in the promulgation and implementation of general policies, some agencies have preferred to use adjudication, or the case-by-case approach. On the whole, this approach provides agency administrators with more flexibility and thus the potential to avoid unnecessary and disruptive regulatory battles. The adjudicative process allows agency officials to assess the entire regulatory picture and to focus on specific problems they perceive as most troublesome. This is especially true if agencies possess the statutory authority to initiate cases. Agency administrators may also prefer the adjudicative approach because it allows them greater flexibility in reversing previous policy directions quickly, without having to advertise and defend their new policy decisions before all interested parties. As mentioned earlier, the courts are more tolerant of agencies reversing previous orders than they are of sudden agency rule reversals.

Agency administrators may also prefer the ordermaking approach over rulemaking because they might be undecided on just what course of regulatory action to take. By proceeding by the case-by-case approach, agency decisionmakers have the flexibility of cautiously building regulatory policies at a time when insufficient data and technical knowledge should rightfully preclude risky, comprehensive policy stands.

In reality, because circumstances differ significantly from one agency to another, the reasons for one agency preferring rulemaking over ordermaking vary greatly. But systems theory does suggest that agency administrators would not only evaluate their choice of policymaking tools on the basis of perceived short- and long-range consequences but also consider which approach appears to be politically best. Since systems theorists maintain that agency survival needs must be considered first, the chances are good that agency officials will normally prefer the policymaking method that can best help them reach their statutory obligations without jeopardizing agency stability or causing any unnecessary headaches.

SUMMARY

It was noted in Chapter 5 that many critics believe that agency rulemaking procedures are not very democratic and, as a result, rules are promulgated that tend to benefit the more influential groups in our society. But this chapter stressed that most scholars hold that rulemaking is a far better method for making public policies, especially those policies aimed at large groups, than is the ordermaking process. Basically, rulemaking is preferred because it is perceived as a much more open, democratic process than ordermaking. That is, while agency adjudications are normally closed to interested outside parties that are not specific litigants in the dispute, the rulemaking process is open to all interested parties who want to influence the drafting of rules. Rules, the product of agency rulemaking, are also favored over orders for promulgating general policies because they are future-general in nature, while orders have a past-specific orientation. Although the rule-making process is generally considered to be the best, agencies such as the NLRB have, nevertheless, relied heavily upon ordermaking. Administrators in these agencies have found ordermaking very convenient, especially when they have felt that it is desirable to make policies gradually and cautiously on a case-by-case basis.

In this chapter an overview of the ordermaking or hearing process was presented with an emphasis on the differences between ordermaking and rulemaking. The differences were stressed in part to clarify why a solid consensus of administrative law and public administration scholars believe that rulemaking should generally be preferred over ordermaking for promulgating public policies. The next chapter focuses on the details of the agency hearing process itself, with this underlying fundamental question in mind: How fair are agency hearings?

NATIONAL LABOR RELATIONS BOARD
V. BELL AEROSPACE COMPANY

---

416 U.S. 267; 94 S.Ct. 1757 (1974)

Facts

The National Labor Relations Board (NLRB) exercised its discretion to use adjudication to determine whether twenty-five buyers for the Bell Aerospace Company (Bell) should be certified as a representative union of buyers under the National Labor Relations Act, 20 U.S.C.S. 158(a)(5 and 1). The NLRB ruled that buyers were covered under the act because they were not "true managerial employees." However, Bell refused to bargain with this union, contending that their buyers functioned in a managerial capacity, creating a conflict of interest since, as buyers, they were serving management and labor interests simultaneously and, because they were managers, were not covered by the act. The NLRB found Bell guilty of unfair labor practices for refusing to bargain with the new buyers union, but the Second Circuit Court of Appeals refused to order the enforcement of the NLRB's order, holding, inter alia, that it was questionable whether the buyers were not managers and that the NLRB had to use rulemaking, not adjudication, to determine whether the buyers should be classified as managers. The Supreme Court granted certiorari.

Justice Powell delivered the opinion of the Court, in which justices Burger, Douglas, Blackmun, and Rehnquist joined. Justice White dissented in part, joined by justices Brennan, Stewart, and Marshall. Only the Court's consideration of the NLRB's choice of adjudication over rulemaking is covered.

This case presents two questions: first, whether the National Labor Relations Board properly determined that all "managerial employees," except those whose participation in a labor organization would create a conflict of interest with their job responsibilities, are covered by the National Labor Relations Act; and second, whether the Board must proceed by rulemaking rather than by adjudication in determining whether certain buyers are "managerial employees." We answer both questions in the negative.

The Court of Appeals denied enforcement. 475 F.2d 485 (1973). . . .

Turning to the merits of the present case, the court acknowledged that there was substantial evidence that the company's buyers were not sufficiently high in the managerial hierarchy to constitute true "managerial employees." Nevertheless, the court denied enforcement for two reasons. First, it was not certain that the Board's decision rested on a factual determination that these buyers were not true "managerial employees" rather than on "its new, and in our view, erroneous holding that it was free to regard all managerial employees as covered by the Act unless their duties met" the conflict-of-interest touchstone. Second, although the Board was not precluded from holding that buyers, or some types of buyers, were not "managerial employees," the court thought that, in view of the Board's long line of cases holding the contrary, it could not accomplish this change of position by adjudication. Rather, the Board should conduct a rulemaking proceeding in conformity with §6 of the Act, 29 U.S.C. §156. The court therefore remanded the case to the Board for such a proceeding.

We granted the Board's petition for *certiorari*. 414 U.S. 816. . . .

The Court of Appeals also held that, although the Board was not precluded from determining that buyers or some types of buyers were not "managerial employees," it could do so only by invoking its rulemaking procedures under §6 of the Act, 29 U.S.C. §156. We disagree.

At the outset, the precise nature of the present issue must be noted. The question is not whether the Board should have resorted to rulemaking, or in fact improperly promulgated a "rule," when in the context of the prior representation proceeding it held that the Act covers all "managerial employees" except those meeting the new "conflict of interest in labor relations" touchstone. Our conclusion that the Board applied the wrong legal standard makes consideration of that issue unnecessary. Rather, the present question is whether on remand the Board must invoke its rulemaking procedures if it determines, in light of our opinion, that these buyers are not "managerial employees" under the Act. The Court of Appeals thought that rulemaking was required because any Board finding that the company's buyers are not "managerial" would be contrary to its prior decisions and would presumably be in the nature of a general rule designed "to fit all cases at all times."

A similar issue was presented to this Court in its second decision in *SEC v. Chenery Corp.*, 332 U.S. 194 (1947) (Chenery II). There, the respondent corporation argued that in an adjudicative proceeding the Commission could not apply a general standard that it had formulated for the first time in that proceeding. Rather, the Commission was required to resort instead to its rulemaking procedures if it desired to promulgate a new standard that would govern future conduct. In rejecting this contention, the Court first noted that the Commission had a statutory duty to decide the issue at hand in light of the proper standards and that this duty remained "regardless of whether those standards previously had been spelled out in a general rule or regulation." The Court continued:

"The function of filling in the interstices of the [Securities] Act should be performed, as much as possible, through this quasi-legislative promulgation of rules to be applied in the future. But any rigid requirement to that effect would make the administrative process inflexible and incapable of dealing with many of the specialized problems which arise. . . . Not every principle essential to the effective administration of a statute can or should be cast immediately into the mold of a general rule. Some principles must await their own development, while others must be adjusted to meet particular, unforeseeable situations. In performing its important functions in these respects, therefore, an administrative agency must be equipped to act either by general rule or by individual order. To insist upon one form of action to the exclusion of the other is to exalt form over necessity.

"In other words, problems may arise in a case which the administrative agency could not reasonably foresee, problems which must be solved despite the absence of a relevant general rule. Or the agency may not have had suffi-

cient experience with a particular problem to warrant rigidifying its tentative judgment into a hard and fast rule. Or the problem may be so specialized and varying in nature as to be impossible of capture within the boundaries of a general rule. In those situations, the agency must retain power to deal with the problems on a case-to-case basis if the administrative process is to be effective. There is thus a very definite place for the case-by-case evolution of statutory standards."

The Court concluded that "the choice made between proceeding by general rule or by individual, ad hoc litigation is one that lies primarily in the informed discretion of the administrative agency."

And in *NLRB v. Wyman-Gordon Co.*, 394 U.S. 759 (1969), the Court upheld a Board order enforcing an election list requirement first promulgated in an earlier adjudicative proceeding in *Excelsior Underwear Inc.*, 156 N.L.R.B. 1236 (1966). The plurality opinion of Mr. Justice Fortas, joined by THE CHIEF JUSTICE, MR. JUSTICE STEWART, and MR. JUSTICE WHITE, recognized that "adjudicated cases may and do . . . serve as vehicles for the formulation of agency policies, which are applied and announced therein," and that such cases "generally provide a guide to action that the agency may be expected to take in future cases." The concurring opinion of MR. JUSTICE BLACK, joined by MR. JUSTICE BRENNAN and MR. JUSTICE MARSHALL, also noted that the Board had both adjudicative and rulemaking powers and that the choice between the two was "within its informed discretion."

The views expressed in *Chenery II* and *Wyman-Gordon* make plain that the Board is not precluded from announcing new principles in an adjudicative proceeding and that the choice between rulemaking and adjudication lies in the first instance within the Board's discretion. Although there may be situations where the Board's reliance on adjudication would amount to an abuse of discretion or a violation of the Act, nothing in the present case would justify such a conclusion. Indeed, there is ample indication that adjudication is especially appropriate in the instant context. As the Court of Appeals noted, "there must be tens of thousands of manufacturing, wholesale and retail units which employ buyers, and hundreds of thousands of the latter." Moreover, duties of buyers vary widely depending on the company or industry. It is doubtful whether any generalized standard could be framed which would have more than marginal utility. The Board thus has reason to proceed with caution, developing its standards in a case-by-case manner with attention to the specific character of the buyers' authority and duties in each company. The Board's judgment that adjudication best serves this purpose is entitled to great weight.

The possible reliance of industry on the Board's past decisions with respect to buyers does not require a different result. It has not been shown that the adverse consequences ensuing from such reliance are so substantial that the Board should be precluded from reconsidering the issue in an adjudicative proceeding. Furthermore, this is not a case in which some new liability is sought to be imposed on individuals for past actions which were taken in good-faith reliance on Board pronouncements. Nor are fines or damages involved here. In any event, concern about such consequences is largely speculative, for the Board has not yet finally determined whether these buyers are "managerial."

It is true, of course, that rulemaking would provide the Board with a forum for soliciting the informed views of those affected in industry and labor before embarking on a new course. But surely the Board has discretion to decide that the adjudicative procedures in this case may also produce the relevant information necessary to mature and fair consideration of the issues. Those most immediately affected, the buyers and the company in the particular case, are accorded a full opportunity to be heard before the Board makes its determination.

The judgment of the Court of Appeals is therefore affirmed in part and reversed in part, and the cause remanded to that court with directions to remand to the Board for further proceedings in conformity with this opinion.

It is so ordered.

MR. JUSTICE WHITE, with whom MR. JUSTICE BRENNAN, MR. JUSTICE STEWART, and MR. JUSTICE MARSHALL join, dissenting in part.

I concur in Part III of the Court's opinion insofar as it holds that the Board was not required to resort to rulemaking in deciding this case, but I dissent from its holding in Part II that managerial employees as a class are not "employees" within the meaning of the National Labor Relations Act. . . .

COMMENTS AND QUESTIONS

Bell is a fairly old, yet classic case focusing on whether administrative law requires rulemaking or ordermaking (adjudication) to be used under certain circumstances by agency officials to promulgate public policies. Although the Second Circuit Court of Appeals held that the NLRB must use the rulemaking approach to decide whether Bell's buyers should be classified as regular employees or managers, the Supreme Court ruled emphatically that the choice between the use of rulemaking or adjudication should be left to the discretion of agency administrators. Even the dissenters agreed on this issue.

Bell draws upon *SEC v. Chenery*, 332 U.S. 194 (1947), to establish the very strong precedent that still stands today. That is, unless specifically prohibited by statute, agency officials have the ultimate authority to choose between rulemaking or adjudication, even though other parties, including the courts, may think that one procedure or approach *should* be used over the other. In fact, the Court in *Bell* suggested that maybe the rulemaking approach should have been used by the NLRB, because rulemaking would have provided "the Board with a forum for soliciting the informed views of those affected in industry and labor before embarking on a new course" (p. 295). Nonetheless, the Court maintained, "surely the Board has discretion to decide" (p. 295).

The vast majority of legal scholars before and after *Bell* have argued, as noted in this chapter, that rulemaking should normally be the procedure of choice when promulgating policies in a democratic society, especially since rulemaking is a much more open process oriented toward making general rules that can be applied industrywide in the future. The Second Circuit Court of Appeals, as well as the Supreme Court, made this point implicitly, if not explicitly, clear.

Yet the Supreme Court acknowledged in *Bell* that under certain circumstances it may be wiser to use the adjudicative approach, especially when unique circumstances would make it difficult to promulgate a general rule that would be valid for the whole industry. The Court admitted that this might be the situation here because buyers may in fact have quite different job descriptions across the industry. Consequently, the Court quipped, it could be difficult for the NLRB to develop "any generalized standard [that] could be framed which would have more than marginal utility" (p. 294). Acknowledging this, the Court thought that it might be best for the NLRB "to proceed with caution" on a case-by-case basis. Accordingly, the Court concluded that "the Board's judgment that adjudication best serves this purpose is entitled to great weight" (p. 294).

It is legally proper to defer to agency expertise and permit the administrative experts to choose between rulemaking and ordermaking. But how should one political system handle agencies such as the NLRB that rely too much on adjudications to make public policies, especially when critics charge that, in the final analysis, this approach is not nearly as open and democratic as rulemaking? Scholars for decades have charged the NLRB especially with being lazy and relying too much upon the adjudicative approach when rulemaking would have been considerably more appropriate and fair. The Court in *Bell* noted that there may be circumstances in which an agency's use of adjudication would constitute an "abuse of discretion," yet the courts almost never so rule. If democratic fairness is promoted more through rulemaking, don't you think that our legislators and judges should do more to urge administrators to use rulemaking as much as possible?

NOTES

1. Cornelius Kerwin, *How Government Agencies Write Law and Make Policy*, 2nd ed. (Washington D.C.: Congressional Quarterly Press, 1999), p. 51.

2. See Kenneth C. Davis, *Discretionary Justice: A Preliminary Inquiry* (Chicago: University of Illinois Press, 1969), chap. 3; Henry J. Friendly, *The Federal Administrative Agencies: The Need for Better Definition of Standards* (Cambridge, Mass.: Harvard University Press, 1962), chap. 1; David L. Shapiro, "The Choice of Rulemaking or Adjudication in the Development of Administrative Policy," *Harvard Law Review* 78 (March 1965); J. Skelly Wright, "Rulemaking and Judicial Review," *Administrative Law Review* 30 (summer 1987); Richard K. Berg, "Re-examining Policy Procedures: The Choice Between Rulemaking and Adjudication," *Administrative Law Review* 38 (spring 1986); Cornelius M. Kerwin, *Rulemaking: How Government Agencies Write Law and Make Policy*, 2nd ed. (New York: Congressional Quarterly Press, 1999), pp. 51–52; David H. Rosenbloom, Robert S. Kravchuk, and Deborah Goldman Rosenbloom, *Public Administration: Understanding Management, Politics, and Law in the Public Sector*, 5th ed. (New York: McGraw-Hill, 2001); Peter L. Strauss, *Administrative Justice in the United States*, 2nd ed. (Durham: Carolina Academic Press, 2002), pp. 258–262; and Michael I. Jeffery, "Intervenor Funding as the Key to Effective Citizen Participation in Environmental Decisionmaking," *Arizona Journal of International and Comparative Law* 19 (2002).

3. Edwin J. Madaj, "Agency Investigations: Adjudication or Rulemaking?—The ITC's Material Inquiry Determinations Under the Antidumping and Countervailing Duty Laws," *North Carolina Journal of International and Commercial Regulation* 15 (1990): 445.

4. David H. Rosenbloom, *Building a Legislative-Centered Public Administration* (Tuscaloosa: University of Alabama Press, 2000). Rosenbloom's book constitutes an important contribution to the public administration literature because his perspective on the traditional line of power separation between the legislative and administrative branches is unique.

5. For one critic's analysis, see William Funk, "Rationality Review of State Administrative Rulemaking," *Administrative Law Review* 43 (spring 1991). Funk skillfully compares the use of the rulemaking approach to making public policies at the state and federal level.

6. Shapiro, "Choice of Rulemaking or Adjudication," pp. 940–941; Kerwin, *Rulemaking*, 2nd ed., chap. 5.

7. Bernard Schwartz, *Administrative Law*, 2nd ed. (Boston: Little, Brown, 1984), pp. 145–149, 191–196; Berg, "Re-examining Policy Procedures," pp. 160–176; and Strauss, *Administrative Justice in the United States*, pp. 258–262.

8. It should be acknowledged that agency decisions, which have great impact on the shaping of regulatory policies, are so informal that they cannot be discussed in the context of the more formalized rulemaking and ordermaking procedures. Nevertheless, basic agency policies are normally made through one or the other, ordermaking or rulemaking. Informal discretionary decisions made outside rulemaking and ordermaking tend only to refine and define basic agency policies.

9. Shapiro, "Choice of Rulemaking or Adjudication," p. 932.

10. Samuel Estreicher, "Policy Oscillation at the Labor Board," *Administrative Law Review*, 37 (spring 1985): 181.

11. Ibid., p. 177.

CHAPTER 7

Agency Hearings

How Fair Are They?

SERVING DUE
PROCESS IN AGENCY HEARINGS

Comments in the last chapter on the difficulty of differentiating rulemaking from ordermaking should not be interpreted to mean that it is never obvious which function is being performed by an administrative agency. When an agency is required by statute to hold a full hearing under specified conditions, the APA outlines how the hearing should be conducted. Section 554 of the act, "Adjudications," sets forth steps and features to be included in formal ordermaking (that is, in a fair hearing). Each year, federal agencies conduct literally millions of hearings, with the Social Security Administration alone conducting well over one million disability disputes, although well over 90 percent are not elaborate formal hearings. If state agencies are included, we can say that public agencies conduct many millions of cases each year.[1] The agency hearing, even a formal hearing, is not expected to be a copy of a formal trial, but hearings should reflect basic court procedures. One fundamental reason for this is that the courts have found that it is easier to review legal points and procedures if the agency hearing process closely resembles actual court proceedings. Judges have found it difficult to review the fairness of hearing procedures when hearings have been "too informal."

Hearings should be conducted in such a way that due process is served. Because administrative agencies decide questions that may place heavy financial or personal hardships on persons who lose, agency hearings are expected to uphold constitutional principles of fair play by not denying anyone freedoms, rights, or property without due process of law. Although due process is mentioned in the

Constitution, it is not defined. But over the years the term has been given some meaning by legislatures and courts, although no clear meaning has been reached. In *Snyder v. Commonwealth of Massachusetts*, 54 S.Ct. 330 (1934), the Court held that due process should meet standards of "fundamental fairness"; in *Rochin v. California*, 342 U.S. 165 (1952), the Court argued that any governmental activity that is "shocking to the conscience" contradicts due process. As Edwin W. Tucker noted, "The constraints of due process are generally shaped by the contemporary collective intuitive sense of what is right and what is wrong."[2] In an important case in the 1980s, the Supreme Court in *Cleveland Board of Education v. Loudermill*, 105 S.Ct. 1487, 1493 (1985), stated: "The point is straightforward: the Due Process Clause provides that certain substantive rights—life, liberty, and property—cannot be deprived except pursuant to constitutionally adequate procedures. The categories of substance and procedure are distinct. Were the rule otherwise, the Clause would be reduced to a mere tautology." The *Loudermill* decision makes clear that once "certain substantive rights" are granted by the legislature, they become "property interests" that cannot be taken away unless minimum due process procedures are employed. Consequently, since Congress and state legislatures have been granting persons more and more legal entitlements or property interests under law, we can expect to see in the future the granting of more hearings to persons, extending to them at least the minimum due process protections.[3] The Supreme Court has, however, held emphatically that *only* administrative or procedural due process (a step down from more elaborate constitutional due process protections) need be provided when property rights are not at stake. In *Board of Curators v. Horowitz*, 435 U.S. 78 (1978), and *Pension Benefit Guar. Corp. v. L.T.V. Corp.*, 110 S.Ct. 2668 (1990), the Court ruled that due process in the form of formal adjudications was not required because property interests were not involved. More recently, the Second Circuit Court of Appeals in *Furlong v. Shalala*, 238 F.3d 227 (2nd Cir. 2001), held that a simple "paper review determination" was appropriate, not a hearing, because no property rights were at stake. Thus, in administrative law the meaning of due process shifts with the kinds of interests at stake. Administrative agencies must be certain about the interests at stake so that they can extend to persons the appropriate due process procedures.

In an attempt to achieve due process in agency hearings, the major provisions of the APA require agencies to (1) provide appropriate persons proper notice as to the "time, place, and nature of the hearing," "the legal authority and jurisdiction under which the hearing is to be held," and "the matters of fact and law asserted"; (2) take into consideration "the convenience and necessity of the parties or their representatives" when scheduling the time and place of the hearing; (3) afford all concerned parties (normally limited to litigants in the dispute) the opportunity to submit and consider all relevant facts, arguments, and proposed settlements or adjustments as time and public interest may permit; and (4) forbid agency employees who have acted as investigators or prosecutors in a case to participate in a hearing decision, except as counsel or a witness in the public proceeding. In addition to these provisions, sections subsequent to 554 strengthen the effort to achieve a fair hearing by legally obligating agencies to (1) allow persons in hearings to be represented by counsel; (2) conclude hearing business "within a reasonable time"; (3) promptly inform interested parties as to the action taken or intended and, in the case of denied requests, the reason why the request was denied; (4) arrive at decisions, rules, or orders in light of the "whole record" or part of the record that is based on "substantial evidence"; (5) provide unbiased and quasi-independent administrative law judges (formerly known as hearing examiners), who can reach decisions fairly and impartially; (6) permit persons to dispute and challenge agency evidence and opinions by providing adequate time and opportunity for persons to present conflicting data, conduct cross-examination, and so on "as may be required for a full and true disclosure of the facts"; (7) keep a complete transcript of the hearing proceedings to constitute the "exclusive record," or reviewable basis for decision; (8) state and substantiate in the record all findings and conclusions; (9) provide for within-agency appeal; and (10) permit and prepare for judicial review of agency actions.

A few relevant cases put contextual meaning and life into the statutory prescriptions of how public agencies ought to perform, and dramatize the importance of administrative due process in the making of public policies through ordermaking. *Morgan v. United States*, 304 U.S. 1 (1938), is a classic administrative law case that focuses on some fundamental requisites that should be included in any fair hearing process. The judicial wisdom displayed in the case was influential in shaping the 1946 APA. The appellant, Morgan, a stockyard operator, argued that the secretary of agriculture had set the maximum rate he could charge in his business without due process of law. The Packers and Stockyards Act of 1921 extended to the secretary of agriculture the power to "determine and prescribe" maximum and reasonable rate charges, but only after a "full hearing." Because Congress realized that it was granting the secretary vast discretionary powers, which could be abused by irresponsible secretaries, the Congress emphasized its intention that rates should never be imposed on stockyard operators without the benefit of a fair hearing. Morgan charged that (1) the secretary's decision was made behind closed doors, (2) Morgan was not given proper notice, (3) specific charges were not made against him, (4) he was not given reasonable time to respond to the general charges made against him, (5) he was never able to see and examine agency evidence to be used against him, (6) he was not allowed to see and make a rebuttal to the department's findings and conclusions, and (7) he was denied an appeal or rehearing within the agency. Originally, Morgan appealed the secretary's order to the district court, which refused to hear the complaint. Morgan then appealed to the Supreme Court. Chief Justice Charles Evans Hughes, speaking for the majority, reversed the district court's decree and declared invalid the secretary's order, arguing that his decision could not stand "as the hearing was fatally defective" on several grounds (p. 22).

In the first place, the Court held that, if liberty is to be retained, administrative agencies must respect and uphold specific directions and intentions of Congress when executing congressional policies:

The vast expansion of this field of administrative regulation in response to the pressure of social needs is made possible under our system by adherence to the basic principles that the Legislature shall appropriately determine the standards of administrative action and that in administrative proceedings of a quasi-judicial character the liberty and property of the citizen shall be protected by the rudimentary requirements of fair play. These demand "a fair and open hearing," essentially alike to the legal validity of the administrative regulation and to the maintenance of public confidence in the value and soundness of this important governmental process. Such a hearing has been described as an "inexorable safeguard." (p. 15)

The Court elaborated further on the nature of a fair hearing:

The right to a hearing embraces not only the right to present evidence, but also a reasonable opportunity to know the claims of the opposing party and to meet them. The right to submit argument implies that opportunity; otherwise the right may be but a barren one. Those who are brought into contest with the Government in a quasi-judicial proceeding aimed at the control of their activities are entitled to be fairly advised of what the government proposes and to be heard upon its proposals before it issues its final command. (p. 18)

The Court was particularly disturbed by the secretary's choice to accept and make "as his own the findings which have been prepared by the active prosecutors for the Government, after an ex parte discussion with them and without according any reasonable opportunity to the respondents in the proceedings to know the claims thus presented and to contest them. That is more than an irregularity in practice; it is a vital defect" (p. 22).

It is important to emphasize that due process entitles parties only to an *opportunity* to be heard but does not require a hearing to be held if the right to a hearing is waived. In *Reno v. Flores*, 113 S.Ct. 1949, 1450–1451 (1993), the Supreme Court, in rejecting the claim that automatic review should be provided in deportation cases, held that "due process is satisfied by giving the detained alien juveniles the *right* to a hearing before an immigration judge" even if the hearing does not take place because the right is waived.

In sum, although in America the meaning of due process has remained relatively stable over time, unquestionably what constitutes precisely due process in, say, agency hearings at a given point in our history depends upon a lot of things. In posing the question, "what process is due," Supreme Court Justices, Souter, White, O'-Connor, and Rehnquist, dissenting in *Burns v. U.S.*, 111 S.Ct. 2182, 2192 (1991), quoted cases to make this point. "Due Process unlike some legal rules, is not a technical conception with a fixed content unrelated to time, place, and circumstances, . . . but is 'flexible' (calling for such procedural protections as the particular situation demands)." In a sociopolitical context, the meaning of due process in general, but in agency adjudications specifically, changes with our political moods as we shift back and forth from relative conservativism to relative liberalism.[4]

ADMINISTRATIVE
HEARINGS VERSUS COURT TRIALS

Overview

The agency hearing process is usually less elaborate or formal than typical court trials. Since parties may suffer substantial losses if they come out on the short end of agency hearings, adjudicative procedures must be elaborate enough to protect persons from blatant or gross denials of due process. However, since only administrative law matters are the subject of agency hearings (for example, license renewals, rate adjustments), it has been commonly argued that agency adjudicative procedures need not approach the rigorous and complex procedures demanded in court trials, in which the litigants may have much to lose. Of course, in criminal cases defendants sometimes literally have their lives at stake. Due process procedures in such cases, especially in a nation that cherishes human rights, are expected to be quite elaborate.

In fact, some observers have argued that many agency disputes involve privileges, not rights, and that the adjudicative procedures should therefore be informal, if granted at all. These critics think it is highly questionable whether hearings should be granted by agencies at all, since persons are not legally entitled to something if only privilege is in question. They feel that an agency is only being generous when it grants a hearing to a party who has a dispute involving a privilege. Actually, this was the position espoused by the court in *Ferraro v. Board of Trustees of Labette County Medical Center*, 28 Fed. Appx. 899 (10th Cir. 2001). In this case Joe Ferraro, an anesthetist, claimed that he had been denied procedural due process rights because, after his suspension was restored as an independent contractor, Labette County Medical Center did not give him back pay, which he regarded as a property right. The court disagreed, holding that Mr. Ferraro's work relationship with the hospital amounted only to a privilege. The court asserted: "Mr. Ferraro had no property rights arising from his independent contractor relationship. Indeed, Mr. Ferraro's privileges at the hospital only provided him a venue and an opportunity to earn income, not a guaranteed" (p. 902).[5]

However, because agencies could avoid confrontations with parties by regarding the matter in question as a privilege instead of a right, thus escaping the obligation of holding an inconvenient and time-consuming hearing, the courts in about the past three decades have been placing an increasing number of areas of controversy in the rights category to protect persons against possible agency abuses. In *Goldberg v. Kelly*, 397 U.S. 254 (1970), the Supreme Court flatly rejected the value of the rights-privileges distinction, arguing essentially that the right to a hearing should not depend so much on whether the claim is considered a right or a privilege, but on the extent to which a person might be expected to suffer a "grievous loss."

Hearings can be more or less formal, but most agency adjudications are quite informal, frequently amounting to nothing more than discussions involving the concerned parties, which lead to a mutually acceptable settlement. However, to protect those involved, Congress has required minimum due process procedures.

Specifically, the Administrative Procedure Act, the most rudimentary law governing administrative procedure, has set forth basic uniform standards that must be followed by agency administrators when conducting hearings. Not only has Congress, through various statutes, compelled agency administrators to honor certain procedural safeguards in adjudications, but pressures to comply with the principles of due process have also come from constitutional provisions, especially the Fifth and Fourteenth Amendments, as well as from the public, the media, the regulated, the courts, and even the agencies themselves. Some of the strictest rules to ensure fundamental fairness in agency adjudications stem from agency rules and regulations governing procedure.

Even so, many agencies have not done a very good job in ensuring that parties in disputes are accorded fair treatment in agency hearings. Some agencies, according to the court, have been content to allow adjudicative procedures that, even in the light of the existence of APA requirements, "are shocking to the conscience" (*Rochin v. California*, 342 U.S. 165 [1952]). As a result, the courts in recent decades have tried to ensure reasonable fairness in agency adjudications by imposing their collective will on agency administrators. In *John R. Gagnon v. Gerald H. Scarpelli*, 411 U.S. 788 (1973), an important precedent, the Supreme Court outlined what is believed should constitute *minimum* due process standards, especially in cases in which severe penalties may be attached to a decision (for example, a revocation of probation resulting in return to prison). In the *Goldberg* case the Supreme Court tried to place into perspective the weights that should be assigned to the obligation of the agency to extend procedural due process to "clients" vs. agency needs to reduce the demands on its limited resources. Although it appears that the Supreme Court would apply the principle more broadly, at least in the context of welfare claimants, the Court held: "Thus, the interest of the eligible recipient in uninterrupted receipt of public assistance, coupled with the State's interest that his payments not be erroneously terminated, clearly outweighs the State's competing concern to prevent any increase in its fiscal and administrative burdens" (p. 266). But three years later, in *Gagnon*, the Court felt that some procedural protections (for example, the agency having to provide counsel to a party) go beyond minimum due process entitlements and tend to place a heavy burden on the limited resources of a public agency and that such procedural safeguards therefore need not always be granted.

In 1976 in *Mathews v. Eldridge*, 424 U.S. 319, the Supreme Court created a three-point analysis test that it felt should be used to determine what due process procedures should be extended to parties under various circumstances.

> First, the private interest that will be affected by the official action; second, the risk of an erroneous deprivation of such interest through the procedures used, and the probable value, if any, of additional or substitute procedural safeguards; and finally, the Government's interest, including the function involved and the fiscal and administrative burdens that the additional or substitute procedural requirement would entail. (at 335)

This three-pronged test demands that agency administrators take a practical approach to agency hearings, realizing that providing certain due process procedures may cost way more than they are really worth.

This cost-conscious approach to due process in agency hearings has survived into the twenty-first century.[6] In *Cleveland Board of Education v. Loudermill*, 105 S.Ct. 1487 (1985), the Court argued that once a property right is granted, the state has the legal obligation to protect it by extending "some kind of hearing" (i.e., at least minimum due process procedures that need not be very elaborate or expensive). In this particular situation the Court held that allowing the employee at least the opportunity to respond to charges against him in a pre-termination hearing "would impose neither a significant administrative burden nor intolerable delays" (p. 1495). In 1991 in *Burns v. U.S.*, 111 S.Ct. 2182, it was noted that the *Mathews* approach to the application of due process is still applied—and very broadly: "Although *Mathews* itself concerned the adequacy of administrative fact finding procedures, we have not confined the *Mathews* approach to administrative contexts. . . . The *Mathews* analysis has thus been used as a general approach for determining the procedures required by due process whenever erroneous governmental action would infringe [on] an individual's protected interest" (pp. 2192–2193). *Mathews* continues to carry considerable weight in the federal and state courts, with a Lexis-Nexis legal search turning up 12,775 positive citations of *Mathews* (see, for example, *Rusu v. INS*, 296 F.3d 316 [2002]; *Foust v. McNeill*, 310 F.3d 849 [5th Cir. 2002]).

The cost-conscious standards espoused by the Court in *Mathews* have unquestionably caused agency administrators to avoid having to provide elaborate hearing procedures or trial-like procedures when they felt they could get away with it. However, over the past two decades or so, as noted, legislative bodies and the courts at the national and state levels have conferred upon persons certain due process rights that they once did not have. This extension of rights, frequently making statutory entitlements property rights, has legally obligated administrators to resolve conflicts involving such rights through elaborate due process hearings. Even applying the cost-reduction analysis recommended in *Mathews*, it cannot be ignored that the Court in *Mathews*, in two of its three points in its three-point analysis test, stressed that the interest at stake must be considered along with the procedural impact upon that interest. Since the interests at stake are now frequently property interests, elaborate trial-like procedures are often granted by administrators to protect them.

Also, judges have often urged administrators to make many hearings more trial-like for selfish reasons. Judges have contended that sensible judicial review of administrative hearings cannot occur if agency hearing procedures fail even to resemble court trials. Judges have maintained that it is next to impossible to determine whether proper due process procedures have been extended in a hearing if no reasonable procedural structure is followed.

Should Agency Hearings Be More Trial-Like?

There is strong reason to suspect that despite the problems associated with the varied interpretations and applications of due process in agency adjudications, it probably would be wise not to formalize the agency hearing process too much. In many respects, the argument that agency adjudicative procedures should become more formalized or more trial-like makes only limited sense. If agency hearing procedures were made more trial-like, judicial review of hearings actions would be facilitated, simply because all procedures leading to agency rulings would be clearly spelled out for the reviewing judges to see. However, the costs of achieving due process in this kind of agency adjudication may be too high, especially when there is no significant evidence to suggest that very many parties participating in administrative hearings are denied fair treatment.

In the precedential case, *Mathews v. Eldridge*, 424 U.S. 319 (1976), the Court reflected on the practical costs of extending hearing rights, especially in making hearing procedures trial-like. The Court noted:

> Financial cost alone is not a controlling weight in determining whether due process requires a particular procedural safeguard prior to some administrative decision. But the Government's interest, and hence that of the public, in conserving scarce fiscal and administrative resources is a factor that must be weighed. At some point the benefit of an additional safeguard to the individual affected by the administrative action and to society in terms of increased assurance that the action is just, may be outweighed by the cost. . . . The ultimate balance involves a determination as to when, under our constitutional system, judicial-type procedures must be imposed upon administrative action to assure fairness. . . . The judicial model of an evidentiary hearing is neither a required, nor even the most effective, method of decisionmaking in all circumstances. The essence of due process is the requirement that "a person in jeopardy of serious loss (be given) notice of the case against him and opportunity to meet it." (p. 348)

Professor Todd Rakoff contends that essentially three models have been used to determine what sort of due process is due in agency hearings.[7] The first model or approach basically requires that administrators provide "some kind of hearing" procedures that minimally satisfy due process requirements as mandated by legislation. That is, administrators employ the minimum due process hearing rights and then ask: "What's wrong with this? Do we need to provide anything else or are these procedures O.K.?" The second model starts from the opposite position and assumes that due process can be obtained only in trial-type hearings that employ the adversary approach. This model poses the question: "Is there justification for departing from a trial-type hearing in deciding the matter?" The third model, adopted by the Supreme Court in *Brock v. Roadway Express, Inc.*, 107 S.Ct. 1740 (1987), applies an unacceptable risk standard, which asks: "Are the procedures used so out of line that due process will be subjected to unacceptable risks," or in the Court's language "contain an unacceptable risk of erroneous decision?" (p. 1749).[8]

This unacceptable risk standard is the new applicable standard and, when applied, would rarely require that administrators must provide trial-like hearing procedures even when property or liberty interests are at risk. Today, in the early twenty-first century, the Court's position is that trial-type hearings should normally not be granted, balancing the interests of the state against property interests, unless they are absolutely sanctioned by specific statutory provisions. Ultimately, due process is protected by making agency hearing procedures subject to judicial review.[9]

Recently, in *Coalition for Fair and Equitable Regulation of Docks v. Federal Energy Regulatory Commission*, 297 F.3d 771 (8th Cir. 2002), the Coalition argued that their due process rights were denied because FERC refused to grant them a full evidentiary hearing or trial-type hearing before an administrative law judge so their complaint regarding the reasonableness of fees charged Union Electric could be heard. The court ruled that under current administrative law the choice of whether to hold an evidentiary hearing is left to the discretion of the agency unless a trial-type hearing is absolutely required by law. Specifically, the court upheld FERC's choice to access the reasonableness of Union Electric's fees through a mere paper review, rejecting "the Coalition's contention that its claim could only be clarified by a discovery and a hearing: 'While trial-type procedural measures may be used to develop a record and resolve issues of fact, they are not intended to be used as a cure for a complaint that fails to inform the Commission completely and clearly as to the issues and factual disputes. . . . ' FERC's decision to deny a hearing on the ground that there were no material factual disputes was within its discretion and did not violate the Coalition's constitutional rights" (p. 779–780).

Some have argued that the Supreme Court since *Goldberg* has gone too far to reduce the procedural protections in agency hearings. Certainly, the High Court's decisions starting with *Mathews* have made it much easier for agency administrators to avoid having to provide elaborate trial-type hearings. But is this necessarily the wrong course to take? The plain truth is that administrative hearings should not be expected to provide formal, court-like procedural protections to litigious parties, because administrative agencies are not supposed to act like courts. The sole function of courts is to hear and decide controversies. This is their only constitutional obligation. The primary role, however, of an administrative agency is to see to it that legislative statutes are faithfully executed. Agencies are not courts of law, and to expect that they should function like courts is to expect too much from the administrative system. It should be understood that lawmakers decided in the 1940s to require agencies to provide hearings so that affected parties could question the procedural soundness and fairness of agency actions.[10] Such a legislative measure was taken to help ensure administrative accountability, but clearly legislators never intended to turn administrative agencies into trial courts.

Agency vs. Court Compassion

Despite the less elaborate due process standards of typical administrative adjudication compared with court trials, some critics believe that persons stand a better chance of receiving fairer, more compassionate treatment from administrative agencies than from courts. According to Victor A. Thompson, this is so because administrative agencies have the luxury of being able to make more "particularistic," as contrasted to "universalistic," decisions than the courts. Therefore,

Thompson concludes, administrative agencies tend on the whole to be more compassionate toward individual parties than the courts. In explanation, Thompson notes:

> A belief persists that an individual can get personalized, compassionate treatment in the courts if it is denied to him by the bureaucracy. Although the belief seems plausible because of the large amount of time and money spent by courts on individual cases, it is not well-founded. In the first place, court treatment is so expensive and time-consuming that most people forego it. Bad as it is, an administrative appeal, or a letter to a congressman, and especially the latter, gives the average individual a better chance of success.[11]

Thompson argues that judges, unlike public administrators, feel compelled to make universalistic decisions or decisions that largely ignore or sacrifice the individual for the sake of upholding the law:

> More important is the fact courts are institutionalized to seek the general principle in the individual case. Justice is blind. The individual is unimportant; only the principle counts. One of the hardest lessons for a young law student to learn is that he must give up his natural, compassionate interest in the outcome and dispositions for the actual persons involved in the cases he studies and that he must concentrate solely on the principle of the law involved.[12]

Therefore, Thompson reasons, "Since courts are staffed with law students grown older and professionally successful, courts are among our least compassionate institutions. They rule by deduction from general principles. . . . Decision by deduction from rules is the least compassionate kind there is."[13] Thompson does not deny that administrative agencies also make impersonal, insensitive, universalistic decisions that are patently unfair to individuals, but he does suggest that due process, when measured in terms of compassion instead of the degree of procedural formality alone, is less likely to be experienced in the courts.

Professors Ernest Gellhorn and Ronald M. Levin argue an opposing view. In sharp contrast, they contend that court decisions are "essentially personal." They hold that agency decisions are bureaucratized because they are "institutional decisions" made by technical experts or bureaucrats way down in the hierarchy where power has been "sub-delegated" to them. They maintain that the impersonal adjudicative decision tends to serve the bureaucracy more than the individual because "it is the product of a bureaucracy rather than of a single person or a group of identifiable people."[14]

A survey of Administrative Law Judges (ALJs) reported in 1994 in the *Administrative Law Review* tends to support Gellhorn and Levin's view. Respondents answered that trial judges make more personal decisions affecting a "person or a few people," while ALJs make decisions that usually affect "many people" and are "national in scope."[15]

In summary, court trial procedures are more elaborate than those normally employed in agency hearings, but one should not necessarily conclude from this that court trials are more apt to reflect the principles of fundamental fairness than agency hearings. But the most important point to reiterate it that administrative agencies are not supposed to function like courts. The chief task of an agency is to administer public policies. Also, agencies are required by statute to handle and resolve many disputes daily. Also, unlike courts, they do not have the luxury of being able to reject cases. As a result, agencies must routinely resolve disputes while attending to their administrative tasks. Thus, agency administrators are frequently forced to forego elaborate hearings for the sake of administrative expediency. Given the very limited human and financial resources characteristic of virtually all governmental agencies in the early 2000s, as well as the much publicized growing budget deficits at all government levels, it is reasonable to assume that Congress does not realistically expect anything else. These realities should be kept in mind in the next few sections, which focus on specific features that characterize administrative adjudications, especially formal hearings.

BIAS, DUE PROCESS, AND REGULATORY EFFECTIVENESS

Administrative Law Judges: The Independence Issue

There are critics who are concerned over the apparent lack of independence of ALJs from agency control and political influence, yet others play down the independence problems as not serious. These defenders of the present regulatory system stress the importance of maintaining an agency adjudicative system that provides for fair hearings, yet simultaneously does not seriously undermine the effectiveness of the regulatory process. Norman Abrams, for example, voices concern about agency influences that might unfairly bias an ALJ's judgment, but nonetheless he understands why an agency would not want to see hearings conducted by adjudicators who are oblivious and insensitive to agency policies, "goals, special regulatory problems, and political considerations." He asks: "Is this inconsistent with the notion of an independent hearing officer?"[16] Also sympathetic to the real problems that agencies face in their efforts to regulate fairly and effectively, Kenneth C. Davis argues especially that the independence of ALJs helps to serve the promotion of objectivity and fairness in agency adjudications, but independence should not be so extreme that it frustrates the policymaking efforts of agency administrators.[17]

It should be understood that administrative agencies, boards, and commissions are not politically neutral institutions. Their leaders are political appointees and they serve, to a greater or lesser extent, political causes. Eleanor M. Fox acknowledges the political nature of agency adjudications in her study of two very different political personalities who chaired the Federal Trade Commission: Michael Pertschuk and James C. Miller, III. Chairman Pertschuk—President Carter's appointee and a liberal who tended to side with the underdog and believed that government should do its best to protect individuals from abuse, especially from big business—reached decisions in agency adjudications that reflected clearly his philosophical perspective. Chairman Miller, in contrast, was President Reagan's appointee and a conservative who sided with the successful, believed that government tended to be the enemy of big business, and felt that governmental intrusion in the private sector tends only to protect the inefficient and weaken society. Chairman Miller's decisions also reflected his predispositions. "At every turn, Mr. Miller drew the inference against the intervention and Mr. Pertschuk drew the inference for it."[18] Regardless of the facts, Fox concluded, "one sees what one is predisposed to see."[19] Commenting on the value of her own research, she noted: "An understanding of the political nature of the FTC chairmanship helps the student of judicial decisionmaking to pierce the myth of the neutral judge applying economic principles dispassionately."[20] It is important to stress that Fox's study serves to acknowledge the political realities of agency decisionmakers, even those serving in a quasi-judicial capacity. She, in actuality, did not condemn the fact that these men let their political philosophies guide them in their jurisprudential role.[21] Possibly Bernard Schwartz summarizes the bias of prejudgment situation best: "If freedom from bias is taken in the broad dictionary sense of absence of preconceptions, no one can ever have a fair trial. The judicial mind is no blank piece of paper; the judge or administrative adjudication starts with inevitable preconceptions. In this sense there is a prejudgment in every case."[22]

Obviously, then, the practical legal question is: How independent should hearing officers be from agency politics, philosophical orientations, outside political pressures, and any other potentially prejudicial influences, if agencies are to provide hearings that are "fair enough"? Predispositions should not bias hearing decisions to such an extent that a mockery is made of due process. To Norman Abrams, for an agency to conduct a reasonably fair hearing, only sufficient impartiality and fair-mindedness should prevail, but not so much that ALJs must separate themselves from agency policy positions or their political ideas.[23] This viewpoint is upheld in a famous bias case, *American Cyanamid v. F.T.C.*, 363 F.2d 757 (1966), in which the court ruled that hearing officers should not be disqualified simply because they express strong attachment to agency policies. In *Rombough v. F.A.A.*, 594 F.2d 893 (2nd Cir. 1979), the court held that it is not inappropriate for agency officials to make hearing decisions that are simply consistent with state agency policy positions. More recently, in *Alma v. United States*, 744 F.Supp. 1546 (S.D. G.A. 1990), the court argued that a hearing official should not normally be disqualified from hearing a case even though the official publicly stated his or her position on the issues.[24] While in *St. Anthony Hospital v. United States HHS*, 309 F.3d 680, 711–713 (10th Cir. 2002), the court acknowledged that it would be a denial of due process if the tribunal was not impartial, yet the court stressed that a "substantial showing" of virtually any kind of bias, prejudice, or predisposition must be shown for the hearing to be judged as unfair or a violation of due process.

Closed Mind Rule

The courts have generally been guided by the "closed mind" rule in bias or prejudgment cases. To prevail before the court the petitioner must prove through "clear and convincing evidence" that the adjudicator has "an irrevocably closed mind on matters critical to the disposition of the proceedings" (*Housing Study Group v. Kemp*, 736 F.Supp. 321, 332 [D.D.C. 1990]). For example, in *Northwestern Bell Telephone v. Stofferahn*, 461 N.W.2d 129, 131 (1990), the South Dakota Supreme Court held that a public utility commissioner should have recused himself, because "clear and convincing evidence" showed that he had an "unalterably closed mind." This commissioner had previously been "a zealous and active opponent of the deregulation legislation" under question and South Dakota law provides that "no commissioner shall participate in any hearing or proceeding in which he has any conflict of interest" (S.D.C.L., Section 49-1-9 [1983]). And in 2000 in *Bird v. Bland County School Board*, 2000 U.S. App. Lexis 553, the Fourth Circuit Court of Appeals held that Bird, a math teacher appealing for reinstatement before the Bland County School Board, was denied due process (i.e., an impartial hearing without prejudgment) because evidence clearly revealed that the board had already decided to terminate Bird's employment before the hearing even began, thus displaying an "irrevocably closed mind."[25]

Prejudgment of Legislative Versus Adjudicative Facts

In deciding bias or prejudgment cases, courts often make a distinction between prejudgment of *legislative facts* and prejudgment of *adjudicative facts*. Legislative facts are general facts pertaining to law or public policy that help officials at the hearing understand the content of the policy or law. Legislative facts have a general and future orientation since disputes involving legislative facts often focus on the likely impact of certain policies. Normally, courts will not rule that hearing examiners or ALJs should have to disqualify or recuse themselves simply because they have taken or prejudged a prior position on laws, policies, or legislative facts unless, as mentioned, the prejudgment is so severe that it is certain that the adjudicator has an "irrevocably closed mind." Thus, the standard for disqualifying hearing officers who have prejudged legislative facts is not tough, because it is assumed that virtually all adjudicators, as public officials, have expressed opinions on public policies.

One of the most famous cases involving prejudgment of legislative facts if *Federal Trade Commission v. Cement Institute*, 333 U.S. 683 (1948). In this case the Supreme Court did not feel that the commissioners on the FTC should have disqualified themselves simply because they had clearly expressed grave doubts about the legality of the Cement Institute's pricing scheme prior to a hearing before the FTC. The Court opined that due process had not been violated, because the Cement Institute was afforded the opportunity to defend its pricing system before the FTC's commissioners, who did not necessarily have an "irrevocably closed mind" on the pricing method (p. 701). In *Stofferahn*, involving prejudgment of legislative facts, the Court upheld standards for determining bias as established in *Cement Institute*, but clear and convincing evidence showed that this particular commissioner has "an unalterably closed mind."

In cases involving alleged prejudgment of adjudicative facts, however, courts have generally applied a much tougher standard to ensure due process. Adjudicative facts, in contrast to legislative facts, do not pertain to general policy-oriented facts, but to the more specific facts in a particular dispute relating to the "who, what, where, and how" questions. Adjudicative facts are the kind of particular and immediate facts that judges and jurors decide (e.g., Did television station KZZZ-TV violate FCC Rule XX by broadcasting such and such a program on such and such a date?). Of course, prejudgment of adjudicative facts in administrative hearings would virtually guarantee that due process would not be served. As a consequence, courts have usually ruled that hearing officials must be disqualified if they have prejudged adjudicative facts.

Possibly the most frequently cited case involving the prejudgment of adjudicative facts is *Cinderella Career and Finishing School, Inc. v. FTC*, 425 F.2d 583 (D.C. Cir. 1970). In this case the D.C. Circuit court argued that Chairman Dixon prejudged not only legislative facts in his public speeches about the finishing school prior to the school's hearing before the FTC but also specific adjudicative facts, precluding any semblance of fair hearing.

In a highly publicized case former baseball star Pete Rose, who was accused of gambling on baseball games including his own team, argued successfully that baseball Commissioner Bart Giamatti had prejudged adjudicative facts by deciding that Rose's involvement in betting on baseball games had occurred. Giamatti had written a favorable letter to a judge on a convicted felon who was to act as an informer against Rose. In the letter Giamatti said he believed that what the informer said about Rose's gambling on games was true. In light of such prejudgment of accusations against Rose (adjudicative facts), the Ohio court ruled that a hearing conducted by Giamatti would deny Rose his procedural due process rights to a fair unbiased tribunal free from "improper prejudice" (*Giamatti v. Rose*, 1989 W.L. 111386, 111447 [Ohio Misc. 1989]).

Personal Bias

Prejudice or personal bias for or against a person by an ALJ or hearing examiner also normally constitutes grounds for disqualification of the adjudicator(s). Personal bias (also called actual bias) is directed toward the person, not the issue. Personal bias can be established by showing that an adjudicator or adjudicators, possibly the whole administrative tribunal, have expressed a strong personal bias either for or against a party that would make a fair and impartial hearing virtually impossible. For example, personal bias was charged in a Colorado case because a hearing examiner had in the past called the plaintiff's lawyer a "nasty little fellow" and a "smart ass" (*Neopolan U.S.A. Corp v. Industrial Claims Appeals Office*, 778

P.2d 312 [Colo. Ct. App. 1989]). Such bias need not be enough to disqualify an adjudicator, however, if a reviewing court believes that otherwise the hearing officer allowed "thoughtful and discriminating evaluation of the facts" (*NLRB v. Pittsburgh S.S. Co.*, 337 U.S. 656, 660 [1949]). Personal prejudice may also be demonstrated if it can be shown that an adjudicator consistently rules against one side (*NLRB v. Miami Coca-Cola Bottling Co.*, 222 F.2d 341 [5th Cir. 1977]).

Conflict of Interest

Courts have held that hearing proceedings may be biased and violate procedural due process standards when conflicts of interest, ex parte contacts, or an appearance of unfairness can be shown. The most blatant conflict of interest can be seen when a hearing official stands to gain or lose something of value personally from the hearing decision. In New Jersey the superior court ruled that a public utility commissioner should have disqualified himself, because he had entered into a clear conflict of interest when he had inquired about possible employment with a utility company involved in a hearing in which he was an adjudicator (*In re Bergen Co. Util. Auth.*, 553 A.2d 849, 853 [N.J. Super. 1989]). In another case, the U.S. Supreme Court in *Ortiz v. Fibreboard Corp.*, 119 S.Ct. 2295 (1999), held that plaintiff's counsel in a class action case could not reach a settlement in the best interests of their clients in a fairness hearing, because at least some of the plaintiff's lawyer's were involved in separate conflicting settlement interests involving legal fees. That precluded the probability that they would try to obtain the best settlement for their present clients in the fairness hearing.

Ex Parte Contacts

Bias or prejudice may also compromise fair hearings as a result of ex parte contacts or communications. Ex parte contacts tend to undermine procedural due process in agency hearings because they allow a particular party or party's representatives to communicate with hearing officials about adjudicative or legislative facts in the absence of the other parties in the dispute, thus giving the party making the contact an unfair opportunity to influence the adjudicator(s). Such ex parte contacts are normally prohibited whether court judges or agency administrators are involved, although ex parte contacts are not necessarily prejudicial if matters related to the case were not discussed (*Romey v. Landers*, 392 N.W. 2d 415,421 [S.D. 1986]). Nonetheless, ex parte contacts are normally frowned upon because such contacts give the appearance of impropriety.

Appearance-of-Fairness Doctrine

An old doctrine known as the appearance-of-fairness doctrine is rooted in common law. Although this standard was at first applied to court trials, the Supreme Court of Washington applied the appearance-of-fairness doctrine to administrative hearings as far back as 1898 in *State ex rel. Barnard v. Board of Educ.*, 52 P

317 (Wash. 1898). The appearance-of-fairness doctrine is made quite clear in *Mordhorst v. Egert*, 223 N.W.2d 501, 505 (S.D. 1974), in which the court, quoting a prior case, wrote:

> A fair and impartial tribunal requires at least that the trier of fact be disinterested . . . and that he also be free from any form of bias or predisposition regarding the outcome of the case. . . . Not only must the procedures be fair, "the very appearance of complete fairness" must also be present. These principles apply not only to trials, but equally, if not more so, to administrative proceedings.

But the truth is that courts are very reluctant to require hearing officers to disqualify themselves solely because of any appearance of bias. Plenty of lip service is paid to violations of the appearance-of-fairness doctrine, but courts are much more likely to enforce this standard when it is coupled with findings of concrete bias.[26]

However, in *1616 Second Ave. Rest v. Liquor Auth.*, 550 N.E.2d 910 (N.Y. 1990), the New York court of appeals held that the Chairman of the state Liquor Authority violated Second Avenue Restaurant's due process rights by failing to disqualify himself after making public statements against the restaurant, thus giving the "appearance of impropriety" that any "disinterested observer" (a popular standard applied by the court) could readily see. Judge Wachtler wrote

> But whether or not he had actually prejudged the matter, his statements nonetheless gave the impression that he had, and that impression lent an impermissible air of unfairness to the proceeding. More importantly, those statements and the message they conveyed to a "disinterested observer" established the Chairman's public position on the issue. (p. 913)[27]

Despite the fact that Judge Wachtler wrote for the majority in this case, Judges Simons, Alexander, and Hancock, writing in dissent, probably reflect better the opinion of most courts today when they held that simply an appearance of impropriety due to alleged bias is not sufficient to justify disqualification; existing law requires, quoting from *Matter of Warder v. Board of Regents*, 53 N.Y.2d 186 (1981), a "factual demonstration to support the allegation of bias and proof that the outcome flowed from it" (p. 914).

Combination of Functions

One other major source of possible bias is from hearing officials who perform a combination of functions. A combination of functions occurs when an administrative agency allows a hearing official or body to perform not only the adjudicatory function but also the investigatory and possibly even the prosecutory function.[28] According to Stephen R. Miller and Larry T. Richardson, "This practice compromises the objectivity of the administrative inquiry, favoring the interests of the agency."[29] They contend further that the "combination of functions is the most obvious source of bias in administrative hearings.[30] Critics, as well as many courts, have argued that combining the investigatory, prosecutory, and adjudicatory functions in the same hearing official or body present a blatant conflict of interest, violating the appearance-of-fairness principle, and, of course, procedural due process. Realizing the procedural due process problems presented by the combination-of-functions problem, many agencies have in good faith tried to separate the investigatory, prosecutory, and adjudicatory roles within their agencies, but some observers charge that this still is not enough to save due process in agency hearings. The reality is, these critics assert, that all these functions are being performed by the same agency's personnel, leading the public to believe that agency officials are working together in a biased manner.

Technically, the federal Administrative Procedure Act, Section 554(d), as well as many state APAs, prohibit agency hearing officials (decision makers) from also serving in a prosecutory and investigatory role. However, Section 554(d), as well as the section's counterpart in most states' APAs, applies only to certain formal hearings, thus allowing the combination of functions to be practiced when formal hearing procedures do not have to be observed, which, of course, accounts for most agency hearings.

Today, although combination-of-functions practices are apparently condemned by most legal scholars and practitioners, the courts have generally not ruled against the use of combination of functions in agency hearings for mostly practical reasons. Courts have normally been sympathetic to agency administrators who have argued that separating functions is costly because it (1) prevents hearing officers from consulting with those who are the most knowledgeable about the case (i.e., those who participated in the investigation); (2) forces the use of more staff to handle cases; (3) causes confusion over what communications among staff are permissible; (4) delays hearing officials from hearing and disposing of cases rapidly; and (5) defies overall practical considerations of administrative efficiency and effectiveness.

In reviewing *In re Deming*, 108 Wash.2d 82 (1987), Stephen Hobbs concluded that one of the reasons that the Washington Supreme Court applied the "weaker" appearance-of-fairness doctrine in ruling that due process was not violated by the state's Judicial Qualifications Commission when it combined investigatory, prosecutory, and adjudicatory powers was because practical administrative factors had to be weighed, specifically, a ruling against the Commission that would require a basic and costly restructuring of the Commission.[31]

To prevail in a combination-of-functions charge, a petitioner must overcome not only concerns of administrative practicality but also the presumption of honesty and integrity. In other words, the petitioner must overcome the presumption that professional and honest administrators cannot serve due process, even if they combine functions.

Rule of Necessity

A controversial doctrine related directly to bias or prejudice cases is the *rule of necessity*. The rule of necessity, based in common law, is controversial because the doctrine appears blatantly to defy common sense. It precludes the disqualification of a hearing examiner, even though the adjudicator may in fact be biased, because no one else is eligible to hear the case. The rule of necessity applies to a single hearing official or an entire administrative tribunal. To many critics, denying due process to a party in an agency hearing this way is wrong, and it certainly points to a problem within the administrative law system. Does it make sense to say "Allowing such bias is clearly unfair and will very likely deny the party procedural due process, but let's do it anyway"? To some courts, the rule does make sense and they have not hesitated to apply it. In *Brinkley v. Hassig*, 83 F.2d 351 (10th Cir. 1936), the court reasoned that when disqualification means that no tribunal will be eligible to hear the case, the public interest must be upheld, even though the individual's rights may be compromised somewhat, by employing the rule of necessity. "From the very necessity of the case has grown the rule that disqualification will not be permitted to destroy the only tribunal with powers in the premises" (p. 357).

It is true that the courts do not like to use the rule of necessity, but certain situations apparently give them little choice. Take, for example, the Federal Trade Commission's situation. Joseph E. Edwards contends that the full FTC would probably never be disqualified, despite prevailing prejudice, because no provision in the Federal Trade Commission Act provides for a change in venue.[32] This means that some commissions could be disqualified because of bias (as was Chairman Dixon in the *Cinderella* case), but never the entire FTC. In fact, in *Marquette Cement Mfg. Co. v. Federal Trade Commission*, 147 F2d 589 (1945), and *FTC v. Cement Institute*, 333 U.S. 683 (1948), the courts said exactly this. In *Cement Institute*, for example, the Court, applying the rule of necessity, concluded: "Had the entire membership of the Commission [been] disqualified in the proceedings against the respondents, this complaint could not have been acted on by the Commission or any other government agencies" (p. 701). It appears, then, that possibly the best way to do away with having to use the rule of necessity, which clearly undermines attempts to achieve due process in agency adjudications, is to make legislators provide sensible hearing alternatives when bias becomes an issue.

CONSIDERING EVIDENCE IN AGENCY HEARINGS

Overview: Common Body of Rules of Evidence Apparently Needed

The issues and questions surrounding the case of evidence in reaching decisions in agency hearings are often very technical and contradictory and thus quite confusing, even to legal experts. A major reason for this is that an accepted body of rules of evidence, which would govern all formal administrative hearings, has not made its debut in administrative law just yet. In contrast, in 1975 federal rules of evidence (FRE) were enacted to govern the handling of evidence by federal courts. The FRE provided common rules of evidence that helped to restructure and order the submission and use of evidence. Michael H. Graham, who believes that modified FRE should be used to guide the handling of evidence in agency hearings, contends that FRE have greatly benefited federal courts and could also benefit agency adjudications. "The enhancement provided by the FRE of pre-dictability and consistency in rulings on admissibility, along with explicit recognition of considerations of waste of time, fosters preparation and orderly conduct of trials."[33] Graham points out that hearings in our federal agencies are somewhat chaotic because they "are governed by more than 280 different sets of regulations controlling the admissibility of evidence."[34] Lack of a common body of rules of evidence also plagues hearings in state agencies. Graham admits that some critics have opposed applying FRE to agency adjudications because they feel that agency proceedings are significantly different from court trials, but he disagrees. "However, the fact is that the FRE apply in federal civil non-jury trials where the need to develop and control an evidentiary record is functionally indistinguishable from the analogous need in administrative adjudications."[35]

Numerous cases have made it clear that a common body of rules of evidence does not apply to administrative hearings at the federal or state level, for example, *Goodridge v. Director*, 337 N.E.2d 927 (Mass. 1978); *Manhattan Scene v. SLA*, 397 N.Y.S.2d 495 (4th Dept. 1977);. *Murphy v. Department of Public Welfare*, 480 A.2d 382 (Pa. Commw. Ct. 1984); *IHC Hospitals v. Board of Comm'rs*, 108 Idaho 136 (1985); and *Walter N. Yoder and Sons v. NLRB*, 754 F.2d 531 (4th Cir. 1985). Once agreeing with Graham, Richard J. Pierce maintained in 1987 that the fact that over 1100 federal ALJs apply 280 different evidentiary rules of evidence has made a mess out of the adjudicatory system. He claimed that the "evidentiary procedure now used in agency adjudications vary substantially along a spectrum from no reference to evidentiary rules at all, to oratory reference to the FRE as a source of guidance, to mandatory incorporation of the FRE."[36] Pierce concluded then that steps should be taken to incorporate uniform codes of evidence into agency hearings, but he urges that newly developed standards should not be so rigid that they would prevent adjudicators from employing their discretion to exclude "unreliable evidence."[37] However, Pierce has changed his mind or at least his emphasis. In his 2002 *Administrative Law Treatise* he argues that ALJs should be respected for their administrative expertise and permitted in adjudication to use their discretion to weigh the reliability of evidence without being restricted by inapplicable FRE. Pierce concludes flatly "that agency adjudications should not be governed by the FRE. As institutions with specialized expertise in the subject matters of the disputes they adjudicate, agencies are entitled to much greater trust than juries."[38]

For public administration, probably the central point regarding evidence is that in a free and open society, evidence employed to justify conclusions in trials or hearings should be gathered, presented, and evaluated in a manner that does not undermine the principles of fair procedure. Focus in the following sections is on how fairly evidence is presented and judged. To provide meaningful insights, once again some comparison are made between procedures employed in administrative adjudications and court trials.

Introduction to Procedural
Due Process Issues Concerning Evidence

Both administrative hearings and court trials have as an ideal reaching decisions that are both rational and fair. But how can one determine whether adjudicative findings (findings are decisions rooted in adjudicative facts) are rational and fair? Surely there are no foolproof tests, but common sense can play a significant role in assessing whether adjudicative decisions are based upon reasonable review and use of the facts and whether procedural due process has been accorded to the disputing parties. In *Bean v. Unemployment Ins. Comm'n*, 485 A.2d 630 (Me., 1984), the court stated that agency findings do not have to be very detailed or technical, but they must be elaborate enough to explain the basis for the decision. Therefore, it is not enough to summarize findings in a single sentence (*Ship Creek Hydraulic Syndicate v. Department of Transportation*, 685 P.2d 715 [Alaska 1984]) or in statutory language in the absence of relevant facts (*Gibson v. Municipal Retirement System*, 683 S.W.2d 882 [Tex. Ct. App. 1985]), or to cause a court to inquire into the thinking of agency adjudicators because they based their finding on a record "so bare as to frustrate effective judicial review" (*Community for Creative Non-Violence v. Lujan*, 908 F.2d 992, 998 [D.C. Cir. 1990]).

It would be a mistake even to lose sight of the immediate and chief purpose of agency adjudications: to resolve disputes. However, it must also be remembered that in agency hearings in which "final decisions" resolve disputes, important public policy decisions are often developed as well. This dual purpose in administrative adjudications undoubtedly causes some ALJs to pay more attention to creating public policies they consider worthwhile than to resolving disputes in the most fair manner. ALJs are cognizant of the reality that agency chiefs can overrule their adjudicative decisions if their decisions run blatantly contrary to agency policies and goals.

Fairness and rationality in adjudicative proceedings depend not only on the factual quality of the evidence entered into the record but also on how the evidence is actually submitted, employed, and evaluated. Thus, the procedural steps used in employing evidence frequently become the main focal point of critics. Most experts agree that it is not the presentation of evidence by each party per se that is most crucial in allowing any tribunal to reach a fair and rational decision; rather it is providing parties in a dispute with the opportunity to scrutinize and challenge the reliability of the evidence the opposing party presents. Kenneth C. Davis, for example, held quite validly a few decades ago that "the central feature of a trial is not affirmative presentation of evidence by each side; it is the opportunity for each side to attack the evidence presented by the other side."[39] Parties can use various tactics in an attempt to diminish the probative worth of the other disputant's evidence, including (1) written and oral arguments; (2) rebuttals; (3) explanatory statements; and (4) cross-examinations. These due process protections apply to agency hearings as much as to court trials.

Proper Notice

A hearing notice is equivalent to a complaint issued in a civil suit. The importance of providing proper notice when procedural due process calls for a full evidentiary hearing or formal hearing "with live witnesses and cross-examination and all the rest of the procedural hoopla"[40] cannot be underestimated. In fact, as Bernard Schwartz exclaims, "The first requirement of such 'procedural hoopla' is that of notice."[41] This is because the quality of evidence presented in one's defense would clearly suffer if proper notice is not given. Put simply, proper notice provides the party with essential and specific information about the complaint and sufficient time to prepare a defense. Under the federal APA, Section 554(b) "Persons entitled to notice of an agency hearing shall be timely informed of (1) the time, place, and nature of the hearing; (2) the legal authority and jurisdiction under which the hearing is to be held; and (3) the matters of fact and law asserted."

Courts have long noted that a part of the right to be heard includes proper notice. In *Goldberg v. Kelly*, 397 U.S. 254 (1970), the Supreme Court regarded notice, specifically "timely and adequate notice detailing the reasons for a proposed (action), as a fundamental requisite of due process." Two decades later a New York court held that "Fundamental due process requires reasonable notice sufficient to allow a party to adequately prepare and present a defense to charges that will be the subject of a hearing" (*Diamond Terminal Corp. v. New York State Dept. of Taxation and Fin.*, 158 A.D.2d 38, 41 [1990]).

In a 1978 administrative law case the Supreme Court placed the role of notice in clear perspective when it said that the "purpose of notice under the Due Process Clause is to apprize the affected individual of, and permit adequate preparation for, an impending 'hearing'" (*Memphis Light, Gas, and Water Division v. Craft*, 436 U.S. 1, 14, 1978). This ruling was in reference to termination of utility service to a customer. The Court argued that the municipal utility company violated due process requirements when it failed to inform the customer of the availability of procedures designed to protect against a termination of utility service. In other situations, due process does not necessarily obligate a public agency to tell parties how to complain. That is, due process does not always require an administrative agency to tell someone specifically how to use the protest procedures, as long as they are available. However, in this case the Court felt that because of the importance of utility termination and the varied educational levels of utility customers in general, due process should have entailed a rather specific explanation to the customer on how to complain (for example, where and when to complain, and to whom specifically).

Proper notice also means that actual fundamental fairness must be accorded, not just the appearance of fairness. In other words, the form of the notice, even though technically correct, may not constitute proper notice in actuality if common sense dictates that the notice did not convey in meaningful terms what should have been conveyed in the notice. That is, procedural due process regarding notice means ideally that the notice should actually or meaningfully notify and not deceive. Of course, courts differ considerably on what constitutes proper or actual notice. Nothing in administrative law seems very certain, even something as apparently so simply as notice. For instance, normally the courts hold that formal, written notice is appropriate, yet some judges have ruled that if it can be shown that parties actually were notified by other means so that they understood the essential facts, "the requirement of notification purposed to inform may be satisfied by actual knowledge, especially when it is acted upon" (*McLay v. Maryland Assemblies, Inc.*, 269 M.D. 465, 477 [1973]). In *Landover Books, Inc. v. Prince George's County*, 566 A.2d 792 (1989), the Court ruled that an adult book store owner had received proper notice because he "appeared and participated in the hearing on the appeal, thus indicating that it [Landover Books] knew the contents of the notice. . . . Under the circumstances presented, we hold that service as in compliance with the substantive requirements of the ordinance despite the technical irregularity since Landover had actual knowledge of the violation" (p. 798).

Other circumstances may allow a public agency to avoid giving any notice. In *Rex Realty Co. v. City of Cedar Rapids*, 322 F.3d 526 (8th Cir. 2003), the court held that the City of Cedar Rapids did not have to give Rex Realty Company notice or a hearing prior to condemnation proceedings, because the taking of the private property for public use was grounded in the government's constitutional power under eminent domain. Rex Realty had claimed unsuccessfully that the City of Cedar Rapids must provide proper notice and a hearing so it could be determined whether the taking is for a legitimate public purpose under eminent domain.

Courts will usually uphold the adequacy of notice if they believe that the record of the hearing clearly indicates that the party knew enough about the charges against him or her and had sufficient time to prepare an adequate defense. Nevertheless, courts have on occasion, possibly too often, upheld notices as proper when they have fallen far short of what a reasonable person would consider proper due process standards. Possibly this is so because proper notice in administrative hearings does not have to be as elaborate or detailed as in criminal complaint, although proper notice for administrative hearings still must be fair enough to allow a party a *sufficient opportunity* to protect his or her rights. Sufficient opportunity is stressed because parties are not guaranteed a right to an adequate defense but only an opportunity through proper notice to prepare an adequate defense. In *Diamond Terminal v. Dept. of Taxation*, 557 N.Y.S.2d 962 (A.D. 3 Dept. 1990), a person appeared unprepared at his hearing because, he contended, he did not have time to prepare, even though the record showed that the hearing officer had offered to give him a thirty-day adjournment to prepare. The court felt that the fact the petitioner was given the opportunity to prepare for his defense, even though he did not take advantage of it, "supports a finding that the notice given was sufficient under those circumstances" (p. 963).

Burden of Proof

In criminal proceedings the burden of proof is always on the state. That is, criminal defendants are presumed innocent until the state proves them guilty beyond any reasonable doubt. However, in administrative adjudications the burden of proof does not always rest on the agency, although it often does. The federal Administrative Procedure Act incorporates the traditional common law practice that places the burden of proof on the party bringing the action (for example, a person applying for a government benefit must prove that he or she is eligible, or an agency charging a company with a rule violation must prove the violation). In short, the mover under the APA normally has the burden of persuading the administrative tribunal that the evidence supports his or her position. The APA, Section 556(d) states: "Except as otherwise provided by statute, the proponent of a rule or order has the burden of proof."

Common sense should suggest that, as a practical matter, it makes a significant difference which side has the burden of proof at a hearing. It is frequently considerably more difficult to prove a charge than to defend against one. Thus, as Barnard Schwartz asserts: "All too often, determining where the burden of proof lies determines who prevails in the case."[42] When the APA does not apply and/or statutes are not clear as to which party has the burden of proof, courts have usually held that agency adjudication should follow customary common law, which assigns the burden to the initiator. However, often court rulings have required agencies to assign burden of proof in such a way that vital liberty and property interests are protected.

In *Esposito v. INS*, 936 F.2d 911 (7th Cir. 1991), the court maintained that Esposito, an alien who had entered the United States through fraudulent and willful misrepresentation, had the burden of proof before the Board of Immigration appeals to show why the board should exclude from consideration its hearing a murder conviction by an Italian court. "The burden of course, is on him to point to exceptional procedural infirmities in the proceedings leading to his convictions, and he has failed to do so" (p. 915). In *Tyra v. Secretary of Health and Human Services*, 9886 F.2d 1024 (6th Cir. 1990), the court acknowledged how the burden of proof can shift from the claimant to the agency. Parenthetically, under some circumstances the burden of proof may shift back and forth several times before a resolution is reached. In *Tyra* the court pointed out that under the Social Security Act, Section 223(d), as amended, 42 U.S.C.A., section 423(d), the "claimant has the ultimate burden to establish an entitlement to benefits by proving the existence of a disability" (p. 1028). In this case Tyra had the burden of proving that he had a severe impairment that prevented him from returning to his previous work. The ALJ ruled that Tyra was impaired enough that he could not return to his past job. However, with this finding the Court noted that the burden of proof shifts to the agency to show what kind of work, if any, the claimant can perform. "At this step in the analysis it becomes the secretary's burden to establish the claimant's ability to work. The secretary must prove that . . . the claimant retains the capacity to perform a different kind of job" (pp. 1028–1029).

Hearsay Evidence and Its Controversial Status

Hearsay ("heard saying")[43] is discussed by many, but my experience has been that few really understand the meaning and uses of hearsay. What is hearsay or hearsay evidence? Hearsay evidence is secondhand evidence, either oral or written, because it does not come directly from those who made the original statement, but from those on the witness stand who claim that they heard another person say it (*Stockton v. Williams*, 1 Doug., Mich. 546, 570 [1845]). Under the New Jersey Rules of Evidence, Rule 63(1)–63(33), which is very similar to Rule 801(c) of the Federal Rules of Evidence, hearsay evidence is defined as "evidence of a statement offered to prove the truth of the matter stated, which is made other than by a witness while testifying at the hearing."

Hearsay evidence carries weaker probative force (i.e., weight in tending to prove something as true) than nonhearsay because it stands either wholly or partly on the credibility and competency of people other than the witnesses (*State v. Klutz*, 206 N.C. 726, 804 [1927]). Such evidence is not subject to cross-examination, because the people who originally made the statements are not present at the hearing. An example of evidence considered hearsay is helpful in clarifying the suspicious nature of such evidence. Imagine that there are three people involved, Green, Black, and White. Green, who is on the witness stand, tells the tribunal that he was told by Black that she saw White, who is on trial for murdering her boyfriend, kill her boyfriend while engaged in a violent argument. Green's statement must be considered hearsay because it is indirect evidence coming from Black who is not present to offer direct testimony. In such a criminal case, the hearsay rule would be applied, thus excluding Green's statement. However, under special circumstances such inferior hearsay evidence has been allowed. In our case, for example, let us say that the court could not subpoena Black to testify because she had died prior to the trial; yet her dying words to Green were that she saw White kill White's boyfriend. Dying declarations have been allowed as a hearsay exception by some courts in the past. Beyond the dying declaration exception, 39 other hearsay exceptions have been noted for criminal law alone (e.g., recorded recollections; expert witness testimony; entry in public record; assertion of pedigree).[44] Nonetheless, because of its obvious inferiority, hearsay evidence is seldom admitted into evidence in criminal trials (*State v. Ah Lee*, 23 P.2 424 [Or. 1890]); *State v. Shaw*, 847 S.W.2d. 768 [Mo. banc 1993]).

Despite the fact that hearsay evidence is rarely allowed to enter the record in court trials, such evidence is accepted in agency hearings. For those of us who want hearing decisions to be based on sound and conclusive evidence, permitting hearsay evidence to be included in the official record, which is used ultimately to substantiate the hearing decision, may seem like kangaroo court nonsense. Hearsay evidence can be reliable and steer tribunals to accurate and just decisions, especially if a preponderance of hearsay all seems to support the same conclusion, *Woolsey v. Nat'l Transportation Safety Bd.*, 993 F.2d 516, 521 (1993). However, hearsay evidence can also be completely inaccurate. The worst thing about hearsay, as implied earlier, is that it is evidence that cannot be tested for its reliability through cross-examination (*Wulfkuhle v. State Dep't of Revenue*, 234 Kan. 241 [1983]; and *Pacific Gas & Electric Co. v. FERC*, 746 F.2d 1383 [9th Cir. 1984]). Since cross-examination appears to most legal scholars to be the single best instrument for bringing the truth to light in disputes, hearsay evidence must be considered far inferior to presented facts that have survived the grueling test of cross-examination unshaken.

Nevertheless, despite the weak probative content of hearsay evidence, the Administrative Procedure Act and the courts have allowed hearsay to be presented and used as evidence in administrative hearings. In *Tyra v. Secretary of Health and Human Services*, 896 F.2d 1024, 1030 (6th Cir. 1990), the court said "relevant evidence not admissible in court, including hearsay, is admissible at an administrative hearing." Section 356 of the APA fails to exclude the use of hearsay evidence by stating that "any oral or documentary evidence may be received." However, although Section 556(d) allows hearsay evidence to be accepted at the discretion of the hearing examiners, it does obligate the agency to exclude as a "matter of policy" all "irrelevant, immaterial, or unduly repetitious evidence," thus discouraging the use of hearsay. Another provision in the same section also discourages hearing examiners from relying too much on hearsay evidence in reaching decisions: "A sanction may not be imposed or rule or order issued except on consideration of the whole record or those parts thereof cited by a party and supported by and in accordance with reliable, probative, and substantial evidence." Since hearsay evidence is rarely considered reliable or probative in content, this section in a sense contradicts its other provision that "Any oral or documentary evidence may be received." Is this section suggesting that hearsay evidence can be received but not used to support hearing decisions?

The controversy surrounding hearsay evidence focuses on two basic questions. Should hearsay be admissible? If it is admissible, what weight should the hearsay evidence be given by agency adjudicators? In criminal law the focus is more on the first question, while in administrative law the focus is more on the second question. That is, because administrative hearings are less formal than court trials, many critics believe that attention should not focus so much on whether the hearsay should be admitted into the hearing record, but on how much weight the hearsay evidence should be given by hearing examiners or ALJs when using it to reach decisions. Courts tend to agree. In *Requero v. Tacher Standards and Practices*, 7889 P.2d 11, 14 (Or. App. [1990]), the court noted that "the hearsay nature of evidence . . . may affect the weight that a fact finder chooses to give it, but does not in itself make it inadmissible. Similarly, the nonexistence of corroborating or independent evidence that tends to prove the same fact as the hearsay evidence is not a prerequisite to admissibility of the hearsay, but bears instead on the weight or sufficiency of the evidence offered."

Common sense must be emphasized to answer both questions. Since hearsay is automatically somewhat suspect or questionably reliable, common sense should dictate whether it should be admitted into the record or not. Without question, the quality of hearsay differs substantially. Some hearsay may amount to wild and false rumor spread by an unreliable person, while other hearsay may be "the kind of evidence on which responsible persons are accustomed to rely in serious affairs" (*NLRB v. Remington Rand, Inc.*, 94 F.2d 862, 873 [2nd Cir. 1938]). Courts have normally upheld the admissibility of hearsay "in administrative proceedings, so long as the admission of evidence meets the tests of fundamental fairness and probity" (*Bustos-Torres v. INS*, 898 F.2d 1053 [5th Cir. 1990]).

In sum, it makes practical sense to use hearsay evidence in agency hearings even though the use of such evidence presents certain problems. However, the problems with hearsay evidence can be drastically minimized if agency adjudicators act professionally and in good faith to see to it that all evidence, including hearsay, is introduced and weighed in a responsible manner so that due process is honored. Or as the court stated recently in *Ramirez-Alejandre v. Ashcroft*, 319 F.3d 365 (2003), "The rules of evidence are not applicable to immigration hearings. Thus, for example, hearsay testimony may be considered. However, the proceeding must be conducted 'in accord with due process standards of fundamental fairness.'"

Making Sense of Hearsay in Light of the Residuum Rule, the Perales Rule, and the Substantial Evidence Test

The residuum rule requires that a finding cannot stand unless it is supported by evidence that would be acceptable in a jury trial. When the residuum rule is applied to hearing decisions, it means that hearsay evidence can be used in helping to reach a decision, but the decision itself must not be supported by hearsay evidence alone but by substantial, nonhearsay evidence. Thomas R. Mulroy, Jr., and Douglas G. McClure provide a frank descriptive definition of the residuum rule: "In other words, hearing officers cannot base their findings on hearsay unless they could have legitimately reached the same result without the hearsay evidence."[45] In *Carroll v. Knickerbocker Ice Co.*, 113 N.E. 507, 509 (1916), the district court, in rejecting a death benefit claim, noted: "Still in the end, there must be a residuum of evidence of legal (i.e., nonhearsay) evidence to support the claim before an award can be made." In *Requero v. Teacher Standards and Practices*, 789 P.2d 11, 14 (Or. App. 1990) the court, quoting Kenneth C. Davis, made clear that

> the residuum rule requires a reviewing court to set aside an administrative finding unless the finding is supported by evidence which would be admissible in a jury trial . . . no matter how reliable the evidence may appear to the agency and to the reviewing court, no matter what the circumstantial setting may be, no matter what may be the evidence or lack of evidence on the other side, and no matter what may be the consequences of refusing to rely upon evidence.

The residuum rule has frustrated and angered many agency adjudicators from the very beginning because it prevents them from reaching decisions based solely upon hearsay evidence, which can be difficult for hearing officials with hefty caseloads who want to reach quick decisions on the basis of what they believe are reliable documents pertaining to the cases in their files (such documents technically constitute only hearsay evidence).[46]

Beyond the practical reasons for rejecting the residuum rule, opponents offer other criticisms. Most of their criticism focuses on the perceived illogical nature of the residuum rule. Critics argue that the residuum rule illogically classifies all hearsay evidence as incompetent regardless of the equality of the hearsay. In legal terms, the residuum rule makes even the highest quality hearsay technically incompetent, and this contradicts reliability standards associated with the admission of evidence. That is, it is argued that properly admitted hearsay (hearsay allowed because any reasonable person would accept it as reliable) must still be considered incompetent or nonsubstantial evidence incapable of supporting a hearing finding. Kenneth C. Davis claims that the most illogical problem with the residuum rule "is the lack of correlation between reliability of evidence and the exclusionary rules of evidence. The exclusionary rules were designed for guiding admission or exclusion of evidence, not for weighing its reliability, and were designed for juries, not for administrators."[47]

However, the attacks on the worth of the residuum rule come mostly from those who believe that its application simply causes unnecessary and costly administrative inconveniences and delays. The residuum rule is not just another stupid rule that makes no sense. In the spirit of justice, it makes a lot of sense. It simply requires that at least some evidence used to reach a hearing decision should be based on more than just hearsay, on at least a residuum of substantial evidence (i.e., nonhearsay evidence). Is that too much to ask to help guarantee fair hearing decisions?

But it appears that residuum rule opponents are not really saying that the rule will not serve administrative justice in agency hearings better. They contend, at least implicitly, that our administrative system cannot afford the luxury of using the residuum rule because its use will increase administrative costs even more in an age when supporting even vital governmental services has become increasingly difficult.

The 1971 Supreme Court decision that stands apparently as the most outspoken word against the value of the residuum rule, *Richardson v. Perales*, 402 U.S. 389, encapsulates the prevalent sentiment of critics that the residuum rule is too impracticable to apply during a time when the administrative burden is so heavy. The *Perales* Court reasoned in rejecting strict reliance upon the residuum rule that

> There is an additional and pragmatic factor which, although not controlling, deserves mention. This is what Chief Judge Brown has described as "the sheer magnitude of the administrative burden," and the resulting necessity for written reports without "elaboration through the traditional facility or oral testimony." With over 20,000 disability claim hearings annually, the cost of providing live medical testimony at those hearings . . . would be a substantial drain. (p. 406)

Ever since the *Perales* decision was handed down in 1971 there has been a fading debate over whether the residuum rule is still applicable law. The controversy still survives today because most legal scholars and court justices insist that the residuum rule is dead, or should be, while a residuum of scholars and justices argue that it is still governing law. Acknowledging the vast criticisms of the residuum rule about a dozen years ago, Bernard Schwartz quipped: "The criticisms referred to ignore the tendency of agencies to exercise little or no control over the admission of evidence. . . . Fear that the residuum rule may be invoked leads agencies to insist on more careful presentation and examination of evidence."[48]

However, ever since Schwartz made these remarks in 1991, a Lexis-Nexis legal search indicates that the residuum rule has lost out to reasons of practicality even at the state level. It appears that a growing number of state courts uphold agency decisions that are rooted entirely in hearsay, ignoring the residuum rule. A Massachusetts court in 2002 seemed to capture the mood of federal courts and most states on the once fashionable residuum rule. In upholding an agency decision based entirely on hearsay, the court reasoned: "The evidence supporting the department's decision in this case was exclusively hearsay. That by itself does not render it not 'substantial'. The so-called 'legal residuum' rule . . . has effectively been rejected. . . . As we stated in *Edward E. v. Department of Social Services* . . . 'the question before us is not whether the administrative decision was based upon uncorroborated hearsay but whether the hearsay presented at the hearing was reliable.' To that we add that reliability must be judged in relation to the significance of the decision being made" (*Covell v. Department of Social Services*, 768 N.E.2d 564, 571 [2002]).

Confusion about applicability of the residuum rule has prevailed since the *Perales* decision over three decades ago because the *Perales* holding conveyed mixed messages about the legal status of the residuum rule. Many legal scholars felt that the *Perales* Court rejected the residuum rule because it upheld a Social Security hearing examiner's decision that was totally rooted in hearsay evidence, not "substantial evidence." The key to understanding the court's decision, however, is in understanding how the Court justified its decision. It then becomes clear that the Court did not flatly reject the residuum rule but only added some flexibility in its use.

In many respects the circumstances in the *Perales* case are unique, and these help explain why the *Perales* Court reached the decision it did. Pedro Perales, a 34-year-old truck driver, claimed that he had become permanently disabled by lifting an object while working. He applied for disability benefits under the Social Security Act. On the whole, his medical records indicated that he was not disabled and could resume work in a matter of months, although one doctor concluded otherwise. In fact, one doctor, Dr. Langston, who had great credibility before the hearing examiner and eventually the *Perales* court, concluded that Perales was clearly not disabled and was faking in order to collect undue disability payments. In fact, Dr. Langston recommended that he should see a psychiatrist. Later, Dr. Bailey, a psychiatrist, and Dr. Mattson and Dr. Leavitt all agreed with Dr. Langston's diagnosis. Beyond this, several other doctors' reports supported Dr. Langston's diagnosis. Only Dr. Morales, a former fellow employee of Perales, perceived as biased by the hearing examiner and eventually the *Perales* court, reached an opposite conclusion.

Given these facts, it is clear from a careful reading of the *Perales* decision that the Court's majority was predisposed to rule against Perales. But the Court also felt that Perales was really treated very fairly by the hearing examiner. What became important to the Court was the fact that Perales, represented by counsel, was given an opportunity to subpoena the doctors so that they could be cross-examined, but that Perales declined the opportunity to do so. The court noted: "Notice was given to claimant Perales. The physicians' reports were on file and available for inspection by the claimant and his counsel. And the authors of these reports were known and were subject to subpoena and to the very cross-examination that the claimant asserts he has not enjoyed" (p. 407).

Given these hearing conditions, then, the *Perales* Court had to decide when and how the residuum rule should be applied and what should really constitute substantial evidence. The Court made a practical decision. It reasoned that it makes sense to suspend the strict application of the residuum rule when the opportunity is given to subpoena documents and witnesses so that the hearsay evidence can be cross-examined. If Perales took advantage of this opportunity, the hearsay evidence would have been transformed into substantial evidence. In effect, the spirit of the residuum rule was not really undermined by the *Perales* Court, because Perales was given the opportunity to subpoena and cross-examine the "hearsay evidence." To the *Perales* Court this failure to take advantage of this opportunity made the hearsay evidence tantamount to substantial evidence.

It is also important to acknowledge that in *Perales* the Court noted that "courts have recognized the reliability and probative worth of written medical reports even in formal trials and, while acknowledging their hearsay character, have admitted them as an exception to the hearsay rule" (p. 405). Is the Court not saying, then, that such medical records really constitute substantial evidence, consistent with the residuum rule, since such evidence, because of its reliability and probative value, is accepted in court trials under a hearsay exception? If so, this is just one more reason to doubt whether the *Perales* Court ever meant to reject the residuum rule.

In sum, the Supreme Court in *Perales* probably did not intend to completely abolish the residuum rule, but it evidently did intend to develop a new flexible standard for applying it. This new standard has become known as the "*Perales* rule." Under the new *Perales* rule, at least the spirit of the residuum rule lives on, which means that hearing officials can use hearsay evidence to substantiate their rulings, but the decision must still be supported by some substantial evidence. This sounds identical to the residuum rule requirements, but the different twist is that the substantial evidence test under the new *Perales* standard can be more easily satisfied. Reviewing courts must now look at the unique circumstances that surround the use of the hearsay evidence in specific cases and fairly judge whether agency adjudicators reached a fair decision based upon reliable evidence reasonable people would conclude constitutes genuine substantial evidence.

The Exclusionary Rule's
Applicability in Administrative Hearings

From approximately the beginning of President Ronald Reagan's administration until the present the exclusionary rule, as applied to criminal law, has come under constant and vehement attack, especially by conservatives. Critics believe that the rule has been used too often to prevent otherwise good evidence from being admitted just because the evidence was seized illegally by police, thus allowing many criminals to get off on mere "procedural technicalities." Simply stated, the exclusionary rule has been used in criminal trials to exclude illegally seized evidence, which has given rise to the "fruit of the poisonous tree" doctrine. In criminal law the doctrine, although it may apply in administrative law, has had the practical effort of making all evidence (and all secondary obtained evidence stemming from it) inadmissible "because procedural steps in obtaining the evidence violated constitutional due process" (*Wong Sun v. United States*, 371 U.S. 471 [1983]). Opposition to the exclusionary rule has evidently influenced the courts because recent decisions have tended to weaken the clout of the exclusionary rule. Recently, in a *Harvard Law Review* article, Charles Fried argued that the courts have been abandoning the exclusionary rule at an increasing rate in search and seizures cases, resulting in "the Court's gradual but determined strangulation of the rule,"[49] while Lars Noah noted in the *Iowa Law Review* that "Judicial nullification may occur . . . when trial judges routinely refuse to apply the exclusionary rule."[50]

The status of the exclusionary rule in administrative hearings is not clear.[51] Some courts have upheld the relevance of the exclusionary rule in agency adjudications, while other courts have not, although in recent years few courts have done so. For example, in a New York case in 1979 the court argued that the exclusionary rule should apply to administrative hearings as well as to criminal trials (*Peccadillo v. Board of Parole*, 48 N.Y. 2d 76, 81). Some federal courts have agreed (e.g., *Knoll Assoc. v. FTC*, 397 F.2d 530 [7th Cir. 1968] and *Navia-Duran v. INS*, 568 F.2d 803 [1st Cir. 1977]). Supporters of the exclusionary rule often maintain that the Fourth Amendment's privacy protections, as well as the Fifth Amendment's protection against self-incrimination, would be upheld whether the government is prosecuting a person for burglary or deciding whether to revoke someone's medical license.

Nevertheless, as in criminal cases, the courts have been increasingly very reluctant to compel agency adjudicators to honor the exclusionary rule. Of course, agency hearings are normally much less formal than court trials, thus making the admission of evidence more flexible. In fact, the federal APA, Section 556(d) says, "Any oral or documentary evidence may be received," and it is well established in administrative law that virtually all admitted evidence, no matter how irrelevant or incompetent, cannot cause "reversible error" or fatally flaw the decision as long as the decision is otherwise supported by substantial evidence.

In sum, in criminal law the exclusionary rule's force has been weakened over the past few decades by the dominance of conservative politics and courts, while in administrative law the exclusionary rule carries very little weight, nor should it, according to Richard Pierce, because agency adjudications need to weigh evidence in a flexible and efficient manner.[52] The U.S. Supreme Court evidently agrees with Pierce. In *Pennsylvania Board of Probation and Parole v. Scott*, 118 S.Ct. 2014 (1998), the court clarified quite comprehensively its position on the application of the exclusionary rule in administrative proceedings, not pleasing those who believe that the exclusionary rule should play some role in agency adjudications. The court argued that various "benefits of the exclusionary rule would not outweigh the costs." The court was particularly concerned with how the force use of the exclusionary rule on administrative agencies would disrupt administrative procedures: "The exclusionary rule, moreover, is incompatible with the traditionally flexible, administrative procedures. . . . Application of the exclusionary rule frequently requires extensive litigation to determine whether particular evidence must be excluded." Consequently, the court concluded that use of "the exclusionary rule would add an additional layer of collateral litigation. . . . The marginal deterrence of unreasonable searches and seizures is insufficient to justify such an intrusion. . . . Because the exclusionary rule precludes consideration of reliable, probative evidence, it imposes significant costs: it undeniably detracts from the truthfinding process" (pp. 2019–2022).

Exclusion of Privileged Evidence

Section 556(d) of the APA does not mean, however, that agency adjudicators can normally go so far as to require that privileged evidence be admitted. As the Revised Model State Administrative Procedure Act, Section 10 states: "Agencies shall give effect to the rules of privilege recognized by law." Privileged evidence is protected either by the Constitution or by statute or, sometimes, by common law. Privileged evidence, for example, consists of attorney-client, husband-wife privilege and other recognized constitutional and statutory testimonial privileges, as well as specifically the privilege against self-incrimination and the use of illegally obtained evidence. As expected, then, in *Southern Cal. Gas Co. v. Public Utils. Comm'n*, 784 P.2d 1373 (1990), the California court upheld the attorney-client privilege in a public utility commission hearing.

It may seem contradictory and confusing to note that illegally seized evidence is considered privileged evidence, yet at the same time point out that the trend, as noted, has been against compelling public agencies to honor the exclusionary rule, thus making them exclude from hearing proceedings illegally obtained evidence that should be considered privileged. The truth is that the situation is contradictory and confusing, but this is not unique to law, especially administrative law. Due to conservative political pressures and other factors, the vast majority of decisions since the early 1980s, although the trend against the exclusionary rule started earlier, have rejected the application of the exclusionary rule under most circumstances. In 1984 the U.S. Supreme Court in *INS v. Lopez-Mendoza*, 468 U.S. 1032, held that the exclusionary rule did not apply to civil deportation hearings, even though, it should be added, losing parties normally suffer a grievous loss. In *Lopez-Mendoza*, employing the most popular reason for throwing out the exclusionary rule, the Court opined that enforcing the use of the exclusionary rule would only minimally deter officials from conducting illegal searches. In *Finkelstein v. State Personnel Board*, 267 Col. Rptr. 133 (Cal. App. 3 Dist. 1990), a California Court assumed for the sake of argument that the briefcase search in question was illegal under both federal and California constitutions, yet nevertheless rejected the application of the exclusionary rule, allowing the illegally seized evidence to be used to terminate a government employee's employment. Comparing *Finkelstein* to a prior ruling by the same court in which the court upheld the exclusionary rule, the court concluded that "in this case there was no search for evidence of crime and no motive to use such evidence for disciplinary purposes. Because of this factual difference, the deterrent effect of the exclusionary rule . . . is lacking here" (p. 138).

What is clear from *Finkelstein* and other cases is that courts are very unlikely to apply the exclusionary rule if they feel that the officials who illegally seized evidence did not know how it would be used later. The logic employed by the courts is that excluding illegally obtained evidence from, for example, an employee termination hearing is not going to deter police officers from conducting illegal searchers when they had no idea that such evidence may be used later in a non-criminal termination proceeding. Do you accept this rationale? This rationale appears more like an excuse to toss out the exclusionary rule than a sensible reason to reject its use. It seems that the best way to discourage any governmental official from conducting illegal searches is to make certain that any illegally seized evidence is excluded from criminal trials or administrative hearings. This makes even more sense when one considers the other chief reason for using the exclusionary rule: The government should not benefit in a criminal trial or an agency adjudication from its own unlawful acts that produced the illegal evidence.

Right to Counsel in Agency Hearings

Courts have insisted that a fair hearing should offer several procedural due process protections, but does the call for fairness require agencies to permit persons in hearings to be represented by counsel, even appointed counsel (paid for by the government)? In 1963 in the now famous *Gideon v. Wainwright* case, 372 U.S. 335, the Supreme Court ruled that in criminal cases defendants have the right to appointed counsel if they cannot afford to pay a lawyer. Later, in 1972, the Court held that the *Gideon* decision applies even to misdemeanor trials from which a possible jail sentence could result (*Argersinger v. Hamlin*, 407 U.S. 25).

The right-to-counsel issue has been settled comfortably in criminal cases, but in agency hearings, it leaves many questions unanswered. During the 1970s a significant number of courts and legal scholars argued that unless legal counsel is actually provided to indigents across the board, blatant inequities in applying administrative justice in agency hearings will inevitably occur. It would on one hand be simpler and fairer in a sense to apply the *Gideon* rule to all administrative hearings than to try to choose the hearings to which it would apply. On the other hand, given the millions of minor hearing cases heard each year by administrators, it became just as clear that it would be very impractical to apply the *Gideon* solution to agency adjudications. The cost to taxpayers would be prohibitive, not only because of the added costs for lawyers but also because these lawyers would unquestionably provide legal defenses that would delay case settlements and place extra financial and staff burdens on agency efforts to prepare, present, and defend their positions.

In *Goldberg v. Kelly*, 397 U.S. 254 (1970), the most influential right-to-counsel case during the 1970s, the Supreme Court stressed the crucial significance to the right to counsel by reiterating an earlier position that "the right to be heard would be, in many cases, of little avail if it did not comprehend the right to be heard by counsel."[53] However, although some applauded the decision as a giant step forward in extending the right to counsel to indigent parties in agency hearings, in fact, the *Goldberg* holding only confirmed a right that the federal Administrative Procedure Act has already granted to federal employees unless specific provisions in federal statutes placed restrictions on the right. Section 555(b) of the APA read: "A person compelled to appear in person before an agency or representative thereof is entitled to be accompanied, represented, and advised by counsel or, if permitted by the agency, by other qualified representatives." But it was also made clear in *Goldberg* that the welfare claimant did not have the right to government-appointed *free* counsel. Many legal scholars and social scientists became irritated by the obvious catch-22 situation posed by the *Goldberg* decision. That is, what good is it to be allowed to obtain counsel if you can't afford to pay for such representation?

Three years after *Goldberg*, in *Gagnon v. Scarpelli*, 411 U.S. 778 (1973), in which the right-to-counsel question was discussed in the context of a revocation of parole hearing, the Court methodically reviewed what should be considered the minimum due process rights in administrative law hearings. Drawing from the precedential case, *Morrissey v. Brewer*, 408 U.S. 471 (1972), the Court acknowledged that even the right to counsel, let alone paid counsel, had not been established in a *de facto* sense as a minimum right. Nonetheless, the Court suggested that the right to government-provided counsel may be advisable under very rare circumstances and when deemed appropriate by the hearing officials.[54] The court did provide guidelines to help hearing officers decide when counsel should be provided, considering, for example, "whether the probationer appears capable of speaking effectively for himself."[55] With great reservation, the Supreme Court in *Gagnon* opened the door just slightly to allow for appointed counsel in cases in which very serious consequences (for example, return to prison, loss of life-sustaining welfare benefits, deportation) would occur to financially and/or educationally deficient persons if adverse rulings were reached.

At the same time, however, the Supreme Court presented in *Gagnon* a strong case for why counsel should not be provided in virtually all administrative hearings, contending that to do so would place a tremendous and unjustifiable burden on administrative tribunals: "Certainly, the decision making process will be prolonged, and the financial cost to the State—for appointed counsel, counsel for the State, a longer record, and the possibility of judicial review—will not be insubstantial" (p. 788). In placing the right to counsel in the context of balancing due process entitlements with agency responsibilities, the Court reasoned that "due process is not so rigid as to require that the significant interests in informality, flexibility, and economy must always be sacrificed" (p. 788).

Despite efforts by the Court to review systematically questions pertaining to the right to counsel, particularly the right to state-supported counsel, the *Gagnon* case left many questions unanswered by creating a vague circumstances test to be applied at the discretion of the hearing officials. Since it is understandable that such hearing officials probably identify somewhat with agency interest, how fair does it seem for the Court to leave the decision on whether persons in hearings should be provided with paid counsel to the very people who will be hearing the case? Would it not take exceptionally fair-minded hearing examiners to grant the request for appointed counsel to parties, knowing the extra time, expense, and headaches it will undoubtedly bring?

A related point is also noteworthy. The APA generally requires agency adjudicators to respect a person's right to obtain legal counsel. However, a loophole in section 555(b) does not obligate agencies to advertise that this right exists. As a consequence, some agencies have, as a matter of official policy, actively discouraged parties from being represented by counsel. At least one state court has spoken out against the administrative practice of not notifying parties that they have not only the right to counsel but also the possible availability of free or low-cost counsel (provided by various publicly and privately supported legal service units). For example, the Tennessee Supreme Court in *Simmons v. Troughber*, 791 S.W. 2d 21, 24 (Tenn. 1990), ruled that the Tennessee Department of Employment Security's failure to inform an employee of the possible availability of free or low-cost legal representation violated her statutory right to a fair hearing.

Beyond agencies simply keeping silent about the right to counsel, the most popular step to discourage representation by counsel is to place a fee limit on what attorneys can charge. For example, the Social Security Administration long ago adopted a rule that placed an absurdly low $10.00 fee limit on how much an attorney could earn while representing Social Security claimants in disability claims. In 1954 Congress set a $10.00 fee limit on the amount an attorney could receive for representing a veteran in a death or disability claim.[56]

Sympathetic to veterans' inability to secure counsel under this fee limitation rule, a district court in 1984 held this fee to violate due process protections (*National Ass'n. of Radiation Survivors v. Walters*, 589 F.Supp. 1302 [N.D. Cal.]). However, the Supreme Court reversed the decision, arguing that due process or "fundamental fairness" had not been violated by the $10 fee limitation (*Walters v. National Ass'n of Radiation Survivors*, 106 S.Ct. 3180 [1985]). Speaking for the high court, Justice Rehnquist asserted that the costs and benefits of extending certain "extra" procedural safeguards must be given serious consideration. Employing the balance test developed in *Mathews v. Eldridge*, 424 U.S. 319 (1976), which basically calls for weighing the costs and benefits of applying the present governmental procedures to the government against the costs and benefits of applying the existing or alternative procedures to the government against the costs and benefits of the existing or alternative procedures to the private party, Rehnquist wrote: "We have emphasized that the marginal gains from affording an additional procedural safeguard often may be outweighed by the societal cost of providing such a safeguard" (p. 3189).

The Supreme Court upheld the *Walters* decision in 1990 in *U.S. Dept. of Labor v. Triplett*, 110 S.Ct. 1428, by holding that even though fee limitations may make attorneys unavailable to claimants, this in itself does not deny claimants due process since they still have the right to counsel. Thus, in reviewing the state court's ruling, the Supreme Court concluded that "the evidence . . . did not remotely establish *either* that black lung claimants are unable to retain qualified counsel or that the cause of such inability is the attorney's fee system administered by the Department. The Court therefore had no basis for concluding that the system deprives claimants of property without due process of law" (p. 1435).

Agencies have also tried to prevent parties from employing counsel by arguing that the use of counsel impairs agency business, especially its investigations. However, this argument has been rejected by many courts since Section 555(b), even acknowledging the section's loopholes, allows agencies to forbid the employment of counsel only under exceptional circumstances. For example, in *Professional Reactor Operator Soc. v. U.S. NRC*, 939 F.2d 1047, 1051–1052 (D.C. Cir. 1991) the court held that the NRC's exclusion of subpoenaed witnesses' counsel during NRC's investigations violates the APA's more weighty right-to-counsel provision.

The right-to-counsel controversy in administrative law cases has been brewing for many years. Scholars seem to be divided on whether this "extra" procedural safeguard would prove too burdensome to the hearing process in our public agencies. Knowing the adversary character of lawyers, no doubt the pressure of legal counsel at administrative hearings would certainly slow things down—in the name of proper legal representation, of course! Several years ago, after examining the right-to-counsel debate, Judge Henry J. Friendly presented a fascinating and provocative idea to resolve the problem many years ago that is still worth attention. Judge Friendly agrees that administrative hearings, handling routine questions pertaining to welfare benefits, school suspensions, and so on, should not be turned into elaborate criminal adversary proceedings. In a now-famous administrative law article entitled, "Some Kind of Hearing," he argues that the adversary hearing approach should be abandoned in many administrative law areas that he categorizes as "mass justice" areas.

These problems concerning counsel and confrontation inevitably bring up the question whether we would not do better to abandon the adversary system in certain areas of mass justice, notably in the many ramifications of the welfare system, in favor of one in which an examiner—or administrative law judge if you will—with no connection with the agency would have the responsibility for developing all the pertinent facts and making a just decision.[57]

In so arguing, Judge Friendly attacks the basic need for counsel on the grounds that the provision of counsel in many administrative law areas cannot be justified in a cost-benefit sense: "The appearance of counsel for the citizen is likely to lead the government to provide one—or at least to cause the government's representative to act like one. The result may be to turn what might have been a short conference leading to an amicable result into a protracted controversy."[58]

Judge Friendly largely rests his call for experimentation in administrative mass justice (that is, doing away with the adversary process in many administrative law areas) on the legal argument that there exists "no constitutional mandate requiring use of the adversary process in administrative hearings unless the Court chooses to construct one out of the vague contours of the due process clause."[59] His nonadversary, investigative model would have the advantage of settling disputes informally and quickly in a conference-like environment. Although Judge Friendly acknowledges that the experiment would represent "a sharp break with our tradition of adversary process," he claims that "that tradition . . . was not formulated for a situation in which many thousands of hearings must be provided each month."[60] Actually, as mentioned, by 2004 the SSA alone hears well over one million disability claims per year.

The whole question of whether claimants actually benefit from having counsel at administrative hearings, the resolution of which would be quite helpful in aiding our decision on whether the Friendly experiment should be tried, was addressed in "Effect of Representation on a Claimant's Success Rate: Three Study Designs," published in 1979.[61] Study results tend to cast great doubt on whether claimants in administrative hearings win more favorable decisions at a greater rate because they are represented by counsel. For example, one empirical study cited revealed that welfare claimants in Wisconsin won at "'about the same' rate without counsel as claimants represented by counsel,"[62] while a 1992 study found that claimants before the SSA won at a 73% rate when represented by counsel, but almost at the same rate, 71%, when not represented by counsel.

In sum, the status of the right to counsel in agency hearings is somewhat clearer in the early twenty-first century than it was in the 1970s. Federal and state courts have made it fairly clear in the past three decades that parties generally have a right to legal counsel, but not guaranteed government-supported counsel. However, the possibility of free or low-cost legal representation is available on a limited basis to indigents through various legal services operations. Courts have normally insisted that proper notice includes informing parties that they have the right to be represented by legal counsel at agency hearings, but courts have been reluctant to push the advertising of legal representation too far, especially requiring agencies to inform parties about the possible availability of free or low-cost counsel. In a few instances the courts have ruled that certain circumstances, usually practical situations upholding a state interest (e.g., an excessive administrative burden), necessitate public agencies to not permit parties to be represented by counsel, particularly if the disputed issue is considered minor. For example, recently the Ninth Circuit court in *U.S. v. Rangel De Aguilar*, 308 F.3d 1134 (9th Cir. 2002), held that Ms. Rangel De Aguilar did not have a right to counsel in a deportation hearing, because, quoting *Michelson v. INS*, 897 F.2d 465, 467–468 (10th Cir. 1990), "a deportation hearing is intended to provide a streamlined determination of eligibility to remain in this country, nothing more. . . . Accordingly, we held in *Michelson v. INS* . . . that the Sixth Amendment right to counsel is inapplicable in the deportation case." However, compare this decision to the Sixth Circuit court's opinion in *Detroit Free Press v. Ashcroft*, 303 F.3d 681 (6th Cir. 2002), in which the court took the opposite view, insisting that the right to counsel in a deportation case, although not at the government's expense, is a very crucial due process right given the "enormity of the interests at stake" so the court "will not lightly find a waiver of that right" (p. 699).

DECISIONMAKING
IN AGENCY ADJUDICATIONS

It has been made quite apparent by now that agency hearings are normally much more informal than court trials at every stage in the proceedings. Not only is evidence accepted and used in a more informal manner in agency adjudications than in court trials, but the process employed in reaching decisions is also considerably more informal in agency hearings. In fact, hearing proceedings are often so informal that evidence may be presented to and evaluated by the hearing officials and a decision reached in a matter of 10 to 20 minutes. However, as noted, some hearings have been very formal and elaborate and have continued for several years. Although court trials can also be short, it is unusual, except in matters involving small claims, for decisions to be reached so quickly because of the more formal requirements associated with handling evidence and reaching decisions in light of the evidence. In this last section principles, doctrines, and rules associated with hearing decisionmaking are reviewed. And, it must be stressed, as it was in *Vollstedt v. City of Stockton*, 269 Ca. Rptr. 404, 408 (Ca. App. 3 Dist. 1990), that "the question of whether the trial was 'fair' encompasses post-hearing actions of the agency as well" (i.e., the post-hearing decisionmaking process).

Applying Standards of Proof in Decisionmaking

There is a qualitative difference between decisionmaking in court trials and agency adjudications. As contrasted with agency hearings, judges or jurors in court trials should root their decisions in more weighty evidence than ALJs in agency hearings. Simply stated, the standard of proof should be higher for court decisions than agency hearing decisions. In criminal cases decisions must be based upon the highest possible standard or the *beyond any reasonable doubt* standard. In an ideal situation, judges or juries cannot convict a person of a crime if a reasonable doubt exists as to whether the person is guilty of the crime. This high standard has posed some problems because some guilty parties have either not been prosecuted or the prosecutors have failed to win their case under this lofty standard, thus allowing guilty parties to go free. Many legal scholars contend, however, that this is a small price to pay for a justice system that honors freedom and individual rights.

There are those who hold that while the criminal justice system is "too fair," permitting many "guilty" parties to escape prosecution or conviction because of "due process technicalities," the administrative justice system is "too unfair," denying parties procedural due process rights while agency administrators rush to dispose of huge case loads as quickly as possible. Critics point out that the failure to honor reasonable due process protections in agency hearings can sometimes cause parties, guilty of no crime, to suffer more harm (e.g., loss of a professional license or business, revocation of parole, deportation) than they would have if convicted of certain criminal acts. This reality motivated Justice Brandeis to conclude many decades ago that deportation decisions, for example, may prove more harmful to persons in deportation hearings than verdicts in criminal trials because adverse deportation rulings may "result . . . in loss of both property and life; or all that makes life worth living" (*Ng Fung Ho v. White*, 259 U.S. 276, 284 [1922]).

Most agency hearing officials have the unenviable task of having to resolve an enormous volume of cases, thus justifying to a certain extent why agencies must restrict procedural due process protections. It is understandable, then, that the standard of proof for reaching hearing decisions falls short of the higher standard of proof required in criminal trials. When reaching decisions in agency hearings, the burden of persuasion is satisfied if the *preponderance of the evidence* supports the decision.

In *Steadman v. SEC*, 450 U.S. 91 (1981), the leading case in this area, the Supreme Court clearly established the application of the preponderance-of-the-evidence standard for administrative hearings governed by the APA. A brief review of this case helps to clarify how the preponderance-of-the-evidence standard became law, especially since the APA does not use the specific rhetoric "preponderance of the evidence." In 1971 the Securities and Exchange Commission (SEC) began disciplinary action against Steadman, charging that he had violated many federal securities laws. After a lengthy on-the-record (evidentiary) hearing before an ALJ and after review by the SEC, which employed a preponderance of evidence test to assess the weight of the evidence, the Commission concluded that Steadman was guilty of violating several anti-fraud, conflict-of-interest, proxy, and reporting provisions of federal security statutes. As a result, it ordered that Steadman be banned permanently from affiliating with any investment companies or associating with any investment companies or associating with any investment advisors, thus prohibiting him from practicing his profession. Steadman sought judicial review, arguing that because of the potentially severe penalties, the SEC should not have used the preponderance-of-the-evidence standard, but should have employed the stricter *clear-and-convincing-evidence* standard to weigh the evidence to substantiate the very serious intent to defraud charges.

However, both the appeals court and the Supreme Court disagreed. The high court reasoned that the substantial evidence requirement in the APA requires that a decision must be supported by a certain "quantity of evidence." The Court was not persuaded by Steadman's argument that the substantial evidence requirement pertains to the "quality" of evidence only. The Court argued that legislative intent was clear from the "House Report, which expressly adopted a preponderance of the evidence standard: Nor is there any suggestion in the legislative history that a standard of proof higher than a preponderance of the evidence was ever contemplated, much less intended" (pp. 101–102). The Court went on to say that "Congress was primarily concerned with the elimination of agency decision making premised on evidence that was of poor quality—irrelevant, immaterial, unreliable and non-probative—and of insufficient quantity—less than a preponderance" (p. 102). Consequently, the Court concluded that through APA provisions Congress has "expressed its intent that adjudicatory proceedings subject to the APA satisfy the statute where determinations are made according to the preponderance of the evidence" (p. 104).

Although the APA preponderance-of-the-evidence standard normally governs agency adjudicators when reaching hearing decisions, specific statutory provisions may override the APA requirement calling for a higher standard of proof. For example, in deportation cases today, as long as the alien entered the country legally, decisions are governed by the higher clear-and-convincing-evidence standard. In *Bustos-Torres v. INS*, 898 F.2d 1053, 1057 (5th Cir. 1990), the petitioner contended that evidence used against him "is not the clear and convincing evidence necessary for deportation." The court acknowledged that "although the government has the ultimate burden of providing deportability by clear and convincing evidence, in a Section 125 (a)(2) case charging deportability of an alien who entered the country without inspection, the government need only show alienage."[63] But recently in *Huerta-Guevara v. Ashcroft*, 321 F.3d 883 (9th Cir. 2003), the court again stressed that the INS must demonstrate clear and convincing evidence to justify deportation, assuming that the alien had entered the United States legally.

There are many critics of the preponderance-of-the-evidence standard. The most prevalent criticism is that the weak standard is applied when common sense should suggest that ALJs should employ stricter or higher due process standards when serious deprivations may result. Justices Lewis Powell and Potter Stewart, the dissenters in *Steadman*, present this criticism well. They argue that when potential penalties are equivalent to or greater than criminal penalties our common law tradition should supersede the APA, especially since the APA does not specifically state that the preponderance-of-the-evidence standard must be applied.

Another criticism is simply that these standards of proof are confusing because they are not clearly distinct. These different standards are used in agency hearings and in court trials to support decisions. But how useful or practical are these tests? Can these standards be applied meaningfully in different situations? Are you convinced that a person of reasonable intelligence could tell you the difference between, say, substantial evidence, preponderance of the evidence, clear and convincing evidence, and evidence that leaves no reasonable doubt? These standards all apply to the *weight* of the evidence, but do you think clear and meaningful distinctions and applications of these standards can be made? When it comes to weighing any evidence, whether in an agency hearing or court trial, the weighing process and the accompanying decision process are quite subjective. What is clear and convincing evidence to one person is not to another. Nonetheless, the preponderance-of-the-evidence standard is the basic standard of proof test used in agency hearings, whatever this standard really means in practice.[64]

Making Decisions on the Basis of the Whole Record

The APA, Section 556(d), requires ALJs to make hearing decisions leading to the issuing of any order only after "consideration of the *whole record* or those parts thereof cited by a party and supported by and in accordance with the reliable, probative, and substantial evidence" (my emphasis). Requiring agency adjudicators to base their decisions on the whole record and not just part of the record seems like a very reasonable and patently fair requirement, yet before the APA was passed in 1946 hearing adjudicators were allowed to substantiate their decisions upon only part of the record. Of course, this permitted hearing decisionmakers to ignore parts of the hearing record that may have contradicted the evidence they used to substantiate their decision. In fact, it clearly gave unscrupulous adjudicators the opportunity to reach outrageously unfair decisions by totally ignoring facts in the record that would cause any reasonable person to reach an opposite decision. Nevertheless, this practice of having to look at only part of the record to satisfy the "one-sided substantial evidence" test was upheld by the courts before the passage of the APA. In *Marzacco v. Lowe*, 58 F.Supp. 900, 903 (D.N.J. 1945), the court remarked: "Under the present prevailing system of administrative law, all evidence to the contrary . . . is a closed book into which this court dare not peek, at least not effectively."

Louis J. Jaffe, among many others, found this narrow and absurd application of the substantial evidence rule horrifying. Rightfully, Jaffe insisted that it is very hard to believe that any truly reasonable and responsible person could, in good conscience, reach rational conclusions by looking at only part of the record.[65] The court reached the same conclusion in *Holo-Krome Co. v. NLRB*, 947 F.2d 588 (2nd Cir. 1991), when the court scolded the NLRB for ignoring important parts of the record (e.g., an ALJ's finding) to justify an unreasonable decision not substantiated by the whole record. The court noted that the whole record must be used in searching a decision, including weighing "evidence opposed to the board's view" (p. 593, quoting from *Local One, Amalgamated Lithographers v. NLRB*, 729 F.2d 172, 175 [2nd Cir. 1984]). In fact, the court concluded that the

NLRB's refusal to consider a critical part of the whole record made "the evidence supporting the Board's decision . . . less than substantial" (p. 592). Consequently, the court ruled that "the Board's decision regarding this evidence was in no way justified by the record before it" (p. 595). In so holding, this federal court relied heavily upon the arguments set forth in the classic case on the whole record requirement, *Universal Camera Corp. v. NLRB*, 340 U.S. 474 (1951), in which the Supreme Court stressed that hearing decisionmakers must base their decisions on the whole record, including conflicting evidence. "The substantiality of evidence must take into account whatever in the record fairly detracts from its weight. This is clearly the significance of the (APA) requirement" (p. 488).

The question of what constitutes the whole record has also been disputed. The dispute is based generally on problems pertaining to definitions of formal and informal evidence and questions over which evidence needs to be included in the "whole" record. Of course, agencies have been charged with keeping incomplete records, failing to note ex parte communications that may influence adjudicators and should therefore be part of the record, and failing to admit certain kinds of evidence (e.g., hearsay, documents and testimony that are "too costly" or "too inconvenient" to obtain). Nevertheless, the whole record requirement is generally honored by responsible ALJs and does not present a significant problem in administrative law. The whole record rule has unquestionably greatly improved the quality of decisionmaking in agency hearings. Probably the best description of the whole record requirement in the context of the substantial evidence rule that agency adjudicators should follow is found in *300 Gramatan v. Human Rights Division*, 45 N.Y. 2d 176, 181 (1978): "In the final analysis, substantial evidence consists of proof within the whole record of such quality and quantity as to generate conviction in and persuade a fair and detached fact finder that, from that proof as a premise, a conclusion or ultimate fact may be extracted reasonably—probatively and logically."

Hearing Decisions Must Be Based on the Exclusive Record

One of the most fundamental principles in administrative law is the "exclusiveness of the record" principle. It is a simple and easy to understand rule, but these simple principles normally carry the most practical weight in law because they are easy to comprehend, follow, and enforce. The exclusiveness-of-the-record principle means that hearing examiners must base their decisions *only* on the evidence produced during the hearing proceeding that constitutes the exclusive record. There are only a few exceptions to this principle. The exclusiveness-of-the-record principle is stated clearly in the federal APA, Section 556(e): "The transcript of testimony and exhibits, together with all papers and requests filed in the proceeding, constitutes the exclusive record for decision."

As noted, the exclusive record principle is and should be a basic maxim that must be followed in a judicial proceeding, whether an agency hearing or a court trial. How absurd it would be if parties in an agency adjudication presented and responded to evidence on the record and then the adjudicators later reached a decision based on evidence not entered as evidence during the hearing when parties had an opportunity to rebut it. The Court in *Mazza v. Cavicchia*, 105 A.2d 545, 554 (N.J. 1954), noted how ridiculous and unfair such adjudicative behavior would be: "Unless the principle is observed, the right to a hearing itself becomes meaningless. Of what real worth is the right to present evidence and to argue its significance at a formal hearing, if the one who decides the case may stray at will from the record in reaching his decision."

Of course, problems develop when agency adjudicators in fact do rely upon information to reach decisions that is not a part of the exclusive record. Ex parte contacts or communications may unduly prejudice hearing decisions because such contacts may provide hearing decisionmakers with information not noted on the record. Ex parte communications are patently unfair and tend to undermine due process in hearing decisionmaking, because the information tends to be one-sided, almost always favoring one party at the expense of the other. And since the ex parte information is not included as part of the record, a rebuttal to it could not be given by the other party in the dispute. Besides, since ex parte evidence is not part of the exclusive record, reviewing courts could never judge the weight adjudicators gave to it when making the decision. It is for these reasons, the court acknowledged in *District No. 1, Pac. Coast Dist., Marine Eng'rs Beneficial Ass'n v. Maritime Admin.*, 215 F.3d 37, 42 (D.C. Cir 2000), that the Administrative Procedure Act, Section 557(d)(1), prohibits off-the-record ex parte contacts in agency adjudications.

Ex parte communications, contacts, or pressures can easily bias or severely contaminate a hearing decision; thus courts have found ex parte influence peddling generating ex parte evidence to be flatly illegal under most conditions. In a leading case, *Sangamon Valley Television Corp. v. U.S.*, 269 F.2d 221 (D.C. Cir. 1959), the court overturned a decision by the FCC allowing a television station to relocate in St. Louis because of improper ex parte influence peddling. The court noted that such ex parte contacts struck at the core of the Commission's quasi-judicial powers, corrupting the process. Fundamental fairness, the court argued, requires that the proceeding be conducted in the open with all the evidence becoming part of the exclusive record. In *English v. Long Beach*, 217 P.2d 22 (Col. 1950), the court held that the exclusiveness-of-the-record rule prohibits talking to a doctor about the extent of injury off the record and outside of the hearing, while in *Cowart v. Schweiker*, 662 P.2d 731 (11th Cir. 1981), the court concluded that the exclusiveness-of-the-record principle had been violated because hearing examiners considered medical reports by doctors submitted after the close of the hearing.

The exclusiveness-of-the-record principle is also violated by the gathering and use of "secret evidence" by hearing officials to help aid their decision. In an old state case, *Carstens v. Pillsbury*, 158 P. 218, 220 (Col. 1916), the court held that to gather secret evidence "and to consider it without even giving the parties an opportunity to . . . meet it in any reasonable way, is contrary to all principles of justice and fairness. It cannot be entertained for a moment." Ex parte "views" or inspections also violate the exclusiveness-of-the-record rule by allowing the viewer (agency adjudicator) to view something (e.g., accident site) outside of the record, preventing the "view" from being cross-examined. Of course, the ex parte view could cause injustices in hearing decisions, especially if the view happened to be a mistaken or incorrect one. In *Feinson v. Conservation Comm.*, 429 A.2d 910 (Conn. 1981), an ex parte view was found to undermine the exclusiveness-of-the-record, because it was not noted on the record and no opportunity was given to rebut the view. But in *Zuniga v. San Mateo Dept. of Health Serv.*, 267 Cal. Report. 755, 761 (Cal. App. 1 Dist. 1990), the court upheld the ex parte view because no prejudice from the viewing was identified and the other party was given sufficient opportunity to respond to the ex parte viewed evidence.

The *Zuniga* decision is rooted in a controversial application of the exclusiveness-of-the-record principle regarding the use of ex parte evidence. Ex parte evidence is sometimes allowed by courts, especially if it can be shown that no prejudice resulted and an opportunity was given to rebut it. In M*arket Street Ry v. Railroad Commission*, 324 U.S. 548, 562 (1945), the Supreme Court argued that in addition to showing that ex parte evidence was received, prejudice must be demonstrated to show that due process violations occurred. The basic criticism of the *Market Street* ruling is that it tends to require opposing parties to prove that ex parte evidence or any extra-record evidence has somehow prejudiced the hearing decision. Since demonstrating such prejudice is frequently very difficult to do, critics contend that such a requirement would really take the thunder out of the exclusiveness of record rule. Consequently, many courts have totally rejected the controversial ruling on the exclusiveness of the record principle espoused in *Market Street*, which is not that difficult since the *Market Street* Court spoke before the federal APA became law. Probably most courts follow the approach adopted in *First Savings and Loan Assn. v. Vandygriff*, 605 S.W.2d 740, 742 (Tex. App. 1980): "It is not the burden of the complaining party to demonstrate harm by showing the extent, if any, to which the official was persuaded by the secret information" (p. 742).

Use of Official Notice in Reaching Decisions

Closely linked to the principle of exclusiveness of the record is the doctrine of *official notice*. In fact, official notice constitutes the most significant exception to the exclusiveness-of-the-record requirement because officially noticed facts (i.e., "very obvious" facts) are permitted to be used by adjudicators to help substantiate their hearing decisions as "extra-record" evidence after the hearing is over. Let's put the use of official notice into perspective.

In reflecting on the appropriateness of evidence employed to justify judicial decisions, Justice Louis Brandeis concluded: "Nothing can be treated as evidence which is not introduced as such." If taken literally, and it never has been, Brandeis's holding would preclude the use of *judicially noticed facts* in court trials and *officially noticed facts* in administrative hearings. To avoid confusion at the outset, it should be made clear that judicial or official notice is not the same as providing "proper notice" to a party. Judicial and official notice refer simply to when a tribunal accepts a fact as obvious and notorious without further proof. When a court notices (recognizes) a fact as indisputably true, the court is judicially noticing the fact. Official notice is the administrative tribunal's counterpart to judicial notice. Therefore, when hearing officers accept facts as unquestionably true, these officials are giving official notice to these facts. Officially noticed facts are normally supposed to be so indisputable or obvious that reasonable people would accept them as common knowledge (for example, Christmas falls on December 25). Officially noticed facts, if they cannot be acknowledged as true on the spot, should at least be easily verified by consulting, say, a calendar or public records. Because of the nature of such facts, officially noticed facts are normally not entered into the record; yet they do form part of the extra-record used by hearing examiners to reach their decisions (*Citizens of the State of Florida v. Florida Public Serv. Comm'n.*, 440 So.2d 371 [Fla. Appl. 1983]; *Dionne v. Heckler*, 585 F.Supp. 1055 [D.Me. 1984]; and *Sykes v. Apfel*, 228 F.3d 259 [3rd Cir. 2000]).

It is easy to justify the use of official notice; for Brandeis's standard to be applied literally would create unnecessary and counterproductive hardships for all tribunals. In administrative agencies, it would slow down to a crawl the disposition of cases. Surely it would be silly to not recognize and use facts that are obvious and helpful to those hearing officials wanting to make fair, reasonable, and practical decisions. It would be a serious mistake for independent regulatory commissioners, for example, to ignore practical and obvious facts when deciding public policy questions that, when implemented in the real world, will have significant social impact.

It would be just as absurd to permit unreasonable and time-consuming challenges to indisputable facts employed responsibly by hearing officials to reach decisions. Although there has been some scholarly and judicial debate over how flexibly official notice should be applied by administrative tribunals, in general, reviewing courts have allowed hearing examiners to officially notice facts that are not obvious to the general public, yet are readily accepted as common knowledge to agency experts who have acquired considerable expertise in specialized areas.[66] The Supreme Court has acknowledged that hearing decisions cannot always be totally supported by the evidence in the record; nor is such support required. Therefore, decisions must ultimately rest in part on facts that are officially noticed by agency experts.[67] But expertise should not be irresponsibly used by agencies to notice facts that cannot be given such status legitimately. This would constitute an abuse of the function of official notice, thus causing the appropriate employment of official notice to "become lost in the haze of so-called expertise."[68]

Although there is no evidence to indicate that official notice has been misused to any significant extent in agency hearings, problems could arise to undermine the extension of fair adjudications if hearing officials acted irresponsibly. Most notably, they could use official notice to recognize facts that are not obviously true, even to the experts. When highly complex, technical questions are involved, giving official notice to facts is less convincing and inappropriate. Even worse, hearing examiners could use facts that are officially noticed only after the hearing proceedings have ended to help substantiate their findings. This practice has bothered reviewing courts because it unfairly prevents any challenges to the validity and use of the officially noticed facts. In *Heckler v. Campbell*, 103 S.Ct. 1952, 1953 (1983), the Supreme Court said that it is a basic administrative law principle "that when an agency takes official or administrative notice of facts, a litigant must be given an adequate opportunity to respond." The Supreme Court still holds to this principle (*City of Erie v. Pap's A.M.*, 529 U.S. 277, 283 [2000]).

Also, the agency that initiates the action normally has the burden of proof. If hearing officers place significant weight on officially noticed facts to substantiate their decisions, even if they allow parties the opportunity to challenge these facts, in effect, the agency is illegitimately shifting the burden of proof from itself to the parties before it. This is so because now the facts are assumed to be accurate unless the parties before an agency show the facts to be untrue.

In sum, few seem to have any serious reservations about the use of official notice, as long as its use does not jeopardize procedural due process protections in agency hearings. For fair procedures to be honored, most experts believe that official notice must be kept limited in its application. According to scholars, responsible employment of official notice would involve (1) making certain that all officially noticed facts are actually obvious and well known to the average person; (2) noticing technical facts not considered common knowledge to the average person only if they are recognized as indisputable knowledge by experts in the field (for example, that recklessly disposing radioactive waste poses a serious health hazard); (3) informing all relevant parties in regard to the officially noticed facts considered to help reach the decision; (4) providing sources to officially noticed facts (for example, agency files); (5) exclusion of *litigation facts* (facts that have emerged in the pending dispute since such facts are presently in question); (6) prohibiting the use of officially noticed facts for establishing principle evidence on which the decision rests; (7) likewise, the preclusion of any officially noticed facts from becoming part of the substantial evidence; and (8) sufficient opportunity to contest all officially noticed facts that could be reasonably challenged (for example, facts in agency files cited but not brought forth). This last limitation seems to be the most vital in preserving fair use of official notice.

Concluding the Hearing Business

The final actions taken by ALJs to conclude hearing business involves the issuance of the written decision. Before the hearing officials write or issue a "recommended, initial, or tentative decision" ("final" decision of the ALJ, but tentative since it can be rejected by the agency head), Section 557(c) of the APA requires that all parties be given "reasonable opportunity to submit . . . (1) proposed findings and conclusions; (2) exceptions to the decisions or recommended decisions . . . ; and (3) supporting reasons for the exceptions or proposed findings or conclusions." Such is normally submitted in the form of legal briefs to the ALJ.

Section 557(c) also specifically requires that the record should "show the ruling on each finding, conclusion, or exception presented." The Section also requires that "all decisions including initial, recommended, and tentative decisions" are part of the formal written record and "include a statement of (A) findings and conclusions, and the reasons or basis therefore, on all the material issues of fact, law, or discretion presented on the record; and (B) the appropriate rule, order, sanction, relief, or denial thereof."

Regarding formal adjudicative decisions, the APA provisions are quite specific and demanding, but evidently the intent of Congress was to force adjudicators to act responsibly in making hearing decisions. Specifically, by compelling ALJs to justify in detail the factual and legal reasons for their findings, Congress in effect is forcing hearings officials to think seriously about its hearing decisions. Of course, this also tends to promote responsible and democratically accountable hearing decisions, as well as a justification for agency orders (public policies) that will make it easier for all affected parties to follow and understand. Possibly most important from a legal standpoint is that detailed justifications for findings and conclusions make judicial review considerably easier and much more effective.

Despite the specific requirement regarding the documentation of hearing decisions, hearing records too often are woefully inadequate, resulting in poorly documented decisions. Many judges still complain that they cannot conduct competent judicial review of agency adjudications because of inadequate hearing records, despite repeated attempts by the courts over the years to make agency adjudicators keep adequate hearing records by complying with APA record-keeping requirements. Observers have maintained that adjudicators still keep poor hearing records because agencies conduct too many hearings and the actual drafting of the decisions has been delegated to lower-level bureaucrats ("opinion writers"). Such opinion writers end up justifying decisions in vague, generic legal reasons, failing to justify in specific legal terms the particular case. Consequently, "the opinion becomes more of a rationalization for the decision than an explanation."[69]

It must be stressed that ALJs do not make final decisions for the agency. Agency heads have the authority to make "institutional decisions" for their particular agency or bureaucracy by overruling the decision reached by an ALJ. This is a legally sanctioned agency right, and it is considered legitimate because agency heads, almost always political appointees, have the obligation of promoting policies that are consistent with the administration's views (i.e., the presidential administration on the federal level and the governor's administration on the state level). As a consequence, an ALJ's decision technically constitutes only a tentative decision or an advisory opinion subject to being overruled by the agency chief. As a practical matter, most hearing decisions are quite routine and "apolitical" and, therefore, become the agency's final decision. However, hearing decisions that are politically sensitive may be reversed by the agency head to make agency policy consistent with the administration's policy. Courts urge that reasonable justifications be given to justify reversing an ALJ's decision, but reasonable justifications are not always given since political reasons do not always seem reasonable in light of the specific facts and law pertaining to a particular case (*Central Transport Inc. v. National Labor Relations Board*, 997 F.2d 1180 [1993]).

The current practice of permitting agency heads inevitably to decide a hearing decision bothers some practitioners and scholars because the practice rejects an old, commonsensical legal principle established in *Morgan v. U.S.*, 298 U.S. 468, 481 (1936), that "the one who hears must decide." In this case Chief Justice Hughes argued that responsible and fair decisionmaking "cannot be performed by one who has not considered evidence or argument" (p. 481). However, increasing hearing caseloads forced a more practical, flexible approach, so in a follow-up case, *Morgan v. U.S.*, 304 U.S. 1, 18 (1938), known as *Morgan II*, the Supreme Court held that the decisionmaker need not be present at the hearing, as long as he "dipped into (the record) from time to time to get its drift." *Morgan II* had the effect of allowing subordinates to hear and decide cases. Today, and for many decades now, agency heads only casually review the tentative decisions reached by ALJs, rejecting those decisions that staffers recommend should be changed to suit administrative policy. As noted, even the ALJs assign out the writing of the decisions to their assistants or "opinion writers," bureaucratizing and impersonalizing the whole process, which at times causes due process to be undetermined.

SUMMARY

Before the passage of the Administrative Procedure Act in 1946, the courts conveyed the clear message, especially in *Morgan v. United States*, 304 U.S. 1 (1938), that public agencies needed to improve their hearing procedures to make them more consistent with constitutional due process standards. Provisions in the APA, however, helped to make agency hearings more fair. Although APA requirements stopped short of demanding that agencies conduct hearings like court trials, court decisions from 1946 to the end of President Jimmy Carter's administration had the impact of making formal agency hearings come closer to mirroring court procedures, especially in regard to giving notice, record keeping, presenting evidence, weighing evidence, and reaching decisions based upon substantial evidence. After *Goldberg v. Kelly*, 397 U.S. 254 (1970), the courts even pondered during the 1970s the question of whether agencies, under certain circumstances, should be compelled to provide persons paid counsel in hearings.

The trend toward making administrative hearings more trial-like has bothered many critics who claim that although moves to make hearings more like court trials have generally improved due process protections in agency hearings, these steps have placed an unduly heavy and costly burden on agency officials and taxpayers. They maintain essentially that public agencies were not designed to act as courts in our political system. They assert also that excessive legal formalism in agency hearings has precluded the possibility of efficient public administration and that it has caused injustices by creating unnecessary administrative delays. For over two decades now conservative politics and conservative courts, especially the U.S. Supreme Court, have had a significant impact on agency procedures,

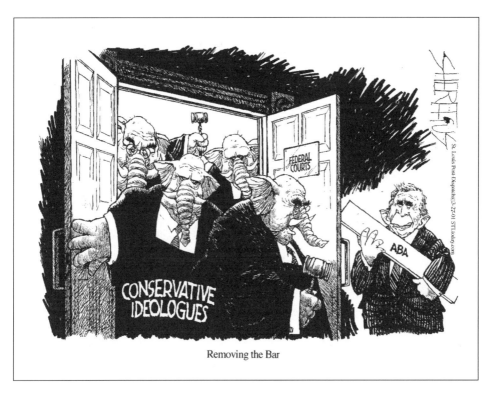

Removing the Bar

Source: Reprinted by permission of John Sherffius and the *St. Louis Post-Dispatch,* March 27, 2001.

particularly agency hearings. The cost-benefit analysis approach to government and judicial decisionmaking has dominated the era. With the federal courts leading the way, many courts in general have used cost-benefit analysis in their decisions to redefine what constitutes procedural due process in agency hearings, arguing essentially that elaborate due process evidentiary hearings from the initial notice stage to the final decision stage must be made cost-effective to our political system. The courts have stressed repeatedly that today's agencies must handle many times more cases than the agencies of yesteryear and, therefore, must be able to resolve disputes expeditiously. This reasoning has allowed the courts in roughly the past two decades to allow agencies to conduct streamlined hearings without all the due process "frills."

Of course, this recent trend has angered the liberals who insist that extending procedural due process protections to parties in hearings is absolutely essential to make hearings fair. However, the conservative response seems equally compelling. They argue that providing elaborate due process protections may be ideal, but the hard reality is that realistically the costs to our system easily outweigh the benefits. Unquestionably, due process is a desirable, yet expensive ideal. In a sense, the more the better. But the real question is: How much due process can we afford?

STATE OF CALIFORNIA V.
FEDERAL ENERGY REGULATORY COMMISSION

329 F.3d 700 (9th Cir. 2003)

Facts

In 2001 the Federal Energy Regulatory Commission (FERC) approved a corporate reorganization of certain subsidiaries of Pacific Gas and Electric Company (PG&E). PG&E sought a quick or urgent approval of the corporate reorganization to avoid possible bankruptcy, because PG&E could not pass on to its customers increases in wholesale power costs. The California state legislature, in an attempt to stabilize electric power costs to consumers, had placed a freeze on retail electricity charges. Petitioners, the State of California, the City of Santa Clara, Transmission Agency of Northern California, and Northern California Power Agency brought suit, maintaining in general that PG&E wanted to reorganize in order to hide millions of dollars in assets from creditors. Petitioners argued specifically that FERC's fast approval of PG&E's restructuring request violated several procedural and substantive due process rights of the petitioners—namely, (1) the right to adequate notice; (2) opportunity for a fair hearing; and (3) proper "public interest" analysis as required by Section 230 of the Federal Power Act, 41 Stat. 1063.

Circuit Judge Ronald Gould delivered the opinion of the court.

This case involves a challenge to the Federal Energy Regulatory Commission's approval of a corporate reorganization of certain Pacific Gas & Electric Co. subsidiaries. The petitioners, the State of California and the Northern California Power Agency, contend that the restructuring was designed to shield assets worth millions of dollars from creditors. The petitioners raise procedural and substantive objections to the Commission's order approving the reorganization. The petitioners argue that the Commission provided inadequate notice of Pacific Gas & Electric's applications, provided inadequate opportunity for a hearing, and failed to conduct properly the "public interest" analysis mandated by §230 of the Federal Power Act. We hold that (1) the Commission's *Federal Register* notice language adequately notified the public of the "essential attributes" of the corporate reorganization, even though the notice language did not disclose the applicant's motive in making the applications or how the applicant would benefit from the reorganization; (2) the Commission's expedited review process, in this case, did not deprive the petitioners of the opportunity to be heard within the meaning of the Federal Power Act or the Fifth Amendment's Due Process Clause; (3) even if the Commission failed to give the petitioners adequate opportunity for a hearing initially, the Commission cured any procedural defect by carefully considering all the evidence and arguments the petitioners offered in their petitions for rehearing and their motions to intervene; and (4) the Commission's decision that the corporate reorganization was consistent with the public interest was supported by substantial evidence and was not "arbitrary, capricious, an abuse of discretion, or otherwise not in accordance with the law" because the Commission properly exercised its discretion to balance factors it deems relevant to the public's energy needs. We deny the petitions.

In the summer of 2000, wholesale electricity prices soared in California. Electricity retailers such as Pacific Gas and Electric Company (PG&E) were unable to pass the increased wholesale power costs on to their customers because the California legislature had imposed a retail rate "freeze" as part of its attempt to restructure the California electricity market. As a result, PG&E incurred billions of dollars of debt. With a possible PG&E bankruptcy looming, three of PG&E's subsidiaries ("the NEG Companies") proposed a corporate reorganization to be consummated in two steps. First, two of the NEG Companies would reincorporate as Delaware corporations. Second, a new company—PG&E National Energy Group, LLC—would be created and interposed between PG&E Corporation and the NEG Companies. This second feature of the reorganization, which PG&E later described as "ringfencing" in its required Securities Exchange Commission disclosures, was intended to improve PG&E's credit rating. Petitioners claim that this was to be accomplished by shielding PG&E assets from creditors in any future bankruptcy proceeding. It was imperative that the reorganization be consummated as soon as possible, according to PG&E, or lenders would stop financing some PG&E entities. If lenders balked, it would threaten PG&E's plan to build new power plants in California and elsewhere—

plants that were needed to increase the electricity supply.

Because the need was urgent, the NEG Companies sought expedited approval for the reorganization in two applications filed with the Federal Energy Regulatory Commission (FERC) in December 2000. The NEG companies filed a first application on December 11, 2000. The Commission published notice of it in the Federal Register on December 19, 2000. The notice stated:

> Take notice that on December 4, 2000, PG&E National Energy Group, Inc., PG&E Enterprises and PG&E Shareholdings, Inc. tendered for filing, on behalf of themselves and their public utility subsidiaries, an application under Section 203 of the Federal Power Act seeking authorization for certain changes to the upstream ownership of their public utility subsidiaries following a proposed intra-corporate reorganization.

Comments on the first application were due on or before December 26, 2000—seven days after notice was published.

The NEG Companies filed a second application on December 28, 2000. The Commission mailed notice of it to the California Governor's Office the same day. The Commission published notice of the application in the Federal Register on January 4, 2001. The notice stated:

> Take notice that on December 28, 2000, PG&E National Energy Group, LLC (NEG LLC) and PG&E National Energy Group, Inc. (NEG) tendered for filing on

behalf of themselves and their public utility subsidiaries, an application under Section 203 of the Federal Power Act seeking authorization for the transfer of all outstanding stock of NEG from PG&E Corporation to NEG LLC.

Comments were due on or before January 8, 2001—four days after notice was published.

Having received no comments or motions to intervene, the Commission approved the NEG Companies' applications in two January 12, 2001, orders. The orders analyzed the proposed reorganization's effects on competition, rates, and regulation and concluded, over a dissent, "that the proposed transactions [are] consistent with the public interest." Hours after the Commission approved the applications, the proposed reorganization was consummated.

After learning of the Commission's approval, the State of California on January 19, 2001, filed a motion for late intervention and requested a hearing. The State urged that it had "very substantial interests in all aspects of the current energy issues involving the State, and with respect to any possible utility bankruptcy." The Northern California Power Agency (NCPA), a public agency that generates and transmits electricity, filed a motion for late intervention and requested a rehearing on February 7, 2001. NCPA stated that it was a creditor of PG&E affected by the transactions. Several other entities, not parties to this appeal, also sought late intervention.

The Commission on February 21, 2001, denied the requests for late intervention and rehearing, holding that it gave adequate notice and opportu-

nity for hearing to members of the public, in light of the urgency of the NEG companies' request. In its February 21, 2001, order, the Commission considered, and rejected, the evidence and arguments offered by the State, NCPA, and other intervenors.

The State, NCPA, and other entities filed for rehearing of the Commission's February 21, 2001, order. The Commission on January 30, 2002, granted rehearing and permitted all the parties to intervene in the proceeding involving the change in upstream ownership (the second application). But the Commission denied the requests to intervene in the proceeding involving the Delaware reincorporations (the first application).

The Commission stated:

For the reasons discussed in the February 21 Order, we find that all interested persons were provided reasonable notice and opportunity to comment in both the Docket Nos. EC01-41 and the EC01-49 proceedings. Nonetheless, in recognition of the special circumstances of the Docket No. EC01-49 proceeding, e.g., the shortened notice period that included a holiday weekend and claims from certain entities that they did not receive notice as required under section 203 of the [Federal Power Act], we will grant the late interventions . . . in Docket No. EC01-49-000. We deny intervention in Docket No. EC01-41 because there has been no showing that reasonable notice was not provided in that proceeding.

The Commission also rejected the intervenors' substantive arguments.

With regard to the petitioners' substantive concerns on rehearing, the pleadings do not raise any new arguments. Therefore, we deny the requests for rehearing of our prior orders, and the request for vacatur of the EC01-49 Order, for the same reasons articulated in the February 21 Order.

The State and NCPA then petitioned us for review.

[1] At the outset, we must decide whether the Commission's notices describing NEG's applications, printed in the *Federal Register*, gave NCPA adequate notice of the essential attributes of the applications under the Fifth Amendment's Due Process Clause. Constitutional due process requires that notice be reasonably calculated to inform parties of proceedings that may directly and adversely affect their legally protected interests. Publication in the *Federal Register* is legally sufficient notice to all interested or affected persons regardless of actual knowledge or hardship resulting from ignorance, except those who are legally entitled to personal notice. . . . We have held that an interested member of the public should be able to read the published notice of an application and understand the "essential attributes" of that application. A member of the public should not have to guess the applicant's "true intent."

Although it is settled that a *Federal Register* notice must disclose an applicant's "true intent," neither we nor our sister circuits have considered the meaning of those words. Must a *Federal Register* notice disclose an applicant's underlying motive or merely its immediate intention? NCPA argues that a *Federal Register* notice must disclose the applicant's underlying motive.

It argues that the notice must disclose not only what the applicant proposes to do, but also what the applicant stands to gain from agency approval. Stated another way, NCPA apparently would require the notice to disclose why the applicant plans to do what it proposes to do. In NCPA's view, the Commission's *Federal Register* notice was insufficient in stating that NEG intended to change the "upstream ownership of their public utility subsidiaries following a proposed intracorporate reorganization" (what NEG planned to do). NCPA contends that the *notice* also was required to state that the underlying motive of the proposed transaction was to improve NEG's credit rating by reducing the likelihood that the assets of the NEG companies would be consolidated in any possible future bankruptcy proceeding (why NEG planned the reorganization).

[2] We reject NCPA's view. A *Federal Register* notice is intended to alert the public to the general nature of a proposed action, not to delineate all the action's possible implications. A *Federal Register* notice must provide basic factual information about what an applicant proposes to do. It need not explain why the applicant proposes a course of action or speculate about the action's significance for others. If an entity requires more detailed information to determine whether, or to what extent, it may be affected by a proposed action, it is the entity's responsibility to seek out that information.

[3] Here, the *Federal Register* notice sufficiently described what NEG intended to do. The notice was not required to do more. Any interested member of the public—and especially

a public utility that participates in a heavily regulated industry and claims to be a substantial creditor of an obviously financially troubled applicant—should have understood that NEG's "intra-corporate reorganization," involving a change in "upstream ownership," might have implications for creditors. If NCPA wanted more information than was provided by the *Federal Register* notices, NCPA should have obtained a copy of NEG's applications. It did not. We hold that the *Federal Register* notices were plainly sufficient to provide notice to all interested persons of the essential attributes of NEG's applications.

We next decide whether the Commission gave the petitioners adequate opportunity for a hearing before approving NEG's applications on an expedited schedule. The State of California argues that the Commission's expedited approval of the NEG applications violated the State's statutory due process rights under § 203 of the Federal Power Act (FPA). NCPA argues that the Commission's expedited approval violated NCPA's constitutional due process rights under the Fifth Amendment's Due Process Clause.

[4] The scope of the "opportunity for a hearing" protected by the FPA has parallels with the "opportunity to be heard" protected by the Fifth Amendment. In both statutory and constitutional due process cases we have relied on the same factors in determining what process is due: the importance of the private interests affected, the value of the claimed procedural safeguards, and the burdens on government of providing those safeguards (the so-called *Mathews v. Eldridge* factors. See

Mathews v. Eldridge, 424 U.S. 319 at 335 [1976]). . . .

[F]irst, the private interest that will be affected by the official action; second, the risk of an erroneous deprivation of such interest through the procedures used, and the probable value, if any, of additional or substitute procedural safeguards, and finally, the government's interest, including the function involved and the fiscal and administrative burdens that the additional or substitute procedural requirement would entail.

Here, the three *Mathews v. Eldridge* factors indicate that the Commission gave NCPA and the State of California adequate opportunity for a hearing before making its initial decision, even though the State had only about four days to respond to the Commission's mailed notice, and NCPA had only seven days and four days to respond to the Commission's two *Federal Register* notices.

[5] First, we consider the private interest affected by the government action. *Mathews*, 424 U.S. at 335. The petitioners argue that the private interest affected is large and important, since the Commission's approval of the applications may have shielded millions of dollars from creditors. The petitioners overstate the significance of their interests. When the commission established the notice periods in December 2000, its approval of the applications would have meant a loss for NCPA only if three future conditions had been met: (1) if NEG declared bankruptcy; (2) if a bankruptcy court decided the transactions were not fraudulent; and (3) if the bankruptcy court approved a reorganization plan

that did not repay petitioners in full. Unless these conditions were met, NCPA's interest as a creditor was secure. NCPA's interest in the transactions thus was speculative. The State's interest in the transactions is also speculative. The State mentions that it has "very substantial interests in all aspects of the current energy issues involving the State, and with respect to any possible utility bankruptcy." The State never specifies what those interests might be, and its general recital of interest does not suggest a need for heightened procedural protections.

[6] Second, we consider the risk of an erroneous deprivation of the petitioners' interest through the procedures used, and the probable value, if any, of additional or substitute procedural safeguards. Id. The Commission allowed only about four and seven days—relatively short time periods—for a response from the State and NCPA. These periods comprised federal holidays and a weekend. Nonetheless, under the circumstances, it does not seem that a longer comment period would have improved the Commission's decisionmaking. Neither petitioner was close to meeting the deadline. The State and NCPA submitted their first pleadings eleven days and thirty days after the deadline expired. By their own admission, the petitioners did not consider filing motions to intervene until they read Commissioner Massey's dissent to the Commission's January 12, 2001, order. It thus appears that the petitioners might not have met even a later deadline. Moreover, the Commission reconfirmed in its January 30, 2002, order—more than a year after the ap-

plications and after much briefing by interested parties—that its original decision was the correct one. Presumably, it would have reached that same correct decision even if it had allowed a few more days for public comment.

[7] Third, we consider the government's interest, including the function involved and the fiscal and administrative burdens that the additional or substitute procedural requirement would entail. Id. Allowing additional time for a response presumably would have cost the Commission little in the way of administrative burdens. But, more importantly, it might have endangered the Commission's administrative mission by preventing it from acting to mitigate the growing California energy crisis. When the Commission received these applications, the commissioners believed they had to act quickly to help NEG secure a better credit rating and financing for subsidiaries. Quick action was crucial, the Commission later explained, so that NEG could continue to construct new power plants that were desperately needed in California. The Commission had a strong interest in reaching a conclusion at the earliest practicable time.

[8] We assess due process case-by-case based on the total circumstances. Given the circumstances here, the Commission's expedited review of the applications did not deprive the petitioners of the opportunity to be heard, either under the Fifth Amendment's Due Process Clause or § 203 of the FPA.

[9] Even assuming *arguendo* that the Commission initially deprived the petitioners of an opportunity for a hearing by approving the NEG applications after only a few days of public comment,

the petitioners still would have no legal basis for complaint. In this case, the Commission provided all the procedural protections required by the Fifth Amendment and FPA when it carefully considered all the evidence and arguments that the petitioners offered in their petitions for rehearing and motions to intervene. . . .

We reach this conclusion by applying the three *Mathews v. Eldridge* factors to the process by which the Commission considered the motions to intervene and petitions for rehearing in this case. As above, we consider the private interest affected, the risk of an erroneous deprivation through the procedures used, and the government's interest in its choice of procedure.

First, we consider the private interest affected by FERC's action. Id. Here, that interest—the petitioners' interest in ensuring full repayment of creditors should the bankruptcy court someday require less than full repayment—was speculative, as explained above.

Second, we consider the risk of an erroneous deprivation of the petitioners' interest through the procedures used, and the probable value, if any, of additional or substitute procedural safeguards. Id. Here, there was little risk that FERC would erroneously deprive the petitioners of their interests by considering their evidence and arguments after its initial decision, rather than before it. Time was not of the essence for the petitioners (unlike for the Commission). The petitioners were not threatened by any imminent or irreparable injury. (Indeed, if the bankruptcy court in the future requires full repayment of creditors, it may appear that the petitioners were never injured.) That the

Commission considered the petitioners' evidence and arguments after its initial decision, rather than before it, was of little practical consequence.

Moreover, the Commission's procedures for considering motions to intervene and petitions for rehearing allowed for thorough consideration of the petitioners' evidence and arguments. The Commission's procedural rules imposed upon the petitioners a duty to include in their motions for intervention and their petitions for rehearing a thorough statement of their objections, including their basis in fact and law. The Commission's Rule 214 provides that "[a]ny motion to intervene must state, to the extent known, the position taken by the movant and the basis in fact and law for that position." 18 C.F.R. §385.214(b)(1). The Commission's Rule 713 provides that

[a]ny request for rehearing must: (1) State concisely the alleged error in the final decision or final order; (2) Conform to the requirements in Rule 203(a) which are applicable to pleadings; and (3) Set forth the matters relied upon by the party requesting rehearing, if rehearing is sought based on matters not available for consideration by the Commission at the time of the final decision or final order.

18 C.F.R. §385.713(c).

The Commission admitted to the record whatever evidence the State, NCPA, and other intervenors submitted with their motions to intervene. And the Commission considered that evidence along with the intervenors' arguments. In its February 21, 2001, order, the Commission stated that it found "no merit in their arguments":

> In their various pleadings, none of the commenters identify flaws in the Commission's analysis. . . . In the absence of any evidence to the contrary, we find that Applicants have adequately demonstrated that the reorganizations are consistent with the public interest.

In sum, the Commission fully considered the petitioners' evidence and arguments. The Commission at all times retained the authority to modify or set aside, in whole or part, its earlier order. 16 U.S.C. § 825l(a). We cannot say that the petitioners' interests would have been better protected had the Commission delayed its initial decision until it heard the petitioners' evidence and argument.

Third, we consider the government's interest. Mathews, 424 U.S. at 335. As we explained above, the government's interest was strong, because delay might have endangered the Commission's administrative mission by preventing it from acting to mitigate the growing California energy crisis.

In light of the private interests affected, the small risk of erroneous deprivation through the procedures used, and the government's strong interest in expedient decisionmaking, we hold that, under the circumstances of this case, the Commission's consideration of the petitioners' evidence and arguments in their motions to intervene and petitions for rehearing gave the petitioners all the procedural safeguards they were due under the Due Process Clause or the FPA.

Our holding today is consistent with our precedent. . . . Moreover, our holding is consistent with the settled administrative law rules that the Commission has wide discretion to select its own procedures and that the Commission's decision not to hold a formal evidentiary hearing is a "virtually unreviewable" exercise of discretion.

We conclude that the petitioners were in fact afforded ample "hearing" on their claims when the Commission considered the petitioners' evidence and arguments in their motions to intervene and petitions for rehearing.

V

Finally, NCPA challenges the Commission's decision on the merits, arguing that the Commission erred in concluding that the PG&E companies' reorganization was "consistent with the public interest." NCPA argues that the Commission's factual findings were not supported by "substantial evidence" and that its legal decision was "arbitrary, capricious, an abuse of discretion, or otherwise not in accordance with law." We reject these arguments.

First, NCPA argues that the Commission's factual findings were not supported by substantial evidence. We disagree. The record contained evidence in the form of an affidavit by an NEG official reciting that ultimate control of the PG&E subsidiaries would not change as a result of the reorganization, that the rates the subsidiaries charged were market-based and would not change, and that the regulatory status of the PG&E entities would not change. A reasonable mind might accept these facts as adequate to support the conclusion that the PG&E reorganization was not harmful to the public interest. The Commission's decision was based on substantial evidence.

Second, NCPA asserts that the Commission erred as a matter of law by "fail[ing] to consider or even discuss the consistency of the reorganization and transfer with the public interest." It also asserts that the Commission "focus[ed] only on the activities of Applicants, and not at all on the effect of the transaction upon the collectability of billions of dollars of unpaid debts of their affiliate PG&E, and the effects of the removal of those assets backing transactions on the California markets in electricity." Both assertions are wrong. In its January 12, 2001, order, the Commission stated that "[a]fter consideration of the particular circumstances presented in this application, it is concluded that the proposed transaction is consistent with the public interest. . . . " In addition, the Commission considered the effects of the reorganization on competition, rates, and regulation. In its February 21, 2001, order, the Commission amplified its earlier analysis, this time noting the transactions' effects on creditors and their bearing on the public interest:

> [T]here is only speculation that the transaction will increase the possibility of non-payment by PG&E and deter non-affiliate suppliers from selling power to PG&E, thus

resulting in diminished power supplies in California. On the contrary, by improving the ability of the NEG companies to obtain higher credit ratings, the reorganization may increase the likelihood that lenders will finance PG&E's electric generation construction projects in California. On balance, to the extent the applications enhance PG&E's ability to construct new generation, we would view the construction of more generation in California to be pro-competitive and consistent with the public interest.

The Commission's order contradicts NCPA's assertions that the Commission failed to consider the public interest and failed to consider the reorganization's effects on creditors. The Commission considered the reorganization's effects on energy markets and creditors and decided, on balance, that the reorganization was consistent with the public interest, based on the relevant factors. Balancing potentially conflicting factors relevant to the public's energy needs is a task for the Commission's discretion that we hesitate to second-guess.

[10] We conclude that the Commission's decision was supported by substantial evidence and that it was not "arbitrary, capricious, an abuse of discretion, or otherwise not in accordance with the law."

PETITIONS DENIED.

COMMENTS AND QUESTIONS

After reading this case, cynics would undoubtedly charge that this represents a classic situation in which the FERC has been captured by the very industry whose regulation it has been entrusted with to promote the public interest. Probably the most serious charge against FERC is not that certain procedural and substantive due process steps had been denied to the petitioners, but that the FERC "focus[ed] only on the activities of applicants, and not at all on the effect of the transaction upon the collectability of billions of dollars of unpaid debts of their affiliate PG&E, and the effects of the removal of those assets backing transactions on the California markets in electricity."

This charge by the State of California et al., is the most serious because it essentially attacks the objectivity of the FERC. California is actually making a charge against a regulatory commission that has been commonly made against regulatory commissions throughout the decades. That is, that regulatory commissions, soon after they are created, start to become infiltrated by industry people via the political appointment process. Within a matter of a few decades, the commissions become completely captured and start handing down orders that do much more to promote the financial interest of the particular regulated industries than to promote the public interest.

Given at least some of the actions by the FERC, even neutral observers might raise their eyebrows and question its rush to approve the reorganization that PG&E sought. In the first place, notice on PG&E's first application was given in the *Federal Register* on December 19, 2000, with comments due on December 26, 2000—one day after Christmas and entirely during the holiday season. How fair was this notice, given the reality that December 23–25 consisted of a weekend plus Christmas Day, while the typical Friday before Christmas is normally consumed by Christmas office parties? This meant that the petitioners had only two to three days during this typically festive period to respond. Certainly, there is reason to suspect that the FERC was trying to do PG&E a "big favor." A second notice on a record application was published on January 2, 2001, giving petitioners only four days to respond. Of course, normally, notice gives a minimum of thirty days to respond, with most notices giving interested parties months, but FERC justified its swift action by contending that PG&E's application for reorganizations was "urgent."

But were PG&E's applications for restructuring that urgent, so urgent that its applications had to be approved, as they were, by FERC orders on January 12, 2001—only about three weeks after the first notice and just a week after the second notice, during most of the holiday season? Various motions by the petitioners were filed to appeal the FERC orders, because they felt that they had "very substantial interests" at stake; yet virtually all procedural appeals were denied, including all "substantive concerns on rehearing." The Ninth Circuit Court of Appeals accepted the arguments by FERC that the commission "provided all the procedural protections required by the Fifth Amendment and FPA where it carefully considered all the evidence and arguments that the petitioners offered." But is not the court just accepting FERC's word for it, deferring to agency discretion? After all, even the court admitted: "We cannot say that the petitioners' interests would have been better protected had the Commission delayed its initial decision until it heard the petitioners' evidence and argument."

One of the petitioners, the Northern California Power Agency (NCPA), challenged the FERC's orders on their merits, claiming that PG&E's reorganization was inconsistent with the public interest, that the commission's decision was "arbitrary, capricious, an abuse of discretion, or otherwise not in accordance with law," and that "substantial evidence" did not support the commissions' factual findings. The court rejected all of these arguments. Would you? Sometimes a regulatory agency must act swiftly to help resolve an urgent problem. In doing so, the regulatory agency must be careful to balance the rights and interests of all parties. In the final analysis, do you think that the FERC sincerely strove in the "urgent" situation to represent all interests fairly? After examining the actions by FERC in support of PG&E's requests, would you be curious to research the backgrounds of these FERC commissioners? Remember, just because the court upheld FERC's actions in this case does not mean that the commission's behavior was good for the political system. As is explained in Chapter 9, the courts have for about twenty years practiced "extreme deference," believing that they should not meddle too far in agency decisions. In this case, the court acknowledged explicitly and implicitly that the FERC, not the courts, has the authority to make discretionary decisions as to procedure, weigh facts to determine "substantial evidence," and judge whether the "public interest has been served." The courts, employing their judicial discretion, will overrule only the most outrageous actions.

NOTES

1. Richard J. Pierce, Jr., *Administrative Law Treatise*, 4th ed. (New York: Aspen, 2002), vol. 1, p. 580.

2. Edwin W. Tucker, *Administrative Law, Regulation of Enterprise, and Individual Liberties* (St. Paul: West, 1975), p. 108.

3. See, for example, *Reeve Aleutian Airways, Inc. v. U.S.*, 982 F.2d 594, 598 (1992); *Levenstein v. Salafsky*, 164 F.3d 345 (7th Cir. 1997); and *Cristin v. Brennan*, 281 F.3d 404 (3rd Cir. 2002).

4. Scholars have noted such shifts. See, for example, Jeremy Rabkin, *Judicial Compulsions: How Public Law Distorts Public Policy* (New York: Basic Books, 1989); Christopher F. Edley, Jr., *Administrative Law: Rethinking Judicial Control of Bureaucracy* (New Haven: Yale University Press, 1990); Pierce, *Administrative Law Treatise*, 4th ed., vol. 2, chap. 9; and William N. Eskridge, Jr., Philip P. Frickey, and Elizabeth Garrett, *Legislation and Statutory Interpretation* (New York: Foundation Press, 2000), pp. 175–181.

5. The court decision is not given an F.3d cite because it is not an officially published opinion and, therefore, does not set binding precedent. To say the least, "unpublished, published" judicial decisions are very controversial, with some legal scholars and judges even claiming that they are unconstitutional. In fact, recently Chief Judge Richard Arnold ruled in *Anastasoff v. United States*, 223 F.3d 898 (2000), that circuit court rules prohibiting citations constituted an unconstitutional encroachment on Article III judicial powers. Some legal scholars also argue that no-citation rules violate the constitutional rights of litigants. I agree and add that the fact is that unpublished opinions are published anyway by Westlaw and Lexis-Nexis and are at least consulted for legal guidance. But how fair is it to litigants in ongoing cases to say that our unpublished decisions are binding for that case yet cannot be cited for legal argument in your case? This sounds like what Mr. K. experienced in Franz Kakfa's *The Trial*. For a scholarly article on the unconstitutional nature of unpublished, no-citation opinions, see Lance A. Wade, "Honda Meets Anastasoff: The Procedural Due Process Argument Against Prohibiting Citation to Unpublished Judicial Decisions," *Boston College Law Review* 42 (May 2001).

6. The obsession with the cost-conscious approach is epitomized by cost-benefit analysis, which became very "popular" during the Reagan presidency. See Christopher M Heiman et al., "Project: The Impact of Cost-Benefit Analysis on Federal Administrative Law," *Administrative Law Review* 42 (fall 1990).

7. Todd D. Rakoff, "*Brock v. Roadway Express* and the New Law of the Regulatory Due Process," *The Supreme Court Review* 4 (1987).

8. Ibid.

9. For an analysis of risk standards in administrative law, see Frank B. Cross, Daniel M. Byrd III, and Lester B. Lave, "Discernible Risk—A Proposed Standard for Significant Risk in Carcinogen Regulation," *Administrative Law Review* 43 (winter 1991).

10. David H. Rosenbloom, *Building a Legislation-Centered Public Administration* (Tuscaloosa: University of Alabama Press, 2000), chaps. 1 and 2.

11. Victor A. Thompson, *Bureaucracy and the Modern World* (Morristown, N.J.: General Learning Press, 1976), p. 114.

12. Ibid.

13. Ibid., pp. 114–115.

14. Ernest Gellhorn and Ronald M. Levin, *Administrative Law and Process in a Nutshell,* 3rd ed. (St. Paul: West, 1990), p. 270.

15. Lloyd Musolf, "Administrative Law Judges: A 1948 Snapshot," *Administrative Law Review* 46 (summer 1994): 265. For an updated study, see Charles H. Koch, Jr., "Administrative Presiding Officials Today," *Administrative Law Review* 46 (summer 1994).

16. Norman Abrams, "Administrative Law Judge Systems: The California View," *Administrative Law Review* 2 (fall 1977): 490–492. Non-ALJs, or administrative judges (AJs), also preside over agency hearings. Although ALJs must hold law degrees, AJs may not have them yet may be technical experts (e.g., physicists adjudicating a Nuclear Regulatory Commission case). Theoretically, AJs are supposed to be used in "less serious" adjudications (e.g., when basic liberties or severe penalties are not at stake), yet this is not always true in practice. For a review of the use of ALJs and AJs today, see Judith Resnik, "'Uncle Sam Modernized His Justice': Inventing the Federal District Courts of the Twentieth Century for the District of Columbia and the Nation," *Georgetown Law Review* 90 (March 2002).

17. Kenneth C. Davis, *Administrative Law Treatise,* 2nd ed. (St. Paul: West, 1980), vol. 3, pp. 325–327.

18. Eleanor M. Fox, "Chairman Miller, the Federal Trade Commission, Economics, and *Rashomon,*" *Law and Contemporary Problems* 50 (autumn 1987): 35.

19. Ibid.

20. Ibid., p. 34.

21. Ibid., pp. 34–35.

22. Bernard Schwartz, *Administrative Law: A Casebook* (Boston: Little, Brown, 1988), p. 510.

23. Abrams, "Administrative Law Judge Systems," p. 491.

24. For a comprehensive review of the independence question and other issues pertaining to the role and performance of ALJs, see Jeffrey S. Lubbers, "The Federal Administrative Judiciary: Establishing an Appropriate System of Performance Evaluation for ALJs," *Administrative Law Journal of the American University* 7 (fall–winter 1994).

25. See note 5.

26. For a solid discussion of the appearance-of-fairness doctrine, see Van Noy, "The Appearance of Fairness Doctrine: A Conflict in Values," *Washington Law Review* 61 (1986).

27. Also see *Grant v. Shalada,* 989 F.2d 1332, 1345 (1993), in which the court stressed that all tribunals "must be unbiased but also must avoid even the appearance of bias." For a critique of *Grant,* see Bernard Schwartz, "Administrative Law Cases During 1993," *Administrative Law Review* 46 (summer 1994). For a thorough analysis of this case, see Edward McGonagle, "Administrative Law," *Syracuse Law Review* 42 (1991).

28. Stephen Hobbs, "Judicial Discipline and Due Process in Washington State," *Washington Law Review* 63 (1988): 732–737.

29. Stephen R. Miller and Larry T. Richardson, "A Central Panel System for Mississippi's Administrative Law Judges: Promoting the Due Process of Law in Administrative Hearings," *Mississippi College Law Review* 6 (spring 1986): 133.

30. Ibid.

31. Hobbs, "Judicial Discipline and Due Process," p. 737.

32. Joseph E. Edwards, "Disqualification of Federal Trade Commission or Members Thereof," *American Law Reports* 8 (1991).

33. Michael H. Graham, "The Case for Model Rules of Evidence in Administrative Adjudications," *Federal Bar News and Journal* 38 (May 1991): 189.

34. Ibid.

35. Ibid.

36. Richard J. Pierce, Jr., "Use of the Federal Rules of Evidence in Federal Agency Adjudications," *Administrative Law Review* 39 (winter 1987): 2–3.

37. Ibid.

38. Pierce, *Administrative Law Treatise*, 4th ed., p. 707.

39. Davis, *Administrative Law and Government*, p. 192.

40. *Altenheim German Home v. Turnock*, 902 F.2d 582, 584 (7th Cir. 1990).

41. Bernard Schwartz, "Administrative Law Cases During 1990," *Administrative Law Review* 43 (summer 1991): 481.

42. Schwartz, *Administrative Law: A Casebook*, p. 553.

43. *Hearsay* represents the modern grammatical construction of the eleventh-century old English expression "saying-hear" and the twelfth century's version, "heard saying." "Hear-saying" was noted by the year 1340, and the term *hearsay* had come into use in the practice of law by the sixteenth century. By the close of the seventeenth century, rules governing hearsay had become firmly established in English law. See Dennis Murphy, "Hearsay: The Least Understood Exclusionary Rule," *Journal of Criminal Justice* 17 (1989).

44. Ibid., p. 269. Because of all the exceptions to the hearsay rule and the controversy pertaining to its use, Eleanor Swift in "Abolishing the Hearsay Rule," *California Law Review* 75 (1987), discusses the consequences of abolishing the hearsay rule. She concludes that we should consider further the many assumptions and values associated with the hearsay rule before thinking of abandoning it.

45. Thomas R. Mulroy, Jr., and Douglas G. McClure, "The Case for Allowing Hearsay in Illinois Administrative Proceedings," *Illinois Bar Journal* (June 1989): 556.

46. It is not uncommon for courts to maintain that reliable documents such as medical reports are only technically hearsay but, for all practical purposes, should be considered substantial evidence because of their high quality and probative value. For example, the Supreme Court in *Richardson v. Perales*, 402 U.S. 406, 407–408 (1971), noted that "although the reports are hearsay in the technical sense, because their content is not produced live before the hearing examiner, we feel" that such evidence can constitute "substantial evidence" because of its "reliability and probative value."

47. Davis, *Administrative Law Treatise*, 2nd ed., vol. 3, p. 242.

48. Bernard Schwartz, *Administrative Law*, 3rd ed. (Boston: Little, Brown, 1991), p. 377.

49. Charles Fried, "Comment: Five to Four: Reflections on the School Voucher Case," *Harvard Law Review* 116 (November 2002), p. 189.

50. Lars Noah, "Civil Jury Nullification," *Iowa Law Review* 86 (August 2001): n. 41.

51. For a lengthy discussion of the exclusionary rule in administrative law, see Scott Meacham, "Evidence: The Exclusionary Rule in Civil Administrative Hearings: *Turner v. City of Lawton*," *Oklahoma Law Review* 40 (1987).

52. Pierce, *Administrative Law Treatise*, 4th ed., pp. 715–716.

53. *Powell v. Alabama*, 287 U.S. 45, 68–69 (1932).

54. A parole revocation seems to many people to be a criminal law matter, not an administrative one, but it is administrative because it involves the question of what to do administratively about a person's prison sentence after that individual has been convicted in a criminal court. Questions concerning the granting or revoking of parole are handled by an administrative tribunal, usually called a parole board.

55. Tucker, *Administrative Law, Regulation of Enterprise, and Individual Liberties*, p. 127.

56. For a review of legal representation at the SSA, see William Justin DeLeonardis, "Representing Your Client at the Social Security Disability Hearing," *Washington State Bar News*, October 1987, pp. 21–23; Joyce Krutick, "Managed Care Grievance Procedures: The Dilemma and the Cure," *Journal of the National Association of Administrative Law Judges* 21 (fall 2001).

57. Henry J. Friendly, "Some Kind of Hearing," *University of Pennsylvania Law Review* 123 (June 1975): 1289.

58. Ibid., p. 1288.

59. Ibid., pp. 1290–1291.

60. Ibid., p. 1290.

61. William D. Popkin, "Effect of Representation on a Claimant's Success Rate—Three Study Designs," *Administrative Law Review* 31 (fall 1979): 451.

62. Ibid., p. 451.

63. In *Woodby v. INS*, 385 U.S. 276 (1966), the Supreme Court reviewed standards of proof but did not discuss how the standards actually differed.

64. Despite exceptions to the preponderance-of-the-evidence standard, the courts are very reluctant to require a higher standard of proof than the federal APA or state APAs minimally require.

65. Louis J. Jaffe, "Administrative Procedure Re-examined: The Benjamin Report," *Harvard Law Review* 54 (March 1943): 732.

66. For a review of this debate, see Stephen G. Breyer and Richard B. Stewart, *Administrative Law and Regulatory Policy*, 2nd ed. (Boston: Little, Brown, 1985), pp. 625–633.

67. *FCC v. Nat'l. Citizens Commission*, 98 S.Ct. 2096 (1978).

68. *Baltimore & O.R. Co. V. Aberdeen & R.R. Co.*, 303 U.S. 87, 91–92 (1986); and *Carson v. Department of Employment Security*, 376 A.2d 355 (Vt. 1977).

69. For an in-depth review of the politicization of Medicare adjudications, see Eleanor D. Kenney, "In Search of Bureaucratic Justice—Adjudicating Medicare Home Health Benefits in the 1980s," *Administrative Law Review* 42 (spring 1990).

CHAPTER 8

Administering Public Policies

Discretionary Agency Actions

It has been stressed in this book that administrative agencies—much to the dismay of those who endorse a clear separation of powers in government—have legislative, judicial, and administrative powers. We have just concluded a discussion of agency adjudication functions, while Chapters 5 and 6 examine rulemaking. In this chapter emphasis is on administrators in their traditional role as administrators of congressionally sanctioned public policies. Here we want to describe and assess the policy implementation powers of agency officials, especially in light of their broad discretionary authority. Because of the major role administrative discretion plays in administrative law, virtually the entire chapter is devoted to discussing the use and misuse of discretionary power, with special attention paid to how sound discretionary actions can be promoted and abuses of discretion can be minimized.

FORMAL VERSUS
INFORMAL AGENCY ACTIONS

Public administrators can follow either relatively formal or informal procedures. Of course, agency actions are not either wholly formal or informal, but a mixture of the two. That is, formal action would consist of decisionmaking processes based solely on the book, in which detailed steps are followed when arriving at decisions. However, since the Administrative Procedure Act or other acts or rules always allow administrators some freedom of choice (discretion) when making decisions, even under the most formalized or structural decisionmaking situations, complete adherence to formal procedures becomes both impossible and undesirable.

Actually, only about 10 percent of all administrative action can be properly classified as formal.[1] A formal agency action normally consists of those actions by administrators that fall well within prescribed (usually written) procedures, as dictated by legislative statutes, court rulings, and/or agency rules and regulations. Formal administrative action, as contrasted to informal administrative action, is characterized by the limited role an administrator's discretion can play in determining what procedures can be followed and what decisions can be reached as the result of following specified procedures. The clearest example of formal agency behavior can be seen when agencies make orders through the holding of formal hearings, which are similar to trial proceedings. Agency rulemaking can also be quite formal if administrators follow the elaborate provisions for making rules as required in Sections 556 and 557 of the APA, discussed previously. Generally speaking, *informal action* refers to any administrative action or inaction (for example, a decision not to act) that does not use a trial-like hearing. Formal rulemaking requires a trial-like hearing and is governed by Sections 556 and 557 of the APA, while informal rulemaking, which does not require a formal hearing, is governed by Section 553 or not by the APA at all. Likewise, adjudications that require a formal trial-like evidentiary hearing are considered formal, while adjudications that occur without a trial-like a hearing are considered informal.

As an academic exercise, it would be futile to try to classify all administrative actions into neat categories as either formal or informal, because in practice administrators interchange formal and informal procedures. For example, hearings range from the very informal to the very formal. But at what exact point does formality begin and informality end? That is, at what precise point does an administrative hearing become formal enough to be considered trial-like? When some traits of a trial are present, yet others are not, it becomes quite difficult to judge just how formal or trial-like the administrative hearing is.

As noted, informal administrative actions are characterized by a broader use of administrative discretion than are formal administrative activities. As the formal-informal agency action continuum in Figure 8.1 illustrates, the more agency actions are controlled by administrative discretion, the more informal the agency action is. Conversely, the more formal the procedural codes (statutes, rules, court orders) that dictate agency actions, the more formal the agency action is considered to be. Of course, agency actions would never, in practice, be completely controlled by formal procedural codes or totally dominated by an administrator's discretion. The extreme ends in the continuum represent only theoretical extremes. Although at times one may not perceive any evidence that an administrator's discretionary decisions are being modified by prevailing legal sanctions, in reality administrators—at least the sane ones—are always cognizant of the need to give in somewhat to environmental pressures to conform to expected patterns of behavior. Systems theory conveys the point that it would be unrealistic to think that administrators could expect to survive in office for long by totally ignoring all prevailing legal and professional sanctions when employing their discretionary powers. An appropriate response to systemic demands would entail keeping the use of discretion within at least minimally tolerable bounds. But this is not to suggest that administrative discretion is not abused. In fact, much of this chapter studies abuses of discretion and methods for controlling them. However, it is maintained that the vast majority of discretionary acts by our public administrators are reasonable, because they are guided by numerous legal, ethical, and professional standards of conduct forced upon them by the system in which they function. Even when reviewing court cases involving the use of discretion, one finds most allegations of discretionary abuse rest on technical legal arguments.

DEFINING ADMINISTRATIVE DISCRETION

Discretionary actions by administrators are informal administrative acts, even though they may be within an administrator's formal authority. According to Kenneth C. Davis, the most authoritative source on the concept of administrative discretion, a public administrator "has discretion whenever the effective limits on his power leave him free to make a choice among possible courses of action or inaction."[2] To Davis, it is important to stress, as is implied above, that "discretion is not limited to what is authorized or what is legal but includes all that is within 'the *effective* limits' on the officer's power."[3] Davis adds that the specific phraseology he employs to describe discretion "is necessary because a good deal of discretion is illegal or of questionable legality."[4]

Davis holds that the lifeblood of the administrative process "is informal discretionary action."[5] Further, he emphasizes that informal discretionary power is enormous, especially when compared to an administrator's quite limited formal powers.[6] Scholars have noted that, although vague and general statutes give rise to discretionary power, these statutes do not effectively control or limit discretion. Consequently, all willful administrators can use their discretionary authority to make themselves far more powerful than their creators, the Constitutional framers and legislators, probably originally intended.[7]

When examining the breadth of informal discretionary power, it is easy to understand why it is considered to be the lifeblood of the administrative process. Informal discretionary powers include such positive functions as "initiating, prosecuting, negotiating, settling, contracting, dealing, advising, threatening, publicizing, concealing, planning, recommending and supervising."[8] But the most awesome discretionary power is the "omnipresent power to do nothing."[9] That is, administrators may simply decide not to initiate, prosecute, negotiate, settle, contract, deal, and so on. These negative discretionary powers in practice provide administrators with more discretionary clout than positive discretionary powers, because it is far more difficult to check the former than the latter. That is, action, simply because it is action, is more easy to control than inaction, since checks are designed mostly to cope with abusive action, not abusive inaction.

For those of us interested in the problems of implementing public policies, the above has obvious implications. Through failing to act, or acting very feebly, administrators can use their discretionary powers to help ensure the failure of cer-

FIGURE 8.1   Discretion in Formal-Informal Agency Actions

tain duly authorized public programs under their jurisdiction that they disfavor. Although Section 706(1) of the APA prohibits abuses of discretion and the courts have ruled that administrators are not free to use their discretionary authority to block the implementation of programs authorized by Congress, or to prevent persons from receiving their statutory entitlements, strong-willed administrators may nevertheless have their way in most instances, especially since forcing administrators to comply with statutory demands through court action is so difficult.[10] As Davis and Pierce, Jr. conclude: "Judicial review of agency action can never be more than a partial solution to the problem of discretion.[11] Federal agencies take millions of actions every year. . . . It is unrealistic to expect courts to identify or to deter each of the occasional cases in which agencies abuse their discretion."[12] Making matters worse, Pierce adds, from 1989 into the early 2000s the Supreme Court has handed down a series of decisions that have greatly weakened the presumption of reviewability of discretionary agency actions.[13] Besides, and if review is given, courts work too slowly, frequently acting after the damage has been done (after the administrator has achieved his or her purpose).

When we think of the discretionary power of administrators, we probably think in terms of how administrative officials may employ their broad discretion to say yes or no to certain major program proposals. For example, in Chapter 4, in *D.C. Federation of Civic Associations v. Volpe,* 459 F.2d 1231 (1971), we reviewed a situation where John Volpe, then secretary of transportation, used his discretion to approve construction of the Three Sisters Bridge, a very controversial project vehemently opposed by many civic associations and environmentalists. Although Volpe's decision essentially constituted an abuse of discretion in the eyes of Judge Bazelon, the *Volpe* case served, inter alia, to demonstrate the vast discretionary powers administrators possess to make final decisions, thus very likely determining the fate of major public programs. It is true that administrators possess great discretionary powers in making final decisions, but Davis holds that an administrator's interim decisions may actually carry more weight than his or her final decisions.[14] Interim actions may be more subtle, but they can nevertheless make or break programs. In essence, interim decisions determine what steps, if any, should be taken to reach some end. Of course, an administrator's interim decisions play a significant role in determining the possible ends that will result. Typically, agency administrators use their discretion to make interim decisions in response to such key questions as: "Shall we investigate the X Company? Shall we institute an investigation proceeding? Shall we make it a prosecutory proceeding? Or shall we make it somewhat one and somewhat the other, allowing its nature to change as it progresses? Shall we give X a chance to escape by agreeing to comply? Or shall we make an example of X? Shall we start a cease-and-desist order proceeding, or shall we recommend a criminal prosecution to the Department of Justice?"[15]

Such interim questions appear to be endless; yet how each question is answered may make a big difference to, say, company X: "X may be vitally affected at every step. Even if it is found guilty of nothing the investigation may cost half a million. Or its license worth millions may be jeopardized. Adverse publicity may cripple its business."[16] Discretionary interim decisionmaking may also play a critical role in determining the fate of public policies. In *Implementation,* Jeffrey Pressman and Aaron Wildavsky held that success in implementing public policy programs depends heavily upon whether administrators make the vital discretionary interim decisions that permit programs to pass the crucial "clearance points" necessary for program survival.[17] In sum, dramatic final actions by public agencies may make front-page news headlines ("Fed hikes interest rates against Bush's wishes"), but the daily, routine, nonnewsworthy interim decisions (Fed decides to discount Labor Department's projection on unemployment) are largely responsible for preventing such agency headline stories from ever occurring.

Thus far, administrative discretion has been defined in the context of substantive decisionmaking, but the scope of informal discretion extends much further. Says Davis: "Discretion is not limited to substantive choices but extends to procedures, methods, forms, timing, degrees of emphasis, and many other subsidiary factors."[18] Actually, because administrative law focuses on procedure, administrative law scholars and the courts are not so much interested in what substantive choices were made, but in how discretion was used by administrators in making their choices. Figure 8.2 illustrates how an administrator can ideally exercise his or her discretion in resolving an administrative problem. The simple model conveys the idea that to resolve an administrative problem, an administrator would first have to employ discretion to discover the relevant facts and then use discretion to search for those applicable laws, rules, and so on that would settle the matter. But this ideal conceptualization is grossly complicated in reality. In the real world, administrators may use their discretionary powers to deny that a problem even exists. This action in itself must be regarded as a powerful exercise of discretion.

But even if an administrator acknowledges the existence of the problem, discretion may be exercised to define it in a particular way. Naturally, the discretion to define the problem in various ways provides administrators with the flexibility to arrive at different possible solutions. In addition, administrators can use their discretion to determine what facts are relevant and what laws, rules, and so on, are pertinent. Of course, the discretion to include and exclude facts that are perceived as relevant or irrelevant allows administrators the opportunity to apply or not apply various laws, rules, and so on, since the facts of a situation obviously determine what laws and rules should be applied. Discretionary decisions are also clouded by administrators' past experiences, present environmental circumstances and pressures, politics, and personal values. Regarding police discretion, Joel Samaha comments: "Discretion creates an enormous gap between what law books say and what law officers actually do, because class, race, economics, and politics influence discretion."[19] Uncertainty also plays an intervening role: "A decision as to what is desirable may include not only weighing desirability but also guessing about unknown facts and making a judgment about doubtful law, and the mind that makes the decision does not necessarily separate facts, law, and discretion. Furthermore, the term "discretion" may or may not include the judgment that goes into finding facts from conflicting evidence and into interpreting unclear law; the usage is divided."[20] In sum, discretionary decisions are very complicated informal administrative actions that involve factors and processes which are extremely difficult to pinpoint and assess. It is partly for these reasons that abuses of administrative discretion are very hard to prove in court.[21]

A HISTORICAL GLANCE AT DISCRETION: THE RULE OF LAW VERSUS DISCRETIONARY POWER

In an enlightening article entitled "Some Reflections on the Anglo-Saxon Heritage of Discretionary Justice," Joel Samaha asserts that the history of discretion is important to examine because the "discretion/law controversy extends back at least as far as 600 A.D."[22] But more important than the duration of the discretion/law dispute, Samaha contends, is the fact that the arguments for and against the use of discretion versus the strict adherence to law, as well as proposed solutions to the discretionary justice problem, have remained practically unchanged. Through the centuries the discretionary justice problem, he notes, has been to balance the need to ensure equality under law through the consistent and objective application of the laws with the need to make the law sensitive to individual cases.

In studying the use of discretion in Anglo-Saxon history, one must stress that discretion has always somewhat challenged the determined efforts by heads of state to make Anglo-Saxon justice based on the rule of law: "Discretion," Samaha has observed "has always been at war with law in Anglo-American history."[23] That is, while rule-of-law government has been associated with the fair and consistent administration of justice in constitutional democracies, the use of discretion in government has traditionally been identified with the unfair, arbitrary, and capricious decisions of absolute leaders in dictatorial systems. Our Anglo-Saxon disdain for the use of discretion may be epitomized best on the Department of Justice building, where a conspicuous engraving reads: "Where Law Ends Tyranny Begins."

FIGURE 8.2   Ideal Exercise of Discretion

But why can we not escape the use of discretion? Is it even desirable to try to abandon our reliance on discretion? Does the engraving on the Justice Department's building represent an overreaction to the possible dangers of discretionary justice? Samaha argues that history has clearly shown that we cannot help but employ discretion, and moreover, that there are sound reasons for incorporating discretion into any governmental system. Even though Samaha notes that the law/discretion controversy dates back to at least 600 A.D., the truth is that the classical Greeks, in the days of Plato and Aristotle, around 400 B.C., recognized the need for discretion to aid administrators in the application of written laws. In a nutshell, it was argued that discretion, although the specific word was not used, gave laws the necessary flexibility to make them viable.[24]

The administration of the Christian penitentials is especially helpful in describing the role of discretion in any system based upon laws. In order to control personal conduct in a manner acceptable to Christian moral principles, a set of books was developed that assigned specific penances for particular sins; these were the *penitentials.* The hope of the Church was that this penitential system could function to minimize the use of discretion by local priests held responsible for enforcing church law (moral codes). However, the priests soon found, as do all who administer regulations of some nature, that a strict adherence to the rules creates many injustices. Exceptions must be made, and the making of exceptions calls for discretion.

Samaha reports that the "combination of severity, disparity, and the individualization of sentences all led to the exercise of discretion in the administration of penance."[25] The harshness of the penalties for sins caused priests to mitigate the penalties, especially for those who could not physically endure the required punishments. Priests also had to exercise discretion to resolve the many apparent contradictions in the books of penitentials. Finally, priests believed that special circumstances should be taken into consideration when evaluating the severity of the sin: "It is to the sinner and not the sin that the priest must look if he is to save a soul and restore a sinner to the congregation. Here arose the great problems posed by tailoring the penalty to suit the offender."[26]

Samaha maintains that the discretionary problems that faced these priests 1,000 years ago were really eerily similar to the discretionary predicaments that plague decision makers in modern times.[27] Do not our regulatory administrators employ discretion when they decide not to impose penalties on, say, companies that have violated their standards, especially if they feel that the companies could not survive the financial strain? In light of the numerous contradictions in various statutes and rules, does not administrative discretion seem essential to keep administrative operations running smoothly? When imposing penalties, or in administration in general, is discretion not used at times by administrators to fit the regulatory action to individual circumstances? In reviewing agency actions, have not the courts acknowledged in numerous opinions over the years how vital the role of administrative discretion is to the stability of normal administrative operations?

Samaha concludes that even the priests' exercise of discretion was attacked for essentially the same general reasons that modern users of discretion are criticized. For instance, priests were charged with abusing their discretionary powers to (1) favor special interests, (2) promote their own personal welfare, and (3) indirectly encourage an increase in violations in society through their arbitrary, capricious, and frequently corrupt administration of the rules and standards.[28] Samaha observed that "the corrupting influence of the wide powers of discretion held by the Anglo-Saxon priests is mirrored in the wholesale assault on the sentencing powers of modern-day judges."[29]

This brief historical view of the use of discretion in the past serves to make the simple point that the exercise of discretion, although absolutely necessary, has always presented a problem for societies, especially those that find rule-of-law principles laudable. To preserve due process under law, many societies have tried to limit the abuses of discretionary power. For example, Bishop Ebo, recognizing that the local priests had to exercise broad discretion in applying the confusing and contradictory books of penitentials, believed that the discretionary justice problem could be resolved by "giving priests proper guidelines to follow so that they would not be left to their own devices in prescribing penance. Specifically, he recommended controlling discretion by rule."[30]

KENNETH C. DAVIS
ON THE PROBLEM OF DISCRETION

No informed student of administrative law could credibly argue that Davis is not the most authoritative source on the subject of discretionary justice. Since the late 1960s, Davis has written three books on the discretionary justice theme: *Discretionary Justice: A Preliminary Inquiry, Discretionary Justice in Europe and America,* and *Police Discretion.* He has also devoted considerable space to the topic in other works, most notably his comprehensive *Administrative Law Treatise.*[31] Because his ideas on discretion have, by his own admission, changed somewhat over the years, various writings of his are consulted so that an accurate and updated review of his thinking on the subject can be presented.[32]

Davis did not decide to devote so much attention to the discretionary justice problem merely for the fun of it. Davis is convinced that the discretionary justice issue poses the most serious threat to individual procedural due process rights. Ten years after his publication of *Discretionary Justice,* a book written to inspire needed research efforts in the areas of discretionary justice, he noted that "the dismal fact is that . . . no major work has attempted either to build on that foundation or to create a new foundation on which to build."[33] Consequently, he still held in his last major work, published in 1994, as emphatically as he did when he wrote *Discretionary Justice* in 1969, that the greatest discretionary injustices are inflicted against individual parties by administrators who abuse their discretionary power when handling these cases. He stresses that "unlimited agency discretion is subject to potential abuse in the form of different treatment of like cases based on impermissible motives or as a consequence of poor institution management or design."[34]

Why does the use of informal discretionary administrative action present such a serious threat to individual liberty? Before responding directly to this question, it is necessary to stress that Davis perceives discretionary justice actions by agency administrators in terms of their impact on individual parties (for example, individuals eligible for welfare, individual associations, and corporations). Public policy–making decisions are excluded from his analysis of discretionary justice because, although they involve discretionary acts (e.g., to deregulate or not to deregulate the airlines), they do not involve discretionary justice decisions, since the decisions are aimed at a larger group (the airline industry) and not a specific party (e.g., Delta Airlines). That is, when a bureaucrat says something is just a matter of policy to a person making an inquiry, the bureaucrat is implying that legislators and agency rulemakers set general policy. The discretionary decisions made to form such policies do not involve discretionary justice. However, in most cases when these general public policies are applied to individual cases, discretionary justice decisions are involved.

Davis thinks several reasons can be given to justify the particularly alarming nature of the discretionary justice problem. Of course, the chief reason is that administrators can easily abuse their discretionary powers when applying general public policies to individual cases. But what makes this problem severe is that the opportunity for discretionary abuses is enormous because, as noted before, about 90 percent of all agency action involves informal agency action (action in the absence of trial-like procedures). Of the 90 percent of agency action that is informal, Davis holds that about 99 percent of it involves the use of discretion. If this discretionary activity were controlled, the discretionary justice issue would not attract so much attention as a problem, but the fact is that this informal discretionary action is largely uncontrolled. Therefore, the problem is really not how to eliminate discretion (although Davis argues that unnecessary discretion should be eliminated), but how to control it. The severity of the discretionary justice problem is given more weight by the reality that this largely uncontrolled discretion is also not practically subject to judicial review.[35] Recall an earlier point made by Richard Pierce that the Supreme Court has recently handed down a series of precedential decisions discouraging the federal courts from even reviewing discretionary agency actions—of course, increasing the odds for abuse of discretion by administrators.

But the discretionary justice question continues to remain the number one problem not only in administrative law but also in the quality of justice rendered to individuals by our government, because too many people have a negative attitude toward our human ability to resolve this very challenging legal problem. However, Davis flatly rejects the viewpoint of such a defeatist position. Such negativism, he contends, has retarded research into 90 percent of all administrative behavior.[36] Consequently, research findings in the area of informal and unreviewable discretionary actions, which could provide useful clues on how to better control administrative discretion so that injustices to individuals can be reduced, are virtually nonexistent. Davis admits that many people will find the study of discretionary justice hopeless, thus forcing them to concentrate on the aspects of administrative law that are more concrete and, therefore, easier to study: "That is why the literature of jurisprudence deals with judges and legislators, not with discretion. That is why administrative law literature has been almost entirely limited to rulemaking, formal adjudication, and judicial review, with hardly any effort to penetrate the discretionary jungle."[37]

Although Davis espoused this comment many years ago, today administrative law scholars and practitioners are even more reluctant to "penetrate the discretionary jungle." This is not because discretionary abuses have gone away. The reality is that discretionary abuses have likely increased because, as Pierce recently asserted, public administrators are now functioning during "a period of diminishing agency resources," which means that practical considerations must prevail.[38] Regrettably, this means that few in our legal-political system are willing to invest the intellectual energy, political or judicial capital, or financial resources to control agency discretion, even if the lack of enthusiasm to control discretionary actions leads to an increase in discretionary abuses. Despite these new twenty-first century realities, it is still worth looking at Davis's views on how discretionary behavior can be controlled to better serve our democratic system, even though, unfortunately, his insights seem today like fantasies for bleeding heart due process types.

Democratizing Discretion: Confining, Structuring, and Checking Discretion

Davis sharply disagrees with William Pitt's immortalized wisdom, "Where law ends tyranny begins." Davis exclaims that "in our system of government, where law ends tyranny need not begin. Where law ends, discretion begins, and the exercise of discretion may mean either beneficence or tyranny, either justice or injustice, either reasonableness or arbitrariness."[39] To Davis, the quotation on the front of our nation's justice building, "Where law ends tyranny begins," is a patently absurd insight into the nature of governmental power. He holds correctly that there has never existed in history a government of laws without the exercise of discretionary power by men.[40] Even if we should observe the behavior of those who work within the Department of Justice, in the building on which Pitt's words are engraved, Davis insists that we would quickly discover these governmental employees using discretion to apply laws. We would even find, he continues, that these Justice Department workers would be "much more occupied with discretion than with law. Not one of them who understands his job would agree that where law ends tyranny begins. Every conscientious employee of the Department of Justice, from the Attorney General on down," Davis emphasizes, "is striving to assure that where law ends, wise and beneficent exercise of discretionary power begins."[41]

But what can be done to ensure that discretionary power does not evolve into a tyrannical force? That is, what can be done to democratize the use of discretion? To minimize injustices as a consequence of the misuse of discretionary power, Davis believes, "we should eliminate much unnecessary discretionary power and that we should do much more than we have been doing to confine, to structure, and to check necessary discretionary power." The goal, he maintains, "is not the maximum degree of confining, structuring, and checking; the goal is to find the optimum degree for each power in each set of circumstances."[42] But in holding that administrative discretion should be confined, structured, and checked, what exactly does Davis have in mind?

Confining Discretionary Power.   Davis explains that sometimes discretionary power can be too restricted, while at other times it can be too broad. If administrative discretion is too limited, injustices can result from the lack of special consideration given to an individual's unique situation or problem. But when discretionary power is too broad, inequitable, and arbitrary, decisions tend to create injustices. As a general rule, in the American administrative system, discretion is rather limited at the lower administrative levels, where red tape tends to restrict severely the decisionmaking alternatives of those workers performing relatively routine tasks.[43] But as the administrative functions become more complex and less routine at higher and higher administrative levels, the scope of discretion broadens. Although Davis acknowledges that injustices occur to individuals because discretion may be too confined, he argues that in the American system most injustices occur because the exercise of discretion is much too broad.[44]

Consequently, discretion must be confined. When Davis speaks of confining discretionary power, he is specifically talking about eliminating and limiting its use. Under ideal conditions, he points out, all necessary discretionary power would be confined within specified boundaries; and all unnecessary discretion would lie outside these parameters. Statutes and rules would ideally provide the guidance needed to keep the exercise of discretion absolutely within these confined boundaries, thus preventing administrators from abusing their discretion by stepping beyond their clear scope of legitimate discretionary authority (see Figure 8.3).

However, Davis holds that this ideal is seldom realized, and consequently, injustices result because administrators exceed their reasonable discretionary powers.[45] Unreasonable discretionary actions are not illegal, however, because administrative discretion has not been properly confined by statutes and rules. Parenthetically, it should be made clear that statutes create administrative discretion through their vague rhetoric (standards), although even the most conscien-

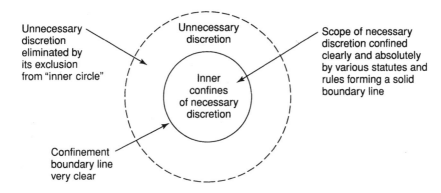

FIGURE 8.3   Ideal Confinement of Necessary Discretion

tious legislators may have a tough time drafting workable statutes (i.e., statutes that do not handcuff administrators) without resorting to nebulous words. In the words of Ernest Freund, written long ago: "A statute confers discretion when it refers an official for the use of his power to beliefs, expectations, or tendencies, instead of facts, or to such terms as 'adequate,' 'advisable,' 'appropriate,' 'beneficial," 'convenient,' 'detrimental,' 'expedient,' 'equitable,' 'fair,' 'fit,' 'necessary,' 'practicable,' 'proper,' 'reasonable,' 'reputable,' 'safe,' 'sufficient,' 'wholesome,' or their opposites."[46] Thus, in the absence of clear statutes and essential rules to guide and confine discretion, unnecessary discretion becomes integrated with necessary discretion, thus opening the door for discretionary abuses (see Figure 8.4). Unless necessary discretion is reasonable, limits of discretion become dangerously confused. Such an atmosphere would not be conducive for promoting fair and consistent discretionary decisionmaking.

Although such critics as Herman Finer, Theodore Lowi, and Richard B. Stewart have seriously questioned the virtues of the legislators' delegating vast discretionary powers to agency administrators through vague statutes,[47] Davis contends that "the chief hope for confining discretionary power does not lie in statutory enactment but in much more extensive administrative rulemaking and legislative bodies need to do more than they have been doing to prod the administrators." In the last clause of this statement, Davis means that legislators need to push administrators into promulgating agency rules that can be used to confine their own discretion. Davis argues that administrators, not legislators, are in the best position to draft rules that are necessary to limit their own discretionary powers, because they know best what specific administrative processes are involved in implementing public policies.[48]

However, for various reasons, administrators are reluctant to promulgate rules that they feel may later tie their hands, especially if they lack confidence in their ability to anticipate the precise consequences of their rules. But such delay in making rules causes vague statutory standards to go unclarified for too long. Davis believes this administrative problem should be and can be corrected: "*The*

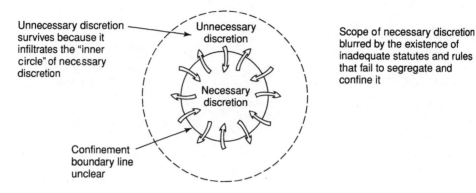

FIGURE 8.4   Actual Lack of Confinement of Necessary Discretion

typical failure in our system that is correctable is not legislative delegation of broad discretionary power with vague standards; it is the procrastination of administrators in resorting to the rulemaking power to replace vagueness with clarity."[49] The best corrective step is to push administrators into using their rulemaking powers earlier and more assiduously so that rules can properly confine discretion.[50]

In Davis's thinking, the administrative rulemaking procedure "is one of the greatest inventions of modern government. It can be, when the agency so desires, a virtual duplicate of legislative committee procedure. More often it is quicker and less expensive."[51] It is also fair, efficient, and democratic, and thus ideally suited for confining administrative discretion, especially when compared to the less democratically sensitive ordermaking process.[52]

Structuring Discretionary Power, Especially Through Openness.   We cannot hope to democratize administrative discretion by simply confining it, although this is an essential initial step. In searching for ways to confine discretionary power, we are basically looking for ways to encapsulate discretion within specified boundaries. This can be accomplished, Davis suggests, "through statutory enactments, through administrative rules, or by avoiding the development of discretionary power beyond the boundaries."[53] However, structuring discretion is aimed toward a different objective. In our attempts to structure discretion, Davis holds, our purpose "is to control the manner of the exercise of discretionary power within the boundaries, and this, too, can be accomplished through statutory enactments, through administrative rules, and by other means."[54] Once again he emphasizes the marvelous attributes of the rulemaking process, noting that rules can be employed to confine discretion as well as to help structure discretionary power (that is, to aid in directing its use within its defined limits). Specifically, according to Davis, structuring discretion involves the tasks of regularizing it, organizing it, and ordering it with the goal in mind of improving discretionary actions toward individual parties so that discretionary justice prevails.[55]

Davis believes that discretionary injustices could be reduced significantly if administrators only cared to take the time to develop viable methods for structuring their discretionary decisions. But just as administrators have been dragging their feet in regard to finding ways to confine their discretionary power, they have also shown great reluctance to take the steps necessary to structure their discretionary actions. Davis perceives most agency decisionmaking as relatively unstructured and, therefore, democratically repulsive. He thinks agency actions tend to violate the canons of democratic government because they are often wantonly inconsistent. Agency decisions tend to be inconsistent, Davis holds, because procedures and standards are applied arbitrarily and capriciously by administrators in reaching decisions from case to case. Employing different methods and criteria allows agency officials to arrive at dramatically different decisions in situations where the facts and circumstances of the cases seem to be quite similar. Unfortunately, this practice tends to make discretionary agency decisions distastefully unreliable.[56]

What compounds the problem for democratic decisionmaking is that the bases for agency decisions are frequently kept secret. For example, in reference to the unstructured manner in which the Internal Revenue Service reaches decisions, Davis points out that the IRS relies on secretive reasons (for example, unpublished rulings) to make decisions that affect the welfare of individual parties. But what is even worse about this "*IRS practice is that it often gives different treatment to two taxpayers who have identical problems, without explanation.*"[57] And further, he notes that the IRS has always held the attitude "that it has no duty either to follow its own unpublished rulings or to explain why it departs from them. Its public position is that unpublished rulings may not be used as precedents."[58] In reality, however, the IRS uses unpublished rulings freely as precedents on which to base future decisions.

The IRS may provide the worst example of inconsistent decisionmaking through its failure to structure its decisionmaking procedures, but the IRS is by no means the only federal agency, or state agency for that matter, that is guilty of employing secretive and nonstandardized procedures to reach inconsistent and, consequently, unpredictable determinations. Such practices are, unfortunately, common throughout the administrative system. The challenging task, then, is to structure agency decisionmaking processes so that similar situations in cases tend to generate similar and expected agency responses. To accomplish this structural goal, Davis recommends that agency discretion should be controlled more by the use of "open plans, open policy statements, open rules, open findings, open reasons, open precedents, and fair informal procedure."[59] He commented that he emphasized the word "open" for an important reason: "Openness is the natural enemy of arbitrariness and a natural ally in the fight against injustice."[60] Davis contends that open procedures should be sought to help structure discretionary power, especially since openness is very consistent with what democratic government demands. However, Davis acknowledges that open methods may sometimes be quite inappropriate for certain governmental tasks, such as decisions involving security secrets or trade secrets. He maintains that openness allows discretionary actions to be placed in the spotlight so that they can stand a better chance of being controlled. How can abuses of discretion be detected and controlled if the reasons justifying discretionary determinations are kept secret?

When agencies have developed policies and rules, Davis argues that it is necessary for the agency administrators to keep us informed by telling us what they are. Publicizing agency policies and rules helps to structure discretionary action simply by keeping open the lines of communication between agency administrators and outsiders, thus allowing healthy and corrective feedback. Also, by placing themselves on public record, administrators would not necessarily commit themselves to certain actions, but they would create for themselves an obligation to follow their publicized courses of action unless they state and publicly justify why they want to change directions. Thus, public disclosure of agency policies and rules would aid in the structuring of discretion by helping to prevent administrators from employing their discretionary power to alter their policies and procedural stands suddenly, secretively, and without sound reasons.[61]

Before formal trial-like hearings agency officials are required by the APA, in reaching decisions, to state systematically their findings of fact and to note in writing their reasoned opinions (why they reached the decisions that they did). But to structure the use of discretion, Davis holds that it would be a good idea to have administrators openly state their findings and reasons in support of their informal discretionary decisions whenever practical. Presently, he asserts, discretionary decisions are too often made without any reasons given for the actions taken.

In introducing Davis's plea for across-the-board openness as a method for controlling possible abuses of discretion, I have presented the fundamental arguments for compelling agencies to follow open precedents. But to reiterate, his chief contention was that consistency can be promoted better if agency officials are obligated to follow established and publicized precedents. Consistency, he maintains, is a highly desirable administrative trait in any government because it tends to reduce arbitrariness, while simultaneously promoting equal treatment under law. Nevertheless, Davis should not be accused of striving for a rigid application of openness in regard to the use of open precedents or any other call for agency openness. The general objective, he asserts, should never be to seek an extravagant application of the rule of law or excessive use of discretion. The goal should be to seek a reasonable balance between the two.[62]

Checking Discretionary Power.   The idea that any form of governmental power should be checked must retain the highest respect in every society that cherishes freedom. But, Davis asserts, the hard reality is that our liberty is threatened by the prevalence of too much administrative discretion that is, for all practical purposes, absolute. Absolute discretionary power, he points out, may not always be employed invidiously, but the potential for evil acts is ever present.[63] He regards such absolute discretionary power as out of character with the principles of democratic government. For Davis, discretionary power is absolute when it is both unchecked and unreviewable: "Absolute discretion means unchecked and unreviewable discretion. When no other authority can reverse the choice made, even if it is arbitrary and unreasonable, discretion is absolute."[64]

The threat absolute discretion poses to our free and democratic system of government is perceived by many others. In *United States v. Wunderlich,* 342 U.S. 98, 101 (1951), Justice William O. Douglas exclaimed: "Law has reached its finest moments when it has freed man from the unlimited discretion of some ruler, some civil or military official, some bureaucrat. Where discretion is absolute, man has always suffered. . . . Absolute discretion . . . is more destructive of freedom than of man's other inventions." In the same year, in *New York v. United States,* 342 U.S. 882, 884 (1951), Douglas wrote: "Absolute discretion, like corruption, marks the beginning of the end of liberty." In an insightful dissenting opinion in *SEC v. Chenery Corp.,* 332 U.S. 194, 215 (1947), Justice Robert Jackson, in direct reference to the need for the Court to keep the administrative leviathan from exercising absolute discretionary powers, argued that the need for administrative discretion cannot "support action outside of the law. And what action is, and what action is not, within the law must be determined by the courts, when authorized to review, no matter how much deference is due to the agency's fact finding. Surely an administrative agency is *not* a law unto itself" (my emphasis). And years later D.C. Circuit judge J. Skelly Wright acknowledged that Davis's concern for the need to check "unchannelled, unreviewable, and untrammelled discretion" is unmistakably legitimate.[65]

Davis holds that the democratic principle of checks and balances is a valuable and practical democratic idea that should be implemented from top to bottom in our governmental system. To him, the principle of check is conceptually simple: "What may be called 'the principle of check' means simply that one officer should check another, as a protection against arbitrariness."[66] He believes that checks are most effective when they are aimed directly at stopping discretionary injustices resulting from arbitrary and illegal administrative behavior. Checks are not very effective when they are indirect, as in de novo review. The problem with de novo review (a new hearing/review) is that it constitutes a fresh or second attempt to check abuses. For this reason de novo review does not check directly. Davis considers de novo review of discretionary action inferior because such review may introduce arbitrariness or illegal actions for the first time. Frequently, these de novo actions are not checked because they are perceived as final agency actions.[67] Therefore, one could say that de novo reviews create only an illusion that misuses of discretionary actions in agencies are ultimately being checked. According to Davis, genuine checks should properly be directed at preventing abuses of discretion in final actions "so that almost all final action is subject to a check for arbitrariness or illegality."[68]

Compared with our very modest successes in confining and structuring discretion, Davis contends, our successes in checking discretion have been much greater, although we must work harder to develop better checks.[69] But how should administrative discretion be checked so that discretionary abuses leading to injustices can be minimized? Davis discusses five methods for checking discretionary power. Discretion can be checked by (1) supervision and review by supervisors, (2) administrative tribunals, (3) legislative committees, (4) ombudsmen, and (5) judicial review of agency action.[70]

A CRITIQUE OF
DAVIS'S DISCRETIONARY JUSTICE

In "Beyond Discretionary Justice," a classic analysis of Davis' *Discretionary Justice*, Judge J. Skelly Wright expressed strong support for Davis's struggle to see to it that administrative discretionary power is appropriately confined, structured, and checked.[71] Wright agrees with Davis that discretion must be controlled if we are to make any significant progress in curbing and eliminating abuses of administrative discretion. Further, Wright acknowledges that Davis has done a brilliant job in placing the American legal system in perspective with the role played by administrative discretion, as well as proposing a tentative scheme for controlling the most outrageous abuses of discretionary power.[72] However, Wright detected serious flaws in Davis' "powerful manifests." Wright's central criticism is simply that Davis's approach is unrealistically and unjustifiably optimistic: "The underlying tone of *Discretionary Justice* is optimistic."[73] He specifically rejects Davis's thinking that "if we have the will to create an effective system of law to guide and channel administrative decisionmaking, then the monster can be tamed."[74]

"The real question," Wright says, "is whether we have the will."[75] He doubts that we do, especially if we are going to rely upon the will of administrators to take the initiative to confine and structure their own discretionary powers. Wright finds Davis surprisingly naive in his belief that administrators will be willing to curtail the use of their own discretionary powers without being forced to do so. This difference in viewpoints between Davis and Wright over possible ways to control behavior represents a classic clash between the perspectives of an idealist and a realist. That is, Davis is essentially arguing that administrators can eventually be relied upon to write their own rules to confine and structure their own discretion, while Wright is asserting that this is utter nonsense since people cannot be expected to surrender their powers voluntarily—in this case, through drafting rules limiting their own discretionary powers.

It is not that Wright does not believe that agency rulemaking cannot help to limit and structure administrative discretion. Clearly, he feels that rulemaking can serve this end. For instance, Wright asserts that Davis is "most convincing when he argues that 'the procedure of administrative rulemaking is . . . one of the greatest inventions of modern government'" and that it can be employed to combat unnecessary and abusive uses of discretion.[76] But Wright deeply disagrees with Davis's main contention that "the chief hope for confining discretionary power' lies in voluntary agency rulemaking."[77] Against this holding by Davis, Wright asserts in typical realistic rhetoric: "If that is true, there may be no hope at all. For the sad fact is that powerful forces are at work which incline agencies toward an ad hoc case-by-case mode of operation. The first of these is simply the bureaucratic imperative of keeping the wheels turning."[78] To keep the wheels turning, administrators generally feel that they need the necessary flexibility in which to function properly. Rules limiting discretion are normally viewed by administrators as irritants that restrict their alternatives. If given the choice, administrators would rather have the freedom to "muddle through" by making ad hoc decisions.[79] In Wright's view, "ad hoc decisions tend to leave the agency freer to change direction at will and allow it to avoid the risks inherent in advance commitments."[80]

Thus, Wright concluded that, given the historical struggle by determined administrators to keep the discretionary powers as broad as possible, "it is unrealistic to suppose that many agencies will dramatically move to confine their own discretion."[81] Emphasizing that "it would be foolish to rely too heavily on voluntary conversion," because, in the final analysis, that is an "unrealizable ideal," he argues that, fortunately, there are more feasible methods that can be employed to make the control of administrative discretion a realizable goal.[82] Wright's solution is rooted in force, however, and not in the blind faith that administrators will be their own reformers. To think that reform can come from within appears ridiculous to Wright. Specifically, he holds that administrators can write their own rules to curb their discretionary power, but only if they are compelled to do so by Congress and the courts, although he believes that the courts must lead the way. In capsular fashion, he notes:

> But while all branches of government must join in the fight to limit discretion, I believe it is the courts which will have to bear the primary burden. Not only must the courts, on occasion, formulate rules of their own which will limit discretion. They must also resuscitate the legal principles which will force sometimes reluctant congressmen and administrators to take action. The courts cannot bear the burden alone; they are not equipped to act as super-administrators, formulating individual rules to govern the thousands of cases heard daily by agencies. But they can reestablish the doctrines which were designed to compel or encourage other branches of government to assume their parts of the task.[83]

Wright further holds that

> more and more legislators have come to realize that the so called 'expertise' of the executive branch is in reality no more than a cloak which hides the raw exercise of untrammeled power. Whereas once it was believed that administrative 'experts' could magically provide a 'scientific' solution to public policy problems, many congressmen now realize that most questions of policy are questions of values, and that the people must determine for themselves the values which they favor. In time, the movement for greater balance between the legislature and the executive promises to bring about the first substantial reallocation of power in almost two generations.[84]

Wright now seems to have been idealistic himself. Since the writing of this article in 1972, Congress has shown some modest, but not unusual, efforts to reinvigorate its controls over the administrative machinery, but with extremely limited success. Most experts, as was pointed out previously in Chapters 1 and 2, argue that given the established and increasing powers of the administrative branch, it would be exceedingly difficult for Congress to successfully reassert the powers they have surrendered to administrators for nearly two hundred years, but especially since the 1930s. Although contempt for technocracy in the 1960s and 1970s led to a call for more control over the discretion of agency experts and an emphasis on participatory, pluralistic, democratic agency decisionmaking, a demand for greater cost-effective administrative efficiency since the early 1980s into the twenty-first century has caused technocrats in public agencies to command new respect, resulting in increased deference to "technocratic discretion" by the legislators and judges.

In any event, Wright maintains that Congress can confine and structure administrative discretion "by reassuming its rightful role as the architect of fundamental administrative policy."[85] Wright means here that Congress should not delegate authority to administrators without attaching standards sufficient to guide agency actions. Although most scholars, including Davis, have pronounced the delegation doctrine dead, Wright believes that the delegation doctrine can still be used as an effective weapon in controlling administrative discretion. In Wright's thinking, by accepting the demise of the delegation doctrine, we are also accepting Congress's unconstitutional right "to vote itself out of business."[86] Unquestionably, he contends, there simply must be limitations placed upon how far Congress can go in transferring its constitutional powers to administrators in the absence of instructions on how these powers can be exercised.[87]

Wright attacks Davis's line of reasoning that the delegation doctrine should be rejected as a method for confining and structuring discretion because it is impractical. We should not accept Davis's position that the delegation doctrine is an impractical weapon in combating discretionary abuses, because, Wright urges, Davis interprets the history of the doctrine to mean that "the legislature either cannot or will not impose meaningful standards on administrative discretion."[88] Wright thinks that "the delegation doctrine retains an important potential as a check on the exercise of unbounded, standardless discretion by administrative agencies."[89]

Even though Davis seeks to confine and structure administrative discretion in a manner more consistent with democratic principles, Wright maintains that Davis's proposed solutions are not so democratic. Consistent with his defense of the constitutional soundness of the delegation doctrine, Wright asserts essentially that it is not in the long-range interests of democracy to argue that administrators should be permitted to make fundamental policy decisions simply because legislators themselves seem unable to set clear policy courses: "An argument for letting the experts decide when the people's representatives are uncertain or cannot agree is an argument for paternalism and against democracy."[90]

Moreover, Wright points out that support for delegating broad powers to administrators is based on the erroneous assumption that conflict over policies can be avoided if policy problems are passed on to administrators. But how can throwing a policy mess into the laps of administrators resolve any problems? He emphasizes that such action can lead only to two unfortunate results: "On the one hand, if the problem is really intractable, it is unlikely that the agency, with all its expertise, will do any better with it than Congress. Indeed, if there is political opposition to any contemplated action, the agency may actually be more vulnerable than Congress."[91] This can only cause an agency to keep blundering along without any real direction or purpose, using discretion in a haphazard way.[92]

Agency actions can be given direction if Congress cares to take the time to perform its constitutional duty by attaching prospective guidelines and standards when delegating powers to administrators. And rulemaking, Wright maintains, can still serve a crucial function in controlling discretionary power, but we should not expect administrators to confine and structure their own discretion. Congress and the courts must force administrators to draft those rules that will help to curtail discretionary abuses. Wright thinks rules, as Davis suggests, can serve to structure discretion by making the intentions of administrators clear to the public. Rules shall be employed in an open political system to give individual parties "fair warning" regarding agency policies and procedures. Wright acknowledges that the purpose of a democratic regulatory system "is presumably to bring primary conduct into conformance with agreed upon social norms. Yet a system operating without rules cannot possibly achieve this goal, since the people being regulated are not informed of what the societal norms are."[93] In the end, the use of discretion in any governmental regulatory operations will inevitably be irrational and arbitrary. Yet the sad reality is, he admits in support of Davis, that we have failed to make our administrators live by rules which force them to exercise their discretionary powers within a due process framework."[94]

While Davis plays down the role the courts can play in helping to confine, structure, and check discretion, Wright, as mentioned, feels that the courts must assume primary responsibility for forcing administrators to limit the application of administrative discretion: "The courts should control discretion by vigorously reasserting their inherent role as the interpreters of legislative enactments and guardians against invidious and irrational exercises of governmental power."[95] More specifically, he believes that the courts must take the initiative and pick up the ball after legislators and administrators have fumbled their attempts to provide the necessary vehicles for placing administrative discretion under safe control. Ironically, Wright notes, in some cases this may require that the courts develop the appropriate standards and guidelines for Congress to attach to statutes when delegating powers to administrators. Wright believes that if we want to take giant steps toward resolving the discretionary justice problem, the courts will have to swing a big judicial stick in the future. Wright, like Davis, wants administrators to possess necessary discretionary powers, but he wants the courts to vigorously oversee and overrule discretionary agency actions that are not within their reasonable authority: "If the agency acts beyond its statutory authority as the relevant statute is interpreted by the courts, the agency action must be reversed."[96] In so doing, Wright concludes that "judges can narrow the scope of agency discretion even if the administrators are unwilling to narrow its scope themselves."[97]

When covering Davis's insights on ways to control administrative discretion, I noted that his views, given the myopic fixation today on ways to cut agency costs, seem like "bleeding heart due process fantasies." Ironically, however, Wright's proposals for controlling agency discretion appear even more unrealistic and utopian because the courts in recent years have only rarely shown any interest in reviewing discretionary agency actions, insisting that enormous discretion is due agency administration to help them streamline agency action to cut their administrative costs. Curbing discretionary abuses and promoting procedural due process seem only minor concerns because, overall, the courts consider the extension of due process protections a luxury that our administrative system cannot afford. How, then, can we expect our courts today to provide a check against discretionary administrative abuses through judicial review when they normally don't even want to review claims of discretionary abuse?

REACTING TO DAVIS: GIFFORD'S MODEL OF DISCRETIONARY DECISIONMAKING

To reiterate, Kenneth Culp Davis believes that administrative discretion is insufficiently confined, structured, and checked. To control discretion for the purpose of curtailing abuses of discretion (arbitrary and capricious decisionmaking made illegal by the Administrative Procedure Act, Section 706[2][A]), Davis urges that agency administrators promulgate standards and rules based on past agency experiences in handling similar factual situations in cases to guide future discretionary administrative decisions. To Daniel J. Gifford, Davis's position is rooted in five basic assumptions. They are

1. The administration of a statute is a learning process for an agency;
2. Repeated application of the statute to differing situations forces that agency to evaluate specifically the various problems faced by regulated subjects;
3. This repeated contact with the regulation in a variety of circumstances helps the agency develop an overview of the problems;
4. The needed narrowing of discretion comes from rules, standards, and precedents that gradually emerge as the agency acquires more information about its tasks; and
5. This information comes, in part, from the repeated decisionmaking.[98]

However, Gifford, among many others whom he cites, seriously doubts whether agency decisionmaking consists of enough recurring common "factual components" to allow standards and rules to be developed within agencies to set precedents for future agency decisions. He points out that many scholars challenge Davis's position, describing "agency work as resolving numerous cases in which the particular factual components rarely repeat themselves. Under this approach, precedents or rules play a smaller role in administrative decisions than in judicial decisions. This is due to the factual variety of cases coming before an agency decision."[99] In particular, Gifford cites an old study by Professor I. L. Sharfman of the Interstate Commerce Commission that found that cases coming before the ICC were almost always so factually unique that they had to be resolved on a case-by-case basis, making virtually impossible the development of general standards and rules to be used as guiding precedents for future resolution of ICC cases.[100] Gifford asserts that this does not mean that Sharfman rejects Davis's pursuit of common rules to confine and structure administrative discretion to promote decisional consistency in public agencies. "Rather, Sharfman's deprecation of rules, precedents, standards, consistency, and predictability results from his different perception of the kinds of cases that form the bulk of the agency workload. The non-repetitious nature of these cases accounts for his emphasis upon the importance of 'the special facts of each controversy' and his belief in the unimportance of precedent in that agency's work."[101] In short, the assumptions of Sharfman and Davis are radically different and miles apart. Simply put, Davis believes that enough repetition of relevant facts occurs in cases in our public agencies to allow our administrators to develop standards and rules to be employed in the future to help confine and structure unnecessary discretion. Sharfman feels such thinking is idealistic and unrealistic, given the great diversity of dissimilar factual cases coming before agencies. Gifford believes that the Sharfman-Davis perceptions regarding the nature of agency caseloads are at opposite ends of a continuum (Figure 8.5).[102]

So the question is: Do relevant facts recur in agency cases frequently enough to permit agency administrators to promulgate those standards and rules worthwhile in curbing unnecessary discretionary actions and thereby promoting fairer, predictable, nonarbitrary, and noncapricious decisionmaking? Attempting to answer this question, Gifford developed a set of criteria to analyze the situation. These consist of the following:

1. The proper guiding, structuring, or confining of discretionary decision-making must be related to the agency's information collection and evaluation processes because authoritative rules or guides ought to be imposed upon decisionmakers only when these rules or guides produce decisions of higher quality than would be the case without them;

2. better informed people tend to make higher quality decisions;

3. the decisionmaking process itself is often a major source of agency information;

4. the value of agency experience in deciding cases and as sources of relevant information for the formulation of standards governing the disposition of future cases is affected by the nature of the agency caseload.[103]

From the application of these criteria, Gifford designed a descriptive model (see Figure 8.6).[104]

Of the variety of cases that come before agencies, only a limited percentage fall into the NE quadrant and thus provide the essential "recurring relevant factors" that promote the development of general standards and rules to guide the exercise of discretionary decisionmaking. As Figure 8.6 illustrates, only in the NE sector are the cases important enough to warrant elaborate justification that also have common factual situations recurrent enough to allow them to be grouped and "class justified"; these cases are appropriate sources of the information needed to develop useful standards and rules to guide administrative discretion. In the SW corner, just the opposite situation exists. Here the agency cases are nonrecurring and perceived as unimportant to the development of agency rulemaking. These cases do not require the attention of top administrators; they simply need to be "managed" or settled (unique justifications are given to dispose of the cases quickly) by lower-level administrators. In the NW quadrant, the cases are perceived as important enough to justify the attention of top-level administrators, but the cases are too unique in character to provide the necessary commonalities absolutely essential to allow for the development of general standards. Those cases in the SE quadrant do recur enough to allow for the formation of general standards and rules to confine discretion, but the cases are regarded as unimportant to the development of agency policy and the fulfillment of agency regulatory goals. Therefore, these cases require only quick decisions with simple to no justifications by lower-level agency officials.

So what does this all mean? The model reveals the complexities of discretionary decisionmaking. It also discloses that the potential to confine administrative discretion through general standards and rules is limited by the kind of cases handled within an agency and by the types of cases various agencies must typically settle. While some agencies may handle a large percentage of cases that could be placed in the NE quadrant, other agencies may find few cases that could appropriately be placed in the NE sector. Gifford concludes that the techniques suggested by Davis for confining, structuring, and checking administrative discretion (namely, rulemaking) have limited application. "The several techniques for confining, checking, and guiding the exercise of discretionary power which he has proposed may be more suitable to some categories of administrative caseloads than to others, and to some levels of bureaucratic hierarchy than to others."[105]

THE COURTS' ROLE IN CONTROLLING DISCRETIONARY AGENCY ACTIONS

As noted in Chapter 2, for the sake of expediency the courts since *Schechter Poultry Corp. v. United States,* 295 U.S. 495 (1935), have generally allowed Congress to delegate increasingly broader discretionary powers to administrators without

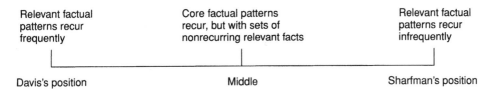

Relevant factual patterns recur frequently	Core factual patterns recur, but with sets of nonrecurring relevant facts	Relevant factual patterns recur infrequently
Davis's position	Middle	Sharfman's position

FIGURE 8.5   Perceptions of Agency Caseloads: Sharfman Versus Davis

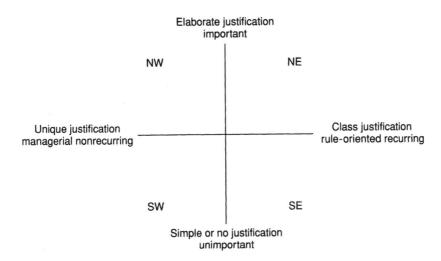

FIGURE 8.6   Gifford's Model of Agency Cases

compelling Congress to limit an agency's administrative discretion by attaching meaningful standards (standards that can be used to guide and restrict the exercise of discretion). However, by the early 1970s some observers detected that a judicial attitude had started to emerge, echoing the mood of many Americans, that the discretionary powers of administrators had grown too threatening for democratic processes and, therefore, had to be better controlled. In 1980, looking back over the 1970s, Bernard Schwartz summarized why the Supreme Court under Warren Burger started to reverse the attitude of earlier Courts toward the power position of administrative agencies: "The changed approach of the Burger Court reflects both the society of the past decade and the period through which it has been passing. Inevitably the malaise about administrative agencies and the manner in which they operate that has increasingly spread through the society has had its effects within the Marble Palace. The present Court's changing administrative law jurisprudence may be seen as a direct response to growing distrust of agencies and their failure to protect that very public interest they were created to serve."[106]

According to Schwartz, the Burger Court took a tough new stand against broad and abusive uses of discretionary power by administrative agencies. He contends that while previous Courts had tolerated vague delegating statutes, which allowed administrators to write their own tickets in regard to what Congress intended, the Burger Court adopted a stricter approach. Schwartz asserts that the Burger Court showed an unwillingness "to look beyond the black letter of delegating statutes and read in implied powers in the light of presumed congressional intent to confer broadside authority."[107] In short, the Burger Court began to reassert the old democratic idea, emphasized by J. Skelly Wright in "Beyond Discretionary Justice," that delegated authority must be transferred in a democratically responsible fashion.

Davis agrees with Schwartz that the overall judicial attitude toward discretionary administrative power changed, but not as much in the high court. Davis claims that this altered judicial perspective since 1970 has increased the potential for petitioners to win cases in agency or judicial appeals on the grounds that administrative discretion has not been properly restrained. Many cases can be cited to substantiate this judicial reversal, but Davis notes that the courts in the immediate future will not necessarily rely upon past precedential decisions but will seek to confine, structure, and check discretion by handing down new precedential rulings of their own: "Judicial disapprovals of uncontrolled discretion often are not based on precedents; judges often create precedents. In the coming years, many questions of first impression about uncontrolled discretion will arise and much new law, not based on specific precedents, will be created.[108]

These views about the present and future efforts of the courts to control discretion, as noted, seem to be based more on high hopes than on actual case law. It is true that the courts in the past few decades have apparently started to rethink their position on what the judicial role should be in controlling discretion. But in too many cases, their *obiter dicta* (comments not necessary to support the holding) denouncing discretionary actions that were encouraged by the existence of virtually standardless statutes ultimately failed to motivate the courts to override the same discretionary activities that they had just denounced. Even Schwartz acknowledges that the courts have too often attacked the discretionary justice problem with mere rhetoric rather than with hard rulings aimed at invalidating illegitimate discretionary behavior. Martin Shapiro asserts that although judges became lay heroes during the 1960s and 1970s when they attacked technocratic administrative discretion in response to public distaste for "rule-by-administrative experts," during the 1980s the courts began to develop a new respect for technocratic administration and once again began deferring to agency expertise. Decisions handed down by the Supreme Court in particular in the past two decades, starting with the famous precedential case, *Chevron, U.S.A., Inc. v. Natural Resources Defense Council, Inc.*, 467 U.S. 837 (1984), have substantiated Shapiro's observation (*Heckler v. Chaney*, 470 U.S. 821 [1985] and *Lincoln v. Vigil*, 113 S.Ct. to 2024 [1993]; *Dickinson v. Zurko*, 527 U.S. 150 [1999]; *U.S. v. Mead*, 533 U.S. 218 [2001]; and *U.S. v. Bean*, 123 S.Ct. 584 [2002]). Ironically, the courts, especially the Supreme Court, has decided to defer broadly to agency expertise/discretion during the same period when suddenly the president and Congress have made efforts to micro-manage the actions of public agencies to make them more democratically accountable.

CASES OVERRULING
DISCRETIONARY ACTIONS

Cases pertaining to the use and misuse of discretion by administrative agencies are numerous, since virtually all administrative law disputes fundamentally involve judgments rooted in discretion. Whether our focus is on formal or informal rulemaking, ordermaking, and so on, discretionary decisions must play a significant role since laws and rules must be interpreted and applied. Thus, if we look hard enough, we can discover legions of cases where the courts apparently tried to limit an agency's use of unlimited discretion by specifically noting instances where an agency had exceeded and/or abused its discretionary authority. In *Germania Iron Co. v. James,* 89 F. 811, 818 (8th Cir. 1898), a case involving the breadth of administrative discretion in adhering to standard procedures in adjudications, the court stated: "What a force the attempt to secure rights in any judicial tribunal must become, if its rules and practice are ignored or applied at the arbitrary will of the judge." In *Vitarelli v. Seaton,* 359 U.S. 535 (1959), the Supreme Court held that administrators are not free to follow agency rules arbitrarily. As Justice Felix Frankfurter succinctly expressed: "He that takes the procedural sword shall perish with that sword" (p. 547). In *Hammond v. Lenfest,* 398 F.2d 705, 715 (2nd Cir. 1968), the appellate court emphasized that a clear abuse of administrative discretion occurs when agency administrators choose to ignore basic rule-of-law principles by arbitrarily violating their own established rules.

In *Environmental Defense Fund, Inc. v. Ruckelshaus,* 439 F.2d 584, 598 (D.C. Cir. 1971), the court insisted that when administrative actions affect the "life, health, and liberty" of individual interests, then the judiciary must subject agency behavior to "strict judicial scrutiny." Specifically, according to the court, close supervision of agency actions in cases involving such personal interests should function to "require administrative officers to articulate the standards and principles that govern their discretionary decisions in as much detail as possible" and "to ensure that the administrative process itself will confine and control the exercise of discretion" (p. 598). A year earlier the same court in *Greater Boston Television Corp. v. FCC,* 444 F.2d 841,850 (1970), held the courts have a legal obligation to scrutinize agency decisions to make certain that agency determinations are based upon "reasoned discretion."

In *Citizens to Preserve Overton Park, Inc. v. Volpe,* 401 U.S. 402 (1971), Secretary of Transportation John Volpe decided to use public funds to build a highway through a public park (Overton Park), even though a statute forbids such construction if a "feasible and prudent" alternative route was available. Volpe argued that his decision to approve construction of the highway was not subject to judicial review, because he had sole discretionary authority to determine whether a "feasible and alternative" route existed. The Supreme Court rejected

Volpe's argument, holding that his informal discretionary action was reviewable under the "arbitrary, capricious" or "abuse of discretion" standards (pp. 413–414). (The courts often make no distinction between these two standards or tests, reasoning that if an administrator acts "arbitrarily and capriciously," the administrator is necessarily abusing his or her administrative discretion.) In *Overton Park* the Court asserted that Volpe's decision should be overruled if "a clear error of judgment" (a new standard) could be found, thus making his informal discretionary action "arbitrary, capricious" or constituting an "abuse of discretion" (p. 416). The high court found such a clear error in his judgment. Recently, the courts have used the "clear error" test as a convenient way to defer more readily to agency discretion. For example, in *Kisser v. Cisneros*, 14 F.2d 615, 618–619 (1994), the court argued that when applying the "arbitrary and capricious" standard to determine whether the agency has abused its discretion, the court should be "highly deferential," presuming "the validity of agency action. . . . We may reverse only if the agency's decision is not supported by substantial evidence, or the agency has made clear error in judgment."

Of course, the courts have held that agencies need to record their "reasoned opinions" to help the reviewing courts decide whether discretion was abused in the decisionmaking process *(Dunlop v. Bachowski*, 421 U.S. 560, 571 [1975]). In *Portland Cement Ass'n v. Ruckelshaus*, 486 F.2d 375, 393 (1973), the appellate court argued that fundamental fairness in rulemaking requires that discretion cannot be employed to allow rules to be promulgated in the absence of inadequate data or on secretive data.[109] A year later, in *National Cable TV Ass'n. v. United States*, 415 U.S. 336, 342 (1974), the Supreme Court, while ruling in favor of the agency's use of discretion, at least paid lip service to the need for discretion to be defined and guided by standards. In *Loyola Univ. v. FCC*, 670 F.2d 1222 (1982), the D. C. Circuit court ruled that an agency acts arbitrarily when the agency can show no reasonable basis for its actions. Discretion is also abused when extraneous considerations (i.e., factors that should have played no role in the decision) are used to support an agency decision, *P.P.G. Corp. v. State Liquor Auth.*, 52 N.Y. 2d 886 (1981).

At an accelerated rate in recent years court decisions have denounced a wide variety of discretionary agency actions, although the courts have not always found it appropriate to overrule the specific agency actions in question or to develop clear and useful standards that could be used to limit the free exercise of administrative discretion. In *White v. Roughton*, 530 F.2d 750, 753–754 (7th Cir. 1976), the court came down hard on an official who had been administering a township assistance program without the guidance of any written standards or rules. The court argued that standards were required to guard against potential abuses of discretion. Because administrator Roughton had established no written rules to guide his discretion, the court held that he could not apply eligibility requirements in a fair and consistent manner. As far as the court was concerned, Roughton, by not limiting his own discretion, allowed himself to possess "unfettered discretion," a clear violation of procedural due process principles.

Two 1979 court decisions attempted to limit the use of discretion by restricting an agency's implied powers. Schwartz held that *FCC v. Midwest Video Corp., 99 S.Ct. 824,* and *NLRB v. Catholic Bishop of Chicago, 99 S.Ct. 1313,* narrowed agency discretion by refusing to permit administrators to expand the scope of their delegated powers by freely and arbitrarily reading into legislation powers that have not been specifically conferred. For Schwartz, these two rulings represented the *McCulloch v. Maryland* (4 Wheat 316 U.S. [1819]) counterpart for administrative law in that the Court was saying that administrative agencies cannot exercise powers that are not specifically delegated to them unless the discretionary use of implied powers can be justified as *necessary* and *proper*.[110] In *Midwest Video Corp.,* the Court held that specific FCC rules were not reasonably necessary to maintain effective TV regulation and therefore constituted an illegitimate extension of their delegated powers, while in *Catholic Bishop* the Court ruled that the NLRB exceeded its statutory discretionary jurisdiction by expanding its regulatory arm to cover lay teachers working for church-governed schools.

In *Sharon Steel Corp. v. EPA,* 597 F.2d 377 (3rd Cir. 1979), and *United States Steel Corp. v. EPA,* 595 F.2d 207 (5th Cir. 1979), the two circuit courts agreed that the EPA can abuse its discretion by using feeble excuses to suspend required notice and comment rulemaking under the "good cause" or "impractical" exception of the APA. The Third and Fifth Circuit courts ruled that the argument by the EPA that APA-required rulemaking procedures had to be suspended because of the EPA's tight schedule did not by itself justify the suspension.

Although Professor Davis expresses serious second thoughts on his assessment of the importance and wisdom of *Morton v. Ruiz,* 415 U.S. 199 (1974), in his 1994 *Administrative Law Treatise,* 3rd edition, coauthored with Richard J. Pierce, Jr.,[111] in his 1978–1984 *Administrative Law Treatise,* 2nd edition, he argued that the Supreme Court in *Ruiz* did an excellent job in helping to confine agency discretion by establishing four important propositions that could be used by lower courts to curb the use of unnecessary and abusive discretionary power. The first was that the authority to implement a program necessarily requires rulemaking (p. 231). Thus, any exercise of discretion in the absence of guiding rules could easily be held invalid in the face of this proposition. Second, agency policies are "ineffective" unless they are rooted in a legislative rule or rules (p. 236). This places obvious restraint on the exercise of discretion by forcing administrators to act within the limits of expressed legislative intent. Third, unpublished ad hoc decisions are prohibited by the APA (p. 236). If honored, this proposition would have a profound impact on the future use of administrative discretion because the decision in fact requires lower courts to overturn virtually all unpublished ad hoc agency decisions, of which there are plenty. And fourth, agency decisions setting eligibility requirements for welfare benefits cannot be determined in an ad hoc manner (p. 232). If this is the case, Davis asserts, "then probably most determinations other than those relating to eligibility for welfare cannot be made on an *ad hoc* basis."[112]

The D.C. Circuit court in *Coal Exporters Association of the United States v. United States,* 745 F.2d 76 (1984),[113] ruled that the ICC had exceeded its "executing discretion" when implementing the vague provisions of the Staggers Rail Act of 1980 (49 U.S.C., Section 10505 [1982]). The court concluded: "Here we admit that the commission has substantial discretion as to how to carry out Congress's instruction concerning the accommodation of shipper and rail carrier interests, but wherever the bounds of discretion are, we have no doubt that the agency's accommodation, as announced and applied in this case, 'is not one that Congress would have sanctioned'" (p. 96). In *Sang Seup Shin v. INS*, 750 F.2d 122 (1984), the same court handed down a similar ruling, holding that the Board of Immigration Appeals of the INS had exceeded the boundaries of its discretion by refusing to "individualize" discretion properly by not reopening a deportation decision even in light of crucial new facts.

The Supreme Court handed down only one major setback for broad use of agency discretion during the 1980s. In *Motor Vehicle Mfrs. Ass'n. v. State Farm Mutual*, 103 S.Ct. 2856 (1983), the high court ruled that the National Highway Traffic Safety Administration abused its discretion by acting arbitrarily and capriciously in rescinding the passive restraint requirement, Standard 208, that required new motor vehicles manufactured after September 1982 to be equipped with seat belts to protect the lives of passengers. Returning in this case to the "clear error in judgment" standard set forth in *Overton Park*, Justice Byron White, speaking for the majority, concluded that the agency was guilty of "clear error" because it failed to support its rescission with any reasonable basis and explanation. "By failing to analyze the continuous seat belt in its own right, the agency has failed to offer the rational connection between facts and judgment required to pass the muster under the arbitrary and capricious standard. . . . While the agency is entitled to change its view on the acceptability of continuous passive belts, it is obligated to explain its reasons for doing so" (p. 2873).

With *Chevron* still serving in the early 2000s as the chief precedential case guiding court decisions pertaining to the exercise of administrative discretion, relatively few judicial decisions have overruled discretionary agency action. However, courts have still set aside blatantly abusive discretionary acts in clear violation of the law. For example, in *ALM Corp. v. U.S. Envtl Protection Agency, Region II*, 974 F 2d 380, 383 (3rd Cir. 1992), the court stressed that there should be "great deference" to agency discretion, but the courts should set aside clear abuses of discretion. In *Haitian Centers Council, Inc. v. Sale*, 823 F. Supp. 1028 (E.D.N.Y. 1993), the court came down hard on Attorney General Janet Reno for abusing her discretion in the handling of Haitian refugees, some having AIDS, who sought to immigrate to the United States seeking political asylum. The court argued that Reno was abusing her discretion by treating Haitian refugees differently from other immigrants just because they were Haitian, many with AIDS. The court held that "the Attorney General has 'broad discretionary power to parole unadmitted aliens,' but she may not exercise that discretion 'to discriminate invidiously against a particular race or group or to depart without rational explanation from established policies.'" (p. 1048).

In recent cases, the court in *St. Luke's Methodist Hospital v. Thompson*, 315 F.3d 984 (2003), ruled against Tommy Thompson, secretary of the Department of Health and Human Services (HHS), because Thompson abused his discretion by applying an obviously inapplicable statute to deny St. Luke's Hospital from receiving an upward adjustment reimbursement for nonroutine costs. Under the APA, Section 706 (2)(A), a court must "set aside" an administrative decision "'if it is arbitrary, capricious, an abuse of discretion, unsupported by substantial evidence, or contrary to law'" (p. 987). Specifically, the court held that Thompson committed a "plainly erroneous" discretionary error in rejecting a fifteen-year-old agency regulation that addresses upward adjustments for nonroutine costs, but choosing to rely on a ten-year-old statutory provision that does not. The court explained: "We are mindful that the secretary is not required to interpret a regulation in the most reasonable manner in order for us to defer to his interpretation. . . . But we are convinced for all of the above reasons that the secretary's interpretation of Section 405.460(f) to deny hospital-based SNFs costs expended within the 'gap' is unreasonable and arbitrary" (p. 989).

Similarly, in *Public Citizen v. Dept. of Transportation*, 316 F.3d 1002(2003), the Court of Appeals for the Ninth Circuit ruled that DOT abused its discretion by ignoring well-established U.S. environment law. Specifically, plaintiffs argued that DOT failed to apply environment impact analyses in promulgating three regulations that would have the effect of allowing Mexican vehicles to travel beyond the border zone limits called for by the North American Free Trade Agreement (NAFTA). The court agreed with the plaintiff, holding that "DOT has failed to demonstrate that its EA contains anything close to the statutorily required 'convincing statement of reasons' sufficient to support a decision not to prepare an EIS" (environmental impact statement). Additionally, the court noted: "We are similarly unpersuaded by DOT's last-ditch argument that, as an agency with no jurisdiction over environmental matters, it need not consider the environmental consequences of its actions" (p. 1027). Accordingly, the court concluded: "We hold that the Department of Transportation acted arbitrarily and capriciously in failing to prepare a full Environmental Impact Statement under the National Environmental Protection At, as well as a conformity determination under the Clean Air Act" (p. 1032).

CASES UPHOLDING DISCRETIONARY ACTIONS

The above sampling of cases might have created the impression that the courts have been busy monitoring and guarding against possible abuses of discretion, but conspicuously absent are recent cases by the Supreme Court denouncing discretionary abuses. The sad truth is, as suggested earlier, that the courts, especially the Supreme Court, have not contributed much to efforts aimed at curtailing abuses of administrative discretion. There are several reasons for this. Of course, the primary reason is that court rulings seem to touch upon only a tiny fraction of discretionary administrative actions. Second, too many court decisions seem too vague, contradictory, filled with loopholes, and consequently, confusing and difficult to comfortably employ in guiding administrative discretion. Third, court holdings have tended to be too narrow and incomplete, applying only to very specific questions of the proper use of discretion, thus making valid generalizations for guiding discretion virtually impossible to infer. And fourth, the Supreme Court, as the judicial leader, has refused to take bold and certain steps toward controlling discretion. As noted, however, the conservative Supreme Court over the past two decades has been very concerned over escalating agency costs. To this Court it seems more cost-effective to defer broadly to agency administrators even if this encourages administrators to skip a few "unnecessary" and more costly due process steps. Maybe this is good because it will save taxpayers money. Is this the Supreme Court's reason? What do you think?

A Supreme Court decision that still receives intense criticism from liberal administrative law critics is *Vermont Yankee Nuclear Power Corp. v. Natural Resources Defense Council, Inc.*, 435 U.S. 519 (1978), which directly reversed two separate and innovative D.C. Circuit court rulings, *Natural Resources Defense Council v. Nuclear Regulatory Commission*, 547 F.2d 633 (D.C. Cir. 1976), and *Aeschliman v. Nuclear Regulatory Commission*, 547 F.2d 622 (D.C. Cir. 1976).[114] Some critics believe the *Vermont Yankee* decision represents an unwise reversal of a progressive judicial trend that had been developing since the mid-1960s at the appellate level led by the D.C. Circuit Court of Appeals.[115] In essence, liberal administrative law scholars and judges had perceived the trend as healthy because the appeals courts were taking a "hard look" (applying a hard look standard) at the use of agency discretion in various areas, especially rulemaking.[116] With the *Vermont Yankee* holding, this all came to an abrupt halt.[117] But what did the Supreme Court say in the *Vermont Yankee* decision to anger the liberal administrative law establishment so intensely?

Briefly, in *NRDC v. NRC* the D.C. Circuit court held invalid a rule promulgated by the NRC and also the commission's decision to grant Vermont Yankee Power Corporation a license to start construction of a nuclear plant. The court rooted its decision in the argument that the NRC's rulemaking procedures were inadequate for proper "ventilation of the issues" *(NRDC v. NRC, 547 F.2d 633, 654; at 644)*. The court reasoned that the NRC failed to employ the available rulemaking methods in a responsible manner, thus precluding the possibility that an adequate representation of facts and opposing views could be presented. The court contended that it is sometimes necessary, in the interest of upholding procedural due process standards, for agencies to follow more elaborate rulemaking procedures than required by Section 553 of the APA, especially when the issues are socially important and technically complex. Short of demanding that the NRC follow certain rulemaking procedures, circuit court judge Bazelon argued that a reviewing court has the responsibility of making sure that agencies provide "a meaningful opportunity [for participation] in the proceedings as guaranteed by due process" (p. 643).

But Justice William Rehnquist, writing the Supreme Court opinion, disagreed. He maintained that if the APA granted agency officials the broad discretionary power to decide which lawful rulemaking procedures to follow, then the judiciary cannot demand that the rulemakers follow more elaborate procedures than required, except in extremely rare situations *(Vermont Yankee Nuclear Power Corp. v. NRDC,* 435 U.S. 519, 543). Further, Rehnquist noted that misunderstanding and uncertainty which would undermine Section 553 of the APA would develop if reviewing courts were allowed to supplement agency procedures with additional procedures not required by existing statutes.

The Supreme Court's decision in *Vermont Yankee* has been subject to heated criticisms by those such as Wright who believe that the courts must take the initiative in devising standards that can be used to help confine and structure agency discretion. For example, Michael J. Perry and Allan F. Wichelman, in separate law review articles, argue that the federal court system is in the most advantageous position, because it is relatively free from the normal political pressures, to insist that crucial public policy issues are given more than superficial attention by regulatory agencies when drafting rules.[118] For a dozen or so years before *Vermont Yankee,* the courts were beginning to take action to limit agency discretion in rulemaking to better ensure that the rulemaking procedures selected were not aimed at satisfying short-run objectives but were directed more at ensuring that the long-term public interest was promoted. But, Wichelman writes, "*Vermont Yankee* calls an abrupt end to this development. Reviewing courts are warned not to 'explore the procedural format' utilized by an agency nor 'to impose upon the agency [the court's] notion of which procedures are 'best' or most likely to further some vague, undefined public good.'"[119] The hands-off principle established in *Vermont Yankee* allows agencies to continue to use their discretion irresponsibly to avoid taking more elaborate rulemaking steps, perceived essential by many, for the healthy development of highly complex and socially relevant public policies: "*Vermont Yankee's* greatest significance lies in its reversal of the trend, especially apparent in the District of Columbia Circuit, toward requiring rulemaking procedures that are more elaborate than those required by Section 553 of the APA when complex and sensitive issues of great public importance are involved."[120]

Kenneth C. Davis claimed, in "Administrative Common Law and the *Vermont Yankee* Opinion," that the Supreme Court's opinion in *Vermont Yankee* was so terrible that he felt it was imperative to stop the printing of the second edition of his *Administrative Law Treatise* so that he could include a commentary on how weak the *Vermont Yankee* decision was. Davis contends that it is necessary that judge-made common law be developed so that abusive discretionary practices can be controlled. He points out that in the past the Supreme Court has been instrumental in developing common law that has been helpful in refining administrative law, as well as other legal areas. However, he claims that the *Vermont Yankee* holding "*essentially forbids lower courts to follow the Supreme Court's example.*"[121] Specifically, the Court's opinion in *Vermont Yankee* is repulsive to Davis because "the main thrust of the opinion is to outlaw new common law that adds to the procedural requirements of Section 553 of the APA."[122] This opinion, Davis holds, is a bad one for many reasons, but what makes the decision particularly unpalatable is that the decision contradicts the legislative history of the APA itself. He notes that the Court's prohibition of common law development "is directly and specifically a violation of the first sentence of section 559 of the APA."[123] Davis asserts that Congress recognized the need for common law to assist the development of administrative law by stating in Section 559 of the APA (originally found in Section 12 of the 1946 APA): "Nothing in this Act shall be held to diminish the constitutional rights of any person or to limit or repeal additional requirements imposed by statute or otherwise recognized by law."[124] Logically, he concludes: "Law that is neither constitutional nor statutory has to be common law."[125]

Apart from this major Court oversight, Davis claims that the high court was also blatantly and pathetically wrong in *Vermont Yankee* in concluding that the courts cannot impose supplemental rulemaking standards, because the APA has already established "maximum procedural safeguards." He makes a credible case that the Supreme Court erred in its decision simply because it was unaware of relevant passages in the APA that clearly convey that the APA had set only minimum procedural standards, not maximum standards.[126]

The *Vermont Yankee* decision still remains controversial in the early 2000s. However, the passage of time has allowed to surface opinions more supportive of *Vermont Yankee*.[127] Today, many still cling to the belief that the *Vermont Yankee* decision was a poor one. Other scholars, as well as judges, maintain that the court in *Vermont Yankee* had no choice but to rule as it did because it is not up to the courts to require agencies to follow more elaborate procedures than the APA requires. As again explained by the Supreme Court in *Chrysler Corp. v. Brown,* 441 U.S. 281, 312 (1979): "We held in *Vermont Yankee* that courts could only in 'extraordinary circumstances' impose procedural requirements on an agency beyond those specified in the APA. It is within an agency's discretion to afford parties more procedure, but it is not the province of the courts to do so."

If the *Vermont Yankee* decision stood alone, then its precedential force might be doubted. But the *Vermont Yankee* case does not stand alone. A few months after *Vermont Yankee,* the Supreme Court handed down another decision, *FCC v. National Citizens Committee for Broadcasting,* 436 U.S. 775 (1978), which again attracted much scorn. According to Daniel D. Polsby, the *NCCB* case must be viewed in light of *Vermont Yankee:* Together they conveyed the clear message to the lower courts that the Burger Court believed that some of these courts, especially the D.C. Circuit Court of Appeals, had gone too far in their efforts to monitor and control agency actions, especially agency use of discretion.[128] In *FCC v. NCCB,* the Supreme Court overruled the D.C. Circuit court opinion that had held that the FCC had abused its discretion by arbitrarily and capriciously defending an outdated grandfather clause pertaining to the licensing of television and radio stations. The Supreme Court said, in sum, that the appeals court had no business trying to limit agency discretion. Judging from the D.C. Circuit court's clear statement on administrative discretion in *Western Coal Traffic League,* cited above, the D.C. Circuit court must have finally received the Supreme Court's message.

In reviewing the *NCCB* case, Polsby admitted that the court of appeals ruling did constitute possibly the boldest judicial attempt to extend judicial influence over agency discretionary matters and that maybe the D.C. Circuit court had indeed gone too far.[129] However, Polsby believes the Court's ruling served to cripple future attempts by the courts to intervene in agency discretionary matters and to develop innovative guidelines that could be used to control discretion. Polsby maintains that it is unquestionable that Congress has left the basic ordering of policymaking values in agency hands, but he holds that administrative discretion should not be so broad that it should be unreviewable and, therefore, virtually uncontrollable, as the Supreme Court appeared to suggest in the *Vermont Yankee* and *NCCB* cases. Acknowledging that the FCC's cross-ownership decision in the *NCCB* case did not constitute what one could consider a "reasoned decision," Polsby asserted that it would be "difficult to imagine how scatterbrained an administrative agency would have to be to entitle a reviewing court to remand a problematic docket for a 'hard look.'"[130]

Although the Supreme Court in 1983 ruled in *State Farm* that the National Highway Traffic Safety Administration abused its discretion in its rescission of a motor vehicle safety standard because it failed to provide an adequate explanation for the rescission, since that holding the high court has repeatedly upheld broad discretionary actions by agency administrators. These decisions have served to establish the clear position of the Supreme Court that broad agency discretion should be honored unless Congress has instructed the courts to scrutinize administrative discretion more carefully, with an eye toward restricting it. In *Capital Cities Cable, Inc. v. Crisp,* 104 S.Ct. 2694 (1984), a unanimous Supreme Court held that when Congress has directed an agency—in this case, the Federal Communications Commission—to exercise administrative discretion, judicial review should be limited to only the question of whether the agency exceeded its statutory authority or abused its discretion by acting arbitrarily.

In possibly the most influential administrative law case handed down in the past few decades, *Chevron, U.S.A., Inc. v. Natural Resources Defense Council,* 104 S.Ct. 2778 (1984), the Supreme Court expanded on its position that agencies should be allowed to exercise broad discretion in making policy choices when executing statutes. Quoting from its decision in *Morton,* the Court stated: "The power of an administrative agency to administer a congressionally created . . . program necessarily requires the formulation of policy and making of rules to fill any gap left implicitly or explicitly by Congress. . . . If Congress has explicitly left a gap for the agency to fill, there is an express delegation of authority to the agency to elucidate a specific provision of the statute by regulation. Such legislative regulations are given controlling weight unless they are arbitrary, capricious, or manifestly contrary to statute. Sometimes the legislative delegation to an agency on a particular question is implicit rather than explicit. In such a case, a court may not substitute its own construction of a statutory provision for a reasonable interpretation made by the administrator of an agency" (p. 2782). Consequently, the Supreme Court concluded that the particular policy choice by the Environmental Protection Agency to control air pollution (i.e., the adoption of the "bubble" concept, previously explained) "is a reasonable policy choice for the agency to make" (p. 2783).

Consistent with its position on discretion developed in *Capital Cities Cable* and *Chevron,* the Supreme Court in *Regents of the University of Michigan v. Ewing,* 106 S.Ct. 507 (1985), ruled in a unanimous decision that universities should be accorded the broadest range of discretion in making decisions pertaining to the academic performance of students. Stating emphatically that this case, involving a student contesting admission to an academic program, should never have been litigated, the Court stressed that to safeguard academic freedom, the courts should stay away from reviewing academic decisions made by faculty members.

That same year the Supreme Court held in *Heckler v. Chaney,* 105 S.Ct. 1649 (1985), that an agency's refusal to act or take enforcement action is unreviewable unless Congress has indicated otherwise. "This Court has recognized that an agency's decision not to prosecute or enforce, whether through civil or criminal process, is a decision generally committed," unless Congress has said otherwise, "to an agency's absolute discretion" (p. 1656). The justification for the Court's holding, as presented by Justice Rehnquist, writing for the majority, has attracted severe criticism. In his reasoning, Rehnquist felt it was necessary to address an apparent conflict between two provisions in the Administrative Procedure Act that has bothered legal scholars for several decades. It is important to understand Rehnquist's perception of the conflict and his resolution of it to grasp the present Supreme Court's posture on judicial review of administrative discretion.

Justice Rehnquist summarized the conflict between Sections 701(a)(2) and 706(2)(A) of the APA by exclaiming that commentators feel that tension exists "between a literal reading of Section (a)(2), which exempts from judicial review those decisions committed to agency 'discretion,' and the primary scope of review prescribed by Section 706(2)(A)—whether the agency's action was 'arbitrary, capricious, or an abuse of discretion.' How is it, they ask, that an action committed to agency discretion can be unreviewable and yet courts still can review agency action for abuse of that discretion?" (p. 1654).[131] Rehnquist's answer is quite simple. He argues that Section 701(a)(1) permits judicial review of agency action only if Congress provides for judicial review, but precludes review of discretionary agency action "if the statute is drawn so that a court would have no meaningful standard against which to judge the agency's exercise of discretion. In such a case, the statute ('law') can be taken to have 'committed' the decisionmaking to the agency's judgment absolutely" (p. 1655). To Rehnquist, this interpretation of Section 701(a)(1) also resolves its conflict with the "abuse of discretion" review standard found in Section 706(2)(A) because "if no judicially manageable standards are available for judging how and when an agency should exercise its discretion then it is impossible to evaluate agency action for 'abuse of discretion'" (p. 1655).

This reasoning by Rehnquist in *Chaney* has baffled and irritated some judicial scholars. One such scholar is Bernard Schwartz. He vehemently argues that this "where there is no law to apply" notion only reiterates the same *Overton Park* heresy, because there is "no place for unreviewable discretion in a system such as ours."[132] As long as the case is justiciable, Schwartz asserts, "all discretionary power should be reviewable to determine that the discretion conferred has not been abused. What the English courts call the *Wednesbury* principle is just as valid in American administrative law. Under it the reviewing court should always be able to determine that the discretion has not been exercised in a manner in which no reasonable administrator would act. To this extent, there is always 'law to apply' and hence reviewable discretion, Section 701(a)(2), *Overton Park* and *Chaney* notwithstanding."[133]

Despite considerable scholarly criticisms of the *Chevron* and *Chaney* decisions, these two cases, especially *Chevron*, have established strong precedent, causing courts since the mid-1980s to defer often and probably too readily to agency expertise, unwilling to scrutinize all but the most blatant abuses of administrative discretion. In *ABF Freight System, Inc. v. N.L.R.B.*, 114 S.Ct. 835, 839 (1994), the Supreme Court, citing *Chevron*, again said emphatically that "When Congress expressly delegates to an administrative agency the authority to make specific policy determinations, courts must give the agency's decision controlling weight unless it is 'arbitrary, capricious, or manifestly contrary to statute.'" And specifically citing *Chaney*, the high court in *Lincoln v. Vigil*, 113 S.Ct. 2024, 2031 (1993), reiterated its position that an agency decision not to act, or specifically not to enforce, is "presumptively unreviewable" because "an agency's 'decision not to enforce often involves a complicated balancing of a number of factors which are peculiarly within its expertise,' . . . and for this and other good reasons, . . . [is] 'committed to agency discretion.'"

Recently, the Supreme Court has built on *Chevron* and *Cheney* to limit its review of discretionary agency actions or to uphold them, and even has creatively reached back to an old case, *Skidmore v. Swift*, 323 U.S. 134 (1944), to aid its cause. In *U.S. v. Mead*, 121 S.Ct. 2164 (2001), the Supreme Court had to concede that the *Chevron* deference standard did not apply, because Congress did not give the U.S. Customs Service any direct statutory authority to determine tariff classifications, obviously preventing the Customs Service from being able to interpret any statutory provision. Nonetheless, the court relied upon *Skidmore*, a 1944 decision that Justice Scalia even believed to have been rendered "anachronistic" by the *Chevron* holding. Determined to defer to agency discretion and expertise, even when *Chevron* could not be applied, the court reasoned the *Chevron* did not prevent the more flexible "choice" standards in *Skidmore* from being used to justify deference to agency discretion if there are reasons that are persuasive. The court was easily persuaded, concluding: "*Chevron* did not eliminate *Skidmore's* holding that an agency's interpretation may merit some deference whatever its form, given the 'specialized experience and broader investigations and information' available to the agency, and given the value of uniformity in its administrative and judicial understandings of what a national law requires (p. 2175). The court continued: "Whether courts do owe deference in a given case turns, for him, on whether the agency action (if reasonable) is 'authoritative.' The character of the authoritative derives, in turn, not from the breadth of delegation or the agency's procedure in implementing it, but is defined as the 'official' position of an agency, and may ultimately be a function of administrative persistence alone" (pp. 2176–2177). In *U.S. v. Bean*, 123 S.Ct. 584 (2002), the Supreme Court continued its consistent recent course in refusing to rule against a discretionary agency "action." Rejecting the presumption of reviewability under Section 706(2)(A) of the APA, which requires a court to rule against agency action if the action is "arbitrary, capricious, and abuse of discretion, or otherwise not in accordance with law," the court argued that the APA does not always apply, especially when it involves an agency inaction. In this case, the Bureau of Alcohol, Tobacco, and Firearms (ATF), acting under the authority of the secretary of the treasury, used its discretion not to act on a firearms application rather than to act and deny the application. The court held that the inaction to be unreviewable. "Application of the APA Standard of Review is predicated upon ATF's dispositive decision: the 'arbitrary and capricious' test in its nature contemplates review of some action by another entity, rather than initial action by the court itself" (p. 588).

Numerous other cases can be cited to substantiate the argument that, on the whole, the courts have done considerably more to promote the broad and potentially dangerous use of discretion than to limit discretion. In the final analysis, despite arguments to the contrary, it seems in general that the courts have thus far tried to control only the most flagrant abuses of discretionary power. This is especially true for the Supreme Court, and the Rehnquist Court is unlikely to shift direction. As we shall see in the next chapter, which focuses exclusively on the role the courts play in reviewing agency actions, judges still cling to doctrines that help them to avoid getting involved in and, according to so many court opinions, disrupting the normal administrative processes. But it seems that normal administrative procedures, unfortunately, too often include the unfair and abusive treatment of individual parties, as well as practices that lead to poorly planned major social policies. To improve administrative decisionmaking in the future, and in particular to help prevent administrative abuses, the courts will have to watch discretionary agency behavior more closely and own up to those actions that reasonable persons would consider repugnant to procedural due process standards. This must be accomplished without imprisoning administrators through undue interference and placing unnecessary restrictions on their discretion.

NONTRADITIONAL ALTERNATIVES TO CONTROLLING ADMINISTRATIVE POWER

We have discussed previously, especially in Chapter 3, methods that have been traditionally employed in the United States for monitoring and controlling administrative behavior. To conclude this chapter, it is appropriate to comment briefly on a few nontraditional alternatives that have been proposed for checking the exercise of administrative power, especially the use of discretion. The following methods are considered nontraditional only because they have not been formally institutionalized on a broad scale in the American political system. Some governmental systems have, however, experimented with these methods with some success.

Administrative Courts

It seems that the present judicial system is ill-equipped to handle all the administrative law conflicts in modern administrative government. Once more, the burden being placed on the judicial system by administrative law questions is increasing daily, as the administrative state continues to expand. For some, the solution would be to develop an administrative court system that could devote its attention only to administrative controversies. As Shane Spellisey advocated recently, "Administrative law involves a rare measure of public policy not present in the resolution of most disputes between parties, mainly because of the role of the State in administrative law as speaking for the interests of the public at large. The fact that the interests of society are so heavily implicated in these disputes speaks to the need for a functioning administrative court system."[134]

The idea that a special judicial system was needed, independent from agency control, yet not connected to the regular court system either, was first given support in America near the turn of this century.[135] In 1910 the Mann-Elkins Act (36 Stat. 539) created a judicial body that embraced the chief features of an administrative court. The purpose of this court was to provide judicial review of actions by the ICC in a more expeditious manner than the appellate courts could.[136] Because of political pressures, the Commerce Court collapsed a few years later, but I. L. Sharfman, one of the former members of the short-lived court, exclaimed: "It is by no means certain that its failure was inherent in the premises upon which it was reared, or that the same need for economy and expertness that led to the development of administrative agencies may not again create a well founded demand for corresponding judicial specialization."[137] The call for judicial specialization in administrative actions has continued well into the twenty-first century. During the 1930s, the President's Committee on Administrative Management and the American Bar Association pushed for an administrative court system similar to the one that had been implemented in France, arguing that such a system was necessary if administrative power was to be kept democratically accountable. However, their recommendations were rejected by the Attorney General's Committee on Administrative Procedure in 1941. This committee was not sympathetic with the argument that the regular court system could not adequately handle administrative law disputes. The second Hoover Commission in 1955 also favored an administrative court system, as did the Ash Council in 1971,[138] the American Bar Association's Standing Committee on Federal Judicial Improvements in 1989, and the Report of the Federal Courts Study Committee (1990).[139]

The Ash Council recommended the creation of a separate administrative court that would function somewhat akin to our Tax Court. While the Tax Court hears only specialized tax cases, the administrative court urged by the Ash Council would review cases only in the areas of energy, securities, and transportation. According to the Ash Report, the advantage of this judicial review arrangement would be that it could provide expert review of technical questions in the areas of energy, securities, and transportation, thus developing over a period of time a uniform and valuable body of administrative law. The Ash Council proposed a three-panel court consisting of fifteen judges serving fifteen-year terms. A year earlier, the Occupational Safety and Health Act of 1970 (84 Stat. 1590) created an administrative courtlike arrangement by separating the judicial and legislative functions. While OSHA, in the Department of Labor, was given the responsibility of setting and enforcing standards, adjudicative matters were assigned to an independent agency, the Occupational Safety and Health Review Commission. According to Neil Sullivan, "the separation of adjudicative and legislative functions between the Review Commission and OSHA is consistent with the recommendations of many groups that have been concerned with improving the administrative process through creation of administrative courts to ensure a strict separation of functions."[140]

Administrative courts would have limited jurisdiction, having authority only over disputes involving governmental agencies. As conceptualized, the use of administrative courts would not preclude judicial review of agency action by the regular courts. Properly used, the administrative courts would reduce the caseload for the regular courts by hearing those time-consuming cases of lesser importance. However, according to a 1990 study by Harold Bruff, administrative courts would reduce the caseload burden only very moderately since administrative cases constituted only 14 percent of the cases in federal courts in 1989.[141] Major issues, especially those involving constitutional and statutory procedural due process questions, would be decided by the regular judiciary. Ideally, while the structural independence of administrative courts helps to ensure unbiased review of administrative actions, the expertise of the reviewing judges helps to provide for effective review of technically complicated cases. If modeled after the French design (likely, since the French administrative court system is considered to be the best), administrative courts would have other advantages over the regular courts. They would be less costly, parties would not necessarily have to retain legal counsel, the administrative court would provide some assistance in helping parties to prepare their cases, and "standing" to bring suit would be easier to obtain. All things considered, supporters of an administrative court system for America hold that it could protect citizens from abuses of administrative powers, especially misuses of discretion, while helping to promote smooth administrative operations through competent review.[142]

Since we do not have an administrative court system in the United States, although one has been variously advocated since before 1900, there may be something wrong with it. Lewis Mainzer notes that "British and American observers worry deeply about the divided jurisdiction of the civil and administrative courts and argue that there is great value in a single, unified system of courts."[143] Harold H. Bruff voices this same concern, arguing that the development of an administrative court system could cause the "loss of the generalist perspective." He believes that this could constitute a serious loss because the wisdom behind generalist courts is that "sound decisionmaking results from exposure to a wide range of problems."[144]

Critics cite other potential problems. Some fear that interest groups would corrupt the appointment process, making sure that judges are appointed to these administrative courts who would likely hand down decisions favorable to their special interests. Administrative courts would be particularly susceptible to political pressures for favorable appointments because these specialized courts would repeatedly hear cases in specialized regulatory areas. "Capturing" judges on administrative courts, critics hold, would be most cost-effective for the special interests, yet at a tremendous cost to the promotion of the public interest.[145] Such judges, protected by long, fifteen-year terms, however, could shun the biased will of special interests, reaching decisions that are fair and objective. And Spellisey warns against the problem of overloading the administrative courts with cases, which is common in the states that use them such as France, Portugal, Germany, Italy, and Greece. When the administrative law system is deluged with cases, he maintains, as regular courts, it will no longer be "able to effectively, efficiently, and fairly review them in a timely manner."[146]

On the whole, however, the administrative court plan has merits that should be given serious attention by our lawmakers. The French administrative court system, despite criticisms, has been at least modestly successful.[147] In America, there is no question that our courts are overburdened, and too frequently with cases that could be much better adjudicated by judges in administrative courts who have expertise in specific administrative areas (for example, nuclear power). Undoubtedly, growth trends in public administration make it very clear that administrative law disputes will contribute to even greater caseload problems for our regular courts in the future. This will mean that unless something is done to alleviate the caseload problem, an increasing number of legitimate administrative law questions, which genuinely need to be resolved, will not be heard. Of course, the courts have in recent years reduced their caseload problem by using an "extreme deference doctrine" to avoid hearing many administrative law cases, some of which probably merit court review. Or if the cases are heard, they will be heard only routinely, without any serious effort exerted to see to it that administrative due process is upheld. A well-designed administrative court system could provide at least part of the answer.

How About an Ombudsman System?

Kenneth J. Meier points out that some observers of public bureaucracy recommend the implementation of some form of ombudsman system in the United States "[b]ecause controlling bureaucracy via other political institutions does not guarantee beneficent administration."[148] Supporters of the ombudsman plan claim that it can be used to keep administrative behavior in check, especially discretionary administrative actions toward individual parties. The ombudsman concept can be traced back to Sweden in 1809. But in more recent times the Danish Ombudsman plan, instituted in 1955, has helped to provide a useful model for other nations or smaller political entities (states, cities) to follow. Since 1955 many nations have incorporated into their system, not necessarily on a national scale, some form of the ombudsman plan. Several works during the 1960s, of which Walter Gellhorn's *Ombudsmen and Others* and *When Americans Complain*[149] probably became the most popular, were quite influential, causing the ombudsman idea to gain widespread popularity in the United States. However, despite the intellectual popularity of the concept, by the 2000s, the ombudsman plan has been implemented only very modestly in the United States, mostly at the state and local levels. Many states have implemented mongrel versions of the Danish ombudsman model in certain state programs and agencies (e.g., health care, judicial response, bankruptcies, social welfare matters), yet only a few states have adopted a comprehensive ombudsman system (e.g., Alaska, Hawaii, Iowa, Nebraska, and New Jersey).

What is an ombudsman?[150] Ombudsman comes from the Swedish word for intermediary or "go-between." An ombudsman may act as a "go-between" and mediate a resolution, but an ombudsman typically exercises only informal, advisory powers. An ombudsman is simply an officer, commissioner, or the like, who is appointed by a governing authority (for example, a congressional or parliamentary body, a state legislature, a city council, a board or commission, or less frequently, an executive official) for the chief purpose of serving as the citizen's defender. Specifically, an ombudsman's office is established so that citizens can voice complaints about public service operations. Ombudsmen are expected to listen to and investigate the complaints and act on those which are legitimate. Typically, ombudsmen are not responsible for running around and discovering the nefarious acts of administrators. Normally, ombudsmen are supposed to start their investigations only after specific complaints have been brought to their attention by citizens, although they may initiate broader investigations of administrative activities that are related to the original complaints. Supporters believe that the ombudsman could be particularly useful for detecting, exposing, and recommending remedies for discretionary injustices committed by public administrators. An excellent definition of an ombudsman is given by Davis: "An ombudsman is a high-level officer whose main function is to receive complaints from citizens who are aggrieved by official action or inaction, to investigate, to criticize, and to publicize findings, but who typically has no power to correct injustice or maladministration except by criticizing and persuading."[151]

The ombudsman concept has been criticized for many reasons. One reason is that an ombudsman system would simply add another costly layer to the already gigantic governmental bureaucracy. In fact, Meier asserts that no comprehensive ombudsman plan has ever been implemented for a government as large as the United

States because to do so "would likely require a bureaucracy as large as many bureaus it would investigate."[152] These critics contend that we already have institutional arrangements to handle citizen complaints about the public service. Specifically, they note that legislative assemblies and the courts are designed to handle such complaints. However, we have already noted that the courts are overburdened and, thus, probably incapable of responding adequately to the beefs that citizens have toward bureaucracy. Besides, to reiterate a well-known point, the courts are too expensive and generally very inconvenient to use, especially to resolve the typical complaints an ombudsman would handle (for example, repeated agency errors, more minor discretionary abuses). In practice, our courts are now primarily used to resolve relatively major legal disputes, but they always must stick to actual legal controversies. Ombudsmen frequently deal, not with complaints that involve illegal administrative behavior, but with actions that fall within the law but need attention to correct agency operations that inconvenience and abuse persons unnecessarily. Such matters are clearly beyond the jurisdiction of the courts.

Hans A. Linde and George Bunn also say legislators are ill-equipped to handle competently the sort of typical complaints an ombudsman's office would process: "Overall, the congressional officers are able to provide assistance to many of the constituents who write for help. . . . Nevertheless, there is much left to be desired in this process of mediating between the citizen and government. A congressional office is simply not equipped to give the type of personal attention which so many of these letters demand, for as dedicated as legislators and their staffs may be, the amount of constituent mail is staggering."[153] These scholars conclude that legislators provide inadequate substitutes for ombudsman offices because, even in responding to citizen complaints, legislators do little to correct the breakdowns in administrative operations on a regular basis.[154]

Walter Gellhorn, once probably the leading American authority on the ombudsman system, basically agrees with the insights of Linde and Bunn. In an interview with this eminent scholar years ago, Professor Gellhorn pointed out for me some of the main arguments for instituting in America an ombudsman system or any similar grievance mechanism. To Gellhorn, ombudsmen should not play an adversary role similar to the role lawyers play in our legal system when defending their clients. He simply perceives an ombudsman's office as a complaint bureau where citizens can come to voice their grievances against public service performance, or say in effect: "I'm not getting proper service and should not someone look into the matter?"[155]

Gellhorn acknowledged that we have traditionally relied upon our national and state legislators to respond to our complaints about how we have been treated by administrators. But he is convinced that legislators normally investigate complaints with only the individual's interest in mind and without proper regard to the actual merits of the complaint. That is, the legislator's approach is often expressed in the attitude that: "By God, I'm going to win this case for my constituent!"[156] But Gellhorn aptly noted that the constituent's complaint is often illegitimate and should not be defended and won. However, he exclaimed:

"But from the legislator's point of view, who is trying to win 'brownie points' from his constituent, winning is the important thing."[157] What Gellhorn wants is "someone to look into the situation from the standpoint of improving administration and not merely [from the perspective of] getting satisfaction for the original complainant."[158] Unfortunately, he confided, legislators are often content with resolving the particular problem for the complainant, while allowing the administrative problem to continue for others.

Gellhorn maintained that an ombudsman would handle the complaint much differently. The ombudsman may not try to resolve an alleged administrative problem in light of a single complaint; but after hearing the same complaint several times, he would be motivated to investigate the reasons for the problem, acknowledging that the frequency of the case points to an administrative breakdown somewhere. Then the ombudsman would be prepared to ask: "Can't something be done to make sure that this problem does not occur again?"[159]

But then, who is really going to act for the individual citizen when he or she is victimized by an administrator's abusive discretionary actions? If an ombudsman's office is designed to defend citizens, should the ombudsman not be concerned primarily with doing just that? It should be pointed out that some critics perceive an ombudsman system as just another typical bureaucratic response to a bureaucratic problem. Robert Miewald emphasizes that an appointed ombudsman would be "expected to be a member in good standing of the bureaucracy."[160] When a citizen has a grievance about how he has been mistreated by some public agency, Miewald exclaims that the last thing this citizen wants is to be given the same runaround by a bureaucratized ombudsman office that instinctively relates more to fellow bureaucrats than to citizens who do not speak or understand the bureaucratic tradition. Consequently, Miewald finds some merit in continuing the old system, under which biased legislators are summoned by citizens to respond to their complaints. He admits critics such as Gellhorn are right in noting that "the greatest failure of the legislators is the lack of impartiality. But who wants impartiality? Impartiality in the bureaucracy means going along with the system. If I have a gripe about the bureaucracy, I am not particularly interested in a sober analysis of the existing rules, especially if those rules have caused my anguish. I do not need an ombudsman to provide me with another explanation of Catch-22. I want some action."[161]

The most serious charge against the viability of the ombudsman concept is that ombudsmen would be unable to alleviate administrative injustices and influence positive administrative reforms because an American ombudsman would not be expected to have any real powers (for example, the power to prosecute) except for the power of persuasion. For instance, in a 2002 law review article, Michele Bertran proudly defends the judiciary ombudsman system in New Jersey, but she admits that the chief complaint is that the ombudsman lacks real power. She observed that people "are disappointed that the ombudsman cannot change the court's decisions or interfere with the adjudication process in any way."[162]

How, then, could ombudsmen's suggestions be expected to carry any weight with those in our political system who have real power? Gerald Caiden, after researching the role played by several ombudsmen offices, concluded that ombudsmen really have limited jurisdictional power, conduct mostly superficial investigations, receive little recognition, and have feeble political clout.[163] In fact, most observers contend, somewhat ironically, that ombudsmen seem to be most "effective" when the system least needs it (i.e., when the existing administrative system is already fairly competent and responsive).[164] Also ironically, Robert D. Miewald and John C. Comer, after investigating the ombudsman system in Nebraska, discovered that the typical ombudsmen clientele needs ombudsmen the least since they are middle-class, relatively well educated citizens who are experienced and sophisticated enough to voice their own complaints.[165]

In *When Americans Complain,* Gellhorn asks: "What is it that makes a critical opinion weighty? Why should an administrator subordinate his judgment to that of a critic, when the critic is known to be toothless?"[166] His response is that opinions carry weight if they are respected in the community. In most situations, ombudsmen would have the respect of the people and, consequently, public officials would be foolish to ignore their criticisms. In light of valid criticisms, he holds that "few administrators have shown dogged devotion to errors that have been persuasively pointed out in an unrancorous atmosphere."[167] Besides, Gellhorn asserts, ombudsmen are frequently placed in the position of being the best defenders of administrative practices when criticisms are unfair. In short, Gellhorn perceptively concludes: "Powerlessness does not necessarily connote unpersuasiveness."[168] Given the apparent virtues of the ombudsman concept, Gellhorn urges America to give the system a try. However, other scholars are not convinced the ombudsman system is worth implementing, but Bertran is. She has concluded that the experimental judiciary ombudsman system in New Jersey has been a success. In general, she contends, the ombudsman system has helped to promote more democratic accountability in government. More specifically, she holds that the judiciary ombudsman program seeks "to guarantee a more responsive, accessible, equal and fair justice system. . . . The ombudsman links citizens with the court by educating the public about its processes and procedures, encouraging communications and interaction and conveying the public's concerns to court leaders." In the final analysis, she concludes, the ombudsman program can discourage unfair, discretionary injustices, announce a commitment to service quality, and promote a better system of judicial administration that "can help the court treat the public fairly, mete out justice speedily, and resolve disputes satisfactorily." Indications are that various ombudsman plans will be experimented with in America in the coming years, especially at the state and local levels.[169]

Resorting to Whistle-Blowers

Various methods have been advanced as feasible for protecting citizens against the arbitrary and ruthless use of administrative power. Of course, the most basic check was provided by our constitutional framers when they established a political system with shared governmental powers. Through the years legislators and judges have proposed and instituted various mechanisms for controlling administrative authority. However, in spite of these efforts to control administrative power, especially the use of administrative discretion, administrators seem to have only increased their relative position of power in our governmental system.

In response to this reality, more innovative ideas such as administrative courts and various ombudsman plans have been proposed by those fearful of the new power of public administrators. Citizen groups, especially consumer protection organizations, have joined the battle by pushing for ways to stop administrative officials from misusing their offices. Some scholars have argued that the best general approach for controlling administrative power is to make sure administrative actions are conducted in the open so that everyone can have an opportunity to see and judge the appropriateness of administrative acts.

But of all the ideas that have been proposed to keep administrative actions democratically accountable and fair to individual parties, probably the most novel idea is to institutionalize whistle-blowing. Because some believe that traditional methods have failed to prevent administrators from abusing their administrative powers, they have argued that we should rely on those inside public agencies to blow the whistle on those whom they discover acting afoul.

The positive social value of whistle-blowing had been recognized by our governmental leaders as far back as 1899 when Congress passed the Refuse Act, which provided that a person who squealed on a polluter was entitled to receive one-half of the assessed fines, even if the squealer worked for the polluting company.[170] Judging from the discoveries of thousands of dumping sites across our land, where both private and public enterprises have dumped toxic chemical wastes presenting serious health hazards, this law makes sense and should still be enforced. Of course, police organizations, frustrated by being confined by institutionalized methods for fighting crime, have also relied heavily on inside informers to blow the whistle on fellow criminals.

In *Whistle Blowing,* Ralph Nader and others make a strong argument for employing whistle-blowers to help keep all public officials acting responsibly. The inherent problem with using external control techniques to control administrative misconduct is that the watchdogs are always outside looking in. However, Nader notes, potential whistle-blowers are inside public agencies where they are obviously in the best strategic position to spot abuses of power. Nader holds that by detecting and blowing the whistle on nefarious official behavior, agency members can provide a valuable public service: "In the past whistle-blowing has illuminated dark corners of our society, saved lives, prevented injuries and disease, and stopped corruption, economic waste, and material exploitation. Conversely, the absence of such professional and individual responsibility has perpetuated these conditions."[171]

Possibly the most famous whistle-blower in recent American history was John Dean, legal counsel to President Nixon. Dean's testimony before the Senate Watergate Committee, which investigated the illegal activities of the Nixon White House, was directly responsible for the fall of the Nixon administration.[172] Nader tells the story of many more whistle-blowers who have served America well in recent years by blowing the whistle on their coworkers and bosses.[173]

Although responsible whistle-blowing can provide Americans with a valuable weapon against such official misconduct as discretionary injustices, Nader is cognizant of the probability that irresponsible whistle-blowing could render a costly disservice to virtually all parties concerned, especially by disrupting needed administrative services. Nader contends that responsible whistle-blowers must consult their conscience after spotting administrative abuses and personally decide whether the apparent misdeed should be reported. To guide their decision to blow or not blow the whistle, he recommends that all civil servants should apply the Nuremberg principle—a principle developed at the trials of Nazis charged with war crimes held during 1946 in Nuremberg, Germany. Basically, the Nuremberg principle holds that individuals, not organizations, are ultimately responsible for preventing injustices. Consequently, he places all those inside bureaucracy on notice "that the defense of 'following orders' is fundamentally defective because there exists with respect to every organization a higher law, a higher principle, a higher morality."[174]

However, Nader's advice could lead to frustrating problems. It should be recognized that morality is difficult to define and, thus, everyone marches to a different moral drummer. During the investigation into the Iran-Contra scandal in the 1980s, Colonel Oliver North lied blatantly to Congress about matters concerning the scandal, evidently believing that he should not blow the whistle on his superiors, but should instead answer to a moral authority higher than the U.S. Congress. In fact, he rooted his 1994 U.S. Senate campaign on his moral choice to defy Congress. He lost.

Due to repeated reports of corruption in our public agencies during the 1970s, pressures were predictably placed on Congress to do something about protecting whistle-blowers. Congress responded by placing some provisions in the Civil Service Reform Act of 1978 (92 Stat. 1111), which gave whistle-blowers limited protection. Basically, the legislation aimed at prohibiting reprisals from being taken against whistle-blowers. More specifically, the act prohibited governmental "officials and employees who are authorized to take personnel actions . . . from taking or failing to take a personnel action as a reprisal against employees who . . . lawfully disclose violations of law, rule, or regulation, or mismanagement, gross waste of funds, abuse of authority, or a substantial and specific danger to public health or safety."[175] To enforce this objective, the act created a special independent council, with members appointed to five-year terms by the president, to investigate any allegations that reprisals have been taken against whistle-blowers and to punish those who have taken reprisal actions.[176]

But critics immediately attacked this law, arguing that the protective provisions were much too weak to really protect whistle-blowers against agency retaliation.

'After All, It's Not Just Any Old Limb He Went Out On'

Source: Reprinted with permission of Tom Engelhardt and the *St. Louis Post-Dispatch,* October 3, 1978.

These critics predicted that the risks to whistle-blowers under this law were so clear that few employees would dare blow the whistle. This prediction proved true, so Congress amended the 1978 Law with the Whistleblower Protection Act of 1989 (103 Stat. 16). These amendments strengthened significantly the protections for whistle-blowers by (1) redefining retaliation, expanding the definition to include even threats of retaliation; (2) making it easier to prove retaliation by having to show only that whistle-blowing was a contributing factor to agency action against them, not a prevailing factor; (3) making it more difficult for the government to defend itself by arguing that the whistle-blower was really being punished for other reasons, not for whistle-blowing (the government now has to base its stand on "clear and convincing evidence" rather than on a "preponderance of evidence") and (4) allowing whistle-blowers to initiate independent action before the Merit Systems Protection Board.[177]

Unquestionably, the Whistleblower Protection Act of 1989, as amended, constitutes a significant improvement over feeble whistle-blower protections found in the 1978 Civil Service Reform Act. Many states have also passed whistle-blower protection laws. However, evidence suggests that whistle-blowing is still risky business.

Whistle-blowers have also experienced unfortunate setbacks in court due to a variety of reasons, including loopholes in whistle-blower legislation and the incompatibility of whistle-blower laws with other state and federal laws, as well as state and federal constitutional provisions. Whistle-blowers have had a particularly frustrating time overcoming in court state and federal immunity protections given to the government/officials, including immunity protections given to states under the Eleventh Amendment (*Gragg v. Kentucky Cabinet For Workforce Development*, 289 F.3d 958, 963 [2002]).

In *Rose v. Stephens*, 291 F. 3d 917 (2002), Gary Rose argued that he was fired as commissioner of the Kentucky State Police in violation of Kentucky's Whistle-blower Act. The Sixth Circuit Court of Appeals affirmed the district court's ruling, holding that Rose's whistle-blower claim cannot be argued in federal district court as the court "lacked jurisdiction over this claim because the language of the act only waived Kentucky's sovereign immunity for claims brought to state court, thus retaining the state's Eleventh Amendment immunity from suit in federal court" (p. 925). In another recent case, *Perez v. Region 20 Educational Service Center*, 307 F.3d 318 (2002), the Fifth Circuit Court of Appeals ruled against Perez, who contended that he was terminated illegally under the Texas Whistleblower Act because he had reported sexual harassment of another employee by management. The Texas Whistleblower Act prohibits a government employer to retaliate against any "employee who, in good faith, reports his employer's violation of law to an appropriate law enforcement agency." Yet without ruling on the merits of the claim, the court simply dismissed the suit, concluding: "Since we hold that Region 20 is an arm of the State of Texas, sovereign immunity bars Perez's claim under the Whistleblower Act" (p. 333). Ironically, even though many, if not most, whistle-blower laws waive government/official immunity protections, commonly the courts find that they somehow do not apply, leaving the whistle-blower vulnerable and unprotected and a loser in an expensive litigation.[178]

SUMMARY

Administrative power is feared by many today because public administrators possess broad discretionary powers that do not appear to be very closely monitored by the other branches of government. Many observers believe that democratic government in America is being threatened by the use of excessive administrative discretion. Specifically, they contend that administrative discretion plays too great a role in shaping and exercising public policy. But the problem of finding the proper dose of unthreatening discretion is as old as democratic government itself. Theoretically, the use of the administrative discretion conflicts sharply with basic rule-of-law principles, since its use seems to place administrators above the law. The exercise of discretion is condemned by strict rule-of-law advocates who maintain that where law ends, tyranny begins. For them, the use of discretion must eventually lead to the decline of liberty and the rise of tyranny.

Kenneth C. Davis, the leading authority on the subject, stresses the seriousness of discretionary injustices against individual parties. Consequently, he urges administrative law scholars to devote considerably more attention to it. However, he does not accept the position that discretion leading to tyrannical rule must start where the law ends. He insists that when the law ends, only the use of discretion begins and that discretion can be employed to preserve democratic institutions and practices. Davis says that most discretionary injustices occur when administrators exercise their broad, informal discretionary powers that fall into their legitimate scope of authority. Such discretion represents approximately 90 percent of all agency actions. He asserts that few injustices occur when administrative actions are formal (structured) and also subject to judicial scrutiny. To guard against abuses of administrative discretion, he suggests that steps be taken to confine, structure, and check informal discretionary agency actions. He believes that administrators should draft their own rules to confine, structure, and check discretionary agency behavior.

However, critics charge that Davis is naive to think that administrators will be willing to place effective restrictions on their own discretionary powers voluntarily, especially since most administrators seek more flexibility in their work. J. Skelly Wright argues that administrative discretion will not be adequately controlled in the future unless Congress decides to reassert its authority to play its proper constitutional role as the chief architect of our laws. But in the final analysis, he feels that the courts must assume primary responsibility for compelling administrators to structure discretion so that its use is more in line with constitutional standards of fair play. But these recommendations also seem to be rooted in naive assumptions. Recent court decisions and congressional behavior do not suggest that judges and legislators are willing to take steps to restrict the exercise of administrative discretion. While Congress has refused to attach meaningful standards to guide agency discretion, *Chevron, Chaney,* and *Mead* stand as major examples of the court's willingness to defer readily to the broad exercise of administrative discretion.

Since traditional political controls have apparently not been able to adequately control the use of administrative discretion, some nontraditional ideas have been proposed for keeping discretionary agency practices within limits that would be safe for democracy. Proposals have called for administrative courts, ombudsmen, and even the institutionalization of whistle-blowing. All of these ideas have been implemented to some extent in the American legal-political system, but each has received mixed reviews and less than enthusiastic support.

LINCOLN V. VIGIL

508 U.S. 182; 113 S.Ct. 2024 (1993)

Facts

In 1985 the Indian Health Service announced that it was discontinuing direct clinical services for handicapped Indian children under the Snyder Act and the Indian Health Care Improvement Act. Instead, the service decided to use lump-sum appropriations from Congress to establish a nationwide treatment program. As a result, handicapped Indian children filed suit against the director of Indian Health Service et al., charging, inter alia, that the service's discretionary decision to cancel clinical services for Indian children violated the Snyder Act, the Improvement Act, the Administrative Procedure Act, the Fifth Amendment's due process clause, and generally, the federal trust responsibility to Indians. The district court and the court of appeals, ruling in favor of the Indian children, inter alia, rejected the service's contention that the decision to discontinue the clinical service was "committed to agency discretion by law" under the APA, Section 201(a)(2). The service appealed and the Supreme Court granted certiorari.

Justice Souter delivered the opinion of the unanimous Court.

For several years in the late 1970s and early 1980s, the Indian Health Service provided diagnostic and treatment services, referred to collectively as the Indian Children's Program, to handicapped Indian children in the Southwest. In 1985, the Service decided to reallocate the Program's resources to a nationwide effort to assist such children. We hold that the Service's decision to discontinue the Program was "committed to agency discretion by law" and therefore not subject to judicial review under the Administrative Procedure Act . . . and that the Service's exercise of that discretion was not subject to the notice-and-comment rulemaking requirements imposed by Section 553.

The Indian Health Service, an agency within the Public Health Service of the Department of Health and Human services, provides health care for some 1.5 million American Indian and Alaska Native people. . . . The Service receives yearly lump-sum appropriations from Congress and expends the funds under authority of the Snyder Act . . . and the Indian Health Care Improvement Act. . . . So far as it concerns us here, the Snyder Act authorizes the Service to "expend such moneys as Congress may from time to time appropriate, for the benefit, care, and assistance of the Indians," for the "relief of . . . distress and conservation of health." . . . The Improvement Act authorizes expenditures for, *inter alia*, Indian mental-health care, and specifically for "therapeutic and residential treatment centers." . . .

This case concerns a collection of related services, commonly known as the Indian Children's Program, that the Service provided from 1978 to 1985. In the words of the court of Appeals, a "cloud of bureaucratic haze" obscures the history of the Program, *Vigil v. Rhoades*, . . . which seems to have grown out of a plan "to establish therapeutic and residential treatment centers for disturbed Indian children." . . .

Congress never expressly appropriated funds for these centers. In 1978, however, the Service allocated approximately $292,000 from its fiscal year 1978 appropriation to its office in Albuquerque, New Mexico, for the planning and development of a pilot project for handicapped Indian children, which became known as the Indian Children's Program. . . . The pilot project apparently convinced the Service that a building was needed, and, in 1979, the Service requested $3.5 million from Congress to construct a diagnostic and treatment center for handicapped children. . . . The appropriation for fiscal year 1980 did not expressly provide the requested funds, however, and legislative reports indicated only that Congress had increased the Service's funding by $300,000 for nationwide expansion and development for the Program in coordination with the Bureau. . . .

Plans for a national program to be managed jointly by the Service and the Bureau were never fulfilled, however, and the Program continued simply as an offering of the Service's Albuquerque office, from which the Program's staff of 11 to 16 employees would make monthly visits to Indian communities in New Mexico and southern Colorado and on the Navajo and Hopi Reservations. . . . The Program's staff provided "diagnostic, evaluation, treatment planning and follow-up services" for Indian children with emotional, educational, physical, or mental handicaps. . . . Congress never authorized or appropriated monies expressly for the Program, and the Services continued to pay for its regional activities . . . out of annual lump-sum appropriations from 1980 to 1985, during which period the Service repeatedly apprised Congress of the Program's continuing operation. . . .

Nevertheless, the Service had not abandoned the proposal for a nationwide treatment program, and in June 1985 it notified those who referred patients to the Program that it was "reevaluating the Program's purpose . . . as a national mental health program for Indian children and adolescents." . . . In August 1985, the Service determined that Program staff hitherto assigned to provide direct clinical services should be reassigned as consultants to other nationwide Service programs . . . and discontinued the direct clinical services to Indian children in the Southwest. . . .

The Service invited public "input" during this "difficult transition," and explained that the reallocation of resources had been "motivated by our goals of increased mental health services for all Indian children." . . .

Respondents, handicapped Indian children eligible to receive services through the Program, subsequently brought this action for declaratory and injunctive relief against petitioners, the Director of the Service and others (collectively, the Service), in the United States District Court for the District of New Mexico. Respondents alleged, *inter alia*, that the Service's decision to discontinue direct clinical services violated the federal trust responsibility to Indians, the Snyder Act, the Improvement Act, the Administrative Procedure Act, various agency regulations, and the Fifth Amendment's Due Process Clause.

The District Court granted summary judgment for respondents. . . . The District Court held that the Service's decision to discontinue the Program was subject to judicial review, rejecting the argument that the Service's decision was "committed to agency discretion by Law" under the Administrative Procedure Act. . . . The court declined on ripeness grounds, however, to address the merits of the Service's action. It held that the Service's decision to discontinue the Program amounted to the making of a "legislative rule" subject to the APA's notice-and-comment requirement, . . . and that the termination was also subject to the APA's publication requirements for the adoption of "statements of general policy." . . . Because the Service had not met these procedural requirements, the court concluded that the termination was procedurally invalid and that judicial review would be "premature." . . . The court ordered the Service to reinstate the Program, . . . and the Solicitor General has represented that a reinstated Program is now in place. . . .

The Court of Appeals affirmed. Like the District Court, it rejected the Service's argument that the decision to discontinue the Program was committed to agency discretion under the APA. Although the court concededly could identify no statue or regulation even mentioning the Program, . . . it believed that the repeated references to it in the legislative history of the annual appropriations Acts, . . . "in combination with the special relationship between the Indian people and the federal government," . . . provided a basis for judicial review. The Court of Appeals also affirmed the District

Court's ruling that the Service was subject to the APA's notice-and-comment procedures in terminating the Program, reasoning that our decision in *Morton v. Ruiz* . . . requires as much whenever the Federal Government "cuts back congressionally created and funded programs for Indians." . . . We granted certiorari to address the narrow questions presented by the Court of Appeals's decision. . . .

First is the question whether it was error for the Court of Appeals to hold the substance of the Service's decision to terminate the Program reviewable under the APA. The Act provides that "a person suffering legal wrong because of agency action, or adversely affected or aggrieved by agency action within the meaning of a relevant statute, is entitled to judicial review thereof," . . . and we have read the Act as embodying a "basic presumption of judicial review." . . . This is "just" a presumption, however, . . . and under Section 701(a)(2) agency action is not subject to judicial review "to the extent that" such action "is committed to agency discretion by law." . . . As we explained in *Heckler v. Chaney*, . . . Section 701(a)(2) makes it clear that "review is not to be had" in those rare circumstances where the relevant statue . . . "is drawn so that a court would have no meaningful standard against which to judge the agency's exercise of discretion." . . . "In such a case, the statute ('law') can be taken to have 'committed' the decisionmaking to the agency's judgment absolutely." . . .

Over the years, we have read Section 701(a)(2) to preclude judicial review of certain categories of administrative decisions that courts traditionally have regarded as "committed to agency discretion." . . . In Heckler itself, we held an agency's decision not to institute enforcement proceedings to be presumptively unreviewable under Section 701(a)(2). . . . An agency's "decision not to enforce often involves a complicated balancing of a number of factors which are peculiarly within its expertise," . . . and for this and other good reasons, we concluded, "such a decision has traditionally been 'committed to agency discretion.'" . . .

The allocation of funds from a lump-sum appropriation is another administrative decision traditionally regarded as committed to agency discretion. After all, the very point of a lump-sum appropriation is to give an agency the capacity to adapt to changing circumstances and meet its statutory responsibilities in what it sees as the most effective or desirable way. . . . For this reason, a fundamental principle of appropriations law is that where "Congress merely appropriates lump-sum amounts without statutorily restricting what can be done with those funds, a clear inference arises that it does not intend to impose legally binding restrictions, . . .

Like the decision against instituting enforcement proceedings, then, an agency's allocation of funds from a lump-sum appropriation requires "a complicated balancing of a number of factors which are peculiarly within its expertise": whether its "resources are best spent" on the one program or another, whether it "is likely to succeed" in fulfilling its statutory mandate; whether a particular program "best fits the agency's overall policies"; and, "indeed, whether the agency has enough re-

sources" to fund a program "at all." As in *Heckler*, so here, the "agency is far better equipped than the courts to deal with the many variables involved in the proper ordering of its priorities." . . . Of course, an agency is not free simply to disregard statutory responsibilities: Congress may always circumscribe agency discretion to allocate resources by putting restrictions in the operative statutes (though not, as we have seen, just in the legislative history). . . . And, of course, we hardly need to note that an agency's decision to ignore congressional expectations may expose it to grave political consequences. But as long as the agency allocates funds from a lump-sum appropriation to meet permissible statutory objectives, Section 701(a)(2) gives the courts no leave to intrude. "To that extent," the decision to allocate funds "is committed to agency discretion by law." Section 701(a)(2).

The Service's decision to discontinue the Program is accordingly unreviewable under Section 701(a)(2). As the Court of Appeals recognized, the appropriations Acts for the relevant period do not so much as mention the Program, . . . and both the Snyder Act and the Improvement Act likewise speak about Indian health only in general terms. It is true that the Service repeatedly apprised Congress of the Program's continued operation, but, as we have explained, these representations do not translate through the medium of legislative history into legally binding obligations. The reallocation of agency resources to assist handicapped Indian children nationwide clearly falls within the Service's statutory mandate to provide health care to Indian people, . . . and respondents, indeed, do not seriously contend otherwise. The decision to terminate the Program was committed to the Service's discretion. . . .

We next consider the Court of Appeals's holding, quite apart from the matter of substantive reviewability, that before terminating the Program the Service was required to abide by the familiar notice-and-comment rulemaking provisions of the APA, 5 U.S.C. Section 553. Section 553 provides generally that an agency must publish notice of a proposed rulemaking in the Federal Register and afford "interested persons an opportunity to participate . . . through submission of written data, views, or arguments." . . . The same section also generally requires the agency to publish a rule not less than 30 days before its effective date and incorporate within it "a concise general statement" of the rule's "basis and purpose." . . . There are exceptions, of course. Section 553 has no application, for example, to "a matter relating to agency management or personnel or to public property, loans, grants, benefits, or contracts." . . . The notice-and-comment requirements apply, moreover, only to so-called "legislative" or "substantive" rules; they do not apply to "interpretative rules, general statements of policy, or rules of agency organization, procedures, or practice." . . .

It is undisputed that the Service did not abide by these notice-and-comment requirements before discontinuing the Program and reallocating its resources. The Service argues that it was free from any such obligation because its decision to terminate the Pro-

gram did not qualify as a "rule" within the meaning of the APA. . . . Respondents, . . . to the contrary, contend that the Service's action falls well within the Act's broad definition of that term. . . . Determining whether an agency's statement is what the APA calls a "rule" can be a difficult exercise. We need not conduct that exercise in this case, however. For even assuming that a statement terminating the Program would qualify as a "rule" within the meaning of the APA, it would be exempt from the notice-and-comment requirements of Section 553. . . . Termination of the Program might be seen as affecting the Service's organization, but "rules of agency organization" are exempt from notice-and-comment requirements under Section 553(b)(A). Moreover, Section 553(b)(A) also exempts "general statements of policy," which we have previously described as "'statements issued by an agency to advise the public prospectively of the manner in which the agency proposes to exercise a discretionary power.'" . . . Whatever else may be considered a "general statement of policy," the term surely includes an announcement like the one before us, that an agency will discontinue a discretionary allocation of unrestricted funds from a lump-sum appropriation. . . .

Our decision in *Citizens to Preserve Overton Park, Inc. v. Volpe* . . . confirms our conclusion that the Service was not required to follow the notice-and-comment procedures of Section 553 before terminating the Program. . . . We held unequivocally that "the Secretary's decision to allow the expenditure of federal funds to build the highway through the park was plainly not an exercise of a rulemaking function." . . .

Overton Park is authority here for the proposition that decisions to expend otherwise unrestricted funds are not, without more, subject to the notice-and-comment requirement of Section 553. Although the Secretary's determination in Overton Park was subject to statutory criteria of "'feasibility and prudence" . . . the generality of

those standards underscores the administrative discretion inherent in the determination (reviewable though it was), to which the Service's discretionary authority to meet its obligations under the Snyder and Improvement Acts is comparable. . . .

The judgment of the Court of Appeals is reversed, and the case is remanded for further proceedings consistent with this opinion.

COMMENTS AND QUESTIONS

This Supreme Court decision is just another in a long series of decisions in which this quite conservative high court has decided that the judiciary should not meddle (i.e., not even review) an agency decision that is properly "committed to agency discretion by law." This case simply involves a dispute over whether an agency or agency director (in this case the director of the Indian Health Service) can spend lump-sum money, appropriated by Congress to the agency for various programs, the way it wants (i.e., at the agency's discretion).

Reiterating the Court's controversial position in *Heckler v. Chaney* (1985), Justice Souter, writing for the unanimous Court, argued basically that unless statutory language specifically forbids an agency from spending or not spending appropriations in a particular manner, that agency has the discretion to spend the money the way it deems appropriate. Specifically, the Court held that the Indian Health Service's decision to discontinue the clinical services for the Indian children was "committed to agency discretion by law" and was, therefore, not subject to judicial review under the APA. According to the Court, the service had every discretionary right to spend lump-sum money appropriated by Congress the way it sees fit to meet statutory objectives, as long as specific legislative intent is not violated. The Court emphasized that decisions as to how to spend money for various agency programs involve balancing many complex factors that only agency experts can do. Courts, Justice Souter stressed, should defer to agency discretion and should not intrude in such agency business. In 2003 the Supreme Court said almost the same thing in *Washington State Dept. of Social and Health Services v. Keffeler*, 537 U.S. 371.

Such extreme deference to agency discretion was well established by the Supreme Court about a decade before in *Chevron* and *Chaney*. *Vigil* simply continued the trend. Ironically, however, lower courts have not always followed the *Chevron* doctrine, refusing to allow agencies to exercise so much unbridled discretion. Of course, one should note that in *Vigil* a unanimous Supreme Court reversed two lower court opinions that refused to permit the Indian Health Service to use its discretion to terminate these Indian services. Do you think the Supreme

Court is wise in allowing agency administrators to exercise so much discretion? Should agency discretion on how to spend lump-sum appropriations from Congress be made virtually unreviewable, as the Supreme Court has ruled? The new conservative politics has pushed for more lump-sum appropriations to agencies and block grants to states that allow administrators in federal and state agencies to exercise considerably more discretion over how tax dollars are spent. Given court reluctance to review such discretionary spending, do you think this is a good idea? Does it encourage fiscal responsibility?

NOTES

1. Richard J. Pierce, Jr., *Administrative Law Treatise*, 4th ed. (New York: Aspen, 2002), vol. 1, p. 24.

2. Kenneth C. Davis, *Discretionary Justice: A Preliminary Inquiry* (Westport, Conn.: Greenwood Press, 1980), p. 4. This book is a reprint of Davis's classic work, first published by University of Illinois Press (Urbana, 1969).

3. Ibid.

4. Ibid.

5. Kenneth C. Davis, *Administrative Law: Cases, Text, Problems* (St. Paul: West, 1977), p. 440.

6. Ibid., pp. 440–47.

7. Kenneth C. Davis and Richard Pierce, Jr., *Administrative Law Casebook* (Boston: Little, Brown, 1994), vol. 3, chap. 17.

8. Ibid.

9. Ibid.

10. For a discussion of such court rulings see, Kenneth F. Warren, "'Spatial Deconcentrating': A Problem Greater than School Desegregation," *Administrative Law Review* 29 (fall 1977).

11. Davis and Pierce, *Administrative Law Treatise*, 3rd ed., vol. 3, p. 105

12. Davis, *Administrative Law: Cases, Text, Problems*, p. 443.

13. Pierce, *Administrative Law Treatise*, 4th ed., vol. 3, p. 1285.

14. Davis, *Administrative Law: Cases, Text, Problems*, p. 442.

15. Ibid.

16. Ibid.

17. Jeffrey Pressman and Aaron Wildavsky, *Implementation* (Berkeley: University of California Press, 1973), chaps. 1–3.

18. Davis, *Discretionary Justice*, p. 4.

19. Joel Samaha, *Criminal Law*, 2nd ed. (St. Paul: West, 1987), p. 14.

20. Davis, *Discretionary Justice*, pp. 4–5.

21. See, for example, the court's arguments in defense of the broad use of discretion in *United States v. International Telephone Corp. and Hartford Fire Insurance Co.*, 349 F. Supp. 22 (1972). It is not as necessary to prove "bad faith" today, because "good faith" cannot be used as a defense when constitutional rights are violated by public officials.

22. Joel Samaha, "Some Reflections on the Anglo-Saxon Heritage of Discretionary Justice," in Lawrence Edwin Abt and Irving R. Stuart, eds. *Social Psychology and Discretionary Law* (New York: Van Nostrand Reinhold, 1979), p. 4.

23. Ibid.

24. See, for example, Plato's discussion of the need for flexibility in the in *The Republic*, trans. F. M. Cornford (New York: Oxford University Press, 1945), book 7, pp. 514a–519e; and Aristotle's call for flexibility in laws in *The Politics*, trans. T. A. Sinclair (Baltimore: Penguin Books, 1962), book 3.

25. Samaha, "Some Reflections on the Anglo-Saxon Heritage," p. 8.

26. Ibid., p. 7.

27. Ibid., pp. 11.

28. Ibid., p. 11–14.

29. Ibid. p. 13.

30. Ibid., pp. 13–14.

31. Davis, *Discretionary Justice*; see also Kenneth C. Davis, *Discretionary Justice in Europe and America* (Urbana: University of Illinois Press, 1976); Kenneth C. Davis, *Police Discretion* (St. Paul: West, 1975); Davis, *Administrative Law Treatise,* 2nd ed. (St. Paul: West, 1980); and Davis and Pierce, *Administrative Law Treatise*, 3rd ed., vol. 3, chap. 17.

32. In his 1979 *Administrative Law Treatise*, vol. 2, p. 160, Davis wrote that the discussion of discretionary justice represents "a mixture of new ideas with ideas drawn from the 1969 book and from the writer's *Police Discretion* (1975) and *Discretionary Justice in Europe and America* (1976)."

33. Davis, *Administrative Law Treatise*, 2nd ed., vol. 2, p. 160.

34. Davis and Pierce, *Administrative Law Treatise*, 3rd ed., vol. 3, p. 102.

35. Davis, *Administrative Law Treatise*, 2nd ed., vol. 2, p. 158.

36. Ibid.

37. Ibid., p. 159.

38. Richard J. Pierce, Jr., "Judicial Review of Agency Actions in a Period of Diminishing Agency Resources," *Administrative Law Review* 49 (winter 1997).

39. Davis, *Discretionary Justice*, p. 3.

40. Davis, *Administrative Law Treatise*, 2nd ed., vol. 2, p. 165.

41. Davis, *Discretionary Justice*, p. 3.

42. Ibid., pp. 3–4.

43. However, this is not always the case. In *Police Discretion*, Davis argues that police officers on the beat possess enormous and significant discretionary powers. Their decisions may have major consequences for individuals.

44. Davis, *Discretionary Justice*, pp. 52–54.

45. Ibid., p. 55.

46. As quoted in Oscar Kraines, *The World and Ideas of Ernest Freund: The Search for General Principles of Legislation and Administration* (Birmingham: University of Alabama Press, 1974), p. 104, appearing in Donald D. Barry and Howard R. Whitcomb, *The Legal Foundations of Public Administration*, 2d ed. (St. Paul: West, 1987), p. 248.

47. Davis, *Discretionary Justice*, p. 55.

48. Norton Long, "Public Policy and Administration: The Goals of Rationality and Responsibility," *Public Administration Review* 14 (winter 1954); Henry Friendly, *The Federal Administrative Agencies* (Cambridge, Mass.: Harvard University Press, 1962); and Davis, *Discretionary Justice*, pp. 56–59.

49. Davis, *Discretionary Justice*, pp. 56–57.

50. Ibid., p. 57.

51. Ibid., p. 65.

52. Ibid., pp. 65–68.

53. Ibid., p. 97.

54. Ibid.

55. Ibid.

56. Ibid., pp. 97–99.

57. Davis, *Administrative Law Treatise*, 2nd ed., vol. 2, p. 207.

58. Ibid.

59. Davis, *Discretionary Justice*, p. 98.

60. Ibid.

61. Ibid., p. 102.

62. For another viewpoint on how to control abuses of administrative discretion, see Ronald A. Cass, Colin A. Diver, and Jack M. Beermann, *Administrative Law: Cases and Materials*, 2nd ed. (Boston: Little, Brown, 1994), pp. 279–293.

63. Ibid., pp. 152–156.

64. Ibid., pp. 152–153.

65. J. Skelly Wright, "Beyond Discretionary Justice," *Yale Law Journal* 81 (January 1972): 575–577.

66. Davis, *Discretionary Justice*, p. 142.

67. Ibid., pp. 142–143.

68. Ibid., p. 142.

69. Davis, *Administrative Law Treatise*, 2nd ed., vol. 2, p. 171.

70. Davis, *Discretionary Justice*, pp. 142–161.

71. Wright, "Beyond Discretionary Justice," pp. 575–577.

72. Ibid., pp. 576–580.

73. Ibid., p. 577.

74. Ibid.

75. Ibid.

76. Ibid.

77. Ibid., p. 578.

78. Ibid.

79. The expression "muddling through" was made famous in the public administration literature by Charles Lindbloom; for his argument that "muddling through" should be seen in a favorable light, see "The Science of Muddling Through," *Public Administration Review* 19 (spring 1959). More recently, Daniel J. Gifford in "Discretionary Decisionmaking in the Regulatory Agencies," pp. 117–121, applies the concept of "muddling through" to his analysis of agency discretion.

80. Wright, "Beyond Discretionary Justice," p. 579. Of course, this view is not profound and is made by virtually every scholar writing on the subject. For a more recent article, see Charles H. Koch, Jr., "Judicial Review of Administrative Discretion," *George Washington Law Review* 54 (May 1986).

81. Wright, "Beyond Discretionary Justice," p. 579.

82. Ibid., pp. 578–579.

83. Ibid., pp. 581–582.

84. Ibid., p. 580.

85. Ibid., p. 581.

86. Ibid., p. 582.

87. Ibid.

88. Ibid., p. 584.

89. Ibid., pp. 583–584.

90. Ibid., p. 585.

91. Ibid.

92. Ibid.

93. Ibid., p. 589.

94. Ibid., pp. 587–593.

95. Wright, "Beyond Discretionary Justice," p. 581; see also Davis, *Administrative Law Treatise*, 2nd ed., vol. 2, p. 173. Basically, Davis argues that the courts provide a poor check against discretionary abuses because of the "practical unavailability" of judicial review.

96. Wright, "Beyond Discretionary Justice," p. 595.

97. Ibid., p. 596.

98. Gifford, "Discretionary Decisionmaking in the Regulatory Agencies," p. 104.

99. Ibid., p. 104.

100. Ibid., p. 105–106. See Isaiah L. Sharfman, *The Interstate Commerce Commission* (New York: Commonwealth, 1931–1937).

101. Gifford, "Discretionary Decisionmaking in the Regulatory Agencies," p. 105.

102. Ibid., p. 106.

103. Ibid., p. 103.

104. Ibid., p. 122.

105. Ibid., p. 135.

106. Bernard Schwartz, "Administrative Law Cases During 1979," *Administrative Law Review* 32 (summer 1980): 411.

107. Ibid.

108. Davis, *Administrative Law Treatise*, 2nd ed., vol. 2, p. 161.

109. Certiorari denied, 417 U.S. 921 (1974).

110. Schwartz, "Administrative Law Cases During 1979," p. 414.

111. Davis and Pierce, *Administrative Law Treatise*, 3rd ed.

112. Davis, *Administrative Law Treatise*, 2nd ed., p. 161. Ironically, in their 1994 *Administrative Law Treatise*, 2nd ed., p. 161, Davis and Pierce reject Davis's earlier analysis, specifically stating that agencies must be allowed to make ad hoc adjustments through adjudications to legislative rules because no

agency can "identify and answer definitively in advance all of the questions that will arise in implementing a regulatory scheme." Common sense, they assert, dictates that *Ruiz*'s restrictions on the application of legislative rule, severally limiting discretion, "is not, and cannot, be the law" (at 274).

113. Certiorari denied, 105 S.Ct. 2151 (1985).

114. For criticism of *Vermont Yankees*, see sources noted by Allen F. Wichelman in "Case Notes: *Vermont Yankee v. NRDC*," *Santa Clara Law Review* 19 (1979).

115. Ibid.

116. The "hard look" standard was developed in *Greater Boston Television Corp. v. FCC*, 444 F.2d 841, 851 (D.C. Cir. 1970), cert. denied, 403 U.S. 923 (1971). It requires reviewing courts to make sure that the decisionmaker took a "hard look" at the facts before reaching a decision.

117. Ibid., p. 803.

118. Michael J. Perry, "Substantive Due Process Revisited: Reflections on (and Beyond) Recent Cases," *Northwestern Law Review* 71 (September–October 1976); and Wichelman, "Case Notes," pp. 801–803.

119. Wichelman, "Case Notes," pp. 803–804.

120. Ibid., p. 807.

121. Kenneth C. Davis, "Administrative Common Law and the *Vermont Yankee* Opinion," *Utah Law Review* (1980): 7.

122. Ibid. p. 10.

123. Ibid.

124. Ibid.

125. Ibid., p. 11.

126. Ibid.

127. Cass, Diver, and Beermann, *Administrative Law*, pp. 546–547; and Pierce, *Administrative Law Treatise*, 4th ed., esp. Vol. 1, pp. 492–497.

128. Daniel D. Polsby, "*FCC v. National Citizens Committee for Broadcasting* and the Judicious Uses of Administrative Discretion," *Supreme Court Review* (1978): 3–5.

129. Ibid.

130. Ibid., p. 36.

131. See, for example, Kenneth C. Davis, *Administrative Law Treatise*, 2nd ed., vol. 5 (San Diego: K. C. Davis, 1984), pp. 274–283.

132. Bernard Schwartz, "Administrative Law Cases During 1985," *Administrative Law Review* 38 (summer 1986): 310.

133. Ibid., pp. 310–311. For a discussion of the Wednesbury principle, as set forth in *Associated Provincial Picture Houses Ltd. v. Wednesbury Corporation* (1948) 1 K. R. at 229, see M. A. Fazal, "Judicial Review of Administrative Discretion: Anglo-American Perspectives," *Trent Law Journal* 9 (1985).

134. Shane Spellisey, "Burning the Idols of Non-Arbitrability: Arbitrating Administrative Law Disputes with Foreign Investors," *American Review of International Arbitration* 12 (2001): 101.

135. Frank Goodnow, in *Comparative Administrative Law* (New York: G. P. Putnam's Sons, 1903), chaps. 1–3, 5, advanced the idea that it would be wise to develop an administrative courtlike system.

136. Neil Sullivan, "Independent Adjudication and Occupational Safety and Health Policy: A Test for Administrative Court Theory," *Administrative Law Review* 31 (spring 1979): 179.

137. Ibid.

138. Ibid., pp. 179–180.

139. Harold H. Bruff, "Specialized Courts in Administrative Law," *Administrative Law Review* 43 (summer 1991): 331.

140. Sullivan, "Independent Adjudication and Occupational Safety and Health Policy," pp. 177–178.

141. Bruff, "Specialized Courts in Administrative Law," p. 331.

142. Stephen Breyer, *Regulation and Its Reform* (Cambridge, Mass.: Harvard University Press, 1982), p. 361. In 1994 President Clinton appointed Stephen Breyer to the Supreme Court.

143. Lewis Mainzer, *Political Bureaucracy* (Glenview, Ill: Scott, Foresman, 1973), p. 54.

144. Bruff, "Specialized Courts in Administrative Law," p. 331.

145. Ibid., p. 331–332.

146. Spellisey, "Burning Idols of Non-Arbitrability," pp. 100–101.

147. Jean-Philippe Colson, "Remedy Discussion Forum: Remedies Discussion Forum," *Brandeis Law Journal* 39 (spring 2001).

148. Kenneth J. Meier, *Politics and the Bureaucracy: Policymaking in the Fourth Branch of Government*, 3rd ed. (Pacific Grove, Calif.: Brooks/Cole, 1993), p. 186.

149. Walter Gellhorn, *Ombudsmen and Others* (Cambridge, Mass.: Harvard University Press, 1960), and *When Americans Complain* (Cambridge, Mass.: Harvard University Press, 1996).

150. Elletta Sangrey Callahan, et. al., "Integrating Trends in Whistleblowing and Corporate Governance," *American Business Law Journal* 40 (fall 2002): 205.

151. Davis, *Administrative Law Treatise*, 2nd ed., vol. 2, pp. 172–173.

152. Meier, *Politics and the Bureaucracy*, p. 187.

153. Hans A. Linde and George Bunn, *Legislative and Administrative Processes* (Mineola, N.Y.: Foundation Press, 1976), p. 608.

154. Ibid.

155. Walter Gellhorn, interview with the author, St. Louis University, March 5, 1980.

156. Ibid.

157. Ibid.

158. Ibid.

159. Ibid. However, Kenneth J. Meier, in *Politics and the Bureaucracy*, argues that the problem with ombudsmen is that they focus on individual complaints and really do not try to resolve the broader, systemic problem in the administrative process.

160. Robert D. Miewald, *Public Administration: A Critical Perspective* (New York: McGraw-Hill, 1978), p. 249.

161. Ibid., p. 250.

162. Michelle Bertran, "Judiciary Ombudsman: Solving Problems in the Courts," *Fordham Urban Law Journal* 29 (June 2002): 2115.

163. Gerald W. Caiden, *Organizational Handbook of the Ombudsman* (Westport, Conn.: Greenwood Press, 1983).

164. Meier, *Politics and the Bureaucracy*, p. 187.

165. Robert D. Miewald and John E. Comer, "Complaining as Participation: The Case of the Ombudsman," *Administration and Society* 17 (February 1986).

166. Gellhorn, *When Americans Complain*, p. 229.

167. Ibid.

168. Ibid., p. 229.

169. Bertran, "Judiciary Ombudsman," pp. 2115–2116.

170. Ralph Nader, Peter J. Petkas, and Kate Blackwell, eds., *Whistle Blowing* (New York: Grossman, 1972), p. 9.

171. Ibid., p. 7.

172. John Dean, in *Blind Ambition: The White House Years* (New York: Simon and Schuster, 1976), chaps. 9–10, provides a fascinating, though possibly somewhat biased, account of this event.

173. Nader, Petkas, and Blackwell, eds., *Whistle Blowing*, chaps. 5–15.

174. Ibid.

175. Quoted in N. Joseph Cayer, *Public Personnel Administration in the United States*, 2nd ed. (New York: St. Martin's Press, 1986), pp. 34–35.

176. Ibid.

177. Robert G. Vaughn, "Consumer Access to Product Safety Information and the Future of the Freedom of Information Act," *Administrative Law Journal* 5 (fall 1991): 699–702.

178. Kathy Wyer, "Recent Developments in Utah Law: Relationship Between Whistleblower Act and Governmental Immunity Act Clarified," *Utah Law Review* (2001). Wyer's analysis makes it apparent that it is not easy to hold governmental employers liable under whistleblower laws.

CHAPTER 9

Judicial Review
of Agency Behavior

JUDICIAL REVIEW: AN OVERVIEW

The courts have expressed over the decades their clear intolerance for administrators who displayed a conspicuous disrespect for principles of procedural due process.[1] It appears that if constitutional democracy is to be preserved, agency administrators cannot be allowed to ignore laws designed to regulate their behavior or use their discretionary powers in a reckless or wanton manner. In our relatively open system of government, as has been acknowledged, there are many formal and informal vehicles that function to help keep the exercise of administrative power under reasonable control and within the realm of minimally acceptable democratic accountability standards. Yet there are those who argue that the judicial system probably provides the best authoritative vehicle for checking administrators who act afoul. The courts hear very few cases, take a relatively long time to act, are expensive, time-consuming, and inconvenient, and are quite particular and frequently unpredictable about the kinds of cases they regard as reviewable. Nevertheless, they do have the power to overrule agency actions and always represent a threat to any administrator who may contemplate acting contrary to the demands of fair and rightful procedure. Under special circumstances, the Congress has made some agency activities unreviewable, but most agency actions are ultimately subject to judicial review, especially since judges have the final say as to what the legislature intended to be reviewable or unreviewable. The courts can also declare unconstitutional various attempts by legislative assemblies to make certain administrative actions exempt from judicial review.

The power of judicial review extends awesome authority to the courts, allowing them to declare legislative and administrative actions unconstitutional, thereby making those acts null and void. **Judicial review,** in the context of administrative law, can be defined accurately as the legitimate sphere of judicial scrutiny of agency actions and the methods that the courts employ to consider the propriety of agency behavior. The power to review the constitutionality of legislative and executive actions makes the courts, in effect, the chief interpreters and defenders (or destroyers) of the Constitution, the basic blueprint that controls our government's way of doing things. In our political system, there exists no higher authority than the Supreme Court on the constitutionality of official behavior. The judicial review power enables nine justices to have the last word on what constitutional and statutory provisions really mean and to have the final say over whether governmental officials, at any level of government, are acting in a way that is consistent or inconsistent with constitutional or statutory requirements. Martin Shapiro stresses that judges exercise enormous judicial discretion, which allows them to actually make law. He argues that "although many judges and a few legal scholars persist in the view that judges only 'discover' or 'interpret' rather than 'make' law, the phenomenon of judicial law-making is widely recognized." Shapiro concludes that judges simply possess the discretion to choose "what law to make."[2]

However, despite the enormous potential power of the courts, most judges have historically been wise enough to exercise their power with caution. No doubt, judges have realized from the beginning, as President Andrew Jackson once reminded them, that the court's greatest strength is in their power to strike down acts by governmental officials; but the court's greatest weakness is that they are completely dependent upon the officials in the other governmental branches to enforce their decisions. Consequently, unreasonable and reckless court decisions would, according to virtually all American government scholars, quickly diminish the prestige and authoritative influence of the courts. Thus, in a very real sense, the judicial review power is very precariously held because, to retain their powers, judges must take care or their decisions will not be respected or upheld by legislators, administrators, interest groups, or the American people in general.

From a systems perspective, the courts must respond to environmental pressures as much as all other political actors in the political system. Political actors retain their power only so long as they can authoritatively allocate values to society. Power does not rest on formal sanctioning alone but on perceived legitimacy and respect. This reality contributes significantly to our understanding of the way courts use their judicial review powers. Despite those who have argued that courts have on occasion played an activist role (have been forceful in pushing for policy changes), in fact, they have almost always made rather conservative decisions. That is, fearing intense reaction to radical court holdings, courts have mostly made conservative decisions that have either upheld the status quo or pushed forward only gradually. Judges walk the same streets and watch the same news programs we do. When making decisions, judges are quite aware of the sort of decisions on social policies governmental institutions and society will tolerate. In Chief Justice William Rehnquist's 2002 book, *The Supreme Court*, he makes the points that judges do not make decisions in a societal vacuum, but are unavoidably influenced by societal feedback and are very cognizant of the impact their decisions will likely have on society.[3] This is one of the chief reasons social reforms proceed at such an incremental pace. The courts refuse to really push hard for needed changes in the areas of civil rights, housing, environmental policy, regulation of nuclear power, and so on. While the courts' historical conservatism allows only the most gradual social change, their practice of judicial self-restraint can be applauded because it has contributed significantly to the stability of the American political system—a trait traditionally valued highly by political scientists.

However, any court decisions, conservative or liberal, because of their perceived impact on society, are unquestionably likely to disturb some group and prove disruptive. Although court decisions that deviate radically from the current social practices would likely prove the most disruptive, court decisions that tend to support the status quo have historically pleased the haves and angered the have-nots. Social inequities can obviously obtain further sanctioning by court decisions that support the status quo.

Of course, the Supreme Court's ruling in *Dred Scott v. Sanford,* 19 Howard 393 (1857), possibly the worst decision ever handed down by the high court, was a decision that supported the status quo but proved extremely disruptive to social order in America. In this case the Court held that blacks could not become United States citizens and that blacks should not be entitled to enjoy the benefits of citizenship. This was a blatantly racist decision, even for the 1850s; and it only served to ignite the controversy surrounding the slavery issue and, consequently, played a key role in making the Civil War inevitable. In an unfortunate and costly way, the *Dred Scott* case serves to demonstrate the major role the judiciary, especially the Supreme Court, plays in influencing American social history.

It should be emphasized that it is exceedingly difficult to have a federal appellate court decision overridden, because the Supreme Court simply lacks the time to review very many appellate court rulings. The Supreme Court may overrule a circuit court decision and the circuit courts may set aside district court holdings; they often do. But it takes a constitutional amendment to overturn a Supreme Court decision on the Constitution. However, if the high court overrules a congressional statute, Congress can void the court's decision by simply passing another statute, as long as only statutory construction is in question, not constitutional issues. Of the tens of thousands of appellate and Supreme Court decisions involving constitutional questions that have been made over the years, virtually all have been allowed to stand by Congress. Congress has amended the Constitution to overrule Supreme Court decisions only five times. For example, the precedential clout of the *Dred Scott* decision was eradicated after the Civil War by the passage of the Fourteenth Amendment. Another reason the courts have possibly been reluctant to flaunt their judicial review powers is that the Constitution did not specifically assign the judicial branch this power. This power was given to the judiciary by Chief Justice John Marshall in *Marbury v.*

Madison, 1 Cranch 137 (1803). By arguing in this case that the courts should have a right to overrule acts of the other branches of government as unconstitutional, he established for the courts the power of judicial review. Marshall's basic contention was that this right was intended by the constitutional framers and was consistent with their perception of the separation of powers doctrine.

Although the authority of judicial review has been accepted as a legitimate judicial power by the vast majority of Americans, it should be pointed out that some still hold, as Judge Gibson did in *Eakin v. Raub,* 12 S.&R. 330 (1825), that the courts should not possess such power. This old Pennsylvania Supreme Court case has become famous for Judge Gibson's repudiation of Justice Marshall's logic in *Marbury.* It is considered to be probably the best argument against the judiciary's review power. Gibson argued, essentially, that the courts should not have the authority to declare congressional acts unconstitutional, because, while the courts are not a very representative (democratic) body, legislative assemblies are much more so. Courts, he maintained, should not be allowed to declare acts that are representative of the wishes of the American people null and void. The judicial review principle, he held, is essentially anti-democratic. But this viewpoint fails to recognize that democratic governments also have the obligation to protect the interests of minorities. Without judicial review, minority rights would likely be subject to the tyranny of majority will. Gibson later reversed his position and supported the concept of judicial review.

THE CHANGING ROLE OF THE COURTS

Observers have pointed out that the role the courts play in American government has changed significantly since the early days of the Republic; but the most dramatic changes have occurred since the 1930s, especially during the decade of the 1970s. Basically, it is argued that the courts once played a relatively restricted role in the American political process because they practiced judicial self-restraint. But today the courts play a major role because they are now practicing judicial activism. However, since the early 1990s the quite conservative Supreme Court, unlike most lower federal courts and state courts, has taken fewer cases and has been less active than it has in several years. Generally, however, this transition from a rather passive judiciary to an activist one has had a profound impact upon the relationship between the courts and administrative agencies.

The Courts' Traditional Role

By and large, the development of the judicial system in the United States has followed an expected course. Its evolution has largely mirrored the transformation of American government from a small, simple, and limited governing structure to a giant, complex, and pervasive governmental leviathan.[4] However, it seems valid to maintain that the court system for most of its history followed the lead of the other two branches but did not play the role as leader itself. In recent decades the courts, although the pace has slowed, have been trying to follow the torrid developmental pace set by the administrative agencies. When the administrative branch's regulatory role began to expand swiftly during the 1930s and 1940s, the courts first took the position that they should, as much as possible, try to leave administrative matters in the hands of the administrative experts. Although this attitude is not quite as strong now, it is argued later in this chapter that the supposedly activist courts today have been noticeably restrained by this still-operative hands-off attitude. This deferential attitude toward public administrators became very evident during the last few years of the Burger Court, and so far it has dominated the thinking of the Rehnquist Court into the 2000s.

The purpose of judicial review under the traditional model was simple. Basically, the job of the courts was to settle specific legal disputes between particular litigants. Typically, the issues that the courts had to resolve were quite simple, narrow, and well-defined, while the solutions appeared fairly obvious and the decisions had very limited social relevance. The legal disputes centered mostly on clear procedural questions. Did Smith receive proper notice? Did the agency deny Jones benefits entitled to him by statute? Few ever denied that it was unnecessary for the courts to protect the public by resolving such questions. For fundamental due process principles to be preserved, it appeared that the courts simply had to at least monitor the procedures that agencies employed while going about the business of implementing public policies.

Under the traditional judicial review perspective, the judiciary should stay as removed as possible from stepping on administrators' toes by hearing cases pertaining to substantive administrative policy questions. During the 1930s the courts, led by the Supreme Court, attempted to avoid ruling on disputes having to do with questions of fact (substantive issues), while concentrating on questions of law. Charles W. Stewart has written: "During the New Deal, the Supreme Court chose to eschew substantive review, permitting most administrative agencies to do business relatively free from concern with court interference."[5] To accomplish this end, judges relied on several legal doctrines to discourage requests for judicial review of substantive agency decisions (discussed later).

The Courts' Modern Role

Most scholars agree that the courts today play a dramatically different role in public administration than they did in the 1930s and 1940s. Most clearly, these changes can be seen in (1) the increased number of administrative law cases handled by the courts; (2) the courts' willingness to step in and hear a much broader variety of administrative law disputes; and (3) the major impact the courts' decisions have upon the shaping of administrative processes and substantive policies, as well as upon American social life in general. Of course, the pervasive and powerful role that the courts now play in American government has caused them to be described in textbooks as activist courts, as contrasted to their once relatively passive and meek role. To some, this new activist judicial attitude is a blessing, while to others it has created some serious problems that might prove dangerously disruptive to administrative operations and thus be harmful to the public interest. In *Judicial Compulsions*, for example, Jeremy Rabkin argues vehemently that the courts' compulsion to intervene in agency business and to too often substitute its public policy–making power for the agency's public policy authority has led to the making of poor and democratically unsanctioned public policies.[6] George Will, a noted columnist, contends that "judicial policymaking" undermines representative government by imposing undemocratically approved social policies on the people[7]; while James Buckley, senior judge on the D.C. Circuit Court of Appeals, condemns judicial activism as constitutionally illegitimate where the court wrongly makes public policy and "in reality substitutes its view of what should be so for the amending process."[8]

The Increasing Caseload. The courts have been asked to settle a growing number of disputes in all areas of law. For various reasons, the American people have turned more and more to the courts to resolve their problems. Today, it seems that few accept "no" as an answer, whether it is an employee who has been denied a promotion or a company that refuses to comply with a governmental regulation. Americans, living in a society that has grown massive and very impersonal, have, more than ever, taken on an exaggerated "what's in it for me?" litigious attitude, resulting in the filing of numerous suits with the promise of winning absurdly favorable settlements. Courts are responding by resolving disputes that judges of yesteryear, practicing judicial restraint, never dreamed they could ever litigate.

The welfare state notion that government should protect its citizens from the cradle to the grave has had its impact on the courts. While once the courts normally heard cases involving major disputes, normally between two private parties, now courts hear cases that involve relatively trivial matters, often between a private party and a public agency. In a sense, the courts have been largely responsible for increasing their own expanding caseloads. Judges have opened the judicial doors to new kinds of cases by ruling that governmental benefits, in an increasing number of situations, should be regarded as *rights* (legal entitlements) and not *privileges*. Regardless of the humanitarian merits of this argument, it has encouraged a plethora of new suits to be filed during the late 1960s and into the 2000s. Increasing educational levels, the affluence of Americans today (which allows so many to afford costly legal services), access to legal services organizations, the availability of free legal services to some, the growing involvement of administrative agencies in the private sector, the growth of citizen and consumer action groups, the courts' new relaxed attitude on standing, and the surplus of lawyers filing nonsense suits because they need the work—all have served to encourage Americans to go to court.

Steven Vago emphasizes that more than ever the American people have come to rely upon the courts to resolve their problems. "Indeed," Vago asserts, "litigation is becoming a national pastime, and more and more people are telling their troubles to a judge."[9] The number of civil cases filed in the district courts, where the vast majority of administrative law cases are heard, went from 59,284 in 1960 to 168,789 in 1980 to 253,354 in 2001, or up 427 percent from 1960.[10] The number of federal judges has also increased dramatically in response to the increasing number of cases filed in federal court. In 1900 there were only 110 federal judges (9 Supreme Court justices, 24 circuit judges, and 77 district judges), while as of June 1, 2000, there were 848 federal judges (9 Supreme Court justices, 179 circuit judges, and 651 district judges), constituting a significant increase of 671 percent, yet one that is dismally failing to keep pace with the much sharper increase in caseloads.[11] To compound this problem, this dramatic increase in civil cases has come during a period when the courts have already been overburdened by criminal law cases. Analysts contend that this caseload problem is acute and must be somehow brought under control.[12]

The Courts' New Eagerness to Hear a Broader Range of Cases.   At one time, the courts were quite selective as to the types of cases they were willing to hear. Courts generally refused to decide cases that they believed were best left to agency discretion. Under the traditional model, the courts refrained from overruling agency actions unless administrators clearly abused their discretionary authority by violating the clear constitutional and statutory procedural due process rights of citizens or reached decisions that were completely unsupported by substantive evidence. However, according to Donald Horowitz, this had all changed by the late 1970s. The courts "have moved beyond protection of the rights of parties aggrieved by administrative action to participation in problem solving and protection of more general public interests against agencies accused of indifference to the public interest. Judicial review has passed from matters of procedure to matters of both procedure and substance."[13]

Today our judges have become society's handymen, available to listen and provide solutions to whatever seems to be bothering us. Consequently, the scope of the judicial review today seems to have virtually no limits. Observers contend that the courts' basic approach to public litigation has changed dramatically. They claim that the typical federal administrative law case today involves many parties seeking solutions to incredibly complex and multifaceted legal disputes that have meaningful social significance. A new twist in the cases commonly heard today is that the judges, unlike those in the past, must concentrate on the likely impact their decisions will have on future public policy directions. Judges have become deeply involved in policy planning, a task performed in the past almost exclusively by legislators and executives. Judges today get significantly involved in the making of public policy by ordering administrators, for example, to bus students to certain neighborhood schools, to perform or stop performing abortions, to leave on or turn off life support systems, and the like.

The Momentum of Judicial Activism.   For the first fifteen to twenty years after the APA was passed, the courts interpreted APA provisions to avoid getting involved with the work of the federal bureaucracy. However, from the early 1960s to the early 1980s, the APA was used by activist courts to enable them to play an active role in the business of administrative agencies. Although not all courts jumped into the administrative thicket to the same extent, the tendency was for judges to perform job tasks related to public policy that were once handled exclusively by agency administrators. Horowitz contends that many judges simply wanted to play, in effect, the role of chief administrator with the final say on matters of public policy.[14]

Horowitz maintains that what was taking place was essentially the judicialization of the administrative process. In so many ways, he notes, administrative agencies started to function like "second-class courts," in that the courts insisted more and more that various agency decision-making processes should become more trial-like, reflecting more closely the procedures used by courts.[15] But this attempt to make administrative agencies function more like courts eventually met with stiff opposition from those who believed that more legal formalism serves mostly to make it virtually impossible for administrators to act in a swift, efficient, effective, and fair manner. Horowitz noted that the change in name from "hearing examiners" to "administrative law judges" during this period symbolized the extent to which agency hearings became more trial-like.[16] To some, administrative agencies were beginning to function more like courts of original jurisdiction than administrative agencies, thus blurring the distinction between the administrative and judicial roles in our governmental system. In a sense, judicial review activities were commencing in agency hearings and continuing on appeal to the appellate courts and possibly even up to the Supreme Court. Acknowledging this basic development, Horowitz asserted: "Judicial review of substantive issues is therefore the aftershock of the judicialization of agency proceedings. Why accept the counterfeit administrative version of a just decision when one can have the real currency, robes and all?"[17]

In short, the courts by 1980 were much more judicially active in the administrative process than they were just two decades before. Judicial activism could probably be seen the best in the courts' growing reluctance to avoid ruling on substantive social policy questions (for example, the feasibility of using busing to achieve racial integration in our public schools) being considered by our public administrators. In numerous opinions judges of yesteryear presented arguments why the courts should not unnecessarily meddle in administrative affairs. However, during the 1960s and 1970s this passive attitude gradually gave way to a new judicial attitude that was supportive of active monitoring of virtually all administrative activities. The reasons most often cited to justify this emerging activist judicial role seem to have been conveyed best by the new action-oriented judges themselves of that era. In *Environmental Defense Fund, Inc., v. Ruckelshaus,* 439 F.2d 584, 598 (D.C. Cir. 1971), the court contended that administrative actions that affect such basic personal interests as "life, health, and liberty" must be closely scrutinized by the courts, while in *Calvert Cliffs v. AEC,* 449 F.2d 1109, 1111 (D.C. Cir. 1971), Judge J. Skelly Wright concluded: "Our duty, in short, is to see that important legislative purposes, heralded in the halls of Congress, are not lost or misdirected in the vast hallways of the federal bureaucracy." In these statements an unmistakable distrust for administrative experts appears to ring loud and clear.

However, the famous 1984 *Chevron* case, *op. cit.*, supposedly set strong precedent by establishing the principle that courts should allow agency administrators to interpret statute and defer to agency expertise/discretion unless the administrative action or inaction is clearly prohibited by statute. Despite the many court decisions that seem to follow the *Chevron* doctrine, which calls for judicial self-restraint, in 1992 Thomas W. Merrill concluded after extensive research into the application of *Chevron* that about half the courts fail to apply the *Chevron* doctrine to resolve deference questions. In fact, his research reveals that "in recent Terms the application of *Chevron* has resulted in less deference to executive interpretations than was the case in the pre-*Chevron* era."[18] In the early 2000s there is no sign that this trend has not continued or that judicial activism does not still dominate the courts despite the practice of judicial self-restraint by some courts and the persuasive intellectual climate against judicial activism.

The remark above requires clarification because it seems to contradict my discussion on judicial deference to discretionary agency actions in Chapters 5–7, pertaining to agency rulemaking and adjudications. This truth is that students and scholars of law are confused over the role judicial activism and judicial self-restraint are actually playing in our courts today. The confusion is heightened by the simplistic notion that the use of deference by the courts represents an accurate barometric indicator of whether the courts are in fact activist or nonactivist courts.

It is held by many, including myself to a certain extent, that the excesses of judicial activism during the 1960s and 1970s came to a grinding halt during President Reagan's administration because of the impact of his conservative appointments to the federal judiciary, followed by the appointment of more conservative judges by President George H. W. Bush. But to say that these conservative appointees to the federal courts killed the practice of judicial activism is to simplify reality and exaggerate the impact these new conservative judges have had on the judicial review process and on agency behavior. In the first place, many liberal judges remain on the federal bench, some left over from the Carter years and many from Clinton's eight-year presidency. We also cannot ignore all of the state courts where many Democratic governors have served appointing many liberals to the judiciary, greatly influencing judicial decisionmaking at the state level. More importantly, it is wrong to simply equate judicial activism with liberals and judicial self-restraint with conservatives. The reality is that both liberal and conservative judges may advance their political agenda by practicing judicial activism or self-restraint, depending upon the circumstances. For example, on one hand, a conservative appellate court could take a case involving the use of agency discretion just to overrule a district court decision in which the judge refused to defer to agency expertise, ruling against the use of agency discretion.

Liberal courts, on the other hand, may defer to agency discretion if they happen to politically support the public policy advanced by the administrative actions. Sometimes conservative courts that have a reputation for practicing judicial self-restraint to advance their political agenda (e.g., deferring to states to settle the dispute because they believe the federal courts should not get involved in state matters) may boldly reverse their philosophical self-restraint position to promote their political will. A blatant example of this occurred in December of 2000 when the conservative majority on the U.S. Supreme Court, after years of preaching the virtues of judicial self-restraint, could not resist acting as "judicial activists" in intervening in Florida's presidential vote count dispute (a controversy that this Supreme Court's majority in the past would have considered a purely state matter, deferring to the state courts to settle), handing down a decision that virtually guaranteed that the conservative Republican candidate, George W. Bush, would win the presidential election.

It also does not make much sense just to count the number of times the courts have deferred to agency actions, because federal and state courts hear a great variety of issues, some of them having considerably more substantive consequence than others and, depending upon the court, some carrying a much greater precedential force than others. It is true that the U.S. Supreme Court has, since *Chevron*, deferred broadly to agency expertise, establishing strong precedent that has had the impact of strengthening the discretionary power of agency administrators and streamlining agency procedures. Yet the Supreme Court hands down only about a hundred or so cases a year, while the lower federal courts decide thousands of cases, not to mention the impact state court decisions have on agency behavior in the states. And the reality is that lower federal courts do not always abide by *Chevron*, as Merrill found, while state courts are not bound by *Chevron*.

All of this is not to suggest that *Chevron* has not had a conservative impact on the use of deference by the courts and ultimately agency actions. It is also not being said that the courts since the Reagan administration and the onslaught of more conservative politics have not been practicing more judicial self-restraint and generally been deferring more to agency expertise. What is being said is that judicial activism is still very much alive and that, at least according to proponents of judicial self-restraint, judicial activism is still causing the courts, even many conservative courts, not to defer to administrative decisions enough.

Recently, for example, conservative circuit judge James Buckley acknowledged that despite the fact that many judicial scholars and judges have called for the practice of deference in the name of judicial self-restraint, probably the majority of judges today, even joined by many conservative judges, play the role of judicial activists, illegitimately pushing their policy agendas on an unwilling public. He cites many recent examples of judicial activism, conveying the point that the "federal courts at every level continue to issue opinions that keep the debate over judicial activism alive, especially when the proclamation of new rights or the expansion of old ones frustrate the popular will."[19]

THE AVAILABILITY OF JUDICIAL
REVIEW OF ADMINISTRATIVE ACTIONS

Judicial review is commonly perceived as the most basic remedy available to those who seek relief because they feel that they have been or will be harmed by *illegal* administrative actions. However, seeking relief through the courts appears much easier than it really is. If courts refuse to review a person's plea for review, as they frequently do, the aggrieved person will simply have to learn to live with the agency decision that motivated the appeal. There are many reasons why a court will not grant review of agency actions, the principle one being that judges usually like to defer to agency authority and expertise because most believe that political legitimacy, reflecting the separation of powers doctrine, requires administrative experts, not judges, to make agency policy decisions. However, a great deal of administrative law deals with the more specific and technical justifications cited by the courts for granting or denying petitions for review of administrative decisions. In the next few sections focus is on the issues, questions, and factors that tend to determine not only what administrative actions are reviewable (reviewability) but also to what depths these reviewable activities should be reviewed (scope of review).

What Is Reviewable?

It is very difficult to answer the question: What is reviewable administrative action? Judges and administrative law scholars have always argued over what should or should not be appropriately considered judicially reviewable agency behavior. Although various legislative and judicial attempts have been made to zero in on what should or should not be subject to review, the painful truth is that the reviewability question has been uncomfortably left unsettled. It would be convenient if we could easily place some agency actions in the reviewable category and others in the unreviewable category, but this simply cannot be done, because it is too unclear as circumstances change from case to case which actions are legitimately reviewable and which unreviewable. The complex and confusing nature of the reviewability question is possibly epitomized best in the intentionally contradictory title of Kim Morris's article, "Judicial Review of Non-reviewable Administrative Action."[20]

It has been my experience that much of the confusion over the reviewability question exists because the distinction between reviewability and scope of review questions is often not made clear. However, it is important to understand that the two concepts pose related, but nevertheless distinct, legal questions. Reviewability is identified with the basic question: Is the matter within the court's jurisdiction for review, thus, according to administrative law rhetoric, making the dispute available for judicial review? While a reviewable issue is within the legitimate jurisdiction of the courts (for example, because a statute specifically provides for review of certain agency decisions), an unreviewable issue is outside the legitimate jurisdiction of the courts (for example, because a statute specifically excludes some action from review, thereby essentially making the decision of agency officials in these unreviewable areas final).

Once a court has answered the necessary questions pertaining to whether or not the case qualifies or is available for review, then the court can determine how far its legitimate scope in reviewing a reviewable case should extend. For instance, once the court decides that a case pertaining to the use of discretion is within the court's proper jurisdiction for review, then the court can ask: To what depth should our inquiry extend into an agency's use of discretion? Obviously, as has been stressed in earlier sections, courts respond to this question quite differently. While courts practicing judicial self-restraint are reluctant to review most discretionary agency decisions, activist courts are more apt to probe deep into an agency's use of discretion.

What determines whether judicial review should be made available to petitioners in administrative law disputes? First, the court must answer *no* to the following basic question: Have applicable statutes prohibited judicial review of the specific administrative action under question? But to the following questions, the court must answer *yes:* Have the relevant statutes explicitly, or at least implicitly, permitted review? Has an eligible party petitioned for review (should the petitioner be given standing to sue)? Has a proper defendant been named in the suit? Is the case ready for review in terms of its timeliness? This question implies three important subsidiary questions. Acknowledging that administrative agencies normally have primary jurisdiction, the court must decide whether it should now intervene (assert its jurisdiction) in the dispute. In seeking relief, has the petitioner exhausted all administrative remedies made available by the agency? Is the case ripe for review (ready for review in the sense that the legal issues are definitive enough, have evolved enough, and have been presented vividly enough to allow the ruling court to reach a clear decision)? And finally, have proper forms of action (specific and technical legal methods for remedial relief, such as request for an injunction) been followed in filing for review? We will return to these questions throughout the remainder of this chapter, especially in the section entitled, "Court Reluctance to Review Agency Actions: Obstacles to Obtaining Review."

The APA and Reviewability.   By 1946 when the Administrative Procedure Act was passed the presumption of reviewability was well established administrative law. The *Stark* decision clearly had a profound impact on the drafting of the APA because the act generally endorses the *Stark* maxim of broad reviewability. Bernard Schwartz once even exclaimed that "the APA codifies the *Stark v. Wickard* principle."[21]

Sections 702 and 704 of the APA uphold the spirit of *Stark.* Section 702 reads: "A person suffering legal wrong because of agency action within the meaning of a relevant statute, is entitled to judicial review thereof"; and Section 704 states: "Agency action made reviewable by statute and final agency action for which there is no other adequate remedy in a court are subject to judicial review." If it were not for the two exceptions to review set forth in Section 701, all federal administrative actions would be subject to review. However, Section 701 states that "Chapter 7—Judicial Review" applies "except to the extent that—(1) statutes preclude judicial review; or (2) agency action is committed to agency discretion by law." But clearly, Congress, in enacting the legislation, intended for the courts to be able to review those agency actions not specifically excluded from review by statutes. Therefore, the APA does establish a strong presumption of reviewability. Actually, legislative intent is very clear in regard to the presumption of reviewability when statutes are silent on the availability of review. A House committee stated that "the mere failure to provide specially by statute for judicial review is certainly no evidence of intent to withhold review."[22]

The cases that uphold the presumption to reviewability under the APA are numerous, but in no decision is the APA's presumption of reviewability better espoused than in *Abbott Laboratories v. Gardner,* 387 U.S. 136 (1967). Justice Harlan, writing for the majority, upheld the contention asserted in *Rusk v. Cort,* 369 U.S. 367, 379–380 (1962), "that only upon a showing of 'clear and convincing evidence' of a contrary legislative intent should the courts restrict access to judicial review" (p. 141). Justice Harlan also maintained, citing *Shaughnessy v. Pedreiro,* 349 U.S. 48, 51 (1954), that the legislative record on the drafting of the APA "manifests a congressional intention that it cover a broad spectrum of administrative actions, and this Court has echoed that theme by noting that the Administrative Procedure Act's 'generous review provision' must be given a 'hospitable' interpretation" (pp. 140–141). The general presumption of reviewability as established in *Stark* and *Abbott Laboratories* was reasserted in *Reno v. Catholic Social Services,* 113 S.Ct. 2485 (1993), and *Forest Guardians v. Babbit,* 174 F.3d 1178 (10th Cir. 1999).

The Presumption of Reviewability Has Been Weakened.   Although the presumption of reviewability still is strong, nonetheless, as Richard Pierce asserted recently, there have been several court decisions that have been handed down in the past two decades that have partially eroded the presumption of reviewability.[23] Although a few Supreme Court decisions began to qualify and weaken the solid presumption of reviewability established by the APA and *Stark* and *Abbott Laboratories,* the case that struck the greatest single blow to the broad presumption of reviewability was *Heckler v. Chaney,* 470 U.S. 821(1985). In the precedential *Chaney* case the court argued that there exists a presumption of unreviewability when courts are faced with the question of whether to review decisions by agencies *not to act* or enforce laws the Congress has specified otherwise.

As mentioned in the last chapter, the *Chaney* decision attracted a lot of criticism since *Chaney* suggests that often when agency administrators use their discretion not to act, the courts must exercise judicial self-restraint and refuse to review the case since there is not law to apply. However, many scholars have and continue to attack the *Chaney* decision, and other decisions that have upheld *Chaney* today, because they argue that it is well rooted in American common law going back to even English common law (e.g., the *Wednesbury* principle) that there is always law to apply. These scholars contend that all discretionary agency decisions should face a presumption of reviewability, whether they constitute agency actions or inactions, because all discretionary actions have the potential to be abusive, which would blatantly violate Section 706(2)(A) of the APA, which these scholars hold prohibits any abuses of discretion, whether they are discretionary actions or inactions. Catherine Zaller also opposes the presumption of unreviewability, because she maintains that agency inactions definitely impact public policy making by public agencies.[24] She comments: "Although the most obvious ways agencies make policy are through positive rulemaking and adjudication measures, agencies also set policy through inaction. . . . Agencies often set policy by not doing anything at all. . . . This inaction is thus itself a form of policymaking in the sense that it prevents the legislative and executive branches from implementing enacted legislation."[25]

Regardless, the present situation on reviewability is this, although, as usual, contradictory court decisions have clouded the status of presumption of reviewability. Generally, the courts recognize a solid presumption of reviewability under Sections 706(1) and 706(2)(A) of the APA, but the courts honor the *Chaney* precedent, which allows agencies to exercise more discretion under the APA than probably Congress originally intended, permitting administrators to escape judicial review under most inaction situations unless specific statutory provisions require positive agency action. For example, in *Oil Chemical and Atomic Workers Int'l Union v. Richardson*, 214 F.3d 1379, 1382 (D.C. Cir. 2000), the court, citing *Chaney*, refused to grant review of the Department of Energy's failure to act on a union contract because "an agency's decision not to prosecute or enforce, whether through civil or criminal process, is a decision generally committed to an agency's absolute discretion."

This basic reasoning was upheld by the U.S. Supreme Court in 2002 in *Barnhart v. Peabody Coal Company*, 123 S.Ct. 748, when the Court held that the failure by inaction of the commission of Social Security to meet a statutory deadline, even though it represented "a default on a statutory deity, . . . may be a wholly blameless one" (p. 665). The court reasoned that the fault was likely excusable in light of the other statutory duties assigned to the Commission. Consequently, the court, rooting its opinion in the presumption of unreviewability and citing its previous decision, *U.S. v. James Daniel Good Real Property*, 510 U.S. 43 (1993), concluded that ". . . if a statute does not specify a consequence for noncompliance with statutory thinking provisions, the federal courts will not in the ordinary course impose their coercive sanction" (p. 666).

Zaller notes that some appellate courts have refused to let agencies off the hook when they have missed statutorily mandated deadlines, while other appellate courts have, leaving the law in this area uncertain. She concludes, however, that the presumption of unreviewability should not be used when agencies fail to act and miss legal deadlines as a result. She asserts: "Statutory deadlines are classified as law. When an agency misses such a deadline, it has unlawfully withheld action.

Therefore, the reviewing court has no choice but to compel agency action in cases of statutory deadlines." For Zaller, courts should uphold agency excuses for missing deadlines only when it is "fiscally impossible" for the agencies to meet them.[26]

Unquestionably, the courts in these cases have stretched the presumption of unreviewability beyond a straight interpretation of *Chaney* to permit agencies to use their discretion to not act to even avoid clear enforcement actions and deadlines statutorily mandated by Congress. This new law represents another step taken by the courts to help agencies reduce their costs by letting them exercise even broader discretion on how they should prioritize agency duties in light of scarce agency resources.

The Reviewability of "Unreviewable" Administrative Actions.   Under Section 701(a)(1)(2) of the APA, agency actions are unreviewable if "statutes preclude judicial review" or "agency action is committed to agency discretion by law." But what do these exclusions mean in practice? Does the first exclusion mean that no matter how absurd administrative action may be, as long as it is protected by statute, it cannot be reviewed? Does it mean that administrators can violate statutory dictates yet remain free from having their actions reviewed? Does the second exclusion mean that administrators can flagrantly abuse their discretionary powers at the expense of claimants yet feel content that their abusive use of discretion can never be reviewed? Unfortunately, the tendency of the courts has been to answer "yes" to these questions because the courts have been generally reluctant to apply the presumption of reviewability to Section 701 exclusions.

However, the illogic of absolutely precluding judicial review of agency actions under Section 701(a)(1)(2) attracted heated criticisms from the very beginning. Judges and legal scholars have argued that at times circumstances justify judicial review of these supposedly unreviewable agency decision-making areas. In 1951 Justice William O. Douglas voiced his opposition to the majority opinion in *United States v. Wunderlich*, 342 U.S. 98, where the Court argued that judicial review of agency action cannot take place even though an administrative determination is shown to be obviously false, as well as reached in an arbitrary and capricious manner, if statutory provisions preclude review. In his dissent, Justice Douglas severely criticized the wisdom of any "finality provisions" in statutes that preclude judicial review entirely, regardless of the circumstances. In response to a specific "finality provision" excluding review of decisions made by contracting officers, Douglas remarked that the majority opinion upholding the validity of the finality provision would have a "devastating effect" and it would tend to make "a tyrant out of every contracting officer" (p. 101).

Douglas's dissenting attitude in *Wunderlich* is slowly winning acceptance, but there remains steady judicial resistance. In *Shaughnessy v. Pedreiro*, 349 U.S. 48 (1956), the Court held that statutory provisions barring review of administrative action should not be interpreted so strictly as to absolutely preclude review. In keeping with the *Shaughnessy* holding, the court held in *Welch v. United States*, 446 F.Supp. 75 (D.Comm., 1978), that a statutory provision, which made all military death benefits claims "final and conclusive" (unreviewable), could be reviewed in matters pertaining to questions of law. In *Owens v. Hills,* 450 F.Supp. 218 (N.D., Ill., 1978), the court ruled that a statutory provision, which made decisions by the HUD secretary "final and conclusive" and "not to be subject to review," should not be applied to totally prohibit judicial review; and in *Ralpho v. Bell,* 569 F.2d 607 (1977), the D.C. Circuit court argued that despite the strong rhetoric precluding judicial review of agency decisions under the Micronesian Claims Act, the "no-review" clause does not preclude judicial intervention to review complaints that the agency has violated either statutory or constitutional mandates. In the district court's view, to absolutely preclude a person's right to seek judicial remedy to correct an agency wrongdoing that has caused the individual harm would cast in doubt how seriously our nation is committed to the promotion of human rights and basic liberties (p. 626).

Although clear law has not been established because various courts have not applied Section 701(a)(1)(2) of the APA consistently, it does appear that a strong consensus of judges nonetheless feel that, despite any "absolute" preclusions of judicial review, ultimately these preclusions themselves are scrutinized by the courts and agency actions are really not final until the courts say they are. As Bernard Schwartz recently concluded, despite judicial decisions that uphold preclusions to review, there still exists "the strong presumption in our law in favor of judicial review. That presumption normally prevails even in the face of statutory provisions that appear to preclude review."[27]

Several cases in the 1990s upheld the basic presumption of reviewability even in the face of provisions precluding review, although the courts may have upheld the particular preclusion in dispute (*Franklin v. Massachusetts,* 112 S.Ct. 2767 [1993]; *Reno v. Catholic Social Services,* 113 S.Ct. 2485 [1993]; and *Kisser v. Cisneros,* 14 F.2d 615 [1994]). Probably no court has summarized the situation on the "unreviewability" of agency decisions better than a New York court in *New York City Dep't of Envt'l Protection v. New York Civil Serv. Comm'n,* 579 N.E. 2d 1385 (N.Y. 1993). In this case a New York statute made the state's Civil Service Commission's decisions "final and conclusive" and "unreviewable." The court noted that the state legislature has the right to preclude review of agency actions and it has clearly done so by statute. But citing a prior case, the court responded: "Even where judicial review is proscribed by statute, the courts have the power and the duty to make certain that the administrative official has not acted in excess of the grant of authority given . . . by the statute or in disregard of the standard prescribed by the legislature (at 1387)." The court held that, despite the statutory preclusion of review, the courts still must look to see whether agency actions were "purely arbitrary." The court stressed that despite the explicit preclusion of judicial review of agency actions by statute, "judicial review cannot be completely precluded." Courts have the responsibility of checking to see whether "the agency has acted illegally, unconstitutionally, or in excess of its jurisdiction" (p. 1387). Or, in the succinct words of the D.C. Circuit court, in our administrative system agency administrators cannot "expect to escape judicial review by hiding behind a finality clause" (*Dart v. United States*, 848 F.2d 217, 224 [D.C. Cir. 1988]).

However, recent court decisions have weakened the precedential force of *Dart*, allowing agencies to escape judicial review if statutes preclude review, allowing agencies to hide behind a crippled finality clause (e.g., *McBryde v. Comm. to Review*, 264 F.3d 52 [D.C. Cir. 2001]; and *Exxon Chems. Am. v. Chao*, 298 F.3d 464 [5th Cir. 2002]). Of course, this trend is not unexpected given the courts' recent propensity to defer more broadly to agency actions.

Court Reluctance to Review Agency Actions: Obstacles to Obtaining Review

As we have seen, judges in general, whether conservative or liberal, since the early 1960s have become more activist, finding it easier to justify intervention in the administrative process to promote their legal-political agendas. Given the highly politicized judicial appointment process, it would be very naive to assume that judges just hand down impartial, politically neutral decisions. Overall, judges are quite astute and politically plugged in and are consequently very aware of the political consequences of their rulings.

Having acknowledged the political context in which judges decide cases, it is important to stress that it is still true that judges, respecting the separation of powers doctrine, try to avoid meddling in the administrative thicket unless they believe that certain conditions compel them to intervene, not excluding political compulsions. Here are some of the basic reasons why the courts would prefer to avoid judicial review of agency actions. One, judges feel that they simply lack the technical knowledge and sufficient time to decide technical questions of fact that they believe could be handled much more competently by agency experts specifically trained to handle such matters. Two, the courts are not interested in interfering with or disrupting normal administrative operations in any way, because undue intervention has the potential to undermine and discredit the administrative process. Three, not only may frequent interventions in administrative business constitute unnecessary judicial meddling, thus influencing public policy making that is best left to the administrative and legislative branches, but such judicial meddling also violates at least the spirit of the separation-of-powers doctrine and encourages parties to file more suits against agency administrators, placing an even greater burden on the already overburdened courts. And four, in recent years the courts have wanted to minimize judicial review of agency actions to help administrators handle agency business in a more cost-effective manner, realizing that diminished agency resources have made it difficult to handle even necessary agency actions.

Over the decades several legal doctrines have evolved that have served both the interests of the courts and the administrative agencies. They have been used to protect the courts from having to hear untimely and unwarranted suits and agencies from hasty, unnecessary, and disruptive judicial excursions in the administrative process. However, for those seeking judicial review of agency actions, these doctrines have often proved to be tough legal obstacles to overcome.

Standing to Sue.   We have considered many complex administrative law subjects; yet possibly the easiest legal principle to comprehend is the basic law of *standing.* In the context of administrative law, fundamental standing law holds that those who are harmed by administrative action should have the opportunity to challenge the legality of the action in court, as long as the action is legitimately reviewable agency action on other grounds. The standing issue essentially asks that the court answer the vital question: Should the petitioner have the right to "stand" before the court and argue his case?

Although the basic standing issue is a very simple one, the importance of the question of standing should not be underestimated. The doctrine of standing poses a prerequisite question. That is, will the court let a person have standing so that the person can have the opportunity to argue the case on the basis of its merits? Standing must be obtained before the petitioner's dispute will be allowed to continue. Many times, especially in administrative law cases, petitioners fail to pass the entryway standing test and are thereby prevented from presenting a possibly solid case before the court on the basis of the merits. Actually, it has been argued that the courts sometimes unreasonably deny standing to petitioners so that they can avoid having to reach an unwanted decision based upon solid evidence and sound legal arguments.[28]

Since the late 1960s, the courts have become in general more lenient in granting standing. While at one time the courts interpreted injury in very narrow terms, thus precluding the possibility that many would obtain standing before the court, broad judicial interpretations of what constitutes a litigious injury have recently eroded many of the traditional barriers preventing parties from obtaining standing to sue. The relaxation of standing requirements in the past few decades has been largely responsible for a new flood of cases in such citizen-consumer areas as consumer, environmental, and housing law. This development is one of the chief reasons that administrative law has become so important to the study of public administration and public policy in recent years.

What tests must a petitioner pass to receive standing? The most basic standing requirement that must be satisfied is a constitutional one. That is, in Article III, Section 2, the Constitution requires that our federal courts can decide only cases of controversy between parties. This means that a genuine dispute must exist, with the court being placed in a position to provide a judicial remedy (relief) to a legally injured party (one who has suffered an "injury of fact") (*Lujan v. Defenders of Wildlife*, 112 S.Ct. 2130, 1992). This constitutional requirement is designed to prevent abstract nonsense suits or to guard against what Justice Oliver Wendell Holmes referred to, in *Giles v. Harris,* 189 U.S. 475, 486 (1903), as "in the air" controversies. Or as the Supreme Court said a few years ago in *Friends of the Earth v. Laidlaw,* 120 S.Ct. 693, 710 (2000), "Standing doctrine functions to ensure, among other things, that the scarce resources of the federal courts are devoted to those disputes in which the parties have a concrete stake."

But what constitutes a cognizable (judicially recognizable) injury? In virtually all cases until the late 1960s, the courts would perceive an injury only as an instance in which one party suffers a direct monetary loss as a result of another's actions. Thus, parties went to court to sue for financial settlements to redress wrongs committed against them. For example, a private company, injured economically by a governmental agency, could sue for financial compensation to cover its losses.[29] Even under this narrow interpretation of standing law, petitioners frequently failed to obtain standing, because they could not demonstrate to a court that their financial loss is or would be different from what others in a group would suffer. In *Perkins v. Lukens Steel Co.,* 310 U.S. 113 (1940), the Supreme Court held: "Respondents, to have standing in court, must show an injury or threat to a particular right of their own, as distinguished from the public's interest in the administration of law" (p. 125). In an earlier suit by a taxpayer challenging the right of the government to spend his tax dollars on a federal program he opposed, the Court ruled that he was not entitled to standing because he could show only that he was suffering in an indefinite way in common with other taxpayers *(Frothingham v. Mellon,* 262 U.S. 477 [1923]). Because of the consequences of ruling otherwise, standing principle as it applies to taxpayers in *Frothingham* has never been reversed. In 1984 the Supreme Court, for example, in *Valley Forge ETC v. American United, ETC.* 102 S.Ct. 752, upheld the *Frothingham* rule by refusing to grant standing to the respondents, Americans United For Separation of Church and State et al., who tried to prevent the secretary of health, education, and welfare from giving surplus government property to a religious organization. The Court argued that the respondents lacked standing as taxpayers because they could not show that they had or would suffer any personal injury any different from any other taxpayer. Quoting from *Frothingham,* the Court said: "The party who invokes the power [of judicial review] must be able to show not only that the statute is invalid but that he has sustained or is immediately in danger of sustaining some direct injury as the result of its enforcement, and not merely that he suffers in some indefinite way in common with people generally" (p. 761).[30]

Pressures placed on the courts in the past quarter century or so by citizen, consumer, and legal action groups have been quite successful in softening standing requirements. The liberalization of standing law is probably best conveyed in a series of public housing opportunity cases during the 1970s, although this liberalization trend can be seen in a host of cases in other public policy areas. In *Warth v. Seldin,* 422 U.S. 490 (1975), the Supreme Court, in a 5–4 decision, denied standing to petitioners challenging a zoning ordinance that they believed discriminated against low- and moderate-income persons, thus depriving them of affordable housing opportunities in Penfield, a relatively affluent white suburban community near Rochester, New York. Although the Court's majority denied standing to the petitioners on the technical grounds that they were third parties (not the low- and moderate-income persons themselves) and, therefore, could not establish a direct, particularized, and "cognizable interest" in the zoned property in question, the majority did imply that parties with a direct stake in the zoning ordinance who could show that they have a "substantial probability" of being harmed by the ordinance's enforcement could obtain standing. The *Warth* decision, although generally perceived as a somewhat conservative decision on standing, nevertheless remains a relatively modern standing case because the Court did at least recognize that standing could be granted to a petitioner on the basis of (1) a claimed noneconomic injury; (2) a substantial probability that the party will be injured by a governmental action; and (3) a denied statutory entitlement.

In *Resident Advisory Bd. v. Rizzo,* 425 F.Supp. 987 (E.D., Pa., 1976), Judge Broderick, building on *Warth,* ruled that those being denied housing opportunities were entitled to standing because they could both demonstrate an actual injury and show how the Court could provide remedial measures. Regarding the Resident Advisory Board, which claimed to be composed of and representing lower-income residents eligible to live in the proposed Whitman public housing project, the court held: "RAB is a proper plaintiff with standing to represent its members. Although there is no allegation that RAB was injured as an organization by the termination of the Whitman project, it is clear that RAB has established actual injury to its members. . . . Clearly, if RAB's claims are legally cognizable, its members have been injured by the failure to build the Whitman project. Those RAB members who live in racially impacted areas of the City of Philadelphia are obviously harmed by the failure to build a scheduled housing project in a non-racially impacted area. Those on the waiting list, which is predominantly Black, have lost the opportunity to live in public housing in a Whitman area" (p. 1012).

In *Village of Arlington Heights v. Metropolitan Housing Corp.,* 429 U.S. 252 (1977), the Supreme Court itself cast doubt on the conservative interpretation of *Warth* by ruling that the Metropolitan Housing Development Corporation, a nonprofit organization wishing to build a housing project for lower-income persons, should be given standing on both economic and noneconomic grounds. The Court also emphasized that the MHDC should be given standing because it would likely benefit from a favorable court ruling. In addition, the Court stressed that "it has long been clear that economic injury is not the only kind of injury that can support a plaintiff's standing" (p. 262).

In *Duke Power Co. v. Carolina Environmental Study Group,* 438 U.S. 59, a non-housing case in 1978, the Supreme Court took a bold step toward eliminating several confusing standing requirements. In reviewing previous standing cases, it concluded: "We . . . cannot accept the contention that, outside the context of taxpayers' suits, a litigant must demonstrate anything more than injury in fact and a substantial likelihood that the judicial relief requested will prevent or redress the claimed injury to satisfy the 'use and controversy' requirement of Act III." In many respects, the liberalization of standing law since the late 1960s threw standing law into terrible confusion. Some standing tests were kept, others tossed aside, while still new ones were invented. The confusion over what standing tests should apply under particular circumstances caused many to call for the virtual abandonment of standing requirements.[31] In the future we can expect, as they already do in the states, that courts will grant standing almost routinely, as long as the plaintiffs can pass the simplest standing test of showing only a fairly reasonable causal connection between an injury or likely future injury and the defendant's action. In fact, in *Clarke v. Securities Industry Ass'n*, 107 S.Ct. 750 (1987), the Supreme Court applied a simple "zone of interest" test to determine whether standing should be granted. The Court explained that "the zone of interest test is a guide for deciding whether, in view of Congress' evident intent to make agency action presumptively reviewable, a particular plaintiff should be heard to complain of a particular agency decision. In cases where the plaintiff is not itself the subject of the contested regulatory action, the test denies a right of review if the plaintiff's interest [is] so marginally related to or inconsistent with the purposes implicit in the statute that it cannot reasonably be assumed that Congress intended to permit the suit. The test is not meant to be especially demanding" (p. 757).

Unquestionably, it is fairly easy today for parties to obtain standing, yet recent decisions demonstrate that courts are still quick to deny standing if basic standing prerequisites are not satisfied. For example, in *Branton v. FCC*, 993 F.2d 906 (D.C. Cir. 1993), the court denied standing to a listener of a radio broadcast where variations of the "f" word were aired ten times. After the Federal Communications Commission failed to act upon the listener's complaint, he filed suit in federal court. However, the court held that he lacked standing because no request for damages or other relief for the "marginal" harm was sought, but instead he wanted sanctions imposed against the radio station "in the hope of influencing another's future behavior" (p. 909). In *Renne v. Geary*, 111 S.Ct. 2331 (1991), the Supreme Court, although it based its decision on ripeness grounds, argued that it is very questionable whether standing can be given to individual members of a committee, because their third-party status does not allow them to sue on behalf of the whole committee. In *INS v. Legalization Assistance Project*, 114 S.Ct. 422 (1993), the high court failed to give standing to Legalization Assistance Project, a legal help organization, which had challenged an INS regulation that placed a limited amnesty on immigrants who had entered the United States illegally. The Court argued that Congress intended standing to be given to parties actually suffering from the illegal wrongs committed by the administrative agency or are "within the 'zone of interests' protected by statute, not by third parties outside the 'zone of interests'" (pp. 423–424). The Supreme Court in *Steel Co. v. Citizens for a Better Environment*, 118 S.Ct. 1003 (1998), refused to grant standing to Citizens for a Better Environment because the organization was not asking for financial damages itself, but just for compensation for bringing the litigation. "Having found that none of the relief sought by respondent would likely remedy its alleged injury in fact, we must conclude that respondent lacks standing" (p. 1020).

In sum, despite some grey areas in standing law, Justice Scalia in *Lujan v. Defenders of Wildlife*, 112 S.Ct. 2130 (1992), did an admirable job summarizing the basic elements of standing. He wrote:

> Over the years, our cases have established that the irreducible constitutional minimum of standing contains three elements: First, the plaintiff must have suffered an "injury in fact"—an invasion of a legally-protected interest which is (a) concrete and particularized; . . . and (b) "actual or imminent," not "conjectural" or "hypothetical." Second, there must be a causal connection between the injury and the conduct complained of—the injury has to be "fairly . . . trace[able] to the challenged action of the defendant, and not . . . the result [of] the independent action of some third party not before the court." . . . Third, it must be "likely," as opposed to merely "speculative," that the injury will be "redressed by a favorable decision."

By particularized, Scalia said, "we mean that the injury must affect the plaintiff in a personal and individual way" (p. 2136). Scalia's insights on standing law in *Defenders of Wildlife* have been cited and upheld in several Supreme Court cases since, including a 2002 case, *Utah v. Evans*, 122 S.Ct. 2191.

Primary Jurisdiction.   A rather simple way for courts to avoid reviewing an administrative controversy is to invoke the doctrine of primary jurisdiction. Bernard Schwartz once pronounced this doctrine "one of the foundations of modern administrative law."[32] The *primary jurisdiction doctrine* serves to allow administrative agencies primary or initial jurisdiction without court intrusion in resolving disputes involving administrative agencies. When Congress has failed to define jurisdiction for a particular matter, the court is confronted with the problem of deciding whether it has primary or initial jurisdiction in the particular question brought to its attention. The court is brought into the controversy initially when an aggrieved party tries to bring legal action against another party in court. In giving consideration to the suit, the court may elect to apply the doctrine of primary jurisdiction; it usually does this, thus dismissing the case. The court will inform the interested parties that a particular administrative agency should have primary or initial jurisdiction in the case. That is, the administrative agency should have first crack at resolving the dispute before the court voices its opinion on the matter. However, a court will occasionally inform the parties that the decision reached by the agency should be considered final, thereby giving the agency both *primary* and *exclusive* jurisdiction. The primary jurisdiction doctrine acknowledges that public agencies should normally be permitted to settle disputes affecting their agencies first unless (1) the agency has ruled previously on a similar question, (2) the regulation or issue in the dispute is patently unreasonable, or (3) the issue poses a question that is clearly within the jurisdiction and competence of the judiciary.

A few cases serve to illustrate how the courts have applied the doctrine in practice. In *Texas and Pacific R.R. Co. v. Abilene Cotton Oil Co.*, 204 U.S. 426 (1907), the Abilene Cotton Oil Company sued the Texas and Pacific Railroad Company because of a perceived rate overcharge. The Supreme Court ruled in essence that the ICC should be given primary jurisdiction in the overcharge dispute. In effect, the Court said that shippers with complaints about rate charges should first take their case to the ICC and then, if necessary, file suit in the district court.

What specific reasons have the courts given for using the primary jurisdiction doctrine? In *Far East Conference v. United States,* 342 U.S. 570, 674–575 (1952), the Court asserted that administrative matters are best handled by administrators, not judges. This is the intent of Congress when it creates agencies. The courts should not ignore this reality. Agencies are best equipped to promote unified regulatory policies through informed opinion and flexible procedures. In *Burlington Northern, Inc. v. United States,* 103 S.Ct. 514 (1982), the Supreme Court ruled that the Interstate Commerce Commission has primary jurisdiction in determining the rates railroads charge shippers. In reversing the D.C. Circuit Court of Appeals, the high court scolded the lower court for interfering with the rate-setting authority of the ICC by vacating an ICC rate order. Speaking for the Court, Chief Justice Burger noted that "the more appropriate course would have been to remand to the Commission for explanation rather than to undertake itself to construe the order, and in so doing to interfere with the Commission's primary jurisdiction contrary to important congressional policies" (p. 522). More recently, the Supreme Court in *Marquez v. Screen Actors Guild,* 119 S.Ct. 292 (1998), held that the National Labor Relations Board, not the federal courts, had primary jurisdiction in resolving a dispute pertaining to an alleged misinterpretation of a 30-day grace provision in the National Labor Relations Act. The court noted that the primary jurisdiction doctrine serves agency interests, specifically because the doctrine helps "to promote the uniform interpretation of the NLRB." The court stressed that plaintiffs cannot circumvent the NLRB's primary jurisdiction simply by claiming statutory violations unless it is argued that the "violation of statute was arbitrary, discriminatory, or in bad faith" (p. 302).

But courts do not always find it appropriate to employ the primary jurisdiction doctrine to dismiss cases involving agencies. In *Nader v. Allegheny Airlines,* 426 U.S. 290 (1976), Ralph Nader sued Allegheny Airlines in federal district court for compensatory and punitive damages after he was bumped from an Allegheny flight for which he had confirmed reservations. Nader specifically charged that Allegheny Airlines' secret overbooking practices were deceptive, thus inconveniencing travelers who believed they in fact had confirmed reservations. Therefore, his suit claimed that Allegheny Airlines was guilty of fraudulent misrepresentation. Should CAB be given primary jurisdiction to settle the claim? While the lower courts said yes and employed the primary jurisdiction doctrine, the Supreme Court said no. It argued: "Referral of the misrepresentation issue to the Board cannot be justified by the interest in informing the court's ultimate decision with 'the expert and specialized knowledge' . . . of the Board. The action brought by petitioner does not turn on a determination of the reasonableness of a challenged practice—a determination that could be facilitated by an informed evaluation of the economics or technology of the regulated industry. The standards to be applied in action for fraudulent misrepresentation are within the conventional competence of the courts, and the judgment of a technically expert body is not likely to be helpful in the application of these standards to the facts of this case" (p. 305).

In *Farmers Ins. Exchange v. Superior Court*, 826 P.2d 730 (Cal. 1992), the California Supreme Court agreed with the U.S. Supreme Court's decision in *Nader*, contending that the primary jurisdiction doctrine applies when practical concerns compel courts to allow administrative agencies the initial opportunity to resolve technical regulatory questions, but not when nonregulatory issues arise such as fraudulent misrepresentation that cannot be resolved appropriately by agency experts (pp. 737–738). This court stressed that primary jurisdiction is a mutually beneficial and practical doctrine, concluding that it "evolved for the benefit of courts and administrative agencies, and unless precluded by the Legislature, it may be invoked whenever a court concludes there is a 'paramount need for specialized agency fact-finding expertise'" (p. 746).

Exhaustion of Available Administrative Remedies.   Closely associated with the primary jurisdiction doctrine is the sister doctrine of *exhaustion of available administrative remedies.* The Tenth Circuit court made this simple distinction between the two doctrines: "The exhaustion doctrine applies where the agency *alone* has exclusive jurisdiction over the case (generally premised on the agency's expertise), whereas primary jurisdiction applies where *both* a court and an agency have the legal capacity to deal with the issue" *(Mountain State Gas Co. v. Petroleum Corp.,* 693 F.2d 1015, 1019–1020). The exhaustion doctrine calls for the courts to stay clear of disputes within the public agencies until the petitioner has completed (totally exhausted) all channels of appeal within and provided by the agency. According to the Supreme Court in *McKart v. United States,* 395 U.S. 185,193 (1969), the exhaustion doctrine "provides 'that no one is entitled to judicial relief for a supposed or threatened injury until the prescribed administrative remedy has been exhausted.'" Thus, if grievant X tries to pull rank on an agency by taking the grievance to court because he or she believes that he or she is getting nowhere with the agency's grievance procedures, the court can use exhaustion to refer the matter back to the agency unless X has exhausted all redress procedures made available to him or her by the agency. The simple exhaustion requirement is that all administrative remedies must be pursued and exhausted by the grievant, "that is, of pursuing them to their appropriate conclusion and, correlatively, of awaiting their final outcome before seeking judicial intervention" *(Aircraft and Diesel Corp. v. Hirsch,* 331 U.S. 752, 767;1947).

The exhaustion doctrine is not controversial. Its usefulness has been recognized since around the turn of the century.[33] Justice Oliver Wendell Holmes applied the doctrine in *United States v. Sing Tuck,* 194 U.S. 161(1904), a case in which the petitioners, who had been denied entry into the United States, decided to appeal the initial agency decision to the courts, even though governing statutes had established remedies for relief within the agency. Holmes noted simply that the courts should not be made available to the petitioners until they had exhausted the administrative appellate process. To allow such petitioners to bypass the available administrative remedies would, in Holmes's view, create an unnecessary burden on the courts to resolve problems that should be decided by the governmental agencies.

The exhaustion doctrine is perceived by virtually all observers as an essential legal weapon. It is designed to prevent an unnecessary disruption of the administrative process by according agencies a certain degree of autonomy. The underlying assumption of the doctrine is that, if left alone, agencies are quite capable of working out most conflicts to the mutual satisfaction of all concerned parties. Even when agencies are in obvious error, it is held that the courts should give agencies an ample opportunity to correct their mistakes. To the Supreme Court in *Bowen v. City of New York,* 106 S.Ct. 2022 (1986), this makes the doctrine of exhaustion "intensely practical" (p. 2032). In *McCarthy v. Madigan,* 112 S.Ct. 1081 (1992), the Supreme Court elaborated on the practical importance of giving administrators ample opportunity to correct administrative errors. "The exhaustion doctrine also acknowledges the common sense notion of dispute resolution that an agency ought to have an opportunity to correct its own mistakes with respect to the programs it administers before it is hauled into federal court. Correlatively, exhaustion principles apply with special force when 'frequent and deliberate flaunting of administrative processes' could weaken an agency's effectiveness by encouraging disregard of its procedures" (p. 1086). The Court also noted that "exhaustion promotes judicial efficiency in at least two ways. When an agency has the opportunity to correct its own errors, a judicial controversy may well be mooted, or at least piecemeal appeals may be avoided . . . and even where a controversy survives administrative review, exhaustion of the administrative procedure may produce a useful record for subsequent judicial consideration, especially in a complex or technical factual context (pp. 1086–1087). A decade later in *Porter v. Nussle,* 122 S.Ct. 983 (2002), the Supreme Court, citing and building upon *McCarthy,* upheld an invigorated exhaustion provision in the Prison Litigation Reform Act, 42 U.S.C.S., 1997e(a), that precluded the federal courts from intervening in cases pertaining to prison conditions until all administrative remedies were exhausted. The court stressed that obviously Congress wanted the exhaustion doctrine to be given the utmost respect by the courts, giving inmates and prison administrators ample opportunity in the exhaustion process to resolve various inmate grievances relating to "prison conditions" before the courts could step in (pp. 988–991). In short, in employing exhaustion, the courts recognize the independent powers and obligations of the autonomous administrative branch, thus paying respect to the more basic separation of powers doctrine.

There are situations, however, where the courts elect not to use exhaustion, believing that circumstances justify judicial intervention before agency remedies have been exhausted. Courts have refrained from using exhaustion and have intervened when it has appeared that an agency has (1) violated (or will surely violate) constitutional due process guarantees; (2) acted (or will act) in an unfair and biased manner; (3) provided (or will inevitably provide) only hopeless and futile remedies (sometimes in bad faith); and (4) delayed remedial relief proceedings unreasonably. For example, in 1969 the D.C. Circuit court elected to intervene because agency remedial action was having a "chilling effect" on the petitioner's First Amendment rights *(National Student Association v. Hershey,* 412 F.2d 1103). In *McCormick v. Hirsch,* 460 F.Supp. 1337 (M.D., Pa., 1978), the court ruled that exhaustion should not be applied when an agency's remedial actions encroach upon constitutionally protected religious freedoms. In *Gibson v. Berryhill,* 411 U.S. 64 (1973), the Supreme Court held that it was improper to apply exhaustion when solid evidence exists showing an agency hearing to be seriously biased. In *Continental Can Co. v. Marshall,* 603 F.2d 590 (7th Cir. 1979), the court refused to apply exhaustion and intervened because it contended that it would be futile for the petitioner to pursue its case in the agency, since the same issues had been heard in the agency before with the same results and with the issue having not yet been satisfactorily resolved. In *Walker v. Southern Ry.,* 385 U.S. 196 (1966), the high court reiterated an old but still applicable rule—that grievants should not be expected to wait indefinitely for agency relief action. In *Sioux Valley Hosp. v. Bowen,* 792 F.2d 715 (8th Cir. 1986), the court held that exhaustion should not be given, because the agency was applying a futile administrative remedy, while in *Luna v. Bowen,* 641 F.Supp. 1109 (D. Colo., 1986), the court ruled that an exception to the exhaustion requirement should be made because the agency demonstrated an adamant commitment to a view against the claimants. Finally, in *Darby v. Cisneros,* 113 S.Ct. 2539 (1993), the Supreme Court held that the courts need not require the exhaustion of "optional appeals" within an agency beyond what is specifically required by statute or agency rules. The Court stated: "Section 10(c) [of the APA] explicitly requires exhaustion of all intra-agency appeals mandated either by statute or by agency rule; it would be inconsistent with the plain language of Section 10(c) for courts to require litigants to exhaust optional appeals as well" (p. 2545).[34] In sum, the exhaustion doctrine should almost always be honored unless certain administrative actions or inactions are clearly depriving parties of adequate and deserved appeal procedures.

The Ripeness Principle. *Ripeness* implies what one would think it implies. When a contested agency determination is ripe, it is mature enough to be ready for judicial review. Just as apples need to ripen before they are edible, disputes with administrative agencies need to ripen before the courts will hear them. If the court perceives a controversy as green, it will regard the controversy as premature and deny review until it reaches maturity. In this regard, then, the ripeness principle is very much a matter of common sense *(Seafarers Int'l Union v. United States Coast Guard,* 736 F.2d 19 [2nd Cir. 1984]).

But when does a challenged agency action become ripe enough for review? Of course, to be ripe, a controversy must satisfy the basic tests we have been discussing.

That is, a petitioner must have a legitimate justiciable dispute, must have exhausted all available administrative remedies, must have satisfied the primary jurisdiction requirements, and must have passed the test for standing. The ripeness test is a broad or umbrella test that goes beyond specific reviewability tests to discover whether the case is totally ripe. Because of the general nature of the ripeness principle, it is frequently confused with other more specific tests, particularly with standing and exhaustion tests. However, while standing and exhaustion ask specific questions, ripeness poses the broad question: What general role should the court play in light of this case? In general, is this the type of controversy that the court should decide?

As do the doctrines just discussed, the ripeness principle also serves a dual purpose. That is, the ripeness principle functions to protect the administrative process from undue interference by the courts, as well as to protect the courts from having to hear controversies that the courts were not designed to decide. In *Abbott Laboratories v. Gardner*, 387 U.S. 136,148 (1967), the Supreme Court asserted that the primary purpose of ripeness "is to protect the courts, through avoidance of premature adjudication, from entangling themselves in abstract disagreements over administrative policies, and also to protect the agencies from judicial interference until an administrative decision has been formalized and its effects felt in a concrete way by the challenging parties."

When the courts test for ripeness, they want to discover, essentially, whether an agency action has had an adverse effect on the petitioner. Bernard Schwartz explains: "The tests of ripeness are adverse effect, concreteness, and imminence. Whether an agency act is sufficiently ripe for review depends primarily upon the effect of the act. If an agency act does have adverse effect upon the person or property of private individuals, then it should be reviewable at the instance of such persons. If, on the other hand, it is only a preliminary or procedural measure, which does not of itself have impact upon them, review should be denied."[35] Employing these tests for ripeness, the Supreme Court in *Thomas v. Union Carbide Agr. Products Co.*, 10a S.Ct. 3325 (1985), decided that the particular dispute in question indeed constituted a case in controversy that could be resolved only by the exercise of judicial powers as authorized by Article III of the Constitution, thus making the case ripe for review (pp. 3332–3333). Justice O'Connor, speaking for the Court, concluded that because possible injury could occur to Union Carbide Agricultural Products Company and other pesticide chemical manufacturers, as the constitutionality of a certain arbitration scheme used by the Environmental Protection Agency under the Federal Insecticide, Fungicide, and Rodenticide Act[36] was in question, the Court could provide "preventive relief" (p. 3333).

As long as all means of appeal have been exhausted, it is not difficult for the courts to determine whether a case is ripe if an administrative agency simply orders a party to act or not to act in a particular manner. It is also easy to see that when a welfare agency makes a final decision to deny a person a welfare benefits claim, the dispute is ripe for review (as long as statutes do not preclude review).

Schwartz notes that cases are clearly ripe for review when decisions (for example, orders, directives) have an immediate impact upon a particular person's "rights and obligations": "Their adverse effect makes them ripe as soon as they are issued, unless there are further administrative remedies to be exhausted."[37]

Problems emerge in judging whether a case is ripe, however, when contested general agency directives are issued that are not aimed at specific parties. The Supreme Court struggled with this problem in the *Abbott Laboratories* case. When the Food and Drug Administration issued a regulation requiring all drug labels to carry particular information, the drug manufacturer brought suit, arguing that the commission had exceeded its authority. The government argued that the case was not yet ripe for review since the regulation had not been enforced and, therefore, the impact of the regulation upon the industry was impossible to assess. But the Supreme Court held the government's "preenforcement" argument to be unreasonable because the regulation created an immediate and obvious hardship on the drug manufacturers, thus making the case ripe for review. Specifically, the hardship was that the drug manufacturers had to comply with the directive or risk prosecution and costly penalties for noncompliance.[38]

However, in 1993, a more conservative Supreme Court in *Reno v. Catholic Social Services*, 113 S.Ct. 2485, apparently restricted its decision in *Abbott Laboratories* by arguing that a "benefit-conferring" rule by an administrative agency is not ripe for review until the petitioner actually has applied for the benefit and is rejected. Under *Abbott Laboratories*, the benefit-conferring rule could actually be challenged as to its fairness and/or legality before the challenger actually applied for the benefit. Bernard Schwartz believes that the Supreme Court's ruling on ripeness in *Catholic Social Services* will unfortunately now "require an untold number of plaintiffs to make unnecessary expenditures of time and money before they can obtain decisions on the validity of rules that may directly affect them."[39]

The Supreme Court in 2001 in *Palazzolo v. Rhode Island*, 121 S.Ct. 2448, devoted considerable attention to summarizing the ripeness principle in an eminent domain case. The court explained that a landowner cannot contest a "takings claim" (i.e., taking of private property under eminent domain) in court until the landowner first follows "reasonable and necessary steps to allow regulatory agencies to exercise their full discretion in considering development plans for the property, including the opportunity to grant any variances or waivers allowed by law." The court stressed an important ingredient of ripeness. Ripeness requires that agencies be given all sorts of opportunities to act and explain their actions, allowing them to reach final decisions, not decisions that could be interpreted as preliminary. For example, in this case the court argued that it could not intervene until the relevant administrative authorities had reached a final decision, making the taking final. "As a general rule, until these ordinary processes have been followed, the extent of the restriction on property is not known and a regulatory taking has not yet been established" (p. 2459). However, federal ripeness standards assume good faith on the part of agencies. Thus, agencies are not free to exploit the perks of ripeness by unnecessarily dragging out the making of final decisions or requiring parties before them to "jump through unjustified bureaucratic hoops" (e.g., "require the submission of further and futile applications") (p. 2462).

The Doctrines of Comity, Abstention, and Full Faith and Credit.   The comity and abstention doctrines are two other doctrines used to stop the courts from meddling in the affairs of administrative agencies. *Comity,* a popular doctrine in international law, obligates one nation to respect and uphold the laws of another; it is applied in principle to administrative law. Comity embraces the broad principle that governmental institutions should generally and initially honor the decisions or judgments of other governmental branches before they become involved. The principle, which can be perceived as a form of respect or courtesy, is an old established one that stands behind the *"full faith and credit"* clause of the U.S. Constitution, which obligates the states to honor the civil statutes of one another. As applied to administrative law, the doctrine constrains the courts to have as their first instinct the notion to honor and respect the wisdom of the decisions reached in administrative agencies.[40] Comity, although not a binding doctrine, has practical significance for administrative law because it promotes a certain mindset in judges that has the impact of discouraging counterproductive judicial meddling in agency activities by avoiding potential conflicts. Edwin Wallace Tucker once remarked: "Relying on comity, a federal court, independent of statutory directives governing its jurisdiction, may forbear taking action while a state proceeding is in progress. By doing so, conflicts are avoided."[41]

Abstention, a judge-made doctrine, supports the spirit of comity. Basically, the doctrine requires the federal courts to respect the independence of state activities. When applied to administrative law, the abstention principle largely calls for the avoidance of unnecessary conflicts between the federal judiciary and state administrative systems. It requests the courts to display "scrupulous regard for the rightful independence of the state governments"[42] by remaining removed from involvement unless there is "danger of irreparable injury."[43] The doctrine functions to prevent disruption of state administrative operations, while simultaneously freeing federal courts from having to adjudicate unnecessary and time-consuming constitutional questions.

From what has been said in this section, it becomes obvious that the courts can rely upon many legal doctrines and principles to deny reviewing contested administrative actions. However, despite the abundance and power of these legal obstacles to review, it is clear that in the past few decades the trend has been generally for the courts to rely upon these legal weapons less and less as a means to deny petitioners their day in court.

SCOPE OF REVIEW

Reviewability and scope of review are associated with each other, but each implies very different questions from the other. Once a court has decided to make review available, the court must decide what its proper *scope of review* should be (to what extent it should review complaints against administrative actions on the basis of the actual merits of the case). Obviously, it would be impossible and unwise for the courts to try to scrutinize the legality of all challenged administrative activities. To emphasize an earlier point, virtually all administrative law scholars believe that unnecessary judicial meddling into agency operations would prove disruptive and counterproductive. Further, the scholars point out, the courts do not have the time or the expertise to competently review the merits of even a tiny fraction of contested administrative actions.

However, at the same time the courts have an obligation to the American people to keep administrative behavior fair, reasonable, and accountable. In its relationship with administrative agencies, this is the judicial system's most basic job task; and it means that the courts' scope of review must be broad enough that those agency actions that exploit individuals and pose serious threats to procedural due process standards can be stopped by judicial intervention. Ideally, the courts should seek a scope of review broad enough to prevent dangerous administrative abuses, yet narrow enough that normal administrative operations are not disrupted by unwanted judicial interference. In *NLRB v. Brown,* 380 U.S. 278 (1966), the Supreme Court reflected upon the judiciary's proper scope of review in reviewing agency activities, in this case actions of the National Labor Relations Board. The Court was specifically addressing what it meant by its conceptualization of "limited judicial review": "When we used the phrase 'limited judicial review' we did not mean that the balance struck by the Board is immune from judicial examination and reversal in proper cases. . . . Courts should be 'slow to overturn an administrative decision' . . . but they are not left to 'sheer acceptance' of the Board's conclusions. . . . Reviewing courts are not obliged to stand aside and rubber-stamp their affirmance of administrative decisions that they deem inconsistent with a statutory mandate or that frustrate the congressional policy underlying a statute. Such review is always properly within the judicial province, and courts would abdicate their responsibility if they did not fully review such administrative decisions. Of course due deference is to be rendered to agency determinations of fact, so long as there is substantial evidence to be found in the record as a whole" (p. 290).

Since the beginning of the growth of big governmental bureaucracy during Franklin D. Roosevelt's presidency, vehement arguments have developed over what the proper scope of review over administrative behavior should be. Although the focal question of the dispute is extremely challenging and remains unsettled today, serious attempts have been made to develop guidelines on what course the courts should follow when faced with the frequently raised question: *To what depth should we probe this contested agency action?* In answering this question, judges are concerned about going too far and overstepping their proper judicial role, as defined broadly in Article III of the Constitution. The maximum constitutional limits of review prohibit the courts from violating the separation of powers doctrine by performing nonjudicial tasks. Thus, reviewing courts could violate the Constitution by extending their scope of review to allow themselves to perform functions that have been duly assigned to only administrators or legislators. For example, in *Federal Radio Commission v. General Electric Co.*, 281 U.S. 464 (1930), the Supreme Court argued validly that a reviewing court should not take the place of administrative agencies by usurping their "purely administrative" functions. It was reasoned that reviewing courts should perform only their rightful judicial role and should not play the role of a "superior administrative agency" by acting as their administrative supervisors. This appears sound, but the guideline is certainly not easy to operationalize. For instance, the courts have always disagreed as to what are purely judicial and purely administrative functions. If the courts decided to drastically restrict their reviewing scope, they could also violate Article III by failing to review legitimate legal controversies. In any event, the courts have the final say in what is within their proper reviewing scope. Consequently, court opinions on scope of review vary greatly from court to court, thus making it very difficult to come to any definitive conclusions as to what agency actions are legitimately within the court's scope of review.

Scope of Review and the APA

During the New Deal era the courts handed down many opinions that provided a fairly clear idea of what generally should be regarded as inside or outside the court's legitimate scope of review. In fact, Section 706, the "Scope of Review" section in the APA, is largely a codification of court opinions on scope of review (see Section 706 of the APA in the Appendix to this text). Although Kenneth C. Davis is very critical of many APA provisions, he believes in general that the scope of review *"provisions themselves have a good deal of clear meaning, and they are a good summary of the law of judicial review."*[44]

Considering the impossible task of trying to define absolutely what should or should not be within the court's legitimate scope of review, Davis is probably correct in concluding that the APA framers did a laudable job in providing useful guidelines for future courts to follow in deciding how far they should go in scrutinizing disputed agency actions. To provide some focus and to avoid unnecessary confusion, we shall examine the more problematical provisions in Section 706; but it is worth summarizing here what the section generally appears to sanction, either explicitly or implicitly. Normally, administrative law scholars and the courts have agreed that agency actions are well within the court's proper scope of review if administrators have (1) clearly violated the constitutional rights of citizens; (2) exceeded their statutory authority; (3) acted in blatant contradiction of previous court rulings; (4) neglected to follow well established procedures of administrative due process; (5) abused their discretionary power in a cruel and obvious fashion; (6) denied fundamental rights, not privileges, to persons; (7) committed "prejudicial error" in reaching decisions; (8) made unreasonable decisions that either have "no basis in fact" or cannot be supported by any "substantial evidence"; (9) reached reckless decisions that totally ignore or blatantly misuse facts; (10) departed for inexplicable or senseless reasons from established agency procedures and prior decisions; (11) brought to question some problem where few, if any, judicial opinions or precedents exist; or (12) otherwise violated clear questions of law.

Seeking the Proper Scope of Review over Administrative Actions

No doubt Section 706 provisions have provided guidelines to help the courts decide what they should review. Unquestionably, however, these provisions are still quite vague and, therefore, wide open to interpretation by those applying them. For example, Section 706 provisions ask the courts to override agency actions that are "arbitrary, capricious, [or] an abuse of discretion" ([2][A]); to declare unlawful administrative behavior that is "in excess of statutory jurisdiction, authority or limitations" ([2][C]); and to set aside agency decisions that are "unsupported by substantial evidence" ([2][E]). Reasonably informed people have a fairly good idea of what these provisions generally mean, but obviously there is still much room for debate over, for instance, what constitutes "an abuse of discretion"; what is "in excess of statutory jurisdiction"; or what should qualify as "substantial evidence" to support an agency conclusion.

Most of the administrative law literature pertaining to scope of review focuses on these kinds of difficult questions. Naturally we should be realistic enough not to expect anyone to arrive at an absolute conclusion as to which administrative actions are "arbitrary and capricious" and which are not and which, therefore, are within or beyond the courts' legitimate scope of review. What is clearly "arbitrary and capricious" behavior to one judge may seem within reasonable limits of administrative discretion to another. The crucial point here is that these different judicial perceptions do play a decisive role in determining whether the courts will review contested administrative actions. Consequently, each court becomes the interpreter of what Section 706 provisions really mean in practice.

Nevertheless, despite the relative vagueness of APA scope of review provisions, it is not unrealistic to expect the meaning of Section 706 provisions to be further clarified. Since 1946, courts have been particularly active in their attempts to refine the meaning of these legal requirements so that they convey a more common meaning and are applied in a more equitable and consistent manner. In so doing, the courts have developed certain rules, tests, and principles to help them employ Section 706 provisions in their efforts to determine their proper scope of review over administrative actions. The more important ones are discussed below.

The Deference Principle.   The *deference principle* is such a basic doctrine in administrative law that it is touched upon in virtually every chapter in this book. It is rooted in the separation of powers doctrine and in plain common sense. In honor of the constitutional separation of powers doctrine and out of respect for the expertise of administrators, judges have relied upon the deference doctrine to guide their interpretations and applications of Section 706, "Scope of Review," dictates. Despite the tendency toward judicial activism, which has brought a general broadening of the court's scope of review, deference to administrative authority and expertise by the courts is still the rule rather than the exception. As the 1980s began, Bernard Schwartz exclaimed: "Of course, the scope of review is normally dominated by the doctrine of deference to the agency. This has not yet been altered by the changed atmosphere that is starting to prevail in the regulatory area."[45] In the context of the Airline Deregulation Act of 1978 (92 Stat. 1075), which called for the gradual dissolution of the Civil Aeronautics Board, the D.C. Circuit court in *Frontier Airlines v. CAB,* 602 F.2d 375, 378–379 (1979), nevertheless acknowledged the applicability of the deference principle by stating: "New era or old, so long as the Board continues to be entrusted by Congress with the primary responsibility for the health of air transportation, it remains true that . . . courts have no special qualifications in this area for second-guessing the Board as to the merits of its determinations, once they have been arrived at within a framework of procedural fair play."

In this assertion the court paid recognition again to the solidly established principle that the courts should normally defer problems involving questions of fact, as contrasted to questions of law, to the judgment of administrators. To recall, questions of fact basically pertain to the factual "what was" or "what is" evidence administrators need to evaluate to reach rational decisions. In contrast, questions of law essentially relate to how laws affect the "what was" and "what is" evidence, that is, how laws apply to the evidentiary facts. Typical administrative law questions pertain to administrative jurisdictional and procedural due process considerations, particularly in regard to the use of administrative discretion, and in the specific context of constitutional, statutory, and common law mandates. Thus, the *Frontier Airlines* case conveys the message that the deference principle is applied to limit the court's scope of review over administrative decisionmaking, just as it was in the precedential case *Gray v. Powell, 314 U.S.* 402 (1941), where Justice Stanley F. Reed, speaking for the Court, wrote: "Where, as here, a determination has been left to an administrative body, this delegation will be respected and the administrative conclusion left untouched. . . . Although we have here no dispute as to the evidentiary facts, that does not permit a court to substitute its judgment for that of the Director" (p. 412).

It was noted in the last chapter that the courts from the 1980s to today, as contrasted to the 1960s and 1970s, have expressed a greater willingness to defer to agency discretionary authority and expertise. This has been especially true for the Supreme Court, as a few cases should make clear. In *United States v. Erika, Inc.,* 102 S.Ct. 1650 (1982), the Supreme Court held that it was the clear intention of Congress to have the courts limit their scope of review by deferring to agency expertise in regard to the determination of benefits under Part B of the Medicare program. In *Capital Cities Cable, Inc. v. Crisp,* 104 S.Ct. 2694 (1984), the high court stressed that courts should defer to agency discretion when Congress has sanctioned such discretion. In the famous precedential case *Chevron, U.S.A., Inc.*

v. Natural Resources Defense Council, 104 S.Ct. 2778 (1984), discussed previously, the Supreme Court deferred to the expertise of the Environmental Protection Agency, contending that "considerable weight should be accorded to an executive department's construction of a statutory scheme it is entrusted to administer, and the principle of deference to administrative interpretations" (p. 2782). And in *Regents of the University of Michigan v. Ewing,* 106 S.Ct. 507 (1985), the Supreme Court emphasized that utmost deference should be accorded academic institutions to protect their academic freedom. "When judges are asked to review the substance of a genuinely academic decision, . . . they should show great respect for the faculty's professional judgment. Plainly, they may not override it unless it is such a substantial departure from accepted academic norms as to demonstrate that the person or committee responsible did not actually exercise professional judgment" (p. 513). However, in *Bowen v. American Hospital Ass'n.,* 106 S.Ct. 2101(1986), the Supreme Court acknowledged that although considerable use has been made of this deference principle, "agency deference has not come so far that we will uphold regulations whenever it is possible to 'conceive a basis' for administrative action" (p. 2112).

As noted in a previous discussion of *Chevron,* the actual impact of *Chevron* on the courts' willingness or unwillingness to defer to agency discretion and expertise is open to question. However, evidence does suggest that despite so much judicial and academic rhetoric supporting the deference principle, as noted, many courts seem to ignore the *Chevron* doctrine and insist on playing an active public policy–making role. And, of course, this is the chief question raised by *Chevron.* Should courts readily defer to agency expertise when statutes seem to be ambiguous, allowing agency administrators to exercise broad discretion in interpreting statues or the intent of Congress, or should the courts take the responsibility of interpreting vague statutes?

Despite some apparent noncompliance with the *Chevron* doctrine by the lower courts, at least the Supreme Court in the 1990s and 2000s has continued to uphold and expand the wisdom of *Chevron.* In *Pauley v. Bethenergy Miner, Inc.,* 111 S.Ct. 2524 (1991), the Supreme Court argued that *Chevron* should be adhered to because the judiciary should play a very limited role in making public policies and because interpreting statutes is very much a part of the public policy–making process, which Congress reserved for public agencies, not the courts. Specifically citing *Chevron,* the Court summarized its position on deference:

> Judicial deference to an agency's interpretation of ambiguous provisions of the statutes it is authorized to implement reflects a sensitivity to the proper roles of the political and judicial branches . . . ("federal judges—who have no constituency—have a duty to respect legitimate policy choices made by those who do"). . . . As *Chevron* itself illustrates, the resolution of ambiguity in a statutory text is often more a question of policy than of law. . . . When Congress, through express delegation or the introduction of an administrative gap in the statutory structure, has delegated policy-making authority to an administrative

agency, the extent of judicial review of the agency's policy determination is limited." (p. 253)

But what perplexes so many about the reasoning in *Chevron* is that it is also true that "the resolution of ambiguity in a statutory text" is often more a question of law than of policy. Such makes applying *Chevron* difficult for some judges, especially those who are predisposed to thinking that it is more up to the courts to interpret ambiguous statutes because, after all, what are the courts for?[46]

Recently, in a ruling that has attracted considerable controversy, the high court upheld the *Chevron* doctrine to limit its review of discretionary agency actions under the deference principle. In *Chevron USA v. Echazabal*, 122 S.Ct. 2045 (2002), the Court rejected Mario Echazabal's claim that he was refused employment at a Chevron oil refinery because Chevron misinterpreted and applied EEOC's regulations in violation of the Americans With Disabilities Act (ADA). Echazabal argued that ADA does permit a company not to hire or retain those with disabilities if the disability may "pose a direct threat to the health or safety of other individuals in the workplace," but ADA does not permit a company not to hire or retain an employee with a disability that could only cause harm to himself, which was the case for Echazabal, who had a liver abnormality. Even though a literal interpretation of ADA did not permit Chevron to deny employment to Echazabal because he would threaten only his own health if hired, the Supreme Court held that *Chevron*'s deference standard allowed Chevron to give broad interpretation to statutes. Specifically, the court ruled that deference should be extended to an agency (in this case a private company responsible for applying federal laws) "so long as it makes sense of the statutory defense for qualification standards that are 'job-related and consistent with business necessity.'"

Some scholars contend that the *Echazabal* holding is a victory for common sense, yet others argue that the Court went too far by allowing a company, Chevron, to stray so far from the literal language of a statute to interpret and apply an action that was not permitted by the statute. Critics charge that Congress could easily amend the ADA to allow companies not to have to hire applicants with disabilities if the disabilities would pose a danger to themselves, but instead the court is making public policy by allowing Chevron to give and act upon an interpretation of statute that does not even seem to be reasonably implied. Now here is another example of a court supposedly practicing judicial self-restraint through deference, yet really engaging in a form of judicial activism by handing down a ruling that makes a public policy that Congress certainly did not make or likely intend.[47]

The Supreme Court continued to give broad deference under *Chevron* in a 2003 case. In *Washington State Department of Social and Health Service v. Guardianship Estate of Keffeler*, 123 S.Ct. 1017, 1027–1029, the court ruled that the Washington Department of Social and Health Services is entitled to very broad judicial deference under *Chevron* to interpret relevant statutes applying to reimbursements to promote a foster child's best interests and the welfare of its foster care program.

Source: Reprinted with permission of John Sherffius and the *St. Louis Post-Dispatch,* February 25, 2001.

Substantial Evidence Rule. The broad deference principle logically supports the more narrow *substantial evidence rule,* which is normally applied to limit a court's scope of review over agency determinations involving questions of fact. The deference doctrine is a comprehensive principle that generally calls for the courts to leave administration to the administrative experts, but it frequently simultaneously implies the use of the substantive evidence rule. The substantial evidence rule essentially requires the courts to see whether there is any substantial evidence supporting challenged agency decisions.[48] Section 706(2)(E) of the APA requires specifically that administrative decisions must be "supported by substantial evidence" on the basis of a record. If a reviewing court asked to review a contested agency decision under Section 706(2)(A) finds that substantial evidence exists to support the agency determination, then the agency has, in effect, passed the substantial evidence test; and the court should withdraw from reviewing the particular matter any further. In so doing, the court is limiting its scope of review, checking only to see whether any reasonable (substantial) evidence exists to support the agency's decision. For example, in *Arkansas v. Oklahoma,* 112 S.Ct. 1046 (1992), the Supreme Court scolded the Court of Appeals for the Tenth Circuit for failing to defer to agency expertise on the basis of the substantial evidence rule. The Court noted that the Court of Appeals "disregarded well-established standards for reviewing the factual findings of agencies and instead made its own factual findings. . . . Although we have long recognized the 'substantial evidence' standard in administrative law, the court below turned that analysis on its head. A court reviewing an agency's adjudicature action should accept the *agency's* factual findings if those findings are supported by substantial evidence on the records as a whole. . . . The court should not supplant the agency's findings merely by identifying alternative findings that could be supported by substantial evidence" (p. 1060).

The application of the substantial evidence rule would be easy enough if the courts only knew what constitutes substantial evidence. But as with so many administrative law principles, rules, and tests, the substantive evidence rule has become difficult for the courts to apply with dependable consistency, because no clear operational definition of substantial evidence has evolved. Attempts to clarify the meaning of "substantial evidence" have proven quite futile since other nebulous terms have been used in definitions. Since the time before the passage of the APA to the present, judicial attempts to define substantial evidence sound uncomfortably similar, indicating that these decades have seen only insignificant progress toward making the substantial evidence rule more viable.

In 1938, for example, the Supreme Court, in *Consolidated Edison Co. v. NLRB,* 305 U.S. 197. 229, said: "Substantial evidence . . . means such relevant evidence as a reasonable mind might accept as adequate to support a conclusion." Since what different 'reasonable minds' would accept to substantiate a conclusion would vary greatly, this definition seems to help very little. A year later in *NLRB v. Columbian Enameling and Stamping Co.,* 306 U.S. 292, 300 (1939), the Court made another attempt by noting that substantial evidence is "evidence which is substantial, this is, affording a substantial basis of fact from which the fact in issue can be reasonably inferred." The thrust of this statement is not really helpful. It simply says judges must in the future determine whether substantial evidence existed to justify an administrator's decision by determining whether the decision rested upon a reasonably substantial basis of fact. Still no help came in 1966, when the Supreme Court asserted in *Consolo v. Federal Maritime Commission,* 383 U.S. 607, 619, that substantial evidence is any "relevant evidence as a reasonable mind might accept as adequate to support a conclusion." For whatever reason, the Ninth Circuit in 1979, in *RSR Corp. v. FTC,* 602 F.2d 1317, believed that somehow the substitution of *realistic* for *reasonable* would resolve the definitional problem: "Substantial evidence means such relevant evidence as a realistic mind might accept as adequate to support the (agency's) conclusion." In 1991 in *Foust v. Lujan,* 942 F.2d 712, 714, (10th Cir.), the court defined substantial evidence as "something more than a mere scintilla but something less than the weight of the evidence," whatever concrete or practical meaning this has! While in 1999 the Supreme Court in *Dickinson v. Zurko,* 119 S.Ct. 1816, traced the confusing history of the substantial evidence standard, noting that it has been a basic threshold test for judicial review, yet acknowledged that its use is difficult since the standard is vague and is even confused with the "arbitrary, capricious, abuse of discretion" standard for review. The court quipped: "Indeed, it apparently remains disputed to this day . . . precisely which standard—'substantial evidence' or 'arbitrary capricious, abuse of discretion'—would apply to court review" (p. 1821).

It may be expecting too much to feel that better operational definitions of substantial evidence can be developed. After all, some abstract concepts have escaped definitive definitions for centuries—for example, justice and love. Sometimes we must rely upon common sense and professionalism to make things work. This is particularly true in the legal field. Kenneth C. Davis suggests that what is important is that judges "generally understand that they may not properly substitute their judgment for administrative judgment except on questions of law on which they are the experts, . . . and that in most cases other factors have a much stronger influence than the words of the formula that is supposed to apply."[49]

If the courts want to expand their scope of review over administrative agencies, it will be difficult to stop them, for they have the judicial discretion necessary to apply such terms as "reasonableness" and "substantial evidence" in whatever "reasonable" manner they see fit. "Despite the statutory formulas," Davis asks, "do not the courts continue as the architects of the scope of review?"[50] Certainly, the vague Section 706 guidelines will not function to prevent judicial meddling in administrative affairs if the courts are determined to intrude. However, it is true that unwarranted lower-court intrusions in the administrative process may be overruled by higher courts.

The "Whole Record" Requirement. Before the passage of the APA, the courts in general had developed an extremely narrow version of the substantial evidence rule. Under this narrow version, any reasonable evidence that tends to support the challenged administrative action should be accepted by the courts. In practice, this application of the substantial evidence rule meant that as long as any plausible evidence was presented to support a conclusion, whether the evidence represented only one side of the picture, or a tiny fraction of the whole record, or all of it, the reviewing court was obliged to honor the agency's right to use such evidence (obviously one-sided) to support its conclusion. It was maintained in those pre-APA days that the courts should not be entitled to weigh the facts to determine whether a "proper" decision was reached, but only to check to see whether any reasonable facts at all were cited by an agency to support its finding. Just prior to the passage of the APA, the Court in *Marzacco v. Lowe,* 58 F.Supp. 900 (D.N.J., 1945), commented on the practical implications of this one-sided substantial evidence test: "Under the present prevailing system of administrative law, all evidence to the contrary . . . is a closed book into which this court dare not peek, at least not effectively" (p. 903).

Louis J. Jaffe found this narrow application of the substantial evidence rule horrifying. Rightfully, Jaffe insisted that it would be absurd to believe that truly reasonable and responsible individuals could, in good conscience, reach rational conclusions by looking at only part of the record: "Obviously responsible men would not exercise their judgement on only that part of the evidence that looks in one direction."[51] However, despite blatant farcical and inequitable consequences of this version of the substantial evidence test, this narrow version of the substantial evidence test managed to survive until after the passage of the APA.

The APA framers were particularly disturbed over the use of this one-sided substantial evidence test. In drafting Section 706(2) of the APA, they made certain that the courts would have to apply the substantial evidence rule in light of the *whole* record. This legislation extended the court's potential scope of review over agency "questions of fact" determinations. Specifically, Section 706(2) created a much broader substantial evidence test for the courts to employ, because the courts were now compelled to judge whether the facts of the case, taken as a whole, would lead a reasonable person to conclude that substantial evidence exists, considering all contrary evidence in the record, to support the agency's conclusion. In *Universal Camera Corp. v. NLRB*, 340 U.S. 474 (1951), the Supreme Court noted the meaning and significance of the whole record requirement. The Court acknowledged that the APA now prohibited the courts from looking at only a part of the record to determine whether agency decisions are supported by substantial evidence and further pointed out that reviewing courts must now examine the whole record, including conflicting evidence: "The substantiality of evidence must take into account whatever in the record fairly detracts from its weight. This is clearly the significance of the (APA) requirement . . . that courts consider the whole record" (p. 488). Courts today still apply the exact same whole record standard as established in *Universal Camera Corp. (Pandrol USA, LP v. Airboss Ry. Prods.*, 320 F.3d 1354 [Fed. Cir. 2003]).

Not surprisingly, the question of what constitutes the whole record has also been disputed. The dispute is generally based in problems pertaining to definitions of formal and informal evidence and questions over which evidence needs to be included in the "whole" record. Agencies have been charged with keeping incomplete records, as has been noted before; this would keep courts from being able to apply the substantial evidence rule adequately. Nevertheless, the whole record requirement has improved the substantial evidence test by broadening the court's scope of review so that fairer and more reasonable judicial review of agency actions can take place. For reviewing courts, what is reasonable has changed from a review of a partial agency record to a complete assessment of the facts supporting conclusions on the basis of the whole record.

The "Fundamental Rights" Requirement.   The scope of review over agency determinations involving questions of fact is usually quite limited by the substantial evidence rule. However, the Supreme Court has ruled that the court's scope of review can be expanded under certain conditions, especially when fundamental rights are at stake. *Fundamental rights*, as they have been interpreted by the courts, normally involve constitutionally guaranteed liberties; but in recent decades some courts have ruled that some statutory entitlements (for example, welfare benefits) should be regarded as fundamental rights.[52]

The famous *Ben Avon* doctrine (also called the "constitutional fact" doctrine), set forth in *Ohio Valley Water Co. v. Ben Avon Borough, 253 U.S. 287* (1920), established that full court review is necessary when constitutional facts are in question. In the *Ben Avon* case, the Pennsylvania Public Service Commission had set a "fair value" rate at a level Ohio Valley Water Company believed was so low that it was confiscatory in nature, thus depriving it of constitutionally protected property rights without due process. While the Pennsylvania court ruled that the court's scope of review was restricted by the substantial evidence rule, the Supreme Court held that full review should be granted and the substantial evidence test made inapplicable, because a constitutional question of fact (property rights) was involved. The Court argued that "if the owner claims a confiscation of his property will result, the State must provide a fair opportunity for submitting that issue to a judicial tribunal for determination upon its own independent judgment as to both law and facts; otherwise the order is void because [it is] in conflict with the due process value" (p. 289).

The *Ben Avon* doctrine has struggled for survival over the decades, but it is clear its spirit lingers, especially in a few states where the doctrine is still cited by the courts to justify their positions on scope of review.[53] Actually, the *Ben Avon* doctrine was expanded by a precedential California decision, *Strumsky v. San Diego Employees Retirement System,* 11 Cal.3d 28 (1974). The emerging *Strumsky* doctrine declares that statutory entitlements, in addition to constitutional guarantees, may qualify for full judicial review. Under the *Strumsky* doctrine, a reviewing court is obliged to grant full review when agency actions deprive persons of statutory entitlements in which they have "a fundamental vested right." As one would predict, the notion of fundamental rights has been expanded by persuasive lawyers who have been able to convince California judges at least that agency decisions involving motor vehicles, stockbrokers, disability benefits, age discrimination complaints, and licenses should receive full judicial review since fundamental rights are at stake. The spirit of the *Strumsky* doctrine has received some recognition at the federal level.

Unquestionably, both federal and state courts have the tendency to expand their scope of review when fundamental rights are at stake. However, the *Ben Avon* doctrine has almost totally been ignored by federal and state courts since 1936 because, very frankly, the doctrine simply demands too much of them. As Kenneth C. Davis and Richard J. Pierce, Jr. assert: "The 'constitutional fact' doctrine could not long survive in a legal system in which many agencies routinely make numerous findings of fact that form the predicates for determining the constitutionality of agency actions. . . . Over time, the Court recognized that it would be absurdly inefficient to require reviewing courts to engage in de novo review of all 'constitutional facts.'"[54] Despite its implicit rejection by the courts, it should be noted, however, that the Supreme Court has never specifically overruled the *Ben Avon* doctrine and still acknowledges that administrative agencies are due less deference when fundamental rights are involved. For example, in *Zadvydas v. Davis,* 121 S.Ct. 2491, 2500 (2001), the Supreme Court, in deciding an immigration case involving an alien, Zadvydas, who the INS was detaining indefinitely at Ellis Island because no country would accept his deportation, acknowledged, "that the Constitution may well preclude granting 'an administrative body the unreviewable authority to make determinations implicating fundamental rights,' Superintendent, Mass. Correctional Institution at *Walpole v. Hill*, 472 U.S. 445, 450 (1985)."

The "De Novo Review" Requirement.   De novo review essentially means a new trial. When a court grants de novo review in an administrative law dispute, it is ordering fresh judicial proceedings so that the arguments and evidence in the controversy can be weighed again by a new, independent tribunal. *De novo* review is rooted in the constitutional requirement that fundamental rights (life, liberty, and property) cannot be taken away without due process of law. In some instances, administrative action does not go far enough in protecting parties from being denied constitutional liberties without adequate due process safeguards. When this happens in the administrative process, a court may order a trial *de novo* so that the case can be heard for a second time.

In the precedential case *Ng Fung Ho v. White*, 259 II.S. 276 (1922), the Supreme Court contended that it is appropriate to grant *de novo* review when an agency action (in this case, a deportation order) may deprive a person of essential liberties "that makes life worth living" (p. 284). In essence, the Court held that extending a court's scope of review is justified when it appears that mere reliance upon the substantial evidence test would likely threaten to deprive a person of a constitutional right without the required due process protections.

At least in general the basic wisdom of *Ng Fung Ho* still stands today. For example, in *City of St. Louis v. Department of Transp.*, 936 F.2d 1528, 1533 (8th Cir. 1991), the court said: "To the extent that the decisions in question rest on findings of fact, we are obliged to uphold them if they are supported by substantial evidence. The agency's interpretation of its governing statutes presents, of course, a question of law, and courts normally review questions of law de novo." However, this should not be taken to imply that *de novo* review is frequently granted by the courts.[55] If this became the case, the courts would begin to assume functions that should be performed by our public agencies. In fact, in an interesting state case, *Bentley v. Chastain*, 249 S.E.2d 38 (1978), a Georgia court held that statutory provisions that sanction de novo review of agency actions are unconstitutional because such provisions ask the courts to perform nonjudicial administrative tasks, while in *Silwany-Rodriquez v. INS*, 975 F.2d 1157, 1160 (5th Cir. 1992), the court paid lip service to the de novo requirement, stating that at least "to the extent it involves a question of law, this is subject to de novo review"; yet it then emphasized that "such review, however, is limited." Bernard Schwartz poses a good question in light of this reasoning: "How can review be both de novo and limited?" He answers sarcastically: "The answer, of course, is that, under *Chevron*, review becomes 'limited' and 'de novo' becomes a ritual incantation devoid of practical content."[56] Schwartz may be exaggerating, because, as mentioned, courts still generally honor the de novo review requirement, yet it is also true that many courts today are trying to limit their burden and one way to do it is to narrow their scope of review by restricting the application of *de novo* review.

COURT ORDERS AND PROBLEMS OF COMPLIANCE

Judicial review is a fundamental process in the American governmental system that makes the judiciary the guardian of the principles of fair play as set forth in statutory and constitutional law. Fortunately, judicial review has so far been used in a flexible manner; it can prevent or prohibit administrative abuses when necessary, yet also allow the administrative process to proceed in an uninterrupted fashion when it is appropriate and expedient to do so. Court decisions resulting from judicial review of agency actions carry great weight and must be honored by administrators, although administrators on occasion may resist and delay compliance with court orders they do not like. If administrators fail to comply with court orders, specific **writs** (orders) may be issued. Writs provide a means (judicial remedies) to protect parties from administrative wrongs. The most commonly issued writs are the (1) **writ of habeas corpus,** which requires an official to present the prisoner in court and justify why the person is being held; (2) **writ of injunction,** which compels or restrains actions by public officials, usually with the purpose of preventing some immediate harm caused by their performance or nonperformance; (3) **writ of mandamus,** which forces an official to carry out certain mandatory functions as required by law; (4) **writ of prohibition,** which orders officials to stop performing activities beyond their legal powers; and (5) **writ of quo warranto,** which makes an official or public agency show the legal authority under which the official or agency functions. If public administrators fail to comply with these writs, they could face fines, jail sentences, or both for contempt of court. If courts did not have this punitive threat, their power to review cases and check administrative abuses would be a hollow one. But because the courts do have this power, judicial review has proven rather effective as a regulatory weapon in our system.

Despite the success of courts in having most of their decisions and court orders carried out, administrators on occasion show flagrant disrespect for the courts by refusing to comply with court decisions and orders. Public officials are particularly apt to violate court orders when they feel that public opinion is on their side, despite the constitutionality or legality of their actions.[57] Although the courts could impose fines or send officials to jail for contempt of court, the administrators know that, historically, the courts have been quite reluctant to take such drastic measures against officials who normally command high respect and popularity in their local areas. For example, public school administrators are not perceived by their communities as criminals. Thus, when they decide not to comply with a court order (for example, a busing order) because they believe it would not be in the best interests of their school system, courts have found it difficult to gain broad respect from the public by having these school officials rounded up and thrown into jail for noncompliance. The general attitude seems to be that jails are for genuine criminals, not for those who believe that a social issue should be handled differently from the way particular courts think it should be done.

Public administrators nationwide have an additional advantage over the courts since injunctions and other court rulings are directed against specific officials. Thus they have the effect of forcing compliance with laws and court orders only in a specific case. For example, if school administrators in Boston refuse to implement school integration plans as ordered by the court, school officials elsewhere can carry out their own segregationist policies, despite their illegality, until the courts finally focus on their school districts and start to direct actions at them. It should be recognized that every time a court decides it should employ every weapon possible to enforce compliance, it risks failure or noncompliance. Judges know failures reflect upon their power, prestige, and image. Consequently, the court's power to demand compliance with their orders is limited by the court's own calculation of the odds of obtaining successful compliance vis-à-vis opposition from administrators and public opinion.

It seems clear that steps should be taken to protect the prestige, power, and credibility of the courts. But this is much easier said than done. Court judges themselves could adopt a get-tough policy and hand out tough sentences for noncompliance, but the judges are already overburdened, and such a move would probably prove futile and counterproductive. The other governmental branches, jealously clinging to their power, may not be ready to create a stronger and more comprehensive court system that would enhance the opportunity for more court-made law. Elected officials are frequently reluctant to endorse an unpopular court decision, fearing that the public may take its revenge at the ballot box. But if public administrators are allowed to defy court orders at an increasing rate in the future, then the ability of the courts to protect against administrative abuses will decline accordingly.

SUMMARY

Courts represent the last hope for redressing administrative injustices for those who feel that they were wronged by agency actions. Despite the inconvenience and expense of redressing wrongs through the judicial system, the courts can provide an effective remedy for persons who have become victims of illegal agency behavior, although the courts can provide no relief for parties who have been victimized by unethical agency practices. The court's power stems from their authority to declare acts of public officials unconstitutional and/or in violation of statute. However, justices have been reluctant to overplay their judicial role since they must rely upon the other governmental branches to enforce their decisions. Most judges are unwilling to jeopardize the good health of the courts by constantly making unpopular decisions against administrators whose actions enjoy broad community support. To survive, the courts, like any other political actor in the political system, must respond appropriately to environmental demands.

It is also true that some judges believe that the courts should exercise restraint in passing judgment on agency actions unless administrators are in clear violation of the law. Actually, during the 1800s and the early 1900s, most judges presumed that administrative actions were unreviewable unless Congress specifically made certain agency actions reviewable. However, for the past half century or so the more activist courts have taken an opposing position and have functioned under the presumption that administrative actions are reviewable unless Congress specifically precludes judicial review. Congress has normally prohibited review of agency behavior when it believes that allowing review would be unnecessarily disruptive to routine administrative processes. Despite congressional prohibitions against review, the judiciary, as the chief interpreter of the Constitution, has given review anyway if it was felt that the statutory preclusion of review had the effect of somehow denying persons basic due process constitutional rights.

Simply, courts consider agency actions reviewable if they perceive administrative conduct to be within their proper jurisdiction. However, parties seeking judicial review of agency actions find that it is not always easy to obtain review. To protect the administrative process from unnecessary and counterproductive judicial meddling, the courts have required petitioners to pass several tests before they will grant review. For a dispute to be ripe for review petitioners must satisfy at least the basic reviewability requirements of standing, primary and exclusive jurisdiction, exhaustion, and mootness.

Once a court has determined whether certain agency actions are reviewable (within its jurisdiction), it must then decide whether the actions are within the court's proper scope of review. In making this determination, the court must decide how far it wants to carry out review in a particular area.

Out of deference to agency expertise, most courts have tried to limit their scope of review, thus leaving most administrative controversies to be resolved by the administrators themselves. Although Section 706 of the Administrative Procedure Act extends broad scope of review powers to the courts, judges have mostly chosen to review questions of law, avoiding questions of fact. This is because the courts do not exist for the purpose of deciding whether agency administrators reach the right decisions, in light of the facts, but whether they use proper procedures in reaching them. It is for this reason that it is said that administrative law deals mostly with questions pertaining to procedural due process in public agencies.

Judicial review is normally restricted to formal agency actions; these constitute only about 10 percent of all agency behavior. As was pointed out in the last chapter, this disturbs many administrative law scholars because, they note, most administrative injustices occur when informal discretionary decisions are involved. In this light, judicial review offers parties only weak protections against abuses of administrative power.

UNITED STATES V. MEAD CORPORATION

---

533 U.S. 218; 121 S.Ct. 2164 (2001)

Facts

The U.S. Customs Service routinely issues at its forty-six port-of-entry offices thousands of import tax or tariff duties on items entering the United States in the form of what are called informal "letter rulings." Under the authority of the Harmonized Tariff Schedule of the United States, 19 U.S.C.S. 1202, the Customs Service's Headquarters Office, in the absence of notice-and-comment rulemaking procedures, issued a letter ruling to Mead Corporation that imposed a 4 percent tariff on its imported "day planners" (day planners were categorized as similar to account books, diaries, memorandum pads). Not having to pay this tariff in the past, Mead Corporation objected and filed suit in the U.S. Court of International Trade, which granted summary judgment for the Customs Service. Mead appealed to the federal circuit court of appeals, which ruled for Mead, holding that *Chevron* deference was not due to letter rulings by the Customs Service nor should any deference be given to such letter-ruling classifications of the day planners. The Supreme Court granted certiorari.

Justice Souter delivered the opinion of the Court, in which justices Rehnquist, Stevens, O'Connor, Kennedy, Thomas, Ginsburg, and Breyer joined. Justice Scalia filed the lone dissenting opinion.

The question is whether a tariff classification ruling by the United States Customs Service deserves judicial deference. The Federal Circuit rejected Customs's invocation of *Chevron U.S.A. Inc. v. Natural Resources Defense Council, Inc.*, 467 U.S. 837 (1984), in support of such a ruling, to which it gave no deference. We agree that a tariff classification has no claim to judicial deference under *Chevron*, there being no indication that Congress intended such a ruling to carry the force of law, but we hold that under *Skidmore v. Swift & Co.*, 323 U.S. 134 (1944), the ruling is eligible to claim respect according to its persuasiveness.

Imports are taxed under the Harmonized Tariff Schedule of the United States (HTSUS), 19 U.S.C. §1202. Title 19 U.S.C. §1500(b) provides that Customs "shall, under rules and regulations prescribed by the Secretary [of the Treasury] . . . fix the final classification and rate of duty applicable to . . . merchandise" under the HTSUS. Section 1502(a) provides that "the Secretary of the Treasury shall establish and promulgate such rules and regulations not inconsistent with the law (including regulations establishing procedures for the issuance of binding rulings prior to the entry of the merchandise concerned), and may disseminate such information as may be necessary to secure a just, impartial, and uniform appraisement of imported merchandise and the classification and assessment of duties thereon at the various ports of entry."

The Secretary provides for tariff rulings before the entry of goods by regulations authorizing "ruling letters" setting tariff classifications for particular imports. A ruling letter "represents the official position of the Customs

Service with respect to the particular transaction or issue described therein and is binding on all Customs Service personnel in accordance with the provisions of this section until modified or revoked. In the absence of a change of practice or other modification or revocation which affects the principle of the ruling set forth in the ruling letter, that principle may be cited as authority in the disposition of transactions involving the same circumstances." §177.9(a).

After the transaction that gives it birth, a ruling letter is to "be applied only with respect to transactions involving articles identical to the sample submitted with the ruling request or to articles whose description is identical to the description set forth in the ruling letter." As a general matter, such a letter is "subject to modification or revocation without notice to any person, except the person to whom the letter was addressed," and the regulations consequently provide that "no other person should rely on the ruling letter or assume that the principles of that ruling will be applied in connection with any transaction other than the one described in the letter." Since ruling letters respond to transactions of the moment, they are not subject to notice and comment before being issued, may be published but need only be made "available for public inspection."

Any of the 46 port-of-entry Customs offices may issue ruling letters, and so may the Customs Headquarters Office, in providing "advice or guidance as to the interpretation or proper application of the Customs and related laws with respect to a specific Customs transaction [which] may be requested

by Customs Service field offices . . . at any time, whether the transaction is prospective, current, or completed." Most ruling letters contain little or no reasoning, but simply describe goods and state the appropriate category and tariff. A few letters, like the Headquarters ruling at issue here, set out a rationale in some detail.

Respondent, the Mead Corporation, imports "day planners," three-ring binders with pages having room for notes of daily schedules and phone numbers and addresses, together with a calendar and suchlike. The tariff schedule on point falls under the HTSUS heading for "registers, account books, notebooks, order books, receipt books, letter pads, memorandum pads, diaries and similar articles," which comprises two subcategories. Items in the first, "diaries, notebooks and address books, bound; memorandum pads, letter pads and similar articles," were subject to a tariff of 4.0 percent at the time in controversy. Objects in the second, covering "other" items, were free of duty.

We granted *certiorari* in order to consider the limits of *Chevron* deference owed to administrative practice in applying a statute. We hold that administrative implementation of a particular statutory provision qualifies for *Chevron* deference when it appears that Congress delegated authority to the agency generally to make rules carrying the force of law, and that the agency interpretation claiming deference was promulgated in the exercise of that authority. Delegation of such authority may be shown in a variety of ways, as by an agency's power to engage in adjudication or notice-and-comment rulemaking, or by some other indication of a comparable congressional intent. The Customs ruling at issue here fails to qualify, although the possibility that it deserves some deference under *Skidmore* leads us to vacate and remand.

When Congress has "explicitly left a gap for an agency to fill, there is an express delegation of authority to the agency to elucidate a specific provision of the statute by regulation," *Chevron*, 467 U.S. at 843–844, and any ensuing regulation is binding in the courts unless procedurally defective, arbitrary or capricious in substance, or manifestly contrary to the statute. But whether or not they enjoy any express delegation of authority on a particular question, agencies charged with applying a statute necessarily make all sorts of interpretive choices, and while not all of those choices bind judges to follow them, they certainly may influence courts facing questions the agencies have already answered. "The well-reasoned views of the agencies implementing a statute 'constitute a body of experience and informed judgment to which courts and litigants may properly resort for guidance,'" *Bragdon v. Abbott*, 524 U.S. 624 (1998) (quoting *Skidmore*, 323 U.S. at 139–140), and "we have long recognized that considerable weight should be accorded to an executive department's construction of a statutory scheme it is entrusted to administer. . . ." *Chevron, supra*, at 844. The fair measure of deference to an agency administering its own statute has been understood to vary with circumstances, and courts have looked to the degree of the agency's care, its consistency, formality, and relative expertness, and to the persuasiveness of the agency's position, see *Skidmore, supra*,

at 139–140. The approach has produced a spectrum of judicial responses, from great respect at one end, to near indifference at the other. Justice Jackson summed things up in *Skidmore v. Swift & Co.*:

"The weight [accorded to an administrative] judgment in a particular case will depend upon the thoroughness evident in its consideration, the validity of its reasoning, its consistency with earlier and later pronouncements, and all those factors which give it power to persuade, if lacking power to control."

Since 1984, we have identified a category of interpretive choices distinguished by an additional reason for judicial deference. This Court in *Chevron* recognized that Congress not only engages in express delegation of specific interpretive authority, but that "sometimes the legislative delegation to an agency on a particular question is implicit." Congress, that is, may not have expressly delegated authority or responsibility to implement a particular provision or fill a particular gap. Yet it can still be apparent from the agency's generally conferred authority and other statutory circumstances that Congress would expect the agency to be able to speak with the force of law when it addresses ambiguity in the statute or fills a space in the enacted law, even one about which "Congress did not actually have an intent" as to a particular result. When circumstances implying such an expectation exist, a reviewing court has no business rejecting an agency's exercise of its generally conferred authority to resolve a particular statutory ambiguity simply because the agency's chosen resolution seems unwise, but is obliged to accept the agency's position if Congress has not previously spoken to the point at issue and the agency's interpretation is reasonable (a reviewing court shall set aside agency action, findings, and conclusions found to be "arbitrary, capricious, an abuse of discretion, or otherwise not in accordance with law").

We have recognized a very good indicator of delegation meriting *Chevron* treatment in express congressional authorizations to engage in the process of rulemaking or adjudication that produces regulations or rulings for which deference is claimed. It is fair to assume generally that Congress contemplates administrative action with the effect of law when it provides for a relatively formal administrative procedure tending to foster the fairness and deliberation that should underlie a pronouncement of such force. Thus, the overwhelming number of our cases applying *Chevron* deference have reviewed the fruits of notice-and-comment rulemaking or formal adjudication. That said, and as significant as notice-and-comment is in pointing to *Chevron* authority, the want of that procedure here does not decide the case, for we have sometimes found reasons for *Chevron* deference even when no such administrative formality was required and none was afforded. The fact that the tariff classification here was not a product of such formal process does not alone, therefore, bar the application of *Chevron*.

There are, nonetheless, ample reasons to deny *Chevron* deference here. The authorization for classification rulings, and Customs's practice in making them, present a case far removed not only from notice-and-comment process, but from any other circumstances reason-ably suggesting that Congress ever thought of classification rulings as deserving the deference claimed for them here.

No matter which angle we choose for viewing the Customs ruling letter in this case, it fails to qualify under *Chevron*. On the face of the statute, to begin with, the terms of the congressional delegation give no indication that Congress meant to delegate authority to Customs to issue classification rulings with the force of law. We are not, of course, here making any global statement about Customs's authority, for it is true that the general rulemaking power conferred on Customs authorizes some regulation with the force of law, or "legal norms," It is true as well that Congress had classification rulings in mind when it explicitly authorized, in a parenthetical, the issuance of "regulations establishing procedures for the issuance of binding rulings prior to the entry of the merchandise concerned." The reference to binding classifications does not, however, bespeak the legislative type of activity that would naturally bind more than the parties to the ruling, once the goods classified are admitted into this country. And though the statute's direction to disseminate "information" necessary to "secure" uniformity seems to assume that a ruling may be precedent in later transactions, precedential value alone does not add up to *Chevron* entitlement; interpretive rules may sometimes function as precedents . . . and they enjoy no *Chevron* status as a class. In any event, any precedential claim of a classification ruling is counterbalanced by the provision for independent review of Customs classifications by the

CIT; the scheme for CIT review includes a provision that treats classification rulings on par with the Secretary's rulings on "valuation, rate of duty, marking, restricted merchandise, entry requirements, drawbacks, vessel repairs, or similar matters." It is hard to imagine a congressional understanding more at odds with the *Chevron* regime.

It is difficult, in fact, to see in the agency practice itself any indication that Customs ever set out with a lawmaking pretense in mind when it undertook to make classifications like these. Customs does not generally engage in notice-and-comment practice when issuing them, and their treatment by the agency makes it clear that a letter's binding character as a ruling stops short of third parties; Customs has regarded a classification as conclusive only as between itself and the importer to whom it was issued, and even then only until Customs has given advance notice of intended change. Other importers are in fact warned against assuming any right of detrimental reliance.

Indeed, to claim that classifications have legal force is to ignore the reality that 46 different Customs offices issue 10,000 to 15,000 of them each year. Any suggestion that rulings intended to have the force of law are being churned out at a rate of 10,000 a year at an agency's 46 scattered offices is simply self-refuting.

Nor do the amendments to the statute made effective after this case arose disturb our conclusion. The new law requires Customs to provide notice-and-comment procedures only when modifying or revoking a prior classification ruling or modifying the treatment accorded to substantially identical transactions; and under its regulations, Customs sees itself obliged to provide notice-and-comment procedures only when "changing a practice" so as to produce a tariff increase, or in the imposition of a restriction or prohibition, or when Customs Headquarters determines that "the matter is of sufficient importance to involve the interests of domestic industry." The statutory changes reveal no new congressional objective of treating classification decisions generally as rulemaking with force of law, nor do they suggest any intent to create a *Chevron* patchwork of classification rulings, some with force of law, some without.

In sum, classification rulings are best treated like "interpretations contained in policy statements, agency manuals, and enforcement guidelines." Christensen, 529 U.S. at 587. They are beyond the *Chevron* pale.

To agree with the Court of Appeals that Customs ruling letters do not fall within *Chevron* is not, however, to place them outside the pale of any deference whatever. *Chevron* did nothing to eliminate *Skidmore*'s holding that an agency's interpretation may merit some deference whatever its form, given the "specialized experience and broader investigations and information" available to the agency, and given the value of uniformity in its administrative and judicial understandings of what a national law requires.

There is room at least to raise a *Skidmore* claim here, where the regulatory scheme is highly detailed, and Customs can bring the benefit of specialized experience to bear on the subtle questions in this case: whether the daily planner with room for brief daily entries falls under "diaries," when diaries are grouped with "notebooks and address books, bound; memorandum pads, letter pads and similar articles. A classification ruling in this situation may therefore at least seek a respect proportional to its power to persuade," *Skidmore, supra*, at 140; . . . Such a ruling may surely claim the merit of its writer's thoroughness, logic and expertness, its fit with prior interpretations, and any other sources of weight.

Underlying the position we take here, like the position expressed by JUSTICE SCALIA in dissent, is a choice about the best way to deal with an inescapable feature of the body of congressional legislation authorizing administrative action. That feature is the great variety of ways in which the laws invest the Government's administrative arms with discretion, and with procedures for exercising it, in giving meaning to Acts of Congress. Implementation of a statute may occur in formal adjudication or the choice to defend against judicial challenge; it may occur in a central board or office or in dozens of enforcement agencies dotted across the country; its institutional lawmaking may be confined to the resolution of minute detail or extend to legislative rulemaking on matters intentionally left by Congress to be worked out at the agency level.

Although we all accept the position that the Judiciary should defer to at least some of this multifarious administrative action, we have to decide how to take account of the great range of its variety. If the primary objective is to simplify the judicial process of giving or withholding deference, then the diversity of statutes authorizing discretionary administrative action must be declared irrelevant or minimized. If, on the other hand, it is simply implausible that Congress intended such a broad range of statutory authority to produce only two varieties of administrative action, demanding either *Chevron* deference or none at all, then the breadth of the spectrum of possible agency action must be taken into account. JUSTICE SCALIA's first priority over the years has been to limit and simplify. The Court's choice has been to tailor deference to variety. This acceptance of the range of statutory variation has led the Court to recognize more than one variety of judicial deference, just as the Court has recognized a variety of indicators that Congress would expect *Chevron* deference.

Our respective choices are repeated today. JUSTICE SCALIA would pose the question of deference as an either-or choice. On his view that *Chevron* rendered *Skidmore* anachronistic, when courts owe any deference it is *Chevron* deference that they owe. Whether courts do owe deference in a given case turns, for him, on whether the agency action (if reasonable) is "authoritative." The character of the authoritative derives, in turn, not from breadth of delegation or the agency's procedure in implementing it, but is defined as the "official" position of an agency, ibid., and may ultimately be a function of administrative persistence alone.

The Court, on the other hand, said nothing in *Chevron* to eliminate *Skidmore*'s recognition of various justifications for deference depending on statutory circumstances and agency action; *Chevron* was simply a case recognizing that even without express authority to fill a specific statutory gap, circumstances pointing to implicit congressional delegation present a particularly insistent call for deference. Indeed, in holding here that *Chevron* left *Skidmore* intact and applicable where statutory circumstances indicate no intent to delegate general authority to make rules with force of law, or where such authority was not invoked, we hold nothing more than we said last Term in response to the particular statutory circumstances in Christensen, to which JUSTICE SCALIA then took exception, just as he does again today.

We think, in sum, that JUSTICE SCALIA's efforts to simplify ultimately run afoul of Congress's indications that different statutes present different reasons for considering respect for the exercise of administrative authority or deference to it. Without being at odds with congressional intent much of the time, we believe that judicial responses to administrative action must continue to differentiate between *Chevron* and *Skidmore*, and that continued recognition of *Skidmore* is necessary for just the reasons Justice Jackson gave when that case was decided.

Since the *Skidmore* assessment called for here ought to be made in the first instance by the Court of Appeals for the Federal Circuit or the Court of International Trade, we go no further than to vacate the judgment and remand the case for further proceedings consistent with this opinion.

It is so ordered.

JUSTICE SCALIA, dissenting.

Today's opinion makes an avulsive change in judicial review of federal administrative action. Whereas previously a reasonable agency application of an ambiguous statutory provision had to be sustained so long as it represented the agency's authoritative interpretation, henceforth such an application can be set aside unless "it appears that Congress delegated authority to the agency generally to make rules carrying the force of law," as by giving an agency "power to engage in adjudication or notice-and-comment rulemaking, or . . . some other [procedure] indicating comparable congressional intent," and "the agency interpretation claiming deference was promulgated in the exercise of that authority." What was previously a general presumption of authority in agencies to resolve ambiguity in the statutes they have been authorized to enforce has been changed to a presumption of no such authority, which must be overcome by affirmative legislative intent to the contrary. And whereas previously, when agency authority to resolve ambiguity did not exist the court was free to give the statute what it considered the best interpretation, henceforth the court must supposedly give the agency view some indeterminate amount of so-called *Skidmore* deference. We will be sorting out the consequences of the Mead doctrine, which has today replaced the *Chevron* doctrine, for years to come. I would adhere to our established jurisprudence, defer to the reasonable interpretation the Customs Service has given to the statute it is charged with enforcing, and reverse the judgment of the Court of Appeals. . . . The Court's new doctrine is neither sound in principle nor sustainable in practice. . . .

As to principle: The doctrine of *Chevron*—that all authoritative agency interpretations of statutes they are charged with administering deserve deference—was rooted in a legal presumption of congressional intent, important to the division of powers between the Second and Third Branches. . . .

Another practical effect of today's opinion will be an artificially induced increase in informal rulemaking. Buy stock in the GPO. Since informal rulemaking and formal adjudication are the only more-or-less safe harbors from the storm that the Court has unleashed; and since formal adjudication is not an option but must be mandated by statute or constitutional command; informal rulemaking—which the Court was once careful to make voluntary unless required by statute, see Bell Aerospace, supra, and *Chenery, supra*—will now become a virtual necessity. As I have described, the Court's safe harbor requires not merely that the agency ha[s] been given rulemaking authority, but also that the agency ha[s] employed rulemaking as the means of resolving the statutory ambiguity. . . .

Worst of all, the majority's approach will lead to the ossification of large portions of our statutory law. Where *Chevron* applies, statutory ambiguities remain ambiguities subject to the agency's ongoing clarification. They create a space, so to speak, for the exercise of continuing agency discretion. . . . *Skidmore* deference gives the agency's current position some vague and uncertain amount of respect, but it does not, like *Chevron*, leave the matter

within the control of the Executive Branch for the future. Once the court has spoken, it becomes unlawful for the agency to take a contradictory position; the statute now says what the court has prescribed. It will be bad enough when this ossification occurs as a result of judicial determination (under today's new principles) that there is no affirmative indication of congressional intent to "delegate"; but it will be positively bizarre when it occurs simply because of an agency's failure to act by rulemaking (rather than informal adjudication) before the issue is presented to the courts. . . .

There is, in short, no way to avoid the ossification of federal law that today's opinion sets in motion. What a court says is the law after according *Skidmore* deference will be the law forever, beyond the power of the agency to change even through rulemaking.

And finally, the majority's approach compounds the confusion it creates by breathing new life into the anachronism of *Skidmore*, which sets forth a sliding scale of deference owed an agency's interpretation of a statute that is dependent "upon the thoroughness evident in [the agency's] consideration, the validity of its reasoning, its consistency with earlier and later pronouncements, and all those factors which give it power to persuade." . . .

Skidmore deference is a recipe for uncertainty, unpredictability, and endless litigation. To condemn a vast body of agency action to that regime (all except rulemaking, formal (and informal?) adjudication, and whatever else might now and then be included within today's intentionally vague formulation of affirmative congressional intent to "delegate") is irresponsible. . . .

There is also no doubt that the Customs Service's interpretation is a reasonable one, whether or not judges would consider it the best. I will not belabor this point, since the Court evidently agrees: An interpretation that was unreasonable would not merit the remand that the Court decrees for consideration of *Skidmore* deference.

Finally, and least importantly, even were I to accept the Court's revised version of *Chevron* as a correct statement of the law, I would still accord deference to the tariff classification ruling at issue in this case. . . .

And here, as in NationsBank, the agency interpretation in question is officially that of the agency head. Conse-quently, even on the Court's own terms, the Customs ruling at issue in this case should be given *Chevron* deference.

For the reasons stated, I respectfully dissent from the Court's judgment. I would uphold the Customs Service's construction of Subheading 4820.10.20 of the Harmonized Tariff Schedule of the United States, and would reverse the contrary decision of the Court of Appeals. I dissent even more vigorously from the reasoning that produces the Court's judgment, and that makes today's decision one of the most significant opinions ever rendered by the Court dealing with the judicial review of administrative action. Its consequences will be enormous, and almost uniformly bad.

COMMENTS AND QUESTIONS

The 2001 *Mead* decision is probably the most significant ruling on the role played by judicial deference since the famous case of *Chevron U.S.A. v. Natural Resources Defense Council*, 467 U.S. 837 (1984). The deference doctrine, as noted in this chapter, is a well-established doctrine that is rooted in plain common sense. What's commonsensical about the doctrine is that unquestionably it makes sense for the courts not to meddle in agency business any more than they should. Thus, when a party files suit and questions an agency action in court, it seems most appropriate under our separation-of-powers system for the court to respect agency expertise by deferring to it unless the agency action has no basis in fact or law. In short, it seems unwise for courts to substitute their opinion for the judgment of agency experts unless the courts have very sound legal reasons to intervene.

This general principle is understood by all administrative law scholars, but arguments continue over *what kind* of deference and *how much* is due agency expertise, discretion, and decisions under various circumstances. The courts have addressed various deference questions over the decades and have tried to establish basic deference standards that have broad application, but the courts, as made clear by *Mead* and especially by the reaction to *Mead* by legal scholars, have failed to develop deference standards that can be applied across the board.

In 1984 in *Chevron* the Supreme Court handed own a very controversial decision that nonetheless seemed to go quite far in developing a general deference standard—obviously not far enough, as we learn from the *Mead* Court. The 1984

*Chevro*n decision established the sweeping "extreme deference" doctrine (the *Chevron* doctrine), which requires essentially that courts defer to agency discretion in decisionmaking (e.g., an agency's interpretation of a statutory provision) unless the agency action is in blatant contradiction of the statute. In subsequent cases the *Chevron* doctrine has been clarified and expanded to allow agency administrators to interpret statutory language very broadly, with the courts not permitted to over-rule any *reasonable* or even *plausible* interpretation of a statute unless the statute clearly prohibits it. Many have criticized such extreme deference, arguing that it can encourage irresponsible administrative behavior and due process violations. But defenders have claimed that such deference prohibits the different courts in the federal system from giving inconsistent interpretations to statutory provisions.

The *Chevron* decision still left several questions unanswered. The *Mead* Court addressed a critical one. That is, is *Chevron* deference due an agency when the agency makes an informal decision such as a "letter ruling" tariff decision with-out any notice-and-comment or adjudicative procedures? The *Mead* Court said no, because Congress essentially did not intend such particularized decisions to carry the force of law and cited authoritatively across the board, although the Court held that the specific letter ruling applying to the Mead Corporation was entitled to deference under *Skidmore v. Swift and Company*, 323 U.S. 134 (1944), as long as the letter ruling was *persuasive*.

In dissent Justice Scalia argues not only that did the *Chevron* decision overrule *Skidmore*—so *Skidmore* should not apply in *Mead*—but that the Court's majority in *Mead* has only confused deference law by making *Chevron's* application am-biguous and impractical. He believes that the majority should have extended *Chevron* deference in a consistent manner, which would permit deference even to letter rulings as long as they were reasonable under law. Which arguments make more sense, Scalia's or the Court's majority? *Mead*, applying *Skidmore*, appears to permit the Courts, if *Chevron* deference does not apply, to judge the applicability of granting deference on a case-by-case basis, depending on the *persuasiveness* of agency justifications for its action. As Scalia asks, Is this practical? Is it wiser for the courts to develop more rigid or more flexible deference standards? What are your value criteria for answering this question?

NOTES

1. In particular, see the scolding of administrative officials by the courts in *Morgan v. United States*, 304 U.S. 1 (1938); *Cinderella Career and Finishing Schools, Inc. v. FTC*, 25 F.2d 583 (D.C. Cir. 1970); *Citizens to Preserve Overton Park v. Volpe*, 401 U.S. 402 (1971); *Motor Vehicles Manufacturers Ass'n. v. State Farm Insurance Co.*, 463 U.S. 29 (1983); *Bowen v. American Hospital Ass'n.*, 10th S.Ct. 2101 (1986); and *St. Luke's Methodist Hosp. v. Thompson*, 315 F.3d 984 (2003).

2. Martin Shapiro, "Discretion" in David H. Rosenbloom and Richard D. Schwartz, eds., *Handbook of Regulation and Administrative Law* (New York: Marcel Dekker, 1994), p. 511.

3. William H. Rehnquist, *The Supreme Court* (New York: Vintage Books, 2002), chap. 1.

4. Owen M. Fiss, "The Bureaucratization of the Judiciary," *Yale Law Journal* 92 (July 1983); and Glen O. Robinson, *American Bureaucracy: Public Choice and Public Law* (Ann Arbor: University of Michigan Press, 1991), pp. 108–110.

5. Charles W. Stewart, "Self-Conscious Interest and the Democratic Process: The Case of Citizens Regulating Agencies and Federal Courts," *Law and Policy Quarterly* 1 (October 1979): 418.

6. Jeremy Rabkin, *Judicial Compulsions: How Public Law Distorts Public Policy* (New York: Basic Books, 1989).

7. George Will, "Who Decides: Judges or People," *St. Louis Post-Dispatch*, November 2, 1994, p. 7B.

8. James L. Buckley, "The Constitution and the Courts," *Harvard Journal of Law and Public Policy* 24 (fall 2000): 189–202.

9. Steven Vago, *Law and Society,* 4th ed. (Englewood Cliffs, N.J.: Prentice-Hall, 1994), p. 190.

10. U.S. Census Bureau, *Statistical Abstract of the United States 2002* (Washington, D.C.: U.S. Government Printing Office, 2002), p. 197.

11. Recent statistics from *United States Government Manual, 2002–2003* (Washington, D.C.: Office of the Federal Register, National Archives and Records Administration 2003), pp. 67–84, table K.

12. Vago, *Law and Society*, pp. 190–194.

13. Donald L. Horowitz, "The Courts as Guardians of the Public Interest," *Public Administration Review* 37 (March–April 1977): 150. Also see Peter L. Strauss, *Administrative Law in the United States*, 2nd ed. (Durham: Carolina Academic Press, 2002), chaps. 7–8; and Mark Seidenfeld, "Getting Beyond Criticism: New Theories of the Regulatory State, Cognitive Loafing, Social Conformity, and Judicial Review of Agency Rulemaking," *Cornell Law Review* 87 (January 2002).

14. Horowitz, "Courts as Guardians of the Public Interest," p. 150.

15. Ibid., pp. 150–151.

16. Ibid., p. 151.

17. Ibid. Also see, Charles H. Koch, Jr., "An Issue Driven Strategy for Review of Agency Decisions," *Administrative Law Review* 43 (fall 1991): 517. Koch does an excellent job in analyzing the impact the new court's role has had on agency administration.

18. Thomas W. Merrill, "Judicial Deference to Executive Precedent," *Yale Law Journal* 101 (March 1992): 970. Ironically, in that same year Michael Hertz, in "Deference Running Riot," *Administrative Law Journal* 6 (summer 1992), reached the opposite conclusion, as implied by the title.

19. Buckley, "The Constitution and the Courts," p. 198.

20. Kim Morris, "Judicial Review of Non-reviewable Administrative Action: Veteran's Administration Benefit Claims," *Administrative Law Review* 29 (winter 1977): 65–86.

21. Bernard Schwartz, *Administrative Law*, 2nd ed. (Boston: Little, Brown, 1984), p. 455.

22. House Judiciary Committee, in *Administrative Procedure Act: Legislative History* (Washington, D.C.: U.S. Government Printing Office, 1946), p. 275.

23. Richard J. Pierce, Jr., *Administrative Law Treatise*, 4th ed. (New York: Aspen, 2002), vol. 3, pp. 1269–1302.

24. Catherine Zaller, "The Case for Strict Statutory Construction of Mandatory Agency Deadlines Under Section 706," *William and Mary Law Review* 42 (April 2001): 1545.

25. Ibid., p. 1573.

26. Ibid.

27. Bernard Schwartz, "Administrative Law Cases During 1993," *Administrative Law Review* 46 (summer 1994): 321.

28. For an argument that the court denied standing to avoid "social unrest," see Kenneth F. Warren, "The Housing and Community Development Act: Two Years after Hartford," *Administrative Law Review* 30 (fall 1978).

29. For example, see *Tennessee Electric Power Co. v. TVA*, 306 U.S. 1181 (1937); *Perkins v. Lukens Steel Co.*, 310 U.S. 113 (1940); *United States v. Caltex Philippines, Inc.*, 344 U.S. 149 (1952); and *Kansas City Power and Light Co. v. McKay*, 225 F.2d 924; cert. denied, 350 U.S. 884 (1955). It should be mentioned that various immunity provisions protect government officials from certain suits—a topic treated in Chapter 10 of this book.

30. The basic argument against granting standing for a generalized taxpayer grievance was upheld in 1974 in *United States v. Richardson*, 418 U.S. 166.

31. Regarding this position, see Justice William J. Brennan's concurring opinion in *Simon v. Eastern Kentucky Welfare Rights Organization*, 426 U.S. 26 (1976), in which he asserts that the application of standing tests are in pathetic confusion (pp. 64–66). See also Mark V. Tushnet, "The New Law of Standing: A Plea for Abandonment," *Cornell Law Review* 62 (April 1977).

32. Bernard Schwartz, "Administrative Law Cases During 1992," *Administrative Law Review* 45 (summer 1993): 269.

33. The first recognized use of the exhaustion doctrine by the Supreme Court was in *Cosmos Exploration Co. v. Gray Eagle Oil Co.*, 190 U.S. 301 (1903).

34. For an insightful critique of *Darby*, see Schwartz, "Administrative Law Cases During 1993," pp. 317–321.

35. Bernard Schwartz, *Administrative Law,* 3rd ed. (Boston: Little, Brown, 1991), p. 563.

36. 7. U.S.C.A., Section 135a(C)(1)(D)(iii).

37. Schwartz, *Administrative Law*, 3rd ed., pp. 563–564.

38. Curiously, a Colorado ruling contradicted the law established in *Abbott Laboratories* by holding that a general regulation has to be actually enforced against a specific party before it can be considered for review (*Colorado-UTE Electric Ass'n v. Air Pollution Comm'n.,* 591 P.7d 1323 [Colo. App. 1978]). This argument, however, was rejected in *Thomas v. Union Carbide Agricultural Products Co.,* 105 S.Ct. 3325 (1985). The reasoning in the Colorado decision was essentially upheld by the U.S. Supreme Court in 1993 in *Reno v. Catholic Social Services*, 113 S.Ct. 2485.

39. Schwartz, "Administrative Law Cases During 1993," p. 324.

40. Before the Supreme Court reversed in *John Parisi v. Philip B. Davidson*, 405 U.S. 34 (1972), out of respect for a military proceeding, the two lower courts relied upon comity to create a "distance" between the federal judiciary and the military justice system.

41. Edwin Wallace Tucker, *Administrative Law, Regulation of Enterprise and Individual Liberties* (St. Paul: West, 1975), p. 134.

42. *DiGiovanni v. Camden Fire Insurance Ass'n.*, 296 U.S. 64, 73 (1935).

43. *Beal v. Missouri Pacific Railroad Corp.,* 312 U.S. 45, 50 (1941).

44. Kenneth C. Davis, *Administrative Law: Cases, Text, Problems* (St. Paul: West, 1977), p. 78.

45. Schwartz, "Administrative Law Cases During 1979," p. 435. Also see Stephen Breyer, "Judicial Review of Questions of Law and Policy," *Administrative Law Review* 38 (fall 1986).

46. For further analysis on *Chevron*, see Cass R. Sunstein, "Law and Administration After *Chevron*," *Columbia Law Review* 90 (December 1990); *ABF Freight System, Inc. v. N.L.R.B.*, 114 S.Ct. 835 (1994); and Einer Elhauge, "Preference-Estimating Statutory Default Rules," *Columbia Law Review* 102 (December 2002).

47. For a critique of *Chevron USA v. Echazabal*, see David Yee, "*Chevron USA, Inc. v. Echazabal,*" *American Journal of Gender Social Policy an the Law,* 22 (2003).

48. The substantial evidence rule was long recognized before the 1946 APA. Its lengthy history dates back to at least 1912, when the Supreme Court in *ICC v. Union Pacific Railroad,* 222 U.S. 541, 548, espoused the rule by maintaining that reviewing courts should "examine the facts . . . to determine whether there was substantial evidence to support the order."

49. Davis, *Administrative Law,* p. 80.

50. Ibid., p. 92.

51. Louis J. Jaffe, "Administrative Procedure Re-examined: The Benjamin Report," *Harvard Law Review* 56 (March 1943): 732.

52. See *Goldberg v. Kelly,* 397 U.S. 254 (1970).

53. Bernard Schwartz, *Administrative Law,* 4th ed. (Boston: Little, Brown, 1994), pp. 864–872.

54. Kenneth C. Davis and Richard J. Pierce, Jr., *Administrative Law Treatise,* 3rd ed. (Boston, Little, Brown, 1994), vol. 3, p. 158.

55. In *Chrysler Corp. v. Brown,* 441 U.S. 281 (1979), the government argued that de novo review should be reserved only for very rare cases. The Court failed to respond to the government's argument, but the position seems sound. De novo review should be limited so that stability in and respect for the administrative process can be maintained.

56. Schwartz, "Administrative Law Cases During 1993," p. 327.

57. Kenneth F. Warren, *In Defense of Public Opinion Polling* (Boulder, Colo.: Westview Press, 2002), chaps. 1 and 7.

CHAPTER 10

Suing the Government and Its Administrators

TORT LIABILITY ISSUES IN A DEMOCRATIC STATE: AN OVERVIEW

Because of the emergence of the administrative state, our entire political system has been affected by efforts to make governmental bureaucracy democratically responsible to the citizenry. The president has created a huge White House staff and extended the informal powers of the presidency in an attempt to keep the administrative system accountable to the national constituency. Congress has also enlarged its staff and created new control mechanisms so that it can retain political control over the administrative machinery. Congress has, in addition, passed major legislation (for example, the APA) in an effort to force public administrators to uphold democratic procedural due process standards. Citizen and consumer organizations have also played a role in checking administrative behavior. Meanwhile, the courts have become more active in recent decades in seeing to it that individual rights, at least in certain areas, are better protected from possible administrative abuses of power. To accomplish this end, the courts have agreed to review a greater variety of administrative law cases, as well as to expand their scope of review in the cases they decide to review.

Since the 1930s the courts have gradually extended procedural due process protections to persons dealing with administrative agencies. Since the late 1960s the courts have turned many citizen *privileges* into citizen *rights,* thus providing individuals with a considerably stronger position than they have heretofore had from which to challenge agency actions toward them. The courts made judicial review of agency actions affecting individuals much more available by liberalizing the standing prerequisites. However, possibly the most significant development occurred during the 1970s when Congress, with the approval of the courts, took from public officials many of the official immunity protections that for so long had made it virtually impossible for citizens to sue public agencies and their officials for grossly irresponsible and malicious conduct. Under present law, it is easier for individuals to sue public administrators for damages caused by "reckless" administrative actions. But is this necessarily a good thing? Can our public administrators function efficiently and effectively as policy implementers if they must always contend with the possibility that they may be found personally liable for their administrative acts? In the implementation of public policies, is it not a given that some citizens will benefit while others will be hurt? This is a reality because governmental administrators are largely responsible for allocating the state's scarce resources. Some will always claim that the pie was divided in a manner that has seriously hurt their interests—so much so that they may be motivated to sue the administrators who caused them injury. Of course, others will want to sue administrators or the government for damages because they believe those administrators have wrongfully denied them due process rights, statutory entitlements, or mistreated them in other ways.

Is it right, however, for a democratic state to employ official immunity to protect administrators from being held responsible for blatantly negligent, exploitative, or malicious actions that cause great harm to individuals or organizations? Should not governmental administrators be held reasonably accountable for their actions? Do not immunity protections tend to encourage irresponsible administrative behavior by eliminating the possibility of damage suits, despite how reckless and harmful the administration may have been? Given the pervasive role administrative power plays in our lives today, would it be in the best interests of ordered liberty to immunize the government and its administrators from liability claims? The central purpose of this chapter is to explore some of the major issues raised by these questions, while examining the specific rights individuals apparently have when they decide to bring tort liability claims against the government or its officers.

THE SOVEREIGN IMMUNITY DOCTRINE

What is the sovereign immunity doctrine, what are its origins, how has it been applied, what are its pros and cons, and why has the doctrine survived so long in American history? The *sovereign immunity doctrine* holds that the government is sovereign and, therefore, cannot be held liable for its actions. More specifically, the doctrine makes it impossible for parties to sue the government for civil damages unless the government permits the suit. The government can permit suits by passing legislation that allows claims to be made against the government under certain conditions. For example, the Tucker Act of 1855 (28 U.S.C.A., Section 1331) confers jurisdiction on U.S. district courts to hear claims against the United States involving contracts (*United States v. Mitchell*, 463 U.S. 206 [1983];

and *Spectrum Leasing Corp. v. United States,* 764 F.2d 891 [1985]); the Federal Tort Claims Act of 1946 (60 Stat. 842) allows persons under certain circumstances to sue the United States government for tortious acts committed against them by its officials (*Dalehite v. United States,* 346 U.S. 15 [1953]; *United States v. Varig Airlines,* 104 S.Ct. 2755 [1984]; and *Christopher v. Harbury,* 122 S.Ct. 2179 [2002]); and Section 702 of the APA, as amended in 1988, permits the federal government to be sued for nonmoney damages in injunctive and mandamus actions. Overall, about forty statutes allow the federal government to be sued for tortious acts under specific circumstances, although only one, the Federal Torts Claims Act of 1946, as amended, has general applicability. But what makes the government sovereign is the very fact that no party can sue unless the government allows the suit. As the Supreme Court made clear in *Federal Deposit Insurance Corp. v. Meyer,* 114 S.Ct. 996, 1000 (1994), the government still enjoys sovereign immunity because, "absent a waiver, sovereign immunity shields the Federal Government and its agencies from suit . . . sovereign immunity is jurisdictional in nature. Indeed, the 'terms of (the United States) consent to be sued in any court define that court's jurisdiction to entertain the suit.'"

From one perspective the sovereign immunity doctrine is "dead" because the federal government has waived its absolute sovereign immunity status, allowing suits against the government under restrictive circumstances. However, from another perspective the sovereign immunity doctrine is still very much alive because in most cases the government still has not allowed itself to be sued, and when it does, the kind of tort suit that can be filed is very limited, normally forbidding or placing caps on money damages and totally prohibiting punitive damage awards. In fact, Harold J. Krent asserted in a recent article that "many have noted that sovereign immunity was never applied as comprehensively in the past as it is today."[1]

The sovereign immunity doctrine has been heavily relied upon by the courts for over two centuries to stop liability suits against the United States government and the state governments. Ironically, however, the use of this doctrine has never been formally sanctioned by our lawmakers.[2] The sovereign immunity doctrine is deeply rooted in America's Anglo-Saxon legal heritage, and it was evidently just assumed that the doctrine should become part of our legal system. The mysterious emergence of the application of the doctrine was recognized by a California court: "How it became in the United States the basis for a rule that the federal and state governments did not have to answer for their torts has been called 'one of the mysteries of legal evolution.'"[3] This mystery has been acknowledged for a long time. About a hundred years ago, in *U.S. v. Lee,* 106 U.S. 196, 207 (1882), the Supreme Court acknowledged that "while the exemption of the United States and of several states from being subjected as defendants to ordinary actions in the courts has . . . repeatedly been asserted here, *the principle has never been discussed or the reasons for it given, but it has always been treated as an established doctrine*" (emphasis mine).

Although the evolution of the sovereign immunity doctrine in American law may be perplexing, the doctrine's historical origins are very clear. As noted, the doctrine is entrenched in our Anglo-Saxon heritage. Actually, it was one of the most fundamental doctrines on which old Anglo-Saxon law was based. Specifically, the sovereign immunity doctrine rests on the medieval argument that the king is sovereign and, therefore, incapable of wrongdoing.[4] But what seems baffling to most scholars is that, although the king-can-do-no-wrong argument may have made sense for a monarchical governmental system, in which the king reigns above the law, it appeared to make little to no sense for a constitutional political system based on the rule of law. Under a rule-of-law system, of course, no one is supposed to stand above the law. Therefore, it was argued, how could a doctrine be employed in American government—a rule-of-law political system—to place governmental officials (for example, public administrators) above the law? Surely, if public officials cannot be sued for their tortious acts because they are protected by the sovereign immunity doctrine, while others in the private sector can be sued because they are not protected by any such doctrine, then the doctrine in effect places these governmental officials above the law.[5]

It should be pointed out that, technically speaking, the sovereign immunity doctrine does not necessarily protect governmental officials from tort liability suits, but only the government. Under common law doctrine, individual public officials could be sued for their tortious acts while functioning as governmental employees. However, for the most part the sovereign immunity doctrine has also been applied in such a way as to provide absolute immunity protections to individual public officials. That is, the courts have until very recently argued that governmental officers performing within their official line of duty shall be granted extensive immunity privileges, if not absolute immunity, so that they will not be vulnerable to liability suits when their official actions may have caused someone harm. For example, in *Barr v. Matteo,* 360 U.S. 564, 571, (1959), the Supreme Court held that public officials should have the luxury of being "free to exercise their duties unembarrassed by the fear of damage suits in respect of acts done in the course of those duties."

Bernard Schwartz is opposed to any governmental immunity system that unfairly and unreasonably prevents those hurt by the government or its officers from being able to sue for justifiable damage claims.[6] Kenneth C. Davis agrees, contending that blanket or sovereign immunity protections are patently unjust. He cites the *Lee* case where the Court explained: "Courts of justice are established, not only to decide upon controverted rights of the citizens as against each other, but also upon rights in controversy between them and the government."[7] But Davis contends that under the sovereign immunity doctrine "the courts are barred from finding facts and applying the law; unless some other tribunal is available, the parties have no means of settling their controversy except by resort to force." He notes further: "When the government is one of the parties, it always prevails because it is always stronger; no private party has an army, navy, and air force."[8]

Davis is also convinced that the sovereign immunity doctrine is un-American and defies plain common sense. For this reason, it had to be abandoned.[9] What sense, he argued, does it make in a modern rule-of-law nation such as the United States for private persons to be subject to liability claims for recklessly running down a person on the street, while the driver of the governmental vehicle is not liable for the same act?

Davis's indictment of the sovereign immunity doctrine is harsh, yet clearly some reasonable arguments to justify the existence of the sovereign immunity doctrine must exist, especially since the doctrine has not only survived into the twenty-first century, but it is even being used more by the conservative federal courts, especially the Supreme Court, to push "federalism revival."[10]

Of course, the traditional arguments in support of the sovereign immunity doctrine are based on the contention that it is potentially very dangerous to allow persons to sue the government for damages that it might cause, because, conceivably, suits brought by enough parties could literally bankrupt and, therefore, destroy the government. For example, if a United States Air Force pilot mistakenly dropped a nuclear bomb on Boston and completely devastated the metropolitan area, should all survivors and their families, businesses, and so on, be given the opportunity to sue the federal government for damages? The humane response might be yes, but the practical response would be no.[11] Actually, the sovereign immunity doctrine has rarely been defended for any other reasons than practical ones. It has probably never been defended on the grounds that it is fair to individuals. Clearly, it is not because the doctrine in fact sanctions individual suffering so that the general public will not suffer. In the imagined Boston tragedy, because liability claims against the federal government would undoubtedly bankrupt and destroy it, the practically minded would contend that the suits should not be allowed. That is, the government should protect itself and the general public against the possibility that the government could be destroyed by massive suits by invoking the doctrine of sovereign immunity. According to supporters of the doctrine, this governmental action would be justified in the reasoning that it is far better for one or a few to suffer than for society as a whole to suffer.

During the heyday of the sovereign immunity doctrine, Justice Oliver Wendell Holmes, speaking for a unanimous court in *Kawananakoa v. Polyfolank*, 205 U.S. 349, 353 (1907), employed traditional logic to defend the doctrine when he explained: "A sovereign is exempt from suit, not because of any formal conception or obsolete theory, but on the logical and practical ground that there can be no legal right as against the authority that makes the law on which the right depends."

But few today believe that the government should remain totally immune from liability suits. The present "liberal perspective" on sovereign immunity is epitomized by Justice Traynor's conclusion in *Muskopf v. Corning Hospital District*, 56 Cal. 2d 211 (1961): "After a re-evaluation of the rule of governmental immunity from tort liability we have concluded that it must be discarded as mistaken and unjust." But Kenneth C. Davis feels that the Supreme Court had made this point about a century ago in *Lee*. In reflecting on how long it has taken for the wisdom in *Lee* to become accepted as law in America as a consequence of Congress's amendments to the APA in 1976, which made the administrative state vulnerable to some kinds of tort liability suits, Davis remarked, "How strange that the Court's 1882 statement never did become clear law until 1976."[12]

But the death of an absolute application of the sovereign immunity doctrine was not unexpected. Since the 1930s social reformers had been pushing to advance the rights of individuals in many areas, but particularly against the administrative state. How could the sovereign immunity doctrine survive without waivers in a new liberal social atmosphere that demanded that individuals be accorded due process protection? Surely, by the 1970s few believed that due process did not include the right of individuals to sue governmental agencies for their tortious acts, especially since it is generally recognized that the government is in a much better position to absorb losses than individual parties. Nevertheless, the sovereign immunity doctrine still lives on in most areas, preventing injured parties in particular from being fairly compensated monetarily for tortious actions against them. Statutes are carefully written to allow only certain liability suits, but they generally preclude major liability claims against the government. Defenders of sovereign immunity argue that such statutory restrictions to liability claims against the government are absolutely necessary to guarantee our government's stability and survival. In the past few decades many states have followed the federal example by amending their sovereign immunity statutes to permit limited damage suits, yet states have also protected their survival by placing strict limitations upon liability suits, limiting financial awards and moving toward "what amounts to a governmental-operated system of mutual insurance for those damaged by administrative action"[13] (discussed later).

It is worth noting that the conservative Supreme Court's majority in recent years, consisting of justices Rehnquist, O'Connor, Scalia, Thomas, and Kennedy, have used the doctrine of sovereign immunity as one of the weapons in its conservative legal arsenal to promote a "federalism revival." Richard Fallon, Jr. in "The 'Conservative' Paths of the Rehnquist Court's Federalism Decisions" argues that these conservative justices have used sovereign immunity very boldly to promote the power of the states at the expense of centralized national power, allowing states to escape having to comply with certain federal laws by using state sovereign immunity as the defense, along with the Eleventh Amendment, which these conservatives justices have held precludes federal jurisdiction in liability suits involving damage claims by private parties against the state.[14]

Fallon contends that the Supreme Court's majority took the boldest step in 1996 in *Seminole Tribe of Florida v. Florida*, 517 U.S. 44, when it broke with established precedent with disdain by ruling "that Congress lacks power under Article I to abrogate the states' immunity from private suits." But possibly the key decision, according to Fallon, came in 1999 in *Alden v. Maine*, 527 U.S. 706, when the Supreme Court "expressly broke new ground by holding that Congress lacks Article I authority to force the states to submit to private suits for damages in state (as well as federal) court, even when the states have violated valid federal law."[15] Of course, the Supreme Court has continued to apply the Eleventh

Source: Reprinted with permission of John Sherffius and the *St. Louis Post-Dispatch,* January 13, 2000.

Amendment and sovereign immunity in state liability cases up to the present to advance the court's federalism revival.[16] Unfortunately, according to Fallon, new creative applications of the sovereign immunity doctrine to promote nineteenth century federalism, which often boldly and briskly break with long-established precedent, have taken the rather simple sovereign immunity doctrine and caused it to become "vastly complex."[17]

SUING GOVERNMENTAL ADMINISTRATORS: THE ROAD TO QUALIFIED IMMUNITY FOR ADMINISTRATORS

Governmental immunity and official (officer) immunity do not mean exactly the same thing. While *governmental immunity* immunizes the government (for example, public agencies) from tort liability suits stemming from of its actions, *official immunity* immunizes the government's officers from liability claims against them arising from their actions. But it seems that the courts have always had a rather difficult time making a practical and functional distinction between the two. In fact, some courts have ruled that governmental and official immunity cannot be distinguished in meaningful substantive terms. In *Larson v. Domestic and Foreign Com-*

merce Corp., 337 U.S. 682 (1949), the Court ruled essentially that suits against governmental officers should be disallowed in most cases, because they are protected by the government's sovereign immunity status. The Court reasoned that a suit against a government's officer was "in substance, a suit against the Government over which the court, in the absence of consent, has no jurisdiction" (p. 688). This judicial opinion set the tone for many other court decisions, thus making it well-nigh impossible for persons to sue either the government or its officers in tort suits.

In an insightful article on the subject of governmental and official immunity in 1963, Louis Jaffe also concluded that "the officer's immunity is the government's immunity as well."[18] Not unexpectedly, however, when some courts began to challenge the validity and fairness of immunity protections in American government, they chipped away at both governmental immunity and official immunity at the same time because of the close relationship between governmental and official immunity. As a result, today the government enjoys only *limited* immunity, while virtually all government officers enjoy only *qualified* immunity. *Limited immunity* for the government means essentially that the government in general is protected under sovereign immunity yet the government's immunity is limited because limited tort liability actions against the government, as authorized by statute, are permitted.[19] *Qualified immunity* for public officials means their immunity protections are not absolute, thus making some of their actions (for example, malicious acts not authorized by statutes) vulnerable to damage claims against them as individuals.[20]

But before the modern qualified immunity doctrine emerged into a position of dominance, the more traditional doctrine of official immunity emerged to dominate American administrative and constitutional law. What justifications were given to justify granting official immunity (virtually absolute immunity) to governmental administrators?

The development of the qualified immunity position for public administrators did not follow an even and clear path. To understand the development of the qualified immunity perspective, it is helpful to divide its development into roughly three stages. These stages convey that initially administrators enjoyed virtually no immunity. Then a trend started that eventually made administrators immune to tort suits. Finally a reaction to the almost absolute immunity status obtained by administrators stimulated liberal reformers to demand that official immunity should be qualified.

Immunity Under Common Law

Under Anglo-Saxon common law, no public official was extended immunity privileges simply because he worked for the government. The reason for this is rooted deeply in our democratic heritage. According to democratic theory, civil servants are perceived to be *ordinary* citizens who are taking their turn serving their government. Because they are still regarded as ordinary citizens under the rule of law, it was held that they should not be entitled to special immunity privileges different from any other citizens. Bernard Schwartz explains the common law logic: "If public officers are not vested with immunity greater than that of ordinary citizens, it follows that they can be sued for the damages caused by their acts, just as a private individual can be, even if the acts were performed in the course of their official work."[21] According to the great British legal scholar, A.V. Dicey, the prohibition against immunity for public servants is entrenched in the concept of legal equality under law, a concept that he noted had been implemented in Britain: "With us every official, from the Prime Minister down to a constable or a collector of taxes, is under the same responsibility for every act done without legal justification as any other citizen."[22]

It should be stressed that under common law public administrators are immune as long as the damaging act was *within their statutory authority.* But which official acts are clearly within the administrator's statutory authority is a subject frequently open to debate, creating a very uncomfortable position for public administrators who must interpret and apply statutes. If they act beyond their statutory authority and cause harm, they may have to fight a damage suit. The famous state case of *Miller v. Horton,* 26 N.E. 100 (Mass., 1891), conveys the message that under common law doctrine even public officials are very vulnerable if they harm anyone through a mistaken application of the law, even if they acted in good faith. In this case, health officers killed a horse that they thought had glanders, a contagious disease the health officers were authorized to combat by destroying all animals infected with it. However, later it was discovered that the horse did not have glanders. The owner of the horse sued for damages, contending that the health officers were authorized to destroy only diseased animals. The court ruled that the officers were in fact personally liable for their actions because they had acted beyond their lawful jurisdiction. In sum, under common law, the government had sovereign immunity, but its officers were not protected from being sued for their tortious acts.

Toward Absolute Official Immunity

The realization by the courts that public officials were placed in a very precarious and probably unfair position under common law doctrine led judges gradually to abandon it so that they could provide governmental officers with reasonable immunity protections from liability suits. It also became clear to the courts that administrators could not perform their duties effectively if they had to worry constantly about the possibility of being sued for any injuries they may cause to persons while implementing the laws.

The *Spalding* Case Breaks New Ground.   To justify granting administrators immunities, the courts began to reason that just as judges need to be free from threatening liability suits to perform their jobs properly, so do administrators. In a precedential case, *Spalding v. Vilas,* 161 U.S. 483, 498 (1896), the Court held

that "the same general considerations of public policy and convenience which demand for judges of courts of superior jurisdiction immunity from civil suits for
damages arising from acts done by them in the course of the performance of their
judicial functions, apply to a large extent to official communications made by
heads of executive departments when engaged in the discharge of duties imposed
upon them by law. The interests of the people require that due protection be accorded to them in respect of their official acts." More specifically, in regard to a
postmaster general facing damage action, the Court commented: "In exercising
the functions of his office, the head of an executive department, keeping within
the limits of his authority, should not be under an apprehension that the motives
that control his official conduct may at any time become the subject of inquiry in
a civil suit for damages. It would seriously cripple the proper and effective administration of public affairs as entrusted to the executive branch of the government,
if he were subjected to any such restraint" (p. 498).

The *Spalding* case is significant for starting the trend toward granting official
immunity to governmental officers. In particular, the Court in *Spalding* acknowledged that discretion does play a necessary role in policy implementation and
that at least high-ranking administrators should not hesitate to use discretion because they fear that they may be sued for their discretionary decisions within
their statutory jurisdiction. The *Spalding* case is also important for the Court's
opinion that top administrators (for example, department heads) should be protected from tort suits against them, regardless of the *motives* that inspired their
actions or whether their conduct was malicious: "The motive that impelled him
to do that . . . is therefore wholly immaterial. If we were to hold that the demurrer admitted, for the purposes of the trial, that the defendant acted maliciously,
that could not change the law" (p. 499). In so ruling, the Court in effect sanctioned the immunization of public officials from damage suits, even if they decide to act maliciously and in bad faith toward individuals with the intention of
harming them. The *Spalding* case raised an interesting question: Can intentional
malicious treatment of persons by administrators in bad faith ever be considered
action within their proper statutory authority?

David Rosenbloom contends that the Court's logic in *Spalding* became more
open to question as the modern administrative state emerged. Rosenbloom considers that the decision in *Spalding* to allow top-level administrators to have virtually total immunity "underestimates the harm that might be done by
administrative officials in a day and age when the penetration by government of
the life of the society is so intense." He maintains that, surely, given the great
powers of administrators today, "at the very least, the citizen needs some protection against a public official such as a department head who is acting in *bad*
faith." But Rosenbloom also believes that the *Spalding* Court failed to understand where the power actually resides in public bureaucracy. That is, in *Spalding*
the Court implied that real decision-making power lies at the top of the administrative hierarchy. To make decisions effectively, the Court reasoned, top-level administrators must be permitted to make executive decisions free from the worry

that they could be held personally liable for damages caused by their decisions. However, Rosenbloom acknowledges that most scholars maintain the middle-range administrators make the most crucial decisions affecting persons: "Consequently, if one is concerned that civil suits 'would seriously cripple the proper and effective administration of public affairs as entrusted to the executive branch', then some provisions for immunity for lower ranking administrators would be necessary."[23]

A Giant Step toward Granting Absolute Immunity to Public Officers: *Barr v. Matteo*.   The courts after *Spalding* did in fact move toward making official immunity more comprehensive. In 1938, in *Cooper v. O'Connor,* 99 F.2d 135 (D.C. Cir.), the court argued that all administrators performing quasi-judicial functions should be given the same immunity protections enjoyed by judges. This is necessary, the court reasoned, because such administrators are entrusted with settling disputes based upon questions pertaining to private rights and obligations.[24]

But is was in *Barr v. Matteo,* 360 U.S. 564 (1959), that the Supreme Court took a giant step in extending absolute immunity to virtually all administrative officials. The case stems from a libel suit filed against Barr, an acting director of the Federal Office of Rent Stabilization, for making public through a press release allegedly libelous remarks about two subordinates. Speaking for the divided Court, Justice John Harlan asserted that the Court had been called upon to consider two questions "of high importance which now and again come into sharp conflict—on the one hand, the protection of the individual citizen against pecuniary damage caused by oppressive or malicious action on the part of the officials of the Federal Government; and on the other, the protection of the public interest by shielding responsible governmental officers against the harassment and inevitable hazards of vindictive or ill-founded damage suits brought on account of action taken in the exercise of their official responsibilities" (p. 565).

The *Barr* case is especially known for the Court's strong, and seemingly extreme, arguments in defense of a public administrator's right to absolute official immunity. The Court's basic argument throughout was rooted in the belief that absolute immunity protections for administrators are in the public interest. Specifically, Harlan acknowledged the validity of the old argument in support of official immunity that governmental administrators must be able to exercise their administrative duties free from the threat of damage suits. According to the Court, such suits "would consume time and energies which would otherwise be devoted to governmental service and the threat of which might appreciably inhibit the fearless, vigorous, and effective administration of policies of government" (p. 571). Drawing from previous court decisions, especially *Gregoire v. Biddle,* 177 F.2d 579 (2nd Cir. 1948), Harlan presented a utilitarian argument to substantiate the Court's conclusion that absolute immunity privileges should be extended to virtually all public officials during the performance of what can reasonably be considered their official duties: "To be sure, as with any rule of law which attempts to reconcile fundamentally antagonistic social policies, there may be occasional instances of actual injustice which will go unredressed, but we think that price a necessary one to pay for the greater good" (p. 576).

It had been argued that the Court in *Barr* was insensitive to the argument that absolute official immunity protections could "open the door to wholesale oppression and abuses on the part of unscrupulous government officials" (p. 576). Harlan asserted that this was a greatly exaggerated and unsubstantiated claim: "It is perhaps enough to say that fears of this sort have not been realized within the wide area of government where a judicially formulated absolute privilege of broad scope has long existed. It seems to us wholly chimerical to suggest that what hangs in the balance here is the maintenance of high standards of conduct among those in the public service" (p. 576).

And finally, the *Barr* decision was instrumental in making it far easier for almost all public administrators to hide under the cloak of official immunity as long as their acts could be justified as barely within the scope of their official discretionary authority. Building upon *Spalding*, the Court reasoned: "The fact that the action here taken was within the outer perimeter of petitioner's line of duty is enough to render the privilege applicable, despite the allegations of malice" (p. 575).

The *Barr* case was highlighted here because its reach was so extensive. In dissenting in *Barr*, Justice William J. Brennan argued that the Court had gone too far in extending absolute immunity privileges to virtually all officials in the federal administrative system. After the *Barr* ruling, federal courts did find it appropriate to apply *Barr* to even relatively low-ranking federal officers.

In *Carter v. Carlson*, 447 F.2d 358, 361 (D.C. Cir. 1971), the court held that a public administrator "is protected by the doctrine of official immunity if the alleged tort was committed in the performance of a 'discretionary' rather than a 'ministerial' function." A *ministerial act* is a straight-line function in which no discretion is involved; rather, orders are only being carried out. However, this distinction has been criticized severely by judges and scholarly critics as too difficult to apply, since it is virtually impossible in practice to make a distinction between "discretionary" and "ministerial" functions. As noted in Chapter 8, Kenneth C. Davis argues that all governmental officials exercise discretion. Thus, by extending official immunity to all governmental officials who exercise discretion, the *Carter* holding, in the spirit of *Barr*, in effect extends official immunity privileges to all governmental administrators. Can you think of any administrator who employs absolutely no administrative discretion in his or her work? If a public official were sued for damages, can you imagine a situation in which the defense attorney could not convince the court that his or her client, as a public official, exercises some administrative discretion? Clearly, any administrator could use discretionary powers to harm citizens.

In sum, the *Spalding-Barr* rationale served to immunize too many administrative actions, thus tipping the delicate balance between the needs of the administrative state and the needs of the citizenry too much in the favor of the former. Under the *Spalding-Barr* rule, David Rosenbloom noted, citizens had no opportunity to recover damages in court for harm done them by even the most malicious administrators. For all practical purposes, he maintained, the application of *Spalding-Barr* makes it impossible for citizens to hold administrators directly accountable for their actions. In short, under Spalding-Barr, "the needs of the administrative state for smooth operation are placed above protections for the citizenry." Because abuses of administrative power were bound to increase under this immunity system, Rosenbloom concluded that "it was only a matter of time before the Supreme Court would have to readdress the concept of *absolute* immunity."[25]

Courts Reverse Direction and Adopt Qualified Immunity Standard: Bivens and After

Virtually every administrative law textbook author cites *Bivens v. Six Unknown Fed. Narcotics Agents, 403 U.S. 388* (1971), as a case that played a major role in eroding the doctrine of absolute immunity and establishing the qualified immunity doctrine. This is because the Court in *Bivens* made it very clear that the judicial doors are always open to those who are victims of flagrant and unconstitutional abuses of administrative power. As Justice John Harlan stated in his strongly worded concurring opinion, judicial remedies should be made available when administrative actions are clearly unjustified and abusive: "Although litigants may not often choose to seek relief, it is important, in a civilized society, that the judicial branch of the Nation's government stand ready to afford a remedy in these circumstances" (p. 411).

These particular circumstances involved a situation where federal narcotics officers broke into the plaintiff's home at 6:30 A.M. without a search warrant and in the absence of probable cause. The narcotics agents handcuffed Bivens, searched his premises, employed excessive force, threatened to arrest his family, subjected him to a visual strip search in the federal court house, fingerprinted, photographed, interrogated, and booked him. When Bivens was brought before a United States Commissioner, however, charges against him were dismissed. Bivens filed against each of the narcotics officers for $15,000 in damages on the grounds that he had "suffered great humiliation, embarrassment, and mental suffering as a result of the agents' unlawful conduct" (pp. 389–390). The high court had to decide whether violation of the Fourth Amendment "by a federal agent acting under color of his authority gives rise to a cause of action for damages consequent upon his constitutional conduct" (p. 389).[26] The Court majority reached a quick decision: "we hold that petitioner is entitled to recover money damages for any injuries he has suffered as a result of the agents' violation of the Amendment" (p. 397).

The Court justified its decision in the logic espoused in the classic case, *Marbury v. Madison,* 1 Cranch 137, 163 (1803), where the Court explained: "The very essence of civil liberty certainly consists in the right of every individual to claim the protection of the laws, whenever he receives an injury." The Court also made clear that "federal courts may use any available remedy to make good the wrong done" (p. 396). An important aspect of the *Bivens* case was the Court's rejection of the argument by the respondents that the claim against the narcotics officers should be treated no differently than a civil action between two private parties in state court. But Justice William J. Brennan, speaking for the majority, contended that such a perspective underestimates the potentially destructive powers of modern administrators. Respondents "ignore the fact that power, once granted, does not disappear like a magic gift when it is wrongfully used. An agent acting—albeit unconstitutionally—in the name of the United States possesses a far greater capacity for harm than an individual trespasser exercising no authority other than his own" (p. 392).

The Supreme Court in *Bivens* expressed only that the actions of the narcotics officers were appalling and that, under the circumstances, the damage suit was appropriate and the federal courts could provide relief by ordering money damages to be paid to Bivens to compensate for his injuries (the denial of Fourth Amendment protections by the narcotics agents). The Court did not decide whether the federal narcotics officers were immune from a liability suit because of their official government position. This question was remanded to the Second Circuit Court of Appeals.

On remand, the court found in *Bivens v. Six Unknown Named Agents,* 456 F.2d 1339 (1972), that these agents were not immune from tort action against them, rejecting the agents' argument that they were engaged in discretionary actions protected by official immunity. Specifically, the appeals court did maintain that governmental officials should be protected by the official immunity doctrine, as established in *Barr,* when they are engaged in discretionary actions "within the outer perimeter of [their] line of duty" (p. 1345). However, in this case the court did not believe that the actions of the narcotics officers could even be considered within that outer perimeter, despite the fact that the court also found the discretionary test not very helpful in legitimately distinguishing discretionary from nondiscretionary acts in most cases. Thus, the court held that the narcotics agents were not entitled to absolute official immunity, "because we do not agree that the Agents were alleged to be engaged in the performance of the sort of 'discretionary' acts that require the protection of immunity" (p. 1343). Further, the court remarked: "It would be a sorry state of affairs if an officer had the 'discretion' to enter a dwelling at 6:30 a.m., without a warrant or probable cause, and make an arrest by employing unreasonable force" (p. 1346). In other words, the court emphasized that federal officers are not entitled to immunity protections in all situations, especially when a damage suit is filed "based upon allegations of violations of constitutional rights" (p. 1347). In so ruling, the appeals court established a qualified immunity standard based on circumstances. A dozen years later in *Davis v. Scherer,* 104 S.Ct. 3012 (1984), the Supreme Court interpreted certain "circumstances" to uphold qualified immunity protections for state officials.

The significance of the Court's action in *Bivens* should not be underestimated, because here the Court, playing a very activist role, radically changed the course of tort law involving public officials by holding that federal agents could be held liable for damages if their actions deprived persons of their constitutional rights even in the absence of federal statutes authorizing such remedies. Drawing from *Bivens* and other cases,[27] the Supreme Court in 1983 said emphatically: "the federal courts' power to grant relief not expressly authorized by Congress is firmly established" *(Bush v. Lucas,* 462 U.S. 367, 374).

Would future courts honor the *Bivens* ruling? They have done so, but with increasing reservations. Actually, the qualified immunity doctrine since *Bivens* has been generally honored by the courts in an effort to provide persons with protections against flagrant abuses of administrative power by public officials insensitive to the constitutional rights of citizens. However, as we shall see, the courts have placed certain restrictions on the *Bivens* remedy, making it somewhat more difficult for plaintiffs to use successfully the *Bivens* action. In *Wood v. Strickland,* 420 U.S. 308 (1975), and *Harlow v. Fitzgerald,* 457 U.S. 800 (1982), the Supreme Court held that public officials were not immune to damage suits under *Bivens,* but plaintiffs had to prove to win a *Bivens* action that such officials "knew or reasonably should have known" that their actions violated established constitutional rights. *Davis v. Scherer,* 104 S.Ct. 3012 (1984), also granted only qualified immunity to public officials, but the Supreme Court made it even more difficult to win using the *Bivens* remedy by ruling that petitioners had to prove that at the time any governmental officer "violated" a person's constitutional rights that the right(s) had to have been "clearly established." The Supreme Court upheld *Scherer* in *Siegert v. Gilley,* 111 S.Ct. 1789 (1991), in which Chief Justice Rehnquist, speaking for the majority, ruled that a former government employee could not pursue a *Bivens* claim against his former supervisor, because he had failed to show that any "clearly established constitutional right" had been violated by his former supervisor, thus failing to satisfy the basic threshold test for a qualified immunity challenge. In *Schweiker v. Chilecky,* 487 U.S. 412 (1988), the high court held that a *Bivens* suit cannot be brought when the government has provided adequate alternative remedies within the administration of the governmental program even if, as in this particular case, administrative wrongs led to the unconstitutional denial of benefits.

Recent court decisions, especially by the Supreme Court, have greatly weakened the applicability or force of the *Bivens* remedy, although on occasion some appellate courts have upheld and even expanded the *Bivens* precedent. For example, in *White v. Lee,* 227 F.3d 1214 (2002), the Ninth Circuit Court of Appeals ruled that HUD employees could be held liable under *Bivens* for harassing citizens for exercising their First Amendment rights in protesting against proposed construction of public housing. However, the Supreme Court in a series of cases has eroded the strength of *Bivens* by (1) refusing to extend *Bivens* to apply to federal agencies; (2) increasing the threshold standards or rationales under which *Bivens* claims can be argued; (3) ruling consistently that if other federal statutory remedies exist, the *Bivens* remedy should not be allowed; and (4) not permitting *Bivens* liability claims to extend to private corporations contracted by the federal government.

Let's look at a few exemplifying cases. In *FDIC v. Meyer*, 510 U.S. 471 (1994), the Supreme Court held that *Bivens* can be used as a remedy for tort claims only against the government itself. Specifically, even though employees of federal agencies may violate constitutional rights, *Bivens* does not permit liability claims to be transferred from agency employees to the federal agencies for which they work. In *Farmer v. Brennan*, 511 U.S. 825, 837 (1994), the Court, building upon the threshold standards to maintain a *Bivens* claim, held that a prisoner cannot win a *Bivens* action against a prison official, arguing that his Eighth Amendment rights were violated by the official, unless it can be demonstrated that the official "knows of and disregards an excessive risk to inmate health and safety." In *Christopher v. Harbury*, 122 S.Ct. 2179, 2190 (2002), the Supreme Court argued not only that were *Bivens* claims inadequately pleaded, particularly because the plaintiff failed to articulate constitutional damage claims under *Bivens*, but also that *Bivens* was not an appropriate remedy since alternate remedies existed—for example, "an action could be maintained under the Federal Tort Claims Act." And in *Correctional Services Corporation v. Malesko*, 122 S.Ct. 515 (2001), the high court refused to apply *Bivens* to a private contractor hired by the federal government even though the contractor, as an agent of the government, violated the petitioner's constitutional rights. Beyond this, the court noted, alternative remedies were available: "The purpose of *Bivens* is to deter individual federal officers from committing constitutional violations. . . . For if a corporate defendant is available for suit, claimants will focus their collection efforts on it, and not the individual directly responsible for the alleged injury. . . . There is no reason to extend *Bivens* beyond this core premise." The Court concluded that the plaintiff, in this case a prisoner, "may not bring a *Bivens* claim against the officer's employer, the United States or the BOP" (Bureau of Prisons) (pp. 521–522).[28]

In sum, it is getting very difficult for plaintiffs today to use the *Bivens* remedy with much success. In general, the courts just do not like to uphold or extend *Bivens*, a decision that most courts, but especially the Supreme Court, regard as a bad decision. Richard Pierce exclaims frankly that "[T]he *Bivens* opinion was a mistake, and the *Bush-Chappell-Chillicky* trilogy suggests strongly that a majority of the Court now recognize that fact."[29] Pierce contends that the Court should simply overrule the *Bivens* decision, but the Court is reluctant to take this giant step because of the respected doctrine of stare decisis. He recommends, however, that the Supreme Court should overrule *Bivens*, which he contends is bad and unfair law because it allows federal officials to be sued and not their agencies instead, and allow Congress to amend the Federal Tort Claims Act "to authorize exclusive damage actions against the government in circumstances in which a citizen previously had a *Bivens* remedy." "That," he adds, "would improve the state of the law significantly."[30]

Applying Provision 1983.   This section deals with Section 1983 liability actions against state and local officials. However, since 1983 suits are statutorily based and permit limited governmental liability as well, many legal scholars regard Section 1983 as superior law to *Bivens*, its "crude" federal counterpart. Matthew Mazefsky, agreeing with Pierce that Congress should draft legislation so the Supreme Court can finally and emphatically overrule *Bivens*, summarizes the distinction between *Bivens* and Section 1983 suits: "It is well established that 1983 provides a damages remedy against state actors that parallel the relief available under a *Bivens* cause of action. However, 1983, unlike the *Bivens* remedy, allows some governmental liability. The availability of governmental liability under 1983 and the lack thereof under *Bivens* could be interpreted as a need for congressional action. Since the present Supreme Court denounced the judicial legislation that led to the implied damage remedy under *Bivens*, perhaps it is time for Congress to legislate a consistent remedy in the federal and state systems that has been lacking."[31]

The original purpose of Section 1983 of the Civil Rights Act of 1871, also known as the Ku Klux Klan Act, was to prevent state and local governmental officials in the Southern states after the Civil War from working with the Klan to deprive newly freed slaves of their civil rights. The Supreme Court in the famous Slaughter-House Cases, 83 U.S. (16 Wall.) 36 (1873) limited Section 1983 to apply to the Act's original purposes. For nearly a century, Section 1983 did not receive much attention, but starting in 1961 Section 1983 was given bold new life in *Monroe v. Pope*, 365 U.S. 167, when the Supreme Court held Chicago police officers liable for damages for conducting an unconstitutional search under Section 1983. The court ruled that the police officers, acting "under color" of state law, could be held liable in federal court bypassing any state remedies as Section 1983 allowed. Pierce notes that "[T]he *Monroe* case opened the way for suing in federal court for violation of the Constitution, even when a state court provided an adequate remedy." *Monroe* started an avalanche of Section 1983 suits to be filed in federal courts. By 1989, state prisoners alone had filed more than 25,000 Section 1983 suits.[32] Section 1983 suits became very popular because state remedies did not have to be sought or exhausted, punitive awards were allowed, and under Section 1988 of the Civil Rights Attorney's Fees Award Act of 1976 (42 U.S.C.), "reasonable" attorney's fees were awarded to successful Section 1983 actions—particularly pleasing and encouraging lawyers to file Section 1983 suits since the awarded attorney's fees on occasion exceeded the Section 1983 damage awards.

The concept of qualified immunity for state officials in a Section 1983 suit was upheld by the Supreme Court in *Scheuer v. Rhodes*, 416 U.S. 232 (1974). In one of the most publicized cases of the 1970s, the petitioners, who represented three students who had been killed by Ohio National Guard troops at Kent State University as they may have protested U.S. involvement in Vietnam, sued Governor James Rhodes of Ohio and others for money damages. The liability suit was predicated on 42 U.S. Code 1983, a provision incorporated into the Civil Rights Act of 1871. The provision states: "Every person who, under color of any statute, ordinance, regulation, custom, usage, or any State or Territory, subjects, or causes to be subjected, any citizen of the United States or other person within the jurisdiction thereof to the deprivation of any rights, privileges, or immunities secured by the Constitution and laws, shall be liable to the party injured in an action at law, suit in equity, or other proper proceeding for redress."

Reversing two lower court rulings, Justice Warren Burger, writing the Court's opinion, argued that qualified immunity should be made available to governmental officials, but only in "varying scope." The variation, he continued, should be "dependent upon the scope of discretion and responsibilities of the office and all the circumstances as they reasonably appeared at the time of the action on which liability is sought to be based" (p. 247). The Court concluded that granting qualified immunity to administrative officials depends on whether they can show that they acted *reasonably* under the circumstances and in *good faith* (p. 248).

The Court in *Davis v. Scherer*, 105 S.Ct. 26 (1984) (noted before and discussed more fully in the next section), handed down a decision that would make it more difficult for plaintiffs to win Section 1983 litigations. To reiterate, in *Scherer* the Court ruled that to win a damage suit under Section 1983, the plaintiff would have to prove that the constitutional and/or statutory rights supposedly violated by public officials were *clearly established* at the time the violations took place. This "clearly established" threshold test or standard for pursuing a Section 1983 suit has proved to be a rather difficult legal obstacle for many petitioners to overcome (*Hunter v. Bryant*, 112 S.Ct. 534 [1991], and *Siegert v. Gilley*).

Section 1983 damage suits have been filed against public officials at such an accelerated pace since the early 1970s that strategies (some very questionable ethically) have been adopted by public officials to stop these suits. In an unusual Section 1983 case, *Town of Newton v. Rumery*, 107 S.Ct. 1187 (1987), the Supreme Court for the first time ruled on whether a prosecutor could enter into a "release-dismissal" agreement where the prosecutor would agree to drop charges against a person (even if the charges were very weak, as it appeared in this case) if the person would agree to not file a damage action suit against the city and its officials under Section 1983. (In this case, police misconduct was alleged; the prosecutor has absolute immunity.) A very divided Supreme Court upheld the "release-dismissal" agreement on the grounds that it was entered into voluntarily, deliberately, and in an informed manner. In addition, the plurality argued, the "enforcement of this agreement would not adversely affect the relevant public interest" (p. 1195). However, the four dissenting justices (Stevens, Brennan, Marshall, and Blackmun) vehemently objected to the plurality's opinion. Speaking for the dissenters, Justice Stevens premised his argument on the contention that no completely innocent persons accused of a crime should "be required to choose between a threatened indictment and trial . . . and surrendering the right to a civil remedy against individuals who have violated his or her constitutional rights" (p. 1198).

Recent Section 1983 Issues.   Recently, the courts have been addressing other new issues in Section 1983 liability suits. One interesting Section 1983 question that has developed deals with whether qualified immunity claims under Section 1983 can be filed against private parties representing or acting in behalf of the government under statutory authorization. The trend toward "privatization" (i.e., the government contracting out all kinds of services to private companies; e.g., a private management firm hired by Housing and Urban Development to manage a HUD housing project) since the beginning of President Reagan's administration has made the liability of such private parties a problematic legal question. Should these private parties, performing contracted job tasks for the government (e.g., private contractors running a prison for a state) be entitled to qualified immunity protections, as government employees, in the face of Section 1983 damage suits against them? The Supreme Court has said "no," yet the Court has been divided on this question.

In 1982 in *Lugar v. Edmondson Oil Company*, 457 U.S. 922, the Supreme Court held that private parties can be said to engage in "state action" through "attachment statutes" if their actions can be "fairly attributable to the state" (p. 937), but the court failed to address the issue of whether private parties should enjoy qualified immunity in Section 1983 suits.

In 1992 in *Wyatt v. Cole*, 112 S.Ct. 1827, a divided Supreme Court addressed this private-party immunity issue, but not very well. In *Wyatt* the Court refused to extend qualified immunity protections to private parties in Section 1983 suits charged with violating a person's constitutional right(s) when engaged in state action or performing job functions as agents of the state. The Court rooted its decision in revised common law reasoning that advanced the notion that immunity should be granted to public officials to protect them from lawsuits so they can vigorously administer public policies in the public interest without worrying about being sued for possible tortious actions. The Court argued that under common law the interest to protect public officials was not applicable to private parties.

Critics reacted immediately, charging that the *Wyatt* decision unfairly leaves private parties engaged in quasi-public activities sanctioned by statutes unprotected and very exposed to potentially devastating Section 1983 damage suits. As Scott C. Arakaki and Robert E. Badger, Jr. exclaim: "By refusing to extend qualified immunity to private defendants, Wyatt increases litigation costs for private parties who are unaware that the statutes upon which they rely will later be declared unconstitutional. The Supreme Court has long recognized that litigation costs present a significant public policy concern."[33] In sum, it is safe to say that the *Lugar* and *Wyatt* decisions have not successfully resolved the private-party liability question and have in fact caused confusion and division in the courts of appeals.[34]

In 1997, a deeply divided Supreme Court in *Richardson v. McKnight*, 117 S.Ct. 2100, upheld *Wyatt* in a 5–4 decision. The Court's slim majority held that two prison guards working for a private company that managed Tennessee's South Central Correctional Center, acting "under color of state law," are not entitled to qualified immunity under Section 1983. The Court spent considerable time reviewing the long history of private firms running prisons for the government, concluding that "we have found no conclusive evidence of an historical tradition of immunity for private parties carrying out these functions. History therefore does not provide significant support for the immunity claim" (p. 2105).

Justice Scalia wrote an emphatic dissent, joined by Chief Justice Rehnquist, Justice Kennedy, and Justice Thomas. Scalia noted that the Court held in *Procunier v. Navarette*, 434 U.S. 555 (1978), that state prison officials, whether serving in management or subordinate capacities, are protected by qualified immunity in a Section 1983 suit. Contending that private prison officials perform the same tasks as government correctional officials "who may be sued for acting 'under color of the state,'" Scalia argued that they need the same immunity protections against Section 1983 suits. Thus, he categorized the majority opinion as "supported neither by common-law tradition nor public policy, and contradicts our settled practice of determining Section 1983 immunity on the basis of the public function being performed" (pp. 2108–2109).

In light of the relentless stream of Section 1983 suits, the courts have also been trying to answer some crucial questions pertaining to punitive damage awards. It is true that Section 1983 may provide parties with their only real chance for recovering punitive damages for having their constitutional rights violated by governmental officials or their "agents" (*Carlson v. Green*, 446 U.S. 14 [1980]), yet key questions remain. What standards should be applied when awarding punitive damages? When are punitive damages excessive? And what are the actual purposes of awarding punitive damages?[35]

In *Larez v. Los Angeles*, 946 F.2d 630 (9th Cir. 1991), an excessive police force case, the circuit court held that punitive damages may be awarded against the Police Commissioners even in the absence of actual malice as long as evidence has shown reckless or callous indifference toward the plaintiff. In *TXO Production Corp. v. Alliance Resources Corp.*, 113 S.Ct. 2711 (1993), the Supreme Court argued that due process does impose caps on punitive damage awards, but the amount that can be awarded can be limited only by the arbitrary "reasonableness" standard. Frequently, courts have held that punitive damages should be linked to a defendant's net worth (which might be substantial if the public official is indemnified by, say, a municipality) and to the need to punish and deter such unconstitutional behavior. Normally, courts have argued that the chief purpose of Section 1983 punitive damage awards is to punish past unconstitutional behavior, to deter future unconstitutional conduct.

In the Rodney King case, *King v. Marci*, 993 F.2d 294 (2nd Cir. 1993), one of the most publicized cases in American legal history, the trial court, as well as the Second Circuit Court of Appeals, accepted King's attorney's summation argument before the jury when he was trying to convince the jury to award punitive damages. King's counsel argued that in light of the brutal beating of Rodney King, his false arrest, and malicious prosecution, punitive damages should be awarded so that the defendant and others in the future ". . . will no longer think they're above the law, so that they won't be arrogant and think they can do whatever they want, so that they won't think that because they have a badge and they have a uniform they can violate people's rights" and that such punitive damages would send "that same message to others in a position to abuse their authority" (p. 298).

In recent years, the courts have ruled against awarding punitive damages under Section 1983 under limited circumstances (*Heck v. Humphrey*, 512 U.S. 477 [1994], where claim for punitive damages was prohibited if judgment would suggest his criminal conviction was invalid), but in general the justification for awarding punitive damages, as articulated in *King*, have been upheld (*Harden v. Potaki*, 320 F.3d 1289 [2003]).

The "Knew or Reasonably Should Have Known" Rule.   The Supreme Court in *Wood v. Strickland,* 420 U.S. 308 (1975), added a new twist that served to make public officials even more vulnerable to tort actions against them. In this case local school board members were sued by high school students who argued that they had been deprived of constitutional due process rights when they were expelled from school for spiking a punch bowl at a school function. Specifically, the students claimed that they should not have been expelled without the benefit of a full hearing. Speaking for the majority, Justice Byron White ruled that the demonstration of good faith does not alone guarantee the extension of immunity to public officials if they were aware, or should have been aware, that their actions, even if within the "outer perimeter" of their duties, would violate the constitutional rights of those involved. Consequently, the Court held that a member of a school board cannot be found to be immune from damage suits *"if he knew or reasonably should have known* that the action he took within his sphere of official responsibility would violate the constitutional rights of the students affected, or if he took the action with the malicious intention to cause a deprivation of constitutional rights or other injury to the students" (my emphasis) (p. 322).

In a 1980 article, David Rosenbloom applauded the *Wood* decision. He maintained on one hand that the "Wood standard goes a long way toward guaranteeing that public administrators will have a sufficient *personal* stake in their actions to force them to avoid engaging in arbitrary unconstitutional actions vis-à-vis members of the general public."[36] But he held that, on the other hand, the *Wood* standard is balanced in that it "is not so general or ill-defined as to invite a rash of unfounded law suits against public officials."[37] Reflecting upon the possible impact of *Bivens* and *Wood* soon after the *Wood* decision was handed down, Bernard Schwartz speculated that these cases may really open the door to liability suits against public administrators "since tortious official conduct can frequently be described in constitutional terms."[38] That is, administrative abuses of all kinds could be rationalized as violating due process guarantees. "If *Bivens* and *Wood* are pressed that far," Schwartz concluded, "it may make for a major extension of liability in cases involving constitutional deprivations by public officers, even those previously immunized under *Barr v. Matteo*."[39] By the mid-1980s it had become clear that in fact the *Bivens, Scheuer,* and *Wood* decisions, buttressed by several other Supreme Court rulings,[40] had led to a host of tort suits against public offi-

cials. Some interpreted this sudden onslaught of tort actions against public officials, especially on the municipal level, as a crisis constituting "the largest threat
to municipalities in the 1980s—expanding tort liability and municipal insurance
unavailability."[41]

According to the *Wood* principle, reiterated in *Harlow v. Fitzgerald, 457* U.S.
800, 818 (1982), under the qualified immunity doctrine public officials (except
for those few given absolute immunity—for example, judges, prosecutors) can
be sued for damages if they "knew or reasonably should have known" that their
actions violated established constitutional or statutory guarantees. But the *Wood*
principle raises an obvious question. What if the statutory or constitutional
rights were not clearly established when the alleged violations took place? This
question was answered by the Supreme Court in 1984 in *Davis v. Scheuer,* mentioned briefly in the last section because it involved a Section 1983 claim. In
Scheuer, Gregory Scheuer, a radio teletype operator for the Florida Highway Patrol, sued his superiors for damages after he had been fired from his job. He
charged that his constitutional due process rights under the Fourteenth Amendment had been violated because he was dismissed without benefit of a pretermination or immediate posttermination hearing. The Supreme Court ruled against
Scheuer, arguing that his claim could not be upheld because at the time of the alleged constitutional violation it had not been *clearly established* that an employee
had a right to a formal pretermination or posttermination hearing. Thus, to the
Court, it would be unfair to allow the damage suit against Scheuer's superiors
since it cannot be shown that they "knew or reasonably should have known" that
they were violating Scheuer's constitutional rights when at the time of the alleged
violation it was not *clearly established* that Scheuer was entitled to such constitutional protections. Quoting from *Harlow,* the Court asserted that public officials
"'are shielded from liability for civil damages insofar as their conduct does not violate clearly established statutory or constitutional rights of which a reasonable
person would have known.' Whether an official may prevail in his qualified immunity defense depends upon the 'objective reasonableness of [his] conduct as
measured by reference to clearly established law.' No other 'circumstances' are
relevant to the issue of qualified immunity" (p. 3017). This new *Scheuer* rule
modifies the old *Wood* rule and serves to make it somewhat more difficult for
plaintiffs to win tort liability claims against public officials, especially in situations where there is some reasonable doubt about the status of statutory or constitutional rights.

In the early 1990s, the Supreme Court in *Siegert v. Gilley*, 111 S.Ct. 1789
(1991), affirmed and expanded upon its decisions in *Harlow* and *Scherer*. The
case involved a former government employee, Siegert, who filed a tort suit
against his former supervisor, Gilley, charging that Gilley, in response to a request for information about his job performance, wrote a defamatory letter in
bad faith that Siegert felt would likely prevent him from obtaining a comparable
job in the future. This, he claimed, violated his constitutional right to due
process. But the Supreme Court, in rejecting Siegert's claim, stressed that the

plaintiff must establish that "clearly established" constitutional rights have been violated before discovery can be granted as a preparation for trial. The Court exclaimed: "One of the purposes of immunity, absolute or qualified, is to spare a defendant not only unwarranted liability, but unwarranted demands customarily imposed upon those defending a long drawn out lawsuit" (p. 1793). The Court, citing its opinion in *Mitchell v. Forsyth,* 472 U.S. 511, 526 (1985), continued: "'*Harlow* thus recognized an entitlement not to stand trial or face the other burdens of litigation, conditioned on the resolution of the essentially legal question whether the conduct of which the plaintiff complains violated clearly established law. The entitlement is an *immunity from suit* rather than a mere defense to liability; and like an absolute immunity, it is effectively lost if a case is erroneously permitted to go to trial'" (pp. 1793–1794). In *Siegert* the Court concluded that it is not enough to argue simply that the constitutional right was deprived with malice, which if shown could make the defendant liable, because first "the substantive defense of immunity controls" (p. 1795). This "heightened pleading standard is a necessary and appropriate accommodation between the state of mind component of malice and the objective test that prevails in qualified immunity analysis as a general matter (p. 1795)."

The Supreme Court built on the *Siegert* and the "clearly established" standard in 2001 in *Saucier v. Katz,* 121 S.Ct. 2151. In this case, an animal rights protester tried to display a protest banner at a military base where the vice president of the United States was speaking, but instead he was seized "forcefully" by military police and shoved into a van. The protester filed suit against the two military police, asserting that he had been denied his constitutional right to protest by having been seized by excessive force in violation of the Fourth Amendment. But the Supreme Court held that the police officers were entitled to qualified immunity from liability suits unless it can be demonstrated that "the officers violated established constitutional rights given the specific factual circumstances."

Unquestionably, the *Saucier* ruling will make it extremely difficult as a practical matter for petitioners to win liability claims against any public officials seeking a qualified immunity defense, because specific application of legal rights are never perfectly clear or "clearly established," given particular circumstances. In fact, this is the very reason why legal scholars and judges argue over how the law should be applied in given circumstances. Acknowledging that the "clearly established" standard amounts to an "impossible" and impractical legal test, Richard Pierce notes: "When an official decides to act, he is confronted not merely with a question of legality in the abstract but with a question of how the law applies to a factual complex. Usually, the application, even of the clearest kind of law, is not clearly established with respect to how it applies to a particular factual complex. Even when the best lawyers are dealing with the clearest law, they may have doubts about how the law applies to unique facts."[42]

Qualified Immunity Should Be the General Rule When Federal Officials Violate Constitutional Rights: The *Butz* Ruling.   Of all the official immu-

nity cases handed down by the courts, none is probably more important, at least from the standpoint of its comprehensiveness, than *Butz v. Economou,* 434 U.S. 994 (1977). In *Butz,* the Supreme Court reviewed virtually all the major official immunity cases decided previously in an effort to link these cases to the Court's present position on official immunity privileges for governmental administrators. The case stems from an action initiated by Earl Butz, the secretary of agriculture, that led to the suspension of Economou's registration privilege, thus preventing him from being able to continue to work as a commodities futures trader. But upon review, the District of Columbia appeals court ruled that the action taken against Economou was improper because adequate warning was not accorded before the suspension. Economou then sued Butz and others for damages, specifically charging that press releases pertaining to the suspension hurt him as a businessman and that the suspension itself was aimed at "chilling" his right to freedom of expression under the First Amendment because he had been outspoken against DOA rulemakers. The Butz defense argued that Butz and his codefendants were entitled to absolute immunity because their actions as top administrative officials were discretionary, not ministerial. Such, they claimed, was well-established federal law.

However, the Supreme Court held that such executive officers as Butz are entitled to qualified immunity only when constitutional rights are involved; therefore, they can be held liable for damages. The *Butz* decision applied the qualified immunity doctrine to federal administrators (except law enforcement officers). Previously, the doctrine had been applied only to state and local governmental officers. The Court contended that "there is no basis for according to federal officials a higher degree of immunity from liability when sued for a constitutional infringement as authorized by *Bivens* than is accorded state officials when sued for the identical violation under Section 1983. . . . Surely, *federal* officials should enjoy no greater zone of protection when they violate *federal* constitutional rules than do state officers" (p. 501).[43]

Arguing that public administrators should be protected against frivolous lawsuits, the Court, nevertheless, concluded "that, in a suit for damages arising from unconstitutional action, federal executive officials exercising discretion are entitled only to the qualified immunity specified in *Scheuer,* subject to those exceptional situations where it is demonstrated that absolute immunity is essential for the conduct of the public business" (p. 507). However, although the Court in *Butz* did establish that public officials should in general enjoy only qualified immunity privileges from damage suits involving constitutional violations, it did insist that absolute immunity protections should be extended to public officers performing quasi-judicial functions (for example, agency attorneys functioning as prosecutors and administrative law judges performing adjudicative functions) to preserve the effectiveness of agency adjudications.

Despite the exclusion of a few types of federal officials from qualified immunity protections, it is clear that *Butz* significantly extended the *Bivens* rule of qualified immunity. The Court did so in an attempt to deter future federal administrators from violating the constitutional rights of citizens. In its decision, the Court noted that it might be a good idea for federal administrators, so as to avoid possible damage suits, be trained more in constitutional law so that they are better equipped to recognize administrative actions that seem to violate constitutional due process dictates.[44] After over a quarter century, the *Butz* ruling, despite some judicial modifications, still remains precedential, being regularly cited. (*Correctional Services Corp. V. Malesko*, 122 S.Ct. 515 [2001]; *FMC v. S.C. State Port Auth.*, 122 S.Ct. 1864 [2002]).[45]

A Concluding Note on *Bivens*: The Good and Bad News on the *Bivens* Remedy. The good news on *Bivens* is that it provides a superior remedy for claimants filing liability actions against federal officials, as opposed to filing a damage action under the Federal Tort Claims Act (FTCA). The bad news, as mentioned previously, is that the federal courts, especially the Supreme Court, have increasingly restricted the application of *Bivens*. Nonetheless, if a claimant is allowed to pursue a *Bivens* remedy, the advantages to the claimant are considerable. Let's summarize the advantages of a *Bivens* remedy.

Supreme Court decisions in the 1980s served to clarify the application of the official immunity decisions of the 1970s. In *Carlson v. Green, 446 U.S. 14* (1980), the Court specifically upheld the qualified immunity doctrine as established in *Bivens,* concluding that "A federal official contemplating unconstitutional conduct similarly must be prepared to face the prospect of a *Bivens* action" (p. 25). In this case, Marie Green sued Carlson, director of the Federal Bureau of Prisons, and others for compensatory and punitive damages, charging that their negligent actions (denying proper medical attention to her son) caused his death. Specifically, Green claimed that these federal prison officials were liable for damage action under *Bivens* because they violated her son's "due process, equal protection, and Eighth Amendment rights" (p. 16).

Carlson and his codefendants argued that the suit against them is inappropriate because the Federal Tort Claims Act (FCTA) provides an avenue for relief. However, the Court replied tersely: "Petitioners do not enjoy such independent status in our constitutional scheme as to suggest that judicially created remedies against them might be inappropriate." Although the Court's upholding of the qualified immunity doctrine, as established in *Bivens, Scheuer,* and *Butz*, is noteworthy, the chief significance of *Carlson* is in the Court's argument on why those seeking damage settlements, when not prohibited by statutes, should be allowed to pursue a *Bivens* remedy, if they choose, instead of an FTCA remedy. Essentially, a *Bivens* action allows public officials to be held personally liable for their unconstitutional administrative actions, while under the FTCA, action is brought against the United States for torts committed by federal administrative officers.

Delivering the opinion of the Court's majority, Justice William J. Brennan maintained that a *Bivens* action should be made available to victims of tortious official behavior, if they so desire, since evidence suggests "that the *Bivens* remedy is more effective than the FTCA remedy" (p. 20). The Court noted that the *Bivens* remedy is preferable to the FTCA remedy in at least four ways. First, since a *Bivens* action allows damage action against individual public officials instead of only the state, as in an FTCA action, it should have a deterrent effect on public officers who contemplate committing tortious acts against citizens: "Because the *Bivens* remedy is recoverable against individuals, it is a more effective deterrent than the FTCA remedy against the United States. It is almost axiomatic that the threat of damages has a deterrent effect" (p. 21). Second, a *Bivens* suit permits punitive damages to be paid to victims, while FTCA action does not. And according to the Court, the payment of punitive damages is "especially appropriate to redress the violation by a government official of a citizen's constitutional rights" (p. 22). Third, under a *Bivens* action a plaintiff is entitled to bring his or her case before a jury, while jury trials are prohibited under an FTCA suit. Although juries would not necessarily favor plaintiffs, Brennan asserted that there is no reason why plaintiffs should not be permitted to choose between a jury and a judge. And fourth, FTCA suits are permitted "only if the State in which the alleged misconduct occurred would permit a cause of action for that misconduct to go forward" (p. 23). However, the Court argued that "it is obvious that the liability of federal officials for violation of citizens' constitutional rights should be governed by uniform rules" (p. 23). *Bivens* allows for such uniformity since cause for legal action is not based on what state laws will allow. The Court reasoned that it made no sense that constitutional violations by public officials created cause for action in some states, but not in others. In sum, the Court held: "Plainly, FTCA is not a sufficient protector of the citizens' constitutional rights, and without a clear congressional mandate we cannot hold that Congress relegated respondent exclusively to the FTCA remedy" (p. 23). But, to reiterate, if the Supreme Court continues to limit the application of *Bivens* by putting up obstacles to a *Bivens* remedy (e.g., precluded by federal statutes, alternate remedies exist such as the FTCA, refusing to apply *Bivens* to federal agencies), the desirable *Bivens* remedy will have little practical utility.

It should be noted that the Supreme Court has never directly applied the *Bivens* remedy to tort claims against state officials, even though state officials may knowingly and maliciously violate U.S. constitutional rights when administering federal programs in their states. Of course the *Bivens* and *Carlson* cases involved tort suits against federal officers. So are state officials liable under *Bivens*? Pierce argues that "[L]ogic requires the answer that state officers are as much under the Constitution as federal officers, but the Supreme Court has never applied the *Bivens* doctrine to state officers."[46] However, they point out that in 1988 in *Schweiker vs. Chillicky*, 487 U.S. 412, 418, the Supreme Court appeared to assume, without actually rendering a decision on the matter, that state officials who implement federal law are subject to *Bivens* suits. Lower courts have been split on the applicability of the *Bivens* remedy in tort suits against state officials.[47] Since state officers can be sued under Section 1983, which provides a remedy similar to *Bivens*, it is probably not that crucial that the Supreme Court rules soon on whether *Bivens* applies to state officers.

The Need to Establish a Direct Causal Connection Between Official Action and Injury in Qualified-Immunity Cases.   In *Martinez v. California,*

444 U.S. 277 (1979), the Supreme Court ruled that, subject to qualified immunity, establishing that the state's action is related directly to the harm caused is necessary to justify a tort claim against a state or its public officials. In this case petitioners had sued California state parole board officials who had paroled a mentally disturbed sex offender who presented a "clear and present danger" to the public. Five months after being released, the parolee tortured and murdered a fifteen-year-old girl. The girl's survivors sued for damages, contending that the negligent and reckless decision by the parole board to parole this dangerous man led to the girl's death. Specifically, the petitioners claimed that the parole board's action deprived the girl of her life without due process of law and, thus, the board's members were liable to pay for the damages caused by the parolee. Also at issue, inter alia, was a California state statute that granted members of the parole board absolute immunity from tort claims.

The Court held that the California statute did not violate due process property rights under the Fourteenth Amendment, because in this case "the State's interest in fashioning its own rules of tort law is paramount to any discernible federal interest, except perhaps an interest in protecting the individual citizen from state action that is wholly arbitrary or irrational" (p. 282). In *Martinez,* however, the Court believed that the parole board's actions were far from being "arbitrary and irrational"; thus it was reasonable for the state to protect such discretionary board decisions from tort suits. In fact, the Court argued that such board action was somewhat similar to judicial decisionmaking and therefore should probably be protected from damage suits. The Court argued that some risk is always involved in paroling prisoners. To subject parole board members to liability claims, the Court maintained, would probably prevent the state from being able to implement any parole program designed to rehabilitate inmates. Besides, the Court held that the action taken by the parolee five months later "can not be fairly characterized as state action. . . . He was in no sense an agent of the parole board" (p. 285). The Fourteenth Amendment, the Court argued, "protected her [the murdered child] only from deprivation by the 'State . . . of life . . . without due process of law'" (p. 284). In short, the Court believed that the relationship between the parolee's action and the parole board's decision was too indirectly related to justify a cause for tort action against the board's officials under the Fourteenth Amendment or any federal statutes (for example, the Federal Civil Rights Act, 42 U.S.C., Section 1983).

The *Martinez* precedent is still cited by the courts when applicable. For example, in a 2002 case, *Gaston v. Houston County,* 196 F.Supp.2d 445, the U.S. District Court for the Eastern District of Texas found *Martinez* directly applicable, ruling: "The situation here resembles *Martinez.* . . . As the death caused by Martinez after his parole was 'too remote a consequence' of the actions by the authorities, so too were the actions of John David Brown" (p. 447).

Liability Claims Not Honored When Congress Has Provided Alternative Remedies.   In *Bush v. Lucas,* 462 U.S. 367 (1983), petitioner Bush, an aerospace engineer working at the Marshall Space Flight Center operated by the National Aeronautics and Space Administration, had often criticized the operations of the space center to the media. Subsequently, Lucas, director of the center, demoted Bush on the grounds that his statements to the media were false and misleading. Although the Federal Employee Appeals Authority upheld his demotion, on further appeal the Civil Service Commission's Appeals Review Board ruled that Bush's demotion had violated his First Amendment guarantees and, thus, recommended his reinstatement to his former position. Bush then filed a damage suit against Lucas, charging that Lucas had violated his First Amendment rights. The Supreme Court refused to grant the remedy sought by Bush. It maintained that Congress had evidently intended to not allow such remedial relief because it had provided appropriate and elaborate alternative remedies under the Civil Service Commission. Speaking for a unanimous Court, Justice Stevens said: "The question is not what remedy the court should provide for a wrong that would otherwise go unredressed. It is whether an elaborate remedial system that has been constructed step by step, with careful attention to conflicting policy considerations, should be augmented by the creation of a new judicial remedy for the constitutional violation at issue" (p. 366). Arguing that Congress is in the best position to develop remedies that would balance the rights of employees with governmental efficiency, the Supreme Court declined to create any new judicial remedy (pp. 380–392). The Supreme Court affirmed this position in the late 1980s in *Schweiker v. Chillicky*, 487 U.S. 412 (1988), yet the high court in 1992 in *McCarthy v. Madigan*, 112 S.Ct. 1081, confused its position in *Bush* and *Chillicky* by holding that a federal prisoner could in fact file a *Bivens* claim even though Congress had provided an alternative remedy under the Federal Tort Claims Act. However, the *McCarthy* decision was made irrelevant by the passage of the Prison Litigation Reform Act of 1995, 42 U.S.C.S. 1997e(a), which requires prisoners to exhaust administrative remedies before bringing suit regarding "prison conditions," as previously discussed. This statute was honored in 2001 by the Supreme Court in *Booth v Churner*, 121 S.Ct. 1819, thus overruling *McCarthy* and reasserting the precedential clout of *Bush-Chillicky*.

In sum, the Supreme Court starting with *Bivens* in 1971 and continuing in such cases as *Scheuer, Wood, Butz,* and *Carlson* did much to destroy the absolute immunity doctrine for public officials as established in *Barr*, while the high court in more recent cases such as *Martinez, Bush, Scheuer, Chillicky*, and *Booth* has conveyed the clear message that it is not willing to proceed recklessly in interpreting the qualified immunity doctrine to make public officials "too" susceptible to tort suits, especially under *Bivens* and Section 1983.

TOWARD INCREASED GOVERNMENTAL LIABILITY AND DECREASED OFFICIAL LIABILITY?

Today, the question of whether public officials or the government should be held liable for tortious acts committed against persons by governmental officers, and under what circumstances, still remains unresolved. Indeed, since the beginning of the republic, our lawmakers and judges have oscillated on this liability question. To recapitulate, at first we drew upon common law to deprive individuals from suing the government for the tortious actions of its officers. But while common law gave the government sovereign immunity, it permitted liability suits to be filed against its officers.[48] However, the courts, with the tacit consent of Congress and state legislative bodies, eventually moved toward making federal and state officials increasingly immune from tort action suits.

But the virtual immunity from liability suits of both the government and its officers created undue hardships for persons abused by public officials committing tortious acts.[49] In response to this unjust situation, legislators developed the doctrines of qualified and limited immunity (for example, the Federal Tort Claims Act), as did judges (for example, the *Bivens* remedy), thus again making public officials more vulnerable to tort actions against them and the government, stripped of its almost untouchable sovereign immunity status, considerably more open to damage suits. Another trend, making public officials less liable and the government more liable to tort suits, has apparently been developing at the national and state levels. In moving gradually in this direction, the government has begun to turn itself into a mutual insurance agency, supported by tax dollars and dedicated to minimizing liability risks to public administrators, while compensating those who are injured by governmental actions.

This step toward a comprehensive liability insurance policy for governmental officers paid for by tax dollars represents an expected extension of the scope of responsibility assumed by the modern welfare state. But as with private insurance policies, the liability policy provides only limited liability coverage. The federal government, as well as state and local governments, are not interested in insuring all forms of tortious acts committed by their officers. The prevailing attitude seems to be that administrative errors that are committed in good faith in the line of duty but that cause unintentional harm to persons should be covered. However, the feeling is that fraudulent, corrupt, or malicious acts by governmental officials should not be given liability protection, especially if not committed in the line of duty. A California statute that substitutes governmental liability for officer liability typifies this modern perspective on liability.[50] The statute obligates the State of California to assume most of the liability risks for its employees, but it still makes its employees liable for their fraudulent, malicious, or corrupt actions. This new concept in governmental liability is based upon the no-fault principle.[51] Thus, compensatory payments will be made to persons injured by governmental activities; but to save court costs, no judicial attempts will be made to prove fault. Overall, this trend away from officer liability to governmental liability represents a movement away from the doctrine of sovereign immunity.

Reasons for Moving Toward Governmental Liability

Why are we apparently moving away from officer liability and toward governmental liability, and why do so many scholars support this trend?[52] From the perspective of the governmental officials, it seems only fair that the government should extend a form of basic liability insurance to its employees. After all, it is argued, these officials are working for our benefit. That is, as a result of their efforts to implement needed governmental programs, society in general benefits. Should we, as a people, make them pay damages out of their own pockets for any innocent mistakes they make in the process of implementing public policies? As Pierce exclaims in his 2002 *Administrative Law Treatise*: "Some of the most flagrant injustice in the legal system occurs when huge judgments are entered against conscientious public employees."[53] As mentioned previously, the use of administrative discretion in making policy implementation decisions almost guarantees that some parties will yell, "Foul!" Besides, it is held, the government is in a much better position to absorb the costs of damage claims than its employees, who are struggling to balance their own family budgets. It is also noted that the vast majority of tortious acts are committed unintentionally and errors that lead to injuries are bound to occur because the workloads of the typical administrator are so heavy and the laws guiding officials are often vague and difficult to understand. Under such conditions agency decisionmakers cannot possibly know for certain when they are violating the law. Yes, the odds are high that administrators will win such suits, but they still may have to fight the expensive and inconvenient tort suit.

From the perspective of the administrative system, as acknowledged before, the omnipresent danger of being sued for wrongdoing would tend to be disruptive to the administrative process because administrators would possibly hesitate to act unless they were certain that their actions were proper and that they would not have to worry about being sued for their acts. This might sound like a good thing, but in reality, in the world of public administration, uncertainty exists behind virtually all administrative acts. Consequently, waiting to make no-risk decisions would probably tend only to promote needless indecision and costly inefficiency in the administrative process. Christopher H. Schroeder feels that this would harm American society greatly, because public administrators must make hard decisions that involve inherently risky modern technologies if we are to advance as a society.[54] And the Supreme Court said in *Scheuer* that the danger of personal liability against public officials would deter their willingness to perform their duties with decisiveness, as is required to promote the public good (416 U.S. 232, 240 [1974]). Thus, despite some of the disadvantages of substituting governmental liability for official liability, it is argued that, on the whole, the substitution is in the public interest because it serves to preserve the essential vitality of the public administration system.

In the 1970s, Kenneth C. Davis argued that transferring tort liability from public officials to the government will have four positive effects. His arguments still make as much sense today. His first two reasons are reiterations of the typical arguments that the shift to governmental liability helps to promote the public interest by preserving the administrative process and that giving immunity to governmental officers is simply the just thing to do. His third and fourth points are more controversial. Davis claims that "the quality of justice to injured persons will be improved in that they will no longer lack a remedy if the officer happens to be judgment proof."[55] To him, "judgment proof" means a public official is too poor to be able to afford to pay a judgment. Also helpful in making an officer judgment proof, according to Davis, is the sympathetic attitude judges and juries hold toward public officials, making them extremely reluctant to conclude that public officials (with families and debts) should be made personally liable for their actions done in the line of public duty. Suits against governments make more sense to him, especially since governments do not elicit particular sympathy and they always have the resources to pay legitimate damage claims. These circumstances tend to make recovery for damages more realistic and fair from the point of view of the injured party. Pierce agrees, noting that "sympathy for the public servant defendant often induces juries to resolve close factual disputes in favor of the defendant and to award lower damages than would otherwise be warranted."[56]

Davis's fourth reason for preferring governmental liability to officer liability is that tort suits filed against the government will deter officials from committing deliberate torts, because the officer charged with committing the tortious act will be reprimanded by his or her superior for causing the governmental unit to fight and possibly pay a liability claim. To substantiate this contention, Davis notes that "all experience shows that subordinates respond more to discipline imposed by superiors than to the possibility that they will be held personally liable."[57] However, he fails to document this very questionable assertion. Justice Brennan, though, argued in *Carlson* that public officials would be more likely to avoid tortious actions if they knew that they might have to suffer the financial consequence of their tortious acts themselves.

Pierce believes that it is so critical to shift liability for tortious actions from public employees to the government that he suggests specific ways for doing it. A few of Pierce's points were mentioned earlier, but they are worth reiterating in a broader context. In particular, he urges Congress to pass a statute that would eliminate *Bivens* claims against federal employees, while also eliminating Section 1983 actions against state and local officials. In addition, he recommends that Congress amend the FTCA by dropping the exemptions for certain intentional torts. Pierce also suggests that Congress should employ its power under the Fourteenth Amendment, Section 5, to make state and local governments liable under Section 1983 suits instead of their officials. Pierce acknowledges that Congress has already shifted liability in specific situations from federal officials to the federal government, but it seems reluctant to pass broad legislation that would shift liability to the federal government for federal employees. He also notes that the courts could do a lot to shift liability to the government at the federal and state and local levels by, for example, specifically overruling *Bivens* and interpreting Section 1983 in such a way that state and local governments would be much more exposed to Section 1983 tort actions than their state and local officials.[58]

Suing the Government Under the Federal Tort Claims Act.   It was not until 1946, when the Federal Tort Claims Act (60 Stat. 842) was passed, that Congress took a significant step toward stripping the federal government of its virtual sovereign immunity status, thus forcing the national government to start assuming some of the responsibility for the damages caused by the tortious actions of its agents. However, in 1946 Congress severely limited the sort of tort action suits that could be filed against the government. Although the FTCA allowed damage suits to be filed against the United States in U.S. district courts "for money only . . . on account of damage to or loss of property or on account of personal injury or death caused by the negligent or wrongful act or omission of any employee of the Government while acting within the scope of his office or employment, under circumstances where the United States, if a private person, would be liable for such damage," other key provisions in the act (1) limited damage claims to only $10,000 or less (this amount has since been abandoned); (2) prohibited jury trials; (3) forbade claims for punitive damages; (4) exempted certain agencies, specific administrative operations, and claims originating in foreign nations; (5) failed to make the act applicable if the claim arises "out of assault, battery, false imprisonment, false arrest, malicious prosecution, abuse of process, libel, slander, misrepresentation, deceit, or interference with contract rights" (Section 421[h]); and (6) prohibited any tort suit "based upon an act or omission of an employee of the Government, *exercising due care, in the execution of a statute or regulation,* whether or not such statute or regulation be valid, or based upon the *exercise or performance or failure to exercise a discretionary function or duty* on the part of a Federal agency or an employee of the Government, whether or not the discretion involved be abused" (Section 421[a]; emphasis mine).[59]

In 1988 Congress passed the Federal Employees Liability Reform and Tort Compensation Act (102 Stat. 4564), which amends the FTCA by (1) broadening the scope of the FTCA to include legislative and judicial branch employees; and (2) transferring to the government liability for common law torts, not constitutional torts, committed by federal officers while acting within the scope of their official duties.[60] These two amendments, although not inconsequential, accomplish less than one may think. In the first place legislative and judicial officials already enjoy absolute immunity from tort suits as long as they are performing legislative or judicial duties. Secondly, Congress did not immunize government officials from liability for constitutional torts committed while carrying out their duties. Since most common law torts can be argued from the standpoint of constitutional torts (i.e., most tortious acts that injure can be presented as a denial of constitutional due process, equal protection, etc.), chances are that federal employees won't gain much added protection from this amendment.

The loopholes in the FTCA are so numerous and broad that many have criticized its practical worth to those who have been victimized by the tortious acts of federal officials. After all, how many times would officers commit tortious acts while performing nonstatutory functions, and in how many cases would you say the exercise of discretion would not be a factor? Section 421(a) basically relieves the government of the burden of being responsible for abusive discretionary acts of its public officials (excluding law enforcement officers) while performing the tasks that they have been hired to carry out.

In fact, in 1953 in *Dalehite v. United States,* 346 U.S. 15 (1953), the Supreme Court applied essentially this interpretation. Filing for recovery of damages under the FTCA, petitioners argued that the negligent handling of ammonium nitrate fertilizer by the federal government caused an explosion that destroyed hundreds of millions of dollars in property, killed 560 people, and injured about 3,000 others. However, the Court had no difficulty in dismissing the hundreds of suits filed, arguing that the FTCA did not permit such suits since "immune discretion" was involved, even if it could be shown that negligence occurred or discretionary authority was abused.

The Supreme Court in 1957, in *Rayonier, Inc. v. United States,* 352 U.S. 315, found the U.S. Forest Service liable for its negligence in providing fire protection services; and in *Indian Towing Co. v. United States,* 350 U.S. 61 (1955), it held that the Coast Guard was liable because it failed to exercise "due care" in maintaining a lighthouse. It returned to the wisdom in *Dalehite* in 1972 in *Laird v. Nelms,* 406 U.S. 797. In *Laird* the Supreme Court ruled that the United States could not be held liable under the FTCA for damages caused by sonic booms resulting from military aircraft that flew over North Carolina at three times the speed of sound. Amazingly, the Court argued that no negligence could be shown in the planning of the flight or in the flight itself. As in *Dalehite,* the Court noted in essence that Congress, in drafting the FTCA, did not intend for a strict liability standard to be imposed upon the government. The Court's majority in *Laird* maintained that the important lesson conveyed "in *Dalehite* is that . . . the Federal Tort Claims Act itself precludes the imposition of liability if there has been no negligence or other form of 'misfeasance or nonfeasance' . . . on the part of the Government" (p. 799).

Thus, as of 1972 the high court had not ordinarily been very generous in permitting tort suits against the federal government. Actually, state court judges have been generally more liberal in allowing tort suits in their respective states, reflecting to some extent the growing trend under state law "making state governments liable upon the same basis as private tortfeasors."[61] The *Laird* decision attracted heated protests from those who believed that the Supreme Court had gone far beyond the intent of the framers of the FTCA in disallowing tort actions against the government. For example, Bernard Schwartz concluded that the *Laird* ruling represented a step backward in tort law. He contended that the damage claim in *Laird* should have been allowed since clearly the FTCA "makes the United States liable for 'negligent or wrongful acts' where a private employer would be. Under applicable tort law, a private person who creates a sonic boom is absolutely liable for any injuries caused thereby. The creation of a sonic boom is thus a 'wrongful act' within the Tort Claims Act, regardless of whether negligence is shown."[62] But possibly the most vehement criticism of the Court's ruling in *Laird* came from justices William J. Brennan and Potter Stewart, who dissented in the case. They argued that the conclusion reached by the Court's majority lacks common sense and clearly contradicts the act's purpose: "Nothing in the language or the legislative history of the Act compels such a result, and we should not lightly conclude that Congress intended to create a situation so much at odds with common sense and the basic rationale of the Act" (p. 809).

But in 1984 in *U.S. v. S.A. Empresa DeViacao Aerea Rio Grandense,* 467 U.S. 797, the Supreme Court again rooted its decision in the restricted line of reasoning developed over thirty years before in *Dalehite.* The legal issue in this case was whether the United States can be held liable under the Federal Tort Claims Act for the negligent certification by the Federal Aviation Administration of an aircraft. Because of an allegedly unsafe trash receptacle, the Boeing 707 caught fire in flight from Paris to Rio de Janeiro and crashed, killing most of the passengers. The airline sued for damages under the FTCA, charging that the Civil Aeronautics Board (the FAA's predecessor) negligently issued a type certificate that in effect approved the lavatory trash receptacle used on the Boeing 707 that really failed to meet applicable air safety regulations.

Consistent with its decision in *Dalehite,* the Supreme Court ruled that the "discretionary function exception" to the FTCA precludes a damage suit against the FAA. Maintaining that the FTCA's discretionary function exception applies to federal agencies as well as to all federal employees exercising discretion, the Court argued that the courts should not intervene and provide relief because "it was precisely this sort of judicial intervention in policymaking that the discretionary function exception was designed to prevent" (p. 820). In explanation, the Court elaborated: "Judicial intervention in such decisionmaking through private tort suits would require the courts to 'second-guess' the political, social, and economic judgments of an agency exercising its regulatory function. . . . FAA employees in executing the 'spot-check' program . . . are protected by the discretionary function. . . . The FAA employees who conducted compliance reviews of the aircraft involved in this case were specifically empowered to make policy judgments regarding the degree of confidence that might reasonably be placed in a given manufacturer, the need to maximize compliance with FAA regulations, and the efficient allocation of agency resources. In administering the 'spot-check' program, these FAA engineers and inspectors necessarily took certain calculated risks, but those risks were encountered for the advancement of a governmental purpose and pursuant to the specific grant of authority in the regulations and operating manuals. Under such circumstances, the FAA's alleged negligence in failing to check specific items in the course of certificating a particular aircraft falls squarely within the discretionary function exception of Section 2680(a)" (p. 820). Given this reasoning, it is difficult to imagine how any plaintiff could win a damage suit under the FTCA. Could not the "discretionary function exception" be used to defeat any claim under the FTCA? If you were injured by a federal agency or its officials, in light of these Supreme Court rulings, what do you think the odds would be of winning a liability claim under the FTCA?

Recent court cases place these odds into perspective, suggesting that the odds of winning a damage award under the FTCA are not very good. The key to winning an FTCA suit seems to be in overcoming the "discretionary function exception." Stated simply, unless the plaintiff can show that a government official caused injury because the tortious action was outside his or her discretionary authority in the administration of some public policy, the plaintiff will not win. For example, in *United States v. Gaubert*, 111 S.Ct. 1267 (1991), the Supreme Court refused to allow tort action under the FTCA brought by a shareholder of an insolvent savings and loan association who charged essentially that negligent regulatory supervision on a day-to-day basis of directors and officers was responsible for the bankruptcy that caused damage to shareholders. Citing *Dalehite* and *Varig Airlines*, the Court held that the discretionary function exemption protects the government from liability as long as "a regulation mandates particular conduct, and the employee obeys the direction. . . . If the employee violates the mandatory regulation, there will be no shelter from liability because there is no room for choice and the action will be contrary to policy. On the other hand, if a regulation allows the employee discretion, the very existence of the regulation creates a strong presumption that a discretionary act authorized by the regulation involves consideration of the same policies which led to the promulgation of the regulations" (p. 1274). Consequently, the Court concluded: "Gaubert asserts that the discretionary function exception protects only those acts of negligence which occur in the course of establishing broad policies, rather than individual acts of negligence which occur in the course of day-to-day activities. . . . If the routine or frequent nature of a decision were sufficient to remove an otherwise discretionary act from the scope of the exception, then countless policy-based decisions by regulators exercising day-to-day supervisory authority would be actionable" (p. 1279).

There are also jurisdictional limitations to the application of the FTCA. In *Smith v. United States*, 113 S.Ct. 1178 (1993), the Supreme Court denied a wrongful death claim brought by a spouse whose husband was killed in Antarctica while working for a construction company hired by the National Science Foundation. The Court dismissed the suit, arguing simply that the FTCA's waiver of sovereign immunity does not apply to tort claims occurring in foreign countries—and Antarctica should be regarded as a foreign country under the FTCA even though it has no recognized government.

Under the FTCA the government is not liable to pay punitive damages. However, in *Molzof v. United States*, 112 S.Ct. 711 (1992), the Supreme Court awarded damages the government argued amounted to "punitive damages" (i.e., future supplemental medical expenses and loss of enjoyment of life). But the Court contended that the FTCA "bars the recovery only of what are *legally* considered 'punitive damages' under traditional common law principles" (p. 718). The Court felt that the award of damages here did not comply with the common law understanding of punitive since the financial award was not awarded to punish the defendant officers for purposeful misconduct.

A few recent representative cases help to illustrate how difficult it is for claimants to win an FTCA suit. In *Popovic v. United States*, 1999 U.S. App. Lexus 7593, a per curiam decision by the U.S. Court of Appeals for the Fourth Circuit in 1999, the court refused to allow Mikulus Popovic, a former National Institute of Health scientist, to argue an FTCA claim against NIH, because the claim was essentially a defamation claim, specifically not allowed under the FTCA. In *O'Toole v. U.S.*, 295 F.3d 1029 (9th Cir. 2002), O'Toole filed an FTCA suit, arguing that his ranch was damaged considerably by negligent maintenance by the Bureau of Indian Affairs (BIA) of a water irrigation system. The court dismissed the FTCA claim on subject matter jurisdictional grounds, holding that "BIA's decision to allow the irrigation system on Bowler Ranch to fall into disrepair to the detriment of neighboring landowners does not fall within the protection of the discretionary function exception to the FTCA" (p. 1037). In a 2003 case, *Muniz-Rivera v. U.S.*, 2003 U.S. App. Lexis 6539 (1st Cir.), Rufino Muniz-Rivera and over a hundred others who owned sixty-seven homes in Salinas, Puerto Rico, filed an FTCA suit, claiming that their homes had been damaged by repeated flooding and that the U.S. government was liable because its officials were largely responsible for situating, planning, and building the houses that frequent flooding damaged. Muniz-Rivera et al. also claimed that federal officials misrepresented the situation by not informing them that they needed to carry flood insurance. The court upheld the dismissal of their claim by the district court under the FTCA's "discretionary" and "misrepresentation" exceptions. "To recapitulate," the court stated, "we hold that the plaintiff's claims that the government negligently failed to warn, to inform of the impending danger, to mandate flood insurance, and to inspect the homes are all barred by the FTCA's misrepresentation exception. We hold that the plaintiff's claims that the government failed properly to supervise the planning and construction of the housing projects and to take appropriate measures to prevent future flooding are barred by FTCA's discretionary function 'exception'" (p. 22).[63]

Suing Municipalities Under Section 1983. We have already reviewed the liability of governmental officials under Section 1983. In this section the liability of municipalities under Section 1983 is discussed. In the early 1960s in *Monroe v. Pope,* 365 U.S. 167 (1961), the Supreme Court, holding to its pro sovereign immunity mood as developed in *Barr* just two years before, ruled that "Congress did not undertake to bring municipal corporations within the gambit of [Section 1983]" (p. 187). However, Supreme Court decisions since have established that municipalities can be held liable under Section 1983 suits under certain conditions.

In *Monell v. Department of Social Services,* 436 U.S. 658 (1978), the Supreme Court, after reexamining the legislative history of the Civil Rights Act of 1871, Section 1983, concluded that the Court in *Monroe* had misread the legislative history and, thus, reached the wrong conclusion about the applicability of Section 1983 claims against municipalities. In *Monell,* the Court reversed *Monroe* in this regard, arguing that "our analysis of the legislative history of the Civil Rights

Act of 1871 compels the conclusion that Congress *did* intend municipalities and other local government units to be included among those persons to whom Section 1983 applies" (p. 690). Consequently, the Court held: "Local governing bodies . . . can be sued directly under Section 1983 for monetary, declaratory, or injunctive relief where, as here, the action that is alleged to be unconstitutional implements or executes a policy statement, ordinance, regulation, or decision officially adopted and promulgated by that body's officers" (p. 690). In addition, the Court held that a municipality can be held liable under Section 1983, like any other "Section 1983 person," if the municipality's official policies can be shown to cause constitutional deprivations. The Court made clear, however, that "Congress did not intend municipalities to be held liable unless action pursuant to official policy of some nature caused a constitution tort. In particular, we conclude that a municipality cannot be held liable *solely* because it employs a tortfeasor—or, in other words, a municipality cannot be held liable under Section 1983 on a *respondeat superior* theory" (p. 691).

But could a municipality escape damage actions against it under Section 1983 for torts that deprive persons of their constitutional rights committed by its officers, even if it contends in defense that its officers acted in *good faith*? The Supreme Court said *no* to this question in *Owen v. City of Independence*, 445 U.S. 622 (1980). The Court's 5–4 majority argued that it would make no sense to allow municipalities a good faith defense since it would leave remediless victims of constitutional violations by municipalities. "Unless countervailing considerations counsel otherwise, the injustice of such a result should not be tolerated" (p. 651). Further, the Court noted, "Section 1983 was intended not only to provide compensation to the victims of past abuses, but to serve as a deterrent against future constitutional deprivations, as well. . . . The knowledge that a municipality will be liable for all of its injurious conduct, whether committed in good faith or not, should create an incentive for officials who may harbor doubts about the lawfulness of their intended actions to err on the side of protecting citizens' constitutional rights. Furthermore, the threat that damages might be levied against the city may encourage those in a policymaking position to institute internal rules and programs designed to minimize the likelihood of unintentional infringements on constitutional rights" (pp. 651–652).

But maybe the most significant aspect of *Owen* is the Court's development of the concept of "equitable loss spreading," which seems to make the *Owen* decision appear very much ahead of its time. In its holding the Court acknowledged that it is crucial for tort law to evolve so that our notion of responsible government is preserved. To the *Owen* Court, "equitable loss spreading" is a fairer principle because it calls for distributing the costs of official misconduct, making no longer "individual 'blameworthiness' the acid test of liability" (p. 657). Basically, the Supreme Court contended that the costs for damages caused by the tortious actions of governmental officials, especially under Section 1983, should be shared by the three principal parties: (1) the victim; (2) the officer(s) who committed the tort; and (3) the public (the governmental unit supported by the citizens' tax dollars, in this case the city of Independence, Missouri). Therefore, the Court concluded: "The innocent individual who is harmed by an abuse of governmental authority is assured that he will be compensated for his injury. The offending official, so long as he conducts himself in good faith, may go about his business secure in the knowledge that a qualified immunity will protect him from personal liability for damages that are more appropriately chargeable to the populace as a whole. And the public will be forced to bear only the costs of injury inflicted by the 'execution of a government's policy or custom, whether made by its lawmakers or by those whose edicts or acts may fairly be said to represent official policy'" (p. 657).

The Supreme Court has attempted to clarify and apply the *Monell* rule that an official's tortious unconstitutional action must have been taken "pursuant to official municipal policy of some nature" before the municipality can be held liable under Section 1983. In *City of Oklahoma City v. Tuttle,* 105 S.Ct. 2427 (1985), the case focused on a *single incident* in which an Oklahoma City police officer shot and killed a man outside a bar where a robbery was reported to be in progress. The plaintiff, the man's wife, filed a Section 1983 suit against Oklahoma City, charging that the city's training and supervisory policies were inadequate and, as a result, had led to the unconstitutional action committed against her husband. The Court held: "Proof of a *single incident* of unconstitutional activity is not sufficient to impose liability under *Monell, unless proof of the incident includes proof that it was caused by an existing, unconstitutional municipal policy, which can be attributed to a municipal policymaker.* Otherwise the existence of the unconstitutional policy, and its origin, must be separately proved. But where the policy relied upon is not itself unconstitutional, considerably more proof than the single incident will be necessary in every case to establish both the requisite fault on the part of the municipality, and the causal connection between the 'policy' and the constitutional deprivation" (p. 2436; emphasis mine).

The key to understanding *Tuttle* is found in the emphasized phrases. A year later in *Pembaur v. Cincinnati,* 106 S.Ct. 1292 (1986), the Supreme Court, drawing on these emphasized phrases, reached a different conclusion in a case involving a single incident. This time the Court upheld the plaintiff's Section 1983 damage suit because it believed that it was clearly shown that the police officers who had violated the plaintiff's constitutional rights had in fact directly followed official county policy, specifically, the county prosecutor's "clear command." The single incident in this case involved a situation where county deputy sheriffs used an axe to gain entry into a room barred by the plaintiff to arrest subpoenaed witnesses employed by the plaintiff at his clinic. However, the deputy sheriffs carried out such action only after they had called the county prosecutor's office and received the "clear command" from the prosecutor to take such action. In light of these facts, the high court ruled that Section 1983 liability may be imposed for a single incident on a governmental unit under such circumstances (p. 1301).

A 1992 case also helps to clarify the scope of Section 1983 liability suits. In *Collins v. City of Harker Heights, Tex.*, 112 S.Ct. 1061, the widow of a sanitation worker employed by Harker Heights's sanitation department brought a Section 1983 suit against the city, claiming that her husband died of asphyxia after entering a manhole to repair a sewer line, because the city had failed to train or warn its sanitation workers of known risks. She argued that such oversight deprived her husband of "life" without "due process of law." The Supreme Court ruled, citing *Monell*, that "the city is not liable under Section 1983 for the constitutional torts of its agents: It is only liable when it can be fairly said that the city itself is the wrongdoer" (p. 1067). In *Monell*, "we decided that a municipality can be found liable under Section 1983 only where the municipality *itself* causes the constitutional violation at issue. *Respondent superior* or vicarious liability will not attach under Section 1983" (p. 1067). Elaborating, the Court explained that inadequate training of employees "could be characterized as the cause of the constitutional tort—if and only if—the failure to train amounted to 'deliberate indifference' to the rights of persons" (p. 1068). Further, "neither the text nor the history of the Due Process Clause supports petitioner's claim that the governmental employer's duty to provide its employees with a safe working environment is a substantive component of the Due Process Clause" (p. 1069). The intent of the Fourteenth Amendment's due process clause, the Court asserted, was "to prevent government 'from abusing (its) power, or employing it as an instrument of oppression'" (p. 1069). Showing some irritation with the claim in the suit, the Court exclaimed that the "petitioner's submission that the city violated a federal constitutional obligation to provide its employees with certain minimal levels of safety and security is unprecedented." Due process does not "guarantee municipal employees a workplace that is free of unreasonable risks of harm" (p. 1071).

Two recent cases have upheld *Collins*. In *Trigalet v. City of Tulsa*, 239 F.3d 1150 (10th Cir. 2001), the City of Tulsa was sued under Section 1983 because three people, including Jean and Myra Trigalet, were killed as result of a "police chase" by Tulsa law enforcement officers. The court held that a municipality can be held liable only "if the City's actions can be characterized as arbitrary or conscience-shocking, in a constitutional sense, even if there are no unconstitutional acts by an individual officer" (p. 1151). The Court dismissed the suit because, it argued, no constitutional violation had been shown since no intentional harm by the officer had been shown. Citing *Collins*, the court concluded: "Therefore, plaintiffs cannot meet the first prong of the test set forth in *Collins v. City of Harbor Heights, Texas* . . . ('proper analysis requires us to separate two different issues when a Section 1983 claim is asserted against a municipality: (1) whether plaintiff's harm was caused by a constitutional violation and (2) if so, whether the city is responsible for that violation')" (p. 1155). Similarly, in *Nix v. Franklin County School District*, 311 F.3d 1373 (11th Cir. 2002), the court dismissed a Section 1983 liability claim against the Franklin County School District because claimants—the parents of Jeremiah Nix, who was accidentally electrocuted to death in a high school electromechanical class—failed to prove a constitutional violation, as established in *Collins*. Consequently, the school district was granted immunity. The Court could find no violation "shocking to the conscience," nor could it find any intent to cause harm. The Court acknowledged the *Collins* court made clear that "the due process clause 'does [not] guarantee municipal employees a workplace that is free of unreasonable risks of harm'" (here applying *Collins* to include high school students). The Court also noted that "both *Collins* and *White* reflect judicial reluctance to second-guess policy decisions about resources to be allocated to safety, which are best left to 'locally elected representatives, rather than . . . federal judges'" (p. 1377).

To conclude, it should be emphasized that Section 1983 suits, while often difficult to win, nonetheless in general have the effect of scaring state and local public officials and the governments that employ them to uphold the constitutional rights of their citizens, because Section 1983 has emerged in modern tort law as a legal weapon with potentially fierce and broad teeth. As Pierce notes in summary, Section 1983

> now authorizes damage actions against state and local government employees based on constitutional torts, damage actions against local governments based on constitutional torts committed while implementing law or official policy, and actions for declaratory and injunctive relief against state and local governments based on violations of either the U.S. Constitution or any federal law that is interpreted to create a judicially enforceable right in an individual. Moreover, because a Section 1983 plaintiff is not required to exhaust state or local judicial or administrative remedies and is often entitled to recover attorney fees under Section 1988, Section 1983 has become the preferred vehicle for obtaining relief based on alleged violations of federal law by state or local officials and institutions.[64]

Optional state and local remedies are seldom used.

Today's Patchwork Quilt.   In the mid-1970s, Walter Gellhorn and Clark Byse, reflecting the sentiment of many administrative law scholars, concluded that "the system of governmental liability resembles a patchwork quilt, and a rather imperfectly constructed one, at that."[65] These scholars, and others, were reacting to a legal system that had failed to produce a clear picture on governmental and official immunity. However, by the 2000s the picture of public tort law is still very blurred, although Congress has made some amendments to public tort law, as noted in this chapter, in an attempt to resolve some issues. Even though some damage actions apply to the states in general (e.g., Section 1983), public tort law at the state level is even more confusing due to specific state enactments limiting sovereign immunity and qualifying official immunity. In fact, Richard Pierce in his 2002 *Administrative Law Treatise*, the most definitive and respected work in administrative law, concludes his chapter on public tort law with a section entitled "Inordinate Confusion and Complexity in Public Tort Law," which seems to encapsulate the problem very well.[66]

After reading this chapter you may feel that you still do not understand public tort law very well. You may feel that you still do not have a very good grasp of the applicability of various liability laws to state, local, and federal officials, as well as to their governments. Well, join the club! After carefully reviewing public tort law in his *Administrative Law Treatise*, Pierce concluded that "the law in this area is so complex and uncertain that no judge or lawyer is likely to be able to address a single dispute in a manner that reflects all of the relevant statutory and decisional law."[67] Pierce, as well as other legal scholars, claims that despite the fact that courts hand down decisions every day pertaining to public liability questions, many, if not most, of the questions they "answer" are really "unanswerable" under our present system of "patchwork quilt" public tort law.[68]

In reading court decisions and the literature on public tort law, it becomes readily apparent that judges and scholars write in tentative, confusing, incomplete, and even contradictory terms. Judicial decisions may sound emphatic and clear in one context, but serious reflection almost always raises questions about how their interpretations would apply in even a slightly different situation or whether another court would give the same interpretation to the exact same questions of tort law and fact and reach the same decision. Public tort law scholars are afraid to draw emphatic conclusions about most issues in public liability law, making their writings confusing, because they normally can't: There are simply no definitive answers to most public tort questions.

Unquestionably, general principles have been developed in the field of public tort law, but applying these principles in specific cases becomes a very difficult and frustrating task because it is not easy to decide, for example, whether the government or its officials are liable or both or neither, which liability laws apply, whether constitutional violations have occurred, whether the constitutional rights violated were "clearly established," whether alternative remedies should preclude the liability suit before the court, whether the discretionary exception should apply, etc. A strong consensus of scholars and practitioners contend that our lawmakers must draft statutes to help clear up the confusion in public tort law because it remains an ugly "patchwork quilt."

THE QUESTION OF
PRESIDENTIAL IMMUNITY

The attitude that certain governmental officials should be entitled to absolute immunity from judicial action against them while performing governmental functions had been well established by 1700 under British common law. Drawing heavily upon the British legal system, our constitutional framers, legislators, and judges in American history at least eventually saw to it that most of our public officials were also extended immunity protections.[69] Our legislators and judges have always enjoyed absolute immunity from judicial actions against them for acts committed in their line of duty.[70] In *Spalding*, in 1896, the Supreme Court gave absolute immunity protection to top executive officers (for example, a postmaster general in this case), while in 1959, in *Barr*, this immunity privilege was extended to cover almost all public administrators.

However, in recent years the courts have abandoned the absolute immunity principle of *Spalding-Barr* and, starting with *Bivens,* replaced it with only a qualified immunity status for federal administrators. But given the unique constitutional and practical position of the president, should our chief executive also be accorded only a qualified immunity privilege? Should the president, like virtually all other public administrators, be made subject to lawsuits arising from official presidential actions or even unofficial actions?[71] Would not the threat of lawsuits prevent the president from providing the nation with effective presidential leadership? Does the Constitution not recognize this and give the president absolute immunity protection?

Although *United States v. Nixon, 418 U.S.* 683 (1974), did not consider the presidential immunity question from the standpoint of whether the president can be brought before a federal court as a defendant in a tort suit, it was an important case for conveying to the public the Supreme Court's perspective on the presidential immunity issue in general. In *Nixon,* Special Watergate Prosecutor Archibald Cox petitioned U.S. District Judge John Sirica for an order that would entitle Cox to obtain from President Nixon certain Watergate tapes required by grand jury subpoena *duces tecum.* However, Nixon claimed executive privilege and filed a motion to have the subpoena dismissed. Judge Sirica denied this motion and then issued an order requesting that specific tapes be released for *in camera* inspection. Nixon appealed, arguing that the "intra-branch dispute" between Cox and himself was a nonjusticiable controversy that precluded court review. In so arguing, Nixon was in effect maintaining that he alone had the authority, under the doctrine of executive privilege, to determine what material should be kept privileged (in this case, away from the grand jury in a criminal prosecution).

The Court ruled essentially that, although it is "in the public interest to afford Presidential confidentiality the greatest protection," the president does not stand above the law (p. 715). According to the Court, the presumption of executive "privilege must be considered in light of our historic commitment to the rule of law" (p. 708). Quoting from *Marbury v. Madison,* 1 Cranch 137 (1803), the Court reasoned that, in order for our governmental system of separation of powers to work, it must be "emphatically the province and duty of the judicial department to say what the law is" (p. 703). Flatly rejecting the argument by Nixon that he should be the only one to determine how the law applies to executive privilege, the Court exclaimed "that the Court has the authority to interpret claims with respect to powers alleged to derive from enumerated powers" (p. 704).

The prevalent attitude in *Nixon* was that executive privilege should never be used without any regard to the impact its use may have on the due process rights of others. The Court argued that it had the responsibility to protect such due process rights. Thus, in the context of the case at hand, the Court asserted that it "must weigh the importance of the general privilege of confidentiality of presidential communication in performance of the President's responsibilities against the inroads of such a privilege on the fair administration of criminal justice." All factors considered, the Court reasoned, the use of executive privilege "cannot prevail over the fundamental demands of due process of law. . . . The generalized assertion of privilege must yield to the demonstrated, specific need" (pp. 711–713).

This forceful decision against Nixon cannot be understood without an appreciation for the atmosphere in which it was made. Public opinion was strongly against Nixon, especially since many citizens believed that he opposed releasing the tapes not for any noble reason but only to hide his criminal involvement in the Watergate affair. Consequently, some scholarly critics at the time contended that the Court might have gone too far in weakening executive privilege, especially since in the public's eye the Court's rhetoric boldly scolded Nixon for perceiving himself above the law.

In *Halperin v. Kissinger*, 606 F.2d 1192 (1979), the D.C. Circuit court considered whether the president should be entitled to absolute immunity from damage suits filed against him.[72] The case stems from a suit filed by Halperin, ex-chief of the National Security Council Planning Group, for money damages. He argued that Nixon et al., had placed an illegal wiretap on his home telephone from 1969 to 1971, violating his Fourth Amendment right to privacy and Title III of the Omnibus Crime Control and Safe Streets Act of 1968.[73] Nixon argued, however, that the president is entitled to absolute immunity in such tort actions. Again, as in the case five years earlier, Nixon's arguments were rejected with judicial vigor.

First, because of the illegal wiretap, the D.C. Circuit court overruled the nominal award of $1 for damages awarded by the district court (424 F.Supp. 838 [1976]). Arguing that such wiretaps require a warrant justifying their use, the Court noted that Halperin and his family were entitled to be paid more than nominal damages because their basic constitutional rights were violated by Nixon et al.: "This court has held that in cases involving constitutional rights, compensation 'should not be approached in a niggardly spirit'" (p. 1208).

Second, rooting its arguments in the reasoning espoused in *Butz*, the Court noted that to accept Nixon's contention that he should be absolutely immune in this suit, "we would have to hold that his status as President sets him apart from the other high executive officials named as defendants to this action. Such a distinction would have to rest on a determination either that the Constitution impliedly exempts the president from all liability in cases like this or that the repercussions of finding liability would be drastically adverse. Because we are unable to make that distinction, we do not believe he is entitled to absolute immunity to a damage action by a citizen subjected to an unconstitutional or illegal wiretap" (p. 1210). The Court acknowledged specifically that the Constitution does not grant the president any special immunities and this should not be interpreted as an oversight, especially since the Founders saw fit to grant legislators certain immunities (p. 1211).

The appeals court also found that it made no sense to allow absolute presidential immunity on what is called "prudential grounds." That is, the Court did not feel that the threat of damage suits against a president would prove disruptive to presidential management. The Court also noted that legitimate suits against the president would be "quite rare" (p. 1212). More specifically, the Court argued that the extra personal burden placed upon presidents by permitting tort suits to be filed against them is not heavy enough to justify extending to them absolute immunity privileges (p. 1213).

The Court in *Halperin* took a very clear stand on the issue of whether presidents should be accorded absolute immunity status. The Court answered with an emphatic "No!" In so ruling, the Court upheld the wisdom of *Butz* that only qualified immunity, not absolute immunity, should be extended to all governmental administrators, except, of course, to those involved in adjudications. Clearly, the Court here refused to place the president in a kingly position by placing him above the law.

However, in *Nixon v. Fitzgerald*, 457 U.S. 731 (1982), the Supreme Court took a radically different stand by ruling that the rule of official liability established in *Scheuer* and *Butz* does not apply to the president because the president, due to his unique office, is entitled to absolute immunity from damage suits (pp. 749–758). Employing a balance test, the Court argued "that a court, before exercising jurisdiction, must balance the constitutional weight of the interest to be served against the dangers of intrusion on the authority and functions of the Executive Branch. . . . When judicial action is needed to serve broad public interest . . . the exercise of jurisdiction has been held warranted. In the case of this merely private suit for damages based on a President's official acts, we hold it does not" (p. 754).

Anticipating that scholars would criticize the Court's decision for apparently placing the president above the law, since this decision now makes presidents absolutely immune from liability suits, the Court argued that alternative remedies and deterrents for presidential misconduct such as impeachment, scrutiny by the press, various formal and informal checks, the desire to earn reelection, the need to retain prestige, and the president's concern for a good name in history "establishes that absolute immunity will not place the President 'above the law'. For the President, as for judges and prosecutors, absolute immunity merely precludes a particular private remedy for alleged misconduct in order to advance compelling public ends" (p. 758). However, Justice White in dissent, joined by Justices Brennan, Marshall, and Blackmun, emphatically disagreed with the majority's holding, arguing that now "a President, acting within the outer boundaries of what Presidents normally do, may, without liability, deliberately cause serious injury to any number of citizens even though he knows his conduct violates a statute or tramples on the constitutional rights of those who are injured. . . . He would be immune regardless of the damage he inflicts, regardless of how violative of the statute and of the Constitution he knew his conduct to be, and regardless of his purpose" (pp. 764–765).

It should be emphasized that in the companion case, *Harlow v. Fitzgerald*, 457 U.S. 800 (1982), the Supreme Court made very clear that, although the president is entitled to absolute immunity from tort liability, his aides are not. The Court concluded that presidential aides, as most other administrators, should be entitled to only qualified immunity. Applying only the "knew or reasonably should have known" rule, the Court held "that government officials performing discretionary functions generally are shielded from liability for civil damages insofar as their conduct does not violate clearly established statutory or constitutional rights of which a reasonable person would have known" (p. 818). It is important to point out that in *Harlow* the Court dropped the good faith-malicious intent factor, arguing that experience has shown that trying to establish the subjective intent of public officials, whether their actions were committed in good faith or bad faith (maliciously), has led to too many long and costly litigations that ultimately fail to prove whether good or bad intentions motivated the alleged tortious actions (pp. 813–815). In sum, *Harlow* established, as confirmed two years later in *Scherer,* that the only question that matters in liability claims against public officials is whether the official "knew or reasonably should have known" that his or her actions were violating clearly established statutory or constitutional rights.[74]

After a very comprehensive review of the amenability of presidents to lawsuits from President George Washington to President George H. W. Bush, Laura Krugman Ray concluded in 1992 that the immunity status of presidents is unclear because the Supreme Court "has failed to meet its institutional obligation to define for the lower courts and for the country the contours of the relationship of presidential power to the legal process."[75] In particular, she found disturbing polar opposite decisions handed down in the 1974 *Nixon* decision and the 1982 *Fitzgerald* holding. The *Nixon* ruling clearly grants only qualified immunity to presidents and places them under the law, while the latter emphatically places presidents above the law by granting presidents absolute immunity while in the performance of their official acts. For Justice White, *Fitzgerald* represents an anomaly because the decision rejects the wisdom espoused in *Nixon* that upholds precedent, history, and the intention of the Founders to make presidents democratically accountable.[76]

In 1994, Paula Jones filed damage claims under Section 1983 and 1985 and state law against President Clinton, seeking $700,000 in damages for sexual harassment (making improper sexual advances) when she was an Arkansas state employee and he was governor. Whether such a damage claim could be filed against a president posed a very interesting question since no court had addressed the question of whether a president could be sued for damages for unofficial actions before he became President. The *Fitzgerald* ruling suggests that a president is absolutely immune from all "merely private suits for damages," but in *Fitzgerald* the Supreme Court was concerned in particular with protecting presidents against apparently all liability suits while performing their official duties while serving as president.

In 1995, a federal district court in Arkansas ruled that Jones' suit cannot be heard until after President Clinton leaves office, although the discovery process could begin. However, in 1996, the Eighth Circuit court reversed, holding that the case can proceed because a president can be sued for his unofficial acts even while in office. Clinton appealed to the Supreme Court, contending that the reasoning applied in *Fitzgerald* should make the President immune from *all* "merely private suits for damages."

In *Clinton v. Jones*, 117 S.Ct. 1636 (1997), the Supreme Court rejected Clinton's arguments, ruling that, despite some evidence and court rulings that have confused the status of presidential immunity, Congress, the U.S. Constitution, or the courts have never definitively given absolute immunity to presidents for civil claims for damages for actions committed before the president even took office. The Court was emphatic in noting that it was not revisiting the *Nixon v. Fitzgerald* question of "whether the President's immunity from damages liability for acts taken within the 'outer perimeter' of his official responsibilities provides a defense" (p. 1640). The Court held that (1) "it was an abuse of discretion for the District Court to defer the trial until after the President leaves office" (p. 1651); (2) it is unpersuaded that its decision to allow the liability suit to continue "will generate a large volume of politically motivated harassing and frivolous litigation, and the danger that national security concerns might prevent the President from explaining a legitimate need for a continuance" (p. 1651); (3) "If Congress deems it appropriate to afford the President stronger protection, it may respond with appropriate legislation"; and (4) "The Federal District Court has jurisdiction to decide this case, like every other citizen who properly invokes that jurisdiction, respondent has a right to an orderly disposition of her claims" (p. 1652).

The Supreme Court in *Jones* seemed to reject the arguments used in *Fitzgerald* to justify giving the President absolute immunity, thus placing the President apparently above the law. In *Fitzgerald*, the court was concerned about the President's "unique position" and the "intrusion on the authority and functions of the Executive Branch" as a result of a "merely private suit for damages." True, the court here was ruling on a suit for "damages based on a President's official acts," but the justifications given for protecting a President from any liability suit while serving in office would seem to be the same if the court is really concerned about advancing "compelling public ends." In any event, the Supreme Court in *Jones* seemed determined to return to the wisdom of *Nixon* where the President is not placed above the law by absolute immunity protection, rejecting the absolute immunity protections granted to the President in *Fitzgerald* by what the *Jones* court referred to as a "thin majority." In trying to understand and reconcile the rather dramatic fluctuations in legal opinions and dicta in *Nixon, Fitzgerald,* and *Jones*, one cannot ignore the political climates of each. Only a naive observer would conclude that such court decisions involving a president are politically neutral.[77]

SUMMARY

Should individuals be able to sue the government and its administrators for their tortious acts in the same manner liability claims can be filed against parties in the private sector? Under the common law doctrine that reflects our Anglo-Saxon heritage, the government was made totally immune from damage suits, while its administrative officers were made quite vulnerable to liability actions against them for tortious behavior. However, some courts did employ the sovereign immunity doctrine to protect the government, as well as its officials, reasoning that the actions of the two could not be separated in practice. But other courts insisted on adopting the old Anglo-Saxon common law argument that the government's administrators should not be exempted from liability suits because to do so would place them above the law, something that is illegitimate in a rule-of-law nation.

The sovereign immunity doctrine is rooted in the old British common law thinking that the king can do no wrong. Although this legal principle was never officially adopted by Congress, it was mysteriously recognized by American courts from the very beginning of the Republic. This was true in spite of the fact that the doctrine, especially when it was used to protect the government's officials, made sense for old monarchical Europe, but virtually no sense for America—a political system based on the rule of law. Regardless of the doctrine's apparent un-American character, it has been only very modestly modified.

Reformers had pushed for the abolition of the sovereign immunity doctrine since at least the 1930s because of its blatantly unfair character. The basic argument was that it was patently unfair to deprive persons of the right to sue the government for its tortious actions against them, especially since the powers of the government placed it in a strategic position to cause injury to parties. Nevertheless, the doctrine survived for so long because proponents of the doctrine, never defending it for being fair to individuals, contended that damage suits had the potential to destroy the government upon which society is dependent. Consequently, the doctrine was justified on the grounds that it is better to allow an individual or a few people to suffer than to permit liability suits to place society in jeopardy.

The development of qualified immunity status for government officials followed an uneven course that can be divided into three basic stages. The first stage lasted until the late 1800s. During this stage the courts generally ruled that the government's administrators could be held liable for their tortious behavior toward citizens. But placing public administrators in such a position was considered unfair since they could ill afford to pay damage claims out of their own pockets. Besides, it was thought that making these devoted public servants vulnerable to tort liability claims tended to disrupt the administrative process.

In 1896 the Court that heard *Spalding* ruled that top-level administrators, who employ considerable discretion in making policy decisions, should not be placed in a position where they would have to worry about whether they could be sued for their official discretionary decisions. But since virtually all administrators employ discretion in the line of duty, it was only a matter of time before the *Spalding* logic was employed by later courts to exempt practically all administrative officials from damage action suits. Indeed, the Supreme Court in *Barr* (1959) applied *Spalding* to cover virtually all governmental administrators. However, scholarly reaction to *Barr* was extremely negative and the courts soon shifted their position. After *Barr* the courts began to find governmental officials at all levels of government increasingly more vulnerable to liability actions against them, especially when it could be shown that they denied clearly established constitutional rights to persons when they knew, or should have known, better (*Scherer* [1984]).

Presently, the government has only limited immunity from liability claims, while its officers enjoy only qualified immunity. In many instances, this allows persons the opportunity to choose between suing the government or its officers, depending upon which course of action would be most beneficial. The courts have made suing the government and its officials easier, creating potentially new financial burdens for the government and its employees. However, new legislation and imaginative new tests created by the courts for overcoming the immunity protection for the government and its officials have made winning tort suits very difficult. Nonetheless, potentially, tort suits can prove to be a financial disaster, especially if publicly insured public officials lose a *Bivens* or Section 1983 claim amounting to awards of millions of dollars in punitive damages. State and especially local governments have been particularly hard hit by the enormous increase in Section 1983 suits that have been filed against them, making it difficult for them to obtain and retain liability insurance at affordable rates. Consequently, state and local authorities have organized to meet what they perceive as the growing crisis in tort liability and insurance unavailability. They have turned to Congress for help, pleading with Congress to pass legislation that would reduce their liability under tort law (for example, doing away with punitive damage claims, placing ceilings on damage awards) and ease their tort liability insurance problems (for example, stabilize rates, prevent insurance companies from canceling liability insurance except for nonpayment or fraud). By the early 2000s, some but not much relief had been provided by Congress, yet the abundance of "anticlaimant" court decisions since the mid-1980s has helped to relieve the liability burden. However, the Supreme Court's decision in *Jones* made one official, the President, more susceptible to tort liability claims.

PORTER V. NUSSLE

---

534 U.S. 516; 122 S.Ct. 983 (2002)

Facts

Ronald Nussle, a Connecticut state prison inmate, filed a Section 1983 grievance suit against prison correctional officers, including Officer Porter, charging that they had singled him out for a brutal beating in violation of the Eighth Amendment's prohibition against "cruel and unusual punishments." Nussle brought his Section 1983 claim directly to federal court without first exhausting state administrative remedies for prisoners, as apparently required by the Prison Litigation Reform Act of 1995 (PLRA), 110 Stat., Sections 1321–1373. While the U.S. District Court for the District of Connecticut dismissed the suit because Nussle had not exhausted the appropriate state remedies, the U.S. Court of Appeals for the Second Circuit reversed, holding that the phrase "prison conditions" under Section 1997e(a) of the amended PLRA did not apply to severe beatings of individual prisoners. The Supreme Court granted certiorari.

Justice Ginsburg delivered the unanimous opinion of the Court.

This case concerns the obligation of prisoners who claim denial of their federal rights while incarcerated to exhaust prison grievance procedures before seeking judicial relief. Plaintiff-respondent Ronald Nussle, an inmate in a Connecticut prison, brought directly to court, without filing an inmate grievance, a complaint charging that corrections officers singled him out for a severe beating, in violation of the Eighth Amendment's ban on "cruel and unusual punishments." Nussle bypassed the grievance procedure despite a provision of the Prison Litigation Reform Act of 1995 (PLRA), 110 Stat. 1321-73, as amended, 42 U.S.C. §1997e(a) that directs: "No action shall be brought with respect to prison conditions under section 1983 of this title, or any other Federal law, by a prisoner confined in any jail, prison, or other correctional facility until such administrative remedies as are available are exhausted."

The Court of Appeals for the Second Circuit held that §1997e(a) governs only conditions affecting prisoners generally, not single incidents, such as corrections officers' use of excessive force, actions that immediately affect only particular prisoners. Nussle defends the Second Circuit's judgment, but urges that the relevant distinction is between excessive force claims, which, he says, need not be pursued administratively, and all other claims, which, he recognizes, must proceed first through the prison grievance process. We reject both readings and hold, in line with the text and purpose of the PLRA, our precedent in point,

and the weight of lower court authority, that §1997e(a)'s exhaustion requirement applies to all prisoners seeking redress for prison circumstances or occurrences.

I

Respondent Ronald Nussle is an inmate at the Cheshire Correctional Institution in Connecticut. According to his complaint, corrections officers at the prison subjected him to "a prolonged and sustained pattern of harassment and intimidation" from the time of his arrival there in May 1996. Nussle alleged that he was singled out because he was "perceived" to be a friend of the Governor of Connecticut, with whom corrections officers were feuding over labor issues.

Concerning the episode in suit, Nussle asserted that, on or about June 15, 1996, several officers, including defendant-petitioner Porter, ordered Nussle to leave his cell, "placed him against a wall and struck him with their hands, kneed him in the back, [and] pulled his hair." Nussle alleged that the attack was unprovoked and unjustified, and that the officers told him they would kill him if he reported the beating.

Then, as now, the Connecticut Department of Correction provided a grievance system for prisoners. Under that system, grievances must be filed within 30 days of the "occurrence." Rules governing the grievance process include provisions on confidentiality and against reprisals.

Without filing a grievance, on June 10, 1999, Nussle commenced an action in federal district court under 42 U.S.C. §1983; he filed suit days before the three-year statute of limitations ran out on the §1983 claim. Nussle charged, principally, that the corrections officers' assault violated his right to be free from cruel and unusual punishment under the Eighth Amendment, as made applicable to the States by the Fourteenth Amendment. The District Court, relying on §1997e(a), dismissed Nussle's complaint for failure to exhaust administrative remedies.

Construing §1997e(a) narrowly because it is an exception "to the general rule of non-exhaustion in §1983 cases," the Court of Appeals for the Second Circuit reversed the District Court's judgment; the appeals court held that "exhaustion of administrative remedies is not required for [prisoner] claims of assault or excessive force brought under §1983." *Nussle v. Willette*, 224 F.3d 95, 106 (2000). Section 1997e(a) requires administrative exhaustion of inmates' claims "with respect to prison conditions," but contains no definition of the words "prison conditions." The appeals court found the term "scarcely free of ambiguity." For purposes of the PLRA's exhaustion requirement, the court concluded, the term was most appropriately read to mean "'circumstances affecting everyone in the area,'" rather than "'single or momentary matters,' such as beatings . . . directed at particular individuals." . . .

The Court of Appeals found support for its position in the PLRA's legislative history. Floor statements "overwhelmingly suggested" that Congress sought to curtail suits qualifying as "frivolous" because of their "subject matter," e.g., suits over "insufficient storage locker space," "a defective haircut," or "being

served chunky peanut butter instead of the creamy variety." 224 F.3d at 105. Actions seeking relief from corrections officer brutality, the Second Circuit stressed, are not of that genre. Further, the Court of Appeals referred to pre-PLRA decisions in which this Court had "disaggregated the broad category of Eighth Amendment claims so as to distinguish [for proof of injury and *mens rea* purposes] between 'excessive force' claims, on the one hand, and 'conditions of confinement' claims, on the other." Id., at 106.

In conflict with the Second Circuit, other Federal Courts of Appeals have determined that prisoners alleging assaults by prison guards must meet §1997e(a)'s exhaustion requirement before commencing a civil rights action. We granted *certiorari* to resolve the intercircuit conflict, 532 U.S. 1065 (2001), and now reverse the Second Circuit's judgment.

Ordinarily, plaintiffs pursuing civil rights claims under 42 U.S.C. §1983 need not exhaust administrative remedies before filing suit in court. Prisoner suits alleging constitutional deprivations while incarcerated once fell within this general rule.

In 1980, however, Congress introduced an exhaustion prescription for suits initiated by state prisoners. This measure authorized district courts to stay a state prisoner's §1983 action "for a period not to exceed 180 days" while the prisoner exhausted available "plain, speedy, and effective administrative remedies." §1997e(a)(1). Exhaustion under the 1980 prescription was in large part discretionary; it could be ordered only if the State's prison grievance system met specified federal standards, and even then, only if, in the particular case, the court believed the requirement "appropriate and in the interests of justice." §§1997e(a) and (b). We described this provision as a "limited exhaustion requirement" in *McCarthy v. Madigan*, 503 U.S. 140 (1992), and thought it inapplicable to prisoner suits for damages when monetary relief was unavailable through the prison grievance system.

In 1995, as part of the PLRA, Congress invigorated the exhaustion prescription. The revised exhaustion provision, titled "Suits by prisoners," states: "No action shall be brought with respect to prison conditions under section 1983 of this title, or any other Federal law, by a prisoner confined in any jail, prison, or other correctional facility until such administrative remedies as are available are exhausted." 42 U.S.C. §1997e(a).

The current exhaustion provision differs markedly from its predecessor. Once within the discretion of the district court, exhaustion in cases covered by §1997e(a) is now mandatory. All "available" remedies must now be exhausted; those remedies need not meet federal standards, nor must they be "plain, speedy, and effective." Even when the prisoner seeks relief not available in grievance proceedings, notably money damages, exhaustion is a prerequisite to suit. And unlike the previous provision, which encompassed only §1983 suits, exhaustion is now required for all "actions . . . brought with respect to prison conditions," whether under §1983 or "any other Federal law." Thus federal prisoners suing under *Bivens v. Six Unknown Fed. Narcotics Agents*, 403 U.S. 388 (1971),

must first exhaust inmate grievance procedures just as state prisoners must exhaust administrative processes prior to instituting a §1983 suit.

Beyond doubt, Congress enacted §1997e(a) to reduce the quantity and improve the quality of prisoner suits; to this purpose, Congress afforded corrections officials time and opportunity to address complaints internally before allowing the initiation of a federal case. In some instances, corrective action taken in response to an inmate's grievance might improve prison administration and satisfy the inmate, thereby obviating the need for litigation. In other instances, the internal review might "filter out some frivolous claims." And for cases ultimately brought to court, adjudication could be facilitated by an administrative record that clarifies the contours of the controversy.

Congress described the cases covered by §1997e(a)'s exhaustion requirement as "actions . . . brought with respect to prison conditions." Nussle's case requires us to determine what the §1997e(a) term "prison conditions" means, given Congress' failure to define the term in the text of the exhaustion provision. We are guided in this endeavor by the PLRA's text and context, and by our prior decisions relating to "suits by prisoners," §1997e.

As to precedent, the pathmarking opinion is *McCarthy v. Bronson*, 500 U.S. 136 (1991), which construed 28 U.S.C. §636(b)(1)(B) (1988 ed.), a Judicial Code provision authorizing district judges to refer to magistrate judges, *inter alia*, "prisoner petitions challenging conditions of confinement." The petitioning prisoner in *McCarthy* argued that §636(b)(1)(B) allowed nonconsensual referrals "only when a prisoner challenges ongoing prison conditions." 500 U.S. at 138. The complaint in *McCarthy* targeted no "ongoing prison conditions"; it homed in on "an isolated incident" of excessive force. For that reason, according to the *McCarthy* petitioner, nonconsensual referral of his case was impermissible.

We did not "quarrel with" the prisoner's assertion in McCarthy that "the most natural reading of the phrase 'challenging conditions of confinement,' when viewed in isolation, would not include suits seeking relief from isolated episodes of unconstitutional conduct." We nonetheless concluded that the petitioner's argument failed upon reading the phrase "in its proper context." We found no suggestion in §636(b)(1)(B) that Congress meant to divide prisoner petitions "into subcategories." "On the contrary," we observed, "when the relevant section is read in its entirety, it suggests that Congress intended to authorize the nonconsensual reference of all prisoner petitions to a magistrate." The Federal Magistrates Act, we noted, covers actions of two kinds: challenges to "conditions of confinement"; and "applications for habeas corpus relief." Congress, we concluded, "intended to include in their entirety those two primary categories of suits brought by prisoners."

"Just three years before [§636(b)(1)(B)] was drafted," we explained in *McCarthy*, "our opinion in *Preiser v. Rodriguez*, 411 U.S. 475 (1973), had described [the] two broad categories of prisoner petitions: (1) those challenging the fact or duration of confinement itself; and (2) those challenging the conditions of confinement." *Preiser v. Rodriguez*, 411 U.S. 475 (1973), left no doubt, we further stated in *McCarthy*, that "the latter category unambiguously embraced the kind of single episode cases that petitioner's construction would exclude." 500 U.S. at 141. We found it telling that Congress, in composing the Magistrates Act, chose language "that so clearly paralleled our *Preiser* opinion." 500 U.S. at 142. We considered it significant as well that the purpose of the Magistrates Act—to lighten the caseload of overworked district judges—would be thwarted by opening the door to satellite litigation over "the precise contours of [the] suggested exception for single episode cases."

As in *McCarthy*, we here read the term "prison conditions" not in isolation, but "in its proper context." The PLRA exhaustion provision is captioned "Suits by prisoners," see §1997e; this unqualified heading scarcely aids the argument that Congress meant to bisect the universe of prisoner suits.

This Court generally "presumes that Congress expects its statutes to be read in conformity with the Court's precedents." That presumption, and the PLRA's dominant concern to promote administrative redress, filter out groundless claims, and foster better prepared litigation of claims aired in court persuade us that §1997e(a)'s key words "prison conditions" are properly read through the lens of *McCarthy* and *Preiser*. Those decisions tug strongly away from classifying suits about prison guards' use of excessive force, one or many times, as anything other than actions "with respect to prison conditions."

Nussle places principal reliance on *Hudson v. McMillian*, 503 U.S. 1 (1992), and *Farmer v. Brennan*, 511 U.S. 825 (1994), and the Second Circuit found support for its position in those cases as well, 224 F.3d at 106. *Hudson* held that to sustain a claim of excessive force, a prisoner need not show significant injury. 503 U.S. at 9. In so ruling, the Court did indeed distinguish excessive force claims from "conditions of confinement" claims; to sustain a claim of the latter kind "significant injury" must be shown. *Hudson* also observed that a "conditions of confinement" claim may succeed if a prisoner demonstrates that prison officials acted with "deliberate indifference," while a prisoner alleging excessive force must demonstrate that the defendant acted "maliciously and sadistically to cause harm." *Farmer* similarly distinguished the mental state that must be shown to prevail on an excessive force claim, i.e., "purposeful or knowing conduct," from the lesser *mens rea* requirement governing "conditions of confinement" claims, i.e., "deliberate indifference." We do not question those decisions and attendant distinctions in the context in which they were made. But the question presented here is of a different order.

Hudson and *Farmer* trained solely and precisely on proof requirements: what injury must a plaintiff allege and show; what mental state must a plaintiff plead and prove. Proof requirements once a case is in court, however, do not touch or concern the threshold inquiry before us: whether resort to a prison grievance process must precede resort to a court. We have no reason to believe that Congress meant to release

the evidentiary distinctions drawn in *Hudson* and *Farmer* from their moorings and extend their application to the otherwise invigorated exhaustion requirement of §1997e(a). Such an extension would be highly anomalous given Congress' elimination of judicial discretion to dispense with exhaustion and its deletion of the former constraint that administrative remedies must be "plain, speedy, and effective" before exhaustion could be required.

Nussle contends that Congress added the words "prison conditions" to the text of §1997e(a) specifically to exempt excessive force claims from the now mandatory exhaustion requirement; he sees that requirement as applicable mainly to "'prison conditions' claims that may be frivolous as to subject matter," 224 F.3d at 106. It is at least equally plausible, however, that Congress inserted "prison conditions" into the exhaustion provision simply to make it clear that preincarceration claims fall outside §1997e(a), for example, a Title VII claim against the prisoner's preincarceration employer, or, for that matter, a §1983 claim against his arresting officer.

Furthermore, the asserted distinction between excessive force claims that need not be exhausted, on the one hand, and exhaustion-mandatory "frivolous" claims on the other is untenable, for "excessive force claims can be frivolous," Smith.

Other infirmities inhere in the Second Circuit's disposition. As *McCarthy* emphasized, in the prison environment a specific incident may be symptomatic rather than aberrational. An unwarranted assault by a corrections officer may be reflective of a systemic problem traceable to poor hiring practices, inadequate training, or insufficient supervision. Nussle himself alleged in this very case not only the beating he suffered on June 15, 1996; he also alleged, extending before and after that date, "a prolonged and sustained pattern of harassment and intimidation by correction officers." Nussle urges that his case could be placed in the isolated episode category, but he might equally urge that his complaint describes a pattern or practice of harassment climaxing in the alleged beating. It seems unlikely that Congress, when it included in the PLRA a firm exhaustion requirement, meant to leave the need to exhaust to the pleader's option. ("It would wholly frustrate explicit congressional intent to hold that [prisoners] could evade this [exhaustion] requirement by the simple expedient of putting a different label on their pleadings.")

Under Nussle's view and that of the Second Circuit, moreover, bifurcation would be normal when a prisoner sues both a corrections officer alleged to have used excessive force and the supervisor who allegedly failed adequately to monitor those in his charge. The officer alone could be taken directly to court; the charge against the supervisor would proceed first through the internal grievance process. Similarly split proceedings apparently would be in order, under the Second Circuit's decision, when the prisoner elects to pursue against the same officers both discrete instance and ongoing conduct charges.

Finally, we emphasize a concern over and above the complexity augured by the Second Circuit's disposition: Scant sense supports the single occurrence, prevailing circumstance dichotomy. Why should a prisoner have immediate access to court when a guard assaults him on one occasion, but not when beatings are widespread or routine? Nussle's distinction between excessive force claims and all other prisoner suits presents a similar anomaly. Do prison authorities have an interest in receiving prompt notice of, and opportunity to take action against, guard brutality that is somehow less compelling than their interest in receiving notice and an opportunity to stop other types of staff wrongdoing? ("Since [the] internal problems of state prisons involve issues so peculiarly within state authority and expertise, the States have an important interest in not being bypassed in the correction of those problems.")

For the reasons stated, we hold that the PLRA's exhaustion requirement applies to all inmate suits about prison life, whether they involve general circumstances or particular episodes, and whether they allege excessive force or some other wrong. Accordingly, the judgment of the Court of Appeals is reversed, and the case is remanded for further proceedings consistent with this opinion.

It is so ordered.

COMMENTS AND QUESTIONS

It has been noted in this chapter and others that the Rehnquist Court, as well as other federal and state courts, has done much during this conservative era to promote administrative efficiency during a period of diminishing resources. The federal courts, but especially the Supreme Court, have also promoted a neofederalist revival, in part by deferring as much as possible to state authority, thus helping to return more power to the states.

The Supreme Court's decision in *Porter v. Nussle* is consistent with this trend, but it also upholds certain basic administrative law principles and traditions. Certainly, this is one reason for the unanimous decision since even the more liberal members of the court, not particularly interested in promoting a neofederalist revival, joined the conservative justices. In *Nussle* the Court settled several issues that were good for prison officials and state prison systems in general but bad for prison inmates seeking relief under Section 1983. Overruling the Second Circuit Court of Appeals, the Supreme Court made very clear that the section on "prison conditions" (1997e[a]) of the Prison Litigation Reform Act applies to *all* prison conditions, whether they have to do with the kind of peanut butter served, chunky or smooth, or the beatings of individual prisoners by guards. The high court ruled that it is unquestionable under Section 1997e(a) that state prisoners must exhaust all state prison administrative remedies before bringing a Section 1983 suit in federal court.

In so holding, the Court accomplished many objectives. As discussed in Chapter 9, the exhaustion doctrine is a fundamental administrative law doctrine, yet historically Section 1983 suits, as the court acknowledged, were excluded from the exhaustion requirement, allowing claimants to skip state remedies and file a damage action directly in federal court. Consequently, Section 1983 suits became a popular remedy, especially with state prisoners. During the 1970s, 1980s, and into the 1990s, thousands of Section 1983 suits, many frivolous, were filed by state prisoners alone, causing extra and costly burdens to the state prison systems, the federal courts, and taxpayers. To curb this heavy tide of Section 1983 damage claims, Congress passed in 1995 the PLRA, as amended by 42 U.S.C. 1997e(a). In *Nussle*, the Court interpreted legislative intent, arguing: "Beyond doubt, Congress enacted Section 1997e(a) to reduce the quantity and improve the quality of prison suits; to this purpose, Congress afforded corrections officials time and opportunity to address complaints internally before allowing the initiation of a federal case."

Not only did the Court in *Nussle* defer broadly to the will of Congress, especially in its interpretation of "prison conditions," but it even stressed the possible advantages of the PLRA (e.g., "corrective action taken in response to an inmate's grievance might improve prison administration"). The Court even answered a question not raised in this suit: Does the PLRA apply to federal prisoners? The Court said emphatically yes, noting that "federal prisoners suing under *Bivens* . . . must first exhaust inmate grievance procedures just as state prisoners must exhaust administrative processes prior to instituting a Section 1983 suit."

Unquestionably, this is a great decision for state and federal prison systems and prison officials. But what practical impact will this have on state and federal prisoners wanting to file legitimate damage actions under Section 1983 on the state level and under *Bivens* on the federal level? If you were a prisoner suffering from unwarranted brutal beatings, what realistic hope would you now have that you could gain timely court review? Have not prison systems had a tainted history of cover-ups? Wouldn't you expect the prison systems to be biased in their favor when hearing complaints? Are you as optimistic as the Court in believing that the PLRA "might improve prison conditions," or would you suspect, given the practical ability for prisons to escape Section 1983 and *Bivens* damage suits, it to actually worsen prison conditions? Do you think that the original framers of Section 1983 back in 1871 would approve of the Court's decision in *Nussle*?

NOTES

1. Harold J. Krent, "Reconceptualizing Sovereign Immunity," *Vanderbilt Law Review* 45 (November 1992): 1530.

2. However, the very fact that our lawmakers allowed the courts to employ the doctrine for so long implies that the legislators gave at least tacit approval to its use.

3. *Muskopf v. Corning Hospital District,* 359 P.2d 457, 458–459 (Cal. 1961).

4. William Bradford, "'With a Very Great Blame on Our Hearts': Reparation, Reconciliation, and an American Indian Plea for Peace with Justice," *American Indian Law Review* 27 (2002–2003): 88.

5. John E. Sherry, "The Myth That the King Can Do No Wrong: A Comparative Study of the Sovereign Immunity Doctrine in the United States and the New York Court of Claims," *Administrative Law Review* 22 (October 1969): 58. Sherry holds that it is the citizen who needs protection, not the state: "Sovereign immunity is at best a judicial protective device created to immunize a weak government against oppressive and insensitive citizen demands. . . . Today it is the citizen who is helpless in the face of growing governmental intrusion into his very life, often with unpredictable and tragic results. . . . Sovereign immunity is dangerous to our democratic institutions."

6. Bernard Schwartz, *Administrative Law,* 2nd ed. (Boston: Little, Brown and Company, 1984), p. 568.

7. Kenneth C. Davis, *Administrative Law Treatise,* 2nd ed. (San Diego: K. C. Davis, 1983), vol. 4, pp. 191–192.

8. Kenneth C. Davis, *Administrative Law and Government* (St. Paul: West, 1975), p. 111.

9. Davis makes this argument in several works, but his best argument against sovereign immunity is in "Sovereign Immunity Must Go," *Administrative Law Review* 22 (April 1970). See also, Davis, *Administrative Law Treatise,* 2nd ed., vol. 4, pp. 191–198.

10. Richard H. Fallon, Jr., "The 'Conservative' Paths of the Rehnquist Court's Federalism Decisions," *University of Chicago Law Review* 69 (spring 2002): 437.

11. This should not imply, however, that the government should not do what it can to provide emergency relief and follow-up care to those harmed in such a tragedy; but the relief provided would be voluntary, not compelled by judicial orders as payment of damages.

12. Davis, *Administrative Law and Government,* p. 220.

13. Bernard Schwartz, *Administrative Law,* 3rd ed. (Boston: Little, Brown and Company, 1991), p. 614.

14. Fallon, "'Conservative' Paths," pp. 429–494.

15. Ibid.

16. See for example, *FMC v. S.C. State Ports Auth.*, 122 S.Ct. 1864 (2002) (state sovereign immunity precludes Federal Maritime Commission from adjudicating private party's grievance that ports authority violated Federal Shipping Act of 1984).

17. Fallon, "'Conservative' Paths," pp. 429–494.

18. Louis L. Jaffe, "Suits Against Governments and Officers: Damage Actions," *Harvard Law Review* 77 (December 1963): 213.

19. *United States v. Caltex (Philippines), Inc.,* 344 U.S. 149 (1952).

20. It should be recognized that the governmental and official immunity doctrine never existed in pure form. In other words, limited and qualified immunity always existed, since the courts have always

honored some exceptions to the sovereign immunity doctrine. Even Congress early in our history recognized that the government should not be completely immune from suits. Congress did establish the United States Court of Claims in 1855, thereby eliminating the government's immunity status in the area of contracts. Thus, limited governmental immunity and qualified immunity imply a significant relaxation of immunity protection occurring in recent years. It should be noted that some authors use the terms *limited* and *qualified* interchangeably to apply to governmental and official immunity. Of course, *limited* and *qualified* do convey the same meaning when applied to immunity. I make the distinction only for the sake of clarity.

21. Schwartz, *Administrative Law,* 3rd ed., p. 598.

22. A. V. Dicey, *Introduction to the Study of the Law of the Constitution,* 9th ed. (London: Macmillan, 1952), p. 193.

23. David H. Rosenbloom, "Public Administrators' Official Immunity and the Supreme Court: Developments During the 1970s," *Public Administration Review* 40 (March–April 1980): 168.

24. The Court in *Butz v. Economou,* 434 U.S. 994 (1978), upheld the validity of extending absolute immunity to governmental administrators who perform quasi-judicial functions, although in general the Court heartily endorsed the concept of qualified immunity for most public officials.

25. Rosenbloom, "Public Administrators' Official Immunity and the Supreme Court," p. 169.

26. The Fourth Amendment guarantees to citizens the right "to be secure in their persons, houses, papers, and effects, against unreasonable searches and seizures." The amendment also states that "no warrants shall [be] issued but upon probable cause, supported by oath or affirmation, and particularly describing the place to be searched, and the persons or things to be seized." These protections, the amendment states, "shall not be violated."

27. *Davis v. Passman,* 442 U.S. 228 (1979); and *Carlson v. Green,* 446 U.S. 14 (1980).

28. For an excellent critique of the *Malesko,* see Matthew G. Mazefsky, "*Correctional Services Corporation v. Malesko*: Unmasking the Implied Damage Remedy," *University of Richmond Law Review* 37 (January 2003).

29. Richard J. Pierce, Jr., *Administrative Law Treatise,* 4th ed. (New York: Aspen, 2002), vol. 3, p. 1471.

30. Ibid., pp. 1471–1472.

31. Mazefsky, "Unmasking the Implied Damage Remedy," p. 662.

32. Pierce, *Administrative Law Treatise,* 4th ed., vol. 3, p. 1174.

33. Scott C. Arakaki and Robert E. Badger, Jr., "*Wyatt v. Cole* and Qualified Immunity for Private Parties in Section 1983 Suits," *Notre Dame Law Review* 69 (1995): 762.

34. Ibid., pp. 737–739, 769–770.

35. Martin A. Schwartz and Eileen Kaufman, "Punitive Damages in Section 1983 Cases," *New York Law Journal,* November 16, 1993, pp. 3–6.

36. Rosenbloom, "Public Administrators' Official Immunity and the Supreme Court," p. 170.

37. Ibid.

38. Bernard Schwartz, *Administrative Law* (Boston: Little, Brown, 1976), p. 560.

39. Ibid., p. 561.

40. *Butz v. Economou,* 434 U.S. 994 (1978); *Carlson v. Green,* 446 U.S. 14 (1980); and *Harlow v. Fitzgerald,* 457 U.S. 800 (1982).

41. National Institute of Municipal Law Officers Mid-Year Seminar, *The Tort Liability and Municipal Insurance Crises,* Executive Committee Report (Washington, D.C., 1986), p. 1. Also see Eric Wiesenthal, "Public Liability Crisis Sparks Reform," *Public Administration Times* 9 (March 1, 1986): 1 and 3. Wiesenthal reports that Section 1983 lawsuits against states and localities have increased from 260 in 1960 to over 38,000 in 1981, causing a crisis for states and localities. To alleviate the crisis, state and local officials have asked Congress to place new regulations on insurance companies to stabilize insurance coverage and rates and to reduce the liability of states and cities and their officials (for example, eliminating or lowering punitive damage awards, shortening the time limit to file damage claims, setting liability ceilings).

42. Pierce, *Administrative Law Treatise,* 4th ed., vol. 3, p. 1418.

43. For a review of the significance of the *Butz* decision, see Robert H. Freilich and Richard G. Carlisle, *Section 1983: A Sword and Shield* (Chicago: American Bar Association, 1983), pp. 60, 301, and 336.

44. Pierce, *Administrative Law Treatise,* 4th ed., vol. 3, p. 1493.

45. Ibid.

46. Ibid.

47. Ibid.

48. See Philip L. Gregory, Jr., "Executive Immunity: For Constitutional Torts After *Butz v. Economou,*" *Santa Clara Law Review* 20 (spring 1980); Schuck, *Suing Government: Citizen Remedies for Official Wrongs* (New Haven: Yale University Press, 1983); and Paul T. Hardy and J. Devereaux Weeks, *Personal Liability of Public Officials Under Federal Law* (Athens: Carl Vinson Institute of Government, University of Georgia, 1985).

49. It could be argued that under social contract theory—as developed through the ages by Thomas Hobbes, Jean Jacques Rousseau, and especially John Locke—citizens should have a right to redress governmental officials' violations of the agreed-upon contract (for example, the Constitution). Under contract theory, the sovereign's power is limited by the contract to certain actions. For example, the sovereign—the U.S. government—cannot, under the Constitution, take away private property without due process of law. Thus, freedom would be severely jeopardized if citizens could not sue the government or its officials for tortious actions against them, since these citizens would be left without remedies short of rebellion (justified, incidentally, by Locke under these conditions) to redress violations of the contract. In short, the undue hardships mentioned above are created, in reality, by unconstitutional actions.

50. Cal. Gov't Code, Secs. 825.4, 825.6.

51. For a fascinating discussion of the pros and cons of the application of this principle, see Richard A. Epstein, *Theory of Strict Liability* (San Francisco: CATO Institute, 1980), especially chaps. 1–3, 8, and 10.

52. I say "apparently" because at this point it is uncertain in which direction we are headed in the area of liability, especially since court decisions in recent years have caused dramatic changes in public tort laws. Pierce in his recent *Administrative Law Treatise,* 4th ed., vol. 3, states that the entire area of tort law is very complex and very confused (p. 1490).

53. Ibid., p. 1391.

54. Christopher H. Schroeder, "Rights Against Risks," *Columbia Law Review* 86 (April 1986). Peter Huber makes an even stronger case for this position in "Safety and the Second Best: The Hazards of Public Risk Management in the Courts," *Columbia Law Review* 85 (March 1985).

55. Davis, *Administrative Law and Government,* p. 218.

56. Pierce, *Administrative Law Treatise,* 4th ed., vol. 3, p. 1392.

57. Davis, *Administrative Law and Government,* p. 218.

58. Pierce, *Administrative Law Treatise,* 4th ed., vol. 3, pp. 1392–1396.

59. Section 421(h) was amended in 1974 (88 Stat. 50) in light of the *Bivens* decision to make law enforcement officers essentially liable for committing the tortious acts specified in Sec. 421(h). That is, the United States is presently liable for assault, battery, false imprisonment, false arrest, abuse of process, or malicious prosecution committed by its law enforcement officers.

60. In *United States v. Smith,* 111 S.Ct. 1180 (1991), the Court ruled that the plaintiff has no remedy if an FTCA exclusion renders the government not liable.

61. Schwartz, *Administrative Law,* 3rd ed., p. 613.

62. Ibid., p. 612.

63. For recent analysis of FTCA issues, see Shawn P. Dontigney, "*McCoy v. United States*: The Eighth Circuit Imposes Excessive Requirements in Administrative Claims and Fails to Apply the Continuous Treatment Doctrine to Properly Postpone a Claim's 'Accrual,'" *Creighton Law Review* 36 (February 2003); and Matthew L. Zabel, "Advisory Juries and Their Use and Misuse in Federal Tort Claims Act Cases," *Brigham Young University Law Review* 2003 (2003).

64. Pierce, *Administrative Law Treatise,* 4th ed., vol. 3, p. 1473.

65. Walter Gellhorn and Clark Byse, *Administrative Law,* p. 377.

66. Kenneth C. Davis and Richard J. Pierce, Jr., *Administrative Law Treatise,* 3rd ed. (Boston: Little, Brown, 1994), vol. 3, p. 276.

67. Pierce, *Administrative Law Treatise,* 4th ed.

68. Ibid., pp. 1490–1496.

69. Keith King, "Indicting the President: Can a Sitting President Be Criminally Indicted?" *Southwestern Law Review* 30 (2001).

70. The courts have generally interpreted "official duty" very liberally, thus assuring legislators and judges very comfortable immunity protections so that they could perform their official duties without

fear that they might have to defend their actions in court. However, in *United States v. Brewster,* 408 U.S. 501 (1972), the Supreme Court argued that legislators should not be immune from prosecution for criminal conduct (for example, accepting bribes) under the speech or debate clause of the U.S. Constitution.

71. It is important to remember that the Court, in *Butz v. Economou,* 434 U.S. 994 (1978), recognized that prosecutors, administrative law judges, and other administrators connected directly with adjudicative processes needed immunity protection to perform their jobs properly. Thus, some administrators today do enjoy absolute immunity privileges.

72. In this case Richard M. Nixon was named as a defendant, along with former national security advisor Henry Kissinger, former U.S. attorney general John Mitchell, and seven others.

73. 18 U.S.C., Secs. 2510–2520 (1976).

74. For a comprehensive analysis of the immunity of presidential aides in light of the *Harlow* decision, see Kathryn Dix Dowle, "The Derivative and Discretionary-Function Immunities of Presidential and Congressional Aides in Constitutional Torts," *Ohio State Law Journal* 44 (1983).

75. Laura Krugman Ray, "From Prerogative to Accountability: The Amenability of the President to Suit," *Kentucky Law Journal* 80 (1991–1992): 813.

76. Ibid.

77. For a comprehensive analysis of presidential immunity from a comparative and theoretical perspective, see Rett R. Ludwikowski, "Politicization and Judicialization of the U.S. Chief Executive's Political and Criminal Responsibility: A Threat to Constitutional Integrity or a Natural Result of the Constitution's Flexibility?" *America Journal of Comparative Law* 50 (fall 2002).

CHAPTER 11

An Administrative Law Challenge

Balancing Societal and Individual Rights

BALANCING: A TOUGH CHALLENGE FOR ADMINISTRATORS

When public administrators take steps to implement public policies, they must cope with the extremely frustrating and challenging question: due process or fair treatment for whom—the individual at issue in any particular case or society? Administrators face a difficult choice because, obviously, what may seem fair for an individual may be unjust for society and vice versa. In short, administrators must make difficult daily choices between the interests of society and those of the individual. And despite how critical these decisions may be to the individual or our society, a viable common value framework has not been developed to guide these choices. Thus, this decisionmaking process, which affects our fundamental liberties, is imperfect at best.

The purpose of this chapter is to highlight some of the issues and difficulties of trying to balance the rights of society with the rights of the individual. This is a vital administrative law topic that should not be understated. Unquestionably, the administrator's task of balancing societal and individual rights when implementing public policies has presented and will continue to present the toughest general administrative challenge.[1] To convey how involved the balancing issue is, I have relied heavily upon relevant and informative court opinions.

PRESERVING INDIVIDUAL LIBERTIES
IN THE FACE OF MASS CONTROL EFFORTS:
AN INTRODUCTORY COMMENT

The social contract theorists (Thomas Hobbes, John Locke, and Jean Jacques Rousseau) once argued that individuals would be willing to surrender some of their personal freedoms to a governmental authority in exchange for peace, security, and order. Essentially, these theorists imagined that society without government was chaotic and full of dangers and human suffering. To escape such a wretched life, reasonable persons would realize that more pleasant living could be attained if governmental institutions were created to order, regulate, and elevate society. Consequently, the prospects of a better life led people to form a "contract" with the government eagerly consenting to the right of government to make the rules necessary to preserve harmony in the social system (to promote "ordered liberty").

For all practical purposes, this conceptualization of the status of individuals in society before government is still accurate today and helps us to comprehend a problem that plagues all modern societies. Fundamentally, as suggested, administrative law implicitly aims at striking an equitable and practical balance between the rights of individual citizens and the rights of the collective citizenry (society). But the intensifying problem in modern American society, especially since "9/11," according to some critics, is that more and more institutional decisions appear to be made to protect group or societal interests at the expense of the individual. It appears that the costs to individuals for the administration of "ordered liberty" in the United States are soaring upward, despite attempts by the American Civil Liberties Union and other such organizations to reverse this trend by fighting to protect the constitutional rights of individual citizens.

We have noted thus far in this text that many relatively recent laws and court rulings have helped to preserve the rights of citizens. But given the rapid expansion of administrative government, some have argued that the preservation and extension of individual rights have not kept pace with the liberties the new administrative state has taken away. Indeed, in 1977 Herbert Kaufman asserted that all the new regulations that have been adopted for the sake of society may have taken too much freedom away from individuals.[2] Of course, September 11 and threats of future terrorist attacks have caused our government to adopt new, bolder restrictions.

It just might be that to uphold its contractual obligation to preserve ordered liberty in our society, the government may have been justified in taking the regulatory steps it has. Increases in crime, terrorism, consumer rip-offs, Internet crimes, securities fraud, and the poisoning of our drinking water by the illicit dumping of toxic wastes provide just a few reasons that increased governmental regulations may have been justified. Nevertheless, the individual freedom we enjoy in America may be in jeopardy; certainly it is already much different from the freedoms of our ancestors. One major problem for administrative law is this:

How can individual liberties still be protected in an atmosphere in which governmental officials are struggling to keep order and continued socioeconomic prosperity in a society increasing in numbers and complexity and in which urban decay, crime, terrorism, environmental pollution, computer and biological viruses, and so on, threaten to disrupt and destroy the nation's welfare?

Every time an administrative agency or a court makes a decision that benefits a larger group at the expense of the individual, another liberty is lost and our way of life changes. For example, because hijacking airplanes was a real threat to air passengers during the 1970s, governmental officials decided in good faith that the public could best be protected if they required each person boarding planes to be searched. The thorough search may involve opening up purses, attaché cases, and even Christmas gifts. Likewise, the increase in drug traffic and threat to homeland security have caused authorities to carry out humiliating searches at border stations, the persons seemingly selected almost at the whim of border officials who try to judge possible smugglers and terrorists. These searches occasionally involve embarrassing naked body searches. Under normal circumstances judges have demanded probable cause before they would issue search warrants permitting particular individuals to be searched. When a search warrant is issued, the signed and dated warrant specifies the place, the person or persons to be searched, and the things to be seized. In the 2000s new satellite remote sensing technology poses a new threat to privacy rights because now the government can conduct broad, invasive "open field" searches using powerful cameras such as the KFA-1000 to view tiny details in objects or on persons from great distances.

In short, although searches administered to protect society against hijackings, drug abuse, terrorism, and the like have a noble purpose, such searches are not specifically aimed at individuals about whom probable cause can be established, but against anyone who boards an airplane or passes through a border station. In many respects, such governmental actions against individuals do not only take away previously enjoyed freedoms; such administrative procedures tend to be insulting and dehumanizing as well. Elaborating, Herbert Kaufman once commented that it is not surprising that the vast majority of decent citizens become resentful of all the abusive rigmarole (red tape) that they must endure so that a tiny fraction may be caught and punished. From this perspective, Kaufman concluded, such governmental rules and regulations, which tend to restrict individual freedom, "are neither justified nor justifiable."[3] But in light of 9/11, he might have been wrong.

The true constitutional legitimacy of such bothersome administrative searches is highly questionable, since the Fourth Amendment clearly prohibits "unreasonable" searches and seizures, and Amendments Five and Fourteen in general call for citizens to be accorded due process. However, despite such infringements upon the constitutional rights of citizens, such administrative practices will probably continue to be allowed so that society can be protected. Whether this will prove beneficial or harmful in the long run, when all costs and benefits are considered, is difficult to judge.[4] But administrative policymakers and reviewing courts, as well as our legislators, must acknowledge the fact that groups are mere *abstractions* and only individuals are *real*. When administrative decisions are made to benefit a large group or society in general, in reality only individuals are affected. This is so because groups, in the final analysis, are made up of nothing more than individuals. Consequently, the critical question for our political system has become: Should we permit public administrators, supposedly for the sake of the public welfare, to execute administrative measures that help to bury our constitutional liberties?

To the late Justice William O. Douglas, by the early 1970s the central question in America had become "whether the government by force of its largesse has the power to 'buy up' rights guaranteed by the Constitution."[5] This had become the crucial question for Douglas because he perceived modern bureaucracy as "not only slow, lumbering, and oppressive; it is omnipresent. It touches everyone's life at numerous points. It pries more and more into private affairs, breaking down the barriers that individuals erect to give them some insulation from the intrigues and harassments of modern life."[6] Thus, one task of administrative law in the 2000s is to seek solutions to societal problems that do not crush individual liberty for the sake of promoting some abstract noble social goal. History should have taught us by now that totalitarian societies tend to emerge when leaders insist that individuals surrender their liberties for the sake of a greater common good. This is not to assert that no sense of a common good or public interest exists. In a free society any state efforts to promote the general welfare should not be achieved by robbing citizens of their inalienable rights. However, in post-9/11 America, preserving freedoms has become more difficult.

ADMINISTRATIVE PRACTICES AND THE BILL OF RIGHTS

What is the Bill of Rights, and what precise relevance does it have to administrative law? The first ten amendments to the United States Constitution constitute the Bill of Rights. State constitutions also have bills of rights. Applicable provisions in the Bill of Rights have been applied to the states by various court decisions over the years. The Bill of Rights places restrictions upon what the government can do while exercising its powers; thus it is quite consistent with the democratic principle of limited government. Actually, the Bill of Rights was added to the Constitution to satisfy those who insisted at the time of its ratification that they would oppose ratification of the Constitution unless a clear statement of rights was attached to specify the personal freedoms individuals would retain under the new government. The Bill of Rights, which guarantees the retention of basic liberties for individuals, has always been considered by constitutional scholars as absolutely essential to the maintenance of a free society.[7]

Specific provisions in the Bill of Rights guarantee American citizens various protections against arbitrary governmental intrusions into their personal life. For example, it protects persons against arbitrary invasions of their privacy by public officials; preserves the right of citizens to state what they think publicly; prohibits the government from stopping citizens from organizing to, say, protest governmental policies; guarantees persons accused of crimes certain due process rights so that they can have an opportunity to prove their innocence; and forbids the taking of life, liberty, and private property without due process under law. In sum, the Bill of Rights places restrictions upon the government by underwriting the principle that individuals should be left alone unless the government can show good legal cause that they should not be.

It should be emphasized that the courts have not interpreted these rights to be absolute. Common sense should dictate that certain circumstances would not justify the absolute extension of these rights, especially if they are used to commit illegal acts that threaten the rights and safety of other citizens. In some situations, Justice Oliver Wendell Holmes argued, the misuse of such rights creates "a clear and present danger" for others or for society. In regard to the acceptable limits of the right of free speech, Justice Holmes remarked: "The question in every case is whether the words used are in such circumstances and are of such a nature as to create a clear and present danger that they will bring about the substantive evils that Congress has a right to prevent. It is a question of proximity and degree." In the same famous decision, he noted, for example, that no one should have the right to yell "Fire!" in a crowded theater and then claim a constitutional right to do so.[8]

The courts have traditionally employed a balancing doctrine to determine whether individuals have abused their constitutional rights, causing an undue threat to the public interest. When the courts employ the balancing doctrine, they are faced with the difficult task of choosing between the rights of the individual and the rights of society. That is, the courts must protect the interests of society while simultaneously preserving the constitutional rights of citizens. This task is becoming more difficult as societal problems become more acute, requiring more intense governmental involvement.

But when making legislation and administering public policies, legislators and administrators must also be guided by the balancing principle. Administrators especially are faced with the daily chore of balancing Bill of Rights guarantees with the apparent needs of society. Although many administrative activities do not involve the application of the Bill of Rights, many do. Administrators are particularly restricted in their regulatory functions by the provisions of the Fourth Amendment, although they must frequently be cognizant of the restrictions placed upon them by the Fifth and First Amendments and, to a much lesser extent, some of the other constitutional amendments.

The remainder of the chapter is an analysis of how well administrative agencies have been doing in preserving Bill of Rights liberties for individuals while implementing public programs aimed at protecting and promoting our nation's general welfare. Only topics not discussed in previous chapters are considered here. The analysis begins with the Fourth Amendment, since it has the greatest relevance to administrative law.

ADMINISTRATIVE ACTIONS
UNDER THE FOURTH AMENDMENT

What does the Fourth Amendment guarantee, and how has it been applied to restrict the behavior of administrative officials? The Fourth Amendment is clearly one of the most important constitutional amendments because it protects individuals "in their persons, houses, papers, and effects, against unreasonable searches and seizures." The amendment specifically prohibits search warrants from being issued except "upon probable cause, supported by oath or affirmation, and particularly describing the place to be searched, and the persons or things to be seized."

Despite its critical relevance to the preservation of individual liberties, this amendment has always been difficult to interpret and apply in practice. What constitutes an unreasonable search and seizure has not always been easy to determine. Generally, the courts have ruled that the particular circumstances surrounding the search and seizure determine the reasonableness of the search and seizure. For example, warrantless searches and seizures have been allowed by the courts when it could be demonstrated that circumstances made it unfeasible to obtain a warrant. Consequently, the constitutionality of certain search and seizure tactics has often been decided on a case-to-case basis, creating great uncertainty in search and seizure law. But one thing is certain: Evidence obtained through illegal searches and seizures cannot normally be used in federal or state courts, although such evidence may be used for questioning witnesses before grand juries.[9] For our purposes, the major question is whether Fourth Amendment protections should be applied to administrative law cases that involve noncriminal, or civil, proceedings.

Historically, the prevalent attitude has been that certain Bill of Rights guarantees, such as Fourth Amendment rights, should only apply to criminal procedures, not to civil procedures. For example, Fourth Amendment safeguards have not been applied customarily to deportation proceedings involving the Immigration and Naturalization Service (INS), because such proceedings are considered civil and not criminal proceedings protected by the Bill of Rights. It was apparently not considered necessary to apply Fourth Amendment protections, as well as other Bill of Rights safeguards, to civil cases because the penalties for civil offenses were not perceived as severe enough to warrant elaborate Bill of Rights protections for individuals. Besides, it was maintained that the government could not afford to absorb the extra administrative costs for such protections and that the extension of such safeguards would make efficient and effective administration impossible.

But it would be patently naive to hold that administrative actions cannot result in the severe deprivation of a person's personal liberties since Congress, as well as state legislatures, has delegated to administrators the power to inflict grave punishments upon individuals or corporate persons without providing them with the benefit of independent judicial judgment.[10] Consequently, concerned observers have begun to question very seriously how fair it is to deny persons constitutional due process protections in certain situations just because the proceedings are labeled "civil" instead of "criminal."[11]

The Administrative Power to Arrest and Imprison

Is it possible in this civilized and free democratic country to be arrested and imprisoned for relatively long periods of time, sometimes for many months, without ever stepping into a courtroom? Shocking as it is, the answer is yes. In *Wong Wing v. United States,* 163 U.S. 228 (1896), the Court held that persons cannot be imprisoned *as a punishment* unless they are first given a criminal trial, according to constitutional requirements, and sentenced by a judicial tribunal. Such a due process safeguard has always been considered essential to any society that cherishes liberty. According to Bernard Schwartz, "the absence of nonjudicial powers of imprisonment sharply distinguishes our legal system from those we disparagingly describe as totalitarian."[12] However, it is crucial for our purposes to point out that the court in *Wong Wing* ruled explicitly that in America persons can be apprehended and sent to jail as long as the incarceration is not done with the intent to punish. In this immigration case, the Court reasoned that immigration administrators can legitimately detain or confine persons temporarily in order to carry out effectively their congressionally mandated legislative functions (p. 235).

Thus, Congress has delegated to administrators the power to arrest and imprison temporarily persons who have not been accused of or convicted of any criminal wrongdoings. But why should Congress want to give administrators the discretionary authority to arrest and imprison noncriminals? In some cases the administrative power to seize and confine persons appears quite reasonable and necessary to protect the larger interests of society, but in other situations the power seems to permit administrators to exploit and punish innocent persons in a patently unreasonable way. On the reasonable side, it seems sensible that public health administrators, to protect the public health, should have the authority to apprehend and confine those who pose a dangerous health threat to a community.[13] In *Ex parte Hardcastle*, 208 S.W. 531 (Tex. 1919), the court asserted that it makes good sense to uphold laws that call for the confinement of those who have been exposed to or are carriers of infectious diseases, even if the laws call for the confinement of such persons without the benefit of a judicial proceeding. Obviously, to protect the general welfare by preventing the spread of a contagious disease, public officials would have to possess powers to enable them to act quickly to stop such individuals from walking freely in the community. For example, the AIDS crisis caused some to recommend the radical step of rounding up and confining those with AIDS to stop the spread of the deadly disease. This suggestion has created much controversy. In fact, early in President Clinton's administration numerous Haitian refugees were detained at Guantanamo Bay Naval Base against their will for long periods of time with U.S. authorities refusing to grant them

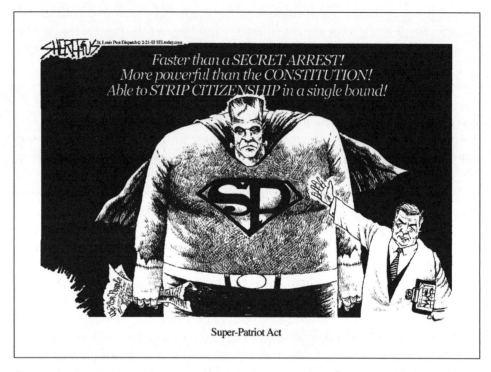

Faster than a SECRET ARREST!
More powerful than the CONSTITUTION!
Able to STRIP CITIZENSHIP in a single bound!

Super-Patriot Act

Source: Reprinted with permission of John Sherffius and the *St. Louis Post-Dispatch,* February 21, 2003.

parole because they had tested HIV-positive. Was this action fair to the refugees? A U.S. district court thought not, ruling that Attorney General Reno and other federal officials had abused their discretion by refusing to grant these Haitian refugees parole simply because they had tested HIV-positive (*Haitian Centers Council, Inc. v. Sale,* 823 F.Supp. 1028 [E.D. N.Y. 1993]). But were Attorney General Reno and the other federal authorities just trying to promote America's public health and safety? In 2003, the threat of SARS spreading rapidly in America cause health officials to consider taking various drastic and restrictive measures to protect Americans.

The vital questions seem to be: When do seizures and confinements become unreasonable and unjustified, even in light of administrative efforts to promote the public interest? How much should the individual be expected to suffer for the good of the public welfare? The public has an interest in a public prosecutor's being able to prosecute a murder case successfully. Therefore, it may be in the interest of the prosecutor to hold a key material witness to a murder in jail until the trial. But how long should the prosecutor be allowed to detain the witness—days, weeks, many months? Continued postponements of trial dates have been known to push trial dates back for months, possibly delaying the trial's outcome for more than a year. Can any society in good conscience hold a material witness, guilty of no crime, in jail for such a long period of time?[14] Should an INS administrator be permitted to seize and incarcerate for months, without benefit of bail, an illegal alien, whose deportability is being determined by the INS? Are not such administrative arrests and detentions flatly contrary to the spirit of the Fourth Amendment, however technically legal they may be in the eyes of the courts?[15] Is not a legal system rather strange if it provides more due process protections from arrests and imprisonment to those accused of violent crimes than to those accused of no criminal conduct at all?

Abel v. United States, 362 U.S. 217 (1960), is an excellent case for conveying the potential dangers behind the use of administrative arrests and detentions. Specifically, the case serves to demonstrate how an administrative official, with powers granted by Congress, can work with law enforcement officers to undermine Fourth Amendment safeguards. Abel was a Soviet spy who the FBI believed was engaged in espionage activities against the United States. Upon learning about his whereabouts, the FBI wanted to arrest him at his hotel, but FBI officers lacked enough evidence against him to satisfy the probable cause requirement needed before a judge would be willing to sign an arrest warrant. To circumvent the constitutional red tape, those FBI agents sought the assistance of INS officials. Having been told by the FBI that Abel was an illegal alien, the district director of the INS made out an arrest warrant. Both FBI and INS officers then went to Abel's hotel with the administrative arrest warrant to make the arrest. This FBI-INS cooperative effort allowed the FBI to obtain an arrest that the FBI alone would not have been able to make if it had to uphold Fourth Amendment due process restrictions. After the arrest, Abel was placed in solitary confinement for five weeks at a detention camp. It was not until criminal charges were finally filed against him that the judicial branch was brought into his case.

The Court in *Abel* had to decide whether the administrative procedures leading to the arrest and imprisonment of Abel were lawful under the Fourth Amendment. Specifically, Abel had charged that the arrest was unconstitutional because the arrest warrant did not satisfy the Fourth Amendment's warrant requirements. However, the court upheld the constitutionality of such "standard" INS arrest procedures (p. 233).

From the very beginning this decision attracted heated protests from liberal critics who believed that the ruling sanctioned actions against individuals that the constitutional framers, in writing the Fourth Amendment, definitely wanted to prevent. In a dissent to *Abel* Justice William J. Brennan argued that the Fourth Amendment was written to prevent such violations of a person's basic rights. Brennan made the point that under this administrative arrest, where no judicial voice was heard, the INS never had to justify any of its actions to an independent judge. Clearly, he maintained, some judicial control over such administrative actions are needed to preserve constitutional due process requirements (pp. 248–256).

However, not all lower courts have always followed the controversial *Abel* holding. For example, in 1994 in *Alexander v. City and County of San Francisco,* 29 F.3d 1355, the Ninth Circuit court ruled that an administrative search warrant

obtained by health inspectors to check for health code violations did not authorize police officers to enter a home to arrest the occupant, actions that actually led
to police killing the occupant. The court stressed that prior cases, including ironically *Abel*, "make it very clear that an administrative search may not be converted
into an instrument which serves the very different needs of law enforcement officials. If it could, then all of the protections traditionally afforded against intrusions by the police would evaporate, to be replaced by the much weaker barriers
erected between citizens and other governmental agencies. It is because the mission of those agencies are less potently hostile to a citizen's interests than are the
missions of the police that the barriers may be weak as they are and still not jeopardize Fourth Amendment guarantees" (p. 1361).

Three years after *Abel*, in *United States v. Alvarado*, 321 F.2d 336 (2nd Cir.
1963), the court upheld the constitutionality of an administrative arrest during
which immigration authorities took even greater liberties with the Fourth
Amendment. This time, acting according to statute, they arrested an alien without first obtaining an administrative warrant.[16] In *Abel*, at least an administrative
warrant was obtained before the arrest was made. Admittedly, the administrative
warrant, as contrasted to a regular judicial warrant, does not go very far in protecting an individual under the Fourth Amendment. Nevertheless, some reasons
must be given to show cause for deportability before the administrative warrant
can be signed by an administrative officer.

What, then, is the real significance of *Abel* and *Alvarado* in light of the Fourth
Amendment? The Fourth Amendment, to reiterate, guarantees essentially that
persons cannot be subjected to "unreasonable searches and seizures." If searches
and seizures were to be carried out, the constitutional framers required probable
cause to be established before search and seizure warrants would be issued, presumably by an independent judicial officer. These quite simple constitutional
procedures seemed to provide the necessary safeguards to ensure that if searches
and seizures were executed, they would be kept within reasonable bounds, consistent with the concept of limited government. The Fourth Amendment emphasizes that its provisions "shall not be violated," and nothing in the amendment
suggests that its provisions cannot be violated by law enforcement officers but
can be violated by other governmental administrators—regardless of how the
courts have interpreted the applicability of the Fourth Amendment.

Circumstances dictate that some reasonable exceptions occasionally should be
tolerated in any laws, but it does appear that the courts went unwisely and too far
in *Abel* and *Alvarado*. The courts in *Abel* and *Alvarado* permitted law enforcement
officers (FBI and U.S. customs officials, respectively) to achieve their search,
seizure, and confinement objectives by calling upon INS agents to do the job that
they were not able to do legally under the constitutional restrictions of the
Fourth Amendment. With the information obtained from the administrative
searches, the FBI and customs officials were then able to build criminal cases
against Abel and Alvarado. Justice Douglas believed such underhanded and tricky
governmental actions defeat the noble purpose of the Fourth Amendment, and

that the facts of the *Abel* case suggest clearly "that the FBI agents wore the mask of INS to do what otherwise they could not have done. They did what they could do only if they had gone to a judicial officer pursuant to the requirements of the Fourth Amendment."[17]

The *Abel* and *Alvarado* holdings conflict with the separation of powers doctrine in that the courts in both cases allowed administrators to act as arresting officers, prosecutors, and judges. Specifically, the courts accepted as constitutional a situation in which officials from the same agency were allowed to (1) decide whether sufficient probable cause existed to justify the issuance of an arrest warrant; (2) issue the arrest warrant itself; (3) carry out the arrest; (4) conduct a general search of the premises to obtain damaging evidence to be used in a criminal trial; and (5) determine whether the arrested person should be confined. Adding further to the consolidation of administrative power under these circumstances, a prior case had upheld a statute giving such administrative officials the power to determine whether bail should be given and, if so, at what amount over $500.[18] Ironically, the courts have allowed such a concentration of power in the hands of administrators because the Fourth and Eighth Amendments were perceived to be applicable, not to such administrative actions, but to police actions against suspected criminals. But regardless of the labels given to these state actions taken against persons, Bernard Schwartz concluded that they "can scarcely conceal the reality of individuals being deprived of liberty without the essential safeguards contemplated by the Bill of Rights."[19]

Today, many legal scholars believe that the United States has gone too far in employing various rationales to deprive persons of their fundamental constitutional due process rights. In a criminal case that has considerable relevance to administrative law, a divided Supreme Court, in 1987, in *United States v. Salerno,* 107 S.Ct. 2095, upheld the constitutionality of the Bail Reform Act of 1984, 18 U.S.C., Section 3142(e), which permits courts to order pretrial detention of persons charged with serious crimes if it is felt, after a pretrial hearing, that they would impose a threat to the community. The *Salerno* holding immediately drew harsh criticism from liberal groups as well as the three dissenting justices in the case (Justices Marshall, Brennan, and Stevens). Justice Marshall started his dissent by addressing the potential tyrannical character of the Bail Reform Act: "This case brings before the Court for the first time a statute in which Congress declares that a person innocent of any crime may be jailed indefinitely . . . if the Government shows to the satisfaction of a judge that the accused is likely to commit crimes, unrelated to the pending charges, at any time in the future. Such statutes, consistent with the usages of tyranny and the excesses of what bitter experience teaches us to call the police state, have long been thought incompatible with the fundamental human rights protected by our Constitution" (pp. 2105–2106).

Justice Marshall objected vigorously to what he felt was the Court's absurd and destructive distinction between *regulatory* and *punitive* legislation, even though a similar distinction and application of the distinction had been made long ago in

Wong Wing. To Marshall, the distinction made by the majority could allow constitutional guarantees to be taken away by the state, under the administrative or regulatory rationale, any time the state felt that certain persons may in the future commit acts that would pose a danger to society. Marshall concluded: "The majority's technique for infringing this right (due process) is simple: merely redefine any measure which is claimed to be punishment as 'regulation,' and, magically, the Constitution no longer prohibits its imposition" (p. 2108). The blatant point that Marshall is making, and it has clear implications for administrative law, is that it is dangerous to uphold laws or regulations, especially when basic constitutional rights are at stake, on the premise that they serve a legitimate regulatory goal of making the community safer. Such could lead to the destruction of our cherished constitutional liberties since virtually all statutes and rules could be justified on such "regulatory interest" grounds.

However, possibly responding to the harsh criticisms it received for its *Salerno* decision, the Supreme Court in *Foucha v. Louisiana*, 112 S.Ct. 1780 (1992), softened the clout of *Salerno* by stating: "It was emphasized in *Salerno* that the detention we found constitutionally permissible was strictly limited in duration. . . . Here, in contrast, the state asserts that because Foucha once committed a criminal act and now has an antisocial personality that sometimes leads to aggressive conduct, a disorder for which there is no effective treatment, he may be held indefinitely. This rationale would permit the state to hold indefinitely any other insanity acquittee not mentally ill who could be shown to have a personality disorder that may lead to criminal conduct. . . . Freedom from physical restraint being a fundamental right, the state must have a particularly convincing reason, which it has not put forward, for such discrimination against insanity acquittees who are no longer mentally ill" (pp. 1787–1788).

But a decade later in *Kansas v. Crane*, 122 S.Ct. 867 (2002), the Supreme Court argued that Kansas' "particularly convincing reason" for civil commitment of a sexual offender need not take an "absolutist approach." That is, the court held that the State of Kansas under its sexually violent predator statute could uphold freedom guarantees under the U.S. Constitution for the sake of civil or administrative commitment of dangerous sexual predator by demonstrating psychiatric proof that the sexual predator poses a serious threat to others because of his inability to control his predatory sexual urges. Specifically citing *Foucha*, the court made clear that the state should be given discretion in the demonstration of that "proof" and that the proof need not be absolute or "demonstrable with mathematical precision. It is enough to say that there must be proof of serious difficulty in controlling behavior. And this, when viewed in light of such features of the case as the nature of the psychiatric diagnosis, and the severity of the mental abnormality itself, must be sufficient to distinguish the dangerous sexual offender whose serious mental illness, abnormality, or disorder subjects him to civil commitment from the dangerous but typical recidivist convicted in an ordinary criminal case" (p. 870).

The Administrative Power to Search and Inspect

From the perspective of administrative law, probably the most serious threat to the guarantees of individual liberty under the Fourth Amendment is posed by the power of administrative officials to employ their discretionary authority to have arrested and imprisoned, in the absence of judicial intervention, persons not charged with any criminal misconduct. Fortunately, however, administrative arrests (seizures) and detentions have been relatively uncommon, although the real threat of terrorism on U.S. soil could make them more prevalent. But administrative searches are very common. For example, at the peak of its regulatory prowess, in fiscal 1976, the Occupational Safety and Health Administration conducted 90,369 work-place inspections.[20] Typically, administrative searches are used to inspect premises (e.g., a person's house or a company's plant), documents (e.g., a person's tax receipts or a corporation's records), and regulated operations (e.g., how a chemical manufacturer complies with federal standards in disposing of its toxic wastes). Such administrative inspections may also present challenges to the right to privacy under the Fourth Amendment.

Why have Congress and state legislatures given administrators the authority to carry out administrative inspections? The reasons should appear quite obvious. As Max Weber acknowledged in his scholarly writing on public bureaucracy, the real strength of bureaucratic organizations resides in the information they collect, store, and use. To function properly, administrative agencies must be able to obtain vital information that can help them perform their assigned regulatory activities. Bernard Schwartz points out that "information is the fuel without which the administrative engine could not operate; the old saw that knowledge is power has the widest application in administrative law."[21] Actually, agencies can obtain most of the information they seek without much difficulty. In fact, much of the data they need can be found by simply referring to their own records, files elsewhere in the governmental bureaucracy, governmental publications, and other readily accessible data sources. Agency staffs can also obtain information through normal research processes that do not involve any direct investigations into the private affairs of individuals and businesses. And even if agency administrators feel that they must obtain certain information from persons and businesses, most times such private parties cooperate rather cheerfully, freely disclosing to these governmental officials what they want to know. There are occasions, however, when individuals and businesses believe that requests for information, frequently in the form of physical administrative inspections, encroach too far upon their right to privacy as protected by the Fourth Amendment. When such resistance occurs, administrators can compel private parties to disclose to them the information they want, sometimes by forcing them to submit to administrative inspections, as long as statutes permit such investigations. Almost all agencies do possess such statutory power. Actually, to protect the administrative investigatory function from possible impotence, virtually all agencies have been given the weapon of the administrative subpoena. It was established in *Cudahy Packing Co. v. Holland,* 315 U.S. 357, 363 (1942), that the administrative subpoena can be employed coercively to subpoena records and witnesses.

A Note on the Record-Keeping Requirement.   Since the beginning of our Republic, it has always been recognized that it is necessary to effective governmental administration to require private parties to keep essential records and present reports to which the government, for the sake of the general welfare, has a legitimate regulatory interest. Consequently, legislated statutes have routinely included record-keeping and reporting provisions.

Obviously, regulatory agencies could not be expected to regulate if the regulated did not need to keep records of its activities. That is, to see whether an industry has been complying with required statutes and rules, the regulatory agency would have to review the industry's records and its reports. For example, how could the FCC decide on whether to renew the license of a television station if the station was not required to keep records and submit reports that help to provide the FCC with valuable information on how well the particular station has complied with approved standards of television broadcasting in the past? To anyone who understands the nature of the governmental regulatory process, it is quite clear that regulatory activities are interrelated and that specific regulatory functions relate to and are dependent upon one another. For instance, record keeping, inspections, and licensing are mutually dependent upon one another. That is, standard and sensible licensing practices require that information pertinent to licensing requirements must be inspected and evaluated periodically so that intelligent decisions can be reached regarding whether licenses should be granted, denied, renewed, or suspended.

The record-keeping and reporting requirements have never faced serious legal challenges.[22] The courts have held in general that the record-keeping requirement does not violate the Constitution as long as "there is a sufficient relation between the activity sought to be regulated and the public concern so that the government can constitutionally regulate or forbid the basic activity concerned, and can constitutionally require the keeping of particular records, subject to inspection by the administration" (*Shapiro v. United States,* 335 U.S. 1, 32 [1948]). Earlier, the Supreme Court held in *United States v. Darby,* 312 U.S. 100, 125 (1941): "The requirement for records . . . is an appropriate means to a legitimate end." According to the high court in *United States v. Morton Salt Co.,* 338 U.S. 632, 652 (1950), even legitimate "official curiosity" can justify agencies to compel parties to keep records because such agencies as the FTC "have legitimate right to satisfy themselves that corporate behavior is consistent with the law and the public interest." Naturally, however, limits must be placed upon an agency's appetite to satisfy its "official curiosity." Once again, the primary task in a democratic system is to try to balance the government's need to obtain information in the public interest with the Fourth Amendment's privacy rights for persons. Regarding record keeping, the only constitutional limitation under the Fourth Amendment seems to be, as expressed in *Shapiro* and many other cases, that record-keeping and reporting requirements be confined to regulatory activities sanctioned by statute. Such records can be required because they are considered in reality *public* records. To satisfy an agency's curiosity, officials cannot require private parties to keep records and submit reports that have no legitimate regulatory value. Such agency requirements would constitute an unfounded invasion of a person's purely *private* affairs.[23]

Fourth Amendment Limitations on Administrative Inspections.   In a genuinely free society (of course, within the limits of what is necessary to maintain socioeconomic and political stability), persons should be protected from unreasonable encroachments upon their personal privacy, whether the intention of the state's search is to uncover criminal evidence or to discover code violations in a person's home or business. Although heated arguments still persist over whether administrative inspections should be restricted by Fourth Amendment provisions, it is clear that personal liberties cannot survive in a nation if governmental officials show wanton disrespect for a person's right to privacy. It is therefore obvious that if personal privacy rights are to be protected, no governmental officials can be allowed to intrude at their discretion into a person's private life, whether the public officials be FBI agents or OSHA inspectors. The Court in *United States v. Martinez-Fuerte,* 428 U.S. 543, 569 (1976), made the point that limits must restrict official intrusions into the private affairs of others or administrative tyranny will surely result. As the Court emphasized in *Wolf v. Colorado,* 338 U.S. 25, 27 (1949), protection against arbitrary invasions of a person's privacy is fundamental to the preservation of a free society; it is at the core of the Fourth Amendment. To permit any public administrator to exercise unconfined, unstructured, and unchecked discretion is to place the liberty of everyone and every business at the absolute discretion of any administrator who has an interest in anyone's personal or business affairs. Such a situation would surely spell the end of freedom. The freedom fighter Justice William O. Douglas conveyed this point succinctly in his dissent in *New York v. United States,* 342 U.S. 882, 884 (1951): "Absolute discretion, like corruption, marks the beginning of the end of liberty." And in *California v. Hodari D.,* 111 S.Ct. 1547, 1561 (1991), dissenting justices Stevens and Marshall, criticizing the Court majority's lack of respect for the Fourth Amendment's protective rights, warned, quoting Justice Brandeis, that our constitutional framers conferred upon us "'the right to be let alone—the most comprehensive of rights and the right most valued by civilized men. To protect that right, every unjustifiable intrusion by the Government upon the privacy of the individual, whatever the means employed, must be deemed a violation of the Fourth Amendment.'"

It should not be overlooked that totalitarian governments retain their position of dominance over their citizenry by allowing their state officers to exercise shockingly broad discretionary powers to spy on persons and business operations, as well as to search and seize individuals and their property. Because personal freedom poses a threat to the survival of totalitarian regimes, governmental laws are typically aimed at destroying individual liberties (for example, freedom of speech, freedom of the press, and the right to be free from unreasonable searches and seizures). In police states, very few, if any, searches and seizures are perceived by governmental authorities as unreasonable. The right to privacy carries little meaning in such regimes, where state rights are considered far superior to individual rights. In reflecting upon the character of totalitarian states, Ronald Bacigal concluded: "Unchecked power to search and seize is crucial to the maintenance of a totalitarian state."[24]

The causes of tyranny were well known and publicized by the founders of our nation. A reading of *The Federalist* would convince anyone of this. The colonists, under British rule, had become quite sensitive to the abuses and excesses of governmental power. As a matter of historical fact, it was largely the reactions by the colonists to oppressive British rule that caused the American Revolution. It is in this context that Justice Felix Frankfurter exclaimed in his dissent to *United States v. Rabinowitz,* 339 U.S. 56, 69 (1950), that the drafting of the Fourth Amendment's "unreasonable searches and seizures" provision must be understood. The precise intent of the constitutional framers in including the Fourth Amendment in the Constitution cannot be known for sure, as no records were kept, but the Supreme Court in *Chimel v. California,* 395 U.S. 752–763 (1969), contended that credible historians have acknowledged that the Bill of Rights's authors, who had suffered at the hands of oppressive British governors, wanted future generations of Americans protected against arbitrary intrusions into their private affairs by any governmental officials.

But how have the courts applied the Fourth Amendment to administrative searches, which mostly involve inspections aimed at discovering whether persons and businesses are complying with various agency regulations in the areas of health (including perceived moral health), safety, and welfare? Once again, because the regulatory activities of the emerging administrative state are relatively new to the American scene, well-established law on how the Fourth Amendment should be applied to administrative intrusions into the private practices of individuals and businesses has not yet developed. Opinions on how the Fourth Amendment should apply to administrative searches have varied greatly from court to court and even within the same courts. In 1971 in *Wyman v. James,* 400 U.S. 309, for example, the Supreme Court said essentially that administrative inspections were not searches restricted by the Fourth Amendment since they are not intended to produce evidence that could be used in criminal prosecutions. However, two decades earlier, in *Rabinowitz,* the high court recognized that search and seizure standards must be applied to administrative officials to prevent capricious and malicious administrative behavior.

To help clarify the Supreme Court's position on the applicability of the Fourth Amendment to administrative inspections, Kevin MacKenzie, several years ago, classified Supreme Court decisions in this area into three general categories. His categories still remain very helpful. In the first category, he includes the cases of *Camara v. Municipal Court,* 387 U.S. 523 (1967), *See v. City of Seattle,* 387 U.S.

541 (1957), and *Marshall v. Barlow's, Inc.*, 436 U.S. 307 (1978). In each of these cases, the Court held that governmental officials must, as a general rule, obtain a search warrant before they can force an individual or company to undergo an inspection. MacKenzie's second category includes the cases of *Colonnade Catering Corp. v. United States*, 397 U.S. 72 (1970), and *United States v. Biswell*, 406 U.S. 311(1972). In these two cases, because the businesses were already closely supervised by regulatory agencies, the Court felt it was reasonable to except such businesses from the normal warrant requirement. MacKenzie includes in the third grouping *United States v. Martinez-Fuerte*, 428 U.S. 543 (1976), and *South Dakota v. Opperman*, 428 U.S. 364 (1976). In these two cases, the Supreme Court also believed an exception to the warrant requirement was justified, but here because adequate administrative safeguards already existed to protect privacy interests in much the same way a search warrant would. A review of what the cases in these three categories seem to establish helps one better understand the present judicial position on the Fourth Amendment's applicability to administrative inspections. The cases MacKenzie places into his three categories are reviewed, along with more recent cases bringing us into the twenty-first century.[25]

Cases Promoting the Administrative Search Warrant Requirement.
Camara, See, Barlow's, Inc., Dow Chemical, Riley, and *Kyllo.* In both *Frank v. Maryland*, 359 U.S. 360 (1959), and in *Ohio ex rel. Eaton v. Price*, 364 U.S. 263 (1960), the Supreme Court took the position that administrative officials could conduct reasonable inspections without first having to obtain an administrative search warrant. However, in *Camara* and *See*, both decisions handed down on the same day, the Supreme Court reversed its attitude toward warrantless administrative inspections and argued that warrantless administrative inspections are unconstitutional because they violate the Fourth Amendment's provision that prohibits the government from carrying out unreasonable searches against persons. The Court held in *Camara*: "except in certain carefully defined classes of cases, a search of private property without proper consent is 'unreasonable' unless it has been authorized by a valid search warrant" (pp. 528–529).

Prior to *Camara* and *See*, it was uncertain whether the warrant requirement of the Fourth Amendment, if applied to administrative searches, should apply to business establishments, as well as to individuals. But in *Camara* and *See* the Court made it very clear that both individuals and businesses have a constitutional right to be protected against warrantless searches by administrators. In *See*, the Supreme Court reiterated what it had just finished saying in *Camara*: "As we explained in Camara, a search of private houses is presumptively unreasonable if conducted without a warrant. The businessman, like the occupant of a residence, has a constitutional right to go about his business free from unreasonable official entries upon his private commercial property. The businessman, too, has that right placed in jeopardy if the decision to enter and inspect for violations of regulatory laws can be made and enforced by the inspector in the field without official authority evidenced by a warrant" (p. 543).

The *Camara* and *See* rulings also answered another vital administrative question that had been left unresolved. By 1967, when the *Camara* and *See* opinions were reached, it had been well established that the Fourth Amendment's guarantee against warrantless searches did apply to criminal investigations, but it was widely questioned whether the Amendment's warrantless search clause should be made applicable to civil or administrative searches. However, the *Camara* Court presented a well-developed, forceful argument that the Fourth Amendment protects persons and businesses against warrantless invasions of their privacy, whether the investigations are civil or criminal in nature.

Rejecting the reasoning in *Frank,* which had upheld the constitutionality of a warrantless administrative inspection of private premises, the Court in *Camara* reasoned that in a free society the Fourth Amendment should be applied broadly so that privacy rights are properly respected. The Court further rejected the majority's contention in *Frank* that administrative inspections such as health and safety inspections are covered only "peripherally" by the Fourth Amendment: "But we cannot agree that the Fourth Amendment interests at stake in these inspection cases are merely 'peripheral.' It is surely anomalous to say that the individual and his private property are fully protected by the Fourth Amendment only when the individual is suspected of criminal behavior" (p. 530). The Supreme Court in *Camara* emphasized that Fourth Amendment privacy rights should be respected in administrative searches because in practice discovered violations may lead to criminal charges, prosecution, fines, and even jail sentences for the offenders. In some cases, the Court noted, refusal to comply with an administrative compliance order is in itself a criminal offense (p. 531). To the Court, warrantless searches, as upheld in Frank, "unduly discount the purposes behind the warrant machinery contemplated by the Fourth Amendment" (p. 532). "The basic purpose of the Fourth Amendment, according to the *Camara* Court, is to safeguard the privacy and security of individuals against arbitrary invasions by governmental officials" (p. 528). Without the warrant requirement in administrative searches, the Court reasoned, privacy rights are threatened unnecessarily by administrative inspectors because "when the inspector demands entry, the occupant has no way of knowing whether enforcement of the municipal code involved requires inspection of his premises, no way of knowing the lawful limits of the inspector's power to search, and no way of knowing whether the inspector himself is acting under proper authorization. These are questions which may be reviewed by a neutral magistrate without any reassessment of the basic agency decision to canvass an area" (p. 532).

In 1978 the Supreme Court, in *Barlow's, Inc.,* affirmed and expanded upon its holdings in *Camara* and *See.* This time the Court ruled that Section 8(a) of the Occupational Safety and Health Act of 1970 (29 USCS Sec. 657[a]), which authorizes warrantless searches by OSHA inspectors, violates the search warrant provisions of the Fourth Amendment. Specifically, the Court rejected the argument by the secretary of labor, in whose department OSHA is housed, that warrantless inspections of business premises are constitutional, although such searches of private dwellings may not be. In an attempt to put to rest the skepticism over whether the constitutional framers intended the Fourth Amendment's provisions to apply to business establishments, the Court built a fairly convincing case to support its contention that the Founding Fathers definitely intended to protect business proprietors against unreasonable invasions of their privacy. Drawing from historians, the *Barlow's, Inc.* Court noted that general administrative search warrants were included in the Virginia Bill of Rights, which the Court noted has been recognized as the basic model for the Bill of Rights. The Court argued that it was common historical knowledge that such legislation as the 1765 Stamp Act, the 1767 Townshend Revenue Act, and the 1773 tea tax were found to be particularly offensive to colonial businessmen and merchants because these acts gave British colonial administrators virtually unlimited discretion to inspect the premises, products, and records of American businessmen and merchants. The Court had noted only a year before, in *United States v. Chadwick,* that "the Fourth Amendment's commands grew in large measure out of the colonists' experience with the writs of assistance . . . (that) granted sweeping power to customs officials and other agents of the King to search at large for smuggled goods" (p. 311). "Against this background," the Court concluded, "it is untenable that the ban on warrantless searches was not intended to shield places of business as well as of residence" (p. 312).

In *Barlow's, Inc.,* the Court was very careful to point out that in obtaining an administrative search warrant, governmental officials do not have to demonstrate probable cause in the same strict manner as is required of law enforcement officers seeking warrants for criminal investigations. To protect the privacy interests of private businesses, the Court held that administrative officials need only show that the searches or inspections are (1) authorized by statute; (2) serve and are consistent with legislative goals and standards; (3) based in a "general administrative plan" necessary to enforce the legislation; and (4) going to be carried out against a specific business cited on the warrant (pp. 309, 320).

The Court in *Barlow's, Inc.,* did a fairly commendable job in placing into a balanced perspective business privacy interests with the legitimate interests of agency administrators trying to perform their mandated regulatory functions. The Court made its position clear: It would not tolerate warrantless searches of the premises of businesses simply because the intrusions into private areas were being conducted for administrative regulatory purposes and not for the collection of criminal evidence. Reiterating much of what was said previously in *Camara* and *See,* the Court stressed the dangers of the warrantless searches and emphasized the value of the Fourth Amendment's warrant requirement. In particular, it noted that the warrantless search allows administrators to enjoy almost unbridled discretionary power as to when, what, and whose premises ought to be searched: "A warrant, by contrast, would provide assurances for a neutral officer that the inspection is reasonable under the Constitution, is authorized by statute, and is pursuant to an administrative plan containing specific neutral criteria. Also, a warrant would then and there advise the owner of the scope and objects of the search, beyond which limits the inspector is not expected to proceed" (p. 323).

The Court did not adopt the general warrant requirement rule for administrative inspections without first considering the possible burden the warrant requirement might have on administrators. It rejected the argument that the warrant requirement would place a heavy strain on the administrative regulatory system and the courts, making administrative regulation in particular less effective. For one thing, the Court noted, most businesses would consent to the inspections without demanding that the administrators obtain a warrant first.[26] In rebuttal to the specific argument that "surprise searches" are necessary to promote "inspection efficiency," the Court pointed out that after inspectors are refused entry, they can then obtain an ex parte warrant and reappear at the business site at any reasonable "surprise time" they desire, since inspectors need not provide any further notice (pp. 317–320).[27] *Barlow's, Inc.* is an important case because it established a strong precedent that under normal conditions (i.e., when special circumstances do not permit a warrantless search) administrative search warrants must be obtained before a search can be conducted (*Dolan v. City of Tigord*, 114 S.Ct. 2309 [1994]; *U.S. v. Tarkowski*, 248 F.3d 596 [7th Cir. 2001]; and *Chao v. Transocean; Offshore Inc.*, 276 F.3d 725 [5th Cir. 2002]). In *Tarkowski*, for example, the court scolded the EPA for thinking it could ignore the Fourth Amendment's search limitations, as developed in *Barlow's*, just because the EPA was "just doing test borings and other investigative work. That such orders must comply with the Fourth Amendment is apparent from *Marshall v. Barlow's Inc.*" (p. 599).

In 1986 in *Dow Chemical Co. v. United States,* 106 S.Ct. 1819, the Supreme Court handed down a decision rooted in what many may perceive as enigmatic judicial logic. Refusing to overrule the warrant requirement for the administrative searches of business premises as established in *Camara, See,* and *Barlow's, Inc.,* yet upholding a warrantless search of the grounds of Dow Chemical Company by the Environmental Protection Agency, the Court ruled that the EPA's warrantless search was lawful because the "search" really didn't constitute a search under the Fourth Amendment. The facts are these. The EPA wanted to conduct an on-site inspection of Dow Chemical's 2000-acre chemical plant that is under tight security and hidden from ground-level public view. However, Dow refused to allow the inspection. Instead of obtaining an administrative search warrant (this is perplexing because such warrants are normally very easy to obtain), the EPA hired an aerial photographer, using a standard aerial mapping camera, to take photographs of Dow's facilities. All photographs were taken at legal altitudes. Learning of the aerial photographic search of its plant, Dow filed suit, charging that the EPA's warrantless investigative actions constituted an illegal search extending beyond the EPA's statutory investigative authority, which violated Dow's right to privacy under the Fourth Amendment.

Unsympathetic to Dow's allegations, the Supreme Court argued that the EPA's aerial search was within the agency's statutory authority, not only because Congress did not prohibit such searches specifically, but also because the EPA must be able to conduct investigations or searches to carry out its mandated regulatory mission (in this case, enforcing the provisions of Section 114(a) of the Clean Air Act). The Court also maintained that the aerial search did not constitute a search under Fourth Amendment protection because the "search" was conducted in lawful navigable air space open to the public and was done with standard aerial photography equipment that only enhanced human vision and was commonly used by aerial mappers. Although the Court found no constitutional problems in the use of this equipment to conduct searches, it implied that more sophisticated aerial spy equipment may pose constitutional problems under the Fourth Amendment (pp. 1823–1824).

It must be stressed that the Supreme Court rested its precedential decision in search law mostly on the contention that the EPA's "search" was not a search subject to Fourth Amendment due process privacy protections because the area "searched" was similar to a public or "open field" where no legitimate demand for privacy can be demanded (p. 1821). Regarding such aerial searches of companies, the Court explained "that the open areas of an industrial plant complex with numerous plant structures spread over an area of 2,000 acres are not analogous to the 'cartilage' of a dwelling for purposes of aerial surveillance; such an industrial complex is more comparable to an open field and as such is open to the view and observation of persons in aircraft lawfully in the public airspace immediately above or sufficiently near the area for the reach of cameras." Therefore, the Court held "that the taking of aerial photographs of an industrial plant complex from navigable airspace is not a search prohibited by the Fourth Amendment" (p. 1827). A divided Supreme Court in *Florida v. Riley*, 109 S.Ct. 693, 705 (1989), also upheld the constitutionality of warrantless aerial searches, even though dissenting justices Brennan, Marshall, and Stevens (Justice Blackmun wrote a separate dissenting opinion) thought such searches could sanction George Orwell's dreaded vision of Big Brother watching us.[28] Although this involved a helicopter police search, *Riley* has implications for warrantless administrative searches because the courts apply less strict Fourth Amendment restrictions when administrative searches are involved.

In sum, the significance of *Dow Chemical* is that it upholds the warrant requirement for legitimate Fourth Amendment searches that normally involve intimate inspections—as established in *Camara, See,* and *Barlow's, Inc.*—because most businesses have a reasonable expectation of privacy, but regulatory agencies do not require warrants for certain kinds of searches that can be classified as nonintimate and nondetailed inspections and that could be conducted by anyone in the general public.

However, Lisa Steele is very concerned that new technologies, and the general judicial sympathy for such searches, will allow invasive, "intimate" warrantless searches, thus bringing "Orwell's vision closer to reality."[29] Since *Dow Chemical*, federal, state, and local governments have been experimenting with various new technologies that have allowed "Big Brother" to get a better peek at what businesses and citizens are doing. For example, sophisticated radar equipment can produce high-resolution radar images (reflections) by sending a high-energy pulse at objects in homes and businesses or within the "cartilage" of these homes and businesses. Infrared sensors have been used to detect infrared light and heat through the walls of homes and businesses, while aerial searches of "open fields" within the "cartilage" of private homes and businesses can be conducted from space by high-tech satellite equipment.

Unfortunately, in recent years courts have used all sorts of rationales, some patently absurd, to justify high-tech governmental searches. Often, courts have argued that such searches are reasonable and the person or place being searched had no reasonable expectation of privacy because the high-tech equipment "only assisted" or "materially enhanced" the natural senses or that the equipment used is "widely available commercially" or that the searched party did not do enough to guarantee privacy, such as stopping detectable heat losses from a structure, or that the person did too much to guarantee privacy, thus creating reasonable suspicion to justify a search warrant, or that the searched party "knew or should have known that he was observable" even if the observation was made from a distance high above the ground.[30] Steele concludes that the courts should carefully examine the implications of such high-tech searches on our Fourth Amendment privacy rights.[31]

However, in 2001, the Supreme Court in *Kyllo v. U.S.*, 121 S.Ct. 2038, ruled that hi-tech searches have their limits under the Fourth Amendment, especially when they are used by governmental officials to conduct searches of a person's home. In this case, an agent from the Department of Interior conducted a warrantless administrative search of Kyllo's home using a thermal imaging device from public streets to scan for "hot spots," which would suggest that high-intensity heat lamps were being used to grow marijuana plants. Although the Department tried to defend the warrantless search on the grounds that such "nonsearches" were allowed under *Dow Chemical* and the search did not reveal intimate details of Kyllo's life inside his home, the Court's slim 5–4 majority vehemently rejected the government's position. Regarding *Dow Chemical*, the majority pointed out several differences, but its main argument was that "Dow Chemical . . . involved enhanced aerial photography of an industrial complex, which does not share the Fourth Amendment sanctity of the home." Furthermore, regarding the government's contention that the thermal imaging search did not expose intimate behavioral details, the majority held that a violation of a person's Fourth Amendment privacy rights in his home has nothing to do with the kind of information found in the search. "The Fourth Amendment's protection of the home has never been tied to the measurement of the quality or quantity of information obtained. . . . In the home, our cases show, *all* details are intimate details, because the entire area is held safe from prying government eyes" (p. 2045).

The *Kyllo* majority made one point very clear: There is a very strong presumption against warrantless searches of private homes. Quoting *Payton v. New York*,

445 U.S. 573 (1980), the Court reiterated: "We have said that the Fourth Amendment draws 'a firm line at the entrance to the house.' . . . The Fourth Amendment is to be construed in light of what was deemed an unreasonable search and seizure when it was adopted, and in a manner which will conserve public interests as well as the interests and rights of individual citizens" (p. 2046) (parenthetically, here is a blatant example of the Court's use the balance doctrine as reflected in this chapter's title).

The *Kyllo* majority also acknowledged that modern technologies present new challenges to Fourth Amendment privacy protections (and they listed many of these new technologies), but the Court insisted that it must follow the restrictive course established in *Katz* because "reversing that approach would leave the homeowner at the mercy of advancing technology—including imaging technology that could discern all human activity in the home" (p. 2044). In sum, *Kyllo* offers some hope that the Supreme Court is concerned about advancing search technologies and the potential for abuses of protected privacy rights by overzealous public officials. *Kyllo*, however, narrowly tailors its decision to only private homes, leaving open the question of how the Court would feel about using modern technologies to breach the walls of businesses that normal vision could not penetrate. Of course, the *Kyllo* Court would not have found anything wrong with the use of thermal-imaging to search Kyllo's home if the DOI agent had obtained an administrative search warrant, which probably would have been very easy to obtain.[32]

A final point on the search warrant requirement is worth noting. It is not always easy for the Court, in light of the specific facts in unique circumstances, to tell, first, whether the search is actually a search under the Fourth Amendment and, second, whether the facts suggest that a search warrant was required. As the Court said in *U.S. v. Nicholson*, 144 F.3d 632 (10th Cir. 1998), quoting *Arizona v. Hicks*, 480 U.S. 321, 329 (1987), "'An apparently small difference in the factual situation frequently is viewed as a controlling difference in determining Fourth Amendment rights'" (p. 640). For example, in *Nicholson*, the Court ruled that a drug enforcement agent violated a bus traveler's expectation of privacy under the Fourth Amendment by not touching his luggage under the acceptable "plain touch" standard but instead "manipulating" his carry-on luggage with his hands in order to feel whether the contents included drugs. The Court held that the traveler's privacy rights were violated because the agent was not free to manipulate the "carry-on bag in any manner."

Cases Upholding Exceptions to the Warrant Requirement When Activities Are Already Tightly Regulated: *Donovan, Pullin, Shoemaker, Krull,* and *Crosby*.   To understand the Court's decision in *Barlow's, Inc.,* clearly, it is crucial to acknowledge that the Court, while upholding *Camara* and *See,* took a rather flexible position over the warrant requirement and did not rigidly hold that it was necessary to obtain an administrative warrant under all inspection or search circumstances. Actually, the Court in *Barlow's, Inc.,* acknowledged (p. 313) that administrative search warrants are not necessary if the businesses subject to searches are already "pervasively regulated" *(Biswell,* p. 316) and "closely regulated" industries which have been under tight governmental control for a long time (*Colonnade Catering Corp.,* p. 76). However, the Court stressed that the *Biswell* and *Colonnade Catering Corp.* decisions represent reactions to "relatively unique circumstances." Therefore, these holdings cannot be applied generally to the more normal situations, as existed in *Barlow's, Inc.,* where it is necessary to protect the privacy interests of businesses by requiring administrative search warrants if consent to search premises, papers, and so on, is refused to inspectors (pp. 313–316).

What were the unique circumstances that existed in both *Colonnade Catering Corp.* and *Biswell* that convinced the Supreme Court that agency officials should be permitted to carry out warrantless searches? How did these circumstances differ from the situation that existed in *Barlow's, Inc.?* In *Colonnade Catering Corp.,* federal inspectors, under federal legislation regulating licensed dealers in alcoholic beverages, forcibly entered a locked liquor storeroom and illegally seized stored liquor. The federal inspectors did this without a search warrant. The Court held that, although the statutes did not provide for forcible entry, inspectors could execute warrantless searches, as authorized by federal statutes, because the liquor business had historically been a heavily regulated industry in order "to meet the evils at hand" (p. 76).

A similar situation existed in *Biswell,* only this time a federal treasury agent searched an unlocked storeroom and seized illegally kept sawed-off rifles. Biswell, a pawnshop operator licensed to deal in sporting weapons, but not sawed-off rifles, at first refused to allow the search but then permitted it after the inspector cited the Gun Control Act of 1968 (18 U.S.C.A., Section 923), which allows such warrantless searches. The chief issue in *Biswell* was whether the statute that authorized warrantless searches was constitutional. The *Biswell* Court believed that the circumstances in *Colonnade Catering Corp.* and *Biswell* were very similar because both cases involved statutes authorizing warrantless searches of federally licensed dealers trading in goods (liquor and firearms) that the federal government historically had a very serious interest in regulating: "Federal regulation of the interstate traffic in firearms is not as deeply rooted in history as is governmental control of the liquor industry, but close scrutiny of this traffic is undeniably of central importance in federal efforts to prevent violent crime and to assist the States in regulating the firearms traffic within their borders. . . . Large interests are at stake, and inspection is a crucial part of the regulatory scheme" (p. 315).

The *Biswell* Court perceived a significant difference between the inspection in *See* and the inspection here. Justice Byron White, speaking for the majority in *Biswell,* pointed out that in *See* a warrantless search was found to be unreasonable and, therefore, unconstitutional under the Fourth Amendment because inspectors sought only to discover whether building codes and the like had been violated, conditions fairly difficult to rectify in a hurry. Thus, the *See* Court concluded rightly that warrantless searches constituted unnecessary intrusions of privacy under the circumstances. But in *Biswell,* the regulation of dangerous firearms is involved. The Court claimed: "Here, if inspection is to be effective and serve as a credible deterrent, unannounced, even frequent, inspections are essential. In this context, the prerequisite of a warrant could easily frustrate inspection; and if the necessary flexibility as to time, scope and frequency is to be preserved, the protections afforded by a warrant would be negligible" (p. 316).

To justify its ruling in *Biswell* that warrantless searches are constitutional in this special area of "urgent federal interest," the Court reasoned: "When a dealer chooses to engage in this pervasively regulated business and to accept a federal license, he does so with the knowledge that his business records, firearms and ammunition will be subject to effective inspection" (p. 316). This reasoning has been severely criticized by many administrative law scholars who hold that it is absurd to maintain that any businessperson knowingly and willfully surrenders Fourth Amendment rights when entering even closely regulated licensed businesses.[33] For example, Kevin MacKenzie argues that it is unsound to base a decision, not upon the genuine reasonableness of the actual inspection, but upon the fictional grounds that those "pervasively regulated" have given their "implied consent" to be, in effect, unreasonably searched. He acknowledges that lower federal courts have already started the dangerous practice of employing the unacceptable "implied consent" rule to settle cases quickly without probing the real constitutional issues.[34]

Several more recent decisions uphold the constitutionality of warrantless administrative searches under the "pervasively regulated" rationale, as established in *Colonnade Catering Corp.* and *Biswell.* In *Donovan v. Dewey,* 452 U.S. 594 (1981), relying heavily on its argument for "pervasively regulated" businesses as developed in *Biswell,* the Supreme Court ruled that the warrantless search of stone quarries, as required by Section 103(a) of the Federal Mine Safety and Health Act of 1977, does not violate the Fourth Amendment. The Court asserted that "it is undisputed that there is a substantial federal interest in improving the health and safety conditions in the Nation's underground and surface mines. In enacting the statute, Congress was plainly aware that the mining industry is among the most hazardous in the country and that the poor health and safety record of this industry has significant deleterious effects on interstate commerce. Nor is it seriously contested that Congress in this case would reasonably determine, as it did with respect to the Gun Control Act in *Biswell,* that a system of warrantless inspections was necessary 'if the law is to be properly enforced and inspection made effective. . . . ' In designing an inspection program, Congress expressly recognized that a warrant requirement could significantly frustrate effective enforcement of the Act. Thus, it provided in Section 103(a) of the Act 'no advance notice of inspection shall be provided to any person.'" In addition, the Court noted that "the Act is specifically tailored to address those concerns, and the regulation of mines it imposes is sufficiently pervasive and defined that the owner of such a facility cannot help but be aware that he 'will be subject to effective inspections'" (pp. 602–603). More recently, the argument presented in *Donovan* that "exigent circumstances" permit exceptions to the warrant requirement was upheld in *O'Brien v. City of Grand Rapids*, 23 F.3d 990, 997 (6th Cir. 1994).

In *Pullin v. Louisiana State Racing Comm'n*, 477 So.2d 683 (1985), the Supreme Court of Louisiana upheld a warrantless search of a race track barn that led to the discovery of drugs prohibited in the horse barns. The seized drugs were then used as evidence in an administrative hearing conducted by the Louisiana Racing Commission that resulted in the suspension of Vernon Pullin, a licensed horse owner and trainer who owned the seized drugs. Pullin sought judicial review of the commission's decision, arguing that evidence seized in the warrantless search of the barn violated his Fourth Amendment rights. Drawing on *Biswell* and *Donovan*, the court held that the warrantless search did not violate Pullin's Fourth Amendment privacy rights because he was in "a closely regulated and licensed business" and, therefore, "consents to certain restrictions on his expectation of privacy" (p. 686). Elaborating further, the court emphasized that "because horse racing is a strictly regulated activity, licenses to participate in the sport are only issued under certain terms and conditions. . . . Among other things, a licensee must agree to being searched within the grounds of a racing association." This type of consent is valid, *despite the element of coercion* (my emphasis) (pp. 686–687).

The Third Circuit Court of Appeals reached a similar conclusion a year later in *Shoemaker v. Handel*, 795 F.2d 1136 (1986), a well-publicized case because several famous horse racing jockeys, including William Shoemaker and Angel Cordero, brought suit against the New Jersey Racing Commission, charging that warrantless random breath and urine testing of jockeys violated their Fourth Amendment privacy protections. The court disagreed, contending that the administrative search exception (reduced privacy expectation) applies in this case because employees in such a heavily regulated business as horse racing have necessarily limited privacy expectations, especially considering the state's strong interest in assuring the public of the integrity of those engaged in the business (p. 1142).

In *Illinois v. Krull*, 107 S.Ct. 1160 (1987), the Supreme Court extended the pervasively regulated rule, established in *Colonnade-Biswell-Donovan* (allowing warrantless searches of liquor dealers, gun dealers, and mine operators, respectively), to cover auto parts dealers (in this case, a wrecking yard dealer selling used auto parts). Under question in this case was the constitutionality of an Illinois statute that required licensed motor vehicle and vehicle parts dealers to permit state officials to carry out inspections at the time of the search. Rooting its argument in *Donovan* in particular, the Supreme Court upheld the statute and the challenged inspection, asserting that the Illinois statute was "directed at one specific and heavily regulated industry, the authorized warrantless searches were necessary to the effectiveness of the inspection system, and licensees were put on notice that their businesses would be subject to inspections pursuant to the state administrative scheme" (p. 1172). The administrative scheme, the Court pointed out, promoted the strong public interest of controlling the theft of automobiles and automobile parts (p. 1172).

The justifications for warrantless administrative searches were articulated quite well by the Eleventh Circuit Court of Appeals in *Crosby v. Paulk,* 187 F.3d 1339 (1999). In this case the Court upheld a warrantless administrative search of nightclubs owned by Joe and Leverne Crosby in Georgia by agents of the Valdosta/Lowndes/Brooks Drug Task Force, investigating illegal alcohol sales to minors and after-hours sales. Citing *Colonnade, Donovan,* and *Krull,* the Court rejected the arguments by the Crosby's that the planned administrative search violated their right to privacy under the Fourth Amendment because a search warrant was required. In the first place, the Court noted that "the privacy 'expectation is particularly attenuated in a commercial property employed in closely-regulated industries.'" The Court also underscored that it has been well established that closely- or pervasively-regulated businesses can be subjected to warrantless administrative searches or inspections under the Fourth Amendment if three criteria are satisfied. That is, the government must (1) have a "substantial government interest" that promotes the "regulatory scheme"; (2) show that the specific warrantless inspection furthers the regulatory scheme; and (3) demonstrate that the "statute's inspection program," as administered, offers a "constitutionally adequate substitute for a warrant" (p. 1346). The Court emphatically rejected the argument by the Crosby's that the agents had sufficient time to obtain a search warrant. The Court asserted not only that the agents did not need to obtain a search warrant under the Georgia Alcoholic Beverage Code but also that "the Crosby's . . . misapprehend the necessity of unannounced regulated businesses as an exception to the warrant requirement. As we have explained, specific notice of the inspection would have frustrated the purpose of the administrative search because the Crosby's would have been alerted to prevent underage sales of alcohol or to secret evidence of after-hours sales under O.C.G.A., Section 3-2-32. The Crosby's were on general notice that such an inspection could occur 'at any time'" (p. 1348).

Martinez-Fuerte and *Opperman* Permit an Exception to Warrant Requirement When Other Acceptable Administrative Safeguards Exist.

In *Barlow's, Inc.,* the Court, in requiring administrative search warrants as a general rule, did not in fact overrule the holdings in *Martinez-Fuerte* and *Opperman* that warrantless searches may be acceptable as long as it can be demonstrated that alternative administrative safeguards exist to prevent inspection searches that are flagrantly offensive to Fourth Amendment privacy rights. The *Barlow's, Inc.,* Court flatly rejected the secretary of labor's argument that if OSHA's warrantless inspections violate the Fourth Amendment, then all regulatory actions involving warrantless searches are unconstitutional. The Court maintained: "The reasonableness of a warrantless search, however, will depend upon the specific enforcement needs and privacy guarantees of each statute. . . . In short, we base today's opinion on the facts and law concerned with OSHA" (pp. 321–322).

Warrantless searches were upheld by the Supreme Court in *Martinez-Fuerte* because the Court believed that the administrative circumstances under which the warrantless searches were carried out provided sufficient alternative safeguards to preclude the need for administrative search warrants. Specifically, the Court held that routine searches of vehicles by the border patrol officers did not require administrative search warrants because, inter alia (1) the searches conducted were reasonably limited in scope; (2) inspection officers had limited discretionary powers; (3) checkpoint authorities were quite stationary and visible; (4) inspection checkpoint stops were placed at fixed and known border locations; and (5) checkpoint sites were selected not by field inspectors but by those officials responsible for making general policy pertaining to the enforcement of immigration statutes (pp. 545–566).

However, in *U.S. v. Santa Maria*, 15 F.3d 879 (9th Cir. 1994), the court refused to extend *Martinez-Fuerte* to allow the Border Patrol to conduct a warrantless search for drugs when the statute only permitted Border Patrol agents to enter private land within 25 miles of the border to find illegal aliens. The Ninth Circuit court concluded "that Section 1357(a)(3) does not authorize the Border Patrol to search only for drugs. The Border Patrol is empowered . . . to conduct administrative searches for aliens. To expand this power to include searches for narcotics is impermissible. Absent probable cause or consent, this search was both unauthorized and a violation of the Fourth Amendment" (p. 883).

During the same year, the high court, in *Opperman,* held that warrantless administrative searches can be constitutional in some situations if administrative procedural checks exist that guard against the possibility that the searches may be administered arbitrarily. This time the Court ruled that warrantless "inventory" searches of automobiles held in police custody are reasonable under the Fourth Amendment because standard procedures for such routine searches are set by high-ranking policymakers in the police department. The Court asserted that such standard operating procedures can easily be assessed by the courts as to their reasonableness under the Fourth Amendment. The Court also noted that it is not necessary for probable cause to be established in such routine caretaker searches: "The probable-cause approach is unhelpful when analysis centers upon the reasonableness of routine administrative care taking functions" (p. 370 n. 5).

In 1990 the Supreme Court in *Florida v. Wells*, 110 S.Ct. 1632, relying upon *Opperman,* declared unconstitutional an inventory search that led officers to open a closed container in Wells' car absent any policy established by the Florida Highway patrol with respect to searching closed containers. The high court noted that "the Florida Highway Patrol had no policy whatever with respect to the opening of closed containers encountered during an inventory search" (p. 1635). Consequently, the court held: "We hold that absent such a policy, the instant search was not sufficiently regulated to satisfy the Fourth Amendment" (p. 1635). The court emphasized that establishing a policy to regulate "inventory searches is based on the principle that an inventory search must not be a ruse for a general rummaging in order to discover incriminating evidence" (p. 1635). And in 1994 in *U.S. v. Andrews*, 22 F.3d 1328, the Fifth Circuit Court of Appeals upheld an inventory search because the court held that established policy regulated sufficiently the discretion that could be employed by the city's police officers in conducting the search. However, the court upheld *Wells* by acknowledging that "the requirement to be distilled from the line of cases culminating in *Wells* is that inventory policies must be adopted which sufficiently limit the discretion of law enforcement officers to prevent inventory searches from becoming evidentiary searches" (p. 1336). Parenthetically, it should be noted that, even though these searches are conducted by police officers, they are technically administrative searches to produce an inventory of items "'to protect the property of the owner and to reduce the potential liability of the police department'" (p. 1336) (also see, *U.S. v. Given*, 320 F.3d 452 [3rd Cir. 2003], and *U.S. v. Shranklen*, 315 F.3d 959 [8th Cir. 2003]).

A Postscript to *Barlow's, Inc.*   In 1973 Roger B. Dworkin remarked in disgust: "The Fourth Amendment cases are a mess!"[35] He essentially meant by this that judicial applications of the Fourth Amendment's warrant requirements to administrative searches and inspections have been too inconsistent to protect either the government's interest or privacy rights. However, the Supreme Court, in *Barlow's, Inc.*, did a great deal to resolve some of the problems that had contributed to the mess. Shortly after the *Barlow's, Inc.*, decision was handed down, Bernard Schwartz predicted that the case promised to become the leading case on administrative inspection power because it went far toward resolving most issues on the subject that the Court had left unanswered in its prior decisions. More directly, he believed that the *Barlow's, Inc.*, Court answered in relatively clear terms the following vital questions pertaining to the basic reasoning for and the scope of the warrantless search/inspection exception: "Did it apply to all regulated businesses or only to those subject to pervasive regulation by an ICC-type regulatory agency? Did it turn upon the fact that the business operated under a license, so that implied consent could be assumed? Or could the legislature authorize warrantless inspections in every case where there was a direct public interest in effective enforcement of the agency's regulatory scheme?"[36]

Professor Schwartz's prediction seems to have come true. Cases handed down since the 1978 *Barlow's, Inc.*, ruling have pretty much followed the Court's thinking on administrative searches of businesses as developed in *Barlow's, Inc.* Fourth Amendment administrative search cases since *Barlow's, Inc.*, have refined *Barlow's, Inc.*, somewhat, but these cases have mainly affirmed the wisdom on administrative case law established in *Barlow's, Inc.* Today, compared to other areas of administrative law, administrative search case law in this specific area is quite well developed, consistent, and clear—so clear that legal scholars should be able to predict with fair accuracy the outcomes of administrative search cases before the courts. Such is the real test for the clarity of any area of law.[37]

Inspections Involving Welfare Recipients

The Supreme Court, in *Barlow's, Inc.,* concluded that administrative search warrants should generally be obtained if business operators refuse entry to inspectors. But what has the Supreme Court said if the premises or papers to be searched do not involve private businesses receiving no direct financial aid from government, but instead those who are receiving public welfare payments? Do welfare recipients have the same privacy rights under the Fourth Amendment as businesses or individuals not receiving welfare benefits?

The answer appears to be a shaky yes, but at a very high price to those on welfare. That is, in *Wyman v. James,* 400 U.S. 309 (1971), the Supreme Court held, in a precedential case that still stands, that warrantless administrative searches cannot be carried out against the wishes of the welfare recipients under the Aid to Families of Dependent Children program;[38] but if entry is refused, welfare benefits may be cut off, as is authorized by statute. In this case, the Court specifically upheld the constitutionality of a New York statute that did require the consent of the welfare recipient before inspectors (caseworkers) could lawfully conduct searches of their homes. However, the statute also authorized public assistance benefits to be discontinued at the agency's discretion if home visitation inspections are refused.

The Court was not sympathetic to the argument by the plaintiff, a mother receiving welfare under the AFDC program, that she had a constitutional right to not consent to the home visitation inspections without having to forfeit her public assistance. She based her argument on the premise that such inspections constituted unconsented-to warrantless searches, in violation of her Fourth and Fourteenth Amendment rights. But the Court disagreed, resting its decision on two major arguments. First, Justice Harry Blackmun, speaking for the 6–3 majority, maintained that home visitation inspections of this nature do not constitute searches within the proper meaning of the Fourth Amendment, since these searches are performed primarily for rehabilitative reasons and not so much for investigatory purposes. Second, even if the home visitation search could be placed under the protection of the Fourth Amendment, Blackmun contended this type of inspection "visit does not fall within the Fourth Amendment's proscription. This is because it does not descend to the level of unreasonableness" (p. 317). To the Court's majority, the home visitation inspection appeared reasonable, mainly because (1) the needs of the dependent children are of paramount importance; (2) the state has a legitimate interest in monitoring how its tax dollars are spent; (3) continuations of benefits should reasonably depend on how public monies are now being spent; (4) visitation inspections are an essential aspect of proper welfare administration; (5) forced entry, entry under false pretenses, entry during unreasonable hours (for example, mid-night searches), and snooping are all prohibited by statute; (6) trained caseworkers making the inspections are friends to those in need, their central objective being to protect the interests of the welfare recipient; (7) the inspection is performed for purely administrative purposes; (8) a warrant under such circumstances would be inappropriate; and (9) refusal to grant entry does not lead to criminal charges but only to the possible denial of future public assistance (pp. 318–324).

The three dissenting judges strongly objected to the majority's holding. Justice William O. Douglas asserted that the government should not be permitted to "buy up" constitutional rights in such situations. In so saying, Douglas meant that a citizen should not have to agree to forfeit one right (for example, Fourth Amendment protection) to receive another (the right to receive public assistance, if eligible) (p. 328). Justices Thurgood Marshall and William J. Brennan also remarked in dissent: "We are told that the visit is designed to rehabilitate, to provide aid. This is strange doctrine indeed. A paternalistic notion that a complaining citizen's constitutional rights can be violated so long as the State is somehow helping is alien to our Nation's philosophy" (p. 343). Quoting Justice Louis Brandeis in his dissent in *Olmstead v. United States,* 277 U.S. 438, 479 (1928), these dissenters noted that over forty years before Brandeis cautioned that "experience should teach us to be most on our guard to protect liberty when the government's purposes are beneficent" (p. 343).

Marshall and Brennan were particularly disturbed over the distinction the majority made between *See* and this case. The majority contended that a *genuine* search was involved in *See* but not in *Wyman.* The majority also noted that in *See* it was a criminal offense to refuse entry, while such was not the case in *Wyman.* However, the dissenters argued that "apart from the issue of consent, there is neither logic in, nor precedent for, the view that the ambit of the Fourth Amendment depends not on the character of the governmental intrusion but on the size of the club that the State wields against a resisting citizen. . . . For protecting the privacy of her home, Mrs. James lost the sole means of support for herself and her infant son. For protecting the privacy of his commercial warehouse, Mr. See received a $100 suspended fine" (p. 340). This implies the major reason for their dissent; it also reflects the chief criticism others have voiced against the *Wyman* decision. That is, the majority's holding in *Wyman,* for all practical purposes, seems to discriminate against the poor in its application of the Fourth Amendment. It is debatable whether this is the case, but Marshall and Brennan thought so, as do legal scholars. Marshall, in writing the dissent in which Brennan joined, concluded: "Perhaps the majority has explained why a commercial warehouse deserves more protection than does this poor woman's home. I am not convinced; and, therefore, I must respectfully dissent" (p. 347).

Kenneth C. Davis agrees with justices Marshall and Brennan that the *Wyman* majority seemed to discriminate against poor parents. However, Davis attacks more the apparent illogic of the decision. He claims that the Court is either discriminating against poor parents, as well as nonpoor children, or—if it does not mean to discriminate—then the Court is saying in effect that governmental inspectors have a right to enter and inspect *all* homes as to various kinds of health, safety, and welfare administrative inspections, since the *Wyman* Court argued that entry was essential to see to it that the needs of the children, which it viewed as of "paramount importance," were being handled adequately. Davis suggests that the *Wyman* Court "may mean that *all* children could be protected by home visits, on the theory that the children give implied consent to visits that are for their own benefit. . . . If that is so, all homes . . . may be entered without warrants."[39] Thus, *Wyman*'s illogic, Davis asserts, could cause one to infer that refusal to allow a social security caseworker to inspect Mr. X's home—to provide another example—might not result in any criminal charges against him, but Mr. X might forfeit his Social Security checks because he insisted on his Fourth Amendment rights.

Because of the illogic of *Wyman,* Davis predicted that the probability that the Supreme Court will continue to follow it in the future appears very unlikely.[40] However, Davis may be right regarding a few specific contentions in *Wyman* but wrong about the general strength of the decision. Although some of the arguments in *Wyman* are admittedly weak, the tone of the ruling in general can be justified in the context of efficient public administration and tight fiscal control over the public treasury. But the *Wyman* Court did leave unanswered one vital question that Davis and others have addressed: Can any private party who receives some form of public assistance (for example, grants, subsidies, unemployment compensation) be placed in the precarious position of having to choose between what it needs from government and its Fourth Amendment rights? In this case, did the Court do a good job in applying the Fourth Amendment to balance the individual's interest with the public interest? Given constant and vehement charges that the government throws our money away, that public bureaucracy is wasteful and inefficient, that too many are on welfare and that too many collect public assistance fraudulently, and that too many children are neglected, would you have ruled differently? Examine carefully the two basic sides to the argument in *Wyman* in the context of the above criticisms and other such criticisms of government. The majority argued that home visitation inspections are necessary for the children's sake and administrative efficiency and effectiveness, while the dissenters argued that such inspections violate the Fourth Amendment. Running a government is often a tough, frustrating, and thankless job.

Although the *Wyman* decision still stands, the case is rarely cited by the courts and, thus, has had limited impact on the development of case law in the area of warrantless searches. Some scholars speculate that *Wyman* is seldom cited because the Supreme Court in *Wyman* was bitterly divided over the decision, the ruling itself constituted bad law that was poorly received by legal scholars, and the decision was forcefully attacked by those who felt that the holding established a double standard that blatantly discriminated against the poor.[41]

A Lexis-Nexis search in the Spring of 2003 turned up only twelve positive cites of *Wyman* and none by the Supreme Court. Obviously, however, a few courts find it appropriate to cite *Wyman*. In fact, as recently as 2002, the Sixth Circuit Court of Appeals in *Marchwinski v. Howard,* 309 F.3d 330, rooted its decision in *Wyman* when holding that requiring welfare applicants and recipients to submit to drug testing does not violate the Fourth Amendment's prohibition against unreasonable searches. The Court argued that Michigan, under its Michigan Family Independence Assistance program, had a right to protect the taxpayers' money by requiring, as a condition of receiving welfare, welfare applicants and recipients to submit to drug tests. The Court concluded: "Our conclusion is premised on . . . the reasoning of the Court in *Wyman v. James*." The Court contended that *Wyman* imposed reasonable and constitutional conditions and here, "we think that the state has made a strong showing that Michigan's program satisfied the *Wyman* factors. . . . Further, the public has a strong interest in ensuring that the money it gives to recipients is used for its intended purposes. The state is not using the information it gathers to institute criminal proceedings. As in *Wyman*, application of the warrant and probable cause requirements would be extremely impracticable. And like the search in *Wyman*, it is consensual in the sense that the recipient may refuse to submit to the test but may not then continue to participate fully in the program" (pp. 337–338). Clearly, the objections the dissenters (Douglas, Marshall, and Brennan) had in *Wyman* would still apply in *Marchwinski*, especially their main contention that receiving welfare should not be conditioned on forfeiting a constitutional right (i.e., the right to privacy under the Fourth Amendment).

THE DECLINE OF THE INDIVIDUAL'S RIGHT AGAINST SELF-INCRIMINATION DURING THE RISE OF THE ADMINISTRATIVE STATE

One clear trait of the modern administrative state is that it has an insatiable appetite for information. Indeed, the state's bureaucratic apparatus needs vast information about people and things to function properly. Nevertheless, free societies have placed limits on how the government can obtain information about its citizens, what information it can legally seize, and how it can use the information it does collect. While the previously discussed Fourth Amendment is aimed largely at prohibiting unreasonable invasions of personal privacy in the face of official efforts to gather information, the Fifth Amendment's self-incrimination clause essentially prohibits the government from forcing persons to implicate themselves in criminal misconduct. Specifically, the Fifth Amendment provides that "no person . . . shall be compelled in any criminal case to be a witness against himself."

Initially the self-incrimination privilege was only used to protect those in court charged with criminal offenses. However, the Supreme Court has extended the privilege to apply to virtually any official proceeding. For example, in *Murphy v. Waterfront Commission of New York Harbor*, 378 U.S. 52 (1964), the Court held that individuals have the constitutional right to avoid being compelled to provide incriminating evidence against themselves in any federal, state, or local proceeding, civil or criminal administrative or judicial, adjudicative, or investigative.[42] But because the guarantee against self-incrimination has been applied quite narrowly in these proceedings, especially since the 1930s, the protection in actuality is not as great as it may seem. In fact, virtually every legal scholar in recent decades has talked about how meaningless the privilege against self-incrimination has become. For instance, in a *Harvard Law Review* article, Justice William J. Brennan once argued that recent court decisions have greatly damaged the protective shield once offered by the Fifth's self-incrimination privilege, as interpreted by the Court in *Boyd v. United States,* 116 U.S. 616 (1886).[43] A lengthy *Harvard Law Review* "Note" takes the position that "values of privacy" have been seriously eroded in modern law by "legal realism." Legal realism, as opposed to the nineteenth century adherence to absolute legal ideals, is characterized by a pragmatic and relativist approach to the application of our legal principles—for example, the privilege against self-incrimination. This modern approach, it is held, has allowed the practical informational needs of the state to be honored increasingly at the expense of the constitutional privilege against self-incrimination.[44] Kenneth C. Davis asserts that the Supreme Court, especially during the 1940s and 1970s, did much to drastically reduce the privacy protections once provided by both the Fourth and Fifth Amendments, the protection against self-incrimination being no exception. He also believes that Fourth and Fifth Amendment privacy protections have been severely compromised to satisfy the practical informational demands of the modern administrative state.[45] In 1993 Joel Cohen concluded, given the present trend of at least the Second Circuit court, that under the new "act of production" doctrine "there will be precious little Fifth Amendment protection covering private documents prepared by individuals."[46] However, Lance Cole asserted in a 2002 law review article that the 2000 *U.S. v. Hubbell,* 530 U.S. 27, decision had the impact of restoring "Fifth Amendment protection to many private papers in the possession of individuals."[47] Let's review the historical development of the application of the Fifth Amendment's privacy protections and its apparent legal protective value today.

Before commencing the analysis of the rise, fall, and possible revival of the Fifth's self-incrimination privilege, a few comments on the logic of the presentation are necessary. In the first place, it is very difficult to discuss the privilege against self-incrimination outside of the context of the Fourth Amendment. This is because the gathering of information, protected under the Fourth, and the use of the gathered information, protected under the Fifth—but also under both, depending upon one's perspective—cannot be neatly separated, even for analytical purposes. In many instances, search and seizure and self-incrimination questions seem to be very intertwined legally. For example, Justice William R. Day, in *Weeks v. United States,* 232 U.S. 383, 392–394, 398 (1914), argued that the seizing and later use of evidence at a trial involves a single evidentiary transaction by the government. Therefore, the defendant has the constitutional right under the Fifth to demand the exclusion of the use of incriminating evidence obtained under the jurisdiction of the Fourth. Justice Joseph P. Bradley had recognized this close relationship between the Fourth and Fifth Amendments' privacy protections years before. In *Boyd,* he declared that "the Fourth and Fifth Amendments run almost into each other" (p. 630). Elaborating, Bradley reasoned that the Fourth and Fifth Amendments "throw great light on each other. For the 'unreasonable searches and seizures' condemned in the Fourth Amendment are almost always made for the purpose of compelling a man to give evidence against himself, which in criminal cases is condemned in the Fifth Amendment; and compelling a man 'in a criminal case to be a witness against himself,' which is condemned in the Fifth Amendment, throws light on the question as to what is an 'unreasonable search and seizure' within the meaning of the Fourth Amendment. And we have been unable to perceive that the seizure of a man's private books and papers to be used in evidence against him is substantially different from compelling him to be a witness against himself" (p. 633).

Although this assertion was made about a century ago, it has survived the test of time. Most legal scholars and justices today appear to recognize the "convergence theory" or "doctrine of mutuality" as established in *Boyd*. Even as late as 1976, in *Andresen v. Maryland*, 427 U.S. 463 (1976), the Supreme Court acknowledged that the Fourth and Fifth Amendments seem to provide more privacy protection when viewed together rather than separately (p. 492). Thus, in the following discussion it is sometimes necessary to consider search and seizure points in order to develop an examination of the Fifth's guarantee against self-incrimination.

It is also necessary to include criminal law cases, as contrasted to purely administrative law cases, since the former help to explain the development of the courts' general attitude toward the applicability of the self-incrimination protection. Besides, as the Court noted in *Boyd,* it is not always fair or practical to draw a sharp distinction between civil and criminal law cases for purposes of applying Fourth and Fifth Amendment protections. In response to the question of whether a governmental prosecutor can deprive citizens of their Fourth and Fifth Amendment rights by seeking desired information under a civil heading rather than under a criminal heading, the Court said not when criminal charges and penalties could result: "The information, though technically a civil proceeding, is in substance and effect a criminal one" (p. 634). In recent years the courts have diminished the worth of the exclusionary rule, a rule designed to exclude illegally seized evidence. For example, the Third Circuit court in 1991 in *U.S. v. Torres*, 926 F.2d 321, 323, held that the fact that "an unlawful search and seizure has occurred does not diminish the probative value of the illegally seized evidence in any way. . . . Evidence seized illegally by state officials" in a criminal matter "may be used in a federal civil proceeding." *Torres* was upheld and expanded in *U.S. v. Acosta*, 303 F.3d 78 (1st Cir. 2002), discussed later in the chapter.

The Fifth Amendment's Protection Against Self-Incrimination Under the Philosophy of Legal Formalism

Nineteenth century legal formalism was a legal philosophy dedicated to the preservation of democratic ideals. And certainly, in the Bill of Rights, which was written near the end of the eighteenth century, many democratic ideals were espoused that needed judicial protection. In the ideal, the Fifth's privilege against self-incrimination meant that individuals should not be compelled to reveal incriminating evidence that can be used by the government against them in criminal cases. This liberty is regarded as necessary in a free society because it places the burden of proof on the state's prosecutor, not on the individual possibly facing criminal charges. But the freedom runs deeper than this in practice. Prohibiting the state from using self-incriminating evidence serves to deter the government from trying to seize incriminating evidence through the use of ruthless inquisitional practices (for example, interrogations continuing for literally days), torture (for example, beating confessions out of individuals), and unreasonable searches (for example, unconscionable warrantless, early-morning bedroom searches). While the legal formalists refused to significantly weaken the coverage of the Fifth's protection against self-incrimination during the 1800s and early 1900s, the emergence of the legal realists brought a rather abrupt end to the thinking that the privacy protections of the Fourth and Fifth Amendments should be applied in any absolute or extreme manner.

***Boyd* Epitomizes the Legal Formalism Perspective.**   Kenneth C. Davis remarked some years ago that "the clear fact is that the law of 1978 is in sharp contrast with the law of *Boyd* (1886) and *American Tobacco* (1924)."[48] To understand why recent judicial applications of Fourth and Fifth Amendment rights differ so dramatically from the application of these rights in *Boyd v. United States,* 116 U.S. 616, or *American Tobacco,* 264 U.S. 298, it is imperative that the different legal philosophies that guided and presently guide judicial determinations be examined and compared. It is worth reviewing the *Boyd* case in relative detail because in its decision, the Court captured the legal formalism perspective that dominated the thinking of so many justices during the nineteenth and early twentieth centuries. One who comprehends the justifications behind the Court's arguments in *Boyd* will become better equipped to appreciate why the demands of contemporary American society pressured the justices of modern America to abandon the rigidity of legal formalism for the flexibility of legal realism. Or, according to Kathryn Urbonya, postmodernist courts today reject the rigid approach of legal formalist judges who tried to root their decision, as the court did in *Boyd*, in "the idea of a singular Truth."[49]

The unanimous Supreme Court ruled in *Boyd* that all governmental efforts to obtain an individual's personal papers violate the Fourth Amendment's prohibition against unreasonable searches and seizures and the Fifth Amendment's protection against self-incrimination (pp. 636–638). In reaching this decision, the Court based its argument in the rationale that the privacy rights of the Fourth and Fifth Amendments are in effect "sacred" and "indefeasible" rights "of personal security, personal liberty and private property" (p. 630). Employing the uncompromising attitude characteristic of legal formalism, the Court maintained that there are certain rights that must be carefully preserved if liberty is to have any concrete meaning. Compromising the privacy protections of the Fourth and Fifth Amendments, Justice Bradley declared in *Boyd,* may serve the ends of despots, but certainly not the ends of those who cherish liberty. He stressed that "any compulsory discovery by extorting the party's oath, or compelling the production of his private books and papers, to convict him of crime, or to forfeit his property, is contrary to the principles of a free government. It is abhorrent to the instincts of an Englishman; it is abhorrent to the instincts of an American. It may suit the purposes of despotic power; but it cannot abide the pure atmosphere of political liberty and personal freedom" (p. 632).

This attitude can be seen somewhat in the Court's decision in *American Tobacco,* although by 1924 the influence of legal formalism was rapidly fading. In *American Tobacco* the Court strongly objected to public agencies (in this case, the FTC) using general subpoena power to permit them to carry out "fishing expeditions" while conducting administrative investigations. The Court exclaimed: "Anyone who respects the spirit as well as the letter of the Fourth Amendment would be loath to believe that Congress intended one of its subordinate agencies to sweep all our traditions into the fire," yet "to allow a search through all of [the American Tobacco Company's] records, relevant or irrelevant, in the hope that something will turn up" would accomplish this (p. 306).

What makes the *Boyd* ruling so characteristic of the legal formalism approach, as contrasted to today's legal realism approach, is the espoused absolutism (i.e., "singular Truth") of the constitutional privacy values set forth in the Fourth and Fifth Amendments. To the *Boyd* Court, protections against unreasonable searches and seizures and against self-incrimination seemed to constitute absolute moral values that should not be questioned as to their rightness in all situations. Rejecting the possible relative nature of these privacy values, depending upon various circumstances, the Court argued that these "sacred" and "indefeasible" rights should not be allowed to be undermined by the government, even for the sake of promoting the general welfare. The question in *Boyd* was essentially the constitutionality of Section A of the 1874 customs law, which authorized a United States court, upon request by government attorney, to compel persons suspected of avoiding customs duties in revenue cases to produce in court relevant personal documents (such as private papers, books, invoices, and the like) or, by not presenting such materials, be faced with in effect admitting to being guilty of the charges.

E. A. Boyd and Sons, an importer of glass, was charged by customs officials with not paying customs duties under the 1874 act on thirty-five cases of imported plate glass. Although the proceeding was on its face a civil or administrative law proceeding, under Section 12 of the act, severe penalties could be imposed on those found to be in violation of the customs laws. Penalties for each offense could include fines of not less than $50 or more than $5,000, or imprisonment not to exceed two years, or both. Additionally, the merchandise would be forfeited.

The Court addressed a few basic Fourth and Fifth Amendment questions. First, is an act constitutional that compels a person to produce in court for inspection evidence that can later be used against him in the prosecution of his case? Second, does not the compulsion of such private and incriminating evidence, for all practical purpose, compel a person to present testimony against himself or herself? And third, does not the forced production of such evidence in effect constitute an unreasonable search and seizure of private property (pp. 621–625)?

To answer these questions, the *Boyd* Court relied heavily upon the arguments presented by Lord Camden in a famous 1765 English case, *Entick v. Carrington and Three Other King's Messengers,* 19 Howell's State Trials 1029, as well as on the American experience that led to the development of the privacy clauses in the Fourth and Fifth Amendments. The contentions of Lord Camden, which embrace the spirit of legal formalism adopted by Justice Bradley in *Boyd,* are worth emphasis. The action under dispute in *Entick* involved a situation where the plaintiff's house was entered by the king's agents, his desks, boxes, and so on, were broken into, and his personal papers were searched and examined with the intention of securing evidence that could be used against him to convict him of a crime (in this case, of seditious libel).

Lord Camden condemned such governmental action as being essentially a violation of the basic social contract, as conceptualized by John Locke and other contract theorists. According to natural law philosophy, quite adequately expressed in the writings of John Locke, individuals possessed certain inalienable rights that the state had no business taking away, even under the social contract. To Locke, to formalist legal scholars such as Lord Camden, and later to Justice Bradley and American capitalist thinkers, the most important of the inalienable rights was the private property right. In fact, Locke asserted that the chief purpose of entering into the social contract was the protection of private property: "The great and *chief end,* therefore, of men's uniting into Commonwealths, and putting themselves under Government, is the *Preservation of their Property.*"[50]

When Locke spoke of private property, he was not referring to merely land or goods; he had a broader meaning in mind. Under the heading of property, Locke included "Lives, Liberties, and Estates."[51] Thus, when Lord Camden defended the property rights of individuals, he applied Locke's conceptualization of private property as extending to personal privacy kinds of property rights.

Echoing Locke's fundamental thinking on property rights, Lord Camden claimed that "the great end for which men entered into society was to secure their property. That right is preserved sacred and incommunicable. . . . By laws of England, every invasion of private property, be it ever so minute, is a trespass" (p. 627). Camden challenged the Crown to show any written laws that allow the government to trespass on private property rights as did the government in *Entick.* Answering his own question, he responded: "I can safely answer, there is none; and therefore, it is too much for us, without such authority, to pronounce a practice legal which would be subversive of all the comforts of society" (p. 628). More specifically, Lord Camden pointed out that no English law permits searches of personal property that would serve to help a person convict himself in either civil or criminal cases (p. 629).

Why did the *Boyd* Court devote several pages of its opinion exclusively to Lord Camden's judgment in *Entick?* A reading of *Boyd* makes it readily apparent that Justice Bradley used Camden's argument to substantiate the point that the constitutional framers intended the Fourth and Fifth Amendments to have the same absolute meaning that Camden had earlier given to such private property freedoms. The Court made evident in *Boyd* that all American political leaders were aware of Lord Camden's monumental defense of such liberties at the time the Constitution was drafted: "As every American statesman, during our revolutionary and formative period as a nation, was undoubtedly familiar with this monument of English freedom and considered it as the true and ultimate expression of constitutional law, it may be confidently asserted that its propositions were in the minds of those who framed the Fourth Amendment to the Constitution, and were considered as sufficiently explanatory of what was meant by unreasonable searches and seizures" (pp. 626–627). One must remember that Justice Bradley considered the privacy clauses in the Fourth and Fifth Amendments to be inseparable. Thus, it must be assumed that Camden's wisdom also stands behind the Fifth Amendment's provision against self-incrimination.

To the *Boyd* Court, it is incredible that the constitutional framers, in light of Camden's condemnation of governmental invasions of sacred private property entitlements under natural law, would have ever signed into law the 1874 customs revenue laws. The Court stressed that for decades the colonists fought the British because they had imposed similar arbitrary and exploitive revenue laws (for example, writs of assistance) that empowered British revenue officers to carry out blatantly unreasonable searches and seizures of private property for the purpose of securing incriminating evidence against colonists. Undoubtedly, the Court contended, the implementation of "writs of assistance in Boston, were fresh in the memories of those who achieved our independence and established our form of government" (p. 625). Consequently, Justice Bradley concluded in *Boyd* that our founders would have flatly rejected, as offensive to the ideals standing behind our Republic, the use of the customs laws in question in this case (p. 630).

In summation, the *Boyd* Court, rooting its judgment in the canons of legal formalism, attacked administrative governmental actions that threatened to erode the privacy protections set forth by the constitutional framers in the Fourth and Fifth Amendments. During this period in American judicial history, the courts adhered to the belief that they had the vital duty of preserving the constitutional rights of individual citizens. Legal arguments, presented mostly by the government, that held that the Bill of Rights should be compromised somewhat so that society in general may benefit were not accepted by formalist justices. Prevailing judicial opinion of the 1800s and early 1900s was that slight encroachments upon the absolute libertarian standards incorporated in the Bill of Rights only served to start the beginning of the end for limited and popular government in America. According to the logic of *Boyd,* "illegitimate and unconstitutional practices get their first footings . . . by silent approaches and slight deviations from legal modes of procedure" (p. 635). Accordingly, the Court in *Boyd* felt that it had to set aside the constitutionality of the 1874 customs revenue laws, which sanctioned unreasonable searches and seizures of private property, as well as permitted the government in effect to compel persons to provide testimonial evidence against themselves.

The *Boyd* decision is particularly noteworthy for its strong endorsement of the use of the *exclusionary rule* as a protective constitutional remedy for citizens. The exclusionary rule allows individuals to have excluded in trials and possibly administrative hearings all incriminating evidence that was obtained improperly (in violation of constitutional or statutory dictates). The logic behind the exclusionary rule, as developed in *Boyd,* is simply that the government has no right to use evidence that was obtained illegally. Wiretaps of home telephones, forced confessions, and administrative or judicial subpoenas that require persons to produce self-incriminating evidence are examples of what courts have considered illegally obtained and, therefore, inadmissible evidence. However, since *Boyd,* the courts have in general permitted the submission of an increasing quantity of evidence that the *Boyd* Court would have considered inadmissible. In the early 2000s, whether in criminal or civil proceedings, the exclusionary rule plays only a minor role in helping to uphold the Fifth Amendment's protections against self-incrimination because the courts have allowed so many exceptions to the exclusionary rule to permit the submission of various kinds of illegally seized evidence[52] (*U.S. v. Payner,* 447 U.S. 727 [1980]; *INS v. Lopez-Mendoza,* 468 U.S. 1032 [1984]; *Pullin v. Louisiana State Racing Comm'n,* 477 So.2d 683 [La. 1985]; *Illinois v. Krull,* 107 S.Ct. 1160 [1987]; *Trinity Industries, Inc. v. OSHRC,* 16 F.3d 1455 [6th Cir. 1994]; and *U.S. v. Keszthelyi,* 308 F.3d 557 [6th Cir. 2002]).

The Erosion of the Fifth Amendment's Protection Against Self-Incrimination Under the Legal Realism Philosophy

After *Boyd* the Supreme Court began to view the Constitution in general less from the perspective of strict constructionalism. Even though the Court since *Boyd* has occasionally interpreted Fourth and Fifth Amendment rights in a rather inflexible and literal manner, the clear trend has been for the Court to reject the rigid or strict constructionalist viewpoint expressed by the *Boyd* Court.[53] A few decades ago, the liberal individual rights philosophy of legal formalism could be seen in the dissenting opinions of Justices William O. Douglas and William J. Brennan.[54] But radically liberal applications of the privacy clauses of the Fourth and Fifth Amendments have accomplished little else except to remind us of how the Supreme Court perceived privacy rights in America's distant past. For all practical purposes, the moral absolutism and democratic idealism that formed the basis of the legal formalist philosophy that guided the unanimous Court in *Boyd* have been almost totally rejected by twentieth and now twenty-first century courts. For example, in *Fisher v. United States,* 425 U.S. 391 (1976), the Court spent considerable time repudiating the underlying philosophy expressed in

Boyd, concluding that "the foundations for the *(Boyd)* rule (against self-incrimination) have been washed away" (p. 109).

For at least the past seven decades, the vast majority of court justices in America have adopted the philosophy of legal realism as the guiding light for their decisions. For many reasons, legal formalism, whether fortunately or unfortunately, was destined to be replaced by the more flexible legal realist philosophy as American society became more complex and the citizenry requested the government to become more deeply involved in the craft of social engineering.

Legal formalism appears, in the context of democratic government, theoretically more sound than legal realism because the principles of legal formalism embrace the principles of democratic ideals much more consistently and comfortably. In fact, legal realism calls for the compromising or rationalizing away of democratic values (e.g., allowing certain "inalienable" property rights to be sacrificed for the good of the whole community). Lord Camden's masterful defense of privacy liberties, in contrast, expressed the legal formalist attitude that democratic values cannot be compromised if limited popular government was to survive. Yet the inflexible principles of legal formalism seemed better suited for the much simpler American society of the 1700s and 1800s. By the early twentieth century, it became evident to most legal and political thinkers that a less formal and more flexible and realistic legal philosophy had to be applied to constitutional issues if the Constitution was to survive. Kenneth C. Davis has noted that modern justices began to recognize that constitutional guarantees could not always be feasibly applied as absolute rights for individuals but had to be balanced so that the interests of both individuals and society could be extended adequate constitutional protections. Davis thinks today's justices are "wise enough to know that such balancing is absolutely essential to keeping the Constitution alive and responsive to the needs of a rapidly changing society and an ever-growing degree of governmental intervention in affairs that were once regarded as private."[55] Once more, he asserts that since government has decided to pick up the regulatory ball, "for better or for worse . . . then what it does must be guided by information and cannot be based on ignorance of the relevant facts."[56]

Therefore, the legal realist school emerged early in the 1900s to replace impractical and outmoded legal formalism and serve modern American government. But the death of legal formalism raised some serious questions about the viability of democracy that should not be overlooked by any student of American government. If the legal formalist philosophy is more sound than legal realism from the standpoint of democratic theory, does the death of legal formalism mean in reality that "genuine" democratic government is a luxury modern America cannot afford because of the pressures modern American society has placed upon its government? Have not fundamental democratic principles, once held to be the vanguard of democratic constitutionalism, been cast aside by the legal realist justices? Does not the legal realist philosophy simply make it too easy for the courts today to rationalize away guarantees promised to individuals in the Bill of Rights? Since legal realism (relativism) has been guiding court decisions, have not the constitutional rights of individuals been severely compromised?[57] In the late 1970s a writer in the *Harvard Law Review* reached this conclusion: "While it is true that balancing need not invariably lead to results undercutting personal privacy, the history of Fourth and Fifth amendment protections since the shift to legal relativism demonstrates that there is no reason to assume balancing will reinforce privacy values."[58] Regarding the privacy protections offered by the Fourth and Fifth Amendments in particular, most legal scholars have concluded that these constitutional guarantees have been drastically reduced, especially in the past seventy years.[59]

Legal Realism in a Nutshell.   By now the general picture of legal realism should be clear. As contrasted to legal formalism, legal realism is a much more flexible and relativistic philosophy. But what is the specific nature of legal realism and how has this philosophical perspective contributed to the quashing of privacy rights for individuals and businesses? Under legal formalism, the argument was posited that privacy protections were absolute rights guaranteed by the Constitution. In regard to the Fifth Amendment's privilege against self-incrimination, this meant that in practice governmental officials could not encroach upon these absolute rights. For all practical purposes, the personal papers, books, and the like of individuals and private business were strictly off limits for governmental officials. But the legal realists rejected the legal formalist contention that any constitutional rights should be perceived as absolute. The legal realists, or relativists, argued that rights vary from one situation to the next. Thus, they advanced the argument that no absolute rights exist. In so arguing, they repudiated the Platonic contention, basic to legal formalism, that absolute rights or standards could be discovered and employed to guide governmental actions. In the *Republic*, Plato maintained that true justice, if it was discovered, would be applicable to all state regulatory situations, since what is just in one situation could not be found to be unjust in another. To Plato, justice was an absolute that could not be compromised and still be preserved. Likewise, for the legal formalists of the 1800s, constitutional privacy rights were also considered absolute values that could not be regarded as right in one situation but wrong in another. The legal formalists believed compromising privacy rights would only serve to destroy them as well as democratic government.

Rooting their thinking in a pragmatic consciousness, the legal realists adopted essentially the Aristotelian notice of moral relativism. That is, they espouse the position that what may be right, proper, moral, or just given one set of circumstances may be found to be quite wrong, improper, immoral, or unjust under other conditions.[60] To philosopher William James, the pragmatic consciousness of the legal realists meant that single perceptions of moral right could not endure from one place at one time to another at a different time: "The true . . . is only the expedient in our way of thinking, just as the right is only the expedient in our way of behaving."[61]

This pragmatic thinking led directly to the idea that, in making judicial decisions, justices had the task of balancing individual with societal rights so that a fair compromise could be reached. Thus, the new legal realist judges became social engineers, entrusted with the difficult task of interpreting the Constitution in such a way that both individual and societal rights were given protection. Whether playing this twofold role is possible remains an unresolved question. In any event, "balancing and accommodating competing societal interests in the pursuit of compromise and expediency emerged as the keynote of the realist approach."[62] This new role for the courts was applauded by some because it prevented justices from forcing their own moral values upon society under the veil of moral absolutism.[63]

The development of legal realism largely paralleled the growth of what Max Weber perceived as scientism and the new rationality in Western society.[64] Weber believed that this new scientism and rationality not only cultivated the growth of modern bureaucracy but also tended to destroy absolute traditional and religious values that were based on faith rather than on empirical observation. In particular, the school of scientism espoused the belief that principles must be verified through empirical scientific testing before they can be accepted as true. But since social principles cannot be easily proved true or false through scientific tests, if at all, it was easy for the legal realists to attack the weak premises on which the principles of the Bill of Rights stood, and then to make the claim that the constitutional ideals should be regarded as guiding standards, not as absolute rights. As Justice Oliver Wendell Holmes, one of the most celebrated legal realists, once remarked, "Such words as 'right' are a constant solicitation to fallacy" (*Jackman v. Rosenbaum*, 260 U.S. 22, 31 [1922]).

To function as viable social engineers, the legal realists had to cast aside the unverifiable assumptions and moral principles underlying the natural law base of legal formalism for a pragmatic consciousness.[65] Adopting the methodology of the "exact" sciences, these legal realist social engineers demanded that democratic principles survive the test of practical social experience, or in the words of Benjamin Cardozo, years before he took his place on the Supreme Court, survive the experiences of "life itself."[66] To pass the practical test of life itself, the application of constitutional principles would have to generate a net benefit for society. Thus, judicial social engineering would involve weighing the costs and benefits to individuals and society according to the facts on a case-by-case basis. For instance, in deciding whether an individual's claim against self-incrimination should be honored under the Fifth Amendment, the court would have to weigh the costs of not granting the individual this privilege against the costs to society if it did. This is exactly what the Court did in reaching its decision in *INS v. Lopez-Mendoza*, 468 U.S. 1032 (1984). In ruling the exclusionary rule inapplicable in deportation hearings, Justice O'Connor, writing the majority opinion, concluded that although it is important to safeguard privacy protections, applying cost-benefit analysis, the social costs of allowing the exclusionary rule to apply in deportation proceedings would be too high. In her words: "In these circumstances we are persuaded that the *Janis* balance between costs and benefits comes out against applying the exclusionary rule in civil deportation hearings held by the INS" (p. 1050).

However, a review of decisions handed down by the legal realist courts conveys the clear message that legal realist justices have a pro-societal welfare bias. In general, when individual rights have clashed with the public interest, the courts have normally opted to reduce the scope of individual rights. For example, in administrative law cases, the courts have become increasingly more supportive of regulatory agency efforts to search for, seize, and use personal materials that were once considered so private that they were placed beyond the reach of administrative officials. But the courts have held that encroachments upon personal privacy are necessary if governmental regulatory activities are to be efficiently handled.

In sum, to the legal realist courts of the twentieth century to this day, the costs to society are weighed much more heavily on the scale of justice than the costs to individuals.

Toward the Virtual Elimination of the Fifth's Privilege Against Self-Incrimination for Business

In 1973, in *Couch v. United States,* 409 U.S. 322, Justice William O. Douglas, dissenting, acknowledged the relentless historical trend toward the elimination of Fifth Amendment privacy protections in the realm of business. He voiced serious concern over the expanded investigatory authority of governmental agencies that had allowed public administrators to pry into the private affairs of businesses, once thought to be sacred and inviolable. Objecting to what the courts had already done to diminish Fourth and Fifth Amendment privacy privileges for businesses, Douglas feared that the courts might go still further in future decisions, causing those in business to not even trust their closest business associates with their business papers. Douglas considered that this would have a crippling impact on democratic society since it would tend to discourage those in the business world from exchanging their *recorded* ideas because of the prevailing risk that such records might at some time be seized by governmental officials and possibly be used to implicate them in some illegal activities. Justice Douglas wrote: "Are we now to encourage meddling by the Government and even more ingenious methods of obtaining access to sought-after materials? The premium now will be on subterfuge, on bypassing the master of domain by spiriting the materials away or compelling disclosure by a trusted employee or confidant" (pp. 341–342). Such, he maintained, "would lead those of us who cherish our privacy to refrain from recording our thoughts or trusting anyone with even temporary custody of documents we want to protect from public disclosure. In short, it will stultify the exchange of ideas that we have considered crucial to our democracy" (p. 342).

How prophetic these words of warning now seem! In light of more recent judicial opinions, especially *Fisher v. United States,* 425 U.S. 391 (1976); *Andresen v.*

Maryland, 427 U.S. 463 (1976); *Matter of Grand Jury Empaneled,* 597 F.2d 851 (3rd Cir. 1979); *United States v. Doe,* 465 U.S. 605 (1984); and *In Re Grand Jury Subpoena,* 21 F.3d 226 (8th Cir. 1994), *Conn. Gen. Life Ins. Co. V. New Images of Beverly Hills,* 2003 U.S. App. Lexis 3958, it now appears that businesspeople have lost virtually all Fifth Amendment protections against self-incrimination in regard to compelled production of private and possibly incriminating business records. That is, it seems that governmental administrators can now compel persons in business to release personal, incriminating business documents unless these things are always kept in their possession and locked safely away.[67]

Earlier Decisions Setting the Stage for *Fisher* and After.   Although the *Boyd* Court held that the government was prohibited by the self-incrimination clause of the Fifth Amendment to compel businesses to produce private and incriminating business documents, not too long after *Boyd* the courts began to restrict its scope. In 1906, in *Hale v. Henkel,* 201 U.S. 43, the Court ruled essentially that the Fifth Amendment's protection against self-incrimination does protect individuals themselves, but not corporations set up by individuals as third parties. The Court reasoned: "The Amendment is limited to a person who shall be compelled in any criminal case to be a witness against himself, and if he cannot set up the privilege of a third person, he certainly cannot set up the privilege of a corporation" (p. 70).

Five years later, in *Wilson* v. *United States,* 221 U.S. 361, 382 (1911), the Court affirmed the *Hale* opinion, asserting that corporations cannot resist attempts by governmental officials to force the production of corporate documents on the basis of the self-incrimination protection. The chief point made by the Court in *Wilson* was that corporate officers do not have the constitutional right to refuse to surrender corporate records to governmental officials even though the records could incriminate them personally. The Court held that "the books and papers are held subject to examination by the demanding authority, the custodian has no privilege to refuse production although their contents tend to incriminate him. In assuming their custody he has accepted the incident obligation to permit inspection" (pp. 381–382). Some legal experts argue that the reasoning of the Supreme Court in *Hale* and *Wilson* is illogical because, despite the fact that the Fifth Amendment prohibits the government from compelling self-incriminating testimony from individuals, the logic of *Hale* and *Wilson* allows the government to use corporations to make individuals in corporations produce incriminating evidence against themselves.[68] Thus, the question raised by *Hale* and *Wilson* is this: Does the spirit of the Fifth Amendment really permit the government to compel individuals to produce self-incriminating records simply because these records also happen to be corporate records?

Whether within the spirit of the Fifth or not, the Supreme Court's answer was yes and has been ever since *Hale*. Actually, the high court since *Hale* and *Wilson* has reached out to prohibit the use of the self-incrimination privilege in other types of organizations. In *United States v. White,* 322 U.S. 694 (1944), decided during a decade when the federal courts struck many severe blows against the privacy protections under both the Fourth and Fifth Amendments, the Supreme Court specifically held that neither an unincorporated labor union nor its officers are entitled to Fifth Amendment self-incrimination privileges in regard to union documents. However, the case is significant because the Court argued that self-incrimination protections should not apply to any associations (incorporated or unincorporated) or their officers in the face of governmental investigations into association records. The Court reasoned that governmental regulatory actions for the sake of the public interest necessitate probings into the books and records of associations. Particularly noteworthy in *White* was the Court's contention that the Fifth Amendment's protection against self-incrimination be restricted to cover only *natural* individuals or persons, as contrasted to *artificial* individuals such as corporations. Although previous courts may have disagreed, the *White* Court asserted that protecting natural persons has been the historic role of the Fifth Amendment's self-incrimination clause: "Basically, the power to compel the production of any organization, whether it be incorporated or not, arises out of the inherent and necessary power of the federal and state governments to enforce their laws, with the privilege against self-incrimination being limited to its historic function of protecting only the *natural individual* from compulsory incrimination, through his own testimonial or *personal records*" (italics mine, at 700–701).

The significance of the Court's phrase "personal records" should not be underplayed, because this dictum set the stage for later courts to really close the door on persons claiming that the self-incrimination clause prohibits the government from using their business records to provide testimonial evidence against them. Davis and Pierce claim that "the language opened the way for a holding that all business records, whether of an individual or an organization, are unprotected by the privilege."[69] *White,* then, established the notable position that the records of corporations, associations, or even the records of individual entrepreneurs, should properly be regarded as business records, not personal records, and, therefore, not protected by the Fifth Amendment's privilege against self-incrimination.

Some questioned whether the *White* Court had meant to include quite small organizations, since very small associations tend to assume a more personal character. Could such small and personal organizations as partnerships among only a few persons or sole proprietorships to some extent escape the regulatory eyes of government by hiding under the Fifth Amendment protection against self-incrimination? In *Bellis v. United States,* 417 U.S. 85 (1974), the Supreme Court answered this question in part by saying no to partnerships. Quoting the language of the lower court, the high court maintained that a partnership consists of more than just an association of a few individuals, that it has "a recognizable juridical existence apart from its members" (p. 87). The specific question in *Bellis* was whether one of the partners in a law partnership, holding the partnership's records in a representative capacity, could guard the partnership's records against

compelled disclosure by asserting his or her rights against self-incrimination under the Fifth Amendment. According to the Court, the partnership had "an established institutional identity independent of its individual partners" because
the partnership constituted a formal institutional structure formed to conduct legal practices, it had a separate bank account in the name of the partnership, sta-
tionery was used in the partnership's name, "and, in general, [the firm] held itself
out to third parties as an entity with an independent institutional identity"
(p. 101). With this being the case, the *Bellis* Court concluded that partnership
records were impersonal enough to be easily classified "partnership property," not
personal property. Since only personal records are entitled to protection against
self-incrimination, such business records had to be excepted from this constitutional protection. The Court left unanswered the question of whether the business records of sole proprietors, which cannot be so easily separated from what
might be considered personal records, should also be excepted from the Fifth
Amendment's protection against self-incrimination.

***Fisher* and *Andresen*.**   By the time the *Bellis* decision was made, the stage had
already been set for the virtual elimination of the Fifth Amendment privilege
against self-incrimination when business and personal records are intermixed.
Court rulings from the 1970s into the 2000s have almost totally destroyed the
idea that governmental administrators could not compel the release of any business records, as long as they were not of a purely personal nature (for example,
one's personal diary). What constitutes records of a purely personal nature has
not been resolved as yet, but with each passing year it seems that the courts have
made more and more records public that previous courts had regarded as strictly
personal records protected by the Fifth's provision against self-incrimination.[70]

Justice Douglas's fears about how "ingenious methods" for obtaining personal
information might evolve in the near future seemed justified in light of *Fisher v.
United States*. In *Fisher*, the Internal Revenue Service was investigating taxpayers
(husband and wife) for possible civil or criminal violations of federal income tax
statutes. Shortly after IRS agents had interviewed the taxpayers, they secured
from their accountants work papers relating to the preparation of their tax re-
turns. Shortly thereafter, they turned their accountants' work papers over to their
attorneys. Upon learning that their accountants' work papers were in the hands
of their attorneys, the IRS subpoenaed the work papers from their attorneys. But
their attorneys refused to produce the documents that the IRS sought. This action caused the IRS to initiate enforcement action. One attorney contended that
forced release of the work papers would violate "the taxpayer's accountant-client
privilege, his attorney-client privilege, and his Fourth and Fifth Amendment
rights," while the other taxpayer's attorney "claimed that enforcement would involve compulsory self-incrimination of the taxpayers in violation of their Fifth
Amendment privilege, would involve a seizure of the papers without necessary
compliance with the Fourth Amendment, and would violate the taxpayers' right
to communicate in confidence with their attorney" (p. 395).

However, the Supreme Court rejected these arguments. The Court reasoned that although the evidence sought was incriminating in nature, the taxpayers were not being compelled to produce the incriminating evidence themselves. The incriminating papers, the Court argued, were being provided by a third party, and the Fifth Amendment's privilege against self-incrimination was only meant to prevent the government from compelling individuals to provide testimonial communications against themselves. Quoting from *Couch,* the Court stressed: "It is extortion of information from the accused himself that offends our sense of justice" (p. 398). The Court continued: "Agent or no, the lawyer is not the taxpayer. The taxpayer is the 'accused,' and nothing is being extorted from him" (ibid.).

Not only did the Court deny that the taxpayer was entitled to Fifth Amendment protections against self-incrimination because he was *not compelled to do anything,* but it also pointed out that the papers were not even the property of the taxpayer. Thus, the Court stated, "the Fifth Amendment would not be violated by the fact alone that the papers on their face might incriminate the taxpayer, for the privilege protects a person only against being incriminated by his own compelled testimonial communications. . . . The accountant's work papers are not the taxpayer's. They were not prepared by the taxpayer, and they contain no testimonial declarations by him" (p. 409). Thus, the Court concluded that attorney-client privilege could not be honored in this instance because the work papers would not even be protected under the self-incrimination clause if they were in the hands of the taxpayer, since they belonged to the accountant (pp. 402–403).

One final point is worth mentioning in regard to the *Fisher* case. The argument was made in *Fisher* that even though the taxpayers transferred the work papers over to their attorneys, irrespective of whether these papers could be lawfully subpoenaed on other grounds, the taxpayers actually retained "constructive possession" of them.[71] But the Court rejected this argument too, maintaining that the transfer of the work papers was not "so temporary and insignificant as to leave the personal compulsion upon the taxpayer substantially intact." In so holding, the Court was suggesting that the "constructive possession" argument would only be upheld as long as the records sought were only very temporarily out of the direct possession of the owner.

During the same term, the Supreme Court, in *Andresen v. Maryland,* immediately affirmed its contention in *Fisher* that the Fifth Amendment's privilege against self-incrimination is not applicable when the individual is *not compelled to do anything* in the production of the incriminating evidence. But this time the Court took the "not compelled to do anything" doctrine one step further. The central question in *Andresen* was "whether the seizure of . . . [personal] business records, and their admission into evidence at his trial, compelled petitioner to testify against himself in violation of the Fifth Amendment" (p. 471). The petitioner had claimed that the "prohibition against compulsory self-incrimination applies as well to personal business papers seized from his offices as it does to the same papers being required to be produced under a subpoena" (ibid.). The petitioner rested his argument on the following contention of the *Boyd* Court: "We have been unable to perceive that the seizure of a man's private books and papers to be used in evidence against him is substantially different from compelling him to be a witness against himself" (ibid.).

However, the *Andresen* Court was unsympathetic to the petitioner's contentions. Citing *Fisher,* Justice Harry A. Blackmun, writing the opinion for the majority, maintained simply that the Fifth's self-incrimination privilege does not apply because, as in *Fisher,* the "petitioner was not asked to say or do anything. The records seized contained statements that petitioner had voluntarily committed to writing. The search for and seizure of these records were conducted by law enforcement personnel. Finally, when these records were introduced at trial, they were authenticated by a handwriting expert, not by petitioner. Any compulsion of petitioner to speak; other than the inherent psychological pressure to respond at trial to unfavorable evidence, was not present" (p. 473). Blackmun also noted that such governmental action was consistent with the principle espoused by Justice Oliver Wendell Holmes in *Johnson v. United States,* 228 U.S. 457, 458 (1913): "A party is privileged from producing the evidence but not from its production." Finally citing *Couch,* Blackmun explained that the Holmes principle "recognizes that the protection afforded by the Self-Incrimination Clause of the Fifth Amendment 'adheres basically to the person, not to information that may incriminate him.'"

Criticism of *Fisher* and *Andresen*.   Critics have harshly attacked the Supreme Court's rulings in *Fisher* and *Andresen* because they claim that these holdings have virtually destroyed individuals' Fifth Amendment protections against being compelled by governmental officials to, in effect, provide the government with self-incriminating personal business records—testimonial materials that, according to William J. Brennan in his dissent in *Andresen,* fall clearly within the "zone of privacy" protected by the Fifth's self-incrimination clause.[72] Justice Brennan asserted that it was unquestionable that the incriminating papers seized from the petitioner's own offices and used as evidence against him were self-incriminating materials protected by the Fifth Amendment. Quoting from *Bellis,* Brennan argued that the Court had only two years before acknowledged that the privilege against self-incrimination "applies to the business records of the sole proprietor or sole practitioner as well as to personal documents containing more intimate information about the individual's private life" (pp. 435–436). Such records, he continued, "are at least an extension of an aspect of a person's activities, though concededly not the more intimate aspects of one's life. Where the privilege would have protected one's mental notes of his business affairs in a less complicated day and age, it would seem that the protection should not fall away because the complexities of another time compel one to keep business records" (p. 436).

According to Brennan, the assault on the self-incrimination protection in *Andresen* is not confined to only narrowing the scope of this privacy protection, because the Court seeks also to circumvent the purpose of this constitutional protection by making "an unjustified distinction between production compelled by subpoena and production secured against the will of the petitioner through warrant" (p. 436). To him, the Fifth Amendment's protection against being compelled to provide the government with self-incriminating material means nothing if all the government has to do to get it is to secure a search warrant and then seize the incriminating evidence. Brennan considers that such incriminating material is compelled in the sense that individuals are not free to stop governmental investigators from searching for and seizing incriminating evidence from their files, as was the case in *Andresen.* Worse yet, as contrasted to the situation in *Fisher,* the individual in *Andresen* had possession of his personal records when they were seized. Brennan noted that the *Couch* Court had recognized rightly that "actual possession of documents bears the most significant relationship to Fifth Amendment protections against governmental compulsions upon the individual accused of crime" (ibid.).

The majority in *Andresen* held that the seizure of the incriminating evidence did not violate the privacy protections under the Fifth Amendment because, not only did the petitioner not have "to do anything" to produce the incriminating evidence, but a legal search warrant was used to secure the records, thus making the search and seizure reasonable. However, Brennan contended that despite what the majority had said, it has never been established that an illegal search and seizure must be executed before the Fifth Amendment's protection against self-incrimination can apply. He pointed out that the Court, in *Gouled v. United States,* 255 U.S. 298 (1921), made "it clear that the illegality of the search and seizure is not a prerequisite for a Fifth Amendment violation. Under *Gouled,* a Fifth Amendment violation exists because the '[accused] is the unwilling source of the evidence,' a matter which does not depend on the illegality *vel non* of the search and seizure" (p. 439).

But in the final analysis, Brennan rested the basis for his dissenting argument in the *Boyd* Court's claim that it could not "perceive that the seizure of a man's private books and papers to be used in evidence against him is substantially different from compelling him to be a witness against himself" (489). Brennan also asserted that he could "perceive no distinction of meaningful substance between compelling the production of such records through subpoena and seizing such records against the will of the petitioner" (p. 435). Emerging from Brennan's argument is the clear viewpoint that men and women and their personal records, business or purely personal, can not be easily separated for the convenient application of the Fifth Amendment's protection against self-incrimination. Obviously, Brennan maintains by implication that personal records represent an extension of the self. That is, what we say, what we write, and what we do reflect what we are. From this line of reasoning, it is quite clear that the Holmes principle does little to strengthen the majority's argument in *Andresen,* since written communications cannot be separated from the person who drafted them. Thus, when a person's personal records are seized by governmental officials and used in court, they can be as self-incriminating as if the person provided direct testimony in court against him- or herself by confessing about what was in the personal records. From this standpoint, echoing the attitude of the Court in *Boyd* and Justice Brennan in *Andresen,* for the government to compel a person to turn over personal records is to compel individuals, in effect, to testify against themselves contrary to the Fifth Amendment's guarantee against self-incrimination. To hold, as the majority did in *Andresen,* that the individual was not compelled "to do anything" to produce the self-incriminating evidence seems absurd.

According to a critique of *Fisher* and *Andresen,* the holdings appear quite shocking from a historical perspective, because these rulings have suddenly, but not without warning, dampened the constitutional privilege against self-incrimination in areas previously enjoyed by individuals under the Fifth: "Historically, the Fifth Amendment was read to allow an individual a privacy interest in his personal business papers. Now the Court has interpreted the Fifth Amendment to allow the government to obtain indirectly the information that it cannot obtain directly from the individual, if the information leaves the individual's possession or is seized pursuant to a search warrant."[73] The *Fisher* and *Andresen* decisions have apparently made virtually all "private" business records the public's business.

In an analysis of these cases in the *Harvard Law Review,* the author maintained that the Constitution has been recast by *Fisher* and *Andresen* so that it now provides "no protection to privacy other than the procedural standards of the warrant clause."[74] Kenneth C. Davis is in comfortable agreement with this insight. He concludes likewise that the judicial propositions developed in *Fisher* and *Andresen* have together reduced "the Fifth Amendment's protection of records to almost nothing."[75] Davis speculates, nevertheless, that future court decisions will likely further erode what few privacy protections remain under the Fifth Amendment in the name of the public interest.

Recent Court Decisions Regarding the Fifth

Less than a year after Davis made this speculation, the Third Circuit Court of Appeals handed down a decision that conveyed that his speculation was on target. In *Matter of Grand Jury Empaneled,* 597 F.2d 851 (1979), this circuit court ruled that a subpoena to produce personal records of a sole proprietor could be served on the proprietor's "trusted employees," to employ Justice Douglas's phrase, without violating the Fifth Amendment's protection against self-incrimination. In previous cases the Supreme Court had left open the question of whether the government could compel the release of business records of sole proprietors because such records, it was commonly believed, were much more personal than other business records, especially those of larger and more impersonal organizations. To recall, in 1911 the Supreme Court in *Wilson* excepted corporate records from Fifth Amendment privacy guarantees. In 1944, in *White,* the business records of associations were excepted by the high court. And in 1974 the Supreme Court excepted partnerships' business records.

The *Grand Jury Empaneled* decision goes far in actualizing some of the fears expressed by William O. Douglas's previously mentioned dissenting opinion in *Couch*. In *Grand Jury Empaneled*, Dominick Colucci, a sole proprietor of a trucking and excavating business that had grown fairly large in its twenty-year history, employed an office manager, Marion DeMato, who kept the business records, specifically, job folders and billing records. The government served subpoenas *duces tecum* on both Colucci and DeMato for the production of Colucci's personal business records. Colucci contended that compelled disclosure of his private business records violated his Fifth Amendment right against compelled self-incrimination.

Finally saying that "a sole proprietor has no legal existence apart from its owner," as contrasted to corporations, associations, or partnerships, the court concluded that Colucci's personal business records are protected by the Fifth Amendment's protection against self-incrimination as long as they are in *his* possession (p. 859). However, the court defeated Colucci's purpose of blocking the compelled release of his business records by ruling that anyone who holds business records in a representative capacity, such as Colucci's office manager, cannot assert the Fifth Amendment privilege. Citing *Fisher,* the circuit court contended that "the Fifth Amendment is a personal right which may be exercised only by the person against whom governmental compulsion is directed. . . . Therefore, Colucci's right under the Fifth Amendment was not infringed by the order and *subpoena* served on DeMato" (p. 860). Thus, employers today lose their Fifth Amendment protection against self-incrimination regarding their personal business papers if they place them in the "hands" of their "trusted employees," even their "personal" secretaries.

Of significance in this case were not only the court's unsympathetic rejection of Colucci's argument that he had "constructive possession" of his business papers but also the general negative tone toward the possible use of constructive possession, as developed in *Couch*. The *Grand Jury Empaneled* court claimed that "possession" for the purpose of the Fifth Amendment "is determined as of the time that governmental compulsion is exerted to produce the documents" (p. 865). At the time the *subpoena* was issued, the business records were in DeMato's possession, thus she was under a legal obligation to produce the papers for the government. On the other hand, "once that official compulsion had been placed on DeMato, Colucci could not rightfully take possession of the records for the purpose of preventing the performance of DeMato's duty called for by the *subpoena*" (p. 865).

The fact that the Third Circuit court rejected the constructive possession argument in this case is very significant because the Supreme Court in *Couch* suggested that the constructive possession doctrine would probably apply in the sort of situation that existed in *Grand Jury Empaneled*. In *Couch* the Court rejected the taxpayer's contention of her tax records because they were in the possession of her accountant, and "the accountant himself worked neither in petitioner's office nor as her employee." But in *Grand Jury Empaneled* the situation exists where

Colucci's business records were kept by his office manager in his office. Despite this, however, the Third Circuit court decided to dismiss *Couch's* suggestive comment regarding the limits of constructive possession as mere dictum (p. 862). Overall, *Grand Jury Empaneled* represents a ruling of major consequence to the status of Fifth Amendment privacy protections for those in business because "the decision limits the operation of the right against self-incrimination to circumstances where the sole proprietor himself prepares and maintains the records, a circumstance unlikely to be found in any but the smallest business."[76]

In 1984 the Supreme Court in *United States v. Doe* reached a decision that limits the protective shield of the Fifth Amendment for businesspeople even more. In *Doe* the Court resolved the question over constructive possession raised in *Grand Jury Empaneled* by simply asserting that the possession question is irrelevant since the only relevant question is whether the self-incriminating records are compelled. Because it is important to capture the precise reasoning of the Court in this complex legal area, it is best to defer to the Court's exact holding: "As we noted in *Fisher,* the Fifth Amendment protects the person asserting the privilege only from *compelled* self-incrimination. . . . Where the preparation of business records is voluntary, no compulsion is present. A subpoena that demands production of documents 'does not compel oral testimony; nor would it ordinarily compel the taxpayer to restate, repeat, or affirm the truth of the contents of the documents sought.' . . . This reasoning applies with equal force here. Respondent does not contend that he prepared the documents involuntarily or that the subpoena would force him to restate, repeat, or affirm the truth of their contents. *The fact that the records are in respondent's possession is irrelevant to the determination of whether the creation of the records was compelled.* We therefore hold that the contents of those records are not privileged" (emphasis mine) (pp. 610–612).

A few key decisions decided in the 1990s and early 2000s reaffirm, clarify, and expand prior case law, especially *Fisher,* establishing current law regarding the Fifth Amendment's privilege against self-incrimination. In 1990 in *Baltimore City Dept. of Social Services v. Bouknight,* 110 S.Ct. 900 (1990), the Supreme Court held that a mother (Bouknight) could be ordered to produce her abused child, which was in her custody and was receiving public assistance, even though production of the child would amount to testimonial, self-incriminating action normally protected by the Fifth Amendment. The Court made clear that the Supreme Court "has on several occasions recognized that the Fifth Amendment privilege may not be invoked to resist compliance with a regulatory regime constructed to effect the state's public purposes" (p. 905). The court, quoting from *Fisher,* argued that "when the government demands that an item be produced, 'the only thing' compelled is the act of producing the (item)" (p. 905). To the high court, the child represented a "required record" that the Department of Social Services had a regulatory right to see or have produced by the mother. The Court noted that "when a person assumes control over items that are the legitimate object of the government's noncriminal regulatory powers, the ability to invoke the privilege is reduced" (p. 906).

The Court in *Bouknight* reaffirmed the "production doctrine," as established in *Fisher*, and developed the "required records exception doctrine" under the Fifth Amendment, first established in *Shapiro v. United States*, 335 U.S. 1 (1948), and elaborated on in *Grosso v. United States*, 390 U.S. 62 (1968). The Eighth Circuit court in 1994 placed these doctrines into clear perspective in *Re Grand Jury Subpoena*, 21 F.3d 226. The only question before the court in *Re Grand Jury Subpoena* was "whether the required records exception applies to an incriminating act of production by a sole proprietor" (p. 228). In this case Spano, a car dealer being investigated for odometer tampering, moved to quash a grand jury subpoena requesting that he produce required business records under federal and state law, including federally required odometer readings. Spano, a sole proprietor, argued that to produce the documents would violate his privilege against self-incrimination under the Fifth Amendment.

However, the court ruled that although the act of production could cause testimonial self-incrimination, in this case the required records exception doctrine applies. In its holding, the Eighth Circuit court did an excellent job summarizing the reasoning behind how the act of production doctrine and the required records exception doctrine applies to privilege against self-incrimination. "We hold that the required records exception applies to Spano . . . , despite the self-incriminating and testimonial aspects of the production for the following reasons: (1) the public interest in obtaining the information necessary to the regulatory scheme outweighs the private interest in disclosure, and if a private individual were able to invoke the privilege the regulatory purpose of the scheme would be frustrated; (2) the individual, by engaging in the regulated activity, is deemed to have waived his privilege as to the production of those records which are required to be kept; and (3) the individual admits little of significance by the act of production because of the public aspects of the documents. We hold that the required records exception to the Fifth Amendment privilege will apply to the act of production by a sole proprietor even where the act of production could involve compelled testimonial self-incrimination" (p. 230).

A 1994 Sixth Circuit court case, *United States v. Ritchie*, 15 F.3d 592, followed almost exactly the decision the Supreme Court rendered in *Fisher*, making it very clear law that the attorney-client privilege does "not prohibit the enforcement of a summons issued by the IRS to the taxpayer's attorney for accounting documents related to the representation" (p. 602). (Presumably, this would apply to any similar summons or subpoena issued by an administrative agency or court.) In this case, Ritchie, a prominent criminal defense attorney, tried to quash IRS summonses that requested Ritchie's law firm to submit records on three of his clients who had paid services by cash amounting to over $10,000 each. The summonses demanded that Ritchie's firm supply names, addresses, and taxpayer identification of these clients, as well as the nature of the services provided to them.

Ritchie contended that forcing him to provide such information would deprive his clients of their Fifth Amendment protection against self-incrimination. Relying mostly upon *Fisher*, the court flatly rejected Ritchie's position, arguing that "the privilege against self-incrimination is a personal privilege . . . and here the client is not the one being compelled. And the attorney may not object that the client may be incriminated by the attorney's testimony; . . . the attorney may, of course, assert the attorney-client privilege if the requested information is actually privileged. Furthermore, the information required must be incriminating or integrally linked with the behavior deemed offensive in order for the Fifth Amendment to be implicated, . . . paying one's attorney in cash does not fall within this category" (p. 602).

In a 2001 case, *SEC v. Dunlop*, 253 F.3d 768, the Fourth Circuit Court of Appeals ruled that Dunlop need not produce SEC-sought records in his personal capacity, because he is protected from doing so under the Fifth Amendment, yet he must produce these records, as business records, in his "business capacity." The SEC suspected Dunlop, as an agent for Southern Financial and Elfindepan (supposedly a Costa Rican financial firm), of violating certain securities laws in an attempt to misrepresent and defraud investors nationwide. The Court reasoned, citing *Bellis*, that the records sought by the SEC would violate Dunlop's constitutional rights because he "possesses a valid Fifth Amendment privilege against production and testimony in his personal capacity." However, "insofar as the Injunction Order's accounting requirement can be satisfied by the production of business records created by Southern Financial in the ordinary course of the its business, Dunlop cannot avail himself of the Fifth Amendment privilege to evade compliance. . . . As the control person of Southern Financial, Dunlop bears responsibility for ensuring that the existing business records are produced" (p. 775).

Further Erosion of the Fifth's Protection Against Self-Incrimination Through the Judiciary's Virtual Rejection of the Exclusionary Rule.

Courts since *Fisher* and *Andresen* have drawn upon these cases to justify their rulings, which generally have had the impact of further limiting the privacy rights of businesspeople and private persons under the closely related Fourth and Fifth Amendments. During the last quarter century, especially, the courts have consistently eroded the use of the exclusionary rule, thus allowing certain self-incriminating evidence to be used against business and private persons in administrative proceedings and trials even though the evidence was illegally obtained. As noted, critics believe that the almost total abandonment of the use of the exclusionary rule has seriously jeopardized the functional value of the Fifth Amendment's protection against self-incrimination. The first case reviewed below is *United States v. Payner*, 447 U.S. 727 (1980). The Court's rejection of the exclusionary rule under the outrageous circumstances in this case is shocking.

In *Payner* the high court ruled that the federal courts' supervisory power does not permit a court to exclude otherwise admissible incriminating evidence, even though the evidence was obtained illegally from a third party not standing before the court (p. 737) (upheld in *U.S. Dept. of Labor v. Triplett*, 110 S.Ct. 1428 [1990]). In this case the Internal Revenue Service had paid a person, Casper,

$8,000 in cash to steal a briefcase (the Supreme Court called the case the "briefcase caper" case) containing incriminating evidence to be later used at trial to help convict another party. Justices Marshall, Brennan, and Blackmun joined in drafting one of the most vehement dissenting opinions ever written by Supreme Court justices.

The dissenting justices concluded that the evidence was illegally obtained by the IRS and, therefore, should not be used to help the government obtain a conviction. But their strong dissent stems from the fact that they perceived the IRS's lawlessness as blatantly evil, conducted in bad faith, and patently offensive to the operations and standards of any righteous democratic government (pp. 738–751). Specifically, the dissenters held that the actions of the paid IRS agent in "stealing the briefcase, opening it, and photographing all the documents inside" were patently violative of constitutional due process standards in regard to the collection and the use of evidence for government prosecutions (p. 746). The three dissenters exclaimed: "If the IRS is permitted to obtain a conviction in federal court based almost entirely on the illegally obtained evidence from its fruits, then the judiciary has given full effect to the deliberate wrongdoings of government. The federal court does indeed become the accomplice of the government lawbreaker, an accessory after the fact, for without judicial use of the evidence the 'caper' would have been for nought. Such a pollution of the federal courts should not be permitted" (pp. 747–748). The dissenters stressed that the IRS had absolutely no case unless it illegally chose "to sacrifice the constitutional rights of one person in order to prosecute another" (p. 748).

In *INS* v. *Lopez-Mendoza,* 468 U.S. 1032 (1984), the Supreme Court ruled that the exclusionary rule does not apply in a deportation hearing. This means that any evidence seized from an illegal arrest or in any other unlawful manner can be submitted as evidence in a deportation hearing. The Court rejected the application of the exclusionary rule on the grounds that the exclusionary rule is used to protect persons in criminal trials, while a deportation hearing is a "purely civil" proceeding "intended to provide a streamlined determination of eligibility to remain in this country, nothing more. The purpose of deportation is not to punish past transgressions but rather to put an end to a continuing violation of the immigration laws" (p. 1039). Although the Court tried to minimize the significance of a deportation hearing, some scholars feel that the stakes for individuals in a deportation case are so high that in reality an adverse decision in a deportation case may result in a more severe deprivation than an adverse decision in a criminal case. This reality motivated Justice Brandeis to conclude many years ago that deportation decisions may be more harmful to persons in deportation hearings than verdicts in criminal trials because adverse deportation rulings may "result . . . in loss of both property and life; or of all that makes life worth living" (*Ng Fung Ho v. White,* 259 U.S. 276, 284 [1922]).[77]

In reviewing the *Lopez-Mendoza* ruling, Bernard Schwartz expressed concern that the *Lopez-Mendoza* decision may signal the end to the use of the exclusionary rule in all administrative proceedings because the Court's rationale to exclude the exclusionary rule in this case could be employed in all other administrative law or civil cases. He argues that "an agency hearing is not just another civil trial, particularly where, as is most often the case, the agency is one of the parties. In addition, in the agency case, the tainted evidence is the fruit of a governmental, not private, crime. The law should not allow a public agency to be the known beneficiary of stolen goods. It is anomalous to enforce opposite rules in administrative and criminal proceedings concerning evidence blighted by the same pollution; an unlawful search violates the identical privacy, whether its fruits are used to convict in a criminal case or to forfeit a personal right in an agency proceeding. An administrative agency, just as any other public organ, is obligated to conduct its activities in conformity with the demands of the Constitution. When its agents exceed those limits, it should not be permitted to avail itself of the fruits of such unlawful activity."[78]

Consistent with the argument made in *Lopez-Mendoza,* the Louisiana Supreme Court in *Pullin v. Louisiana State Racing Comm'n* (1985), *op. cit.,* ruled that even if the evidence were obtained illegally, the evidence should not be excluded from the administrative hearing before the Louisiana State Racing Commission under the exclusionary rule because the hearing was only a civil proceeding, not a criminal trial. In the court's tongue: "Even if the evidence were illegally seized, no purpose is served by excluding it in a civil administrative proceeding" (p. 690).

In 1994 in *Trinity Industries v. OSHRC* the Sixth Circuit court seemed to employ an illogical argument to allow illegally seized evidence to be used in an Occupational Safety and Health Review Commission proceeding. The court noted that a "full-scope" physical OSHA inspection that produced incriminating evidence was conducted without probable cause and in clear violation of the requirements for administrative inspections as set forth in Barlow's and, thus, should normally cause the evidence to be excluded. The court also rejected OSHA's argument, based upon *Lopez-Mendoza,* that the exclusionary rule should not apply because the benefits of including the illegally seized evidence outweigh the costs to Trinity Industries. Further, the court asserted that the exclusionary rule does not apply to agency enforcement actions for the purpose of correcting violations, but does apply when the objective of the administrative inspection is to gather evidence for the purpose of assessing penalties for violations, which was OSHA's objective in this case. Nonetheless, despite noting such objections to the illegally seized evidence, the Court held that the evidence should not be suppressed under the exclusionary rule because the inspectors acted in "good faith" under a restrictive search warrant and, therefore, the "good faith exception" to the exclusionary rule should apply. Given all of these "exceptions" to the application of the exclusionary rule, it is really difficult to imagine when the exclusionary rule would apply, especially in administrative proceedings.

As we start the new century, there is no indication that the drubbing of the exclusionary rule has subsided. For example, in 2002 in *U.S. v. Acosta* the First Circuit Court of Appeals emphatically upheld *Torres,* ruling: "Given the great weight of the precedent and following the unanimous, reasoned approach of our sister circuits, we hold that the exclusionary rule does not bar the use of evidence seized in violation of a defendant's Fourth Amendment rights" (p. 86).

It should be emphasized that the chief reason for the exclusionary rule is to deter the government from using its law enforcement and administrative officials to gather and use incriminating evidence against businesses and individuals in an unconstitutional manner. Supposedly, such governmental officers would find it cost-ineffective to illegally gather information if the illegally seized evidence could not be used. Unfortunately, the courts, employing the legal realist philosophy to an extreme, have very often handed down decisions that tend to encourage the illegal gathering and use of information much to the dismay of civil libertarians who believe that the Fourth and Fifth Amendment privacy rights are worth saving. The practical question remains: How far should we drift from upholding "pure" constitutional principles to catch and punish those who violate our laws and rules?

"ADMINISTRATIVE" SEARCHES AND SEIZURES SINCE THE TERRORIST ATTACKS OF 9/11 AND THE PASSAGE OF THE USA PATRIOT ACT

Let me pose the last question again, but now in light of the terrorist attacks of September 11, 2001: How far should we drift from upholding "pure" constitutional principles to catch and punish those who violate our laws and rules? Or, more specifically in light of our focus on administrative searches and seizures: Should we permit increasingly bolder and more invasive searches, even if in the spirit of a national emergency rationale, to the point where the Fourth Amendment has been so hopelessly gutted that we are left without any protective privacy shield? Obviously, a review of recent scholarly journal articles reveals that many scholars believe so. That is, they contend that the terrorist attacks of 9/11 and the threat of future terrorist attacks should change the way we view civil liberties. Many scholars and practitioners now maintain that the potential for devastating terrorist attacks in the future has shaken not only our democratic republic but also other democratic nations worldwide, because terrorism is clearly not just an American concern—it is a terrifying global problem that must be addressed and defeated. Although my focus is on the American political-legal system, the reality is that all democratic countries face the challenge of fighting terrorism to protect their people while trying to preserve their civil liberties at the same time. This balancing act is a much more difficult problem than it may seem because, as many scholars contend, it may be impossible to combat terrorism effectively without having to seriously erode or even eliminate certain constitutional rights and freedoms that we have long cherished and honored.

Before evaluating the status of Fourth Amendment privacy rights since 9/11, a few points should be reiterated and stressed. One, when illegal searches violate individual or business privacy rights under the Fourth Amendment, chances are high that, practically speaking, Fifth Amendment protections are being violated as well, since incriminating evidence illegally seized tends to violate one's rights against self-incrimination, although not all courts have held such. As the *Boyd* Court reasoned, the Fourth and Fifth Amendments are so closely related that it is difficult to ignore their interrelated character. Two, remember that it is not always easy to distinguish between an administrative search and a criminal search because routine administrative surveillances or searches by, say, the INS may uncover documents and activities that may later be used in criminal trials. We are going to critique in this section searches and seizures under the USA PATRIOT Act, 115 Stat. 272 (2001), which was passed as emergency legislation only about six weeks after 9/11. But the question is, what does the PATRIOT Act really authorize, administrative or criminal searches? The act seems to authorize general administrative searches to help our intelligence community collect intelligence information so agencies involved in intelligence information gathering can carry out their regulatory mission (e.g., reviewing bank transactions, especially involving individuals and businesses involved with transactions with foreign individuals and organizations; scrutinizing the cargo of individuals entering the United States; checking on the whereabouts and activities of aliens in our country; keeping an eye on suspicious individuals, businesses, and groups that may pose a threat to U.S. security interests). But, as we shall see, the information gathered for intelligence purposes, mostly through warrantless searches without any significant judicial supervision, may end up being used as evidence in criminal prosecutions. Not only is it difficult to categorize these searches as administrative or criminal searches, helping to confuse us all, but it is also troubling to many civil libertarians, since using warrantless administrative searches to collect evidence that will be used in criminal prosecutions makes, for all practical purposes, a farce out of Fourth and Fifth Amendment privacy protections.

In a sense, this chapter is ending where it began, but on a much lower or less optimistic note for civil libertarians. In the past, we have used the balance doctrine to balance the rights of individual citizens against the rights or needs of society with, of course, our government acting for the interests of our society. However, only a few years ago terrorists did not pose a realistic threat to our society or to the American way of life. That is, terrorism on a limited scale has always existed and, in fact, terrorist attacks have been carried out against Americans and U.S. interests from, for example, the assassination of President Abraham Lincoln to the Oklahoma City bombing. However, the terrorist attacks of 9/11 shocked civilized society in America and abroad and they have served as a horrific wake-up call. We now realize that these new terrorists present a real danger to the sociopolitical and economic stability of the world. Many terrorist organizations are not only sophisticated but very well financed and globally situated. They also have access to weapons of mass destruction, having the potential to kill millions of people with biological, chemical, or nuclear weapons. We have also begun to realize that democratic countries such as ours are particularly vulnerable to terrorist attacks because terrorists have been able to take advantage of the openness and freedoms that have allowed them to move rather easily in and out of democratic countries and, because of privacy protections, remain pretty free to do what they want in the almost total absence of any governmental scrutiny or surveillance.

The PATRIOT Act:
A Response to "Blood in the Streets"

Jennifer Collins, reflecting upon the problem terrorism poses for democratic government, started her analysis by paraphrasing an old insight into democracies: "democracies respond when there is blood in the streets."[79] Collins, analyzing the USA PATRIOT Act of 2001, urges our government to respond with the PATRIOT Act, despite the fact that she seriously doubts the constitutionality of various provisions in the act. She focuses upon the Act's provision that permits once very secret grand jury information to be disclosed and shared with the intelligence, counterintelligence, and, for all practical purposes, law enforcement agencies. Of course, this shared information with law enforcement authorities, often quite incriminating, can then be used eventually as evidence in criminal prosecutions. And this disclosure and sharing of grand jury testimony and subpoenaed documents does not require meaningful preapproval by the courts or any significant postdisclosure reports. She exclaims, "In its starkest terms, therefore, this legislation, for the first time, gives the Central Intelligence Agency . . . and our nation's other intelligence and defense agencies entry into the grand jury—one of the most powerful and secretive domains of domestic law enforcement. Moreover, this access to the grand jury is essentially unsupervised."[80]

Of course, this legal development poses new threats to the actual functional value of the Fourth and Fifth Amendments' privacy protections, especially in light of findings in the 1970s that found plenty of Fourth and Fifth Amendment abuses when intelligence agencies and their information mixed with domestic law enforcement agencies wanting to use any evidence they could get their hands on, regardless of its constitutional legitimacy, to help them with criminal arrests and prosecutions. Collins acknowledges all of this but nonetheless concludes that September 11 changed how we must look at our laws and the freedoms that they once permitted. She argues that we must allow the "intelligence" information that we collect through routine administrative searches and seizures, even documents obtained through grand jury subpoenas, to be shared with appropriate state officials to prevent future terrorist attacks, even if the information circumvents the Fourth and Fifth Amendments and is used in criminal prosecutions. She holds: "The twenty-first century terrorist threat implicates—in a powerfully intertwined way—both domestic law enforcement and foreign intelligence concerns. Information obtained by defense and intelligence officials increasingly will form the basis for, or at least be used in, criminal prosecutions. . . . The continuing threat of terrorism, therefore, necessitates carefully and thoughtfully lowering the wall of separation between the grand jury and other agencies of the government to improve coordination and the sharing of national security information—with the goal of safeguarding the nation's security and its citizens."[81]

Collins is far from the only scholar who recognizes the unconstitutionality of many of the PATRIOT Act's provisions (at least if we apply traditional interpretations of the Constitution to the act), yet she believes nonetheless that conventional constitutional standards should be abandoned so we can prevent future terrorist attacks. For instance, Stephen Tountas reviews the FBI's "Carnivore" program, which operated in relative secrecy before 9/11 to sift through the e-mail of those suspected of some form of cybercrime (e.g., plotting terrorist attacks, securities fraud, child pornography).[82] However, once Carnivore's secret cover was blown by the media, it was severely criticized by the American Civil Liberties Union (ACLU), Electronic Privacy Information Center (EPIC), and other civil liberties organizations as violating Fourth Amendment privacy rights because the routine administrative monitoring of "pen registers" had the potential to obtain more content-oriented information than the court approved surveillance warrants allowed. Technically, a pen register just records a listing of telephone numbers or e-mail addresses of the caller/sender and the recipients. However, Carnivore functions more like a wiretap than a true pen register, continuously collecting and recording information that can also be easily "hacked" to screen the content.[83]

But the PATRIOT Act greatly expands the surveillance prowess of Carnivore, essentially allowing the program to be used to collect information transmitted over the Internet and by computer networks with little to no court supervision. Since the PATRIOT Act classifies Carnivore as a pen register search program, it gives the program Fourth Amendment cover by sanctioning warrantless searches under the rationale that those subject to pen register searches have no expectation of privacy.

Tountas notes that "Congress's enactment of the Patriot Act clearly demonstrates its view that the security of the United States must come before the security of personal information."[84] Although he believes that online crime poses a threat to our security interests, he does "wonder whether this particular national security concern should trump the Fourth Amendment," especially considering that it gives our government "a means by which law enforcement agencies freely dispose of constitutional liberties."[85] However, Tountas does conclude that "given the devastation of September 11, . . . it is in Congress's best interest to disregard Carnivore's constitutional issues. The only alternatives are either to abandon electronic surveillance or develop a new form of technology that passes constitutional muster." But facing future hostilities, he holds that "both options are seemingly impractical." Prioritizing practical necessity over preserving the Fourth Amendment guarantees against unreasonable searches and seizures, he concludes, as has our government, that "Carnivore remains the only effective way to combat cyber crime and should properly continue in its regulation of both electronic and wireless technology."[86]

The PATRIOT Act was passed with enormous alacrity as a response to the terrorist attacks of 9/11. It was passed as emergency legislation after an informal declaration of war by President George W. Bush. The name "USA PATRIOT Act" is a clever acronym for "*U*niting and *S*trengthening *A*merica by *P*roviding *A*ppropriate *T*ools *R*equired to *I*ntercept and *O*bstruct *T*errorism Act." Signed into law on October 26, 2001, the act is amazingly complex and comprehensive. Legal scholars and practitioners are overwhelmed by the act's 342 pages, covering 350 subject areas and applying to 40 different agencies.[87] To summarize, the act delivers on its promise to strengthen "tools to intercept and obstruct terrorism"; whether the tools are appropriate from a democratic and constitutional perspective remains a hot debate. In addition to greatly increasing the power of federal agencies to conduct administrative/criminal searches and seizures through the use of a variety of traditional and high-tech electronic surveillance means, the act, as mentioned, severely limits judicial review of these searches. The PATRIOT Act breaks dramatically with past legal practices and allows information obtained through "intelligence" searches and grand jury proceedings to be shared by the intelligence and law enforcement communities. As noted, this allows prosecutors to use this information as evidence in criminal prosecutions. The act's provisions, inter alia, also compel more comprehensive financial disclosures of individuals and businesses and allow for the freezing of the financial assets of those suspected of being terrorists or dealing with terrorists or terrorist organizations. The act, in addition, delegates enormous discretionary powers to the president, giving him very broad discretion to interpret and implement many of its provisions as he believes appropriate, turning the presidency once again, according to Melissa Mathews, into "the Imperial Presidency."[88] Likewise, the act gives the attorney general broad discretionary powers to, inter alia, interpret and apply the meaning of what constitutes a terrorist or terrorist group under the act; decide whether certain persons or organizations should be targeted in terrorist investigations; determine whether the financial assets of suspected terrorists, terrorist organizations, or those supporting terrorists or terrorist groups should be frozen; and whether certain aliens should be detained or deported because they are suspected of being terrorists or having ties with terrorists.[89]

Michael McCarthy acknowledges that the enormous powers delegated to the president and Justice Department have attracted many critics who argue that the PATRIOT Act's provisions are excessive, providing for unreasonable searches, seizures, and detentions, making a mockery of the Fourth and Fifth Amendment privacy protections. Unquestionably, McCarthy maintains, as do others, the vast delegated power opens the door for potential abuse. However, McCarthy asserts: "Any resolution of the debate over whether the USA Patriot Act is appropriate or excessive . . . is premature, since the effects of the Act depend on how the executive branch exercises its broadened authorities. Instead of labeling the Act's provisions as 'good' or 'bad' based on their potential for misuse, a more useful analysis of the legislation looks at how the Act balances the need for a more powerful executive to fight terrorism with congressional and judicial oversight to protect individual rights."[90]

McCarthy's spin on the PATRIOT Act is positive, yet not unreasonable because most of the criticisms of the act are rooted in the pessimistic assumption that our governmental officials will use their awesome discretionary power and new grants of authority under the act to sabotage many of our constitutional freedoms. Regarding our focus, critics fear that governmental administrators, given new powers to "sneak and peak" in order to gather intelligence and counterintelligence information, will exploit this opportunity by "sniffing out" all sorts of unreasonable information on people and organizations to be later used against them in criminal prosecutions. Of course, the findings of the Church Committee, as mentioned, tend to support this pessimistic perspective on how the PATRIOT Act may be used. These cynical insights seem to be rooted in the old adage "Power corrupts and absolute power corrupts absolutely."

A final comment on McCarthy's optimism: He claims that the delegation of these vast discretionary powers, with new "appropriate tools," are tempered by congressional and judicial oversight, which will presumably prevent abuses of civil liberties from occurring. But not only has history revealed that the legislative and judicial processes have not always functioned very well to prevent abuses, especially during emergencies (e.g., the Civil War, World War I, World War II, the Cold War, and the Vietnam War), but recent and present legislative and judicial practices suggest that it would be naive to count on Congress or the courts to adequately thwart abuses of power by the administrative branch. Remember the lessons of earlier chapters. That is, once great powers are delegated to administrators, legislative oversight historically has not proved very effective.[91] Additionally, judicial oversight has also been considered a weak check, because not only is judicial review inherently a passive power—meaning that judges cannot actively search for abuses and then act to eliminate them—but even when reviewing administrative actions, they have seemed obsessed in recent decades with applying *Chevron*'s extreme deference doctrine to defer to administrative actions as long as these actions do not specifically contradict statute. Thus, since virtually no administrative actions (e.g., authorized searches and seizures) would likely contradict statutory provisions of the PATRIOT Act, given the enormous discretion given to various administrators to interpret these provisions, it is highly unlikely that the courts would overrule the acts of administrators unless their abuses were gross and flagrant abuses of statutory authority.

In fact, Congress and the courts so far have been very reluctant to say much negative about the PATRIOT Act or do anything to undermine the act's clout. Yes, a few U.S. representatives and senators have expressed some reservations about the its provisions, but others even talk about strengthening the act with a new Super PATRIOT Act.[92] Many even assure Americans that the PATRIOT Act has a limited life anyway because it is subject to sunset provisions. However, it should be recalled from our discussion of sunset provisions in Chapter 3 that they have been notoriously impotent in preventing programs and statutory provisions from being continued. Plus, critics of the PATRIOT Act point out that some of the most "abusive" provisions of the act (e.g., surveillance and handling of immigrants) are not sunset. Also, opponents claim that it was foolish to pass such constitutionally dubious legislation so hastily shredding Fourth Amendment protections, and then attaching such distant sunset restrictions, allowing such unconstitutional practices to continue for several years to come. Stuart Taylor feels that, given the failure of Congress to scrutinize very carefully the PATRIOT Act in rushing to pass it, it would have been more appropriate to subject the act to sunset after just six months rather than not subjecting it to sunset scrutiny until 2005. Given the enormous powers delegated to administrators to conduct dubiously constitutional searches, etc., Taylor comments: "I wrote at the time that I thought they should have a six-month sunset. The idea being there isn't time to think about this now, not so much six months because we won't need it in six months, but six months to think about it and do it over more carefully."[93]

Administrative Detentions Under the PATRIOT Act

One very controversial measure under the PATRIOT Act pertains to the discretionary power given to the Justice Department, specifically the attorney general, to subject aliens and others suspected of terrorist connections to administrative detention for a period not to exceed seven days and without the benefit of a habeas corpus proceeding, which would require the government to show cause for the detention. This may not seem that unreasonable because the detention gives the government time to conduct an investigation of the person's background to see whether this person is connected to terrorist organizations and poses a genuine threat to U.S. security interests and the safety of America. Of course, if you were being held against your will for seven days with no opportunity to talk to an attorney or to appeal your detention to a judge, you would probably consider this extremely unreasonable.

However, the administrative seizure and detention situation is worse than it might first appear. The act gives the attorney general broad discretion to extend the seven-day limit to an extra six months. Still worse, this six-month extension can be extended limitless times without any charges being filed and without the opportunity for the detention to be reviewed by a court. Why our legislators decided to allow this flagrant abuse of basic civil liberties, even in emergency times, is baffling. It is interesting to note that Israel's Emergency Powers (Detention) Law of 1979,[94] even though Israel has been the recipient of repeated deadly terrorist attacks for decades, does not permit such draconian detentions.[95]

Under the Israeli detention law, during times of emergency the minister of defense is granted the discretionary power to detain a person under a "detention order" for up to six months, but only if reasonable grounds are established by the government that it is necessary to hold the person for national security reasons and/or the individual poses a public safety risk. Although this alone differs from administrative detentions under the PATRIOT Act, overall the Israeli emergency detention law is considerably more sensitive to civil liberties (i.e., to denying people their basic right to freedom) than its U.S. counterpart. As Professor Emanuel Gross of Haifa University explains,

> In my opinion, the significant difference between the PATRIOT Act and the Israeli law concerns the issues of judicial review. Contrary to the position in the United States where the power of the Attorney General is not subject to judicial review, the power of the Minister of Defense in Israel is subject to routine scrutiny. First, a person arrested under this law must be brought before a judge within forty-eight hours of the day of his detention. If a judge authorized the detention, the law requires the President of the District Court to reconsider the matter of the detention every three months. Moreover, the law enables a detainee to appeal the decision of the President of the District Court before the Supreme Court. No such provision exists in the Patriot Act.[96]

Gross contends that the courts in Israel have actually used their review power to crack down on the Israeli government for unreasonably detaining people. For example, he notes that in 2000 the Israeli Supreme Court ordered the release of Lebanese detainees held under administrative detention because the court felt that the detainees posed no actual danger to national security or public safety and that the detainees were only being held as leverage in seeking release of Ron Arad, an Israeli navigator. This was not a valid reason to hold these Lebanese people under the Emergency Powers Law.[97] Gross concludes that the fact that in Israel "no steps are taken to prevent the judicial review of the detention of a person even in times of emergency, allows Israel to pan the test of democracy in time of crisis with greater success than the United States."[98]

Courts Uphold PATRIOT Act's Emergency Powers, Despite Significant Encroachments on Civil Liberties

Few court decisions have addressed the PATRIOT Act thus far, but those few have upheld the act's bold intrusions on civil liberties. The PATRIOT Act, under the banner of protecting Americans from terrorism, has authorized (1) freedom-robbing administrative arrests; (2) indefinite administrative detentions without habeas corpus and judicial review protections; (3) extraordinary and dubiously "constitutional" administrative searches and seizures; (4) grand jury "secrets" to be shared and, given the problem of leaks, made public; (5) financial assets of those suspected of being terrorists or those suspected of dealing with terrorists to be frozen without any real proof and short of judicial review; (6) information gathered by intelligence and counterintelligence officers, absent Fourth and Fifth Amendment privacy protections, to be shared with law enforcement agencies, allowing this information to be later used as evidence in criminal prosecutions; (7) the president and attorney general to exercise very broad, democratically tenuous, and virtually unsupervised and unchecked discretionary powers to fight terrorism; and (8) sunset of some of the act's provisions years down the road, while not subjecting some of the most draconian provisions to sunset at all.

Nonetheless, our courts, legally obliged to protect our civil liberties, have found nothing in the PATRIOT Act thus far to be constitutionally objectionable. This seems remarkable since many organizations concerned about civil liberties, from the American Civil Liberties Union to the American Library Association, have vehemently spoken out against the act and even defied some of its provisions. These groups contend that, although fighting terrorism is essential to protect America, several of the Act's provisions clearly are unconstitutional, severely and unreasonably encroaching upon basic civil liberties. While the ACLU attacks the constitutionally unreasonable Carnivore searches under the act, the ALA opposes and has even openly resisted searches under the PATRIOT Act which allow federal authorities to conduct secret "administrative" searches of library records which, in turn, permits them to scrutinize what resources library patrons have used from books and articles to Internet sites they have "hit" in order to profile reading habits. The act prohibits libraries from notifying patrons that their reading habits are being monitored. Yet many librarians have protested this invasion of privacy by posting warning notices that "anything you read is now subject to secret scrutiny by federal agents." Some librarians have also destroyed in protest library records on patron use of books, periodicals, and computers.[99]

A summary of a few court decisions on the PATRIOT Act helps to clarify how the courts viewed the constitutional status of the act just a year or so after it became law, especially regarding searches and seizures. In *Global Relief Foundation, Inc. v. O'Neill*, 207 F.Supp. 779 (2002), the U.S. District Court for the Northern District of Illinois, Eastern Division, upheld FISA, as amended by the PATRIOT Act, rooting its argument basically in the government's position that the intention of Congress in passing the PATRIOT Act was not to punish individuals or organizations but to provide tools to administrators to fight terrorism so as to prevent future terrorist attacks. Global Relief Foundation is a U.S.-based Islamic charity specializing in helping to fund humanitarian relief programs in Muslim countries, although it has provided relief assistance to non-Muslim countries, including the United States. On December 14, 2001 a warrantless search, authorized by the deputy U.S. attorney general, was conducted of Global Relief's Illinois Office and private residence of Global Relief's executive director. Much was seized from the Global Relief office, as well as the director's private home, including computers, servers, modems, diskettes, tapes, U.S. mail, foreign currency, cellular phones, video and audio equipment, photographs, receipts, and other documents and records. As a result of the search and seizure, the government temporarily blocked or froze the financial assets of Global Relief. Global Relief brought suit, arguing among several other things that the government's actions violated many constitutional guarantees, including prohibitions of Bill of Attainder and *Ex Post Facto* laws, due process violations, and Fourth, Fifth, and Sixth Amendment privacy and trial protections.

The Court was completely unsympathetic with Global Relief's claims, rejecting every one. Let's summarize the court's ruling. One, the Court acknowledged that Global Relief had been designated as a possible "terrorist organization," allowing the government to seize property and freeze its financial assets, but the Court reasoned that such did not constitute a Bill of Attainder because such a bill is a law directed against specific parties with an intent to punish without due process (i.e., a trial). The Court concluded that the legislation did not target Global Relief specifically and the temporary seizure of property and freeze on financial assets were not intended to punish but to help prevent future terrorist attacks. The Court opined that the Office of Foreign Asset Control's "identification of Global Relief as one to be investigated for possible support of terrorism and its temporary blocking of Global Relief's assets does not constitute 'punishment' within the meaning of the Bill of Attainder Clause." Additionally, the government's "actions seem motivated by a desire to protect the health and well-being of the nation by reducing the likelihood of future terrorist attacks" (pp. 799–800).

Two, the Court applied a three-pronged test to determine whether the search, seizure, and freeze on assets under the PATRIOT Act constituted an ex post facto law: "(1) the legislation must be penal or criminal in nature; (2) the legislation must be retrospective; and (3) the legislation must 'disadvantage the offender affected by it.'" The Court held, as noted in another context, that the purpose of the act was not to punish, in a criminal manner; the act was definitely future in nature not only because the search, seizure, and freeze placed upon Global Relief's assets came after the passage of the PATRIOT Act, but because the act's purpose was to prevent future attacks; and (3) "the USA Patriot Act is not 'unquestionably a law that alters the legal rules of evidence, and receives less, or different, testimony, than the law required at the time of the commission of the offense," and the seizure is only temporary, thus it does not disadvantage Global Relief (pp. 801–802).

Three, under the violation of due process, Global Relief argued, inter alia, that its Fourth and Fifth Amendment privacy rights were violated by an unconstitutional search and seizure of Global Relief's Illinois office and home of its director. Regarding Global Relief's Fourth Amendment claim, the court held: "We reject Global Relief's argument because FISA's safeguards provide sufficient protection for the rights guaranteed by the Fourth Amendment in the context of foreign intelligence activities" (p. 807). The Court, however, failed to say what those safeguards FICA, amended by the PATRIOT Act, provided.

Finally, Global Relief felt its Fifth and Sixth Amendment due process protections had been violated because of the use of compelled seized evidence used against Global Relief and because it was required to answer for a capital crime without being presented with charges or indicted by a Grand Jury. Additionally, Global Relief maintained it was denied a speedy and public trial by an impartial jury and without being provided with an opportunity to defend itself by examining and cross-examining evidence in light of formal charges and by being able to provide evidence and witnesses in its defense. The Court summarily rejected these arguments, holding that they were rooted in the false assumption that it was facing criminal charges. "In this case, Global Relief is not being 'held to answer for a capital or otherwise infamous crime.' . . . It also does not currently face a 'criminal prosecution. . . . ' Consequently, the protection afforded by the amendments do not apply to Global Relief" (pp. 807–808). What the court is saying is that Global Relief is only the target of administrative actions against it, thus not protected by the usual constitutional protections that those being subjected to searches and seizures for the purpose of criminal prosecutions would enjoy. Of course, Civil Libertarians, as discussed previously, are very critical of the government being able to circumvent the Constitution by essentially saying it can do so because it is only engaging in administrative actions (e.g., administrative searches, seizures, and detentions), not criminal actions. But this blatant denial of due process protections under the banner of "just conducting administrative actions not aimed at punishing" constitutes a due process flaw in our constitutional democracy. As expressed previously, what practical difference does it make to the victim of a governmental search, seizure, and even detention whether these actions are carried out as administrative or criminal actions? The victim of such actions still suffers from invasions of privacy, loss of property (even if "temporary"), and freedom if held against his will. How can the courts possibly rationalize the injustice, as in Global Relief, by arguing that Global Relief was not punished? How would judges like it if they had their businesses and homes searched, property seized, and financial assets frozen in the absence of due process protections under the justification that actions against them were mere administrative searches and seizures with no intent to punish? Clearly, to any person who respects civil liberties at all, this injustice must be purged from our political system, even as we fight terrorism, or our country, as Professor Emanuel Gross eluded, will start taking on the character of a dreaded police state.[100] Parenthetically, the district court's decision was affirmed by the Seventh Circuit Court of Appeals in *Global Relief Foundation, Inc. v. O'Neill*, 315 F.3d 748, December 31, 2002.

Possibly the most important case reviewing the constitutionality of searches and seizures under the Foreign Intelligence Surveillance Act (FISA), 50 U.S.C. Sections 1801–1862, as amended by the PATRIOT Act, is *In re: Sealed Case No. 02-001*, 310 F.3d 717 (2002). This is a unique case where a special court established under FISA called the Foreign Intelligence Surveillance Court had its decision reviewed by the Court of Review. In this case, the United States government challenged the FISA Court's ruling that placed certain restrictions on the way the government can conduct surveillance to gather intelligence information, especially if the intelligence officials are working with and sharing the information with law enforcement officers wanting to obtain and use the gathered information in criminal prosecutions.

In re: Sealed Case represents the first time a FISA Court decision was appealed to the Court of Review, and it doesn't read like a normal opinion because it does not involve two parties, but just the government's appeal of the FISA Court's restrictive decision. The Court of Review's long and tedious justifications for overruling the FISA court's ruling are quite complex, but what came through loud and clear was that it supported giving our government FISA, as amended by the PATRIOT Act, virtually unrestricted powers to conduct intelligence searches even when working with law enforcement officers and even when the "intelligence" information gathered is shared with the law enforcement community and used in criminal trials to prosecute the accused.

The ACLU filed an amicus curiae brief opposing the government's position. Specifically, the ACLU argued that not only does a FISA order fail to "qualify as a warrant within the meaning of the Fourth Amendment," but "that any government surveillance whose *primary purpose* is criminal prosecution of *whatever kind* is per se unreasonable if not based on a warrant" (p. 737).

However, the Court of Review disagreed. It rejected the ACLU's first contention as merely an erroneous assumption. Regarding the ACLU's second contention, it argued that Congress, in amending FISA, changed "primary purpose" to read "a significant purpose," thus clearing the way for the government to conduct surveillances and gather intelligence information even if its "primary purpose" was not to obtain intelligence information but to gather evidence to be used by law enforcement officials in criminal prosecution. As long as "a particular purpose" was to obtain intelligence information, even though it was not the government's "primary purpose," the search was legal under FISA, as amended by the PATRIOT Act, as well as under the Fourth Amendment. The Court of Review exclaimed: "The important point is . . . the Patriot Act Amendment, by using the word 'significant,' eliminated any justification for the FISA court to balance the relative weight the government places on criminal prosecution as compared to other counterintelligence responses. If the certification of the application's purpose articulates a broader objective than criminal prosecution—such as stopping an ongoing conspiracy—and includes other potential non-prosecutorial responses, the government meets the statutory test" (p. 735).

The problem here is that the court is ruling in favor of allowing our government to conduct surveillances or searches, inside or outside the United States, as long as terrorist-related activity of some kind is suspected, without the protections of the Fourth Amendment, even if the "primary purpose" of the search is to collect evidence to be used later in criminal prosecution. This encroachment on the Fourth Amendment the FISA court did not permit. Presumably, before the PATRIOT Act's amendment to FISA, a wall existed between intelligence gathering by the intelligence community for intelligence purposes and evidence gathering by the law enforcement community for the purpose of arresting and prosecuting suspected criminals. Civil Libertarians charge that now, under the PATRIOT Act, and with the blessings of the Court of Review in *In re: Sealed*

Case, the investigative activities of both the intelligence and law enforcement communities can merge, something that prior to the PATRIOT Act was strictly prohibited. As it stands now, law enforcement officials can even work with intelligence officials to gather the incriminating evidence they need for criminal prosecutions while doing a side-step around the Fourth Amendment's warrant requirements.

The *In re: Sealed Case* Court recognizes this to a point but argues that allowing such "Fourth Amendmentless" searches are acceptable under the "special needs" exception as recognized by the Supreme Court in *Vernonia School Dist. v. Acton*, 515 U.S. 646 (1995). The Court of Review explained: "The distinction between ordinary criminal prosecutions and extraordinary situations underlies the Supreme Court's approval of entirely warrantless and even suspicionless searches that are designed to serve the government's 'special needs, beyond the normal need for law enforcement'" (p. 745). The court continued by asserting that the government certainly has a "special need" now, concluding that since 9/11, "it is hard to imagine greater emergencies facing Americans. . . . Our case may well involve the most serious threat our country faces. Even without taking into account the President's inherent constitutional authority to conduct warrantless foreign intelligence surveillance, we think the procedures and government showings required under FISA, if they do not meet the minimum Fourth Amendment warrant standards, certainly come close. We, therefore, believe firmly, applying the balancing test . . . that FISA as amended is constitutional because the surveillance it authorizes are reasonable" (p. 746). Accordingly, the court lifted the restrictions imposed by the FISA Court on the way government can conduct intelligence surveillance and work and share the information with law enforcement agencies.

Concluding Thoughts on Searches, Seizures, and Detentions in the Context of the PATRIOT Act

Oh, how far we have regressed since 1789 in our defense of our civil liberties! The founding fathers believed that certain liberties are absolutely essential if freedom is to survive. The writ of habeas corpus requires that government should show cause before a court for why the person should be seized and detained against his will. Many civil libertarians hold that habeas corpus is the most essential component of liberty because, after all, what else protects us against that dreaded knock at our door and being dragged away to a Kafkaian nightmare of prolonged secret detention? Yet the PATRIOT Act allows this, thus attracting the scorn of those committed to preserving civil liberties.

In *Ex parte Merryman*, 17 F.Cas. 144 (Cir. Ct., D. Md.), Justice Taney vehemently ruled against President Abraham Lincoln's order suspending the writ of habeas corpus, which allowed Lincoln to eventually imprison over 13,000 citizens, including journalists, lawyers, judges, legislators, draft resisters, and others whom Lincoln, at his discretion, felt somehow obstructed his war efforts. Taney wrote: "I can see no ground whatsoever for supposing that the president, in any emergency, or in any state of things, can authorize the suspension of the privileges of the *writ of habeas corpus*, or the arrest of a citizen, except in aid of the judicial power" (p. 149). Taney regarded such actions by Lincoln as blatantly undemocratic, unconstitutional, and dictatorial, usurping the power of Congress and flagrantly denying citizens of a fundamental freedom. However, Lincoln paid no attention to Taney's ruling. In 1862, the Supreme Court in the Prize cases,[101] 67 U.S. 635, narrowly upheld Lincoln's actions in a 5–4 decision, yet limited the suspension of habeas corpus to situations involving actual armed invasions of the United States. Of course, the 9/11 terrorist attacks could fall momentarily into this category, but should the ongoing "war" warrant the suspension of habeas corpus and the continued secret detentions? I am not certain the founding fathers would think so.

The creators of our Constitution also felt that the Fourth and Fifth Amendments in particular were essential to guarantee that the United States does not become a police state. Yet as documented in this chapter, the Fourth and Fifth Amendments have been seriously eroded over the decades. Civil libertarians argue that it is understandable that the Fourth and Fifth Amendments' privacy protections should be compromised for short durations during times of national emergencies to protect the public health and safety, but they maintain that the United States too often goes too far in encroaching unnecessarily on civil liberties. Just look at the buzz words used by the court of Review in *In Re* to justify the demolition of Fourth and Fifth Amendment privacy protections under the PATRIOT Act. The court tried to convey that the draconian searches, seizures, and secret detentions are permissible under the Constitution because Americans are facing no "greater emergencies" than 9/11; that the court applied a "balancing test" that the warrantless searches under FISA may not meet the minimum Fourth Amendment warrant requirement, but they "certainly come close"; and, therefore, such administrative actions "are reasonable."

But how arrogant must a court be to think reasonable people could accept such nonsensical dicta and logic? Given what the *In Re* court permits under the PATRIOT Act, if it did apply a "balancing test," it certainly gave no weight to any privacy protection concerns under the Fourth and Fifth Amendments, yet total weight to our "emergency" situation. And how absurd it is to conclude that surveillances under FISA, as amended by the PATRIOT Act, "are reasonable" because "if they do not meet the minimum standards," they "certainly come close." As virtually all legal scholars have concluded in their law review articles, the searches, seizures, and detentions under the PATRIOT Act do not come close to satisfying constitutional standards. Many of these scholars support the PATRIOT Act's harsh measures to fight terrorism, but few actually try to argue, as the *In Re* court does, that these measures are constitutional.

President Lincoln is honored as a great president for taking bold steps to preserve the Union, yet Lincoln probably overreacted by taking too many unconstitutional steps, such as suspending the writ of habeas corpus. Lincoln's unconstitutional actions, even for a war situation, set bad precedent for our democracy because Lincoln would have very likely won the Civil War without having to unconstitutionally seize and imprison thousands of people, many of whom were only imprisoned because they disagreed and/or protested Lincoln's public policy positions toward the war. Justice Taney argued credibly in *Ex Parte Merryman* that Lincoln was setting a dangerous precedent for our democratic republic by his unconstitutional overreactions. Unfortunately, Lincoln's precedent-setting unconstitutional oversteps were narrowly upheld by the Supreme Court in 1862, thus solidifying this bad precedent for future generations faced with deciding what to do with constitutional freedoms when facing national emergencies.

Unfortunately, as Oren Gross contends, "experience shows that when grave national crises are upon us, democratic nations tend to race to the bottom as far as protection of human rights and civil liberties, indeed of basic and fundamental legal principles, is concerned. Emergencies suspend, or at least redefine, *de facto*, if not *de jure*, much of our cherished freedoms and rights."[102] Just as the unconstitutional, unconscionable, and inhumane detention of Japanese Americans during World War II constitutes a blatant and tragic example of overreaction during a period of national crisis, so does the PATRIOT Act today, which has been responsible for, inter alia, numerous warrantless searches and prolonged secret detentions of American Muslims and others suspected of possibly having terrorist ties. Scott Alexander points out, for example, that the PATRIOT Act "has had, and continues to have, a devastating impact on the actual freedom of U.S. Muslims. Of particular concern are the act's provisions for 'enhanced surveillance procedures' (Sections 201–225)—especially the provisions allowing considerable delay in the notice of the execution of a warrant for search and seizure—and the act's 'enhanced immigration provisions' (Sections 411–418)—especially the provision severely limiting petitions of habeas corpus and review by additional courts. These provisions have resulted, among other things, in surprise raids on the homes of U.S. citizens who happen to be Muslim, widespread ethnic profiling, and investigations of the borrowing records of Muslim citizens from public libraries."[103] Alexander stresses that "American Muslims, like other Americans, understand the need for increased security and extraordinary measures in these troubled and confusing times."[104] However, he maintains, as others do, that the PATRIOT Act simply is an overreaction and goes too far in stripping people of their basic freedoms.

It all boils down to this reality, as Senator Russ Feingold (D.–Wis.) said when acting as the lone U.S. senator to vote against the PATRIOT Act: Unquestionably, it is easier in a "police state" to nab terrorists.[105] Sure, but we must resist turning our government into a police state, because our free society is what makes the United States so desirable to live in. The problem with the PATRIOT Act, as succinctly put by Kerby Anderson, is that "in fighting terrorism, the bill also seems to be fighting liberty."[106] As Americans, we must learn to respond to national emergencies in a democratic way—not in a way that will jeopardize our survival but in a manner that ensures our survival yet simultaneously prevents the quashing of our cherished liberties. Unfortunately, thus far we have not learned from our history, because we keep overreacting and trashing our constitutional freedoms during crises, while not always restoring liberties after the crises. It is appropriate to conclude with Justice Brennan's insight: "There is considerably less to be proud about, and a good deal to be embarrassed about, when one reflects on the shabby treatment civil liberties have received in the United States during times of war and perceived threats to the national security. . . . After each perceived security crisis ended, the United States has remorsefully realized the abrogation of civil liberties was unnecessary. But it has proven unable to prevent itself from the repeating the error when the next crisis came along."[107]

SUMMARY

Systems theory has made it quite clear that public administrators are constantly faced with the frustrating problem of satisfactorily balancing the conflicting demands of their environments. Without much doubt, probably the most difficult task for our administrators, especially for those who make significant public policy choices, is balancing fairly the rights of individual parties with the rights and apparent needs of society. To perform their functions properly, they must carry out certain administrative actions which necessarily invade the privacy interests. Such administrative behavior makes administrators vulnerable to criticisms from opposite sides. If administrators become overzealous in gathering essential regulatory information, individuals may bitterly attack them, possibly in court, for illegally encroaching upon constitutionally protected privacy rights, as protected by the Fourth and Fifth Amendments. On the other hand, if regulatory officials fail to obtain information which is considered crucial for proper regulatory operations, legislators, the media, citizen action groups, and the general public may charge that an agency has favored special parties and, in so doing, failed to act responsibly in promoting the public interest. Since 9/11 Attorney General John Ashcroft has found himself in such a precarious position. There are those who criticize Ashcroft for not doing enough to prevent future terrorist attacks, while others charge that he has gone too far in fighting the war against terrorism by conducting unreasonable searches and seizures and subjecting individuals to long administrative detentions without due process.

In this chapter special attention was devoted to assessing how well administrative officials have been doing in upholding Fourth and Fifth Amendment privacy guarantees, while serving as regulators. The Fourth Amendment provides individuals with protection against unreasonable searches and seizures. Convincing historical evidence suggests that the constitutional framers incorporated these privacy protections into the Bill of Rights in reaction to the unreasonable searches and seizures that they had to endure while under British colonial rule. The Fifth Amendment protects individuals from being compelled to be a witness against themselves. Ideally, this constitutional guarantee was supposed to prevent governmental officials from forcing individuals to produce testimonial evidence, either oral or written, which would be self-incriminating. At first it was questioned whether the Fourth and Fifth Amendment privacy rights should be made applicable to only criminal cases, but the courts soon extended these constitutional privacy protections to apply to civil matters (for example, administrative inspections).

During the 1800s administrative power was severely restricted and administrators seldom violated Fourth and Fifth Amendment privacy rights. When administrators did appear to transgress upon these privacy protections, the courts were usually quick to overturn such administrative intrusions into the private affairs of individuals and private businesses. In a famous nineteenth century case, *Boyd v. United States,* 116 U.S. 616 (1886), the Supreme Court, guided by the prevailing philosophy of legal formalism, argued essentially that constitutional privacy rights were absolute and should not be compromised by administrators. Legal formalism, which espoused the basic belief that Bill of Rights guarantees should be strictly upheld if the democratic liberties were to be preserved, reigned as the major philosophical force guiding judicial decisionmaking until the early 1900s.

As society became more complex and the need for more comprehensive and rigorous governmental regulation increased during the twentieth century, the courts began to turn to the philosophy of legal realism to guide their judgments. Legal realism seemed better suited to the demands of the emerging administrative state. Basically, it is a pragmatic legal philosophy which has had the effect of permitting administrative agencies to gather and use information which appears necessary if they are to competently perform essential regulatory functions for the good of society. In practice, this has allowed the courts to uphold administrative searches and seizures, as well as to permit agencies to use self-incriminating evidence, especially as applied to the use of personal business papers.

In response to the growing complexities of modern technological society and new threats to homeland security, the administrative agencies have felt compelled to gather and use more and more information so that they can function as effective regulators. Adequate information on what is being regulated, administrative officials argue, provides the key to regulatory success. The courts, sympathetic to the regulators' plight, have been charged in recent decades with employing the balance doctrine to favor agency regulatory interests, while freely permitting the dangerous erosion of constitutionally protected privacy guarantees. Critics admit that the regulatory problems which confront our administrators are massive and real, but they maintain that the judiciary has gone too far in sanctioning agency actions which have clearly violated Fourth and Fifth Amendment privacy rights.

In recent cases the Supreme Court has upheld unscrupulous, invasive, and illegal methods for obtaining material to be used as incriminating evidence against individuals. These rulings indicate that the high court, at least, has little respect for the exclusionary rule and, as a result, is unwilling to make decisions that would discourage administrative agencies from adopting investigative and prosecutorial procedures that clearly undermine the intent of the Fourth and Fifth Amendments' privacy protections. Further, the federal courts' decisions in *Global Relief* and *In re: Sealed Case* provide blatant examples of the willingness of the

Board of Education v. Earls

federal courts to uphold provisions of the PATRIOT Act that boldly threaten due process privacy protections.

Democracy is a fragile governing mechanism that can be preserved only if governmental officials, while carrying out the tasks of government, respect and uphold fundamental constitutional liberties reserved for private parties. Probably the chief difference between democratic and totalitarian governments lies in how each regards and treats individuals, especially in regard to personal privacy rights, even in times of emergency, such as after 9/11. Judging from recent trends in regulatory behavior in America, we must act together as a society to make regulatory procedures more administratively effective and at the same time more sensitive to personal privacy rights. Since the survival of genuine democratic governmental practices in America depends upon our commitment to this task, we cannot afford to not accept this challenge.

BOARD OF EDUCATION V. EARLS

---

536 U.S. 822; 122 S.Ct. 2559 (2002)

Facts

The Tecumseh, Oklahoma, School District instituted the Student Activities Drug Testing Policy sanctioned by the Oklahoma Secondary Schools Activities Association. The policy demands that all middle and high school students who participate in any extracurricular activities (e.g., sports, choir, band, any academic competition such as debate) submit to warrantless, suspicionless urinalysis drug tests. Teachers would monitor the giving of urine by waiting outside bathroom stalls and then collect the urine samples. Students had to provide a list of any prescription drugs being taken before the urine was tested for controlled substances. Results were kept confidential, although parents were notified, along with possible recommendations for drug counseling. The test was considered an administrative search because students were not subject to arrest, although they could be eventually dismissed from school if tests were repeatedly positive and they refused counseling.

Lindsay Earls and other students brought suit in federal district court arguing, inter alia, that the drug-testing policy subjected them to unreasonable searches in violation of the Fourth Amendment to the U.S. Constitution. While the U.S. district court granted summary judgment in favor of the school district, the Tenth Circuit court reversed, holding that the school district failed to demonstrate a need for the search. The Supreme Court granted certiorari.

Justice Thomas delivered the opinion of the divided court. He was joined by justices Rehnquist, Scalia, Kennedy, and Breyer. Justice O'Connor, Ginsburg, Stevens, and Souter joined in dissent.

The Student Activities Drug Testing Policy implemented by the Board of Education of Independent School District No. 92 of Pottawatomie County (School District) requires all students who participate in competitive extracurricular activities to submit to drug testing. Because this Policy reasonably serves the School District's important interest in detecting and preventing drug use among its students, we hold that it is constitutional.

The city of Tecumseh, Oklahoma, is a rural community located approximately 40 miles southeast of Oklahoma City. The School District administers all Tecumseh public schools. In the fall of 1998, the School District adopted the Student Activities Drug Testing Policy (Policy), which requires all middle and high school students to consent to drug testing in order to participate in any extracurricular activity. In practice, the Policy has been applied only to competitive extracurricular activities sanctioned by the Oklahoma Secondary Schools Activities Association, such as the Academic Team, Future Farmers of America, Future Homemakers of America, band, choir, pompom, cheerleading, and athletics. Under the Policy, students are required to take a drug test before participating in an extracurricular activity, must submit to random drug testing while participating in that activity, and must agree to be tested at any time upon reasonable suspicion. The urinalysis tests are designed to detect only the use of illegal drugs, including amphetamines, marijuana, cocaine, opiates, and barbiturates, not medical conditions or the presence of authorized prescription medications.

At the time of their suit, both respondents attended Tecumseh High School. Respondent Lindsay Earls was a member of the show choir, the marching band, the Academic Team, and the National Honor Society. Respondent Daniel James sought to participate in the Academic Team. Together with their parents, Earls and James brought a 42 U.S.C. §1983 action against the School District, challenging the Policy both on its face and as applied to their participation in extracurricular activities. They alleged that the Policy violates the Fourth Amendment as incorporated by the Fourteenth Amendment and requested injunctive and declarative relief. They also argued that the School District failed to identify a special need for testing students who participate in extracurricular activities, and that the "Drug Testing Policy neither addresses a proven problem nor promises to bring any benefit to students or the school."

Applying the principles articulated in *Vernonia School Dist. v. Acton*, 515 U.S. (1995), in which we upheld the suspicionless drug testing of school athletes, the United States District Court for the Western District of Oklahoma rejected respondents' claim that the Policy was unconstitutional and granted summary judgment to the School District. The court noted that "special needs" exist in the public school context and that, although the School District did "not show a drug problem of epidemic proportions," there was a history of drug abuse starting in 1970 that presented "legitimate cause for concern." The District Court also held that the Policy was effective because "it can scarcely be disputed that the drug problem among the student body is effectively addressed by making sure that the large number of students participating in competitive, extracurricular activities do not use drugs."

The United States Court of Appeals for the Tenth Circuit reversed, holding that the Policy violated the Fourth Amendment. The Court of Appeals agreed with the District Court that the

Policy must be evaluated in the "unique environment of the school setting," but reached a different conclusion as to the Policy's constitutionality. Before imposing a suspicionless drug testing program, the Court of Appeals concluded that a school "must demonstrate that there is some identifiable drug abuse problem among a sufficient number of those subject to the testing, such that testing that group of students will actually redress its drug problem." Id., at 1278. The Court of Appeals then held that because the School District failed to demonstrate such a problem existed among Tecumseh students participating in competitive extracurricular activities, the Policy was unconstitutional. We granted *certiorari* and now reverse.

The Fourth Amendment to the United States Constitution protects "the right of the people to be secure in their persons, houses, papers, and effects, against unreasonable searches and seizures." Searches by public school officials, such as the collection of urine samples, implicate Fourth Amendment interests. We must therefore review the School District's Policy for "reasonableness," which is the touchstone of the constitutionality of a governmental search.

In *Vernonia*, this Court held that the suspicionless drug testing of athletes was constitutional. The Court, however, did not simply authorize all school drug testing, but rather conducted a fact-specific balancing of the intrusion on the children's Fourth Amendment rights against the promotion of legitimate governmental interests. Applying the principles of Vernonia to the somewhat different facts of this case, we conclude that Tecumseh's Policy is also constitutional.

We first consider the nature of the privacy interest allegedly compromised by the drug testing. As in *Vernonia*, the context of the public school environment serves as the backdrop for the analysis of the privacy interest at stake and the reasonableness of the drug testing policy in general. . . .

A student's privacy interest is limited in a public school environment where the State is responsible for maintaining discipline, health, and safety. Schoolchildren are routinely required to submit to physical examinations and vaccinations against disease. Securing order in the school environment sometimes requires that students be subjected to greater controls than those appropriate for adults. . . . And apart from education, the school has the obligation to protect pupils from mistreatment by other children, and also to protect teachers themselves from violence by the few students whose conduct in recent years has prompted national concern.

Respondents argue that because children participating in nonathletic extracurricular activities are not subject to regular physicals and communal undress, they have a stronger expectation of privacy than the athletes tested in *Vernonia*. . . .

In any event, students who participate in competitive extracurricular activities voluntarily subject themselves to many of the same intrusions on their privacy as do athletes. Some of these clubs and activities require occasional off-campus travel and communal undress. All of them have their own rules and requirements for participating students that do not apply to the student body as a whole. For example, each of the competitive extracurricular activities governed by the Policy must abide by the rules of the Oklahoma Secondary Schools Activities Association, and a faculty sponsor monitors the students for compliance with the various rules dictated by the clubs and activities. This regulation of extracurricular activities further diminishes the expectation of privacy among schoolchildren. . . . We therefore conclude that the students affected by this Policy have a limited expectation of privacy.

Next, we consider the character of the intrusion imposed by the Policy. . . .

Under the Policy, a faculty monitor waits outside the closed restroom stall for the student to produce a sample and must "listen for the normal sounds of urination in order to guard against tampered specimens and to insure an accurate chain of custody." The monitor then pours the sample into two bottles that are sealed and placed into a mailing pouch along with a consent form signed by the student. This procedure is virtually identical to that reviewed in *Vernonia*, except that it additionally protects privacy by allowing male students to produce their samples behind a closed stall. Given that we considered the method of collection in *Vernonia* a "negligible" intrusion, the method here is even less problematic.

In addition, the Policy clearly requires that the test results be kept in confidential files separate from a student's other educational records and released to school personnel only on a "need to know" basis. Respondents nonetheless contend that the intrusion on students' privacy is significant because the Policy fails to protect effectively against the disclosure of confidential information and, specifically, that the school "has been careless in protecting that information: for example, the Choir teacher looked at students' prescription drug lists and left them where other students could see them." . . .

Moreover, the test results are not turned over to any law enforcement authority. Nor do the test results here lead to the imposition of discipline or have any academic consequences. Rather, the only consequence of a failed drug test is to limit the student's privilege of participating in extracurricular activities.

Given the minimally intrusive nature of the sample collection and the limited uses to which the test results are put, we conclude that the invasion of students' privacy is not significant.

Finally, this Court must consider the nature and immediacy of the government's concerns and the efficacy of the Policy in meeting them. This Court has already articulated in detail the importance of the governmental concern in preventing drug use by schoolchildren. The drug abuse problem among our Nation's youth has hardly abated since *Vernonia* was decided in 1995. In fact, evidence suggests that it has only grown worse. As in *Vernonia*, "the necessity for the State to act is magnified by the fact that this evil is being visited not just upon individuals at large, but upon children for whom it has undertaken a special responsibility of care and direction." The health and safety risks identified in *Vernonia* apply with equal force to Tecumseh's children. Indeed, the nationwide drug epidemic makes the war against drugs a pressing concern in every school.

Additionally, the School District in this case has presented specific evidence of drug use at Tecumseh schools. Teachers testified that they had seen students who appeared to be under the influence of drugs and that they had heard students speaking openly about using drugs. A drug dog found marijuana cigarettes near the school parking lot. Police officers once found drugs or drug paraphernalia in a car driven by a Future Farmers of America member. And the school board president reported that people in the community were calling the board to discuss the "drug situation." . . .

Respondents consider the proffered evidence insufficient and argue that there is no "real and immediate interest" to justify a policy of drug testing nonathletes. The School District has provided sufficient evidence to shore up the need for its drug testing program.

Furthermore, this Court has not required a particularized or pervasive drug problem before allowing the government to conduct suspicionless drug testing. For instance, in Von Raab the Court upheld the drug testing of customs officials on a purely preventive basis, without any documented history of drug use by such officials. Likewise, the need to prevent and deter the substantial harm of childhood drug use provides the necessary immediacy for a school testing policy. Indeed, it would make little sense to require a school district to wait for a substantial portion of its students to begin using drugs before it was allowed to institute a drug testing program designed to deter drug use.

Given the nationwide epidemic of drug use, and the evidence of increased drug use in Tecumseh schools, it was entirely reasonable for the School District to enact this particular drug testing policy. We reject the Court of Appeals' novel test that "any district seeking to impose a random suspicionless drug testing policy as a condition to participation in a school activity must demonstrate that there is some identifiable drug abuse problem among a sufficient number of those subject to the testing, such that testing that group of students will actually redress its drug problem." . . .

Respondents also argue that the testing of nonathletes does not implicate any safety concerns, and that safety is a "crucial factor" in applying the special needs framework. They contend that there must be "surpassing safety interests," or "extraordinary safety and national security hazards," in order to override the usual protections of the Fourth Amendment. Respondents are correct that safety factors into the special needs analysis, but the safety interest furthered by drug testing is undoubtedly substantial for all children, athletes and nonathletes alike. We know all too well that drug use carries a variety of health risks for children, including death from overdose.

We also reject respondents' argument that drug testing must presumptively be based upon an individualized reasonable suspicion of wrongdoing because such a testing regime would be less intrusive. In this context, the Fourth Amendment does not require a finding of individualized suspicion, and we decline to impose such a requirement on schools attempting to prevent and detect drug use by students. Moreover, we question whether testing based on individualized suspicion in fact would be less intrusive. Such a regime would place an additional burden on public school teachers who are already tasked with the difficult job of maintaining order and discipline. A program of individualized suspicion might unfairly target members of unpopular groups. The fear of lawsuits resulting from such targeted searches may chill enforcement of the program, rendering it ineffective in combating drug use. In any case, this Court has repeatedly stated that reasonableness under the Fourth Amendment does not require employing the least intrusive means, because "the logic of such elaborate less-restrictive-alternative arguments could raise insuperable barriers to the exercise of virtually all search-and-seizure powers." . . .

Finally, we find that testing students who participate in extracurricular activities is a reasonably effective means of addressing the School District's legitimate concerns in preventing, deterring, and detecting drug use. While in *Vernonia* there might have been a closer fit between the testing of athletes and the trial court's finding that the drug problem was "fueled by the 'role model' effect of athletes' drug use," such a finding was not essential to the holding. *Vernonia* did not require the school to test the group of students most likely to use drugs, but rather considered the constitutionality of the program in the context of the public school's custodial responsibilities. Evaluating the Policy in this context, we

conclude that the drug testing of Tecumseh students who participate in extracurricular activities effectively serves the School District's interest in protecting the safety and health of its students.

Within the limits of the Fourth Amendment, local school boards must assess the desirability of drug testing schoolchildren. In upholding the constitutionality of the Policy, we express no opinion as to its wisdom. Rather, we hold only that Tecumseh's Policy is a reasonable means of furthering the School District's important interest in preventing and deterring drug use among its schoolchildren. Accordingly, we reverse the judgment of the Court of Appeals.

It is so ordered.

JUSTICE GINSBURG, with whom JUSTICE STEVENS, JUSTICE O'-CONNOR, and JUSTICE SOUTER join, dissenting.

Seven years ago, in *Vernonia School Dist. v. Acton* (1995), this Court determined that a school district's policy of randomly testing the urine of its student athletes for illicit drugs did not violate the Fourth Amendment. In so ruling, the Court emphasized that drug use "increased the risk of sports-related injury" and that Vernonia's athletes were the "leaders" of an aggressive local "drug culture" that had reached "epidemic proportions." Today, the Court relies upon *Vernonia* to permit a school district with a drug problem its superintendent repeatedly described as "not . . . major," to test the urine of an academic team member solely by reason of her participation in a nonathletic, competitive extracurricular activity—participation associated with neither special dangers from, nor particular predilections for, drug use.

"The legality of a search of a student," this Court has instructed, "should depend simply on the reasonableness, under all the circumstances, of the search." Although "'special needs' inhere in the public school context," those needs are not so expansive or malleable as to render reasonable any program of student drug testing a school district elects to install. The particular testing program upheld today is not reasonable, it is capricious, even perverse: Petitioners' policy targets for testing a student population least likely to be at risk from illicit drugs and their damaging effects. I therefore dissent.

A search unsupported by probable cause nevertheless may be consistent with the Fourth Amendment "when special needs, beyond the normal need for law enforcement, make the warrant and probable-cause requirement impracticable." *Griffin v. Wisconsin*, 483 U.S. 868 (1987). In *Vernonia*, this Court made clear that "such 'special needs' . . . exist in the public school context."

The *Vernonia* Court concluded that a public school district facing a disruptive and explosive drug abuse problem sparked by members of its athletic teams had "special needs" that justified suspicionless testing of district athletes as a condition of their athletic participation.

This case presents circumstances dispositively different from those of *Vernonia*. . . . Concern for student health and safety is basic to the school's caretaking, and it is undeniable that "drug use carries a variety of health risks for children, including death from overdose."

Those risks, however, are present for all schoolchildren. *Vernonia* cannot be read to endorse invasive and suspicionless drug testing of all students upon any evidence of drug use, solely because drugs jeopardize the life and health of those who use them. Many children, like many adults, engage in dangerous activities on their own time; that the children are enrolled in school scarcely allows government to monitor all such activities. If a student has a reasonable subjective expectation of privacy in the personal items she brings to school, surely she has a similar expectation regarding the chemical composition of her urine.

The . . . commonality to which the Court points is the voluntary character of both interscholastic athletics and other competitive extracurricular activities. "By choosing to 'go out for the team,' [school athletes] voluntarily subject themselves to a degree of regulation even higher than that imposed on students generally." Comparably, the Court today observes, "students who participate in competitive extracurricular activities voluntarily subject themselves to" additional rules not applicable to other students.

The comparison is enlightening. While extracurricular activities are "voluntary" in the sense that they are not required for graduation, they are part of the school's educational program; for that reason, the petitioner (hereinafter School District) is justified in expending public resources to make them available. Participation in such activities is a key component of school life, essential in reality for students applying to college, and, for all participants, a significant contributor to the breadth and quality of the educational experience. . . .

Voluntary participation in athletics has a distinctly different dimension: Schools regulate student athletes discretely because competitive school sports by their nature require communal undress and, more important, expose students to physical risks that schools have a duty to mitigate. For the very reason that schools cannot offer a program of competitive athletics without intimately affecting the privacy of students, . . .

In short, *Vernonia* applied, it did not repudiate, the principle that "the legality of a search of a student should depend simply on the reasonableness, under all the circumstances, of the search." Enrollment in a public school, and election to participate in school activities beyond the bare minimum that the curriculum requires, are indeed factors relevant to reasonableness, but they do not on their own justify intrusive, suspicionless searches.

Vernonia initially considered "the nature of the privacy interest upon which the search [there] at issue intruded." The Court emphasized that student athletes' expectations of privacy are necessarily attenuated. . . .

Competitive extracurricular activities other than athletics, however, serve students of all manner: the modest and shy along with the bold and uninhibited. . . .

On "occasional out-of-town trips," students like Lindsay Earls "must sleep together in communal settings and use communal bathrooms." But those situations are hardly equivalent to the routine communal undress associated with athletics; the School District itself admits that when such trips occur, "public-like restroom facilities," which presumably include enclosed stalls, are ordinarily available for changing, and that "more modest students" find other ways to maintain their privacy. . . .

In this case . . . Lindsay Earls and her parents allege that the School District handled personal information collected under the policy carelessly, with little regard for its confidentiality. Information about students' prescription drug use, they assert, was routinely viewed by Lindsay's choir teacher, who left files containing the information unlocked and unsealed, where others, including students, could see them; and test results were given out to all activity sponsors whether or not they had a clear "need to know."

In granting summary judgment to the School District, the District Court observed that the District's "Policy expressly provides for confidentiality of test results, and the Court must assume that the confidentiality provisions will be honored." The assumption is unwarranted.

Finally, the "nature and immediacy of the governmental concern" faced by the Vernonia School District dwarfed that confronting Tecumseh administrators. *Vernonia* initiated its drug testing policy in response to an alarming situation. . . . Tecumseh, by contrast, repeatedly reported to the Federal Government during the period leading up to the adoption of the policy that "types of drugs [other than alcohol and tobacco] including controlled dangerous substances, are present [in the schools] but have not identified themselves as major problems at this time." . . .

Not only did the Vernonia and Tecumseh districts confront drug problems of distinctly different magnitudes, they also chose different solutions: Vernonia limited its policy to athletes; Tecumseh indiscriminately subjected to testing all participants in competitive extracurricular activities.

At the margins, of course, no policy of random drug testing is perfectly tailored to the harms it seeks to address. The School District cites the dangers faced by members of the band, who must "perform extremely precise routines with heavy equipment and instruments in close proximity to other students," and by Future Farmers of America, who "are required to individually control and restrain animals as large as 1500 pounds." . . . Notwithstanding nightmarish images of out-of-control flatware, livestock run amok, and colliding tubas disturbing the peace and quiet of Tecumseh, the great majority of students the School District seeks to test in truth are engaged in activities that are not safety sensitive to an unusual degree. There is a difference between imperfect tailoring and no tailoring at all.

The Vernonia district, in sum, had two good reasons for testing athletes: Sports team members faced special health risks and they "were the leaders of the drug culture." No similar reason, and no other tenable justification, explains Tecumseh's decision to target for testing all participants in every competitive extracurricular activity. . . .

Even if students might be deterred from drug use in order to preserve their extracurricular eligibility, it is at least as likely that other students might forgo their extracurricular involvement in order to avoid detection of their drug use. Tecumseh's policy thus falls short doubly if deterrence is its aim: It invades the privacy of students who need deterrence least, and risks steering students at greatest risk for substance abuse away from extracurricular involvement that potentially may palliate drug problems.

To summarize, this case resembles *Vernonia* only in that the School Districts in both cases conditioned engagement in activities outside the obligatory curriculum on random subjection to urinalysis. The defining characteristics of the two programs, however, are entirely dissimilar. The Vernonia district sought to test a subpopulation of students distinguished by their reduced expectation of privacy, their special susceptibility to drug-related injury, and their heavy involvement with drug use. The Tecumseh district seeks to test a much larger population associated with none of these factors. It does so, moreover, without carefully safeguarding student confidentiality and without regard to the program's untoward effects. A program so sweeping is not sheltered by *Vernonia*; its unreasonable reach renders it impermissible under the Fourth Amendment.

It is a sad irony that the petitioning School District seeks to justify its edict here by trumpeting "the schools' custodial and tutelary responsibility for children." In regulating an athletic program or endeavoring to combat an exploding drug epidemic, a school's custodial obligations may permit searches that would otherwise unacceptably abridge students' rights. When custodial duties are not ascendant, however, schools' tutelary obligations to their students require them to "teach by example by avoiding symbolic measures that diminish constitutional protections." "That [schools] are educating the young for citizenship is reason for scrupulous protection of Constitutional freedoms of the individual, if we are not to strangle the free mind at its source and teach youth to discount important principles of our government as mere platitudes." *West Virginia Bd. of Ed. v. Barnette*, 319 U.S. 624 (1943).

For the reasons stated, I would affirm the judgment of the Tenth Circuit declaring the testing policy at issue unconstitutional.

COMMENTS AND QUESTIONS

The *Earls* decision is another in a long list of Supreme Court decisions over roughly the past two decades in which the Court has upheld a search of dubious constitutionality under the Fourth Amendment's prohibition against unreasonable searches and seizures. As documented in this chapter, the federal courts, led by the Rehnquist Supreme Court, have employed creative and imaginative reasons to justify all sorts of warrantless, suspicionless "administrative" searches, angering many civil libertarians who claim that, sadly, the Fourth Amendment today has only feeble protective force.

The *Earls* case involves a warrantless suspicionless search of the urine of Tecumseh middle and high school students who participate in any extracurricular activity. The slim majority on the high court upheld the search, giving as their chief argument that the drug testing policy helps to promote student health and safety and is reasonably rooted in a "special need"—that is, that the school district has a drug problem that needs to be solved. Of course, as civil liberty groups have noted, all a court has to do is cite a "special need" to justify a search and, bingo, the Fourth Amendment's protection against unreasonable searches and seizures disappears.

Given the vehement dissent, the dissenters apparently believed that the majority's search for justifications for their decision appeared even more unreasonable than the search of student urine that they were judging. Justice Ginsburg, writing the dissenting opinion with whom justices Stevens, O'Connor, and Souter joined, rejected virtually every reason given by the Court's majority for upholding the constitutionality of the drug testing policy for Tecumseh students. First, the majority argued that this case was similar to the circumstances involving the testing of student athletes in *Vernonia School District v. Acton*, 515 U.S. 646 (1995). But the dissenters disagreed, noting that the circumstances in this case are "dispositively different from those of *Vernonia*." In *Vernonia* the search was limited only to students participating in student athletics, while in *Earls* all students participating in any extracurricular activity were subjected to urine drug tests. This intrusive testing was done to Tecumseh students, Ginsburg asserted, despite any real proof that any significant drug problem existed among Tecumseh students, the district's justification for the drug testing program under the "special need" standard. In *Vernonia*, she pointed out, it had been demonstrated that the school district faced "a disruptive and explosive drug problem sparked by members of its athletic teams," justifying the "special need" for an invasive, suspicionless search via urinalysis drug testing, while in the Tecumseh School District, Ginsburg exclaimed, even the school system's superintendent repeatedly downplayed the drug problem as "not major."

The dissenters also felt that Tecumseh's drug testing policy was too broad to survive constitutional challenges under the Fourth Amendment. Historically, the Supreme Court has ruled against various governmental policies, including searches, that were not "narrowly tailored," subjecting unnecessarily and unfairly too many citizens to various restrictions and tests. In *Earls*, the dissenters believed the drug testing went too far, stripping unfairly too many students of their privacy rights under the Fourth Amendment. Specifically, the dissenters thought, if Lindsay Earls—a member only of the band and academic team, not a participant in school sports—"has a reasonable subjective expectation of privacy in the personal items she brings to school, . . . surely she has a similar expectation regarding the chemical composition of her urine" (p. 822).

The dissenters were also very critical of the majority's reasoning in *Earls* that the drug testing policy was acceptable because these extracurricular activities were voluntary and thus students could, presumably, avoid being subjected to drug testing by simply not participating in these extracurricular activities. The dissenters adamantly rejected this depiction of participation in school-sponsored and taxpayer-supported extracurricular activities. They maintained essentially that such activities may not be required per se to graduate, but students realistically are expected to participate in them, especially if they plan on applying to college, because "they are part of the school's educational program" (p. 845).

Other objections were or could have been raised by the dissenters (e.g., promised confidentiality was breached; drug tests could eventually be used to expel students and/or used in criminal prosecution; the district court should never have granted summary judgment when so many "doubtful matters should have been resolved in favor of the judgment seekers"), but the bottom line is that it appears that the Supreme Court has shown very little respect for privacy rights in recent times and has been quite blatant about using the balancing test to strengthen the police powers of the government at the expense of individual freedoms.

Unquestionably, the Supreme Court's majority is right when asserting that Tecumseh's school children, as well as school children elsewhere, need protection from the horrors of drug use. As the dissenters argue, however, this still does not justify interpreting *Vernonia* to permit "invasive and suspicionless drug testing of all students upon any evidence of drug use, solely because drugs jeopardize the life and health of those who use them" (p. 844). As the dissenters acknowledge, unfortunately children, as well as adults, engage in dangerous behavior, but does this necessarily justify the government declaring a "special need" to compromise various basic constitutional freedoms by invasively monitoring all of our "risky" activities? Should not teachers be spending less time and fewer tax dollars testing students for drugs and more time and money on actually teaching students? The Supreme Court in recent years has been quick to rule against various agency due process procedures deemed to be cost-ineffective. Well, how cost-effective do you think it is to test for drug use among virtually all students in a school system when the percentage of students actually using drugs is very low? Don't you think parents, not the government, should take the responsibility for testing their children for drugs if they suspect their children are using them?

NOTES

1. Of course, in drafting public policies and resolving disputes in court, legislators and judges must also choose between societal and individual rights. Consequently, one could validly say that seeking an equitable balance to these frequently competing rights is government's single biggest task.

2. Herbert Kaufman, *Red Tape* (Washington, D.C.: Brookings Institution Press, 1977), p. 19.

3. Ibid.

4. For a thorough analysis of the costs and benefits of preserving protected interests, see Richard J. Pierce, Jr., *Administrative Law Treatise,* 4th ed. (New York: Aspen, 2002), vol. 1, chap. 4; col. 2, chap. 1.

5. Dissenting in *Wyman v. James,* 400 U.S. 309, 328 (1971).

6. Ibid., at 335.

7. Michael J. Perry, *The Constitution, the Courts, and Human Rights: An Inquiry into the Legitimacy of Constitutional Policymaking by the Judiciary* (New Haven: Yale University Press, 1982), especially chaps. 3 and 4; Ronald C. Kahn, *The Supreme Court and Constitutional Democracy* (Ithaca, N.Y.: Cornell University Press, 1984); Bruce A. Ackerman, "The Storrs Lecture: Discovering the Constitution," *The Yale Law Journal* 93 (May 1984); and Richard Sobel, "The Degradation of Political Identity Under a National Identification System," *Boston University Journal of Science and Technology Law* 37 (winter 2002).

8. *Schenck v. United States,* 249 U.S. 47 (1919).

9. *Weeks v. United States,* 232 U.S. 383 (1914); *Mapp v. Ohio,* 367 U.S. 643 (1961). Recently, however, courts have been ruling that illegally seized evidence can be used in a variety of imaginative ways. For example, evidence illegally seized by state authorities may not be usable in state proceedings, but be in federal civil proceedings (*United States v. Torres,* 926 F.2d 321 [1991]).

10. Bernard Schwartz, *Administrative Law,* 3rd ed. (Boston: Little, Brown, 1991), pp. 94–107.

11. Ronald F. Wright, "The Civil and Criminal Methodologies of the Fourth Amendment," *Yale Law Review* 93 (May 1984). Also see the dissenting opinions in *United States v. Salerno,* 107 S.Ct. 2095 (1987).

12. Schwartz, *Administrative Law,* 3rd ed., pp. 98–99.

13. See Walter Gellhorn, Clark Byse, Peter L. Strauss, Todd Rakoff, and Roy A. Schotland, *Administrative Law: Cases and Comments,* 8th ed. (Mineola, N.Y.: Foundation Press, 1987), pp. 673–701.

14. Several years ago, there was a good deal of publicity about the case of a Spanish-speaking immigrant who had witnessed a murder in Boston shortly after he had moved to the United States. Because he was regarded as an unreliable witness (one who might vanish before being called to testify), the prosecutor's office ordered that he be detained in the Suffolk County Jail, a jail known for its deplorable conditions, until he could testify at the trial. His story received media attention when it was learned that he had been kept in the jail for six months and that, because the defense had just been granted another postponement of the trial date, it appeared that the unfortunate witness, guilty of no crime, would likely have to spend at least another half year in jail. Public comment centered on the quality of welcome to the country that this man had received.

15. Incidentally, a writ of habeas corpus would not be used to obtain the release of individuals lawfully held by administrators. A writ of habeas corpus can be employed only to obtain the release of persons *illegally* held by administrators.

16. An immigration statute, 8 U.S.C., Sec. 1357(a)(2), permits immigration officials to make an arrest without an administrative warrant if it is thought that the alien would likely "escape before a warrant can be obtained for his arrest."

17. Justice William O. Douglas, dissenting in *Abel,* p. 245.

18. *Carlson v. Landon,* 342 U.S. 524 (1952). This decision may be questioned under the Eighth Amendment's provision guaranteeing persons the right to be released after posting reasonable bail. For conservative and liberal thinking on the use of bail, see *United States v. Salerno,* 107 S.Ct. 2095 (1987).

19. Schwartz, *Administrative Law,* 3rd ed., p. 107.

20. U.S. Department of Labor, *Annual Report* 37 (Washington, D.C.: U.S. Government Printing Office, 1976). This figure dropped to 59,932 in fiscal 1977 because of public reaction to the quantity of OSHA inspections. To systems theorists, the reduction in inspections from 1976 to 1977 points out perfectly how agencies adjust to the feedback demands from their environments. OSHA has had to make appropriate adjustments to survive (U.S. Department of Labor *Annual Report* 48 [Washington, D.C.: U.S. Government Printing Office, 1977]). As reported earlier, OSHA inspections dropped off dramatically during the Reagan administration.

21. Schwartz, *Administrative Law,* 3rd ed., p. 110.

22. Ibid.

23. For a commentary on the "required records" doctrine, see Unauthored Note, "Organizational Papers and the Privilege Against Self-Incrimination," *Harvard Law Review* 99 (January 1986). As record keeping applies to banks, see Jill Brenner, Brittany Nelson, and Daniel Chudd, "Financial Institutions Fraud," *American Criminal Law Review* 39 (spring 2002).

24. Ronald J. Bacigal, "Some Observations and Proposals on the Nature of the Fourth Amendment," *George Washington Law Review* 46 (May 1978): 559.

25. Kevin I. MacKenzie, "Administrative Searches and the Fourth Amendment: An Alternative to the Warrant Requirement," *Cornell Law Review* 64 (1979).

26. The Court acknowledged that its decision in this case would cause more businesses to demand in the future that inspectors go back and obtain a search warrant before they allowed the inspection. However, since the warrants can be obtained very easily, I doubt whether many astute businesspeople, who have some understanding of human psychology, would want to irritate administrative inspectors, who can exercise vast discretion in spotting violations, by inconveniencing them and forcing them to get warrants. For a zoologist's fascinating view of how we make certain responses that tend to elicit hostile attitudes in others, see Desmond Morris, *The Naked Ape* (London: Corgi Books, 1967), chap. 5. To avoid being cited for so-called extra violations, Morris's advice to business managers would be to take on a noncombative, submissive role in an effort to avoid putting the inspectors in positions in which they feel compelled to demonstrate their power and dominance. Morris says that once animals (including humans) establish dominance, they no longer feel compelled to act aggressively, since the challenge has been met.

27. It should be noted that surprise inspections probably have little value in the administrative regulatory process, as compared to the criminal law area, because, minor violations aside, serious violations cannot normally be kept hidden from inspectors (for example, cracks in the walls of nuclear power plant chambers or unhealthy and unsafe working conditions).

28. Three of the four dissenting justices have left the Supreme Court, thus leading to the speculation that now the more conservative court would most likely find most aerial searches constitutional under the Fourth Amendment. See Susan M. McDonough, "The Fourth Power? Administrative Searches vs. The Fourth Amendment," *New England Journal on Criminal and Civil Confinement* 20 (winter 1993).

29. Lisa J. Steele, "The View from on High: Satellite Remote Sensing Technology and the Fourth Amendment," *High Tech Law Journal* 6 (fall 1991): 302–333.

30. Ibid.

31. Ibid., pp. 333–334. Also, see Lisa J. Steele, "Waste Heat and Garbage: The Legalization of Warrantless Infrared Searches," *Criminal Law Bulletin* 29 (January–February 1993).

32. For a review of the implications *Kyllo,* see Heather K. McShain, "Not Quite Bradbury's *Farenheit 451:* The Uncertain Future of Sense-Enhancing Technology in the Aftermath of *United States v. Kyllo,*" *West Virginia Law Review* 105 (fall 2002).

33. Justice Potter Stewart presents an argument against the use of implied consent to take away a person's Fourth Amendment rights in his dissenting opinion in *Donovan v. Dewey,* 101 S.Ct. 2534 (1981).

34. MacKenzie, "Administrative Searches and the Fourth Amendment," p. 867.

35. Roger B. Dworkin, "Fact Style Adjudication and the Fourth Amendment: The Limits of Lawyering," *Indiana Law Journal* 48 (spring 1973): 329.

36. Bernard Schwartz, "Administrative Law Cases During 1978," *Administrative Law Review* 31 (spring 1979): 146.

37. For recent articles on the Fourth Amendment and administrative searches, see, for example, Allison M. Sgroi, "Federal Food and Drug Act Violations," *American Criminal Law Review* 39 (spring 2002); Rachael M. Dockery, "*Atwater v. City of Lago Vista*: A Simple, Bright-Line Holding Results in Future Fourth Amendment Confusion," *Arkansas Law Review* 55 (2002); and Jeffrey S. Grand, "The Blooding of America: Privacy and the DNA Dragnet, *Cardozo Law Review* 23 (August 2002).

38. AFDC ended in 1998 and was replaced by state welfare "reform" programs receiving federal subsidies.

39. Kenneth C. Davis, *Administrative Law Treatise*, 2nd ed. (San Diego: K. C. Davis, 1979), vol. 1, p. 261

40. Ibid., p. 262.

41. For an article that places *Wyman v. James* into perspective with Fourth Amendment administrative searches, see Christopher Slobogin, "The Poverty Exception to the Fourth Amendment," *Florida Law Review* 55 (January 2003).

42. Actually, as far back as *Boyd v. United States,* 116 U.S. 616 (1886), the Court recognized that Fourth Amendment protections should sometimes be extended to cover civil proceedings since civil proceedings frequently assume a quasi-criminal nature, especially when refusal to comply with requests under civil laws can lead to criminal charges and eventual fines or imprisonment (pp. 634–635).

43. William J. Brennan, Jr., "State Constitutions and the Protection of Individual Rights," *Harvard Law Review* 90 (January 1977): 495.

44. Note, "Formalism, Legal Realism, and Constitutionally Protected Privacy Under the Fourth and Fifth Amendments," *Harvard Law Review* 90 (March 1977).

45. Davis, *Administrative Law Treatise,* 2nd ed., vol. 1, p. 299.

46. Joel Cohen, "Are John Doe's Personal Papers Protected by the Fifth Amendment Any More?" *New York Law Journal* 210 (September 21, 1993): 1 and 4.

47. Lance Cole, "The Fifth Amendment and Compelled Production of Personal Documents After *United States v. Hubbell*—New Protection for Private Papers?" *American Journal of Criminal Law* 29 (spring 2002): 124.

48. Davis, *Administrative Law Treatise,* 2nd ed., vol. 1, p. 299.

49. Kathryn R. Urbonya, "A Fourth Amendment 'Search' in the Age of Technology: Postmodern Perspectives," *Mississippi Law Journal* 72 (fall 2002): 465.

50. John Locke, *Two Treatises on Civil Government,* intro. Peter Laslett (Cambridge, England: Cambridge University Press, 1960), p. 368.

51. Ibid.

52. Deborah Connor, "Criminal Procedure Project: The Exclusionary Rule," *Georgetown Law Review* 82 (March–April 1994).

53. Several Supreme Court decisions have supported the *Boyd* ruling at least in principle (specifically, the holding that a person should not be compelled to produce self-incriminating evidence), although in practice the decisions served to undermine the application of the *Boyd* principle. See *Wilson v. United States*, 221 U.S. 361 (1911); *Wheeler v. United States*, 226 U.S. 478 (1913); *United States v. White*, 332 U.S. 694 (1944); *Couch v. United States*, 409 U.S. 322 (1973); and *Bellis v. United States*, 417 U.S. 85 (1974).

54. See Douglas's dissenting opinions in *Abel v. United States*, 362 U.S. 217 (1960); *Warden v. Hayden*, 387 U.S. 294 (1967); *Wyman v. James*, 400 U.S. 309 (1971); and *Couch v. United States*, 409 U.S. 322 (1973). In *Fisher v. United States*, 425 U.S. 391, 414 (1976), Justice Brennan, concurring, voiced strong objections to the Court's majority opinion regarding compelled production of one's private papers. He maintained that it struck another crippling blow to the privilege against self-incrimination. In his own words: "It is but another step in the denigration of privacy principles settled nearly 100 years ago in *Boyd v. United States*, 116 U.S. 616 (1886)."

55. Davis, *Administrative Law Treatise,* 2nd ed., vol. 1, pp. 299–300.

56. Ibid.

57. See "Formalism, Legal Realism, and Constitutionally Protected Privacy Under the Fourth and Fifth Amendments," pp. 979–991; Steven T. Wax, "The Fourth Amendment, Administrative Searches and the Loss of Liberty," *Environmental Law* 4 (summer 1988); Thomas M. Blumenthal, "Judicial Activism—The Politicization of the Right of Privacy," *Saint Louis University Public Law Review* 11 (fall

1992); and William R. Huhn, "Teaching Legal Analysis Using a Pluralist Model of Law," *Gonzaga Law Review* 36 (2000–2001).

58. "Formalism, Legal Realism, and Constitutionally Protected Privacy Under the Fourth and Fifth Amendment," p. 932.

59. For an excellent analysis of how the employment of "balancing" has compromised Fourth and Fifth Amendment private protections see, Ronald F. Wright, "The Civil and Criminal Methodologies of the Fourth Amendment," *Yale Law Journal* 93 (May 1984). Basically, Wright contends that when the balance test (i.e., balancing between the privacy rights of an individual and the public interest) is applied by the courts, it is easier to rule in favor of the public interest, whereas if a more "concrete" standard is used (for example, showing probable cause), it is more difficult to side with the public interest. Like most legal scholars addressing this issue, he believes that the increased use of balancing has unfortunately resulted too often in individuals being denied their Fourth and Fifth Amendment privacy rights.

60. For discussions of this theoretical background, see Morton Gabriel White, *Social Thought in America* (Mineola, N.Y.: Foundation Press, 1957), p. 7; and Edwin Wilhite Patterson, *Jurisprudence* (Mineola, N.Y.: Foundation Press, 1957), p. 472.

61. William James, *Pragmatism: A New Name for Old Ways of Thinking* (1907; reprint, New York: Green and Company, 1947), p. 222.

62. "Formalism, Legal Realism, and Constitutionally Protected Privacy Under the Fourth and Fifth Amendments," p. 966.

63. Ibid.

64. Reinhard Bendix, *Max Weber: An Intellectual Portrait* (New York: Doubleday, 1962), chaps. 3, 12–15.

65. Roscoe Pound, "The Scope and Purpose of Sociological Jurisprudence," *Harvard Law Review* 25 (April 1912): 514.

66. Benjamin N. Cardozo, *The Nature of the Judicial Process* (New Haven: Yale University Press, 1921), p. 113.

67. For a review of some key decisions since *Boyd*, see Cohen, "Are John Doe's Personal Papers Protected by the Fifth Amendment Any More?"

68. Pierce, *Administrative Law Treatise*, 4th ed., vol. 1, pp. 193–249.

69. Ibid., p. 234.

70. In *United States v. Osborn*, 561 F.2d 1334, 1338 (9th Cir. 1977), the court noted that records kept by persons who are connected with an industry regulated by the government (for example, bank accounts, utility bills, sales transactions of personal property, tax statements) are not personal records. Since government regulation is so pervasive today, it appears that only a few of our records could be classified as purely personal.

71. In this case "constructive possession" means that the taxpayer actually retained legal possession of the work papers, even though he had temporarily transferred them from his hands to his attorney's.

72. Justice Thurgood Marshall also wrote a separate dissenting opinion, in which he supported Brennan's basic position that the seized personal business records should have been suppressed at the petitioner's trial.

73. Comment: "Fifth Amendment: Compulsory Production of Incriminating Business Records," *Journal of Criminal Law and Criminology* 71 (1980): 52.

74. "Formalism, Legal Realism, and Constitutionally Protected Privacy Under the Fourth and Fifth Amendments," p. 978.

75. Davis, *Administrative Law Treatise*, 2nd ed., vol. 1, p. 284.

76. "Fifth Amendment: Compulsory Production of Incriminating Business Records," p. 53.

77. This is not an exaggerated statement. During the Iranian hostage crisis that plagued the last year of the Carter administration, Carter ordered many Iranians in the United States, many of them students, sent back to Iran. However, many of these Iranians feared that their lives would be in danger if they were sent back to Iran, because many of them and their families in Iran (some of their family members had already been killed) were bitter and vocal enemies of Iran's new leader, Ayatollah Khomeini, and friends and even aides of the deposed shah. Consequently, several Iranians in the United States vigorously fought their deportation in INS hearings. Haitians seeking political asylum in the United States during the Clinton administration had similar fears regarding being returned to Haiti, as have certain Cubans recently seeking political asylum in the United States during George W. Bush's administration.

78. Bernard Schwartz, "Administrative Law Cases During 1984," *Administrative Law Review* 37 (spring 1985): 141.

79. Jennifer M. Collins, "And the Walls Came Tumbling Down: Sharing Grand Jury Information with the Intelligence Community Under the U.S.A. Patriot Act," *American Criminal Law Review* 39 (summer 2002): 1261.

80. Ibid.

81. Ibid., p. 1285.

82. Stephen W. Tountas, "Carnivore: Is the Regulation of Wireless Technology a Legally Viable Option to Curtail the Growth of Cybercrime?" *Washington University Journal of Law and Policy* 11 (2003).

83. Ibid., pp. 363–374.

84. Ibid., p. 374.

85. Ibid., p. 376.

86. Ibid., pp. 376–377.

87. Collins, "And the Walls Came Tumbling Down," pp. 1262–1267.

88. Melissa K. Mathews, "Restoring the Imperial Presidency: An Examination of President Bush's New Emergency Powers," *Hamlin's Journal of Public Law and Policy* 23 (spring 2002).

89. Michael T. McCarthy, "USA Patriot Act," *Harvard Journal on Legislation* 39 (summer 2002): 435.

90. Ibid., p. 436.

91. Ibid., pp. 435–453.

92. Ibid.

93. Stuart Taylor, Jr., "Panel Discussion: The USA Patriot Act and the American Response to Terror: Can We Protect Civil Liberties After September 11?" *American Criminal Law Review* 39 (fall 2002): 1509.

94. 33 L.S.I. 89 (1978–1979).

95. Emanuel Gross, "The Influence of Terrorist Attacks on Human Rights in the United States: The Aftermath of September 11, 2001," *North Carolina Journal of International Law and Commercial Regulation* 28 (fall 2002): 70.

96. Ibid.

97. Ibid., pp. 70–71.

98. Ibid., p. 71.

99. Rene Sanchez, "Libertarians Won't Stay Quiet About the Patriot Act," *Washington Post National Weekly Edition,* April 21–27, 2003, pp. 30–31.

100. Gross, "The Influence of Terrorist Attacks on Human Rights in the United States," pp. 1–101.

101. Named after several ships, the brig Army *Warwick*, the schooner *Crenshaw*, the barque *Hiawatha*, and the schooner *Brilliante*, which were captured and taken as prizes.

102. Oren Gross, "Chaos and Rules: Should Responses to Violent Crises Always Be Constitutional?" *Yale Law Journal* 112 (March 2003): 1019.

103. Scott Alexander, "Inalienable Rights?: Muslims in the U.S. Since September 11," *Journal of Islamic Law and Culture* 7 (spring–summer 2002): 114.

104. Ibid.

105. Kerby Anderson, "Amend the Patriot Act?" *Kerby Anderson's Commentaries* (January 11, 2002), www.probe.org/docs/c-patriot.html.

106. Ibid.

107. Quoted in Oren Gross, "Chaos and Rules: Should Responses to Violent Crises Always Be Constitutional?" p. 1020.

Federal Administrative Procedure Act (as amended as of 2003)

TITLE 5, U.S. CODE

Chapter 5—Administrative Procedure

§551. Definitions

For the purpose of this subchapter—

(1) "agency" means each authority of the Government of the United States, whether or not it is within or subject to review by another agency, but does not include—

(A) the Congress;

(B) the courts of the United States;

(C) the governments of the territories or possessions of the United States;

(D) the government of the District of Columbia; or except as to the requirements of section 552 of this title;

(E) agencies composed of representatives of the parties or of representatives of organizations of the parties to the disputes determined by them;

(F) courts martial and military commissions;

(G) military authority exercised in the field in time of war or in occupied territory; or

(H) functions conferred by sections 1738, 1739, 1743, and 1744 of title 12; chapter 2 of title 41; subchapter II of chapter 471 of title 49; or sections 1884, 1891–1902, and former section 1641(b)(2), of title 50, appendix;

(2) "person" includes an individual, partnership, corporation, association, or public or private organization other than an agency;

(3) "party" includes a person or agency named or admitted as a party, or properly seeking and entitled as of right to be admitted as a party, in an agency proceeding, and a person or agency admitted by an agency as a party for limited purposes;

(4) "rule" means the whole or a part of an agency statement of general or particular applicability and future effect designed to implement, interpret, or prescribe law or policy or describing the organization, procedure, or practice requirements of an agency and includes the approval or prescription for the future of rates, wages, corporate or financial structures or reorganizations thereof, prices, facilities, appliances, services or allowances therefor or of valuations, costs, or accounting, or practices bearing on any of the foregoing;

(5) "rule making" means agency process for formulating, amending, or repealing a rule;

(6) "order" means the whole or a part of a final disposition, whether affirmative, negative, injunctive, or declaratory in form, of an agency in a matter other than rule making but including licensing;

(7) "adjudication" means agency process for the formulation of an order;

(8) "license" includes the whole or a part of an agency permit, certificate, approval, registration, charter, membership, statutory exemption or other form of permission;

(9) "licensing" includes agency process respecting the grant, renewal, denial, revocation, suspension, annulment, withdrawal, limitation, amendment, modification, or conditioning of a license;

(10) "sanction" includes the whole or a part of an agency—

(A) prohibition, requirement, limitation, or other condition affecting the freedom of a person;

(B) withholding of relief;

(C) imposition of penalty or fine;

(D) destruction, taking, seizure, or withholding of property;

(E) assessment of damages, reimbursement, restitution, compensation, costs, charges, or fees;

(F) requirement, revocation, or suspension of a license; or

(G) taking other compulsory or restrictive action;

(11) "relief" includes the whole or a part of an agency—

(A) grant of money, assistance, license, authority, exemption, exception, privilege, or remedy;

(B) recognition of a claim, right, immunity, privilege, exemption, or exception; or

(C) taking of other action on the application or petition of, and beneficial to, a person;

(12) "agency proceeding" means an agency process as defined by paragraphs (5), (7), and (9) of this section;

(13) "agency action" includes the whole or a part of an agency rule, order, license, sanction, relief, or the equivalent or denial thereof, or failure to act; and

(14) "ex parte communication" means an oral or written communication not on the public record with respect to which reasonable prior notice to all parties is not given, but it shall not include requests for status reports on any matter or proceeding covered by this subchapter.

§553. Rule making

(a) This section applies, according to the provisions thereof, except to the extent that there is involved—

(1) a military or foreign affairs function of the United States; or

(2) a matter relating to agency management or personnel or to public property, loans, grants, benefits, or contracts.

(b) General notice of proposed rule making shall be published in the Federal Register, unless persons subject thereto are named and either personally served or otherwise have actual notice thereof in accordance with law. The notice shall include—

(1) a statement of the time, place, and nature of public rule making proceedings;

(2) reference to the legal authority under which the rule is proposed; and

(3) either the terms or substance of the proposed rule or a description of the subjects and issues involved.

Except when notice or hearing is required by statute, this subsection does not apply—

(A) to interpretative rules, general statements of policy, or rules of agency organization, procedure, or practice; or

(B) when the agency for good cause finds (and incorporates the finding and a brief statement of reasons therefor in the rules issued) that notice and public procedure thereon are impracticable, unnecessary, or contrary to the public interest.

(c) After notice required by this section, the agency shall give interested persons an opportunity to participate in the rule making through submission of written data, views, or arguments with or without opportunity for oral presentation. After consideration of the relevant matter presented, the agency shall incorporate in the rules adopted a concise general statement of their basis and purpose. When rules are required by statute to be made on the record after opportunity for an agency hearing, sections 556 and 557 of this title apply instead of this subsection.

(d) The required publication or service of a substantive rule shall be made not less than 30 days before its effective date, except—

(1) a substantive rule which grants or recognizes an exemption or relieves a restriction;

(2) interpretative rules and statements of policy; or

(3) as otherwise provided by the agency for good cause found and published with the rule.

(e) Each agency shall give an interested person the right to petition for the issuance, amendment, or repeal of a rule.

(Added Sept. 6, 1966, P.L. 89-554, §1, 80 Stat. 383.)

§554. Adjudications

(a) This section applies, according to the provisions thereof, in every case of adjudication required by statute to be determined on the record after opportunity for an agency hearing, except to the extent that there is involved—

(1) a matter subject to a subsequent trial of the law and the facts de novo in a court;

(2) the selection or tenure of an employee, except a [an] administrative law judge appointed under section 3105 of this title;

(3) proceedings in which decisions rest solely on inspections, tests, or elections;

(4) the conduct of military or foreign affairs functions;

(5) cases in which an agency is acting as an agent for a court; or

(6) the certification of worker representatives.

(b) Persons entitled to notice of an agency hearing shall be timely informed of—

(1) the time, place, and nature of the hearing;

(2) the legal authority and jurisdiction under which the hearing is to be held; and

(3) the matters of fact and law asserted.

When private persons are the moving parties, other parties to the proceeding shall give prompt notice of issues controverted in fact or law; and in other instances agencies may by rule require responsive pleading. In fixing the time and place for hearings, due regard shall be had for the convenience and necessity of the parties or their representatives.

(c) The agency shall give all interested parties opportunity for—

(1) the submission and consideration of facts, arguments, offers of settlement, or proposals of adjustment when time, the nature of the proceeding, and the public interest permit; and

(2) to the extent that the parties are unable so to determine a controversy by consent, hearing and decision on notice and in accordance with sections 556 and 557 of this title.

(d) The employee who presides at the reception of evidence pursuant to section 556 of this title shall make the recommended decision or initial decision required by section 557 of this title, unless he becomes unavailable to the agency. Except to the extent required for the disposition of ex parte matters as authorized by law, such an employee may not—

(1) consult a person or party on a fact in issue, unless on notice and opportunity for all parties to participate; or

(2) be responsible to or subject to the supervision or direction of an employee or agent engaged in the performance of investigative or prosecuting functions for an agency.

An employee or agent engaged in the performance of investigative or prosecuting functions for an agency in a case may not, in that or a factually related case, participate or advise in the decision, recommended decision, or agency review pursuant to section 557 of this title, except as witness or counsel in public proceedings. This subsection does not apply—

(A) in determining applications for initial licenses;

(B) to proceedings involving the validity or application of rates, facilities, or practices of public utilities or carriers; or

(C) to the agency or a member or members of the body comprising the agency.

(e) The agency, with like effect as in the case of other orders, and in its sound discretion, may issue a declaratory order to terminate a controversy or remove uncertainty.

§555. Ancillary matters

(a) This section applies, according to the provisions thereof, except as otherwise provided by this subchapter.

(b) A person compelled to appear in person before an agency or representative thereof is entitled to be accompanied, represented, and advised by counsel or, if permitted by the agency, by other qualified representative. A party is entitled to appear in person or by or with counsel or other duly qualified representative in an agency proceeding. So far as the orderly conduct of public business permits, an interested person may appear before an agency or its responsible employees for the presentation, adjustment, or determination of an issue, request, or controversy in a proceeding, whether interlocutory, summary, or otherwise, or in connection with an agency function. With due regard for the convenience and necessity of the parties or their representatives and within a reasonable time, each agency shall proceed to conclude a matter presented to it. This subsection does not grant or deny a person who is not a lawyer the right to appear for or represent others before an agency or in an agency proceeding.

(c) Process, requirement of a report, inspection, or other investigative act or demand may not be issued, made, or enforced except as authorized by law. A person compelled to submit data or evidence is entitled to retain or, on payment of lawfully prescribed costs, procure a copy or transcript thereof, except that in a nonpublic investigatory proceeding the witness may for good cause be limited to inspection of the official transcript of his testimony.

(d) Agency subpoenas authorized by law shall be issued to a party on request and, when required by rules of procedure, on a statement or showing of general relevance and reasonable scope of the evidence sought. On contest, the court shall sustain the subpoena or similar process or demand to the extent that it is found to be in accordance with law. In a proceeding for enforcement, the court shall issue an order requiring the appearance of the witness or the production of the evidence or data within a reasonable time under penalty of punishment for contempt in case of contumacious failure to comply.

(e) Prompt notice shall be given of the denial in whole or in part of a written application, petition, or other request of an interested person made in connection with any agency proceeding. Except in affirming a prior denial or when the denial is self-explanatory, the notice shall be accompanied by a brief statement of the grounds for denial.

§556. Hearings; presiding employees; powers and duties; burden of proof; evidence; record as basis of decision

(a) This section applies, according to the provisions thereof, to hearings required by section 553 or 554 of this title to be conducted in accordance with this section.

(b) There shall preside at the taking of evidence—
(1) the agency;
(2) one or more members of the body which comprises the agency; or
(3) one or more administrative law judges appointed under section 3105 of this title.

This subchapter does not supersede the conduct of specified classes of proceedings, in whole or in part, by or before boards or other employees specially provided for by or designated under statute. The functions of presiding employees and of employees participating in decisions in accordance with section 557 of this title shall be conducted in an impartial manner. A presiding or participating employee may at any time disqualify himself. On the filing in good faith of a timely and sufficient affidavit of personal bias or other disqualification of a presiding or participating employee, the agency shall determine the matter as a part of the record and decision in the case.

(c) Subject to published rules of the agency and within its powers, employees presiding at hearings may—
(1) administer oaths and affirmations;
(2) issue subpoenas authorized by law;
(3) rule on offers of proof and receive relevant evidence;
(4) take depositions or have depositions taken when the ends of justice would be served;

(5) regulate the course of the hearing;

(6) hold conferences for the settlement or simplification of the issues by consent of the parties or by the use of alternative means of dispute resolution as provided in subchapter IV of this chapter

(7) inform the parties as to the availability of one or more alternative means of dispute resolution, and encourage use of such methods;

(8) require the attendance at any conference held pursuant to paragraph (6) of at least one representative of each party who has authority to negotiate concerning resolution of issues in controversy;

(9) dispose of procedural requests or similar matters;

(10) make or recommend decisions in accordance with section 557 of this title; and

(11) take other action authorized by agency rule consistent with this subchapter.

(d) Except as otherwise provided by statute, the proponent of a rule or order has the burden of proof. Any oral or documentary evidence may be received, but the agency as a matter of policy shall provide for the exclusion of irrelevant, immaterial, or unduly repetitious evidence. A sanction may not be imposed or rule or order issued except on consideration of the whole record or those parts thereof cited by a party and supported by and in accordance with the reliable, probative, and substantial evidence. The agency may, to the extent consistent with the interests of justice and the policy of the underlying statutes administered by the agency, consider a violation of section 557(d) of this title sufficient grounds for a decision adverse to a party who has knowingly committed such violation or knowingly caused such violation to occur. A party is entitled to present his case or defense by oral or documentary evidence, to submit rebuttal evidence, and to conduct such cross-examination as may be required for a full and true disclosure of the facts. In rule making or determining claims for money or benefits or applications for initial licenses an agency may, when a party will not be prejudiced thereby, adopt procedures for the submission of all or part of the evidence in written form.

(e) The transcript of testimony and exhibits, together with all papers and requests filed in the proceeding, constitutes the exclusive record for decision in accordance with section 557 of this title and, on payment of lawfully prescribed costs, shall be made available to the parties. When an agency decision rests on official notice of a material fact not appearing in the evidence in the record, a party is entitled, on timely request, to an opportunity to show the contrary.

§557. Initial decisions; conclusiveness; review by agency; submissions by parties; contents of decisions; record

(a) This section applies, according to the provisions thereof, when a hearing is required to be conducted in accordance with section 556 of this title.

(b) When the agency did not preside at the reception of the evidence, the presiding employee or, in cases not subject to section 554(d) of this title, an employee qualified to preside at hearings pursuant to section 556 of this title, shall initially decide the case unless the agency requires, either in specific cases or by general rule, the entire record to be certified to it for decision. When the presiding employee makes an initial decision, that decision then becomes the decision of the agency without further proceedings unless there is an appeal to, or review on motion of, the agency within time provided by rule. On appeal from or review of the initial decision, the agency has all the powers which it would have in making the initial decision except as it may limit the issues on notice or by rule. When the agency makes the decision without having presided at the reception of the evidence, the presiding employee or an employee qualified to preside at hearings pursuant to section 556 of this title shall first recommend a decision, except that in rule making or determining applications for initial licenses—

(1) instead thereof the agency may issue a tentative decision or one of its responsible employees may recommend a decision; or

(2) this procedure may be omitted in a case in which the agency finds on the record that due and timely execution of its functions imperatively and unavoidably so requires.

(c) Before a recommended, initial, or tentative decision, or a decision on agency review of the decision of subordinate employees, the parties are entitled to a reasonable opportunity to submit for the consideration of the employees participating in the decisions—

(1) proposed findings and conclusions; or

(2) exceptions to the decisions or recommended decisions of subordinate employees or to tentative agency decisions; and

(3) supporting reasons for the exceptions or proposed findings or conclusions.

The record shall show the ruling on each finding, conclusion, or exception presented. All decisions, including initial, recommended, and tentative decisions, are a part of the record and shall include a statement of—

(A) findings and conclusions, and the reasons or basis therefor, on all the material issues of fact, law, or discretion presented on the record; and

(B) the appropriate rule, order, sanction, relief, or denial thereof.

(d) (1) In any agency proceeding which is subject to subsection (a) of this section, except to the extent required for the disposition of ex parte matters as authorized by law—

(A) no interested person outside the agency shall make or knowingly cause to be made to any member of the body comprising the agency, administrative law judge, or other employee who is or may reasonably be expected to be involved in the decisional process of the proceeding, an ex parte communication relevant to the merits of the proceeding;

(B) no member of the body comprising the agency, administrative law judge, or other employee who is or may reasonably be expected to be involved in the decisional process of the proceeding, shall make or knowingly cause to be made to any interested person outside the agency an ex parte communication relevant to the merits of the proceeding;

(C) a member of the body comprising the agency, administrative law judge, or other employee who is or may reasonably be expected to be involved in the decisional process of such proceeding who receives, or who makes or knowingly causes to be made, a communication prohibited by this subsection shall place on the public record of the proceeding:

(i) all such written communications;

(ii) memoranda stating the substance of all such oral communications; and

(iii) all written responses, and memoranda stating the substance of all oral responses, to the materials described in clauses (i) and (ii) of this subparagraph;

(D) upon receipt of a communication knowingly made or knowingly caused to be made by a party in violation of this subsection, the agency, administrative law judge, or other employee presiding at the hearing may, to the extent consistent with the interests of justice and the policy of the underlying statutes, require the party to show cause why his claim or interest in the proceeding should not be dismissed, denied, disregarded, or otherwise adversely affected on account of such violation; and

(E) the prohibitions of this subsection shall apply beginning at such time as the agency may designate, but in no case shall they begin to apply later than the time at which a proceeding is noticed for hearing unless the person responsible for the communication has knowledge that it will be noticed, in which case the prohibitions shall apply beginning at the time of his acquisition of such knowledge.

(2) This subsection does not constitute authority to withhold information from Congress.

§558. Imposition of sanctions; determination of applications for licenses; suspension, revocation, and expiration of licenses

(a) This section applies, according to the provisions thereof, to the exercise of a power or authority.

(b) A sanction may not be imposed or a substantive rule or order issued except within jurisdiction delegated to the agency and as authorized by law.

(c) When application is made for a license required by law, the agency, with due regard for the rights and privileges of all the interested parties or adversely affected persons and within a reasonable time, shall set and complete proceedings required to be conducted in accordance with sections 556 and 557 of this title or other proceedings required by law and shall make its decision. Except in cases of willfulness or those in which public health, interest, or safety requires otherwise, the withdrawal, suspension, revocation, or annulment of a license is lawful only if, before the institution of agency proceedings therefor, the licensee has been given—

(1) notice by the agency in writing of the facts or conduct which may warrant the action; and

(2) opportunity to demonstrate or achieve compliance with all lawful requirements.

When the licensee has made timely and sufficient application for a renewal or a new license in accordance with agency rules, a license with reference to an activity of a continuing nature does not expire until the application has been finally determined by the agency.

§559. Effect on other laws; effect of subsequent statute

This subchapter [5 USCS §§551 et seq.], chapter 7 [5 USCS §§701 et seq.], and sections 1305, 3105, 3344, 4301(2)(E), 5372, and 7521 of this title, and the provisions of section 5335(a)(B) of this title that relate to administrative law judges, do not limit or repeal additional requirements imposed by statute or otherwise recognized by law. Except as otherwise required by law, requirements or privileges relating to evidence or procedure apply equally to agencies and persons. Each agency is granted the authority necessary to comply with the requirements of this subchapter through the issuance of rules or otherwise. Subsequent statute may not be held to supersede or modify this subchapter, chapter 7, sections 1305, 3105, 3344, 4301(2)(E), 5372, or 7521 of this title, or the provisions of section 5335(a)(B) of this title that relate to administrative law judges, except to the extent that it does so expressly.

CHAPTER 7—JUDICIAL REVIEW

§701. Application; definitions
§702. Right of review.
§703. Form and venue of proceeding.
§704. Actions reviewable.

§705. Relief pending review.
§706. Scope of review.

§701. Application; definitions

(a) This chapter [5 USCS §§701 et seq.] applies, according to the provisions thereof, except to the extent that—
  (1) statutes preclude judicial review; or
  (2) agency action is committed to agency discretion by law.
(b) For the purpose of this chapter
  (1) "agency" means each authority of the Government of the United States, whether or not it is within or subject to review by another agency, but does not include—
    (A) the Congress;
    (B) the courts of the United States;
    (C) the governments of the territories or possessions of the United States;
    (D) the government of the District of Columbia;
    (E) agencies composed of representatives of the parties or of representatives of organizations of the parties to the disputes determined by them;
    (F) courts martial and military commissions;
    (G) military authority exercised in the field in time of war or in occupied territory; or
    (H) functions conferred by sections 1738, 1739, 1743, and 1744 of title 12; chapter 2 of title 41; subchapter II of chapter 471 of title 49; or sections 1884, 1891–1902, and former section 1641(b)(2), of title 50, appendix, and
  (2) "person," "rule," "order," "license," "sanction," "relief," and "agency action" have the meanings given them by section 551 of this title.

§702. Right of review

A person suffering legal wrong because of agency action, or adversely affected or aggrieved by agency action within the meaning of a relevant statute, is entitled to judicial review thereof. An action in a court of the United States seeking relief other than money damages and stating a claim that an agency or an officer or employee thereof acted or failed to act in an official capacity or under color of legal authority shall not be dismissed nor relief therein be denied on the ground that it is against the United States or that the United States is an indispensable party. The United States may be named as a defendant in any such action, and a judgment or decree may be entered against the United States: Provided, that any mandatory or injunctive decree shall specify the Federal officer or officers (by name or by title), and their successors in office, personally responsible for compliance. Nothing herein (1) affects other limitations on judicial review or the power or duty of the court to dismiss any action or deny relief on any other appropriate legal or equitable ground; or (2) confers authority to grant relief if any other statute that grants consent to suit expressly or impliedly forbids the relief which is sought.

§703. Form and venue of proceeding

The form of proceeding for judicial review is the special statutory review proceeding relevant to the subject matter in a court specified by statute or, in the absence or inadequacy thereof, any applicable form of legal action, including actions for declaratory judgments or writs of prohibitory or mandatory injunction or habeas corpus, in a court of competent jurisdiction. If no special statutory review proceeding is applicable, the action for judicial review may be brought against the United States, the agency by its official title, or the appropriate officer. Except to the extent that prior, adequate, and exclusive opportunity for judicial review is provided by law, agency action is subject to judicial review in civil or criminal proceedings for judicial enforcement.

§704. Actions reviewable

Agency action made reviewable by statute and final agency action for which there is no other adequate remedy in a court are subject to judicial review. A preliminary, procedural, or intermediate agency action or ruling not directly reviewable is subject to review on the review of the final agency action. Except as otherwise expressly required by statute, agency action otherwise final is final for the purposes of this section whether or not there has been presented or determined an application for a declaratory order, for any form of reconsideration, or, unless the agency otherwise requires by rule and provides that the action meanwhile is inoperative, for an appeal to superior agency authority.

§705. Relief pending review

When an agency finds that justice so requires, it may postpone the effective date of action taken by it, pending judicial review. On such conditions as may be required and to the extent necessary to prevent irreparable injury, the reviewing court, including the court to which a case may be taken on appeal from or on application for certiorari or other writ to a reviewing court, may issue all necessary and appropriate process to postpone the effective date of an agency action or to preserve status or rights pending conclusion of the review proceedings.

§706. Scope of review

To the extent necessary to decision and when presented, the reviewing court shall decide all relevant questions of law, interpret constitutional and statutory provisions, and determine the meaning or applicability of the terms of an agency action. The reviewing court shall—
(1) compel agency action unlawfully withheld or unreasonably delayed; and
(2) hold unlawful and set aside agency action, findings, and conclusions found to be—
(A) arbitrary, capricious, an abuse of discretion, or otherwise not in accordance with law;
(B) contrary to constitutional right, power, privilege, or immunity;
(C) in excess of statutory jurisdiction, authority, or limitations, or short of statutory right;
(D) without observance of procedure required by law;
(E) unsupported by substantial evidence in a case subject to sections 556 and 557 of this title or otherwise reviewed on the record of an agency hearing provided by statute; or
(F) unwarranted by the facts to the extent that the facts are subject to trial de novo by the reviewing court.
In making the foregoing determinations, the court shall review the whole record or those parts of it cited by a party, and due account shall be taken of the rule of prejudicial error.

§1305. *Administrative law judges*

For the purpose of sections 3105, 3344, 4301(2)(D), and 5372 of this title and the provisions of section 5335(a)(B) of this title that relate to administrative law judges, the Office of Personnel Management may, and for the purpose of section 7521 of this title, the Merit Systems Protection Board may investigate, prescribe regulations, appoint advisory committees as necessary, recommend legislation, subpoena witnesses and records, and pay witness fees as established for the courts of the United States.

§3105. *Appointment of administrative law judges*

Each agency shall appoint as many administrative law judges as are necessary for proceedings required to be conducted in accordance with sections 556 and 557 of this title. Administrative law judges shall be assigned to cases in rotation so far as practicable, and may not perform duties inconsistent with their duties and responsibilities as administrative law judges.

§3344. *Details; administrative law judges*

An agency as defined by section 551 of this title which occasionally or temporarily is insufficiently staffed with administrative law judges appointed under section 3105 of this title may use administrative law judges selected by the Office of Personnel Management from and with the consent of other agencies.

Glossary
Key Legal Terms*

Ad Hoc For this special thing or purpose (e.g., *ad hoc* committee).

Adjective Law The *procedural laws/rules* under which *administrative agencies* function.

Adjudicate To hear, listen to, or judge.

Adjudication A decision, *judgment,* or recording of a judgment in favor of one side in a *dispute*.

Adjudicative Facts "Who, what, where, when" facts involving persons in *dispute* in an agency *hearing*. They contrast sharply with *legislative facts*.

Administrative Agency An administrative sub-division or unit of *government* (also may be called a board, bureau, commission, department, office, etc.) having the primary purpose of executing governmental *laws*.

Administrative Arrest The official seizure of a person for administrative reasons (e.g., questioning, material witness). Administrators can hold persons for lengthy periods without justifying the detention before a judge, unlike with criminal arrests.

Administrative Board A courtlike body assigned to conduct agency *hearings*.

Administrative Discretion Flexibility, sometimes great, of administrators to act or make decisions that are not covered precisely by *laws* or *rules*. To some, the problem of achieving *discretionary justice* is the most significant challenge of *administrative laws*.

Administrative Expertise Specialized knowledge of agency administrators. Judges frequently employ the *deference principle* so they can defer to agency expertise, especially when they want to avoid meddling unnecessarily in the administrative process or feel they cannot handle adequately difficult technical *questions of fact*.

Administrative Law *Law* pertaining to the operation of *administrative agencies,* especially as they interact with citizens, related interests, and other branches of *government*. Administrative law is concerned primarily with achieving *procedural due process* in *public administration*.

---

*The definitions in the glossary are presented in simple, abbreviated prose. The glossary is not intended to be complete but only to provide students with convenient, short, and understandable definitions of legal terms often used in administrative law. For more help on legal definitions, it is strongly recommended that the student consult a legal dictionary. The best and most complete is *Black's Law Dictionary,* published by West. However, many good paperback law dictionaries are available. Please note that words in italics are defined elsewhere in this glossary.

Administrative Law Judge One who presides over agency *hearings,* but unlike court judges, has limited judicial powers, especially the authority to reach final decisions. Formerly called *hearing examiners* on the federal level, but still are called hearing examiners in some states. Also referred to as presiding officers in some federal agencies.

Administrative Procedure Act of 1946 The chief federal law establishing procedural standards governing how *administrative agencies* must perform their regulatory business. Many states have passed administrative procedure acts. Most follow closely the federal example.

Administrative Remedy Relief provided by an *administrative agency.* All administrative remedies must be *exhausted* before judicial *remedies* can be sought.

Administrative Search A search, often called an inspection, carried out by an *administrative agency* for a regulatory purpose. A *search warrant* is sometimes required. To be lawful, an administrative search must conform with a legislatively sanctioned *administrative scheme* or purpose.

Administrative Scheme An administrative plan or reason. To obtain an administrative *search warrant,* it is required that administrators must demonstrate to a magistrate that there exists an administrative plan, scheme, or purpose.

Advisory Opinion A formal opinion expressed by a judge, but not as part of a *lawsuit,* on a legal question. Judges provide advisory opinions when, for example, public officials request judges to give their opinion on a *question of law.*

Advocate A party who argues for or tries to fight for a cause or another party. Ralph Nader is a consumer advocate who tries to defend consumer causes before public agencies and courts.

Affirm To confirm, establish, ratify, or uphold, especially in regard to upholding the judgment of an agency or a lower court.

Affirmative Action Legal requirements that compel organizations (e.g., universities) to take positive actions to remedy past discriminatory practices, especially against minorities and women, in education, hiring, etc. Affirmative action programs are not to be confused with equal opportunity programs, since the former provides for special advantages to be given that have led to charges of reverse discrimination.

Aggrieved Party A *person* who has suffered a loss or has been injured. An aggrieved party is one who has had his or her *privacy* or *property rights* violated.

Alia Other persons or other things.

Alienable Rights Those *rights* that can be taken away. These rights contrast sharply to *inalienable rights.*

Allegation A factual assertion in a *pleading* that a party in a *dispute* is prepared to prove.

Ambulatory Changeable, movable, or revocable.

Amend Action to correct or change, especially with the purpose of improving something. The U.S. *Constitution* has been amended many times.

Amendment A correction or change, usually an improvement in something (e.g., U.S. Constitution) brought about through an amendment process.

Appeal A request for an adverse decision to be reviewed by higher agency authority, a court, or a higher court. The Supreme Court is the court of final appeal. The party who initiates the appeal is called an *appellant* or *petitioner,* while the party who must respond to the appeal is called the *appellee* or *respondent.*

Appellant One who appeals a *case* to a higher court.

Appellate Court A higher court that hears *appeals* from a lower court.

Appellate Jurisdiction The authority of an appeals or higher court to hear and decide *cases* already heard by a lower court.

Appellee One who responds to an appeal taken in a *case* taken to a higher court. The appellee *(respondent)* is normally the winner of the lower court's decision.

Arbitrary Behavior Action that is not guided by *laws,* principles, or *rules,* but taken impulsively according to a *person's* whim. In *administrative law,* arbitrary and capricious behavior (the two terms almost always appear together) are prohibited by the *Administrative Procedure Act* and other laws because such actions conflict with *rule of law* principles.

Arguendo To assume true for the sake of argument.

Argument The persuasive presentation of *facts* and legal reasoning to support a contention/position in a legal *controversy,* usually before a judicial body.

Association A group of people joined together for a specific and mutual reason(s).

Authority Authorized power to perform actions.

Bad Faith Willful failure to act in an honest or legal manner. Public officials acting in bad faith may be held *liable* for *damage* actions against them.

Balancing Test A practical constitutional doctrine (test) used by courts to help them reach fairer decisions that reflect the weighing of the rights of an individual (for example, to privacy, freedom of speech, equal protection) against the rights of government to protect and promote the public interest.

Benefit A *privilege* or advantage, but not a *right.*

Best Evidence Rule A rule of evidence requiring the best evidence available (e.g., the actual tapes and not transcripts of them) to be presented in judicial proceedings.

Bias Preconceived opinion that precludes the possibility of impartial judgment in judicial proceedings.

Bill of Attainder A legislative act that punishes *persons* without the benefit of a trial. Such an act is prohibited by the U.S. Constitution, Article I, Section 9.

Bill of Rights The first eight *amendments* (some say first ten) to the U.S. Constitution that set forth individual *rights.*

Bona Fide Real and in good faith without fraud or deceit; genuine. *Bona fide* agreement is one made in good faith.

Burden of Proof The requirement to substantiate an *allegation* in a judicial proceeding. In criminal law the burden of proof is placed on the *state,* while in *administrative law* the burden of proof may carry the *risk of nonpersuasion.*

Case An action or *controversy* to be settled, usually before a judicial body.

Case Law *Common law* established through judicial decisions, not legislative acts. That *law* that comes from the whole body of judicial opinions.

Cause of Action Legal charges set forth sufficient enough to warrant judicial involvement. Such charges, rooted in *facts,* must be sufficient enough to justify judicial intervention or the complaint will be dismissed.

Certiorari A *writ* by a higher court to a lower court to send up for review its proceedings on a case. *Writs of certiorari* are requested by parties wanting to appeal a judicial *judgment* to a higher court. In many *states,* a *writ of certification* accomplishes the same purpose.

Chilling Effect Where a person voluntarily refuses to exercise First Amendment freedoms out of the fear that the application of a *law* (e.g., loyalty oath) may lead to his/her prosecution.

Civil Law That body of *law* (e.g., *administrative law*) which deals with noncriminal matters.

Class Action An action *(lawsuit)* initiated by representative members of a larger group on behalf of all of the members of the group.

Code A systematic compilation of *laws, rules,* and *regulations.*

Code of Federal Regulations Where all federal *rules* and *regulations* are codified. *States* publish similar codes of regulations.

Comity A doctrine of courtesy and respect. Courts may use comity to defer to the jurisdictional authority of another (e.g., court, *state*).

Common Law A system of jurisprudence based on judge-made *law* originating in England. Common law is rooted in custom, tradition, and common sense and subject to sudden change under new conditions. Consequently, common law is considerably more flexible, but less stable, than laws made by legislators. Probably about ninety percent of *administrative law* is judge-made.

Complainant One who initiates judicial proceeding by bringing a *cause of action.* Also called *petitioners* and *plaintiffs.*

Conflict of Interest A situation where a public official's official actions are affected by or conflict with his/her personal interests. Various laws try to prevent conflicts of interest by making such conflicts illegal.

Constitution An initial body of *laws* in a country (e.g., U.S. Constitution), organization, or *state* that sets forth fundamental governing principles and laws.

Controversy A legal dispute over an *issue* where an *allegation* is set forth and a defense is made.

Corporation An association of shareholders that exists under *law* as an artificial *person,* as contrasted to a natural person. For legal purposes, it is created as a separate legal entity from the people (natural persons) in it, thus protecting them from personal *liability* resulting from corporate acts.

Damages Monetary compensation awarded under *law* to one who has been harmed by the actions of another. Public officials committing tortious acts against persons may have to pay damages.

Dannum Absque Injuria Harm or a loss in the absence of a legal injury, thus preventing the harmed party from being able to sue in court for *damages.* A *public administrator* may cause harm to an individual when implementing lawfully certain *public policies,* yet the *law* provides no legal *remedies.*

Declaratory Judgment A judicial determination on a legal question or the *rights* of parties short of awarding *damages* or ordering any actions to be taken. Parties may seek declaratory judgments if a genuine, not a theoretical, legal problem exists.

De Facto In actuality, fact, or reality. A *person* who in fact performs the duties of an administrative post, yet does not legally hold the position, is serving in a *de facto* capacity, as contrasted to a *de jure* capacity.

Defendant The party that must respond or offer a defense against a *civil* or criminal *cause of action.*

Defense Answers, arguments, denials, and pleas used to repudiate charges brought by the party initiating the *controversy.*

Deference Principle Employed commonly by the courts when they want to yield (i.e., defer) to the *judgment* of *administrative expertise.* Critics argue that the courts too often defer to agency expertise, thus escaping the problem of reviewing difficult cases, especially ones involving technical *questions of fact.*

De Jure Lawful, legitimate, or sanctioned. A public official performing in a *de jure* capacity has lawful title to his office and is functioning with legal sanctioning, as opposed to one who is performing in a *de facto* capacity.

Delegation Doctrine The *doctrine* applied by the courts that permits the legislature to transfer (delegate) some of its powers, especially its lawmaking power, to *administrative agencies.*

De Minimis Frivolous, minute, or insignificant. Courts cannot be bothered with *de minimis* questions.

Demurrer A legal *allegation* that holds that the case (facts and arguments presented by the other side), even if correct, is insufficient to permit the *dispute* to continue any further in court, thus constituting grounds for dismissal.

De Novo Fresh, new, renewed, or revived. A *de novo hearing* is a fresh, new hearing being heard for the second time, as if the first hearing had not taken place.

Discretionary Justice The end sought in the fair and proper use of *administrative discretion.* The phrase was made popular by the prolific writings of Kenneth C. Davis. To him, discretion has to be "confined, structured, and checked" if discretionary justice is to be achieved.

Discrimination The treatment of people in an unequal manner. Some discriminatory practices (e.g., sex discrimination) are illegal.

Dismiss To terminate a case before it has been completed. See *demurrer.*

Disposition The final result. Final action *(judgment)* of a court in a *case.*

Dispositive Facts Weighty *facts* that clearly resolve a legal *dispute.*

Dispute A *controversy* between parties over *rights* and legal *issues.*

Dissent To disagree or differ from another's opinion. Judges give dissenting opinions in *cases* when they disagree with the *majority opinion.*

Doctrine A legal principle, *rule,* or tenet. Various doctrines (e.g., *exhaustion doctrine)* are used by judges to guide judicial behavior.

Domain Control and ownership, especially by the public. National parks are part of the public domain.

Duces Tecum Bring with you. See *subpoena duces tecum.*

Due Just, lawful, or proper. For example, proper *notice* is due notice.

Due Process of Law Due process is a vague phrase required by the U.S. Constitution. The due process clause protects against the *arbitrary* deprivation of "life, liberty, or property without due process of law." Constitutional due process standards have been incorporated into *administrative law.* Constitutional due process differs from *procedural due process.*

Ejusdem Generis Of the same kind, type, or general nature.

Eminent Domain The *government's* constitutional *right* to take private property for public use, as long as just compensation is paid.

Enabling Legislation *Laws* that permit public officials to have powers to perform certain actions. Critics charge that legislators have irresponsibly *delegated* vast powers to public administrators through enabling statutes, thus giving to them dangerously broad *administrative discretion.*

En Banc Full bench. Where the whole court is sitting rather than the regular quorum of judges. In the United States Circuit Courts the judges normally sit in panels (normally three), but the court may be expanded to include the whole court for important cases (for example, a school desegregation case) where they would sit en banc.

Entrapment A very controversial governmental action where public officials (normally law enforcement officers) induce a *person* to commit a crime. The purpose is to catch persons who would be predisposed to commit crimes.

Entitlement A complete or absolute *right* to something under *law* as long as legal requirements are satisfied. See *statutory entitlement.*

Equal Protection A constitutional provision that calls for the *government* to treat all *persons* equally. Statutes also prohibit unfair and unequal treatment of persons. In implementing *public policies* (e.g., housing programs), *public administrators* must be careful not to violate equal protection provisions.

Equitable What is fair, just, or right for particular situations. *Public administrators* are obligated to administer *public policies* in an equitable fashion.

Ergo Therefore.

Erratum Mistake.

Estoppel A bar or preclusion that stops an unfair act from taking place. For example, the equitable estoppel doctrine can be employed to prevent a party from denying the truth or a commitment to another *person,* especially if harmful misrepresentation is involved.

Evidence Any information, documents, testimony, etc. that is entered at a judicial proceeding to move or disprove *allegations* and facts. Rules of evidence are stricter in court trials than in administrative *hearings.* For example, *hearsay evidence* is rarely permitted in court trials, but is allowed in administrative hearings.

Exclusionary Rule Used to prohibit the submission of *evidence* that would ordinarily be admissible, but becomes inadmissible because it was obtained illegally. Some argue, for example, that evidence obtained through *entrapment* methods should be considered inadmissible evidence.

Executive Branch The administrative arm of *government,* broadly including the president and the bureaucracy on the national level.

Executive Privilege Consists of the *privilege* (possibly a *right)* of executive officials to withhold "privileged" information or refuse to appear before a court or legislative committee. Executive privilege does not give the president total *discretion* in deciding what should remain privileged information *(United States v. Nixon,* 418 U.S. 683; 1974).

Exhaustion of Administrative Remedies To obtain *judicial review,* a party must exhaust all *remedies* within an *administrative agency* before the *controversy* can be appealed to a court. Courts employ the exhaustion doctrine to help reduce the court's *case* load and to allow agencies ample opportunity to settle *disputes.*

Ex Officio By virtue of the power of the office alone. A *person,* only because of the office he/she holds, may be entitled to sit *ex officio* on a governing board.

Ex Parte Where only one side is present or represented. *Ex parte* contacts with *public administrators* are considered unfair by many because only one side is given the opportunity to peddle influence.

Ex Post Facto Literally means after the fact. *Ex post facto laws* are prohibited by the U.S. Constitution because they make certain actions illegal that were not unlawful at the time they were committed. Common sense dictates that such laws are patently unfair.

Ex Rel Literally means on relation or report. It is used often in *case* cites. *Ex rel Smith v. Brown* simply means that the state is bringing suit against Brown for Smith.

Fact Something that is real, took place, or exists. An act or event. *Questions of fact* pertain to what happened. Facts are real and not opinions or imaginary events. Facts provide important *evidence* and are carefully scrutinized in legal *disputes.*

Fair Hearing What administrative agencies supposedly provide when they follow trial-like procedures or at least full *hearing* requirements as required by *law*.

Feasance Performance of an act or duty.

Federal Register Where all administrative agencies publish their *proposed and final rules*.

Fiat A command or *order*. The president can issue an executive fiat or order.

Final Rule A *rule* by an *administrative agency* that has been finally adopted and put in effect or scheduled to become effective, usually within about thirty days after the final rule is published in the *Federal Register*.

Finding A decision reached by a judge, jury, or *administrative law judge*, after weighing *evidence*. A finding of *fact* occurs when a decision is reached in regard to a *question of fact*.

Fishing Expedition An unethical or illegal practice where someone (e.g., administrative official) carries out a general search. *Administrative searches* should be limited to particular items specified on the administrative search warrant so fishing expeditions cannot unnecessarily invade someone's privacy.

Good Cause Nonarbitrary, legally justifiable.

Good Faith Honest and fair intentions. A public official is acting in good faith if his or her actions are honest, sincere, and well intended.

Government A governing force, body, or political unit entrusted with implementing *public policies*. Governments differ radically in governing styles and political purposes.

Governmental Immunity In *tort law*, a situation where the *government* cannot be sued or held *liable* because of the tortious actions of its officers.

Headnote A summary of a court case preceding the published *case*.

Hearing An informal or formal trial-like adjudicative proceeding within an *administrative agency*. Not to be confused with a *public hearing*.

Hearing Examiner See *administrative law judge*.

Hearsay Evidence *Evidence* that is secondhand. What John Smith said in a *hearing* about what Joe Doe said is an example of hearsay or secondhand evidence. If the *best evidence rule* was invoked, Joe Doe would have to appear at the hearing himself to give testimony. Hearsay evidence is considered somewhat suspect and unreliable since the *evidence* rests upon the credibility of the *person* presenting it.

Held Decided or concluded. *Cases* are concluded with what the judicial body holds or decides when they hand down a decision. "We hold that . . . "

Holding What a judge or judicial body decides. The essence of a written judicial opinion/decision in a case. Holdings establish legal *precedents*.

Hornbook In *law*, a book that covers fundamental principles of a single legal topic.

Hybrid Rulemaking Rulemaking that combines legislative and adjudicative proceedings. Hybrid rulemaking is controversial because critics hold that the *Administrative Procedure Act* distinguishes between *rulemaking* and *adjudication* and authorizes one process or the other, but not a combination of the two.

Imminent Threatening or just about to occur or take place.

Immunity In *tort law*, a situation where a *person* (i.e., public official) is made exempt from tort *liability* suits. See *governmental, official,* and *sovereign immunity*.

Impeach To call into question. To charge a public official with misconduct in office, with a crime, or with a misdemeanor.

Inalienable Rights Those *rights* considered so basic that they should not be taken away. To some, those rights set forth in the *Bill of Rights* should be regarded as inalienable.

In Camera In chambers, particularly in a judge's office (chamber). *In camera* inspections, usually of sensitive materials, are often carried out in the privacy of a judge's office.

Inchoate Incomplete, partial, or unfinished, as in an inchoate record or document.

Indefeasible Right A *right* that cannot be defeated, taken away, or revoked.

Indemnify To compensate a party who has suffered *damages* or losses. To insure against future losses.

Influence Peddling An unethical or possibly an illegal situation where a *person* tries to influence someone (e.g., agency administrator) to see it his/her way in order to receive an unfair benefit for himself/herself or a party he/she is representing.

In Haec Verba In these same words.

In Re Literally, in the matter of. *In Re* is a prefix attached to a *case* dealing with a thing (e.g., a business) and not a *dispute* involving named persons. For example, *In Re International Business Machines Corp.,* 618 F.2d 923 (2d Cir., 1980).

Inter Alia Among other things.

Interpretative Rule A *rule* that is open to interpretation by the Courts because it is promulgated in the absence of *clear legislative intent* (i.e., direct statutory sanctioning). Unlike *legislative rules,* interpretative rules are often invalidated by the courts because of their questionable statutory sanctioning.

Intervenor A party who voluntarily involves oneself in a legal *dispute.*

In Toto Totally, completely, wholly.

Inure To become effective, operative, or to the benefit of a person.

Ipso Facto Literally, by the fact itself. By the simple fact that.

Irreparable Injury Injury (harm) that cannot be appropriately fixed by money or any other *remedy.* See *reparable injury.*

Issue Specific *questions of fact* or *law* disputed by opposing parties in a legal *controversy.*

Judgment Decision or verdict by a judicial body in a *case.*

Judgment-Proof Where a money *judgment* against a *person* would have no significance because they cannot pay or are protected from having to pay. A *tort* suit against a poor public official may prove futile since the official may likely be judgment-proof.

Judicial Review The power of the courts to review and interpret governmental *laws* and actions to determine their constitutionality. The judicial power to declare laws unconstitutional.

Juridical Pertaining to judicial practices or the judicial system.

Jurisdiction The physical or nonphysical area in which judges or public officials have legal authority.

Jus Justice. *Law* or an entire body of law.

Justiciable A *controversy* that is within the proper jurisdiction of a court.

Knowingly Acting willfully or with full knowledge of.

Law Legal principles, *rules,* and standards set forth by a governing authority (e.g., United States government) that must be obeyed or *punishments* may be imposed. Law also refers to an area of legal study or practice (e.g., *administrative law*).

Lawsuit A judicial proceeding *(civil* action, not a criminal action) employed to enforce a legal *right.*

Legal Formalism A prevailing nineteenth century legal philosophy that held essentially that those *rights* set forth in the *Bill of Rights* were *inalienable* or absolute and should not be compromised by judges in their decisions.

Legal Realism A dominant twentieth-century legal philosophy that holds that those *rights* in the *Bill of Rights* are not absolute and should be interpreted in the context of socioeconomic, political, and psychological factors. The application of this philosophy has made it considerably easier for *government* to extend its regulatory arm.

Legislative Facts General *facts* that serve to guide agency *rulemaking* and policy positions. They contrast sharply with *adjudicative facts.*

Legislative Intent What legislators meant (intended) when they passed a *law.* Since laws are often vague, legislative intent is often difficult for both administrators and judges to determine. Much of *administrative law* is concerned with determining whether administrators have carried out what legislators intended.

Legislative Purpose In light of the past *law,* what the new law seeks to change. As with *legislative intent,* what administrators and judges look for when interpreting *statutes.*

Liability A legal debt, obligation, or responsibility. See *liable* and *tort law.*

Liable The state of being held responsible for something. In *tort law,* a *public administrator* may be held liable for tortious actions that cause harm to a *person* and may be required to pay *damages.*

Magistrate A judge with limited judicial functions/powers. Sometimes magistrates perform "less significant" judicial functions (e.g., signing *administrative search warrants)* to free judges so they can focus on "more significant" judicial tasks.

Majority Opinion The opinion held by the court's majority when handing down a *judgment* in a *case.*

Malfeasance Wrongdoing. Malfeasance of office involves the performance of an illegal act.

Malicious Behavior Intentional conduct done with bad motives and without moral or legal reasons.

Ministerial Action Following *orders* without employing *administrative discretion* to make choices. While lower level public officials (e.g., clerks) perform mostly nondiscretionary ministerial functions, higher level officials (e.g., agency heads) employ significant discretion in making policy decisions.

Misfeasance Improper performance. Misfeasance of office involves the improper execution of duties, although the acts may be otherwise legal.

Municipal Corporation City or municipality.

Natural Law Basic moral *law* as opposed to *positive state law.* Such law is perceived as higher, universal law fundamental to human behavior, therefore, natural. It is discovered through reason.

Negligent Behavior Careless, reckless, or unreasonable conduct that causes harm to another party, thus giving possible grounds to the injured party to bring *tort* action.

Nonfeasance Failure to perform a required function. A *public administrator* may be charged with nonfeasance of office if he or she fails to perform official duties.

Notice Formal notification, usually through written communication, alerting an interested party to information, an action, or a proposed action. In *administrative law,* proper notice is sometimes required so *procedural due process* can be extended to persons, especially those involved in *hearings.*

Obiter Dicta Rhetoric or side remarks of minor significance. Judges engage in *obiter dicta* when they digress from their central argument in a case.

Official Immunity In *tort law,* a situation where governmental officials are granted immunity from *tort liability* suits against them. Today, governmental officials enjoy only limited immunity.

Official Notice Where an administrative tribunal recognizes (accepts) a commonly known *fact* (e.g., Christmas falls on December 25) without further verification, thus allowing a party in a dispute to not have to formally enter the fact as *evidence*. Similarly, judges give judicial notice.

Ombudsman One who listens to complaints from citizens about governmental operations. An ombudsman, in an official capacity, can investigate and voice complaints, but normally has no power to prosecute.

Order The result of an agency's *ordermaking* or adjudicative process. A general command or *fiat*, especially by a court or a high executive officer.

Ordermaking The adjudicative process used by *administrative agencies* to make *orders*.

Per Curiam Literally means by the court. A *per curiam* decision is one supported by all of the judges, yet normally appears without a judge's name attached to it.

Peremptory Absolute or conclusive, requiring no justification to be given.

Per Se Standing by itself, in and of itself, or taken alone.

Person In *law*, a natural individual or an artificial party (e.g., a *corporation*) who can sue or be sued.

Petition A written request, usually to a court, asking for some action to be taken.

Petitioner One who initiates a judicial proceeding by presenting a petition to a judicial body. An *appellee* or *respondent* responds to the petitioner's *cause of action*.

Plaintiff One who initiates a judicial proceeding by bringing a *cause of action* in an effort to seek a *remedy* to an injury or a denial of *rights*.

Pleading A logical, legal statement of the *facts* in a *dispute* that constitutes the petitioner's *cause of action* and the *respondent's defense*.

Plenary Full or complete.

Police Power A basic governmental power to establish and enforce the *laws* and *rules* of the *government* for the purpose of promoting the *public interest* and preserving societal order.

Positive Law The *laws* of the *state* passed by a legislative body as opposed to *natural law*.

Precedent A decision by a judicial body on a *question of law* that helps establish judgemade or *common law* that can be drawn upon in the future to aid decisions on similar legal questions in *dispute*.

Preemption A Supreme Court-drafted *doctrine* that holds that certain national concerns have priority over state and local matters, thus allowing national laws to preempt state and local laws whenever they conflict. For example, states cannot pass regulations that contradict federal regulatory standards.

Prejudice A preconceived *judgment* or opinion in support of one side in a *dispute*. Such a *bias* precludes the possibility of impartiality during judicial proceedings.

Prior Hearing A *hearing* within an *administrative agency* that is sometimes required before an adverse action can be taken that may harm a *person*.

Privacy Right Basically, the *right* to be able to enjoy life free from governmental intrusions. Privacy rights are protected especially by the Fourth and Fifth Amendments.

Privilege An advantage given to a party short of a legal entitlement (*right*). Unlike rights, privileges can be more easily denied and carry considerably less weight in *controversies* before judicial bodies.

Probable Cause According to the Fourth Amendment, the valid reasons that must be given before a judge or *magistrate* can issue a *search* or seizure *warrant*. Probable cause standards are less demanding for *administrative searches* and seizures than for criminal searches and seizures.

Probative Tending to substantiate or prove something, as in a probative *fact*.

Procedural Due Process A vague phrase that implies that *public administrators* should employ fundamental fairness principles (*due process of law*) when implementing *public policies*. Although there is a difference between procedural due process (administrative due process) and constitutional due process, the former reflects closely the spirit of the latter.

Procedural Law Essentially, administrative *rules* and processes used to implement *substantive law*. *Administrative law* focuses on procedural law with the hope of achieving *procedural due process*.

Promulgate To officially produce or publish. *Public administrators* promulgate *rules* in the *rulemaking* process.

Property Right The right to own or to be entitled to something. In recent times "new property rights" have included *statutory* entitlements (e.g., welfare benefits).

Proposed Rule A *rule* that an *administrative agency* intends to promulgate. A proposed rule, under most circumstances, must be published in the *Federal Register* so interested parties are given *notice* and can then comment on the proposed rule. *Final rules* follow.

Public Administration The administrative activities carried out by *public administrators* aimed at implementing *public policies*. Public administrative functions are governed in part by *administrative law*.

Public Administrator One who works for a public agency and is responsible for executing the *laws, rules,* and *orders* of the *government*.

Public Hearing A proceeding used by *administrative agencies* to propose an agency action (e.g., *rule),* display something, or listen to public comments and criticisms on various agency-related matters.

Public Interest That which is in the interest of the people of a *state* as a whole. Some argue that a singular public interest (common good) does not exist, but that there are many public interests.

Public Policy Strategic actions taken by the *government,* which ideally represents the will of the people, to resolve present and anticipated future social problems. Public policies are ideally aimed at promoting the *public interest* or public health and safety.

Punishment Penalties (e.g., fines, imprisonment, death) assessed for not complying with the *government*'s criminal *laws* and *administrative rules* and *regulations*.

Quasi-Judicial The *ordermaking* or adjudicative power of an *administrative agency.*

Quasi-Legislative Power The *rulemaking* or "lawmaking" power of an *administrative agency.*

Question of Fact A disputed factual statement that a judicial body may resolve. Questions of fact differ from *questions of law,* although the two questions are often almost impossible to distinguish. Courts mostly focus on questions of law.

Question of Law A disputed legal *issue* that a judicial body may resolve. In *administrative law,* a question of law usually pertains to some *procedural due process* question. In *controversies,* courts focus on questions of law, placing less emphasis on *questions of fact.*

Quid Pro Quo Something given in exchange for something, such as in a *quid pro quo* agreement.

Quo Warranto Where a court questions the right of, for example, a *public administrator* to hold a particular office or perform specific actions.

Reasonable A very vague and flexible word employed frequently in *law.* The word takes on its practical meaning when placed in context (e.g., reasonable action, reasonable care, reasonable force, what a reasonable person would accept). Reasonableness tests are commonly used to help judicial bodies weigh evidence and reach decisions.

Record A formal, usually recorded or written, account of official proceedings (e.g., administrative hearings, court cases). A complete record would include all pertinent documentation. The Administrative Procedure Act has a whole record requirement. A public record is open to public scrutiny.

Regulation A quasi-law. See *rule.*

Regulatory Agency An *administrative agency* that promulgates *rules, regulations,* and *orders* for the purpose of controlling various socio-economic activities.

Remand To send back, as when a higher court sends down a *case* on remand for further review.

Remedy A means to redress a harm done or a right denied. *Administrative agencies* provide *administrative remedies,* while courts provide judicial remedies.

Reparable Injury An injury that can be fixed by monetary compensation. Contrasts sharply with an *irreparable injury.*

Residuum Rule In *administrative law,* it requires that a residue of hard *evidence,* outside of *hearsay evidence* or other evidence that would be inadmissible in court, must exist to support a *hearing* decision.

Res Judicata A thing or *controversy* that is finally decided and cannot be reheard.

Respondeat Superior A legal obligation making the employer responsible for the conduct of an employee while in the service of the employer. From Latin, meaning literally "let the Master answer."

Respondent One who responds to a *cause of action* in an *appeal.* The respondent (*appellee*) may have been a *defendant* or *plaintiff* in a lower court.

Restraining Order An order by a judge to a *person* (e.g., public official) that prohibits that person from acting until a *hearing* can be held to resolve certain questions.

Reviewability Pertains to whether a court believes it has the authority or jurisdiction to review a *case.* See *scope of review.*

Right A legal *entitlement,* not a *privilege,* that is *due* a party.

Ripe A ripe *case* is one that is mature enough and thus ready for review. The ripeness doctrine is used by courts to turn down cases they believe have not been sufficiently developed at the agency level.

Risk of Nonpersuasion *Burden of proof* whereby the party bringing action will lose the *case* if the *hearing examiner* or judge is left unconvinced (not persuaded).

Rule The result of an agency's *rulemaking* or "lawmaking" process.

Rulemaking The lawmaking process used by *administrative agencies* to promulgate *rules.*

Rule of Law Phrase connotes a high democratic principle that places all governmental actions under *law.* Rule of law prohibits any *person* in the political system from acting arbitrarily or in any way above the law.

Scope of Review Pertains to the depth to which a court will review an *issue* after it has agreed to review the issue. See *reviewability.*

Search Warrant Written permission granted by a judge or *magistrate* for police to search for particular items at a specific place. Police must establish *probable cause* before the *warrant* can be issued. *Administrative search* warrants do not require probable cause to be established as long as an *administrative scheme* or purpose can be shown.

Separation of Powers A basic constitutional principle that holds that legislative, judicial, and administrative powers should not be concentrated in a single branch, but shared among the branches so that governmental power can be checked. Some charge that the separation of powers doctrine is threatened by the exercise of all three governmental powers by administrative agencies.

Sine qua non An indispensable condition, practice, or thing.

Sovereign Immunity In *tort law,* a situation where the *government* enjoys absolute *immunity* from *tort liability* suits. The sovereign immunity doctrine is based on the old British *common law* assumption that the "king can do no wrong." Today, governments in the United States enjoy only qualified immunity.

Standing The legal *right* to sue another party in court. This right is only given by a court after the petitioning party has shown that he, she, or it would suffer a legal injury if a *lawsuit* could not be pursued.

State A political unit (e.g., Britain, France, United States) or a political sub-division (e.g., Missouri).

Statute A *law* passed by a legislative body.

Statutory Entitlement Something that one has a *right* to receive under *statute.* If eligible, a *person* is entitled under statute to receive welfare benefits.

Subpoena A judicial *order* requiring a *person* to appear in court to provide *evidence* or give testimony.

Subpoena Duces Tecum Where, under *subpoena,* a *person* is required to appear before court with specific documents.

Substantive Law Basic written *law* pertaining to *rights* and duties. Substantive law is enforced through *procedural law.*

Tort A civil *wrong* committed against another *person* that causes legal harm or injury.

Tortfeasor A person who commits a *tort.*

***Ultra Vires* Actions** Acts beyond the legitimate scope of one's authorized or official activities. Applied particularly to *corporations.*

Undue Illegal or unethical.

Vel Non Or not.

Veto Where a president, governor, or other high ranking executive refuses to sign into *law* a bill passed by a legislative body.

Warrant A legal document issued by a judge or *magistrate,* after certain warrant requirements have been satisfied, that authorizes searches, seizures, and arrests.

Warrantless Search A search without a *search warrant.* In criminal law, search warrants are almost always required. However, in *administrative law, public administrators* under several circumstances can carry out administrative searches without a *warrant.*

Whistle-Blower A *person* working for an agency who discloses to the public administrative inefficiencies or wrongdoings.

Wanton Behavior *Malicious,* reckless, or ruthless conduct. A public official may treat citizens with a wanton disregard for their *privacy rights,* thus giving the harmed party grounds for a *tort* suit.

Writ An *order* issued by a judicial body that compels something to be done or authorizes something to be done. See, for example, *writ of mandamus.*

Writ of Certification See *certiorari.*

Writ of Habeas Corpus A *writ* that demands that governmental officials, almost always police officers, justify before a judge why a *person* is being held. The *writ* is mostly applicable to criminal law.

Writ of Mandamus A court *order* that compels a public agency or official to do something (normally, to perform official duties as required by *law*).

Writ of Prohibition An *order* that calls for an action to be stopped or for actions not to be carried out.

Wrong An action that violates a party's legal rights.

Case Index

Name Index

Subject Index